Brief Contents

Contents

Part 1   Examining Personality

Chapter 1   What Is Personality?   2

Chapter 2   Research in Personality Psychology   38

Part 2　**Parts of Personality**

Part 3 **Personality Organization**

Chapter 8   **How the Parts of Personality Fit Together**   272

Chapter 9   **Dynamics of Action**   316

Preface for the Student

I wrote this book in order to provide you with the very best textbook in personality psychology that I could imagine. The book has been motivated by my own lifelong curiosity about—and deep caring for—the field of personality psychology, as well as my optimism regarding the future of the field.

The most typical way to teach personality psychology today is by covering a series of theoretical perspectives on personality first laid out in the early to middle twentieth century by figures such as Sigmund Freud, Carl Jung, Carl Rogers, and others. With such books, a student learns the psychodynamic approach, the trait approach, and other theoretical approaches covered in Chapter 3 of this book. The problem with such an approach, to me, is that it relies on a somewhat outmoded, early twentieth century way of thinking about psychology. The present textbook employs a new scientific framework that uses all the above theories together to focus on a single, integrated picture of personality. The textbook and the new scientific framework were developed together. As I developed this book, I wrote a series of journal articles addressed to my colleagues about how the field should be reorganized, and why.

In the process of publishing those journal articles, I received a great number of peer reviews by colleagues commenting on my suggested reorganization of the field, sometimes positively and sometimes negatively. That peer review allowed me to rethink areas of the outline, revise my ideas, and, in a couple of cases, publish new articles that the field needed before a book such as this could be written.

I also received invaluable feedback from my students—both from undergraduate students who took the course and were free with their comments about what worked and what didn't, and from graduate students who were teaching assistants for the course, or who taught the course themselves with the evolving book.

The new outline for the field, on which *Personality: A Systems Approach* is based, is called the *systems framework for personality psychology,* and divides the study of personality into four major topics:

1. What (and where) is personality? Personality is in the person somewhere, perhaps, but where more precisely?
2. What are personality's parts? Shyness? Sociability? Emotionality?
3. How are those parts organized into a whole? How is personality structured, and what sorts of dynamics take place within it?
4. Finally, how do the parts and the whole develop and change over time?

These four topics—defining personality, learning about its parts, its organization, and its development—can provide an overview of the whole field of personality psychology, and the four parts of this textbook mirror those four topics.

As you read and study personality psychology with this book, you will enjoy:

- *The Liberal Use of Case Examples.* Wherever possible, examples of personality are drawn from real people's lives.

- *A Variety of Study Aids.* These include:
  - central questions at each chapter's opening
  - marginal glossary terms
  - supplemental boxed features, including case studies, interdisciplinary connections, looks inside the field, and interesting research findings
  - study questions at the conclusion of each chapter

In addition to my own ideas, this textbook reflects the comments, needs, and hopes of students who have taken the personality course with me in past years. I hope you will find this book both interesting and inspiring, and for those who continue to be interested by personality psychology, an ongoing resource in understanding the field.

A Vision

Our field grew out of a vision. The discipline of personality psychology was intended to integrate the findings from the rest of psychology in a coherent, broad picture of how an individual's mental life operated. This picture of personality would be global enough to permit discussion of the important questions about being human such as: "Who am I?" and "How should I live my life?" and yet would be rigorous enough to promote scientific research (Alexander, 1941; Allport, 1937; Greebie, 1932; Wundt, 1897).

Maintaining that vision throughout the field's history has been challenging. The advent of the grand theories of personality during the early part of the twentieth century captured the imagination of many scholars. Enticing as those grand theories were, however, they diverted attention from the painstaking but gradual accumulation of research findings in the field. Many courses on personality psychology became courses about the personality theories of Freud, Jung, Maslow, and others (see e.g., Hall & Lindzey, 1978). Each theory used a different language, and many denied the validity of the other theories. Thereafter, a return to a unified picture of the personality system and to the original vision of the field faced certain obstacles. Moreover, a sense of how to begin to reintegrate the accumulating research in the field—and to teach it—was lost (see e.g., Mendelssohn, 1993).

To be sure, some tried to integrate the field. Robert Sears (1950) hoped to return the field to a systematic view of personality. To do so, he laid out the topics he believed one should study when looking at a whole system: "Structure, Dynamics, and Development," as he put it. Unfortunately, the terms he employed went undefined, and even those psychologists who wanted to use his approach remained confused as to how to apply his vision (e.g., Messick, 1961).

In the fifty-odd years since Sears's simple formula, several advances have occurred that enabled this book to effectively and fully align itself with that powerful vision of the founders of the field.

- The first advance was the recognition that the grand theories of personality are not as contradictory as they first seemed. In fact, many such theories have been translated into one another's terminology, and, increasingly, a common terminology in the field is employed (e.g., Dollard & Miller, 1950; Erdelyi, 1980; Mayer, 1993-1994; 1995a; 1995b; 1998; 2001; 2004; 2005; Westen, 1991; 1998).

- Second, research has grown at a consistent rate, guided by mini-theories specifically relevant to the issues being researched. This, in turn, has led to a new and sizeable research base for the field—so that, when one describes what is known about personality, there is a fair amount to say.

- Third has been the development of the systems framework that is used in this book. The framework allows for personality to be discussed as a system without needing to be constrained by the jargon of general systems theory, cybernetics, and similar approaches. Rather, talking about personality as a system can be done simply and directly (Mayer, 1993–1994). The systems framework for personality has been published as a series of peer-reviewed articles. One of those articles was also the subject of public peer commentary. The development of this book has been greatly enhanced by such continuous and open review (Craik, 1998; Emmons, 1998; Funder, 1998; 2002, p. 5; Hogan, 1998; Mayer, 1993–1994; 1994; 1995a; 1995b; 1998a; 1998b; Mayer & Carlsmith, 1997; McAdams, 1998; Singer, 1998; Tennen & Affleck, 1998).

> Only the fairy tale equates changelessness with happiness. Permanence means paralysis and death. Only in movement, with all its pain, is life.
>
> Jacob Burckhardt

With these developments, the stage has been set for a new integrated approach to personality psychology. It is my hope that this textbook will itself become a touchstone in the reorganization—and revitalization—of the field of personality psychology. I believe that this reenvisioning of the field can return us to the original conceptions and purposes for which the field was created, and integrate the most up-to-date and highest quality theory and research available.

Organization of the Book and the Course

Personality psychology is often taught today by examining a number of theoretical perspectives on the system such as the psychodynamic, behavioral, trait, and so on. This leads to a fragmented approach—and one that becomes strained when attempting to fit in current research.

Personality: A Systems Approach evolved from an intentional re-focusing on the central mission of personality psychology: To directly describe the personality system and its major psychological subsystems. The framework that organizes this textbook divides the study of personality into four areas. These proceed from: (1) describing personality and the discipline of personality psychology, to (2) examining personality's parts, (3) personality's organization, and (4) personality's development. The framework's four topics, and the chapters that accompany each, appear in Table P.1.

Using the New Book

One natural concern for an instructor is, "How much time will it take to use this new book, and how easy is it to convert to this new organization?" Two qualities make it relatively easy to convert to this new approach. First, the book maintains some of the traditional content of the course. This means that one can use many materials that one has become accustomed to using with any course in personality psychology—just in a new order. Second, a variety of materials are available to assist instruction of the course—including a complete set of lecture outlines in PowerPoint—that make the switch as easy as possible.

TABLE P.1 Four Topics of This Book and the Chapters' Organization			
Exploring Personality	**Parts of Personality**	**Personality Organization**	**Personality Development**
1. What Is Personality? 2. Research in Personality Psychology 3. Perspectives on Personality	4. Motivation and Emotion 5. Interior Selves, Interior Worlds 6. Mental Abilities and Navigating the World 7. The Conscious Self	8. How the Parts of Personality Fit Together 9. Dynamics of Action 10. Dynamics of Self-Control	11. Personality Development in Childhood and Adolescence 12. Personality Development in Adulthood

Using Current Lectures in a New Order

The counterpoint of specialization is always organization—organization is what brings specialists . . . into a working relationship with other specialists for a complete and useful result.

John Kenneth Galbraith

The first aspect of the book that makes a switch to it easy is that many lectures commonly employed in a theories approach can be used with this new book. That is because the emphasis of this new book is on re-organization and integration. Examples of some common lectures from personality psychology that can be employed with only modest modification are shown in Table P.2. There, such common topics as lectures on Freudian defense mechanisms, Murray's work on the Thematic Apperception Test, Jung's archetypes, Costa and McCrae's Big Five personality traits, George Kelly's personal constructs, and other topics, are arranged as they might be for a specific course using this textbook.

A Full-Featured Instructor's Manual

A second quality that makes this textbook easy to switch to is the full-featured online Instructor's Manual that accompanies it. It includes: (a) a sample syllabus for the course, (b) complete PowerPoint lecture notes for those new to the course, (c) a test bank, (d) recommended demonstrations and class interactions, and (e) a suggested group of films, among other features. The Instructor's Manual is available through the Instructor's Resource Center at www.ablongman.com/irc.

Organization Advantages

The new format employed here permits a rational progression of study that focuses on the best elements of the field, while employing a clear, organized pedagogy. The book's organization and associated pedagogy lead to a set of advantages for the instructor in the classroom. These advantages include holding student interest, coping with students from different majors, and focusing on the best of the field. Examples of the specific manner in which the text addresses the challenges of teaching the personality course are outlined in Table P.3.

TABLE P.2	How Perspectives-Oriented Lectures (e.g., Psychodynamic, Trait, Humanistic, etc.). Can Be Used with This Book

Common Lecture Topic(s) in Personality Psychology	Placement of the Lecture Using This Textbook
· Defining personality and describing the field	Chapter 1: What Is Personality?
· Reliability and validity	Chapter 2: Research in Personality Psychology
· Introduction to the different theories of personality (e.g., introduction to the psychodynamic, trait, humanistic, sociocognitive, and other perspectives)	Chapter 3: Perspectives on Personality
· Murray's Thematic Apperception Test (TAT) · Eysenck's model of neuroticism and extraversion	Chapter 4: Motives and Emotions
· Kelly's personal constructs · Jung's archetypes · Markus's possible selves · Higgins's ideal and actual selves	Chapter 5: Interior Selves, Interior Worlds
· Adler's creative personality · Standard lecture on intelligence	Chapter 6: Mental Abilities and Navigating the World
· Freud's ego; Jung's ego · Free will versus determinism	Chapter 7: Consciousness
· The Big Five traits · Mischel's model of person-situation interactions · MacLean's triune brain · The conscious versus unconscious	Chapter 8: How the Parts of Personality Fit Together
· Mood-congruent phenomena · Interaction of motives · Personal strivings, personal projects · Latent versus manifest content of behavior	Chapter 9: Dynamics of Action
· Freud's mechanisms of defense · Hypnotic phenomena · Feedback loops · Auto-suggestion	Chapter 10: Dynamics of Self-Control
· Erikson's eight stages of development · Attachment theory · Birth order · The identity crisis	Chapter 11: Personality Development in Childhood and Adolescence
· Levinson's stages of adult development · Adult relationships and marriage · Maslow's self-actualized person · Erikson's generativity versus despair	Chapter 12: Personality Development in Adulthood

TABLE P.3   **Advantages of Using the Systems Approach in the Classroom**

The Issue in Brief	The Issue in the Classroom	How This Text Addresses the Issue
Raising the interest level	Students become bored with coverage of one theorist after another, or one experimental research topic after another.	Students are interested in human personality, and this book shifts the focus from theory and research to the personality system itself. The book's organization incorporates favorite student topics from emotions to hypnosis to the unconscious. It also includes the liberal use of up-to-date case examples to illustrate material.
Different student interests	Some students want to understand theories of personality. Others, with more science background, want to learn about research studies.	Both the theory and empirical research of personality are integrated and applied to the topics of the parts of personality, personality organization, and the development of personality.
Drawing in diverse student majors	Many students who take the course come from other majors such as sociology and English, and applied fields such as social work and nursing.	Interdisciplinary text boxes connect personality to other fields. Material is developed with high levels of clarity so that everyone can understand.
Improving the presentation of the field	Professors and their students feel let down by constant contradictions between one theory and another.	Those views of personality are emphasized that are most plausible and have garnered the best research support—in an even-handed fashion.
Addressing commonly used statistics in the field	Current personality psychology involves discussion of advanced mathematics such as factor analysis; these can be difficult to convey in class.	Students learn how to read mathematical techniques such as factor analysis. The "reading research" treatments are carefully worked over to ensure their clarity, and are presented at a level accessible to most students. This gives students something they can understand relatively quickly that will help them evaluate substantive issues in the course.
Students want to learn something about their lives	Students face the developmental task of fitting into the world both in creating bonds with others, and occupationally. They look to this course for answers.	Students learn about how personality relates to life throughout the book. For example, they learn about motivational and emotional traits, mental models of the self and the world, personal themes in relationships, and how the individual fits into society across the life span—with special attention to the tasks of emerging adulthood that many of them now face.

Outstanding Features

The most outstanding feature of *Personality: A Systems Approach* is how its cumulative approach integrates theory and research in the field. This is best appreciated by carefully examining actual selections from the book itself. That said, a few central advantages are summarized here.

Cumulative Approach

Each part of the book lays the groundwork for the next. The study of the field's scope, methods, and theories (Part 1), lays the groundwork for the study of the parts of personality (Part 2). The study of personality's parts prepares a student to understand structural divisions and dynamic processes of personality (Part 3). Finally, the student is prepared to appreciate how personality's parts and its organization develop and grow over time (Part 4).

A Balanced, Thoughtful Use of Theories

Personality perspectives are introduced in Chapter 3 as part of the book's first section. Thereafter, the book draws on parts of those theories when needed to explain how a part of personality functions, rather than the theories being covered as whole topics in and of themselves. Relevant portions of different theories often appear together where their complementary perspectives often enrich discussion of a given topic. For example, the discussion of models of the self draws on the concepts of Freud's ego-ideal, Higgins's actual, ideal, and ought selves, and Markus's possible selves, and integrates such ideas with contemporary research.

Personality theories that are no longer making important research contributions to the field are deemphasized. Where a theory is of some historical interest but no longer motivates contemporary research, it is mentioned along with the new research that now carries along its tradition or addresses the same questions. Portions of older theories of continued central importance to the field are dealt with fully, for example defense mechanisms. The book's narrative guides students through the complexities and contradictions of the field, commenting freely on them. This smoothes the student's way and enhances the learning experience.

Contemporary Research Coverage

The systems organization makes it easy to fully integrate contemporary research in personality. Nearly 1,400 original sources of theory and research are cited across the twelve chapters of the book. This is competitive with that of any other textbook of its length. Moreover, a large portion of those sources date from 1980 forward, with many articles from the past several years. The research coverage is carefully organized according to whether it pertains to personality's definition, the parts of personality, personality organization, and/or personality development.

The textbook covers personality research that has not always appeared in personality texts before despite its obvious relevance to the field, including research on hypnosis, cognition and affect, intelligence and creativity, and self-regulation.

The Liberal Use of Case Examples

Wherever possible, the discussion of personality is clarified and enlivened by the use of examples from real people's lives. Some of these are historical and some are contemporary. For example, Chapter 4, Motivation and Emotion, opens with the case example of a reporter who is high insensation-seeking. Chapter 5, Interior Selves, Interior Worlds, explains mental models using a real-life interaction between a student and her professor (from Epstein, 1998). In the same chapter, another example describes a basketball player who imagined herself as someone else so as to improve her performance on the court. Examples are both integrated within the text and presented in *Case Study* boxes.

Addressing Contemporary Issues

The book is sensitive to such current issues of concern as personal versus social responsibility, group and ethnic diversity, cross-cultural psychology, and evolutionary psychology.

> **Life seems to take a zigzag course, instead of following a direct line toward what appears to be its goal. Growth too often proceeds by a series of maladjustments and corrections, by groping in the dark rather than by moving straight onward. The highest function of education is to conserve the life forces, to produce the best results with the least expenditure of energy.**
>
> Edwin Diller Starbuck

Pedagogical Features

There are many good ways for faculty to teach and for students to learn. This book is constructed so that it provides a foundation for the different ways of teaching and learning that are employed by highly trained faculty and their diverse students (Benassi & Fernald, 1993). Each chapter contains carefully planned pedagogical features to support the overall organization of the book and to support a variety of different approaches to learning and teaching:

- *An Advanced Organizer for the Chapter.* Each chapter begins with a list of central questions introducing what the chapter will cover.
- *Connecting Windows.* These windows connect material across different portions of the book without interrupting the flow of the narrative. They help the student find earlier, prerequisite material for understanding a section or find out more about a topic from a later section of the book.
- *A Floating (Marginal) Glossary.* Key terms are defined in the margins of the text as they are introduced.
- *Floating (Marginal) Quotations.* Relevant quotations are arranged in the margin alongside material to stimulate thinking about a topic.
- *Supplemental Boxed Features.* Each chapter is accompanied by boxes that enrich the main narrative with engaging features from the world of personality psychology. Examples of the four types of boxes follow.

Case Study

The Mysterious Social Activities of Robert Leuci

Consider the case of Robert Leuci, a former Chicago police officer. His personality shows signs of emotional stability, sensation-seeking, and extraordinary social skill. But that doesn't quite tell us everything about the individual. Rather, we want to know how these components are integrated together dynamically. They are rather like beads: but what sort of a beaded necklace do we get: one that goes from red through the colors of the rainbow to violet? Or, one where all the colors are haphazardly intermixed? Dynamics address this issue. An emotionally stable, sensation-seeking, high-achieving, socially adroit police officer, for example, might decide, through good works, to seek a promotion and use his social skills to lead his own team of officers.

What if, however, the police officers around him were corrupt? He might move to a different force, or he might do what Leuci did. Leuci became an undercover informant—a police officer working for federal prosecutors to try to clean up the police force around him. He was up against criminal corruption among police officers and attorneys, which blended into an underworld of bail bondsmen, dope pushers, and members of organized crime.

He coupled his desire for excitement with his social adroitness in astonishing ways. For example, at one point he was starting a meeting with a suspected criminal named DeStefano. They were together in a bar and DeStefano was becoming increasingly wary of whether Leuci was an informant.

Leuci chose a daring way to deflect suspicion from himself. As they were choosing their seats, Leuci said:

"Let's not sit next to the jukebox tonight, because I am not getting any kind of recording."

"That's not funny," said DeStefano. Adding to the provocation, Leuci elaborated on his theme, bragging, and craftily insisting he was working for the government. He pointed to a barmaid across the room, and said his transmitter was stuffed in her private parts. As Leuci later recounted it, "They all laughed, but DeStefano's laugh was dry." (Daley, 1981, p. 101)

As the psychologist Paul Ekman observed:

Leuci ridicules DeStefano by brazenly telling the truth—he really can't make a good recording near the jukebox, and he is working for the government. By admitting it so openly, and by joking about the waitress also wearing a concealed recorder . . . Leuci makes it difficult for DeStefano to pursue his suspicions without seeming foolish. (Ekman, 1985, p. 38)

The point to be made here about dynamics is that the parts of Leuci's personality really don't tell us about how he puts them together—the way he chooses to string together those qualities to perform his actions. Thus, at some point, it is useful to move beyond the discussion of individual parts alone, or even in combination, to begin to describe the individual's dynamics.

• *Case Study* boxes contain case studies of individuals (or behaviors) that illustrate points discussed in the text.

Research in Focus

The New Research on Developing Self-Control

A new era of research concerns how to best use and develop self-control. This research has important applications. The research conveys a new idea: that the best form of self-control to use will depend upon the situation—and even on a person's age and other factors. Three brief examples are given here: of eating, of thinking positively, and of pain control.

In regard to eating, recent research indicates that optimal strategies may change from childhood to adulthood. Recall that children in Mischel's study on self-control were presented with a treat they hoped to resist. The most successful children in the original preschool study succeeded by distracting themselves from the treat. Studies on adults who diet, however, suggest that actually concentrating on food can assist those who are on a weight loss plan. For example, Polivy and her colleagues (Polivy, 1976; Polivy, Herman, Hackett, & Kuleshnyk, 1986) found that when people trying to diet distracted themselves from eating, they sometimes ate more than they otherwise would. On the other hand, having people self-monitor their eating—actually writing down everything they eat—serves to reduce the amount eaten (Herman & Polivy, 1993; Prokop et al., 1991).

Trying to think positively also benefits from focused attention—but the specific matter one focuses on is important as well. Wenzlaff and

Bates (2000) wanted to help participants to think positively. They gave participants six scrambled words and asked them to make a five-word positive sentence out of them. For example, the scrambled words, "have life succeeded failed I at" could be unscrambled as, "I have succeeded at life," rather than the less desirable "I have failed at life." In one condition, participants were told to concentrate on composing only positive sentences. In another, they were told to avoid making any negative sentences. Later on, Wenzlaff and Bates discovered that those participants who concentrated on making pleasant sentences had far fewer intrusions of negative thoughts from the sentences, compared to the avoidance group and a control group.

But such focused concentration does not work the same way in pain relief. Fauerbach and colleagues (2002) divided hospital patients who were still in pain after receiving medication to try one of three strategies (in three experimental conditions): ignore the pain, imagine the pain as something positive, or distract themselves by listening to music. In such conditions, listening to music was by far the most effective method of self-control (Fauerbach et al., 2002).

As psychologists learn more about such methods of self control, the possibility arises that most of us or all of us will learn to feel, think, and act, more like we would wish to.

• *Research in Focus* boxes cover individual research issues or particular studies in detail.

- *Disciplinary Crossroads* boxes show how personality psychology interacts with other disciplines such as political science, literature, religion, and the sciences.

Disciplinary Crossroads

Deception in Myth and Literature

Psychologists may draw on human myth, history, and literature for a more global understanding of the ways dynamic actions are carried out. Military histories and literature tell us that acting and deception have been a part of human existence and played a critical role in human history for centuries. One of the most dramatic examples of such stories is that of the Trojan horse in the battle between Greece and Troy. According to Homer in the *Iliad*, and supplemented by fragments of other epics, Troy was an ancient city with great walls, lofty gates, and fine towers. One of Troy's rulers, Paris, during travel to Greece, eloped with Helen, a relation to the most powerful king in Greece of that time, Agamemnon. Helen was reputed to be the most beautiful woman in the world. Paris and Helen traveled back to Troy, the Greeks rounded up assistance and set off to reclaim her and sack Troy.

A series of inconclusive military engagements ensued for the next ten years. The Greeks patiently waited, because it had been foretold by a seer that their fortunes would change in the tenth year. In that year, the Greeks played a trick on the enemy. They built a hollow wooden horse, and placed within it several of their greatest warriors. They then burned their own camps at the outside of Troy, got in their ships, and set sail (but only out of eye-shot). When the Trojans found the horse, they interpreted it as a peace offering (along with the fact that the Greeks had left) and took the horse within their walled city and celebrated. At midnight, though, the warriors crept outside the horse, unleashed shots to signal the Greek fleet's return, and in the interim killed all the male firstborns in the city (Wood, 1985, pp. 21–26). For many years, Troy was thought to be a mythical place until an amateur archeologist, Heinrich Schliemann, finally unearthed it

(Wood, 1985). The course of the war, of course, is still told only by epics. Still, there exist no shortage of histories of actual wars played out with deception and surprise.

Individual deception was well known by Elizabethan England. One of the most beautiful juxtapositions of dramatic scenes occurs in Shakespeare's *Macbeth*, when King Duncan tells his son, Malcolm, about how he was betrayed by a follower. King Duncan instructs his son that he could not, nor could anyone, detect the follower's deceit until it was too late. He warns his son:

> There's no art
> To find the mind's construction in the face:
> He was a gentleman on whom I built
> An absolute trust. (Shakespeare, 1606/1936;
>   Act I, Scene IV)

The lesson is apparently well taken. Shortly after, Malcolm awakes at Macbeth's Castle, hearing a commotion. King Duncan, his father, has been murdered. Macbeth and his wife express their shock at the news—fraudulent shock, as Macbeth is the murderer—and accuse the King's attendants of the deed. As Malcolm and his brother, Donaldbain, watch, the audience cannot help but recall the late King's words to his son. Will Malcolm have learned not to trust appearances? Indeed, Malcolm pauses contemplatively over the scene. He and his brother remark to themselves, ". . . there's daggers in men's smiles . . ." and off they proceed, separately, for safety, to England and Ireland (Shakespeare, 1606/1936, Act II, Scene III). Recognizing they are unable to see behind the others' smiles, they depart to make time to better understand what has transpired and plan how to counter it. Later they succeed reclaiming the throne for themselves.

- *Inside the Field* boxes provide a special "inside edition" report of the field. These are designed to illustrate important characteristics of the field through descriptions of its contemporary and historical figures, of its debates, of its societies and associations.

Inside the Field

Funder's Laws

"Please do not memorize these laws," the personality psychologist David Funder has written. "I haven't memorized them myself. They are just my attempt to distill into a few aphorisms some observations of which, for some reason, I am particularly fond" (Funder, 2004, p. 9). I realized these laws had come of age during a thesis defense I chaired. In response to a question I asked the doctoral candidate about her thesis, she quoted one of Funder's laws (the Fourth) to explain, modestly, why her data was not as good as some of her committee members believed it to be. I was very impressed that she both knew and could apply Funder's laws in such a useful fashion. Funder's laws are not all about research methods, but the second, third, and fourth are. The page numbers all refer to Funder (2004).

Funder's Second Law: *There are no perfect indicators of personality; there are only clues, and clues are always ambiguous* . . . when you try to learn about or measure personality, you cannot base this endeavor on just one kind of information. You need many kinds (p. 19).

Funder's Second Law reflects the potential complexity of the personality system. Its many parts may be expressed through language, posture, and acts. Personality's expression may take place over a few seconds in a relatively straightforward situation, or take place according to strategic, long-term plans, or according to many other variations. For that reason, each

research finding about personality is a clue in a broader mystery story. Continuing along the same line, consider:

Funder's Fourth Law: *There are only two kinds of data.* The first kind is Terrible Data: data that are ambiguous, potentially misleading, incomplete and imprecise. The second kind is No Data. Unfortunately, there is no third kind, anywhere in the world (p. 49).

I do think our data are often better than both Funder—and the (now) Ph.D. who quoted the Fourth Law—make them out to be. Still, any single measure is certainly insufficient to tell a complete story about an individual. If you begin to despair about the research process, however, you can take some solace from Funder's Third Law. The Third Law reflects why research psychology is so important, even though it often is imperfect:

Funder's Third Law: *Something beats nothing, two times out of three.* . . . The only alternative to gathering information that might be misleading is to gather no information. That is not progress (p. 21).

I enjoy reading through these and other laws by Funder, which collectively provide a sophisticated perspective on a challenging field. David Funder is a personality psychologist currently at the University of California, Riverside, where he studies, among other topics, people's ability to accurately observe others' personalities.

- Each chapter concludes with a chapter review that briefly summarizes its content and poses questions with which students can test their knowledge.
- The book makes liberal use of graphics, diagrams, and pictures.

Supplements

An extensive Instructor's Manual and Test Bank, which includes syllabi, downloadable lectures, classroom demonstrations, exam items, and other instructional support, is available through the Allyn & Bacon Instructor's Resource Center at www.ablongman.com/irc. A computerized test bank (using TestGen software) and PowerPoint presentations are also available through the Instructor's Resource Center.

Go to www.ablongman.com/Mayer1e to view the companion website to *Personality: A Systems Approach.*

An associated book of readings, "Reading Personality Psychology" offers students guidance as to how to read different kinds of articles in the field, and provides sixteen original selections.

John D. Mayer received his B.A. from the University of Michigan and his M.A. and Ph.D. from the doctoral program in psychology at Case Western Reserve University. After obtaining his doctorate, he taught his first course in personality psychology at Case Western using Hall and Lindzey's classic text, *Theories of Personality*. Although he loved the book, the problems of teaching personality psychology by studying various theories led him to a career-long search for a better way to teach—and more generally, think about—personality psychology.

Dr. Mayer examined the contributions of mental abilities to personality in his postdoctoral work at Case Western Reserve, and the interactions of emotion and thought within personality, as a postdoctoral scholar at Stanford University.

Dr. Mayer returned to teaching personality psychology with his first faculty position at the State University of New York at Purchase. There he resumed his search for a better way to teach the course. In 1989, Mayer moved to the University of New Hampshire and began to publish a series of articles on the "systems framework for personality," a new approach to integrating the study of the discipline. The framework elaborated in those articles provides the basis for this new textbook.

While developing the systems framework and this textbook, Dr. Mayer published over ninety articles, chapters, books, and psychological tests. His 1990 articles on emotional intelligence, with Professor Peter Salovey of Yale University, are often credited with beginning scientific research on the topic. Dr. Mayer is coauthor of the Mayer-Salovey-Caruso Emotional Intelligence Test (MSCEIT), and coeditor, with J. Ciarrochi and J. P. Forgas of *Emotional Intelligence in Everyday Life: A Scientific Inquiry*.

Dr. Mayer has served on the editorial boards of *Psychological Bulletin*, the *Journal of Personality*, the *Journal of Personality and Social Psychology*, and the *Review of General Psychology*. He has been the recipient of an Individual National Research Service Award from the *National Institute of Mental Health*, and has been a senior research fellow of the United States Army Research Institute. In addition to many years of teaching university classes, Professor Mayer also has lectured to diverse audiences throughout the United States and abroad on topics related to personality psychology.

Acknowledgments

The idea of writing a personality textbook emerged most consciously for me in 1986 when I was a beginning instructor at the State University of New York. There, I encountered Joseph Jansen III of Norton Publishers, who took an interest in my views on the field, and the original handouts that I was using with my students. Mr. Jansen suggested those handouts might form the basis of a book, although I am not sure he could have foreseen how many years it would take until the book's first edition was completed.

I drew on many skills I learned from many teachers to create and complete this textbook. I was particularly fortunate to have parents, Edna and Arthur Mayer, who encouraged my learning and education. I attended the Ardsley, New York public schools, where I was privileged to learn from such wonderful instructors as Vincent Carravaglio, John Conroy, and Robert Clancy, among many others. At the University of Michigan, I encountered more excellent educators including professors Bert Hornbeck, Peter Ferran, and Warren Hecht.

At Case Western Reserve, where I received my Ph.D., a number of faculty members fostered my education in psychology, and in personality. These included Sandra Russ, Irving Weiner, Douglas Schultz, and especially Douglas Detterman. My learning continued under the sponsorship of Gordon Bower at Stanford University where I was a postdoctoral scholar.

As my classroom notes gradually evolved into this book, my undergraduate students provided much helpful feedback, and I later was the beneficiary of comments from a string of highly talented graduate students including Marc Brackett, Elise Cantor, Kevin Carlsmith, Heather Chabot, Mike Faber, Glenn Geher, Zorana Ivcevic, Dennis Mitchell, Alex Stevens, and Xiaoyan Xu.

I also am grateful for the many colleagues who provided support for the project. At the University of New Hampshire these included almost everyone, but especially Victoria Banyard, Victor Benassi, Ellen Cohn, Peter Fernald, Michelle Leichtman, Kathleen McCartney, Edward O'Brien, David Pillemer, and Rebecca Warner. Beyond UNH, my colleagues and friends, Peter Salovey and David Caruso, provided further support and encouragement.

In the Fall of 2001, I was fortunate enough to have lunch with Nancy Forsyth, then the president of Allyn & Bacon, who inquired about any book plans I had. By Spring, 2002, the book was under contract with Allyn & Bacon, with plans to issue classroom-test editions through Pearson Custom Publishing, so as to prepare the book for more general release. With the help of Grace Sullivan, then my local A&B representative, I began my collaboration with a series of Pearson Custom editors including Tanja Eise, Kim Brugger, Rebecca Faber, and Scott Salesses, who, together, ushered the developing book through three editions. Several University of New Hampshire students, among them Elise Cantor, Nicole Frechette, and Kate Edwards helped assemble those volumes.

Professors Marc Brackett, Robert Eckstein, Zorana Ivcevic, and Dubravka Vidmar all used the books in their classrooms, and provided very helpful suggestions for revisions.

The professionals at Allyn & Bacon continued to guide the volume editorially. My acquisitions editors included Carolyn Merrill, Karon Bowers, and Susan Hartman, and my developmental editors included Mary Connell Hanson, Richard Wilcox, and Christine Poolos.

The book received a final go-ahead from Karon Bowers in the Spring of 2005. A new group of editorial experts and other specialists then began work, including my internal production editor, Claudine Bellanton, and project coordinator, Denise Botelho. Others contributed to the book's design, photographs, and copyright permissions. These included especially Jean Hammond, Laurie Frankenthaler, Deb Hanlon, and Robert Tonner.

Pamela Laskey helped develop the marketing plan for the book. My father, Arthur C. Mayer, lent his considerable professional expertise to help refine some of the marketing copy for the book. I would like to thank the reviewers as well: Timothy Atchison, West Texas A&M University; Barbara R. Beaver, University of Wisconsin at Whitewater; Robert K. Bothwell, University of Louisiana at Lafayette; David N. Entwistle, Malone College; Dean Frost, Portland State University; Sandra M. Harris, Troy State University; Deborah L. Jones, Barry University; Seth Kalichman, University of Connecticut; Travis Langley, Henderson State University; Patricia L. Mather, Illinois Central College; Diane Mello-Goldner, Pine Manor College; Leslie Minor-Evans, Central Oregon Community College; David W. Shantz, Oakland University; and David Wasieleski, Valdosta State University.

The last, most special thanks go to my wife and daughter, who were so patient and supportive during the long development of this book. My wife, Deborah, read and commented on portions of the manuscript, helping especially with its clarity and tone in key places. She and my daughter helped me find the time to write this book, and bore with me as it was revised, rerevised, and entered the final publication process. They also insisted, on occasion, that I take time off from working on the book. They taught me that when I take the time to enjoy life with them, the book I write is the better for it.

I extend my grateful and heartfelt thanks to all those mentioned, and anyone I omitted either inadvertently or due to space constraints. This book cannot possibly reflect the quality of all the wonderful teaching, guidance, and support I have received, for I am an imperfect student, but I believe that the book's quality has been immeasurably strengthened by what others have provided me.

Part 1
Examining Personality

*P*art 1, Examining Personality introduces the personality system, and the field
that studies it. Many people think about their own and others' personalities.
Psychologists, though, have developed formal theories and research methods to help
them study personality. Their approach provides a scientific basis for their
understanding of the personality system. In this first part of the book, personality is
defined, and some of the theoretical perspectives and research methods employed in
its study are discussed.

Chapter 1

What Is Personality?

What questions motivate the study of personality? What is personality? How did the field of personality psychology start, and how did it develop? What can be learned from a course in personality psychology? These questions are the departure point for the book. Understanding personality can help you better understand yourself and others.

- **What Are the Fundamental Questions Addressed by Personality Psychology?**
  "Who am I?" and "What is my future?" are just two of the questions from antiquity that still motivate the field today. These questions can be used to trace some of the intellectual history of personality psychology—and to help identify some of its current concerns.

- **What Is the Personality System?**
  Figuring out what to study starts with a consideration of what personality itself is. Personality has been defined in somewhat different ways throughout history, but the consensus view is that it is a system—the system that organizes all the other psychological subsystems such as perception, memory, and emotions.

- **What Is the Field of Personality Psychology?**
  To study personality, we will draw on theory and research from the field of personality psychology. The discipline appears to be growing and many people recognize it to be of considerable importance. How someone becomes a personality psychologist, and what such individuals do, are examined.

- **Why Study Personality Psychology?**
  What makes the study of personality important? From its study one can hope to learn a bit about oneself and others with whom one interacts. Some examples of research that inform such learning are discussed.

- **How Should One Study Personality?**
  In this book we will briefly examine personality methods and personality theories. Then, we will continue by looking at personality's parts, its organization, and its development.

What Are the Fundamental Questions Addressed by Personality Psychology?

Big Questions and Science

Psychology: A scientific discipline that studies how the mind works.

Personality Psychology: A scientific discipline that addresses the questions, "Who am I?" and "Who are others?" Personality psychology involves the study of a person's mental system, with a focus on its largest, most important parts, how those parts are organized, and how they develop over time.

Who am I? What is my future? Big questions such as these have motivated an intellectual odyssey from humanity's earliest times to the present. How did the universe begin? What is life? Over time, sciences evolved to address such questions. Astronomy examined the universe; biology examined life; and psychology examined the mind. As each science took on its modern form, each became a sophisticated field dealing with hundreds of topics. But many of the sciences also retained a branch or branches that reached back to the basic questions of philosophy. For example, the area of astronomy called cosmology addresses how the universe began, and certain areas of biology deal with the origins of life (Rosenberg, 2000).

Psychology, too, addresses such big fundamental questions. **Psychology** is a scientific discipline concerned with the question of how a person's mind works. That includes such questions as how a neuron works, how the eyes sense, the structure of the brain, and how people understand language. **Personality psychology** is a discipline within psychology that asks how the major psychological processes such as motives, emotions, and thoughts, operate together—and what those processes mean for a person's life. The personality psychologist's specialty is looking at the person comprehensively (see Hall & Lindzey, 1978; Funder, 2004; Little, 2005).

> All inquiries carry with them some element of risk.
>
> Carl Sagan

Because personality psychologists examine an individual's mental life by taking a very broad, big picture perspective on the individual, they provide a critical connection between the science of psychology, on the one hand, and the philosophical questions about human nature and how to live one's life, on the other. That is, personality psychologists, in particular, are responsible for addressing big questions such as "Who am I?"

Many of the fundamental questions identify problems of practical importance. Developmentally speaking, the "Who am I?" question often arises for people as they enter young adulthood (Erikson, 1963; Marcia et al., 1993). Questions such as "Who am I?" often emerge out of conflicts felt by the individual asking them (Alexander, 1942; Woodhouse, 1984, p. 4). Here are some versions of the "Who am I?" question from students who wrote into an advice column called, "Big Questions, Real Answers":

- "My school has kids of all different races, but I'm afraid to make friends with them. Am I a racist?" (Perry, 2001b)

- "I daydream a lot. Does that mean I'm lazy?" (Perry, 2001c)

- "My older brother is always calling me stupid, a moron, a loser. I try to ignore it, but sometimes it gets to me and I think I am stupid. What can I do?" (Perry, 2001a)

Though these questions are about "Who am I?" they also reflect an important variation of the question, "Who am I in the eyes of others?" The answer may vary depending upon who the others are (Jopling, 2000, p. 166).

Questions and Inquiry

We can regard questions such as "Who am I?" as generating an intellectual path from antiquity to the present. That path can be followed so as to help understand the history behind personality psychology. There are a number of such big questions about identity and mental life that personality psychologists have sought to address in their research. Three questions in particular can help organize these ideas (though others are possible): "Who am I?" (and "why is it so hard to know ourselves?"); "Why are people different?"; and "What is my future?" Asking and wondering about such questions can organize and help our learning (Bonwell & Eison, 1991, pp. 7–31; Hamilton, 1985). These questions sensitize us to the personal and intellectual quests that helped establish the foundations of personality psychology in advance of the contemporary field (Roback, 1928; Winter & Barenbaum, 1999).

> One does not get to know that one exists until one rediscovers oneself in others.
>
> Goethe

Who Am I?

Knowing Ourselves

Consider: "Who am I?" During the years from 800 BCE to approximately 200 CE, a temple stood at Delphi in ancient Greece, erected to the God Apollo (La Coste-Messelière,

The Temple at Delphi was where ancient Greeks went to ask the Oracle to prophesize about the future. "Know Thyself," was engraved on a column near the entrance to the shrine—an early expression of the value of self-understanding.

1950). At its entrance was the command, "Know thyself," carved into a column by Chiron of Sparta (Diodurus, 1935/1960, Book IX, 9, 10). The ancient Greek philosopher Socrates refers to the command and asked why it was so prominent. Socrates agreed with the command—in fact, he professed to be interested in self-knowledge above all else (Griswold, 1986, p. 68). For Socrates, asking "Who I am?" is a moral necessity if one is to lead a good life (Griswold, 1986, pp. 2, 7; Jopling, 2000, p. 1).

Implicit Personality Theory: The informal, often unnoticed or unconscious system of beliefs an individual holds about how his or her own personality operates, and how the personalities of other people operate.

As we develop an understanding of ourselves we construct an **implicit personality theory**—our own informal, and sometimes unstated, theory of who we are and how others behave (Bruner & Tagiuri, 1954). For example, students beginning the personality psychology courses come in with fairly elaborate implicit theories—as featured in the Research in Focus box. These theories, which we build up from our own experience and observation, may become quite sophisticated—but they may not necessarily conform to any standards of scientific inquiry.

Why Is It So Hard to Know Ourselves?

Although at first it seemed that knowing oneself was simply a matter of desiring to do so, later thinkers regarded self-understanding as more tenuous and challenging. By the time of the middle ages, an individual's personality seemed driven by all sorts of mysterious forces—even at times by a spirit or devil. In 1775, Father Johann Gassner, an exorcist of the time, claimed that he could cure many illnesses by expelling the devil from people he believed to be possessed. He mounted a number of public demonstrations in which he cured people suffering from tremors, tics, and fatigue (Ellenberger, 1981, pp. 53–57).

Personality can never develop unless the individual chooses his own way, consciously and with moral deliberation.
Carl G. Jung

Research in Focus

Casual Thinking and Scientific Thinking about People

Understanding others is often crucial to our social well-being. Most people recognize different types of people around them—the warm type, the brain, the jock, and so forth—and act differently depending upon who they are dealing with. Knowing another person closely also invites predictions of how the individual will react or behave. Just before we tell our jealous friend about her ex-boyfriend's misfortune, we might suspect, "This will make her happy." Most people's judgments are intuitive—a kind of casual collection of information drawn from personal experience, observation, and the ideas of others.

These informal theories, although often unstated and even unnoticed, help people to predict how others will behave. Bruner and Tagiuri (1954) introduced the term *implicit personality theory* to describe the person's unstated sets of assumptions or ideas about their own and others' behaviors. Implicit personality theories are often a research topic themselves.

To help identify your own implicit theories of personality it helps to ask yourself, "What questions do you sometimes ask yourself when meeting a new acquaintance?" (Anderson, Rosenfeld, & Cruikshank, 1994.) The answer to that question—what you consider important to know about someone—may indicate what you think motivates others, or simply what you like and enjoy in others (or wish to avoid). After you mull that over, you might consider how intensely personal the answer to the question is. That is, your concerns will be quite different from the concerns of someone else (Kelly, 1955).

In a survey of beginning personality psychology students at the University of Central Florida, Alvin Wang (1997) found that student's assumptions about personality varied in

a number of important ways. First, about 53 percent of the students believed in the importance of watching actions, rather than listening to what a person says, whereas the remainder were interested in listening. As another example, about 27 percent of the students thought that people (and their personalities) existed on earth for a higher purpose. Only 12 percent of the students thought personality was heavily influenced by genetics. Eighty-five percent believed in unconscious influences before starting the course, and about the same percent also believed people were very complex to study. Only about 25 percent thought personality could easily change.

Anderson and colleagues (1994) asked students in a personality course to develop their own theories of personality as a semester-long project. As they did so, the students began to realize that many of the parts of the theories about others were unconnected to one another. For example, their theory might include the idea that other people sometimes get defensive, but without understanding the motivation behind the defensiveness. In addition, students often discovered that the assumptions they made about personality were contradicted by research evidence.

This course is designed to help you improve your implicit theory of personality by providing some established research findings about people that can be worked into it. Even trained psychologists' theories often start with their own implicit ideas (Monte, 1999, p. 26; Wegner & Vallacher, 1977, p. 21). By bringing more formal personality theories to light and studying them using the scientific method, the best of those ideas can be collected together and used with greater confidence.

As the biological and social sciences grew, however, scientific explanations supplanted the idea that people were possessed. Anton Mesmer, for example, discovered "animal magnetism" or "animal gravity"—a means of influencing other people that today we refer to as hypnosis. Mesmer was able to perform cures similar to those of Gassner using animal magnetism. Although Mesmer's animal magnetism was only poorly understood at the time, his attempt to create a scientific basis for such cures opened the door to the empirical examination of suggestibility and the unconscious.

> No man can climb out beyond the limitations of his own character.
>
> John Morley

A century later, the philosopher Schopenhauer (1819/1966) portrayed individuals as driven by blind instincts and deluded by their own wills. Furthermore, he said, the will blocks out what is unpleasant to it, and this may be responsible for mental illness. Soon after, Eduard Von Hartmann (1869) published the "Philosophy of the Unconscious," in which he collected examples of how people deceive themselves, surprise themselves, and otherwise pit nonconscious ideas against the conscious (cited in Ellenberger, 1981, pp. 208–210). Just two decades later, Freud would create an even more comprehensive theory of the unconscious. Still today, contemporary research makes clear that the problem of self-knowing is considerable (Dunning, 2005; Vogt & Randall, 2005; Wilson & Dunn, 2004).

How and Why Are People Different?

People often ask not only, "Who am I?" but also, "Who are you?" The answers are different because people differ. The ancient Greek Theophrastus wondered, "Why it is that while all Greece lies under the same sky and all the Greeks are educated alike, it has befallen us to have characters variously constituted?" (cited in Roback, 1928, p. 9). From Theophrastus's question first emerged **characterology**, a literary endeavor to describe the different sorts of individuals who existed. An example of a character description from Theophrastus concerned the flatterer. The flatterer, as Theophrasus defined him, was someone who engaged in a degrading form of companionship that might, however, bring him or her profit.

Characterology: A literary tradition in which an author writes a series of short descriptions about the different character types he or she has recognized. Each description of a type is designed to bring forth a definite feeling of recognition in the reader that he or she has seen an example of that type of person as well.

> The flatterer is a person who will say as he walks with another, "Do you observe how people are looking at you? This happens to no man in Athens but you. A compliment was paid to you yesterday. . . . More than thirty persons were sitting there; the question was started, Who is our foremost man? Everyone mentioned you first, and ended by coming back to your name. . . . (cited in Roback, 1928, p. 10)

As writers outlined the different characters, early physicians tried to explain how those differences came about. One early scientific approach to this question involved the study of temperament. **Temperament** refers to the physiologically based motivational and emotional styles people exhibit. In the fourth century BCE, the great Greek physician Hippocrates, and later, Galen, developed a four-fold classification of personality, dividing people into cholerics, melancholics, phlegmatics, and the sanguine.

Temperament: The study of different, largely innate, motivational and emotional styles that are repeated across people.

Choleric: One of four ancient personality types. The choleric type is quick to action, has a short temper, and is lean.

In the four-fold system, the **choleric** type was described as tall, thin, and easily irritated. Such a person easily became enraged and tended to hold grudges as well;

Melancholic: One of four ancient personality types. The melancholic type is slow to move, self-preoccupied, and most distinctly, unhappy and depressed.

Sanguine: One of four ancient personality types. The sanguine type is cheerful, lively, and easy-going.

Phlegmatic: One of four ancient personality types; the phlegmatic type has little energy, is prone to eating too much, and is somewhat indifferent in disposition.

this was all a consequence of too much yellow bile. The **melancholic** type was contemplative in a sad, resigned way; he or she lacked energy and expected the worst in everything; this was a consequence of too much black bile. The best personality type was thought to be the **sanguine** type. This even-tempered individual was generally cheerful and hopeful and displayed a ruddy complexion. He or she could be assertive but not angry or vindictive. The sanguine type's pleasant disposition was a consequence of more blood than the other types. The worst personality type was probably the **phlegmatic** type, who slept too much and was perceived to be dull, cowardly, sluggish and overweight. This individual suffered from an excess amount of phlegm (think about how you feel when you have a cold!).

Although starting out as a purely literary endeavor, philosophers carefully examined such works and drew out their implications. Francis Bacon, for example (1561–1626), suggested that some people's minds would be better suited to certain occupations than others. Some people, he said, excel at thinking about many matters at once, whereas others' minds are suited to focusing on just a few matters; some people do things very quickly, whereas others are more suited to work on projects that take a great deal of time (Bacon, 1861/2001; Book VII, Chapter 3). Today, many areas of personality psychology study these variations from person to person, termed individual differences, and the implications such differences hold for a person's life.

What Will My Future Be?

Finally, consider "What will my future be?" To the extent that one has control over it, philosophers ask how one can lead one's life to the fullest and act in the best ways possible. For example, in fifth century BCE China, Confucius worked out a system—the Analects—for instructing people on how to bring about harmony in a socially chaotic world. Aspects of Confucianism involve the importance of education and overcoming the self (Stevenson & Haberman, 1998, pp. 32–38). There are many other such systems developed throughout the world. This question of how a given life pattern can influence one's future is one that contemporary personality psychology also addresses.

To return to the temple at Delphi for a moment, one of the reasons ancient Athenians and Spartans traveled there was to have the future foretold. Within the shrine an oracle—a young woman from the town—sat amidst vapors in a cavelike area. She spoke in tongues, probably under the influence of ethylene, a volcanic gas with hallucinogenic effects (Spiller, Hale, & De Boer, 2002).

Both assessing people—and foretelling something about their future—is facilitated through the use of mental testing. The first reliable records of mental ability tests indicate their use in the second century BCE in China. There, the tests were employed as civil service examinations, so as to place people in government positions; a more limited use of mental tests arose in ancient Greece (Bowman, 1989; Doyle, 1974). From their beginnings in the Middle Ages, European universities awarded degrees and honors on the basis of formal examinations. Psychological testing continued to focus on mental ability through the beginning of the twentieth century (Goodenough, 1949). Then it broadened into tests of attitudes, temperamental styles, and personality more generally as the twentieth century progressed.

The advent of personality tests contributed to such issues as, "Who am I" and "How are people different?" for as soon as measurement was possible, clarifications

Inside the Field

Does Becoming a Personality Psychologist Influence How You View Others?

"One of the downsides of attending dinner parties," wrote one personality psychologist, "is telling people I am a psychologist and then hearing them say things such as, 'I bet you're trying to figure me out,' or 'Oh, good, maybe you can tell me what makes my husband (wife, son, daughter, friend, etc.) tick'" (McAdams 1965, p. 368).

Is there something about studying how the mind works that changes a personality psychologist's outlook on other people? Let us begin at one end of the spectrum of psychologists in this regard—the psychotherapist—whose job it often is to listen to others and analyze their mental lives. Farber and Golden (1997) described the outlook of a typical therapist-in-training:

> Gradually, my classmates and I are being initiated into a unique culture in which psychological mindedness reigns . . . [we are with those] who share our fascination with human nature and with other people's inner worlds . . . I now listen both to patients and to myself, trying to hear what is said and what is not said, as if I were a third party . . . At a recent party with friends, someone joked about needing a drink to combat the stress of everyday life. Everyone laughed in implied agreement, then went on with social pleasantries. My inclination was to pursue the comment but social dictates held me back. (pp. 212–215)

At the other end of the extreme are some psychologists—those who study, say, the immune system, or learning in various animal species—whose outlook toward people may not be much different than that of computer scientists, educators, or engineers. (There is, of course, wide variability both among therapists and researchers.)

Along this continuum of outlooks, personality psychologists probably fall somewhere around the middle. Much of the time, personality psychologists may simply notice an individual's most visible traits: Whether the person is outgoing or shy, conscientious or not, warm or hostile. Most people detect such differences, but perhaps personality psychologists add clearer labels to them (some of which you will learn in this course).

Although personality psychologists are commonly researchers and teachers, they do sometimes become analytical about relationships. The personality psychologist Dan McAdams (1996) wanted to explore what it meant to know someone. As an example, he described how, while driving home, his wife and he had analyzed the personality of a woman they met at a party from which they were returning. The two of them discussed how their feelings about the woman changed over the evening (they ended up liking her), things they learned about her, and hypotheses about how her personality operated. "My wife and I," he wrote, "were enjoying the rather playful exercise of trying to make sense of persons. In the professional enterprise of personality psychology, however, making sense of persons is or should be the very raison d'être of the discipline" (McAdams, 1995, p. 368).

Although personality psychologists do try to understand others, most of them come to it with a considerable sense of humility as to what they can and cannot know about others. Many would endorse this comment, also by an eminent personality psychologist:

> It is difficult for humankind to view itself objectively. What is needed . . . [is] an ability to face who we are and, in particular, how we practice our science, and to do this with courage, honesty, and with an absence of illusion, which is no simple matter given our all-too-human nature. (Epstein, 1997, p. 7)

Test Yourself: How Psychologically Minded Are You?

People who are psychologically minded ask a lot of questions such as "Who am I?" and "Who are you?" Psychologists have become interested in psychological mindedness. Are you the sort of person who asks these questions? Find out by answering these six items from a longer scale, as shown here.

	1 = Strongly disagree	2	3	4 = Strongly agree
1. I really enjoy trying to figure other people out.				
2. I am always curious about the reasons people behave as they do.				
3. I am willing to change old habits to try a new way of doing things.				
4. Talking about your worries to another person helps you to understand your problems better.				
5. Usually, if I can feel an emotion, I can identify it.				
6. Understanding the reasons you have deep down for acting in certain ways is important.				

Scoring: Calculate your total score by simply adding up the responses you made. The range of average scoring lies between 13 and 15 points. The more you agree with these statements, the higher your psychological mindedness is.

Source: Test items adapted from Shill & Lumley (2000), pp. 140–141. Reproduced with permission from *Psychology and Psychotherapy: Theory, Research and Practice* © The British Psychological Society.

could be made to the understanding of how people differed, and, through statistical reasoning and techniques, future prediction became possible. For example, once good measures of sociability were in place, it became possible to compare the future life patterns of those who were high in sociability versus those who were low in sociability. In this way, psychology began to address how personality influenced an individual's future. Knowing the future remains relevant to psychology today, each time we predict from personality to life outcomes (Lubinski, 2000). Together, the questions "Who am I?" and "What will my future be?" can also be interpreted as reflecting a more personal desire to be more than one is, to ask, "How shall I make myself more of a person?" (Greenbie, 1932, pp. 1, 21).

Different Kinds of Answers

The exact answer to the question "Who am I (or you)?" or "How should you live your life?" or any other question will be dependent upon the circumstances in which it is asked and the person who is asked (Gasking, 1946; Hamblin, 1967, p. 49). A friend might tell us that we are kind or caring or have more strengths than we know. During an argument, however, that same friend may tell us that we are stubborn and thick-headed. Over time, comments from parents, friends, and others lead us to build up a particular view of ourselves. Seeing ourselves as others see us is sometimes referred to as the looking-glass self (Cooley, 1902; G. H. Mead, 1934; Tice, 1992).

Psychological Mindedness: A person's trait or predisposition to analyze one's own and others mental characteristics, and how those mental characteristics lead to a person's behaviors.

Of course, some things remain hidden inside. Researchers such as David Funder (1995; 1999) have found that observers are fairly accurate in perceiving readily noticeable traits such as how talkative, lively, and sociable a person is. For more internal sorts of qualities, however, such as intelligence, observers are less accurate.

Psychologists sometimes refer to people who are interested in such questions as psychologically minded. **Psychological mindedness** refers to an interest in understanding relationships among psychological processes and how they influence a person's life (Shill & Lumley, 2000). If the questions here—and the types of answers provided by personality psychology—are of interest to you, then you may wish to continue by considering the question of what personality is. You can also take some items from a scale of psychological mindedness in the Test Yourself feature.

What Is the Personality System?

A System of Systems

In 1887, Wilhelm Wundt founded the first psychological laboratory in Leipzig, and that is often taken as the date modern psychology began. Experimental psychologists of the time addressed such issues as "What is sensation?" "What is perception?" and "What is learning?" Wundt saw that smaller psychological systems—to which those questions were addressed—built into larger ones in a hierarchy of complexity. For example, at the middle level of complexity were systems such as motivation, emotion, and intelligence. At the most global, highest level, for Wundt (1897, p. 26) might be the "total development of a psychical personality." For Wundt and others the level of psychical personality was where the answers to the larger personal and social questions would be found.

Molecular-Molar Continuum (or Dimension): A dimension or continuum along which various scientific systems of study can be located, from those that are smallest to those that are largest.

Molecular Systems: Systems that are relatively small, such as atoms and molecules.

Molar Systems: Systems that are relatively large, such as the economy or the ecosphere.

Scientists often employ a **molecular-molar continuum** to organize what is being studied within a given field, and across fields as well. The molecular-molar continuum is one that divides smaller objects of study from larger ones. **Molecular** things are relatively small. Examples of smaller, molecular, psychological processes include sensing the color orange, feeling a momentary pang of envy, or thinking that an apricot is a fruit (see Figure 1.1, bottom row). These mental processes or events are small because they involve individual sensations (e.g., of orange), emotions (e.g., envy) and cognitions (e.g., of an apricot). More **molar** psychological processes are larger and combine smaller processes. For example, feeling envious of a friend who owns a beautiful painting of a bright orange apricot combines the smaller psychological processes just discussed into a larger whole (see Figure 1.1, row 2). The larger whole is molar relative to the individual parts.

FIGURE 1.1

Wilhelm Wundt's Personality Psychology

Wilhelm Wundt, one of the founders of modern psychology, saw personality as the global system that integrated other major psychological subsystems.

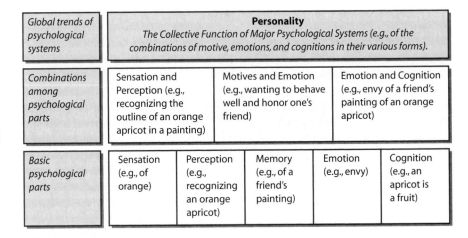

Global trends of psychological systems	**Personality** *The Collective Function of Major Psychological Systems (e.g., of the combinations of motive, emotions, and cognitions in their various forms).*				
Combinations among psychological parts	Sensation and Perception (e.g., recognizing the outline of an orange apricot in a painting)		Motives and Emotion (e.g., wanting to behave well and honor one's friend)	Emotion and Cognition (e.g., envy of a friend's painting of an orange apricot)	
Basic psychological parts	Sensation (e.g., of orange)	Perception (e.g., recognizing an orange apricot)	Memory (e.g., of a friend's painting)	Emotion (e.g., envy)	Cognition (e.g., an apricot is a fruit)

Even feeling envious over a painting is still fairly modest in size compared to some larger psychological processes. Consider that the person might momentarily think of taking the envied painting and at the same time experience a moral correction and decide to leave the painting where it is. Together, such a reaction represents the collective action of many psychological subsystems: perception, emotion, motivation, morality, and a sense of self.

For Wundt and those who came after, understanding the combined operation of all the major psychological systems together—the most molar level of psychology—involved the study of personality psychology (Wundt, 1897, pp. 25–26). Figure 1.1 shows how Wundt saw the more molecular psychological processes building into personality psychology. Wundt's definition was a systems definition at a time when scientists had become increasingly interested in systems (Whitehead, 1929; Laszlo, 1975). And, Wundt concluded, it was the study of personality that would best allow psychology to address the big questions about identity and how to live.

What Is a System?

Simply put, a system is any set of interrelated parts. As applied to personality, the parts might be mental mechanisms such as short-term memory, mental models such as one's view of oneself, or a trait, such as whether or not one is sociable. These parts are interrelated, as for example, if one is sociable, one will learn and remember different things about oneself than if one prefers more solitary activities.

Systems can be simple or complex, rational or haphazard-seeming. An example of a physical system which is comprehensible in many ways is the solar system. The solar system follows many rules—rules that make it possible to construct charts of planetary orbits, to predict such things as eclipses, and to calculate the possibilities for space travel (see Figure 1.2). By contrast, there are many other systems that are less predictable and more challenging to fathom. Rube Goldberg, an early twentieth-century cartoonist, took delight in imagining new versions of mechanical systems of his time. His *Automatic Dishwasher* was inspired by the already-workable versions of dishwashers then available. Goldberg's model included certain departures from what was then typical, however. For example, it relied on the activity of a mouse (See Figure 1.3, letter B). The photo caption explains how the system works from start to finish, and also sug-

The Solar System
Some systems can be elegant and highly predictable, such as the movement of the planets within our solar system.

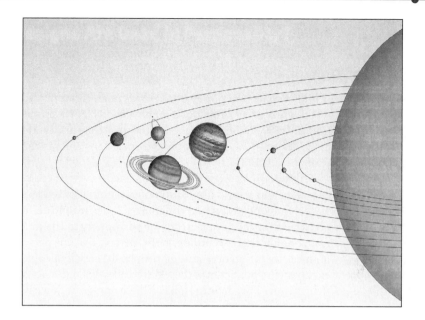

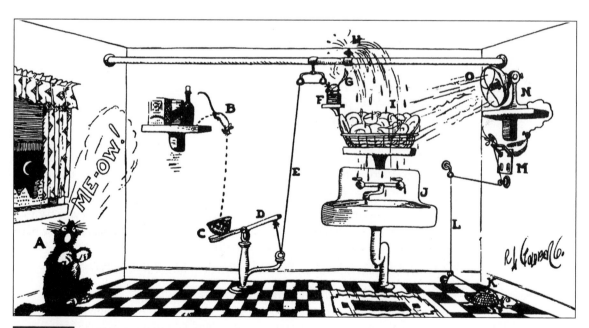

Automatic Dishwasher

Some systems are irregular, as is this *Automatic Dishwasher,* envisioned by Rube Goldberg, an early twentieth-century cartoonist, who wrote: *When spoiled Tomcat (A) discovers he is alone he lets out a yell which scares mouse (B) into jumping into basket (C), causing lever end (D) to rise and pull string (E) which snaps automatic cigar-lighter (F). Flame (G) starts fire sprinkler (H). Water runs on dishes (I) and drips into sink (J). Turtle (K), thinking he hears babbling brook babbling, and having no sense of direction, starts wrong way and pulls string (L) which turns on switch (M) that starts electric glow heater (N). Heat ray (O) dries the dishes. . . . If the cat and the turtle get on to your scheme and refuse to cooperate, simply put the dishes on the front porch and pray for rain.*

gests a backup plan in case of a malfunction. The personality system is a bit more regular and rational than Goldberg's dishwashing system—but probably more complex.

Defining Personality

Wundt's definition of personality as a system that organized psychological systems was the first of a number of similar versions. For example, the psychoanalyst Prince (1921, p. 532), referred to personality as: "the sum-total of all the biological innate dispositions . . . and the acquired dispositions and tendencies . . ." (cf. Allport, 1937, p. 48; Lewin, 1935).

Although the systems definition had the widest currency in personality psychology, there was a loyal opposition of psychologists who wanted to define personality as the study of individual differences. The **individual differences** definition emphasizes that the proper study of personality is the analysis of how people differ from one another. According to this perspective, the personality psychologist should (a) measure differences among people, (b) classify people according to these differences, and (c) predict how these differences will influence a person's behavior at a particular time. This definition has the advantage of describing accurately what a great number of personality psychologists do; it does, however, have certain disadvantages.

> **Individual Differences:** A topic of scientific study that addresses the questions of how one person differs from another. Some people use this as an alternative definition of personality psychology.

One of the drawbacks of this definition is that it reduces personality psychology to a single focus—the study of individual differences. Some personality psychologists, however, are interested in describing consistencies in personality across all individuals (e.g., Freud believed most everyone had an ego). In a widely repeated passage, Kluckhohn and Murray noted that each individual is in certain ways:

> like all other people
> like some other people, and
> like no other people. (1953, p. 53)

Personality research addresses all three of these possibilities at one time or another. That is one reason that the individual differences approach is incomplete.

Pervin (1990) noted that, in his own textbook, he struggled between using an individual differences approach and a more general systems approach:

> . . . it is my sense that . . . [the study of an organization of parts] is what is truly distinctive about the field, and that recognizing this would lead to a greater emphasis in research on the system aspects of personality functioning. (p. 12)

Wundt, Allport, and many others' system definitions are similar to the one used here in this text, which states,

> **Personality:** Personality is the organized, developing, psychological system within the individual that represents the collective action of that individual's major psychological subsystems.

> **Personality** is the organized, developing, system within the individual that represents the collective action of that individual's major psychological subsystems.

A more light-hearted definition of personality comes from the mid-century physician and psychiatrist, Karl Menninger, who said that

> . . . it means the individual as a whole, his height and weight and loves and hates and blood pressure and reflexes; his smiles and hopes and bowed legs and enlarged tonsils. . . . (1930, p. 21)

Menninger's description is delightful; but should definitions of personality psychology really include bowed legs and enlarged tonsils? To find out we need to consider more carefully where the personality system is located.

Locating the Personality System

The Molecular-Molar Dimension

Sciences commonly identify their subjects of study according to a series of more-or-less universal dimensions that describe them. For example, Wundt had employed the molecular-molar dimension to describe how personality was a global system made up of smaller psychological subsystems. Let us now extend that molecular-molar dimension to more completely connect personality to other scientific areas of study.

The vertical dimension of Figure 1.4 shows an extended version of the molecular-molar continuum first shown in Figure 1.1. This time, the lowest level begins with biological processes on the bottom, which include neurons communicating, the function of brain areas, and the like. The middle level shows personality psychology—the study of larger psychological systems. Specific details of individual psychological processes—individual sensations, emotions, and cognitions—are omitted to keep the picture simple. The molecular-molar dimension can be extended upward past personality to larger systems, as well. Recall that personality is the most molar topic at the psychological level. More molar systems than personality, therefore, involve groups of personalities—as would be found in a family, or other small groups, or a larger community. The larger social groups of which the person is a member are depicted at the top of Figure 1.4.

Personality's location on the molecular-molar dimension tells us that it will be influenced by systems "underneath" or "underpinning" it, including the brain and influences on the brain. It will also be influenced by organizations "above" or "including" it—social systems such as the family and society.

The Internal-External Dimension

Internal-External Continuum (or Dimension): As applied to personality psychology, a dimension or continuum that separates the internal parts of personality ("beneath the skin") from the external aspects of personality (behavior, environment).

Many sciences also make use of an **internal-external continuum (or dimension)** to further distinguish their objects of study (Henriques, 2003; Mayer, 1995a; Singer, 1984). The personality system is internal to the person, inside the skin, with perhaps the innermost part of personality being consciousness itself. The internal personality is joined to the outside world through the sensory-motor boundary. Most signals traveling from personality to the outside world are communicated by the person's motor systems through speech, posture, and actions. Conversely, information from the outside environment must be sensed and converted into symbols before they can reach personality.

Personality's location on the internal-external dimension means that it is a set of private internal psychological processes existing literally within the individual's skin. This can be distinguished from the expression of personality through language and other motor activities. Outside observers can typically see only our external expression. Only an individual has access to his or her interior self. Personality operates internally, but it also operates in the external, ongoing social situations in which it finds itself. This internal-external dimension is represented by the horizontal dimension of Figure 1.4.

FIGURE 1.4

FIGURE 1.4

Personality's Location
Personality can be viewed amidst its neighboring systems of scientific study. In this diagram, personality is related to those systems according to a molecular-molar dimension (vertical) and an internal-external dimension (horizontal). Biology is molecular relative to personality, the social situation is external, and larger social systems incorporate both personality and the external situation.

Source: From Mayer (2004), adapted with permission of the American Psychological Association.

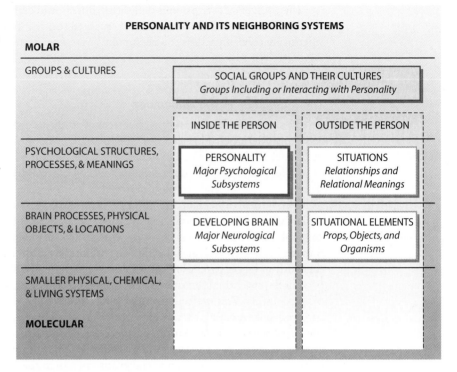

PERSONALITY AND ITS NEIGHBORING SYSTEMS

MOLAR		
GROUPS & CULTURES	SOCIAL GROUPS AND THEIR CULTURES *Groups Including or Interacting with Personality*	
	INSIDE THE PERSON	OUTSIDE THE PERSON
PSYCHOLOGICAL STRUCTURES, PROCESSES, & MEANINGS	PERSONALITY *Major Psychological Subsystems*	SITUATIONS *Relationships and Relational Meanings*
BRAIN PROCESSES, PHYSICAL OBJECTS, & LOCATIONS	DEVELOPING BRAIN *Major Neurological Subsystems*	SITUATIONAL ELEMENTS *Props, Objects, and Organisms*
SMALLER PHYSICAL, CHEMICAL, & LIVING SYSTEMS		
MOLECULAR		

The Time Dimension

A third dimension is that of time. Personality develops; it changes over time, from infancy to childhood, from adulthood to maturity. Personality is different during each life epoch, and this too is important in locating the system. This volume will address adult personality, but it will refer frequently to how personality develops during childhood.

So, personality is a global system of smaller psychological systems. It is inside the person but interacts with the outside situation, and it develops from infancy to maturity.

What Is the Field of Personality Psychology?

What Is a Field of Science?

A field of science such as personality psychology can be considered a body of knowledge, created and renewed by an organized group of individuals who produce knowledge about it. Its people include scientists who study a common group of problems and are recognized as belonging to that group, the colleagues with whom they consult, and, especially, the students they educate, some of whom go on to become the next generation of scientists.

These people are organized and represented within institutions such as colleges and universities, and other research bodies. Most colleges and universities include in their psychology areas one or more psychologists who study personality psychology.

Similarly, granting agencies often designate funds for the study of personality. Moreover, there exist professional associations that tie such individuals together.

Personality psychologists produce knowledge about how the personality system operates. Using a variety of scientific methods, these individuals discover relationships, test hypotheses, and publish their results in research publications. Personality psychologists publish their articles in peer-reviewed journals, in chapters in edited books, in full-length books, and as educational communications in magazines and newspapers as well. The next sections provide a brief overview of the emergence of modern personality psychology to further explain what the discipline is all about.

The Emergence of Modern Personality Psychology (1890–1949)

Recall that at the close of the nineteenth century, Wilhelm Wundt had envisioned personality as the study of person's major psychological subsystems. In the years immediately following Wundt's vision, the first personality psychologists arose. Many of them, like Sigmund Freud, Carl Jung, Alfred Adler, and others, attempted to synthesize all that was known at the time into a single, grand theory of personality. (Wundt's term "personality" was not yet regularly employed, and Freud and his colleagues employed a number of terms alternative to personality for their studies.)

Freud was preeminent among those who designed such comprehensive theories. In the late nineteenth and early twentieth centuries, he synthesized considerable early writings on hypnotism, psychopathology, and his own case analyses to arrive at a novel understanding of how personality operated, called psychoanalysis or "Psychodyanmic Psychology"—how one part of the mind influenced another. Carl Jung wrote on psychoanalytical psychology; Alfred Adler wrote on individual psychology. These various "psychologies"—views of personality, really—were sometimes arranged helter-skelter with studies of sensation, memory, and other topics (e.g., Murchison, 1930).

Others organized and recorded what had been written earlier about personality—and the burgeoning new theories of Freud and others. Much of this activity took place in the 1920s in and around Boston.

Among those who helped review and consolidate the field, perhaps the foremost early contributor was Arthur Roback. Roback (1927) noted that by the mid-1920s, in the Boston area, courses in personality psychology were underway on a regular basis. The clearly intended purpose of his book, *The Psychology of Character,* was to be a first textbook in personality psychology (Roback, 1927). To accomplish this, Roback provided an exhaustive review of studies in character, temperament, and mental conflict, including the works of Freud. Another key figure in the area, Gordon Allport, had taught such a personality course in 1924 and 1925 at Harvard (Winter & Berenbaum, 1999, p. 10).

Twelve years later, Allport and others published a cluster of new textbooks in the field—Gordon Allport's (1937) *Personality Psychology,* Henry Murray's (1938) *Explorations in Personality,* and Ross Stagner's (1937) *Psychology of Personality,* and with that the discipline of personality psychology had officially begun (Craik, 1993). For his volume, Allport had collected together dozens of meanings of the term *personality,* and took considerable care in explaining why it was a good term for the discipline.

In 1938, Gordon Allport, a professor at Harvard University, wrote one of the earliest textbooks on personality psychology used in the United States.

Murray's *Explorations,* focused on motives—both conscious and unconscious, and Stagner's book focused a bit more on systems and behavior.

By the end of World War II, still more new theories were emerging. Allport had introduced a theory of traits; Murray a theory of needs. Humanistic psychologists such as Abraham Maslow and Carl Rogers emphasized the human potential for growth and positive mental health, and described how people could attain it. Social cognitive psychologists examined learning about the world as a part of personality.

Each of these theories employed its own language and terminology, and many arose to critique or supplant other theories. The action in the field was taking place at a theoretical level rather than at a level of trying to understand personality through research. This wasn't necessarily a bad thing: there was great intellectual excitement in these diverse theories.

This and the further background of the field is depicted in the timeline of personality psychology shown in Figure 1.5.

Connecting Window *Early Personality Theory*
The early theories of personality were gradually developed into broader theoretical perspectives—the psychodynamic, trait, and humanistic approaches among others. These are covered in Chapter 3, Perspectives on Personality.

Influences on the Field	Events in the Field

"PERSONALITY" BEFORE PERSONALITY PSYCHOLOGY

Influences on the Field	Events in the Field
551–479 B.C.E. Confucious and followers lay out rules for behavior in Ancient China.	
460?–377 B.C.E. Hippocrates develops the first recorded theory of temperament	
427–322 B.C.E. Plato and Aristotle lay out rules for behavior in Ancient Greece	
206 B.C.E.–220 C.E. Han Dynasty (China) implements first mental examinations as part of civil service requirements	
372?–287 B.C.E. Theophrastus (Athens) writes the first character sketches in *Characters*	
1214–1294 C.E. Roger Bacon suggests people fit into society in different ways depending upon their character	
1588–1679 C.E. Thomas Hobbes formulates the idea of a social contract	
1734–1815. Mesmer discovers animal gravity (hypnosis)	
1859. Charles Darwin publishes his theory of evolution	
1879. Wilhelm Wundt founds the first psychological laboratory	

CONSOLIDATION OF THE FIELD AND SYNTHESIS OF WHAT CAME BEFORE

Influences on the Field	Events in the Field
1898. Wilhelm Wundt envisions the role of personality psychology in relation to general psychology	1893. Sigmund Freud and Joseph Breuer publish "Studies on Hysteria"—a first general theory of psychology
	1900, 1901. Freud publishes the "Psychopathology of Everyday Life" and "Interpretation of Dreams"
	1905. Alfred Binet publishes article on the first successful intelligence test
1920–1960. Behavioral learning theories ascend in importance in American psychology	1927. Arthur Roback publishes *The Psychology of Character*, a textbook for the burgeoning courses in personality
	1937–1939. In quick succession, Gordon Allport, Henry Murray, and Ross Stagner publish three personality textbooks

THE GROWTH OF THEORIZING AND THE IMPORTANCE OF THEORIES

Influences on the Field	Events in the Field
1948. Norbert Weiner proposes the field of cybernetics	
	1950–1970. Humanistic personality psychology emerges through the efforts of Carl Rogers and Abraham Maslow
	1950. Robert Sears reviews the field of personality for the Annual Review
1953. Watson and Crick publish "A Structure for Deoxyribose Nucleic Acid"—thereby discovering DNA	
	1958. Hall and Lindzey publish the first successful "Theories" book of personality
	1960. Dollard and Miller translate Freudian psychology into the language of behaviorism

GRADUATE TRAINING GAINS MOMENTUM AND RESEARCH ACCELERATES

Influences on the Field	Events in the Field
1960–1980. The ascent of cognitive viewpoints in psychology	1968. Walter Mischel questions the stability of human personality
	1981–1990. Trait theory reemerges in popularity with the advent of the Big Five
	1981–1990. Cognitive psychology investigates the Freudian unconscious and other forms of unconscious

CONTINUING A TREND FROM THE 1950S, THE FIELD DEVELOPS A COMMON LANGUAGE; INTEGRATED FRAMEWORKS OF THE FIELD ARE DEVELOPED

Influences on the Field	Events in the Field
1991–2000. Advances in biology lead to new research techniques with relevance to personality psychology, including brain scans, and new means of linking genes to neurotransmitters	1991–2000. Major trends: Increased influence of psychoevolutionary and social cognitive theory
	1991–2000. A period of continuing integration and crossdiscipliinary study; Frameworks for integrating personality psychology are introduced
	2000–Present. A renewed emphasis on predicting from personality measures to an individual's behavior

FIGURE 1.5   **Personality Psychology: A Timeline**
A Timeline of Selected Events and Trends Critical to the Development of the Field of Personality Psychology

Evolving Viewpoints on the Field (1950 to the Present)

Throughout the latter part of the twentieth century, as more and more students were attracted to the area, research blossomed, and the field was rich with both theory and empirical findings. Today, typing the word *personality* into PsycINFO—the database for psychological literature—returns over a quarter-million responses. Hence, a central problem for the field was to develop a good approach to organizing and teaching its expanding understanding.

The way a field of science understands itself—the lens through which it understands its own work—can be referred to as a discipline's fieldwide framework. The framework of a field is important because it is employed to understand what the field ought to be studying and explains and organizes the research in the field. Of considerable importance to those taking a course in personality psychology, the framework also is used to organize textbooks in the area. In a sense, the framework represents a field's identity (Mayer, 1993–1994, 1998).

During the second half of the twentieth century, the major framework for the field was a perspective-by-perspective approach. Calvin Hall and Gardner Lindzey (1957) introduced a personality textbook that presented, in historical order, a balanced coverage of the global psychological theories of Freud, Jung, Adler, Rogers, Maslow, Angyal, and many others with whom you may be less familiar. Each chapter focused on presenting a personality theory, and then concluded with an evaluation of the theory and any research evidence for it. Several generations of students were exposed to this approach to personality psychology and it is still used today.

Over time, the number of theories increased, and gradually, textbooks evolved to discuss broader theoretical perspectives rather than individual theories. For example, theories that emphasized a biological approach were grouped together, as were trait theories, and theories with a psychodynamic orientation that had stemmed from Freud's work. Clustering individual theories together this way exposed students to the early twentieth century theories of personality in some depth and retained a philosophical orientation that focuses on big questions. By grouping individual theorists together, textbooks in the field still conveyed some of the flavor of original theorists of the field, while making room to incorporate the burgeoning new research relevant to the field.

There is, however, a considerable amount of research in the field today that does not pertain to one theoretical perspective or another. For example, it would be difficult to understand human personality adequately without understanding how the emotions system works. Yet, studies of emotions emerged as a topic of study independent of psychobiological, psychodynamic, and humanistic theories. Second, such books leave the individual with the question of which perspective is best. The answer, of course, is that each one (or at least most of them) contributes to a different understanding of personality. Still, psychologists and their students often hope for something more integrated.

A new framework for the field—the one used here—has emerged to address such issues. It is called the systems framework for personality psychology (Mayer, 2005). The **systems framework** for personality is a new outline for the field that focuses directly on the personality system itself (as opposed to theories). Its four major topics of study are: (1) the identification and location of personality; (2) the parts of per-

Systems Framework: The systems framework is an outline of the field of personality psychology that divides it into the study of (a) the definition and location of personality, (b) personality parts, (c) personality organization, and (d) personality development.

• FACTS • AT • A • GLANCE •

The Key Ideas of the Most Highly Cited Personality Psychologists of the Early-to-Mid Twentieth Century

Name and Location	Dates of Major Works	Some Key Ideas They Developed
1. Sigmund Freud *Vienna, Austria*	1890–1939	. . . that human instincts, feelings, and thoughts are often unconscious; that the individual often struggles between personal, biological needs, on the one hand, and the expectations and rules of society, on the other.
2. Carl Rogers *Rochester, NY; California*	1940–1979	. . . that empathizing with another person can encourage that person's positive personality development; that people need to develop their true selves.
3. Albert Bandura *Stanford, CA*	1960–2000	. . . that people are influenced in what they do by watching others behave and seeing what happens to them; that a person's own confidence level can determine what he or she does.
4. B. F. Skinner *Cambridge, MA*	1930–1989	. . . that what people do is exclusively a function of their biology and the patterns of reinforcement around them. For that reason, it is unnecessary to be concerned with internal mental processes.
5. George Kelly *Columbus, OH*	1950–1969	. . . that a person behaves much like a scientist who is trying to discover and control his or her own world; that a person develops his or her own theories about the world, and that these personal theories differ dramatically from person to person.
6. Gordon Allport *Cambridge, MA*	1930–1959	. . . that a person's traits, such as his or her generosity, honesty, and aggression, influenced and account for much of his or her nature.
7. Alfred Adler *Vienna, Austria*	1900–1969	. . . that a person often feels inferior about a part of him or herself and will try to overcompensate for it—by masking fear with unusual courage, for example.
8. Abraham Maslow *Waltham, MA*	1940–1970	. . . that as people's physical and social needs are met, they attempt to develop their own psychological selves. The culmination of this can be an especially healthy psyche.
9. Carl Jung *Zurich, Switzerland*	1920–1959	. . . that the types of people who appear in myths—heroes, magicians, rulers, and healers—are near universally recognized across humanity, and that people may try to act out such mythic types in their own lives.
10. Hans Eysenck *London, England*	1940–2000	. . . that human personality can be described according to "supertraits"—broad, general traits such as Neuroticism, that are composed of smaller clusters of traits, such as anxiety, mood swings, and sensitivity.
11. Karen Horney *Berlin, Germany; New York*	1930–1969	. . . that people develop characteristic ways of relating to others, such as moving toward or against others; that women's mental lives are distinct in some ways from men's and need to be understood, at least in part, on their own terms.

Source: Rankings and dates from Mayer & Carlsmith (1998).

TABLE 1.1	Representative Career Paths of Personality Psychologists

A professor of personality psychology.   Most professors who teach personality psychology began by earning an undergraduate degree in psychology or a related field. They then went on to obtain a graduate degree (Ph.D.) in a field of psychology. Most often, the degree would be in personality psychology itself or a joint program in personality and social psychology. People from other subfields of psychology, notably developmental psychology and clinical psychology, sometimes switch into personality psychology as well. Once they have obtained a faculty position, these individuals teach a variety of courses and sometimes conduct research in personality psychology and areas related to it.

A clinical psychologist who studies personality psychology.   Some clinical psychologists also work in the area of personality psychology. Most began by earning an undergraduate degree in psychology or a related field. They then went on to obtain a professional degree related to conducting psychotherapy and psychological assessment (a Ph.D. or Psy. D.). They may work solely in private practice or hold an adjunct appointment, or be a faculty member at a college or university. Such individuals can draw on their clinical experience with patients to inform their theorizing and research in personality psychology.

A psychiatrist who studies personality psychology.   Psychiatrists in medical settings also have developed personality theories. Such individuals receive medical training, and after obtaining their M.D.'s, may go on for further training in psychology. Throughout the twentieth century, postdoctoral training in psychoanalysis was very popular among M.D.'s. This training focused on techniques of psychotherapy, as they had been initially described by Freud, and then further developed by his followers. Physicians also were exposed to psychological theory as undergraduates. They often bring to bear their experience observing their patients in psychotherapy when writing about personality psychology.

A human resources officer who studies personality psychology in an organization.   A human resources officer typically works in larger business, governmental, or educational settings. Although those in human resources deal with a variety of issues, some focus on selection and development of personnel. Such individuals have typically earned a bachelor's degree, and possibly an M.B.A. in organizational behavior, or they have psychological training at the undergraduate or graduate level. They are often certified to give psychological tests measuring personality. Such individuals may select tests for the purposes of hiring or developing the skills of staff members. Those in human resources also may administer such tests, and may conduct research into how test scores can be used to predict an individual's performance in the organization. They may also engage in coaching employees to make them more effective.

sonality; (3) personality organization, and (4) personality development. Each major topic has been carefully defined over a series of reviews, and subsidiary divisions under each topic also have been developed. This new approach is one among several that have been developed to integrate the study of personality psychology (Cervone, 2004; Henriques, 2003; Pervin, 1990; Sternberg & Grigorenko, 2001). It is this new framework that, in part, makes this new textbook possible (Mayer, 1993–1994; 1995a; 1995b; 1998; 2005). New as this framework is, its mission is still to address, in part, the questions that began this chapter: "Who am I?" "How are people different?" and "What is my future?"

Although this framework is new, it draws on Wundt's founding vision of personality as organizing a person's psychology (e.g., Pervin, 1990; Sears, 1950; Mayer, 2005). It also owes its existence to a small but intrepid group of psychologists who translated the terminology of one major theoretical perspective to another—thus building unity into the contemporary discipline. Such psychologists translated Freudian dynamics into behavioral terms (e.g., Dollard & Miller, 1950), or cognitive terms (Erdelyi, 1985), with many variations (Mayer, 1995; Westen, 1990). Many others experimented with alternative frameworks of note (e.g., Maddi, 1972; McAdams, 1996).

Training and Research in Personality Psychology

The end of World War II saw a growing demand for a college education. During the 1950s, a new generation of personality psychologists was hired to teach the subject. By the 1960s, the field of personality psychology began to take on a shape that would be familiar today.

By the 1960s, graduate study in psychology had become popular. Government agencies such as the National Institutes of Mental Health, and private foundations such as the Ford Foundation funded research in psychology. Graduate students were trained and then hired as new professors—or went to work in business, education, and government.

The first several decades of training in personality psychology, from the 1940s to the 1970s, were often allied with clinical programs (programs that train psychotherapists), which made sense because many personality theories of the time had important implications for how to assess the individual and how to conduct psychotherapy. Over the years, however, graduate training programs in personality have become more closely allied with social psychology (e.g., Swann & Seyle, 2005). Both personality and social psychology address normal personality, use similar research methods, and are concerned with how people behave in social situations. Social psychology, however, studies people's attitudes toward the world, and the world's influence on the individual. Personality psychology, as we have seen, is concerned with how the personality system operates and its implications for a person's life. Academic and other career paths for personality psychologists are described in Table 1.1.

Professors of personality psychologists taught undergraduates and trained graduate students, some of whom became the next generation of professors. This training and research cycle has resulted in an explosion of research in personality psychology and related disciplines. Each year, hundreds of studies are carried out in the discipline and more data is collected related to how personality operates. Many lines of personality research have taken on lives of their own, independent of one personality theory or another. Figure 1.6 on page 26 shows the number of articles mentioning the term *personality* by decade, as indicated by a search of *PsycINFO*—one of the field's central databases. There were 192 such articles between 1901 and 1910, and a gradual rise over the decades of the twentieth century to 72,107 such articles in the 1990s alone.

Today every fall and early spring, undergraduates apply to graduate programs in psychology or related fields throughout the world. In the United States and Canada, about fifty-five graduate programs train students specifically in personality psychology (American Psychological Association, 1996). If you are interested in a career in psychology—and perhaps in personality psychology—you can visit the American

Case Study

The Careers of Two Personality Psychologists

Case study boxes examine the lives and activities of individuals so as to bring certain concepts or areas to life. Here, the spotlight turns toward the lives and careers of two personality psychologists whose work will be covered in this book.

Dr. Nancy Cantor

The "Distinguished Scientific Award for an Early Career Contribution to Psychology" is one of the highest honors the American Psychological Association can bestow on a member. On the occasion of winning the award in 1985, Nancy Cantor revealed that some of the questions discussed in the opening of this chapter—such as "Who am I?"—had helped motivate her as a youth (Committee on Scientific Awards, 1986).

Cantor was born in New York City in 1952. She had a working mother (once president of the Gerontological Society of America) to whom she often professed her dislike for careerism. "As an adolescent in the 1960s," she commented, "I took . . . the struggle for identity to new heights, or to new depths as my parents might add." Her mother was patient with her daughter's stated desire to get married and have ten children. Despite her early conviction, Cantor became quite serious in school. Her father

was a former union organizer, and his example filled her with the desire to become a social activist.

When Cantor attended Sarah Lawrence College, she encountered a number of great teachers and became interested in psychology. She entered graduate school at Stanford University and found a mentor in the prominent personality psychologist Walter Mischel, whose work stressed that people could be flexible and exert some control over their own lives.

For Cantor, answering questions of identity doesn't happen only through self-reflection: "from my viewpoint," she states, "personality develops and grows through the individual's participation in struggles with [life] tasks (Pervin, 1996, p. 297)." In her work with John Kihlstrom, Cantor has studied the social tasks young people engage in and the social intelligence they develop as they carry out those tasks. She and Kihlstrom studied how undergraduate students create social knowledge of how to function in their four years of college. Whatever personal project that a student is working on—getting into graduate school, getting married, or getting a good job after graduation—the more expertise they develop in the area and the more they use that expertise rather than simply

Psychological Association's website at www.apa.org, or that of the American Psychological Society at www.psychologicalscience.org. Both sites contain a great deal of information for students who are thinking about becoming psychologists. The American Psychological Association also publishes regularly updated books such as *Careers in Psychology* and *Graduate Study in Psychology*. More specific information about the field of personality psychology can be found at the website for the Society for Personality and Social Psychology: www.spsp.org. At present the site is weighted heavily toward social psychology, but some information there pertains to personality psychology as well.

relying on preferred styles of behavior, she found, the better they end up doing (Cantor and Kihlstrom, 1987, p. 241). Other aspects of Cantor's work have addressed how people may be flexible and growing, even when others perceive them according to stereotyped traits.

Cantor's teaching career began at Princeton University. She then moved to the University of Michigan and later became chancellor at the University of Illiniois.

Dr. David Buss

David Buss was the 1988 winner of the high honor, the "Distinguished Scientific Awards for an Early Career Contribution to Psychology" (Committee on Scientific Awards, 1989). On the occasion of his award, Professor Buss also revealed his own engagement, early on in his life, with the "Who am I?" question. Buss was born in Indianapolis in 1953. He originally dropped out of high school, where his only good subject (he said) was mathematics, and worked at a truck stop in New Jersey, where he pumped gas and changed tires. There, he says, he enjoyed an invaluable opportunity to study personality close up, by observing the ex-policemen, alcoholics, retired army personnel, and criminals who stopped to tell him their stories.

After a while, he says, he decided that there must be a better way to make a living, and he went back to school. He earned his high school diploma in night school and then returned to his hometown to attend the University of Texas at Austin. While there, his interest in psychology grew more powerful. This led him to attend graduate school at the University of California, Berkeley, where he studied with such luminary personality psychologists such as Jack and Jeanne Block, Kenneth Craik, and Richard Lazarus. He was married there and now has two children. He completed his Ph.D. in 1981 and taught at Harvard, then moving to the University of Michigan, and then returning to the University of Texas as chair of the Psychology Department.

Buss's best known works apply evolutionary psychology to personality development, particularly in the areas of courting behavior and mate selection. A central aim of Buss's work has been to establish psychoevolutionary theory as a central method for understanding human behavior. His provocative work has been used to explain cross-cultural consistencies in preferences among men and women for features in their prospective partners (Buss, 1989). He is also known for his research with Kenneth Craik on the measurement of "act frequencies," that is, self-reported acts such as "paying someone a compliment to get a favor," that can be measured and combined to study traits.

Why Study Personality Psychology?

The discipline of personality psychology's task is to catalog, unify, and organize information from the rest of psychological inquiry and apply it to questions of individual uniqueness and human nature. Whereas many subdisciplines of psychology concern one part of mental life or another, personality psychology is devoted to providing an overview of the most important findings concerning mental life and its operation. Personality psychology, as the broadest of the subdisciplines of the study of mental life, also serves as a bridge between psychology and philosophy, as well as

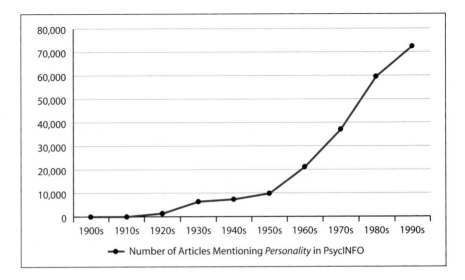

**The Growth of
Research in
Personality
Psychology**
The number of articles in
PsycINFO with mentions of
personality, by decade of the
twentieth century.

between personality and other sciences such as neurobiology, educational theory, anthropology, and sociology.

The "Who Am I?" Question—A Part of Scientific Inquiry

Returning to the question "Who am I?" some have argued that understanding oneself and others is a value in and of itself—knowledge for knowledge's sake (Jopling, 2000, p. 3). In its role as a science, personality psychology provides some tools to analyze oneself: methods for measuring features of the individual, a sophisticated language for the parts of personality and their organization, and procedures for studying lives over time. Rather than just describing ourselves as shy and intelligent, we may develop a richer way of thinking about our own characteristics. For example, we might learn we are "introverted" rather than shy. There is a subtle difference between the two: shy people want to be with others but are socially avoidant; introverts often prefer being alone. We might suddenly realize that, along with other introverts, we love to read and watch movies, and seem somewhat more sober than our more sociable friends. The "who am I?" question is also refined through related questions.

> Personality has unconditional value . . . No abstract idea of the good can be put above personality.
> Nicolas Berdyaev

The "How and Why Are People Different?" Question—Asked in Personality Assessment

The question "Why and how are people different?" is highly related to *personality assessment.* Personality assessment refers to learning about a person. It could be called the "art of 'sizing up' people," and is something that we do all the time to ensure smooth interpersonal relationships (Kleinmuntz, 1982, p. 1). In the hands of a trained psychologist, however, personality assessment is more than an art.

Today, clinical personality assessment is growing in importance. This field is focused on how to outline the qualities of a person. Personality assessment typically consists of observing and interviewing a person, and then administering a set of psychological tests. The assessment setting may be a medical complex or psychologist's office in which the person is interviewed and takes psychological tests. Children are sometimes assessed at school. Alternatively, the setting of the assessment may be an assessment center—a specially constructed environment (typically, offices)—in which a person is asked to perform various tasks and sometimes interact with others in simulations of on-the-job behavior.

Using data from the observations, interviews, and tests, the psychologist then composes a narrative description of the personality under study, discussing personality's parts, organization, and development: and also, typically, answering a specific question about the individual. The question about the person typically depends on the setting. In a legal setting, the tests may indicate something about whether the person had moral capacity at the time of committing a crime. In an organizational setting, the assessment may deal with the strengths that an individual can bring to a job. In a clinical setting, psychological assessments may deal with why a person is experiencing life difficulties, and the areas in which a person can improve (Butcher, 1995).

The "What Is My Future?" Question—Prediction, Selection, and Change

Prediction and Selection

"What will my future bring?" orients us toward our future selves. Personality psychology also serves a predictive, or forecasting, purpose. It can identify likely

Psychological testing is increasingly conducted by computer. Whether the test is administered by a computer or a person, however, the goal is the same: to understand the key parts of an individual's personality, how those parts work together, and what that might say about the person's current needs and future functioning.

No predictions are perfect, but psychological testing often can help select better candidates for job positions. This can be particularly important when the position is crucial to carrying out an organization's mission, such as that of law enforcement.

(Speaking in) Probabilistic Terms: Speaking in terms of events that are most likely (i.e., probable) to occur, typically using statistical techniques to enhance the accuracy of those accounts.

outcomes of the ways we are and the things we do (Funder, 2000). People probably have been making decisions about the others around them from the beginning of time. The choice of a good hunting partner was probably a life or death decision for our ancient ancestors (Buss, 1991). When research on testing is conducted with groups—say with a group of applicants for a job—it is possible to draw conclusions about who will do the job more or less well, in probabilistic terms. Personality psychologists usually speak in **probabilistic terms**—that is, they speak in terms of events that are most likely to occur, using statistical techniques to make their accounts as accurate as possible. Such testing and selection may also be used to select people who might benefit from training in a particular area (for example, benefit from training in social skills).

Consider the selection and training of police officers. Such selection begins with assessments, and then moves from performance in an assessment situation to predicting who will do well on the job. Dayan, Kasten, and Fox (2002) examined candidates for the police force in an assessment center setting. In the assessment center, the police candidate went through simulations of on-the-job encounters—everything from handing out a traffic citation to searching a suspect. The candidate's performance was observed and assessed by his or her peers and by judges. Those ratings and evaluations turned out to be highly valid for predicting later on-the-job performance (Dayan et al., 2002). In addition, part of those officers' assessments involved taking psychological tests, which also predict on-the-job performance. For example, higher scores on tests of general cognitive ability, and on tests of conscientiousness, generally predict better on-the-job performance (Black, 2000; Cortina et al., 1992; Dayan et al., 2002). In one study, officer candidates who scored low on scales of maturity, low on commitment to values, and low on self-control were found to be at greater risk for serious breaches of confidence on the job, such as the use of undue force and

Disciplinary Crossroads

What Does Personality Psychology Offer Other Fields?

Disciplinary Crossroads boxes examine personality psychology's relationships to other fields in the arts and sciences. For example, personality theory has long been an inspiration for works of art and literature. Theories developed by Sigmund Freud and Carl Jung, among others, have been illustrated in countless films representing both popular entertainment and high art. In the science fiction film, *Forbidden Planet,* a lost civilization builds a mental amplifier that causes their Freudian "Ids" (instinctual energy) to aggress against the world around them and end up destroying themselves. In turn, personality theorists have often taken their inspiration from works of art. The ancient Greek myth of Oedipus Rex formed the basis for Freud's idea of an Oedipal complex. That psychological complex involved aspects of the love a young boy feels toward his mother, and his fear of his father.

What other fields find personality psychology important? The economist John Maynard Keynes, whose theories underlie many governmental policies, wrote that personality factors were essential to economic progress, stating, "if the [person's] animal spirits are dimmed and the spontaneous optimism falters . . . enterprise will fade and die (Keynes, 1936, pp. 161–162). Bearing out that thought, a psychoeconomic study by Austin, Deary, and Willock (2001) recently related social energy and other factors to success among Scottish farmers.

Personality is regarded as critical in politics, diplomacy, and war. During World War II, General William J. Donovan commissioned a psychiatrist to study Adolph Hitler's personality and predict his behavior if he began to lose. The psychiatrist, Walter Langer, correctly predicted that with each loss Hitler would become more enraged and brutal, lose confidence, and would ultimately lock himself in a "symbolic womb" and commit suicide (Langer, 1972, p. 212). As the war drew to a close, Hitler indeed locked himself inside an underground bunker and killed himself (but other predictions have not been as accurate).

President Jimmy Carter carefully read through detailed studies of the personalities of Israeli Prime Minister Begin and Egyptian President Sadat, compiled by the intelligence community, before negotiating the Camp David peace accords with the two leaders. He formed a clear image of each one's personality, including especially each one's motivations, and used these images to successfully broker a peace accord between the two in 1979 (Carter, 1982, p. 320).

Looking toward the future, engineers have devoted considerable attention to the question of whether or not expert computer systems, and now robots, should be endowed with built-in emotions and personalities. One research team recently created an emotionally empathic operating system to help reduce human users' frustrations (Klein, Moon, & Picard, 2002).

likelihood of corruption (Hargrave & Hiatt, 1989). The employment of tests and assessment centers can meaningfully increase the quality of a given workforce. The widespread use of psychological assessment, selection, and training applications can help members of occupations, and the organizations to which they belong, function in a smoother, more competent and professional manner.

Applications to Personality Change

A final reason to study personality is to gain knowledge so as to change oneself, others, or one's relationships. Personality psychology highlights areas a person might want to change, whether it is because a part of one's own personality is causing the person problems, or because personality psychologists hold out models of optimal functioning, and some people aspire to make themselves better if they can. Let us shift examples from one of occupational selection and training to a topic of interest to anyone in a relationship.

Observe all men; thyself most.
Benjamin Franklin

After studying the constructive and destructive patterns of couples over many years, Gottman and Silver (1999) made a number of recommendations to help people better handle their interactions in relationships. The recommendations were modeled on what successful couples did. The researchers noted that such simple routines as asking your companion how his or her day went, and reminding your companion you notice his or her positive aspects, were both important to maintaining a good relationship. Other recommendations included doing things together during good times and being sure to talk to one another during bad times. They recommended focusing on the relationship itself—that is, "What is good for us?"—separately from focusing on each other as individuals. In arguments, members of the couple should proceed gently, repair hurt feelings, and not let emotion take over. And if you can't do a lot of this? Well, personality psychology has also contributed importantly to the methods used in learning to improve oneself.

These are some of the applications and contributions that personality psychology has made within the discipline. Other disciplines also draw on personality psychology, as illustrated in the Disciplinary Crossroads box.

How Is This Book Organized and What Will You Learn?

Some Cautions and a Beginning

Who am I? What is my future?—We now have an idea of some of the questions that led up to the discipline. Personality psychology is not the only discipline that addresses such questions. Asking "Who am I?" of a biologist could elicit a commentary on the similarities and differences among animal species and their evolutionary progression. Asking "Who am I?" of a theologian will obtain answers that involve the relationship between an individual and a spiritual force or supreme being (e.g., Heschel, 1965, pp. 91–92). Asking "How shall I live?" of an ethicist will elicit an answer related to what is good and right to do (Marinoff, 1999).

Personality Psychology's Answers

As a science, personality psychology focuses on issues of function—explaining how something works. Of the "Who am I?" question, personality psychology takes the portion of it that is answered by "How does a mind work?" (Marinoff, 1999). Of "How should I lead my life?" personality psychology takes the portion of it that is answered by "Given that a person is a particular way, how will that impact his or her life?" Most centrally, personality psychology addresses: "How does a person's psychology work and what implications does it have for the individual's life?"

To address such questions, this book is organized into four topics: What (and where) is personality? What are the systems parts? How is personality organized? And, How does personality develop? These topics are the topics of the systems framework for personality described earlier. To get a sense of how these four topics will work—and to provide an overview of what you will be studying—let's begin by analyzing a specific person using the four topics. This "getting to know the person" example will provide an example, in miniature, of how the book works.

Identifying Personality

The first topic of the systems framework—and of Part I of this book—concerns defining and identifying personality. As we put personality in context, we can also examine the context of an individual's personality.

For example, by recognizing personality as a collection of major psychological systems, and placing it in context, it is next possible to go out and find examples of personality and how it relates to a person's life—that is, real-life data. As we'll see in Chapter 2, Research in Personality Psychology, data about personality may be generated by the personality itself or may come from observers or institutions surrounding the individual. An example of data generated by the individual would be a memoir. A memoir is a written document that presents a self-description of the person, his or her personality, and the individual's development over time.

An example of such a personal history is that by Linda Greenlaw (1999), who was captain of a fishing ship when she wrote of a year in her adult life. To identify and locate Greenlaw's personality, one can begin by asking about her physical characteristics, the settings in which she functions, her interactions with others, and her social memberships. As with any examination of personality, the answers we arrive at always will be approximate and incomplete; yet, they begin to address the question.

At the time of her memoir, Greenlaw was captain of a fishing ship. She was strong and healthy enough to carry out the physically strenuous activity of offshore fishing. She further tells us that she was able to operate on relatively little sleep in relation to most people, which is lucky considering the demands of her job.

Greenlaw's most usual social settings during the year of her memoir included the small Maine town in which she grew up, the Massachusetts fishing town of Gloucester, from which she set sail, and the boat on which she sailed, the *Hannah Boden*. She had frequent interactions with Bob Brown (her boss and the owner of her boat), the captains of other boats, and the sailors on her boat. She doesn't speak of spending much time in organized group activities, although she mentions in passing that she has been awarded a law degree.

We will learn in Chapter 2 that studying an individual's life such as Greenlaw's, as we are doing here, means using the case study method, and that there are other methods available for studying personality as well. One strength of the case study is that we can see the richness of a person in all his or her uniqueness; one drawback is that the individual studied in a case may not be representative of others; for that reason, whatever is learned specifically may not be applicable to people more generally.

Chapter 3 examines theories of personality. Theories direct us to examine special phenomena within the person. Trait theory, for example, is concerned with people's traits—distinct consistencies in their mental lives and behaviors, such as their sociability or happiness. As a second example, humanistic theories focus us on how individuals grow and attain their potential.

Part I of this book gets the reader underway, introducing some basic research and outlining some theoretical perspectives on the person. This will prepare the reader for further understanding.

Parts of Personality

The second part of the book focuses on the parts of people's personalities: their motives, emotions, relationships, and other qualities. A **personality part** or **component** is a discrete mental quality or area of mental function within a person (Mayer, 1995b, p. 828). Certain parts of Greenlaw's personality stand out during her ship-captaining years. One such part is her need to achieve and meet high standards. For example, although it caused her some conflicts, she chose to work with a difficult and demanding boss. The boat owner

Personality Components (or Parts): Individual instances of personality function, content, or processes are known as personality's parts or components. These components or parts may be biological mechanisms such as a *need for thirst,* or learned contents such as the *multiplication tables,* or thematic ways of feeling, thinking, and acting, such as *shyness,* among others.

> was an amazingly clever person . . . [he] was a top-notch mechanical and electrical troubleshooter. As for determination . . . he would take his boat to Mars if he thought there might be a fish to be caught there. . . . My only real problem with Bob, I thought . . . was that he demanded so much of people . . . Bob's approval was something I strove for, and seldom achieved . . . [yet] [o]ur relationship worked. (Greenlaw, 1999, p. 3)

Linda Greenlaw, captain of the deep sea fishing boat the Hanna Boden, *wrote an eloquent memoir of a deep-sea fishing trip. Her memoir can be used to help understand her personality.*

Their relationship worked in part because Greenlaw was one of the top captains on the East Coast. Another sign of her need for excellence is her competitive quality. She explained:

> When I wish a fellow captain "Good luck" on the radio and tell him that I hope he loads his boat with fish the next day, I am sincere, and hope that only I will beat him. (Greenlaw, 1999, p. 136)

Another part of Greenlaw's personality concerns her mental models related to fishing and fishing boats. Most people would probably struggle to come up with something to say about cooking on fishing boats in bad weather. Greenlaw's personality, however, is chock full of ideas about that. She recounts that:

> It is absolutely expected and acceptable to hear the cook screaming profanities while getting a meal together in rough seas. If there are no obscenities heard, there is probably no cooking going on, in which case all shipmates fend for themselves. Peanut butter sandwiches and Pop-Tarts are common heavy weather meals. (Greenlaw, 1999, p. 63)

Other parts of personality concern mental abilities. Cognitive intelligence is crucially related to a person's occupational and even marital status. Greenlaw holds a law degree, is a successful ship captain, and is able to write a lively memoir. Her capacity to navigate a number of intellectually challenging endeavors strongly suggests that she is above average in a number of intelligences (an intelligence test score would provide further information).

Finally, some parts of personality concern self control and a sense of personal choice or agency. Is Greenlaw's (or anyone's) life a product of her choices, or is it determined by fate? How much control can we exercise over ourselves? A person's agency refers to the capacity of personality to make decisions and exert influence on its surroundings, independent of the environment. The existence of human agency is a controversial topic; not all scientists believe such parts exist.

In Part 2 of this book, Chapter 4 examines the motivational and emotional traits and other parts of personality. Chapter 5 examines a person's mental models (e.g., how cooks talk on ships). Chapter 6 examines intelligences and other mental abilities. Finally, Chapter 7 examines consciousness, will, agency, and related parts of personality.

The second part of the book acquaints readers with many different, varied parts of personality. At this point, the reader will be able to recognize many different aspects of his or her own personality and the personalities of others. Still, the student may feel a bit overwhelmed, because as of yet there is no way to put the parts together. The view of personality at this point is beginning to develop, but still it may seem fragmented and disjointed.

Personality Organization

The third topic in studying personality asks how the parts of personality are organized. Are there sensible ways to divide up personality so we can ensure we have an overview of its most important functions? Beyond that, how do the parts do things and act together to bring about personality dynamics?

One dynamic that characterized Greenlaw's personality at that time was her social tact and skill, and, in general, her admirable honesty both with herself and with those around her. The one possible exception was in the case of competitive situations. When those arose she was sometimes willing to bend the truth. After a particularly good day of fishing, for example, Greenlaw was in radio contact with several other ships' captains. She intentionally understated her catch, so as to discourage other boats from coming closer, and reflected, "I lied for the sake of my livelihood, my crew, my boss, and myself, but mostly I lied because . . . getting to the top was a painful journey, and I planned to stay there . . ." (Greenlaw, 1999, p. 185). Dynamics of action concern how what goes on in a person's hidden, private personality is translated into a person's actions.

Another sort of dynamic concerns the dynamic of self control. One of Greenlaw's truly remarkable aspects is the gentle and wise means by which she controls herself. She reports that, as the *Hannah Boden* sailed away from port on her voyage, there came a point when she checked her charts and found she was about as close as she would come to her hometown and family for months. She felt overwhelmed by sadness, and she imagined her own self as a child watching herself at that moment, and saw the child cry. She notes, "All I had to do was twist the knob on autopilot, turning the boat around 180 degrees," but she didn't. She reported that "Each time I sailed by the island, I felt the possibility of ever changing my life getting more remote" (Greenlaw, 1999, pp. 49–50).

Structural Organization:
This aspect of personality organization refers to the relatively long-term, stable positioning of one part of personality in relationship to another.

Dynamic Organization:
Personality dynamics involve trends of causality across multiple parts of personality, in other words, how the parts of personality influence one another. For example, dynamics of action describe how a person's urges end up being expressed in the individual's actions.

There are three chapters on personality organization. Chapter 8 examines the structural organization of personality. **Structural organization** refers to the long-term basically stable divisions of the personality system. Knowing these makes it easier to think about the personality system piece by piece. **Dynamic organization** refers to the major causal pathways that bring about important consequences across the personality system. Chapter 9 covers the dynamics of action. It examines how a person moves from being motivated, to acting on a motive. Chapter 10 examines the dynamics of self-control. It examines the different forms that self-control takes and what types of self-control may be particularly effective.

If this section has begun to paint a picture of Captain Greenlaw as a whole, the same can be said of the third section of the book. Now readers will be able to use powerful ways of putting personality together—that is, personality structure and dynamics—to integrate what they had earlier learned about a person's specific parts of personality.

Personality Development

The fourth and final topic asks how personality develops. Personality does not spring from the mother's womb fully grown but develops through childhood and adulthood. Greenlaw tells us little about her growing up, except to emphasize a generally happy childhood on a small island, and her fascination with and captivation by the sea, which leads her to study and interact with the ocean. The environmental influences in such an upbringing seems far more likely to produce a ship's captain than, say, growing up in the middle of Chicago might.

Greenlaw's position as a ship's captain seemed stable and secure to her. Yet both environmental and internal mental processes can lift a person out of a set pattern of existence and into a new one. A series of events, including the sinking of her sister ship in a catastrophic storm, the death of her ship's owner, and her own assessment that her needs were not being met by deep sea fishing, led Greenlaw to make some changes in her life. In the end, she gave up her ship to return to lobstering closer to home.

Personality development concerns how the personality system grows and changes over the course of a lifetime. Chapter 11 examines lifespan development, with a focus on children and adolescence. Chapter 12 examines areas of emerging adulthood, adult development, and maturity, examining what is stable and what changes in a person's life.

At the conclusion of the final part of the book, the reader should have a whole overview of how to envision a personality—from its location, to its parts, to its organization, and through its development.

The course provides the opportunity for increased self-understanding, the potential for predicting one's own and others' thoughts and feelings, and for some tools of change. It is fair to ask whether the questions personality psychology addresses are worth understanding, whether the field has applications of importance, and whether we can better understand ourselves and each other through a study of the discipline. We personality psychologists believe, and I hope this book will show, the answer is yes.

> **Personality Development:** Personality development concerns how the personality system develops over the individual's life span.

Reviewing Chapter 1

The primary goal of this chapter is to introduce you to the field of personality psychology. It covers contemporary issues such as how people become personality psychologists, and it is designed to help you understand a bit of the field's history. Finally, the chapter is aimed at providing you with an overview of what will come next in the book. To help ensure that you have learned the more important points of the chapter, please review the following questions, which are arranged according to the major sections of the chapter:

What Are the Fundamental Questions Addressed by Personality Psychology?

1. Can you describe the sorts of questions addressed by personality psychology?

One way to get the big picture of a field is to understand the sorts of questions that motivated its creation. "Who Am I?" is a basic question that in part organizes and

motivates personality psychology. What are some related questions?

2. What was an early typology of human personality developed by Hippocrates?

The early temperament theory of personality—the fourfold classification of humours worked out by Hippocrates—is important to our contemporary understanding of personality (as we will see later). Can you describe each of the four personality types, sanguine, choleric, melancholic, and phlegmatic?

3. What events contributed to an understanding of unconscious processes?

Before Sigmund Freud and modern psychology came on the scene, a number of individuals had studied phenomena related to the unconscious. These included studies of animal magnetism (mesmerism). What has become of the research today?

What Is the Personality System?

4. Do you know the definition(s) of personality? Definitions of personality tend to stress the fact that it is an organized system of parts. Who was the first to suggest such a definition? How could personality psychology contribute specifically to the field of personality? Note how personality is defined specifically in this textbook. There exist other definitions of personality as well, including those that stress individual differences. What are some of the drawbacks (if any) of these alternative definitions? What are some of their advantages?

5. Can you relate personality to its surrounding scientific systems?
The personality system does not exist in isolation. Rather, it is embedded in other surrounding systems. Personality is "located and identified" amidst other systems of scientific study in this chapter. It is distinguished from its biological bases and from more complex systems such as social groups. Two of these dimensions are the molecular-molar dimension and the internal-external dimension. Can you explain what these are? What is yet another dimension?

6. What are personality's neighboring systems?
Using some of the dimensions to arrange personality amidst its neighbors, what are the various systems that can be arranged around personality, and where can they be placed in a dimensional system?

What Is the Field of Personality Psychology?

7. What activities characterized the establishment of modern personality psychology?
In 1890, Wilhelm Wundt recommended the establishment of the discipline. Between that time and the 1920s, two trends occurred: consolidation and synthesis. Consolidation involved collecting what was then known about personality psychology. Synthesis concerned integrating what was known into grand theories. Do you know the role of Sigmund Freud, Arthur Roback, and Gordon Allport in such activities?

8. Views of the field.
In the middle twentieth century, how was personality psychology taught? Gradually, the field has become more integrated across theories. This has depended upon several lines of work including translating the language of one theory into another, increasing research, and better defining the central topics of personality psychology. Do you know the first major translation of one theory into another?

9. Why did research in the field increase so dramatically?
After World War II, more Americans than ever decided to seek a college education. Psychology became an important major on campus. A number of foundations began funding psychological research in general and personality research in particular. Today, graduate students often apply to psychology departments to study personality psychology. Do you know to which area(s) of specialization they apply?

10. How are personality psychologists trained?
The training of personality psychologists varies; early personality psychologists came from a variety of disciplines, but personality training programs are of increasing importance. What are some characteristic career paths of personality psychologists today?

Why Study Personality Psychology?

11. What are some reasons for studying personality psychology?
One can study personality psychology simply to seek knowledge for its own sake. In addition, personality psychology has a number of applied uses: for personality assessment, selection, and prediction. Can you give an example of how personality assessment works? What about selection and prediction?

How Should One Study Personality?

12. What are some of the limits of personality psychology?
Can personality psychology really answer questions such as "What is the best way to live?" or "Who am I?"? Why or why not? What are the limits involved in studying a complex system such as personality psychology? Although these limits exist, studying personality can still be a rewarding, exciting experience, and personality has important practical applications.

13. What are personality components and why are they useful to study?

How are personality components defined? The section on personality parts will examine motives and emotions; mental models of the self, world, and relationships; thinking with those models; and the more mysterious parts of personality including free will and consciousness.

14. What is personality organization?

Personality organization refers to how the parts of personality are related to each other. Organization can be divided into two parts. Structural organization refers to the stable, long-term arrangement of personality's parts. Dynamic organization refers to how the parts of personality interact with one another.

15. What is personality development?

Personality development refers to how the parts of personality and their organization change over time. Personality development is often divided between personality origins and growth in childhood and development in adulthood.

Chapter 2

Research in Personality Psychology

*N*ow that we have defined the personality system, it is useful to take a look at the sorts of data personality psychologists study and the sorts of methods that personality psychologists use. Personality psychologists use many research designs common to psychology more generally. The nature of the personality system, with its many internal parts, and its many connections to biological and social systems, however, shapes the methods that are most commonly used. In particular, psychologists have developed practices that help them to measure personality's many features, and to manage many measurements together. Learning about these methods provides a foundation for better understanding the work of the field.

- ### Where Do Data Come From?
  No matter if we are theorizing or researching, we must start with some observations on the personality system itself. But where is that data going to come from? It can come from external sources, such as institutional records or observer reports, or from personal reports—data emanating from inside the individual. Research findings then begin to prompt more questions about personality and how it operates.

- ### What Research Designs Are Used in Personality?
  Research designs indicate what data must be collected to answer given theoretical questions. Personality psychologists use a broad range of research designs, each of which contributes in a different way to the knowledge of the field.

- ### What Does It Mean to Measure Personality?
  No matter what research design is used, it will become necessary at some point to take measurements of a person. But what, exactly, is measurement and how does one carry it out? The field of psychometrics addresses such questions.

- ### How Do Personality Psychologists Study So Many Variables?
  Personality psychologists like to take a broad view of personal functioning, so they often want or need to collect many different measurements on a person. The problem then becomes how to organize the variables that have been collected. Several mathematical techniques are available for that purpose, notably factor analysis and structural equation modeling.

Where Do Data Come From?

Olympian Issues

The Olympic competitions bring together some of the best athletes in the world and foster their abilities in a highly demanding sports competition. The best athletic performances are then rewarded with bronze, silver, and, best of all, gold medals. The idea of ranking athletes on a scale of bronze, silver, and gold arose in ancient Greece, with Plato's idea, in the *Republic,* that people in a society differed from one another, with some "men of bronze," some "of silver," and some "of gold."

The 2002 women's figure skating competition in Salt Lake City pitted vibrant sixteen-year-old Sarah Hughes against the superb veteran performer, Michelle Kwan. As Hughes and Kwan competed, Olympic officials collected data about them. Some data was measured objectively with electronic timers, other data involved evaluations of the competitors' style, artistry, athleticism, level of skill, and all-around quality. The judges observed the skaters throughout their competitions. Hughes, Kwan, and others were rank ordered according to their performance. The Olympic officials awarded the gold medal to sixteen-year-old Sarah Hughes, who unexpectedly surpassed Michelle Kwan; that night, Kwan won the Bronze.

This athlete gazes toward a monitor that displays measurements— judges' evaluations— of her performance along a number of dimensions.

We might wish to understand more about this competition than just who won. As personality psychologists, we might be interested in data about the competitors' states of mind. How did Kwan and Hughes feel about each other as the competition began? Did their feelings and thoughts influence their competitive performance? For example, as a beginning skater, Hughes idolized Kwan. What about the gold (and other) medals Kwan and others won in national and international competitions both before and after the 2002 Olympics (Park, 2002)? Is Kwan's performance reliably different than Hughes's over time? More generally speaking, we may wonder how good an indicator any single bronze, silver, or gold medal is of athletic performance during a particular competition.

In psychological research, as in the Olympics, data about people are collected and evaluated to make important decisions—and psychologists need to understand the merits and drawbacks of different kinds of data. In the Olympics, data reflecting the timed duration of a performance are different in nature than the subjective evaluations of athletic performance by Olympic judges. For example, the music played as part of a skating routine can influence the judges, independent of the athletic merit of the performance. Other extraneous factors may enter in as well. In the 2002 Olympic figure skating competition, one judge was investigated as to whether or not her objectivity had been compromised by political considerations. All together, the accuracy of judges' ratings is subject to many factors, and important to explore (Swift, 2002).

Data concerning an individual's personality, like data concerning athletic performance, comes in different forms, and each much be evaluated on its own merits. That data can then be used in a variety of research designs, and through it, we can begin to understand the personality system.

Observer Data

Observer or Informant: Data: A type of data about the person that comes from observers of the person such as specially trained raters, acquaintances, or friends.

In the Olympic case, the judges provide us with a kind of data known generally as **observer** or **informant data**. This kind of data come from observers directly evaluating the personalities (and sometimes performance) of people they know (and sometimes, whom they don't know). Studies concerning the accuracy of observer data have focused on a variety of variables.

Observer data tends to be particularly useful if the trait being measured is readily seen and easy to recognize by those around the individual. Athletic performance in the Olympics is one such example. In the psychological realm, some mental qualities can be discerned easily by observers if they concern outward behavior. One such trait is extraversion. This makes sense because extraverts often behave in sociable, outgoing ways, seeking social contact, whereas shy people may tend to look nervous or to look away from others. Not all mental traits, however, can be readily gauged. For example, people are notoriously bad judges of less visible qualities such as people's intelligence.

Under ideal circumstances, the observer is under little pressure to perceive things one way or another. Under some circumstances, however, such as social pressure, observers can be biased in small or not-so-small ways. In a study of judges of competitive figure skating championships, for example, there was evidence that judges brought their rankings of final events closer to the other judges after seeing the posted results in earlier competitions (Wanderer, 1987). Judges also appear to favor athletes from their own countries, or from countries that are aligned with their own (Seltzer & Glass, 1991).

The relation a person has to the person being judged may also affect the information. For example, supervisors may perceive an employee differently than their coworkers, even though both are observing the same individual. In one study, managers who scored high on tests of integrative complexity were rated by two groups of observers: their own supervisors and their coworkers. Integrative complexity is the capacity to see things from different perspectives, and it is crucial to the success of creative architects, scientists, and writers.

The supervisors rated employees high in integrative complexity as relatively high in initiative and as being relatively objective about themselves compared to those who scored lower on the test. Their co-workers, however, rated them as higher on narcissism and saw them as somewhat antagonistic. Observer ratings are often said to reflect a person's reputation, and, plainly, these managers had different reputations among their supervisors and coworkers (Tetlock, Peterson, & Berry, 1993).

The Life Sphere and External (Life) Data

Observer ratings are just one type of data about an individual. There are many such sources of data. These sources of data can be organized first according to where they come from. In Chapter 1, we saw that personality is surrounded by such neighboring systems as its neurobiological environment (e.g., the brain), and the external setting, including the person's location and nearby objects and people. The surrounding systems further include the interactive social situation (e.g., being with friends), as well as the larger groups in which the person is a member. Personality and those surrounding systems are shown in Figure 2.1, much as they were in Chapter 1.

The systems surrounding personality make up what has been referred to as the person's life space (Lewin, 1935, pp. 172–173; Cattell, 1965, p. 60; Mayer, Carlsmith,

Data Sources Drawn from Personality and Its Surrounding Systems

Data that pertain to personality can come from the personality system itself (e.g., self-report data) or from the systems surrounding it, such as institutional and observer data.

Source: From Mayer (2004), adapted with permission of the American Psychological Association.

& Chabot, 1998). Data related to that life space (and to personality) have been superimposed on Figure 2.1, arranged according to where they come from.

Data that arises external to personality, from the life space—from biology, settings, interactions, and institutions—are referred to as **external-source** or **life-data.**

External-Source Data (or Life Data): A type of data about the person that comes from a person's surrounding life, for example, from institutional records and the observations of others.

Such external-source or life data include any data that emerge from sources external to personality: from a person's outside life. Observer data of the type we just discussed is one such example of this external data. Such external-source data can also include information such as one's medical status and history, grades in school, how others view one's character, and whether one keeps a neat or disorderly room (Cattell, 1965, p. 60; Mayer, 2004).

Rather than directly observe a person, for example, one could collect data about the individual's social setting (called setting data). One study collected information about how clean and how well-decorated a person's bedroom was. Individuals with comfortable, clean, organized bedrooms were higher in the psychological trait of conscientiousness than others, as independently assessed by a psychological test. In the same study, the participants with decorated, distinctive bedrooms with many different kinds of books were higher in cultural openness—again, as assessed by an independent test. Thus, a person's living space and other surroundings provide important data that reflect on their personalities (Gosling, Ko, Mannarelli, & Morris, 2002, p. 391).

Personal-Report Data: A type of data of that the person generates himself or herself. This kind of data is often generated in interviews, while taking a test, or in similar activities.

Personal-Report Data: Self-Judgments, Criterion-Convergence, and Thematic-Report

Whereas external source data come from the areas surrounding personality, **personal-report data** come from the individual. Personal report data are data that the indi-

Data on the individual may come from multiple areas of a person's life space: home life, on the job, and leisure activities, among other areas.

Self-Judgment (or Self-Report) Data: A type of data about the person that the person generates himself or herself, and that typically involves some judgment of his or her own qualities and features.

Process-Report Data: Data that arise from a person's description of his or her mental processes as those processes are unfolding at the moment they are being described.

vidual communicates, discloses, or otherwise reports to a psychological investigator. Interviews and questionnaires yield personal report data, as do more elaborate psychological tests. We can briefly introduce a few main categories of such data (e.g., Funder, 2004; Mayer, 2004; 2005).

Self-judgment (or self-report) data arise when the individual is asked to describe or explain something about him or herself. For example, a person might go through a series of statements such as, "I like mechanics magazines" or "Most people think of me as shy," and indicate how much each one applies to his or her personality. This kind of data directly measures an individual's self-concept. Tests of self-concept and tests of personality traits such as extraversion and neuroticism are of this type.

A variation of self-judgment data is **process-report data**. Process-report data involve the individual's report of an ongoing mental process, such as an emotion or a thought. For example, test items such as "Are you happy right now?" and "Are you trying to avoid how you feel right now?" would generate process report data. Process report data are often of value because they track ongoing mental states, and therefore do not depend on an individual's memories as much as some self-judgment data.

Criterion-Report (or Mental Ability) Data: A type of test data in which the person must solve problems or engage in tasks, and then his or her performance is judged against a standard.

Thematic-Report Data (or Projective-Report Data): A type of test data in which a person constructs a response to an ambiguous stimulus, and that is often thought to reflect important motivational, affective, and cognitive processes in personality.

Criterion-report (or mental ability) data arise when the individual answers a test question with a response that will be judged against a criterion of correctness. Criterion-report items ask questions such as, "If four people begin work at 9:00 A.M., at what time would they complete a sixteen-hour job?" and "What does *Ocean* mean?" Educational achievement tests, memory tests, and tests of intelligence often employ criterion-report data.

A third kind of data, **thematic-report data (or projective-report data)** arise when the individual responds to an ambiguous stimulus, such as an inkblot, and is asked to say what it looks like or to tell a story about it. The responses may be scored according to a given theme—such as how well the person constructs reality, or to what degree an individual expresses a specific motivation, such as acquisitiveness, in response to the ambiguous stimulus.

Any or all of these sources of data may be drawn upon when considering a research design to study a problem. Some interesting research issues arise concerning which data is right for a given purpose. For example, some researchers have asked whether self- or observer-judgments are more accurate in assessing personality. Some of the debate is shown in the Research in Focus box.

Research in Focus

Are Self-Judgments or an Observer's Judgments More Accurate?

Let's say you want to find out something about another person. One very basic methodological question is: "If you really want to know the nature of a person, who should you ask—the person, or an observer?" Certainly, both are legitimate data sources. Psychological tests can be based on self-report or the judgments of informants. Both can be reliable. But which is most valid? Which tells us the most about who a person really is?

Freud argued that observational data is crucial to understanding another person. He believed that the more extensive observations a person carried out, the more accurate their conclusions regarding the individual would be. Funder and his colleagues have been approaching this problem in the context of a decade-long research program in the judgment of traits—long-term characteristics such as extraversion, friendliness, and neuroticism (e.g., anxiety and self-consciousness). The accuracy of observers, it

turns out, is dependent upon a number of factors. Recall that Freud said that judge's knowledge could be enhanced by regular, long-term, observation. Research indicates that is the case.

For example, Paulhus and Nadine (1992) assigned participants to sixteen groups of about six members each. Each participant took a scale measuring such traits as Extraversion, Openness, and Friendliness. Then the participants in each group were assigned to meet with one another for a short time each week for seven weeks. They rated one another after the first week (before they knew one another well), and through the seventh week on a rating scale of the same traits (e.g., Extraversion, etc.). Would the self- and observer ratings agree more as time went on? They did, significantly rising from correlations of .21 to .30.

Similarly, Funder and Colvin (1988) brought participants into the lab and had them rate one another on a variety of individual test items.

What Research Designs Are Used in Personality?

Types of Research Designs

The exact data one chooses to collect will in part be a function of the research design one is using. Research designs are often divided into three broad areas: case studies and observationism, correlational research, and experimental research. Loosely speaking, case studies involve observing a person. The correlational approach involves quantifying the relationship between two or more variables. The experimental method, on the other hand, involves manipulating a variable to determine its influence on another variable. These research designs will be described in greater detail, and ideas about them will be refined, next.

The Case Study Method

Case Study Design: A scientific research design in which one person ("the case") is studied in depth.

Case Studies and the Scientific Method

A **case study design** involves the intensive examination of a single person—the "case"—over some period of time. Whenever we consider a given individual and his or

---

When they had done so, each participant was asked to bring a friend who knew him or her well to the laboratory. The friends, of course, had known the participants much longer than the strangers. The friends rated the people they knew and others they did not (in each case, the friends were assured that the people they rated would not find out what they said). Friends' ratings agreed relatively highly with the people they knew, and very low with the people they did not. Kenny and colleagues (1994) qualify these consistencies by arguing that increased correspondences may be due to discussions between the people rather than actual observation.

Still, in both studies, judges were more accurate when they described traits that are called "subjectively observable"—that is, traits that people believe they can "see" or "read" relatively easily in another person. For example, most people find extraversion to be highly visible, and judges were better at identifying extraversion in their targets than almost any other trait. Some readily visible traits are "physically attractive,"

"talkative individual," "values intellectual and cognitive matters," and "has social poise." Some difficult to judge qualities include "is subtly negative," "has persistent preoccupying thoughts," "is generally fearful," and "compares self to others" (Funder & Colvin, 1988). When only subjectively visible traits are studied, agreement between observers and targets is fairly high, with correlations in the $r = .40$ level.

Still, there is some disagreement between self-reports and judges. These disagreements can be lessened a bit by combining judges (Kolar, Funder, & Colvin, 1996). Even so, it remains, and so the question arises: who is correct? The answer: it depends. Self-reports are more often better predictors of matters such as day-to-day moods and social behavior (Spain, Eaton, & Funder, 2000). Still, friends can sometimes outperform in predicting social behavior, particularly when raters are combined, and certain kinds of judges outperform others (Christiansen et al., 2005; Kolar, Funder, & Colvin, 1996).

her life, we are potentially employing a case study design. Case studies serve three functions (McAdams & West, 1987; Sears, 1959). The first is *exemplification,* meaning that the case can be used to illustrate, display, and provide examples of a particular psychological part or dynamic. Case studies are often easily understandable, requiring of the reader little or no knowledge of methodology or statistics. Therefore, they communicate well. Moreover, the best case studies can be colorful and interesting in making their points. The description of a person's life, the obstacles he or she contends with, and the ultimate success or failure the individual faces can often bring to life a concept in a way a table of statistical results cannot. One reason this textbook employs a number of case studies is to provide such lively examples of concepts and ideas.

> Science has radically changed the conditions of human life on earth. It has expanded our knowledge and our power but not our capacity to use them with wisdom.
>
> J. William Fulbright

A second function is to *evaluate* comparative explanations of personality by testing hypotheses according to whether they are plausible. For example, if one wanted to evaluate a theory that both competitive drive and social support contribute to good performance at the Olympic Games, one could try to apply it to the cases of Michelle Kwan and Sara Hughes to see if there were any differences in the competitors' competitive levels and the support they received. In this instance, one would examine each skater's family support and desire to achieve and see how those led to their professional, graceful, and at times joyous performances (Swift, 2004, p. 48). Of course, a case study by itself is not enough to decide whether a theory is sound, but it can help illustrate the value of a theory in certain instances.

A third function of case studies is *discovery.* This involves learning about new problems that scientists may not have encountered before. Because case studies include a great deal of rich, "unfiltered" information, they can be a great source for hypothesis generation. Small details included in the case may trigger new ways of thinking about a problem and may suggest new causes of behavior.

The disadvantages of case studies, however, are also quite important to recognize. The individual in a case study is not a randomly selected representative of a group. Quite the contrary, the individual may have become the object of study precisely because she or he is a colorful character, faces unusual circumstances, or is otherwise unrepresentative. That limits one's confidence in generalizing from the individual case to a more general group. Second, the observer(s) of a case are subject to individual biases and social pressures. Moreover, even the most forthright and honest of observers may miss key aspects of the person studied in a case, because human nature is so complex and, at times, so subtle. Even so, case studies are of considerable use to the personality psychologist.

Using Case Studies to Study Personality Psychology

A recent case study was conducted of Dodge Morgan, a wealthy man who sought—successfully—to circumnavigate the globe on a sailboat by himself. As a boy, Morgan had worked in a boatyard owned by his uncle, and as a youth had accumulated a remarkable 25,000 miles of sailing experience. After sailing from Maine to Ketchikan, Alaska (through the Bahamas) he returned to his native Massachusetts to take up work with a high-tech firm; some years later he bought a company that was spun off from it, called Worcester Controls Corporation (WCC). As owner of WCC, he amassed a small fortune.

Then at age fifty-four, although in a successful marriage and raising a son and daughter, Morgan decided to sail around the world in an easterly direction, on a solo, nonstop voyage to be completed in 180 to 220 days (Morgan, 1989, p. 191; Nasby & Read, 1987, p. 827). In June of 1984 he had completed a seventeen-page description of the project. A portion of it provided a self-assessment of his own mental and emotional factors:

> My mental faculties are more than adequate. My emotional status is sound. I have a strong will and singular determination to succeed. I do not easily give up. I can concentrate well over long periods of time and can focus a natural impatience on realistic objectives, satisfied with inches of progress if that is the order of the day or task. I know how to sort priorities and do not become confused by too many details. I know well the power of planning and time to reach an objective. I am very happy in my own company and can find loneliness a rather delicious feeling. And I don't suffer from seasickness. (Morgan, 1989, p. 200)

He was driven, he said, to find out, "How much more is there?" to life, and driven by the irresistible sense that "It is time to try again to find out. There is so little time left" (Morgan, 1984, cited in Nasby & Read, 1987, p. 827). Against the advice of his wife and friends, he commissioned a boat to be built in record time and departed shortly after its completion. In a letter to the psychologists, he wrote that voyage was an opportunity to bring about profound personal change (Nasby & Read, 1997, p. 884).

It is noteworthy that although Morgan completed his voyage successfully in 150 days, the psychological transformation he had hoped for himself did not take place exactly as he had expected. Instead, the journey left him somewhat unsettled, confused, and worried: "If anything," he wrote, "I feel more isolated than ever. I feel I have less in common with others than ever . . . I understand the need for compassion in people more than I did but find myself less able to practice it . . ." (Nasby & Read, 1997, p. 1040).

Recall that cases are useful for exemplification, evaluation, and discovery. Some have used Morgan's personality as an instance of a contradiction found more generally among certain difficult people: Morgan's traits of independence, aggression, and rejection of others puts him in the "most socially undesirable of all interpersonal categories." At the same time, he provides a nearly heroic example of achievement to many (Wiggins, 1997, pp. 1076–79).

The case can also be used for evaluation of theories. One theory of psychology is that people's lives reenact the lives of recurring characters in myths, such as heroes. Building on the heroic themes of Morgan's story, some have related it to mythical notions of the hero. They note that Morgan's voyage reenacts the myth of the hero, in

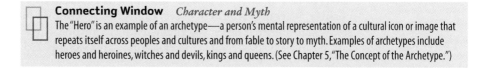

Connecting Window   *Character and Myth*
The "Hero" is an example of an archetype—a person's mental representation of a cultural icon or image that repeats itself across peoples and cultures and from fable to story to myth. Examples of archetypes include heroes and heroines, witches and devils, kings and queens. (See Chapter 5, "The Concept of the Archetype.")

Dodge Morgan sailed solo around the world and was the subject of an intensive case study of personality.

which the hero must separate from others, face an arduous task, and understand its meanings upon his return. This interpretation would predict that although Morgan had not yet discovered his truth, he would discover it in the future (Nasby & Read, 1997). Other theories, beyond the scope of this methodological review, have also examined the case. Does this short case study suggest any areas of research that might be worth further study? If so, the case fulfilled its role in encouraging discovery.

The Method of Observationism

Observationism: A scientific approach in which multiple case studies are studied, and principles are deduced and tested from examining what has gone across the cases, and what is similar or different across them.

Observationism is an outgrowth of the case study method. Instead of one case examined in depth, this method involves multiple, repeated examinations of many different cases (Mayer & Bower, 1986). Observationism can be defined as the intensive investigation of multiple cases with the intention of drawing generalizations from them that can be applied to a general population. The early personality psychologists were often physicians or clinical psychologists by training, and their observations went hand-in-hand with their attempts at treatment (Mayer & Bower, 1986; Mayer & Carlsmith, 1998).

Sigmund Freud was a physician by training and argued persuasively for the use of observationism as he examined his patients and first began to define the use of the method (Gay, 1988, pp. 295–305). First, Freud believed that a high frequency and duration of observation created a kind of magnifying lens for the quality of personality data. He observed his patients for an hour a day, four, five, or six days a week. Where possible, he continued these observations for between six months to two years. It seems plausible that observing and listening to anyone with such frequency and duration can yield considerable information (Gay, 1988, pp. 295–305).

Second, for Freud, observationism was helped by employing a consistent environment in which to observe the individual. Freud was quick to realize that an individual will react sensitively to various environments. When observing his patients, therefore, he retreated to the background—literally sitting behind a couch (on which a patient lay while speaking) out of sight—and keeping his own remarks to a minimum. The combination of being (relatively) unseen and unheard was intended to create the sense of a blank slate on which the patient could record his or her associations with minimal interference. We know today that by creating such an unconstrained situation, in which the patient could say anything, Freud also maximized the variety of individual differences he observed (Caspi & Moffitt, 1992).

Free Association: A method of case-study observation in which a person is asked to talk aloud about anything that enters his or her stream of consciousness, however trivial or even embarrassing it might seem.

A third aspect of observationism, for Freud, was more unique to his own research in psychoanalysis. It involved a primary concern with internal psychological processes as revealed through the technique of free association. **Free association** is a method by which patients are instructed to tell the therapist/observer whatever comes into their minds, no matter how personal, nonsensical, or even embarrassing the thoughts are. The idea was that people were to associate freely from one thought to the next. In doing so, they would reveal (we would say today) the structure of their memories and their mental models of the world. The result would allow a therapist such as Freud to track down the causes of certain thoughts by following their associations from present concerns back to an earlier time in their lives. Although other psychologists shared with Freud a belief in using repeated observation and keeping the observational setting a constant, they did not all use free association. Carl Rogers, for example, employed a technique that involved empathic listening in which the counselor repeated key feeling statements made by the individual to help clarify them (Rogers, 1951, pp. 27–30).

Freud believed that observationism represented a potential pinnacle of the scientific method for personality psychology. The natural sciences had made great strides by enhancing observational techniques. Modern biology had employed the microscope to discover the first one-celled organisms. Modern astronomy had developed the telescope to discover craters on the moon and spots on the sun. Freud believed that the repeated observation of the same individual could be psychology's microscope or telescope—a new instrument with which to study personality in detail. (See the Case Study about Emmy Von N. for an example of how Freud used observationism.)

The Observational Method and the Development of the Discipline

In many respects, the method of observationism and the early discipline of personality psychology grew together. The advantages and problems that observationism presents have truly shaped the discipline.

Connecting Window   *Freud's Observational Work*

Through his observational work, Freud was able to outline many of the central conflicts between an individual's psychological urges and the often opposing demands of society. Freud constructed his psychodynamic theory on the basis of this observational work. For example, he concluded that when people suppressed certain urges they felt, it was because those urges were in conflict with the requirements of society (see Chapter 3, "Psychodynamic Theory Views the Person").

Case Study

Freud's Case of Emmy von N.

Frau Emmy von N. was Freud's first psychological case study. The case of Frau Emmy von N. dates back to the late 1900s in Victorian-influenced Austria. Its setting is one of horse-drawn carriages, high infant mortality, experimental hypnosis, and great mysteries surrounding the mind.

The case emphasizes the relation between what is conscious versus what is unconscious and hidden in a person's mind; it also explores treatments for mental illness. In the case of Frau Emmy von N., the uncovering of what is hidden occurs through the use of hypnosis. Even examining just a few portions of the original, lengthier case, we can see Freud (and Frau Emmy von N.) arriving at some of the chief insights of psychodynamic theory before our eyes: (a) present pathological symptoms are caused by the memories of earlier events; (b) by addressing these early memories, the present symptoms can be improved; and (c) these memories are not always available in a conscious state.

Freud describes Frau Emmy von N. as follows:

> This lady, when I first saw her, was lying on a sofa with her head resting on a leather cushion. She still looked young

and had finely cut features, full of character. Her face bore a strained and painful expression, her eyebrows were drawn together and her eyes cast down. (Freud, 1893, p. 83)

Emmy von N. was easily disturbed and frightened by the events around her. Her anxiety was so great that she frequently stammered, screamed, fainted, begged others to leave her alone, and had epileptic-like fits. Freud begins to connect childhood memories to present symptoms in his questioning of Frau Emmy under hypnosis:

> I asked her why it was that she was so easily frightened, and she answered: "It has to do with memories of my earliest youth." "When?" "First when I was five years old and my brothers and sisters often threw dead animals at me. That was when I had my first fainting fit and spasms. But my aunt said it was disgraceful and that I ought not to have attacks like that, and so they stopped. Then I was frightened again when I was seven and I unexpectedly saw my sister in her coffin; and again when I was eight and my

Throughout his life, Freud continued to claim that observationism was the best of all psychological research methods. In fact, when an American psychologist wrote to Freud to tell him he had gathered experimental evidence to support the concept of the mental defense called "repression" (the forgetting of unpleasant material), Freud wrote that he appreciated the gesture, but that it was really unnecessary. Freud's observational studies had already confirmed the concept's existence and any further experimental evidence was unnecessary (Rosenzweig, 1941).

The Limits of Observationism

Freud's claim that observationism is a secure, useful method was based in part on the idea that any two people practicing it would confirm what one another saw. Not only did Freud suppose that different observers would agree, but also that there ought to

brother terrified me so often by dressing up in sheets like a ghost; and again when I was nine and I saw my aunt in her coffin and her jaw suddenly dropped." (Freud, 1893, p. 87)

Frau Emmy von N.'s direction of the questioning toward childhood memories encouraged Freud to urge her to go back to the earliest time she could remember having each symptom. In essence, Freud traced the psychological history of the symptom. Here he reports on her stammering, again from his case notes:

I had asked her the origin of her stammering and she had replied, "I don't know." I had therefore requested her to remember it by the time of today's hypnosis. She accordingly answered me today [under hypnosis] without any further reflection but in great agitation and with spastic impediments to her speech: "How the horses bolted once with the children in the carriage; and how another time I was driving through the forest with the children in a thunderstorm, and a tree just in front of the horses was struck by lightning and the horses shied and I thought: 'You must keep quite still now, or your screaming will frighten the horses even more and

the coachman won't be able to hold them in at all.' It came on from that moment." (Freud, 1893, p. 93)

Freud wondered whether he could alter the memories under hypnosis, and whether that might, in turn, improve the symptoms.

I extinguished her . . . [emotional reaction to the] memory of these scenes, but asked her to imagine them once more. She appeared to try to do this and remained quiet as she did so; and from now on she spoke in the hypnosis without any spastic impediment. (Freud, 1893, p. 93)

Case histories help us gain a feel for the richness of psychological phenomena. The case of Emmy von N. is a fascinating drama as complex as life itself. After a first successful treatment, Emmy von N. relapsed. She tried some unsuccessful and possibly destructive treatment by local physicians and then returned to Freud's care. The treatment was again successful, but her reprieve was short-lived. Not long after her second course with Freud, Emmy von N. endured watching her own daughter go mad. The tragedy proved too much for her to bear, and she once again reverted to a state much like the one she was in before treatment.

be agreement with the person being observed—the patient. In fact, the patient was ultimately expected to verify certain conclusions about his or her condition. Grunbaum (1986) has referred to this as the tally argument. The idea is that those points on which the patient and therapist/observer are in agreement will be considered true, and the remainder will be discarded as false.

The tally argument, however, may be subject to theoretical bias. Those who share the same bias may agree; those who don't may disagree. At first, Freud's claim for the consistency of observational data received some support. He trained a number of colleagues and students who at first reported seeing much the same things he did. After a while, however, some of Freud's colleagues developed alternative theories and observed different phenomena than he had. Notably, Carl Jung said he was unable to trace conflicts to the same sexual motivations as Freud had, even though he used the same free-association technique. Similarly, Otto Rank traced neurotic conflicts to conflicts between wanting to live and wanting to die. These defections seemed to argue in the face of observationism.

A disagreement doesn't mean a method is all bad. After all, astronomers disagreed for centuries over whether the lines they saw on Mars were natural structures or canals built by Martians—but they didn't throw out their telescopes simply be-

---

Inside the Field

Funder's Laws

"**P**lease do not memorize these laws," the personality psychologist David Funder has written. "I haven't memorized them myself. They are just my attempt to distill into a few aphorisms some observations of which, for some reason, I am particularly fond" (Funder, 2004, p. 9). I realized these laws had come of age during a thesis defense I chaired. In response to a question I asked the doctoral candidate about her thesis, she quoted one of Funder's laws (the Fourth) to explain, modestly, why her data was not as good as some of her committee members believed it to be. I was very impressed that she both knew and could apply Funder's laws in such a useful fashion. Funder's laws are not all about research methods, but the second, third, and fourth are. The page numbers all refer to Funder (2004).

Funder's Second Law: *There are no perfect indicators of personality; there are only clues, and clues are always ambiguous* . . . when you try to learn about or measure personality, you cannot base this endeavor on just one kind of information. You need many kinds (p. 19). Funder's Second Law reflects the potential complexity of the personality system. Its many parts may be expressed through language, posture, and acts. Personality's expression may take place over a few seconds in a relatively straightforward situation, or take place according to strategic, long-term plans, or according to many other variations. For that reason, each

research finding about personality is a clue in a broader mystery story. Continuing along the same line, consider:

Funder's Fourth Law: *There are only two kinds of data.* The first kind is Terrible Data: data that are ambiguous, potentially misleading, incomplete and imprecise. The second kind is No Data. Unfortunately, there is no third kind, anywhere in the world (p. 49).

I do think our data are often better than both Funder—and the (now) Ph.D. who quoted the Fourth Law—make them out to be. Still, any single measure is certainly insufficient to tell a complete story about an individual. If you begin to despair about the research process, however, you can take some solace from Funder's Third Law. The Third Law reflects why research psychology is so important, even though it often is imperfect:

Funder's Third Law: *Something beats nothing, two times out of three.* . . . The only alternative to gathering information that might be misleading is to gather no information. That is not progress (p. 21).

I enjoy reading through these and other laws by Funder, which collectively provide a sophisticated perspective on a challenging field. David Funder is a personality psychologist currently at the University of California, Riverside, where he studies, among other topics, people's ability to accurately observe others' personalities.

cause they couldn't settle the issue. Rather, they admitted the limitations of their research tools and sought new ones to settle the debate. In 1958, Erik Erikson, a renowned child psychoanalyst, described some of the virtues and limits of the observational approach in a detailed description of his use of the procedure. At the time, however, there was little empirical support for the approach.

Clinical psychologists and others continue to use observationism (e.g., Singer, 1997). A number of researchers have also asked, "Exactly how good are we at understanding other people by observing them?" They have studied observationism in the laboratory, and find good reason to be optimistic about it as a method (Funder, 1999). Meanwhile, psychologists of Freud's time, and those of today, have gone on to establish other research methods with complementary powers and drawbacks. For some amusing commentary on the strengths and weaknesses of data, see the Inside the Field box on Funder's Laws.

The Correlational Research Design

The Nature of Correlational Research Design

Variable: A feature of a person, situation, or other entity, which can take on more than one value. For example, level of creativity, number of siblings, and height are all variables.

The purpose of the correlational design is to find the relation between two or more personality variables. A **variable** is a characteristic that changes its value across people. For example, extraversion is a personality variable, as is creativity. The number of parties a person goes to in a week is also a variable—one related to personality. Some correlational studies examine a variable from inside personality in relation to the person's performance in the outside world or life. This would be the case with a study that looked at the relation between extraversion and the number of parties a person attended in a month. Once one knows the interrelation between the two variables one can predict the action of one variable from another. The central part of the correlational design always is to assess the relationship between two or more variables.

For example, Totterdell (1999) examined the moods and the performances of professional male cricketers. Cricket is one of most popular sports in England and is played by two teams of eleven players each, with balls, bats, and wickets. Totterdell hypothesized that a player's mood would change as a function of his performance in the game. In this case, the two variables that Totterdell employed were mood and performance on the field. Totterdell found that, in general, as a player became happier and more pleased, he would play better. Thus positive moods were seen to correlate with better performance on the field.

Correlation Coefficient: A statistic, ranging from −1 to +1, that describes the relation between two variables.

Note that such a relationship does not tell us whether better playing caused a positive mood, or whether a positive mood caused better playing. Correlations speak of relationships, not causation. The **correlation coefficient** is a statistic that measures the degree of association between two variables, such as mood and performance.

(Co-)Relating Two Measurements: A Review

You have probably encountered the concept of correlation coefficients before in your other psychology courses, but it may be helpful to refresh your memory before going on. A correlation refers to the "co-relation" between two variables, for example, between two sets of scores on tests. So, if a group of people took tests X and Y, we might want to know how their scores on the two tests are related. For example, look at the scores obtained by the five people shown in Table 2.1.

TABLE 2.1	Scores of Five Participants on Tests X, Y, and Z		
Participant	**Test**		
	X	Y	Z
Erin	0	2	4
Abigale	2	0	6
Max	3	3	3
Tyler	4	6	0
Glenn	6	4	2

Consider just Tests X and Y for a moment. You can see that as people scored higher on Test X, they generally scored higher on Test Y as well. These might be tests of confidence and mental toughness among athletes (Gould, Dieffenbach, & Moffett, 2002). Mental toughness is defined as a tenacious motivation to meet one's goals. Table 2.1 indicates that Erin and Abigale scored lowest on both tests, Max scored in the middle, and Glenn and Sarah scored highest on both tests. In this sample of athletes, as scores on test X (confidence) go up, they also go up on test Y (mental toughness). The relation is not perfect, but it is plainly present. When this occurs, scores are said to be positively correlated.

Now compare tests X and Z. Test Z might measure nonconformity. It is negatively correlated because, in this sample, as scores on test X go up, scores on test Z go down. Erin and Abigale scored lowest on test X (confidence) but highest on test Z (nonconformity), Max scored in the middle, and Glenn and Sarah scored highest on test X (confidence) but lowest on test Z (nonconformity). From measures like these we could say that confidence and mental toughness are positively correlated, whereas confidence and non-conformity are negatively correlated among samples of athletes.

The degree of correlation is typically represented by a product-moment correlation coefficient, or Pearson's r. The correlation, r, varies between -1.00 and $+1.00$. When $r = -1.00$, a perfect, negative relationship exists. For example, an $r = -1.0$ exists between tests T and U in Table 2.2. A positive $r = 1.00$ exists between tests T and V.

The $r = -1.0$ relation reflects that the higher the test T score, the lower the test U score. Similarly, the $r = 1.0$ between tests T and V exists because the higher the test T score, the higher the test V score. The relation between tests T and V is said to be perfect (and therefore $r = 1.0$) because an increase of one in test T equals an increase of the same interval in test V. Notice the same is true between tests T and W. For example, as test T goes up 1, test W goes up 5. An increase of 1 in T always predicts an increase of 5 in W; because the prediction from one to the other is always perfect and linear (would graph as a straight line), the two tests are considered perfectly correlated, $r = 1.0$.

Correlations and Scatterplots

A given correlation between two variables is sometimes represented as **scatterplot**. In this context, a scatterplot is a diagram representing pairs of measurements on two variables, X and Y. The plots are displayed in a two-dimensional space in which the

Scatterplot: A graphical depiction of points, in which each point represents a pair of observations, such as the achievement-motivation score on a test, and the earned income of that individual. The magnitude of one variable is represented on the horizontal, X axis; the magnitude of the other variable is represented on the vertical, Y axis.

TABLE 2.2	Scores of Five Participants on Tests T, U, V, and W			
Participant	**Test**			
	T	U	V	W
Erin	1	8	2	10
Abigale	2	7	3	15
Max	3	6	4	20
Tyler	4	5	5	25
Glenn	5	4	6	30

horizontal dimension represents the X variable; the vertical dimension, Y. For example, we can set up an X and a Y axis and plot the points as illustrated in Figure 2.2 adding a few more test-takers. The X axis represents scores on test T, the Y axis represents scores on test V. Each point in the plot represents a pair of scores that one person received on two tests. For example, there is a "dot" at the pair of points (1,2), representing the fact that Erin received a 1 on Test T, and a 2 on Test V. Plotting the two tests for the participants in Table 2.2, along with a few more test-takers, makes clear the perfect relation between the two tests. That is, one test can be predicted perfectly from the other. The same is true when $r = -1.0$, as it does in Figure 2.3, where Tests T and U are plotted for the test-takers in Table 2.2 and a few others.

If the tests were imperfectly related (which is most often the case), the points would no longer form a straight line, but rather would hover around a hypothetical straight line. That was the case with the correlation between tests X (confidence) and Y (mental toughness) in the earlier table, which is shown graphed in Figure 2.4 along with a few more test-takers, yielding a correlation of, approximately, $r = .75$. If the two

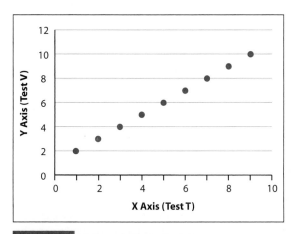

FIGURE 2.2   **A Correlation of +1.0.**

A correlation of +1.0 indicates a perfect relationship, in that as one variable goes up (or down) so does the other.

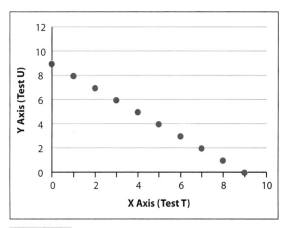

FIGURE 2.3   **A Correlation of −1.0.**

A correlation of −1.0 indicates a perfect *inverse* relationship, in that as one variable goes up, the other goes down, or vice versa.

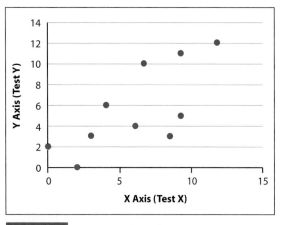

FIGURE 2.4   A Correlation of +.75

A correlation of +.75 indicates a positive but imperfect relationship between two variables. As one variable goes up (or down), the other tends to do the same.

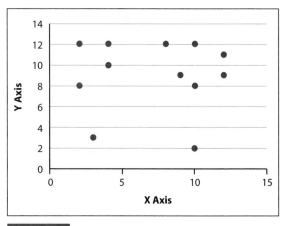

FIGURE 2.5   A Correlation of .00

A correlation of zero indicates that two variables are entirely unrelated; you cannot predict one from the other.

scales were entirely unrelated, then the correlation between them would be $r = 0$, and the points would form a random, haphazard pattern, as in Figure 2.5.

Correlational designs are important to personality psychology. They stress the relationship between variables. At the same time, they don't necessarily reveal whether one variable might be causing another. To examine that question, it is valuable to manipulate one variable and assess its influence (if any) on another variable. Variables are manipulated in experimental designs.

Natural Experiments

Natural Experiments: An experimental design in which the treatment of the experimental group (also known as the experimental manipulation) has already occurred naturally, rather than being randomly assigned. For example, in a comparison of airline pilots with middle managers, "profession" is manipulated, but the individuals have already chosen their profession, and so profession has not been randomly assigned.

Experimental designs in personality research take two general forms: **natural experiments** (also known as quasi-experiments), and **true experiments**. In natural experiments, people pursue their lives—find jobs, get married—all without experimental controls and randomization. Later, personality psychologists divide people into groups, such as employed or unemployed, and try to identify the factors that led the people to arrive at a particular destination in life. In experiments, two or more groups are examined. The experimental group or groups have received a **treatment** or "manipulation;" the control group has not. The two groups are then compared on a dependent (outcome) variable.

The "natural" part of a natural experiment refers to the fact that the group(s) who received the treatment were not randomly assigned. Rather, uncontrolled and perhaps unknown circumstances led to their group membership. For example, Carter (1998) employed a natural experimental design to examine anabolic steroid use among athletes. Anabolic steroids are synthetic versions of the male sex hormone, testosterone. Athletes and others use the drug to increase their muscle strength. They do so at some risk, however, because such drug use is illegal, considered cheating in competitions, and can result in serious medical complications.

True Experimental Design:
A formal plan for carrying out an experiment, usually by comparing control and experimental groups on a dependent variable. Members of the experimental group receive a treatment, which is hypothesized to alter their level on the dependent variable, relative to the control group.

Treatment: In regard to experiments, the specific procedure employed to manipulate the independent variable.

Carter recruited ninety-six male body builders from several health clubs who she classified into three groups. Thirty were current steroid users, thirty were former steroid users and thirty-six had never used steroids. The "treatment" in this case was anabolic steroid use. The control group consisted of those who did not receive the treatment, that is, the thirty-six who had never used steroids. The outcome measure of interest was personality—or more specifically, certain personality traits. All the participants were asked to take psychological tests to measure those traits. Carter was interested in personality differences between drug users and nonusers.

This is a natural experiment because the participants had decided whether to take the drugs in the present, in the past, or not at all (as opposed to the experimenter). Carter found that those who had used steroids tended to be lower in conscientiousness, more anxious, and more resentful, relative to the control group. Current steroid users also exhibited increased depression, obsessive-compulsiveness, and hostility.

The value of natural experiments is that they tell us about the personality differences among real groups of people—in this case, people who do or do not use steroids to improve their athletic performance. The drawback is that differences across groups may not be caused by the treatment studied. We might wonder, for example, whether some participants in Carter's control group might actually have taken steroids but preferred to say they had not. In such a case, the researcher might be observing differences between steroid users who are candid and open about it, versus those who are not. Another concern is that the admitted steroid users might have been engaged in other illegal activities besides steroid use that accounted for some of the group differences. To avoid such issues of interpretation, psychologists use true experimental designs.

> The revolution which the experimental method has affected in the sciences is this: It has put a scientific criterion in the place of personal authority.
>
> Claude Bernard

True Experimental Designs

True experimental designs involve the random assignment of people to groups. Then, the experimental groups are administered a treatment decided upon by the experimenter. The control group receives no treatment. After the intervention, the people are assessed to see if there is a change in some other variable of interest—the dependent variable.

Life would be a bit easier for personality psychologists if they could employ experimental treatments that dramatically and convincingly altered an individual's personality for short periods of time. Then they could study such interesting ideas as the impact of conflict with a parent on later personality. In fact, when psychologists have tried to do this it is not always convincing. In one line of research, investigators hypnotized participants and suggested to them that they possessed disturbing memories of conflicts with their mothers. After the memories were implanted hypnotically, they found that participants behaved in a more pathological fashion (e.g., Kubie, 1939; Luria, 1932).

Ecological Validity: In regard to personality experiments, the degree to which the treatment brings about a change in personality that is similar to the actual personality phenomenon being studied in the real world. For example, the degree to which experimentally introducing a mental conflict approximates an actual mental conflict.

The problem with such experimental approaches is one called **ecological validity.** Ecological validity concerns the degree to which the experimental treatment or manipulation approximates real life. It seems unlikely that a suggested memory of conflict can closely approximate a real-life conflict in all its particulars. People who have real, disturbing, conflicts with parents probably are different from those who have conflicts hypnotically induced in two respects. First of all, real conflict arises from something in the person himself or herself in interaction with his or her parent. Second, conflicts with parents evolve over decades, reinforcing certain feelings, memories, and behavioral patterns throughout the personality system. This is likely to have a more extensive, general impact than an experimental induction of a personal conflict that lasts for just an hour or so.

> The great tragedy of Science—
> the slaying of a beautiful
> hypothesis by an ugly fact.
> T. H. Huxley

There do exist, however, certain parts of personality—including mood and learning—that can be convincingly manipulated. Experimental manipulations that improve a person's abilities are especially interesting, because they suggest that a person can improve his or her condition in life. Twenty-seven members of the United States Figure Skating Association participated in a true experiment to see if their skating ability could be improved. Skaters in the experimental group were assigned a mental rehearsal treatment. They imagined a real skating competition, seeing themselves on the ice, visualizing their coach at the skating door, as well as the judges.

Disciplinary Crossroads

The Measurement of Length in the Physical Sciences

Personality measurement has evolved, and the concepts of reliability and validity have been successfully applied in the field. Measurement in other sciences has evolved as well. Consider how to measure length. True, in the twenty-first century, one is apt to take such a direct physical measurement for granted. Yet, even the measurement of such an obvious quality did not spring full-grown; rather, it evolved alongside science and technology. The following historical description is based on an earlier compilation by Jones (1971, pp. 338–340).

The earliest units of length—thought to be employed as long ago as 7000 B.C.E.—used parts of the human body as standards. Thus, the cubit (also known as the elbow or ell) was the length of the forearm from the point of the elbow to the tip of the outstretched middle finger. Another such length was the digit, which was the breadth of a finger. Because people undoubtedly varied in size in 7000 B.C.E. as they

do today, these units probably varied according to who was doing the measuring.

Next, attempts were made to create standards of certain lengths. By about 2300 B.C.E., the Babylonians employed cords in which knots were tied at five-cubit intervals. By 1500 B.C., a cubit rod with subsidiary measures on it was employed by the Egyptians (and is on display at the Louvre in Paris).

As modern governments evolved in Europe, they took on the responsibility of standardizing measurements. Thus, Edward I, King of England, decreed in 1305 that "Three grains of barley dry and round make an inch; twelve inches make a foot; three feet make an ulna; five and a half ulnae make a rod; and forty rods in length and four in breadth make an acre." Although the King's decree mentioned grains of barley, measurement was in fact standardized against a single iron rod designated as one ulna in length. The barleycorn-unit remains in use today—it is the unit in which shoe sizes are

As they imagined this, their own skating music was played, and they drew their movements on a page. The skaters in the control group were assigned stretching exercises for the same period of time. Results showed that, in a subsequent skating competition, mental rehearsals improved rated performance of the experimental group relative to the control group, for jumping, spins, and connecting moves (Garza & Feltz, 1998).

There are many other opportunities for experimental changes in personality. For example, considerable experimental work has been devoted to changing peoples' moods through mood manipulations and seeing what influence that has on their thoughts (e.g., Forgas, 2001). Other research has instructed people to control their thoughts in various ways so as to examine what is most effective in blocking out unwanted ideas (e.g., Wegner, 1989). Still other research has involved experimentally inducing fear (through threatening electrical shocks) to examine which kinds of people recognize they are afraid, and which don't (Weinberger, Schwartz, & Davidson, 1979). Experiments play an important role in understanding how personality functions.

measured. That is, a shoe size 9 is one barleycorn longer than a shoe size of 8.

As the industrial age progressed, increasingly accurate measures were needed. People recognized that iron rods expanded and shrank with temperature. In 1835, a gunmetal bar was designated the "imperial yard." It remains today, defined as correct at 62 degrees Fahrenheit with a barometer at thirty inches of mercury.

Scientific measurement proceeded at a different pace in different places. As late as 1800 in France, for example, the Arabic hashimi cubit (about two feet) was a measure of length—and three distinct standards were said to have been used within the city of Bordeaux alone.

In 1791, to remedy such difficulties, the French Academie of Sciences proposed a metric standard as one ten-millionth of the earth's polar quadrant passing through Dunkirk and Barcelona. This standard was compulsory in parts of France and Italy, in Austria, and in Germany. A seventeen-nation treaty, known as the Convention of the Meter and signed in 1875, used a standard platinum-iridium meter bar, stored in a vault at the International Bureau of Weights and Measures in Sevres, France.

Within the metric system, the centimeter itself was redefined for even greater precision. The Eleventh General Conference of Weights and Measures, meeting in 1960 with thirty-eight countries represented, agreed upon an international meter that was precisely 1,650,763.73 vacuum wavelengths of monochromatic orange light emitted by a krypton atom of mass 86. The measurement of length had come quite a distance!

Concerns such as standards, and conditions of measurement, apply across disciplines. For example, measurement standards are set in psychology by examining test averages on many people (called standardization). People's scores are compared according to whether they are above or below the mean. Conditions of measurement are important because, for example, a person must be awake, well, and free of distraction to concentrate on the questions at hand. Psychological measurement must be repeatable (reliable) and measure a person's actual attributes.

What Does It Mean to Measure Personality?

The Psychometric Approach

What Is Measurement?

Whether the research design employed is a case study, a correlational design, or a true experiment with random assignment, some measurement of human attributes must take place. But what is measurement? We never really measure an object itself, but rather a property of an object. For example, we do not measure tables, diamonds, or races. Rather, we measure the *length* of a table, the *weight* of a diamond, or the *duration* of a horse's run around a track. In the same way, we don't measure personality, but rather, we measure the *intelligence, extraversion,* or *emotionality* of a personality.

Personality Measurement: A research procedure in which numerals are assigned to features of a personality in a systematic fashion.

Personality measurement is the assignment of numerals to the various features or properties of personalities according to some orderly system. By a property or attribute of a person we mean any characteristic that can vary. The properties that vary are referred to as variables.

At the outset of the twentieth century psychologists commonly doubted that measurement of such abstract qualities as intelligence, extraversion, or emotion was possible. Only after the 1920s did experts come to agree that such measurement could be carried out adequately. Some landmarks in the first one hundred years of testing are shown in Table 2.3. The evolution of psychological measurement is typical of many disciplines in that progress required many innovations and considerable time. Even measuring length is not so straightforward as it seems today—as illustrated in the Disciplinary Crossroads box.

Fundamentals of Measurement

Psychometrics: A branch of psychology concerned with measuring mental and behavioral attributes.

Psychometrics is the field within psychology devoted to the measurement of the psychological attributes of a person. The psychometrician is a person who studies, develops, and applies psychometric theory. Psychometric theory enables us to interpret test scores; that is, to figure out what they mean for the individual who obtains them. The theory also enables us to evaluate a test according to preestablished criteria so that we can decide how good or bad it actually is.

Test (or Scale): In psychometrics, a defined group of questions or tasks (called items), to which a person can respond, that is intended to measure one or more attributes of the person.

Psychometricians often use psychological tests to measure a person's attributes. A **test** (or **scale**) can be defined as a systematic procedure in which individuals are presented with a set of constructed stimuli, called "items," to which they respond in some way. Test items come in a variety of forms, from "Do you like broccoli? (Yes/No)" to "How many uses can you think of for a teaspoon?"

Classical Test Theory (CTT)

Classical Test Theory: A theory underlying much psychological measurement, classical test theory is notable for its clarity and powerful predictions. Also known as classical true-score theory and classical reliability theory.

Most of the standard procedures for creating and evaluating tests are based on a set of assumptions that has come to be called **classical test theory**. Classical test theory is a set of assumptions and mathematical derivations that describe much of the basic thinking about tests in use today. There also exist more contemporary developments of the theory but the classical version provides a good beginning to the field (Allen & Yen, 1979; Bechger et al., 2003; Cronbach et al, 1965; Murphy & DeShon, 2000; Novick, 1966).

• FACTS • AT • A • GLANCE •

Selected Milestones in One Hundred Plus Years of Personality Testing

1904   The first major textbook on educational and psychological measurement, *Introduction to the Theory of Mental and Social Measurement* is published by E. L. Thorndike.

1905   The first intelligence test is published by Binet and Simon—forming the basis of the intelligence tests that would come later.

1910   The first word-association test designed to study the mental complexes of psychiatric patients is published by Carl Jung.

1917   The first group intelligence tests are used to place enlistees by the U.S. Army in World War I.

1921   Herman Rorschach introduces the world to the inkblot test, with the publication of *Psychodianostics: A diagnostic test based on perception,* in German.

1927   The first career-interest tests are published by Strong.

1936   The Graduate Record Exam is first used to screen applicants to graduate school.

1938   Henry Murray and his colleagues introduce the Thematic Apperception Test—a projective test, often used for measuring motives.

1942   The Minnesota Multiphasic Personality Inventory—a test of abnormal personality—is introduced

1952   The APA's Committee on Test Standards publishes the first technical recommendations for psychological measures.

1956   Paul Meehl publishes "Wanted—A good cookbook" in the *American Psychologist,* in which he summarizes the convincing evidence that test evaluations outperform clinical judgment in assessments of people.

1959   Hans Eysenck introduces the Maudsley Personality Inventory, the first scale designed to measure a person's Extraversion and Neuroticism—the first two dimensions of (what would later become) the Big Five trait approach.

1961   Tupes and Christal publish the first consistent findings of what became known as the Big Five personality traits in a U.S. Air Force technical report.

1966   The first *Standards for Educational and Psychological Tests and Manuals* is published jointly by the American Psychological Association and the American Educational Research Association.

1968   Walter Mischel publishes "Personality and Assessment," in which he finds that many tests (excluding intelligence tests) have an upper limit of around $r = .30$ in predicting single behaviors. The figure was later revised upward to $r = .40$ or .45 by others.

1980   Seymour Epstein publishes "The Stability of Behavior: II. Implications for Psychological Research" in the *American Psychologist,* in which he demonstrates how tests perform better than Mischel thought (see the previous) when predicting aggregated (groups of) behaviors.

1993   Lewis Goldberg publishes "The Structure of Phenotypic Personality Traits" in the *American Psychologist,* indicating that the Big Five personality traits had come of age.

1994   By 1994, over 3,009 mental tests are in print, a sizeable number measuring personality attributes from achievement motivation to Xenophobia, with self-esteem and qualities such as the Big Five traits in between.

2001   Psychological tests are found to be comparable in accuracy to medical tests.

2005   By 2005, a search in PsycINFO for the term "personality test" brings up more than 2,500 scientific articles.

Sources: From Aiken (2003), p. 5; Meyer et al. (2001); Murray (1938; 1994); Peterson, (1997), and general sources.

The fundamental hypothesis of classical test theory is that a person's score on a test is made up of a combination of an ideal "true" score and an "error" score. So, if Michael receives a score of 60 on a test of extraversion, that score reflects some portion of his true level of sociability, and some error. In terms of an equation, the fundamental assumption of classical test theory is this:

$$X = T + E,$$

Obtained Score: In psychometrics, the score a person obtains on a test.

True Score: In psychometrics, a hypothetical score a person would obtain on a test that has measured the person perfectly; that is, the score that reflects the real level of the attribute in the person who is being measured.

Error Score: In psychometrics, a hypothetical score that reflects mistakes in measurement that are either positive or negative. Positive error scores reflect testing that gives the respondent too much credit; negative error scores reflect testing that has not given the respondent enough credit.

X = an **obtained score** on a test.
T = a person's **true score** on a test.
E = a person's **error score** on a test.

So, Michael's true level of extraversion might be $T = 50$. Given that his obtained score was $X = 60$, that means his score included an error of $E = 10$; that is, he scored 10 points too high. How could that happen? Well, right before walking into the test, he might have been among a group of friends and had an enjoyable, lively conversation with them. As he answered questions on the extraversion test such as "Do you like being with groups of people?" his memory might have been biased by that recent experience, which caused him to inflate his enjoyment of such activities. You can see that Michael's score could have come out too low, at 40, as well, if he had had some unpleasant experiences with his friends; in that case his error score would have been $E = -10$.

Criteria for Good Measurement

One of the purposes of psychometric theory is to permit us to decide whether a test is an adequate measure of a concept. Psychometrics has two primary criteria of whether a test works: Whether the test is reliable, and whether it is valid.

Reliability

What Is Reliability?

Reliability: In psychometrics, the consistency with a test measures. More technically, the correlation between people's obtained score on a test and their corresponding true scores.

A commonsense understanding of **reliability** equates it to stability, predictability, dependability, and consistency. For example, a bathroom scale that gives you the same weight when you step on it twice or three times in a row is reliable. A reliable test will yield the same score for people with the same level of a given attribute each time it is given. A test is judged to be reliable when it is found to measure whatever it measures with consistency.

Further insight into reliability is offered by recalling the concepts of obtained, true, and error scores from classical test theory. Recall that the obtained score equals the true score plus the error score, or, $X = T + E$. In classical test theory, tests are more reliable when the error is small. In fact, when the obtained score equals the true score, there is no error ($X = T$), and the test is considered to be perfectly reliable. Actually, test reliability is defined as the correlation coefficient between the test's obtained score and true score across the sample. Of course, it is unusual for the obtained score to equal the true score exactly. There is usually some error (E). When the error is small, however, the correlation between the obtained score and true score may be as high as $r = .80$ or $.90$. If the error is large, however, the

> Science is the attempt to make the chaotic diversity of our sense-experience correspond to a logically uniform system of thought.
>
> Albert Einstein

reliability may approach zero. When the obtained scores on the test equal only error (X = E), the test is said to possess no reliability at all, $r = 0$. (Reliability coefficients typically range from zero to 1.0; they do not commonly fall into negative territory.)

Estimating Reliability

There exists no way to directly calculate a reliability by, say, correlating obtained scores with true scores. The reason? True scores are theoretical entities and cannot be known directly. It is relatively easy, however, to *estimate* reliability using any of several methods. Derivations from Classical Test Theory indicate that these methods provide closely equivalent estimates of reliability under many conditions. They do, however, vary a bit, for reasons discussed next.

Types of Reliability

Parallel Forms Reliability

Perhaps the most straightforward way to judge a test's reliability is to write two strictly parallel tests and intercorrelate them. Parallel tests have comparable items between the forms. For example, an item on one test might ask, "Are you moody?" whereas the corresponding item on its parallel test might ask, "Does your mood go up and down?" Other items would be similarly parallel across forms. In such an instance, the reliability of either test is equal to the correlation between the two tests. This is known as **parallel forms reliability**. Although this method is sometimes used, it is often considered labor intensive in that one must produce two tests when often only one is needed.

Parallel Forms Reliability: A reliability coefficient calculated by developing two parallel forms of the same test and correlating them.

Internal Consistency Reliability

Another way to determine a test's reliability is to estimate its internal consistency. This is known as **internal consistency reliability**. The simplest form of internal consistency is a split-half reliability. The split-half method involves first dividing a test into parallel halves. Although one is dealing with a single test, one considers the two halves as representing parallel forms of one larger test (see parallel forms reliability, above). For example, the test might be divided into its odd-numbered items and even-numbered items. The correlation of the two halves is a direct estimate of the reliability of half the test. It must be corrected upward to get a reliability of the whole test, and this can be done by employing a special correction.

Internal Consistency Reliability: A type of reliability estimated by examining the intercorrelations of items on a test. Examples include split-half and coefficient alpha reliability coefficients.

One limitation of split-half reliability is that there is usually more than one way to split a test in half—into odd and even halves, but also, say, into first and second halves. Each different split can potentially yield a somewhat different estimate of reliability (although for longer tests, the estimates are very similar). To get around this problem, most psychologists employ coefficient alpha, which is roughly equivalent to the average of all the split-half reliabilities. Coefficient alpha is the most commonly employed reliability estimate today.

Test-Retest Reliability

A final way to calculate reliability is to administer the same test at two different points in time to find out whether the taker's scores stay the same over time. This method, known as **test-retest reliability**, works well for tests that measure characteristics that are expected to stay relatively constant over a period of months or years, such as intelligences or attitudes. One cannot use the test-retest method with, say, hunger levels

Test-Retest Reliability: A type of reliability that is estimated by giving the same test to a group of people at two points in time, typically a few weeks apart, and then correlating the scores across administration.

because the changes in test scores between one occasion and the next might result from actual shifts in the person's hunger rather than from the test's unreliability. In such instances, internal consistency approaches to reliability work better.

Note that test-retest reliability tells us something more than just about the test itself. It tells us both that the test is consistent, and that the quality being measured is stable over time. In essence, the reliability coefficient is telling us when it is appropriate to use a given test and the scores it produces: It is telling us the score will indicate something stable over time. This application of reliability to more general problems of measurement provides a basis of one of the more recent developments of classical test theory (e.g., Cronbach et al., 1965; Murphy & DeShon, 2000).

Evaluating Reliabilities

For basic research, a reliability of r = .50–60 is not uncommon, but r = .70 or higher is considered desirable. For other personality assessments where the test may be used to help determine someone's future, reliabilities of at least r = .85 are considered desirable, because reliability influences how accurately one's predictions about the individual student will be.

Recall that reliability assesses whether a test measures *something* with consistency. Reliability is a necessary attribute of a good test. For a test to truly work, however, it must also measure what it is intended to measure. This aspect of a test's performance is called validity.

Validity

Validity: In psychological measurement, the fact that a test measures what it claims to measure.

Validity refers to whether a test measures what it is intended to measure. The validity of a test is based on many types of evidence. Some evidence for a test's validity may be based on logical argument, whereas other evidence may come from empirical studies. A test may be valid for some purposes but not for others—that is, it may measure the right thing in some circumstances but not others. A test needs to possess the right kinds of validity to accomplish the task it was designed for. The kind of validity that is most important may vary depending upon whether the test was designed as an assessment instrument, or to predict a criterion, or to test a theory (Landy, 1986). Some of the more important forms of validity are covered next.

Content Validity

Content Validity: A type of validity a test exhibits when its items are systematically selected from the areas the test claims to measure. For example, if the test measures U.S. history from 1900 to 1950, and its items sample history questions from the five decades in question, that would reflect content validity.

Content validity refers to whether the given test measures the content that it is supposed to measure. For instance, if one wants the test to measure "hostility," then it is important to define hostility, and write test items to measure each of its aspects. A. H. Buss and Durkee (1957) defined hostility as including: (a) assaults on others, (b) indirect hostility (e.g., not helping a person who would otherwise be harmed), (c) irritability, (d) negativism, (e) resentment, (f) suspicion, and (g) verbal hostility. They then wrote a scale that carefully included items to measure each of the foregoing areas. That process helped insure that their scale had content validity.

Criterion Validity

Criterion Validity: A type of validity a test exhibits when it correlates with a criterion of interest.

Criterion validity refers to the fact that a test correlates with a criterion. A criterion is a standard of performance or an outcome that one wants to predict; it might be grades, behaviors, or good health. For example, because intelligence tests correlate with school grades, they are said to have criterion validity for predicting school grades. When intelligence tests are found to correlate with students' current grades they are said to have *concurrent* validity because they are predicting to a criterion that is occurring at (roughly) the same time as the testing. When intelligence tests are found to correlate with future school performance they are said to have *predictive* validity because they are correlating with a future criterion. Tests with criterion validity are often used to diagnose people or to select people for particular positions in organizations for which their skills and tendencies are a good fit. For example, tests of sociability might help a person decide that sales would be a possible career for him or her, because more sociable people tend to enjoy sales more.

Structural Validity

Structural Validity: A type of validity a test exhibits when its items form a number of groups (as determined empirically by a technique such as factor analysis) that correspond to the number of things the test as a whole claims to measure. For example, if research indicates a test has three distinct groups of items, and those groups correspond to three scales that claim to measure three things, the test has structural validity.

Another form of validity is called **structural validity**. The "structural" part of structural validity refers to how many independent variables the test measures. This is decided by examining the structure of the data produced by the test. For example, one can mathematically accumulate evidence that a test is measuring one thing, two things, or more things, even without knowing what those things are. When you measure the height and width of a window, for instance, you know that you are measuring two different things in part because height and width vary separately. When test items vary separately, that indicates that the items are measuring separate things as well.

The idea behind structural validity is that a test should measure the number of things it says it does (Loevinger, 1967). If a test author says the test measures two things and it does, then it is structurally valid. If the test measures only one variable or four variables, however, it would lack structural validity because the test would fail to match the theory on which it is based. In practice, a test maker might claim his or her test measured only extraversion. A structural analysis of the test, however, might indicate that it measured three different scores—none of which were related to the other. In such a case, the test would lack structural validity. Structural validity is determined by using factor analysis, a mathematical technique that is described later in this chapter.

Construct Validity

Construct Validity: The degree to which a test measures the concept it is supposed to measure. Construct validity must be established on the basis of considering other forms of validity: content, criterion, and structural; if everything indicates the measure is assessing people as it should, then construct validity can be established.

Construct validity refers to whether a given test behaves as you would want or expect it to, given what it claims to measure. The "construct" really refers to the *concept* of the test (in fact some theorists believe it is indistinguishable from the concept of validity itself). Let us say, for example, that we have a test that measures a person's honesty in a variety of situations. For the test to have construct validity, it should give higher scores to those people who are honest in more areas of their lives relative to others. So, for example, an investigator might give the test to clergy, to a general sample, and to felons serving out their jail time. If the researchers found that the test rated the clergy most honest, the general sample somewhere in the middle, and the felons most dishonest, the outcome would give you confidence that the test measured what it was supposed to.

Next the investigator might create an experimental manipulation in which students in the lab took a test about celebrities in a room with a current *People* magazine plainly in view. If the high scorers on the honesty test refrained from opening the

Test Yourself: From Magazine Quizzes to Psychological Tests

For many years, magazines and newspapers across the United States have published personality-related quizzes for their readers to take so as to evaluate themselves. *Esquire, Cosmopolitan,* the *Utne Reader,* and many others have all included such quizzes at one time or another. Often, such scales are presented in the form of a psychological test, and they promise to describe some of the qualities of their readers' personalities—helping them to gain self-knowledge.

The best of such quizzes are breezy, fun, and informative. Jennifer Lawrence, a writer who works with horses and teaches riding and aerobics, wrote the following quiz to help people think about their approach to fitness (Lawrence, 2000). Take it and see how you do.

Fitness Aptitude Quiz

1. Your idea of a great workout is …
    a. Taking the dog for a hike in the woods.
    b. Beating your opponent in a blistering one-on-one game of tennis, racquetball, etc.
    c. Going to the gym and not having to wait in line to use any of the equipment.
    d. Enjoying a gentle yoga class.
    e. Shopping at the outlet mall the day after Thanksgiving.
2. Your favorite pair of shoes are …
    a. Hiking boots
    b. The latest in pump, gel or air technology
    c. Cross-trainers
    d. Sturdy, comfortable walking shoes
    e. Faux leopard bedroom slippers
3. Congratulations! You've just won a vacation to an all-inclusive Jamaican resort. The first thing you do is …
    a. Try parasailing
    b. Sign up for a beach volleyball tournament
    c. Do some laps in the pool
    d. Stroll on the beach in the tropical sunshine
    e. Take advantage of the swim-up bar
4. After a hard week of work, you've finally got a morning all to yourself. You can't wait to …
    a. Bike up to the mountains to see the sun rise
    b. Meet your friends at the courts for a game
    c. Hit the gym, then go shopping for new workout clothes
    d. Putter in the garden
    e. Unplug the phone and alarm clock and sleep in.
5. Your favorite sporting event is …
    a. The X-Treme Games
    b. The Super Bowl
    c. The Boston Marathon

Test Yourself *(Continued)*

    d. Figure Skating Championships
    e. Channel Surfing
6. One of your favorite sayings is . . .
    a. A rolling stone gathers no moss
    b. You gotta be in it to win it
    c. Rome wasn't built in a day
    d. Slow and steady wins the race
    e. Good things come to those who wait

Here is how readers were instructed to evaluate their test responses:

If you scored mostly A's, you're an Outward Bounder. You enjoy being outdoors, breathing fresh air and using the outdoors as your gym. Who needs a treadmill when you've got the open road?

If you scored mostly B's, you're a Rockin' Jock. You have a tough competitive nature and may already be an avid sports participant. Others describe you as the one to beat.

If you scored mostly C's, you're a Gym Dandy. You are self-motivated, fairly disciplined and enjoy working out several times a week. Although you may not feel totally confident in the hows and why of your routine, at least you've got one.

If you scored mostly D's, you're an Easy Spirit. You're not against getting physical, but you don't want to push yourself too hard. You may have some limitations, health issues or maybe you're just older and wiser.

If you scored mostly Es, you're a Channel Surfer. You're honest enough to admit that you're among the majority of Americans who, while not necessarily sedentary, aren't doing anything physical to improve their health. But the fact that you've read this far is a good sign.

Compare this quiz to a psychological test . . . This quiz, first published in *Vegetarian Times* maga-zine, is similar in many ways to a psychological test. The author created a theory of fitness types: Outward Bounders, Gym Dandy's, and Rockin' Jocks, among others. She then selected questions related to people's fitness attitudes and styles, and provided them with the kinds of responses to choose from that reflect people's fitness attitudes: (e.g., "You can't wait to . . . meet your friends at the courts for some games"). She then classified each response as indi-cating one or the other of her fitness types. Her scoring system is rational and logical.

The clarity and logic of this quiz make it an unusually good instance of a magazine quiz (and it compares favorably with many psychological tests, as well). So what more is needed to make a psychological test? To fully develop a psychological test, data must be collected so as to evaluate the measure's reliability and validity as discussed in the "What Does It Mean to Measure Personality" section of this chapter. Modifications may then be introduced to improve the scale's performance.

People magazine, whereas the low scorers did look for hints, the test's construct validity would be further supported. Finally, the test of honesty might be intercorrelated with a test of lying, and a negative correlation would be expected. If the test performed as expected in each of these situations then it would be gathering evidence to support its construct validity (Cronbach & Meehl, 1955).

Evaluating Validity

There is no single way to evaluate validity. Some tests have content validity in that their items measure all the right areas of a concept, yet they may still fail to predict a criterion of interest; hence, they would be said to lack criterion validity. Some tests are valid for some purposes but not for others. Intelligence tests, for example are valid for predicting grade-point average, but invalid for predicting good moods. Some tests are valid in some settings but not in others. For example, a self-report test of honesty might work when it is filled out anonymously, but almost everyone might claim to be honest most the time if they had to put down their names. To pick the right test for the right purpose requires understanding concepts of validity and how a specific test will perform in a particular situation. Do you think tests in magazines, such as the one in Test Yourself can meet the criteria of reliability and validity?

How Do Personality Psychologists Study So Many Variables?

Multiple Variables and Multivariate Techniques

Many variables must be measured to fully assess how the personality system is operating. Let's say a researcher wants to predict performance on the job. What personality variables should be measured? Well, motivation, of course, and then there is emotional style, and intellectual competence, and styles of coping for when things get tough, and interpersonal styles . . . and, in this way, the variables multiply. Even taking coping style by itself, we may wonder how many coping styles there are and how many need to be measured to get a sense of how someone copes.

Multivariate Statistical Technique: A statistical technique designed especially to answer questions about more than two variables at a time.

Factor Analysis: A mathematical technique for grouping variables together based on their inter-correlations. Factor analysis is used to reduced large numbers of variables to smaller sets, and also for determining structural validity; that is, how many things a test measures.

To help cope with so many variables, psychologists have developed **multivariate statistical techniques.** These techniques are, basically, extensions of simpler statistics such as a correlation, to larger numbers of variables. Knowing how to use and fully interpret a multivariate statistical technique is typically the subject of an advanced undergraduate or graduate level statistics course. We can introduce the subject here, though—by fostering a beginning understanding of one such technique, **factor analysis**, that is widely employed in the field to organize multiple variables. Many examples of factor analysis will appear in forthcoming chapters because a considerable amount of our present-day understanding of parts of personality relies on the technique.

The Logic of Factor Analysis

Factor analysis is the oldest and best developed of the techniques for organizing many variables. It can be used to group similar traits according to their similarities. For example, it tells us that thrill-seeking, liveliness, and sociability are all part of extraversion. The purpose of factor analysis is to help a psychologist understand how many things the items on a test measure, or, in other uses, how many things multiple tests measure. As an introduction to the technique, we will focus on the factor analysis of a small set of items from a single test. Recall from the earlier section on test validity that structural validity refers to how many things a test measures. Factor analysis is the mathematical technique that determines answers to that question.

The logic of factor analysis is straightforward. If two test items are always answered the same way, then they are said to measure the same thing. For example, if people who say they always cope by "doubling their efforts" also say they "changed something so as to make it better," and if other people who rarely "double their efforts," also rarely "change something to make it better," then the two items are answered the same way and are said to measure the same thing. If test items are answered differently, however, then they are said to measure different things.

In one study, people answered a longer test with four items similar to those shown in Table 2.3 (Anshel, Williams, & Williams, 2000; Folkman et al., 1986).

> **Mathematics, rightly viewed, possesses not only truth, but supreme beauty—a beauty cold and austere, like that of sculpture, without appeal to any part of our weaker nature, without the gorgeous trappings of painting or music, yet sublimely pure, and capable of a stern perfection such as only the greatest art can show.**
>
> Bertrand Russell

Participants were asked to recall a recent stressful event, one in which they might lose the affection of someone important, or appear uncaring or unethical, or need to cope with harm to a loved one. Then participants answered questions by agreeing or disagreeing with statements describing their typical responses to the situations. For example, the respondent might, for item A, agree or disagree with the idea that he or she had "doubled my efforts to work things out; I knew what had to be done," or (for item B) "changed something so things would turn out right." Both of these items seem to describe a proactive, effortful response to stress and it seems likely people who would use one strategy would use the other. A person who would respond to A with a "4" (agree) might also respond to B with a "4." A person who used some other coping strategy, however, such as doing nothing, would tend to disagree with both items (responding with a "1" or "2," to disagree). Therefore, items A and B would be answered in much the same way. According to the logic of factor analysis, they would be measuring the same thing. When two or more items are said to measure the same thing, that thing is referred to as a factor. Thus, in the terminology of factor analysis, we would say that Items A and B—"doubled efforts," and "changed something"—are two items that measure one factor.

Now consider item C, "accepted sympathy and understanding from someone," and item D, "discussed my feelings and thoughts with someone I knew well." These items both reflect seeking support from others. It also seems likely that people would answer these two items in similar ways. After all, a person who likes to get help from others would both accept sympathy from others (item C) and talk about his or her feelings (item D), and mark 4 (agree) or 5 (strongly agree) for both items. If items C and D are answered in the same way as well, they also would be measuring the same thing according to the logic of factor analysis. Again, one would conclude that items C and D are two items that measure one factor.

Finally, compare items A and B with items C and D. Some proactive copers (who endorse items A and B) might also seek support from others (endorse items C and D). Other proactive copers, however, might cherish their independence and avoid

---

TABLE 2.3   A Coping Test

Test Instructions: Please answer the following questions using this scale:
   1: strongly disagree; 2: disagree; 3: neutral; 4: agree; 5: strongly agree

A. _____   Doubled my efforts to work things out; I knew what I had to do.

B. _____   Changed something so things would turn out right.

C. _____   Accepted sympathy and understanding from someone.

D. _____   Discussed my feelings and thoughts with someone I knew well.

Source: Abridged and adapted from Folkman & Lazarus (1986), p. 8. Reprinted with permission of Mind Garden, www.mindgarden.com.

seeking help from others (disagree with C and D). That is, answers to items A and B tell us little or nothing about answers to items C and D. For that reason, items A and B are said to measure something different from what items C and D measure. That is what this particular logical analysis leads us to conclude—but is it an accurate reflection of how these test items really work?

Factor analytic techniques involve an empirical check of such logic. The first step of a factor analysis involves taking a set of test items, administering them to a group of people, and then finding the correlations among the items. For example, the four-item test described above (i.e., [A] "doubled efforts," [B] "changed something," [C] "accepted sympathy," and [D] "discussed feelings") might be given to one hundred people, and then test data would be collected that looked like those in Table 2.4.

TABLE 2.4   Raw Data Matrix for the Coping Test

	Item A Doubled efforts	Item B Changed something	Item C Accepted sympathy	Item D Discussed feelings
Person 1	5	5	1	1
Person 2	5	4	4	5
Person 3	1	2	3	3
Person 4	5	5	5	4
. . .	. . .	. . .	. . .	. . .
Person 100	1	1	1	1

Source: Abridged and adapted from Folkman & Lazarus (1986), p. 8. Reprinted with permission of Mind Garden, www.mindgarden.com.

TABLE 2.5	**Correlations among the Coping Items**			
	Item A Doubled efforts	Item B Changed something	Item C Accepted sympathy	Item D Discussed feelings
A. Doubled efforts	1.00			
B. Changed something	.40	1.00		
C. Accepted sympathy	.10	.10	1.00	
D. Discussed feelings	−.13	−.01	.39	1.00

Source: Abridged and adapted from Folkman & Lazarus (1986), p. 8. Reprinted with permission of Mind Garden, www.mindgarden.com.

Table 2.4 suggests that people tend to give answers to items A and B that are similar to one another; they also tend to give the answers to items C and D that are similar to each other. On the other hand, their answers to Items A and B seem unrelated to their answers on items C and D.

The exact degree to which people give the same answers to various item pairs are indexed with a correlation coefficient. The higher the correlation, the more people tended to give the same answers. The correlations among items A, B, C, and D are shown in the correlation matrix in Table 2.5. A correlation matrix is a table that has a set of variables across the top, and the same set of variables down the side. A given correlation coefficient—say between items A and B—can be found where column A intersects with row B.

Like any correlation matrix, only one half of the matrix is shown (in this case, the lower triangle of correlations) because the other half would be identical. The diagonal (the diagonal line of numbers that slopes across the table) is all 1.00s, indicating that each variable correlates with itself perfectly. The remaining correlation coefficients indicate the relationships among the variables we have just discussed. The (A) "doubled efforts" item correlates substantially with the (B) "changed something" item ($r = .40$). The (C) "accepted sympathy" and (D) "discussed feelings" items correlate highly as well ($r = .39$). But neither the (A) "doubled efforts" nor the (B) "changed something" items correlate with the (C) "accepted sympathy" item ($r = .10$ and .10, respectively) or the (D) "discussed feelings" item ($r = −.13$ and $−.01$).

But why don't the items that we thought might measure the same thing correlate with each more highly, close to $r = 1.0$? Instead they seem to correlate closer to $r = .40$. This occurs because each test item alone is very unreliable. Individual items can be thought of as the shortest possible test one can construct—and they are also the least reliable. Because the items are so unreliable by themselves—they contain so much error variance—their correlations with other similar items are relatively low.

Even though these correlations of around $r = .40$ are low, they are still relatively higher than the remainder of the correlations which seem very close to zero—between −.15 and +.15, in fact. The correlation matrix is another way of showing what we have already discussed: that items A and B seem to measure one thing, and items C and D measure a second, different thing. But note that we have now collected data that support our guess that "doubled efforts" and "changed something" are related. Factor analysis will sort the items based on these empirical relationships into separate groups: "doubled efforts" and "changed something," on the one hand, and "accepted sympathy" and "discussed feelings," on the other.

Reading the Results of a Factor Analysis

If all the results were as clear as those in the correlation matrix above, the analysis could stop here. But when a researcher is dealing with hundreds of items rather than four, and when the correlations are closer together, the second step of factor analysis becomes very important. This second step involves understanding how the original variables—the items on the test, in this case—relate to the factors. The outcome of this step can be understood apart from its mathematical method which is lucky because the mathematics employed are complex and outside the scope of this course in personality psychology. Even the name of the step: "extracting factors" or "estimating parameters" is a bit off-putting. To return to the point of this step: it is to rearrange mathematical information, so that the relations between each of the original test items, and the factors which now group the test items, are clear.

To do this, a table is created in which the original test items are listed down a column on the left-hand side, and the factors are numbered across the top. This arrangement is shown in Table 2.6. Table 2.6 is referred to as a "factor-loading table." It provides: (a) the original items, (b) the number of factors (things) the test measures, and (c) the correlation of the original variables with the factors, which are called **factor loadings**.

In Table 2.6, the four coping test items (on the left) are shown in relation to two factors (designated by roman numerals). The original items measuring "doubled ef-

Factor Loading: The correlation between an observed variable and a hypothetical variable called the factor (representing a group of variables).

TABLE 2.6 Factor Results for the Coping Scale		
Original Test Items	**Factor**	
	I	II
A. Doubled my efforts to work things out; I knew what I had to do.	.71	−.05
B. Changed something so things would turn out right.	.59	.13
C. Accepted sympathy and understanding from someone.	.15	.57
D. Discussed my feelings and thoughts with someone I knew well.	−.08	.56

Source: Abridged and adapted from Folkman & Lazarus (1986), p. 8. Reprinted with permission of Mind Garden, www.mindgarden.com.

forts" and "changed something," are highly correlated with, or load on, the first factor (.71 and .59), and the second group of original items "accepted sympathy," and "discussed feelings" are highly correlated with (that is, load on) the second factor (.57 and .56). Based on these results, the first factor was named "planful problem solving" and the second factor "seeking social support." The factor names are given by the researchers based on their judgment of the group of items that load on the factor (Folkman, Lazarus, Dunkel-Schetter, et al., 1986).

Today, many factor analyses are carried out as part of a broader mathematical technique called *structural equation modeling*. In the context of that newer technique, this second step of factor extraction is called parameter-estimation, and is represented in a figure rather than a table. Such a diagram is shown in Figure 2.6. There the original test items are represented in boxes and the factors are represented as ovals. The variables are connected to the factors by lines, and the factor loadings appear next to each line. So, much of the information remains the same: the same items are there; the same factors. The factor loadings, which had been found in the table, are instead transferred next to the line in the figure connecting the given item to the factor. For example, the factor loading of r = .71, which represented the relation between the "doubled my effort" item and the planful problem solving factor in Table 2.6, is found in Figure 2.6 on the line connecting the original item (in the square) and the factor (in the oval).

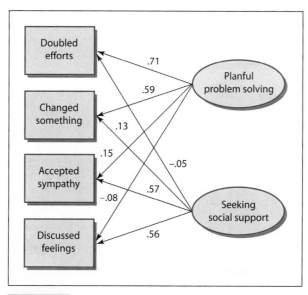

FIGURE 2.6   **A Factor Analysis Represented in Structural Equation Modeling**

In structural equation modeling, boxes represent observed variables, and ovals represent factors (or latent variables, more generally). This provides a pictorial representation of the data in Table 2.6.

Source: Abridged and adapted from Folkman & Lazarus (1986), p. 8. Reprinted with permission of Mind Garden, www.mindgarden.com.

Researchers often prefer this newer approach to factor analysis, because it makes it easier to compare different theoretical models by adding or altering lines between items and factors—and to test which models are better than others (e.g., Bentler, 2000; Gorsuch, 1983; Jöreskog & Sörbum, 1999); Maruyama, 1998; Raykov & Marcoulides, 2000.

High versus Low Correlations in the Correlation Matrix versus in the Factor Table

A few additional clarifications can complete this picture of factor analysis. Recall that the initial correlations among test items often included a fair number of low correlations in the correlation matrix. These correlations had resulted because the individual test items are often unreliable. You might wonder, then, why the individual items have far higher loadings on factors. The reason the correlations between items and factors are so much higher in the factor loading table (or diagram) is that this phase of factor analysis corrects for the unreliability of items. Typically, those items with loadings of $r = .40$ to $.90$ are considered good indicators of the factor; those items with loadings below $r = .30$ are considered relatively independent of the factor.

Bipolar Factors and Negative Correlations

What about negative correlations among items? To find out, let's return to the coping scale we first examined and add a negatively correlating item: test item E, "did nothing because I was confused about what to do," as illustrated in Table 2.7.

Let's suppose that planful problem solvers (who agree with items A and B) will tend to disagree with item E. Conversely, people who endorse item E, "did nothing," do not actively plan, and will disagree with A and B. If that is so, then item E will correlate *negatively* with items A and B, because as E goes up, A and B will go down, and vice versa. If we test this empirically, it will turn out to be the case. We would obtain a correlation matrix such as the one in Table 2.8.

TABLE 2.7	The Extended Coping Test

Test Instructions: Please answer the following questions using this scale:

1: strongly disagree; 2: disagree; 3: neutral; 4: agree; 5: strongly agree

A. _____ Doubled my efforts to work things out; I knew what I had to do.

B. _____ Changed something so things would turn out right.

C. _____ Accepted sympathy and understanding from someone.

D. _____ Discussed my feelings and thoughts with someone I knew well.

E. _____ Did nothing because I was confused about what to do.

Source: Abridged and adapted from Folkman & Lazarus (1986), p. 8. Reprinted with permission of Mind Garden, www.mindgarden.com.

TABLE 2.8	Correlations among the Items from the Extended Coping Test				
	Item A Doubled efforts	Item B Changed something	Item C Accepted sympathy	Item D Discussed feelings	Item E Did nothing
A. Doubled efforts	1.00				
B. Changed something	.40	1.00			
C. Accepted sympathy	.10	.10	1.00		
D. Discussed feelings	−.13	−.01	.39	1.00	
E. Did nothing	−.49	−.40	.07	−.03	1.00

Source: Abridged and adapted from Folkman & Lazarus (1986), p. 8. Reprinted with permission of Mind Garden, www.mindgarden.com.

Table 2.8 still indicates that only two factors are being measured: Planful problem solving and seeking social support. Why? The high negative correlations between E, and A and B (i.e., $r = -.49, -.40$) mean that there is a strong negative relationship between actively problem solving, on the one hand, and not doing anything, on the other. They are just the opposite sides of the same coin. Moving on to the second step of the factor analysis, the factor table would look like Table 2.9. "Did nothing" appears—with a fairly high negative correlation—on the planful problem solving factor. (When a variable correlates with a factor, we often say the variable "loads on" or "appears on" the factor.)

Table 2.9 indicates that whenever planful problem solving is present, action is present, and inaction is missing, and vice versa. In the last section, the factor analyst

TABLE 2.9	Factor Results for the Extended Coping Scale		
Original Test Items		**Factor**	
		I	II
A. Doubled my efforts to work things out; I knew what I had to do.		.71	2.05
B. Changed something so things would turn out right.		.61	.03
C. Accepted sympathy and understanding from someone.		.15	.57
D. Discussed my feelings and thoughts with someone I knew well.		−.08	.56
E. Did nothing because I was confused about what to do.		−.65	−.12

Source: Abridged and adapted from Folkman & Lazarus (1986), p. 8. Reprinted with permission of Mind Garden, www.mindgarden.com.

Bipolar Factor: In factor analysis, a factor that has both positive and negative variable loadings.

Unipolar Factor: In factor analysis, a factor that has only negative, or only positive variable loadings.

named the first factor "planful problem solving" and the second factor "seeking social support." Seeing the performance of the "did nothing" item, the analyst might want to rename the first factor "planful problem solving versus inaction," to reflect the fact that it has variables that define both extremes of coping. Sometimes a factor that displays this double-sided quality is referred to as a **bipolar factor**. Otherwise, the factor is referred to as a **unipolar factor**.

A Critique of Factor Analysis

Factor analysis is a useful technique for clustering variables according to their similarities. But factor analysis cannot substitute for good theories and careful thought about an area of measurement; it may sometimes group together items that, although highly correlated, are clearly theoretically distinct (Mayer, Salovey, Gomberg-Kaufman, & Blainey, 1991). For example, height and weight are highly intercorrelated—the taller people are, the more they weigh. And yet physicians would have overlooked very important aspects of personal health had they merely grouped height and weight together as a general size factor rather than noting, for example, that short

The direction a person takes in life is the product of many personality variables (and variables in the environment, as well). For that reason, personality psychologists have developed methods that enable them to deal with large numbers of psychological and other variables. By examining many variables together, scientists can do a better job of understanding the choice of direction a person finally takes.

height and high weight co-occur in obesity. Factor analysis more or less mindlessly clusters together intercorrelated variables. For some purposes that is the right thing to do; for other purposes, as with height and weight in medicine, it may well be the wrong thing to do. Only careful theoretical consideration can make a final determination of when it is right, and when it is wrong.

There are many opportunities for data collection and studying the relations among variables. Psychological tests ask many good questions. Factor analysis is an invaluable tool for organizing similar items together into factors so as to simplify the research task.

Reviewing Chapter 2

The aim of this chapter is to introduce you to how research is conducted in personality psychology. After examining the sorts of data available to the psychologist, several research approaches to personality psychology have been discussed, including case studies and correlational designs. Whatever design a psychologist uses, some measurement must be taken of the individual and/or his or her surroundings. Some elements of psychological measurement have been covered, particularly the fundamental ideas of psychometrics, including reliability and validity. Finally, personality psychologists often like to examine a number of personality variables together. The last section has examined the multivariate technique of factor analysis. Can you answer the following questions, arranged by the major sections of the chapter?

Where Do Data Come From?

1.   What are some of the places data come from?
Data about the person can come from the person's life sphere or life space. That data is often called Life data, or L data. Data from the person's life sphere may include institutional information from school records, biological information from medical tests, and observer-ratings. Data can also come from within the person, for example, from personal reports. Data from within the person include self-judgments. What other kinds of data come from the person himself or herself?

What Research Designs Are Used in Personality?

2.   What is the point of case studies?
Probably the earliest method used in personality psychology is the case study approach. When one describes a single person, one is using a case study method. What can case studies accomplish that other methods can't do as well? What are some of the drawbacks of case studies?

3.   What is observationism?
How is observationism similar to the case study? How is it different? What historical events in the field led to a deemphasis on observation?

4.   What is a correlational design?
What does correlational design involve? What does the method tell us? A correlation coefficient indicates the relationship between two variables. It is of central importance to conducting studies using correlational designs. These coefficients have a range from -1 to 1. Can you say what a coefficient of 1.0 means? What about 0.0 and $-.70$?

5.   What is a full experimental design and how does it compare to a natural experiment?
In an experiment, two groups are compared, and hypothesized to be different in relation to an outcome, called the dependent variable. Typically, the two groups

are called the experimental and the control groups. The experimental group has been changed through a treatment. The treatment is a manipulation of some sort that is expected to make the experimental group different from the control group. In a full experimental design, people are randomly assigned to the control and experimental groups, and then the treatment is applied to the experimental group. In a natural experiment, however, two groups that are naturally different are selected, such as two different occupational groups. What is the advantage of a full experimental design relative to a natural experiment? Given that superiority, why are natural experiments considered so useful in the study of personality?

What Does It Mean to Measure Personality?

6. What is the psychometric approach?
The field of psychometrics is concerned with creating workable mathematical models for measuring people's qualities. One doesn't measure a person, rather, one measures the attributes or features of a person. The fundamental theorem of psychometrics is that $X = T + E$, or, in words, that any observed score (X) reflects both a person's true quality (T) on the attribute, and some degree of error (E). What happens if an error is positive, or, if it is negative?

7. What is reliability?
Reliability is a property of all adequate measurement and concerns the degree to which tests measure with consistency. There are several different ways of assessing reliability, including the parallel test, internal consistency, and test-retest methods. Can you define each of these?

8. What is validity?
Validity refers to whether a test measures what it claims to measure. There are a number of types of validity, including content, criterion, structural, and construct validity. Can you define each of them?

How Do Personality Psychologists Study So Many Variables?

9. Why do personality psychologists study so many variables?
Personality is a comprehensive system, including many individual parts, their organization, and their development. Measuring enough aspects of personality to make

sense of it (and enough aspects of the life sphere to make sense of that) requires large numbers of individual observations. What is it about how we think of personality that encourages measuring so many different variables?

10. How do personality psychologists study so many variables?

Statistical techniques that examine many different variables are called multivariate techniques. A widely used method of looking at multiple variables is called factor analysis. When multiple variables are used, one often begins by calculating a simple index of relationship between each pair of variables. What statistic tells us about how two variables are related?

11. What is factor analysis?

Factor analysis concerns studying how many things a test measures. It can be used to reduce the number of variables of a test, and also to demonstrate a type of validity. Do you know which sort of validity it helps determine? If you were presented with a test that claimed to measure five things, and a factor analysis said it only measured three things, would you be able to conclude anything about the test's validity?

12. How do you read a factor analysis?

Basically, findings from a factor analysis are presented as follows: A list of original variables forms a left-hand column. To the right are columns representing factors, each labeled with a roman numeral. The columns themselves contain a correlation between an original variable and its factor. Do you know what the correlation between a test item and a factor is called?

13. What about the dimensions that factor analysis produces?

Factors with only positive (or negative) loadings are considered unipolar and are designated with one name (e.g., *Extraversion*). Factors with both positive and negative loadings are called bipolar and are designated with two opposing names: (e.g., *Extraversion-Introversion*). Seeing a factor table, would you be able to read a factor analysis and name the factors?

Chapter 3

Perspectives on Personality

*T*heoretical perspectives provide a way for psychologists to look at personality and to generate research questions about how personality operates. Some theoretical perspectives center on the psychological parts central to personality functioning and the dynamics among those parts. Other perspectives emphasize the contribution of the brain and its biology to personality. Still others focus on society's influence. Today, personality psychologists use such outlooks together to develop an integrated view of the person.

- **What Are Perspectives on Personality?**

  Questions about personality often stem from a particular point of view—such as that personality is influenced by biology or by the social world. Such outlooks are called perspectives on personality.

- **What Is the Biological Perspective?**

  The idea that personality is closely connected to the brain and other biological influences is known as the biological perspective. This perspective highlights the brain's contribution to personality, and how some personality mechanisms may have evolved.

- **What Is the Intrapsychic Perspective?**

  Intrapsychic perspectives, on the other hand, emphasize how one psychological part of personality influences another. For example, trait theorists may be interested in understanding which psychological qualities contribute to extraversion. Psychodynamic theorists are interested in how parts interact—and often conflict—with one another.

- **What Is the Sociocultural Perspective?**

  The idea that people are who they are because of the situations they face and the culture within which they are embedded forms a key part of the sociocultural perspective.

- **What Is the Temporal-Developmental Perspective?**

  Taking the long view on an individual—beginning by seeing what he or she is like as an infant, a child, an adolescent, and then an adult—is at the core of the temporal-developmental perspective.

- **How Does One Cope with Multiple Theories?**

  Each perspective has been responsible for focusing research efforts on a particular question about personality. The research hypotheses generated by such theories can be organized according to whether they address the parts, organization, or development of the personality system.

What Are Perspectives on Personality?

Frameworks, Perspectives, and Theories

Personalities come in a startling variety of forms and types. For example, Paul Erdos was a mathematician who published 1,475 academic papers in mathematics, some of monumental importance, with more than 485 coauthors. In the later decades of his life, he traveled to and from the homes of different colleagues, living from a suitcase and relying on a network of trust of colleagues, their students, and relatives. He supported himself through academic lectures and gave away most of his money to various charities, while encouraging young mathematicians and trying to keep up the spirits of those who were aging. Of Erdos, it was said that he could pose just the right problem for a fellow mathematician—just far enough ahead of his or her thinking to be challenging, just near enough to his or her abilities to be solved (Hoffman, 1998, pp. 7–10, 13, 42).

Why did Erdos devote his life to mathematics? How did his abilities arise? Was it in his genes, or due to his environment? What qualities did he possess that encouraged others to collaborate with him, and to host him? Have you ever imagined yourself completely devoting yourself to a single project or aim in your life?

Generating hypotheses about personality and testing them is at the heart of the science of personality psychology. Creating an explanation is often fostered by the use of one or more specific points of view, called theoretical perspectives or theories about how personality operates. These theoretical perspectives focus attention on a specific aspect of how and why personality functions as it does. Recall that a **framework** for a discipline—like the systems framework used in this book—divides personality into topics of study such as its parts, organization, and development. Frameworks, however, do not directly explain or account for the phenomena of the personality system, nor do frameworks create specific hypotheses to test. Theoretical perspectives do that. Such theoretical approaches range in scope from the very broad perspective, to the more focused theory, to the pragmatic micro-theory.

Framework (of a field): A framework for a field is an outline of that field's most important topics.

Perspectives on Personality

At the broadest theoretical level are the perspectives on the field. Concretely, the term *perspective* refers to the fact that, when one stands in a particular place, one can see some things and not others. Similarly, a perspective provides us with a special view of the personality system in which some things can be seen well and other things are, perhaps, a bit more obscured. A theoretical perspective, then, involves a "a place from which to view" certain parts of personality.

Using this knowledge, we can create a more formal definition of a personality perspective: A **personality perspective** is based on a set of assumptions or beliefs about what the most important influences on personality are. These influences are often classified according to the body of knowledge they draw on, be it knowledge of personality or one of the neighboring systems that surround it and influence it (Larsen & Buss, 2002, pp. 15–16). The systems we have discussed that surround and involve personality are biological, psychological, and sociocultural in nature. From that, it is possible to "deduce" that the major perspectives of study will be biological, psychological, and sociocultural, and to represent the time dimension) temporal—that is, developmental. These perspectives are, indeed, widely used, although the exact names and labels given to the perspectives vary (cf., Larsen & Buss, 2002; Funder, 2001; Mischel, 1998). The perspectives are shown in the top portion of the diagram in Figure 3.1.

Personality perspective: A manner of looking at personality that is made up of a number of related theories that emphasize certain influences on personality, and share in common certain assumptions. Examples include the psychodynamic perspective and the trait perspective.

The perspectives give us a hint as to where to look in understanding personality—to biology, or culture, for example—but they are not explicit in telling us how personality operates or how it came to be. For example, the biological perspective directs us toward an area of expertise that will be helpful to understanding the system. The perspective itself, however, exists at too broad a level to generate specific hypotheses for scientific testing. For that reason, many psychologists find it useful to go beyond a perspective on personality, to a theory of personality.

Personality Theories

Each general perspective has connected with it several more specific theories. In this chapter, each perspective is illustrated with one or two more specific theories. A

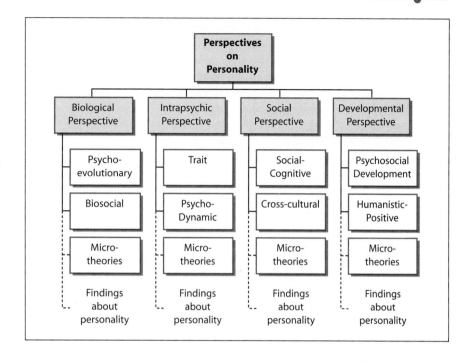

FIGURE 3.1

A Hierarchy of Theoretical Thought on Personality
Scientific thought about personality ranges from the general to the specific. These are arranged here as a hierarchy from general perspectives (near the top; e.g., Biological, Intrapsychic) to the empirical findings they help explain (at the bottom). In between are specific theories (e.g., Psycho-evolutionary, Biosocial, Trait), and micro-theories, which make the most specific predictions about how personality operates.

Theory of personality: A theory of personality is a set of statements or assumptions about human mental life or behavior that explains why people are the way they are.

theory of personality contains a set of statements or assumptions about how personality operates. It develops this series of assumptions into a picture of the individual. Next, a good theory will contain rules for relating those assumptions and definitions to real, observable, empirical events. That is, the theory makes guesses or predictions, called hypotheses, about how personality operates. The hypotheses are tested with empirical research, and that research may either bear out the entire theory, portions of it, or none of it (Hall & Lindzey, 1978, pp. 17–18). Thereafter, the theory may be modified to make it more accurate. The better the theory operates, the more weight it will be given.

In personality psychology, some theories are expressed in a logical organized fashion. For example, the social-cognitive theorist George Kelly (1955a) began his personality theory with a central postulate (roughly, that a person is like a scientist trying to discover and predict the world), and then set out additional assumptions that elaborated his views. Most larger personality theories, however, are developed over a series of publications. Freud's twenty-plus volumes of writings represent an evolution of his theory, and, to some extent, he left it to others to systematize it (Rapaport, 1960).

> **Theory helps us to bear our ignorance of facts.**
> George Santayana

Each theory makes predictions about people. For example, Kelly explained that if you asked a person to reconsider what he or she is thinking at the right time, it should bring about desired change in therapy (Kelly, 1995b, p. 1090). If Kelly's predictions seem fairly general, it is typical. The predictions of other major theorists, including Freud, Jung, and Rogers were also general. Many personality theories employed descriptions of behavior that were so general that, in the form they were proposed, they were not useful in motivating direct scientific investigations. Some theories are shown in the middle portion of Figure 3.1. Note that there are many different theories and many theories are sufficiently broad that there is more than one way to classify them. Some psychologists now prefer to talk about "approaches" rather than theories, believing that the original personality theories were misnamed (e.g., Funder, 2001). Whether or not that is the case, a better bridge between such approaches/theories and research work was still needed. So-called micro-theories create this bridge.

Micro-Theories and Research

The general theories—or approaches—to personality were too large, diffuse, and sometimes self-contradictory to be accessible to scientific test (e.g., Hall & Lindzey, 1978; Larsen & Buss, 2002; Mendelsohn, 1993). So, something more specific was needed to connect a theory (or approach) to actual research. This more specific level of theorizing—a level that addresses specific, relatively narrow problems in personality rather than trying to explain the whole personality—is here called the *micro-theory* level (Johnson et al., 1980). It is shown near the bottom right of Figure 3.1. Elsewhere, it has gone by the name of *mid-level theory*, and *limited-domain theory* (e.g., Maddi, 1993, p. 89; Schulz & Schulz, 2001, p. 445).

Micro-theories often arose in the research laboratory. Personality psychologists committed to conducting high-quality, rigorous research often preferred to develop smaller theories that took pieces of larger theories, such as those of Freud and Kelly, and turn them into research questions. The smaller micro-theories the researchers articulated could then be reasonably tested in the laboratory. In addition, researchers often raised some important theoretical questions of their own in their micro-theories. They certainly didn't want to be excluded from theorizing just because they preferred not to theorize about all of personality. The micro-theory level is crucial, because that is the theoretical level at which most personality research takes place.

Each micro-theory is empirically tested, and then results are obtained and interpreted. Typically, these results have implications for an understanding of personality's parts, organization, and development, as shown at the very bottom of Figure 3.1. It is these findings, drawn from across various theories, that we will employ to describe each of the remaining topics of this book: the parts of personality, personality organization, and personality development.

First, however, it is worth learning something of the theories that motivate some of the research discussed. Only the briefest sketch of each perspective and its theories can be presented in a single book chapter. However, the theories and their contributions will be repeatedly treated and further developed in the later chapters of the book. That said, those interested in the personality theories themselves are directed to any of the excellent textbooks devoted to them (e.g., Hall & Lindzey, 1978; Funder, 2001; Monte, 1999; Ryckman, 2004). The sketches provided here provide sufficient information to at least introduce these important theoretical influences on the field.

What Is the Biological Perspective?

The biological perspective emphasizes the influence of biology on an individual's mental and social functioning. Among the most influential biological approaches and theories are the psychoevolutionary theory and the biopsychological approach.

Psychoevolutionary theory emphasizes that much of the way an individual feels, thinks, and behaves is due to a long-standing evolutionary process. For example, we have emotions and memories because they have assisted our survival. The psychobiological perspective investigates the direct influences of the brain on mental life. The two approaches are complementary to one another. As people evolved, so did the direct influences exerted by the nervous system and brain on behavior.

Evolutionary Theory Views the Person

From an evolutionary perspective, each of us is the product of a very long line of ancestors. If any one of our ancestors in that great long chain had failed to survive and reproduce, we would not be here. The fossil record was full of organisms, most notably dinosaurs, that had become extinct. The same fossil record showed that other organisms that are with us today have gradually changed over time. Long before evolutionary theory was developed, it was understood that animal species—including the human species—changed over time.

Evolutionary theory helps explain how it is that some organisms survive and reproduce and others do not. Charles Darwin was the first to propose a theory of natural selection that described the process by which this occurs. In Darwin's original formulation, the evolution of species took place according to two processes: natural selection and sexual selection.

Natural and Sexual Selection

Natural selection describes how organisms with certain characteristics are better able to adapt to hostile forces of nature than are others. Because they are better adapted, they are most apt to survive and to reproduce. At one time, for example, the giraffe's ancestors had shorter necks. Over generations, competitor species began eating the lower growing leaves of the trees on which giraffes fed. Because the giraffes with longer necks were able to eat the high-growing leaves that the other animals could not reach, they were more likely to survive and reproduce. In each generation, giraffes with longer necks fared better, and, as a consequence, the species gradually developed the long neck as an adaptation to the environmental change imposed by the competitor species.

Adaptive responses to challenging environments, however, appear insufficient to explain all evolutionary phenomena. It is not enough for organisms to merely survive in order to reproduce; they must also attract mates. Consequently, some adaptations evolve for the purposes of sexual selection. The peacock's extensive and colorful feathers are not adaptive in the context of natural selection. In fact, they create a problem for the peacock because they are very noticeable to predators. They are adaptive, however, in terms of mate selection. The plumage attracts the peahen and thus increases the likelihood of sexual reproduction.

This simple model is the one that Darwin proposed in 1850. Since that time, some important elaborations have been added. Modern evolutionary theory is called "inclusive fitness theory" (Hamilton, 1964). It is concerned not solely with an individual and his or her genes, but also with the broader gene pool to which the individual belongs. Modern evolutionary theory better takes into account the way that an organism can benefit from helping a relative to survive and to mate. Brothers, for example, share 50 percent of their genes in common. For that reason, if one brother helps another survive (say, by protecting him against bullies), then that brother has enhanced the survival of his own genes as well. Psychoevolutionary theorists describe the existence of certain mental mechanisms—such as preferences for helping relatives—as a consequence of natural and sexual selection (Tooby & Cosmides, 1990).

A Micro-Theory about Jealousy and Evolution

The broader evolutionary perspective gives rise to more specific micro-theories concerning the different strategies men and women employ in relationships. For example, one of the central issues driving relationships between men and women from an evolutionary perspective concerns the certainty of parenthood. The condition of men and women in this regard is quite different. For example, mothers have an essentially 100 percent likelihood of knowing who their true children are. They give birth to them, after all. For fathers, however, the chances that they know their true offspring are somewhat less than 100 percent. It is always possible that a newborn might be the offspring of another man. From a psychoevolutionary perspective, such an outcome for a male—raising another man's child—would have disastrous consequences because it would mean that one's genes failed to survive another generation. Thus, evolutionary theory would predict that men should be very wary of possible threats to the sexual fidelity of their mates.

The woman's situation is different. She knows that her genes have been passed along to the next generation. She, too, is dependent upon her partner—but more for material resources than for assurances of reproductive success. She wants to prevent the loss of her mate's resources should he leave for another woman. The woman still knows her children are her own, even if the man has other sexual partners. On the other hand, if the man becomes emotionally committed to another woman, he might leave and in the process withdraw his resources: help with children, food gathering, and protection.

This reasoning leads to the conclusion that mental mechanisms should differ between men and women in response to infidelity in a relationship. From the evolutionary perspective, it would make sense for men to have developed mechanisms for monitoring their partners and preventing them from having other sexual liaisons. On the other hand, it would make sense for women to have developed mechanisms aimed at preventing men from straying from their emotional commitments. Such monitoring will help protect them from any intention on the man's part to withdraw commitment and resources. In short, men should jealously guard their mate's sexual fidelity; women should jealously guard their mate's emotional fidelity.

In a series of studies on sexual versus emotional jealousy, participants were asked to imagine a strong, committed, romantic relationship they had had in the past. Then, they were asked to rate how distressed they would feel if their partner "formed a deep emotional attachment" to someone else, or if their partner "enjoyed passionate sexual intercourse" with someone else. In keeping with the evolutionary hypothesis, 60 percent of all men reported more sexual than emotional jealousy. On the other hand, 80 percent of all women reported more emotional than sexual jealousy. This pattern is consistent across several Western cultures (Buss, Larsen, Westen, & Semmelroth, 1992; Buunk et al., 1996).

In this case, evolutionary psychology appears to offer a compelling and straight-forward explanation for an otherwise difficult-to-explain difference in mating behavior. The limitation of this perspective is that it is sometimes difficult to prove that evolution is at work rather than some other causal mechanism, such as some form of cultural learning. In addition, evolutionary psychology seems focused on universal adaptive and reproductive differences. It can predict the existence of individual differences (diversity increases survival), but it focuses less on telling us what those specific individual differences are, who has them, and how one should behave under the circumstances. For answers to these questions, other perspectives are helpful.

Biopsychology Views the Person

The biopsychological approach to personality views the individual's mental phenomena through the lens of how the nervous system and its surrounding biology influence a person's mental life. The nervous system is divided into two parts: the peripheral nervous system, which extends throughout the body, and the brain.

The brain itself has sometimes been described as composed of three layers representing three phases of its evolution. The innermost part is called the reptilian brain because its central structures are shared by most reptiles. The layer surrounding the reptilian brain is the old- or paleo-mammalian brain, so-called because its central structures are found in all mammals. Finally, the outside layer is called the neo-mammalian brain because it is found only in the most complex mammals, reaching its fullest development in human beings. From the biopsychological perspective, much or all of everything a person wants, feels, and thinks, is a product of the functioning of this central nervous system. Some of the key features of the biopsychological approach can be seen in Table 3.1, where it is compared to the evolutionary approach.

Connecting Window   *Trilogy-of-Mind*
One important historical division of the mind has been into motivational, emotional, and cognitive areas. Some psychologists recognize a rough correspondence between motivation and the reptilian brain, emotion and the old-mammalian brain, and cognition and the neomammalian brain. Such relationships are important to deciding how personality is structured, and are picked up again in Chapter 8, "The Trilogy and Quaternity of Mind" and "A Brain to Match?"

The Nervous System and Its Influences on Psychology

The nervous system and brain influence mental experience and psychological action through four means: a person's brain structure, neurotransmitters, hormones, and the immune system.

Brain Structure

The link between brain structure and personality was first made in the 1790s but early connections were mostly speculative and research after that was slow (Allport, 1937, p. 79). Today, information about brain structure has become dramatically more accessible due to modern brain imaging techniques. For example, Magnetic Resonance Imaging (MRI) is an extremely sensitive technique that scans the brain for

TABLE 3.1	The Biological Perspective: A Comparison of the Psychoevolutionary and Biopsychological Theories	
	Psychoevolutionary	**Biopsychological**
View of Personality	• Personality is the result of a long genetic line of ancestors, each of whom successfully met the challenges of survival and reproduction. • Personality is made up of many mental mechanisms that enhance survival.	• Personality is the direct result of neural structure, activity, and associated chemical influences. • The individual's motives, feelings, and thoughts are formed by the action of their underlying biological systems.
Central Issues	• How have evolutionary pressures shaped human nature? • What are evolved mental mechanisms?	• How does the brain bring about personality? • What biological changes will affect personality?
Typical Research Approach	• Comparisons across species; survey approaches with human beings to identify universal preferences.	• Brain scans, studies of patients with neurological disorders, studies of psychoactive drugs, experimental brain studies in animals.

magnetic fields surrounding the atoms of its tissues. This and other techniques provide a view of the brain's structure and can uncover individual differences of interest in anatomy.

Given that brain size increases across species, scientists have speculated that larger brains are more intelligent. In studies of human beings, the results of such analyses have been controversial. On the one hand, numerous studies have pointed to a relationship between head size and IQ. On the other hand, critics point out that it is difficult to assess brain size from the skull's outside dimension; the critics have raised legitimate concerns that scientists might have been influenced by their desire to see a relationship that is not, in fact, there (e.g., Gould, 1981). Rather than measure brain size from the outside (through measures of the skull), MRI brain-scanning techniques permit direct measures of the brain independent of the skull. Such measures add to the preponderance of evidence that brain size is consistently, if modestly, related to intelligence (e.g., Andreasen, et al., 1993; Bigler, Johnson, & Blatter, 1999; Pennington et al., 2000). Other scanning techniques permit further insights into how the brain operates in support of personality (e.g., Phelps & Mazziotta, 1985).

Brain Neurochemistry

A second way that the brain influences personality is through its neurochemistry. Neurons are information-processing cells that operate according to principles of both electrical and chemical transmission. The neuron is made up, in part, of a series of branches, called dendrites, that lead into the cell body. It is also made up of an axon that leads away from the cell body toward the dendrites of other neurons (see Figure 3.2). The neuron's axon ends at a synapse, where it meets the dendrite of the next neuron. The space between the end of the axon and the beginning of the next

FIGURE 3.2

Diagram of a Neuron
The neuron is one of the building blocks of the nervous system, receiving information from its dendrites, transmitting it down its axon, and then releasing chemical transmitters across the synaptic cleft.

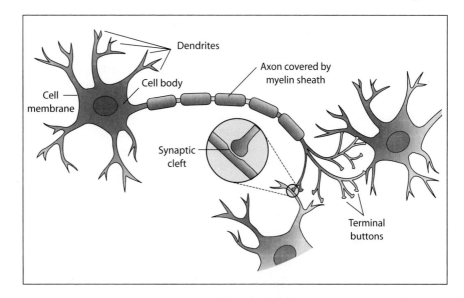

An actual neuron. To the left, its dendrites collect signals from neighboring neurons (not shown). These are collected into the cell body (the dark spot, center left). To the right, the cell's axon carries messages to other neurons.

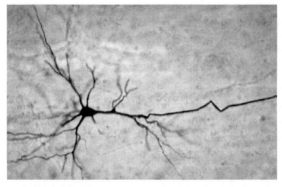

Neurotransmitters: Chemicals secreted by neurons at the presynaptic sac that influence neighboring neurons.

neuron's dendrite is called the synaptic cleft. This area is important because chemicals—called **neurotransmitters**—are transmitted across the synapse (see Figure 3.2).

Neurotransmitters are chemicals that transmit neural impulses from one neuron to the next. Many psychoactive chemicals are manufactured in the brain and body themselves. The different neurotransmitters, hormones, and immune system chemicals influence certain areas of the brain more than others, and influence certain areas of function more than others. The amount of such chemicals present are partly under genetic influence (Grigorenko, 2002; Zuckerman, 1991, pp. 200–201). Although hundreds of such chemicals are active in the brain, there exist a small "classical group" of neurotransmitters and hormones, so-called because they were discovered decades ago and have been more intensively studied than others. This classical group includes serotonin, which is involved in stress reactions and depression, and dopamine, which is implicated in attention and other cognitive functions. Also included are glutamate and acetylcholine, which have been found to play a role in memory. Endorphins, meanwhile, are natural opiates that modulate pain and are often studied in relation to drug addictions.

Hormones: Chemicals secreted by the endocrine organs into the bloodstream that can also influence brain function.

Neurotransmitters are secreted by the neurons of the brain, but they are not the only chemicals that influence neural transmission. Many **hormones** act as neurotransmitters as well (McEwen, 1991). Hormones are secreted by endocrine organs into the bloodstream. Hormones primarily influence specific target cells in certain organs, including the heart, the liver, and the pancreas, and also certain regions of the brain. Hormones that influence personality include sex hormones such as estrogen and androgen. Estrogen is secreted by a woman's ovaries and activates the reproductive system by stimulating the uterus, enlarging the breasts, and by stimulating the brain to increase interest in sexual activity. In the male, androgens stimulate the maturation of sperm and increase both a male's motivation for sexual activity and his aggressiveness. Both men and women produce estrogen and androgens; it is simply that the concentration of estrogen is relatively higher in women and that of androgen is relatively higher in men. Hormones influence behavior in many positive ways. One thought-provoking finding, however, is that, among men imprisoned for crimes, individuals convicted of violent or coercive sexual crimes such as rape and child molestation have higher testoterone levels than others on average (Dabbs et al., 1995).

Disciplinary Crossroads

The Use of Psychiatric Drugs to Improve Personality

How important is our real personality and how might we go about changing it? In his best-selling book, *Listening to Prozac,* Peter Kramer (1994) raised the possibility that various psychopharmacological agents could be used "cosmetically"—to make already healthy personalities even more desirable. In 1998, a team of researchers reported in the March issue of the *American Journal of Psychiatry* that even people who were not depressed felt less blue and were more socially cooperative when they were taking the drug Paxil (related to Prozac).

The use of drugs to improve personality is, in one sense, something that goes on all the time. People use caffeine to keep themselves alert, alcohol to better relate to others, and even chocolate to feel better. Yet the advent of psychopharmacological drugs that alter personality vastly broadens the scope of possibility. Can people resist the temptation to change their personalities this way? Should they?

Some people find the prospect frightening. Paul K. Ling, a leader in a Massachusetts group of clinical psychologists called the Consortium for Psychotherapy, detects overtones of "Brave New World" in the prescription of these drugs for individuals who aren't really suffering from psychological illness, but who may merely be subject to the common anxieties of modern life. In an interview he noted "I think there are many governments in this world who would like to have a docile population" (Kong, 1998, p. C4).

Dr. Carl Elliot, a bioethicist, is also concerned that people will undergo medical procedures to make them feel and think differently, so as to respond to the social norms and marketing pressures of the day. He goes on to say, "Today, it is very easy to speak of any disagreeable personality trait as if it were an illness—and even some that are not so disagreeable, like shyness, which is being discussed more and more often in the ethical and psychiatric literature as if it were some kind of mental disability . . . We have redefined identity as illness" (Kong, 1998, p. C4).

The Immune System

The latest research on psychopharmacology is now paying particular attention to the immune system. Originally, the brain and the immune system were viewed as fairly independent of one another. More recently, the connection between psychological stress and illness has become clearer (Dunn, 1989). For example, Cohen and colleagues (1991; 1998) have conducted an impressive series of studies indicating that psychological stress alters the immune system—making it more likely, for example, to catch a cold. There is much more to learn in this area (Guyton, 1991).

Beyond such research, many biological factors appear unrelated to personality. For example, no connections have been found between blood type and personality, despite several large studies of the relationship (Wu, Lindsted, & Lee, 2005).

A Micro-Theory That Traits Are Inherited

Twin Studies: A type of study where people with different genetic overlap (e.g., identical and fraternal twins, siblings, cousins, and unrelated people) are compared as to their similarity on a given trait.

Monozygotic (identical) twins: Twins who develop from a single fertilized egg, and thus share all their genetic material in common.

Dizygotic (fraternal) twins: Twins who develop from two different eggs and thus share 50 percent of their genetic material in common.

The biopsychological perspective gives rise to many important micro-theories. Some of those micro-theories concern the influence of genetics on personality. For example, researchers have hypothesized that two people who share more genes in common will be more psychologically similar, on average. Such a prediction can be tested empirically with twin studies. **Twin studies** examine pairs of people with high genetic similarity, such as twin brothers or sisters, and compare them to pairs of people with less genetic similarity, such as cousins or strangers, to see whether those with higher genetic similarity are more similar on a given trait. If pairs of people who are genetically similar are also similar on a given trait, that provides evidence that a genetic influence may underlie the similarity.

At one end of genetic similarity is the identical or **monozygotic** twin. Identical twins share 100 percent of their genetic materials in common, as they are born from one egg that divides early in reproduction. Such individuals can be contrasted with fraternal or **dizygotic** twins, who develop from two different (but simultaneously fertilized) eggs, and share only 50 percent of their genetic material in common. Siblings, too, share 50 percent of their genetic material in common. First cousins share 25 percent of their genetic material in common, and strangers, share 0 percent of their genetic material in common. According to the logic of twin studies, the degree to which identical twins exceed fraternal twins in similarity indicates the degree to which genetic material is controlling development. Some understanding of the role environment plays in personality can also be gained this way. For example, one can examine adopted siblings—children who, like strangers, have little genetic material in common, but who, unlike strangers, are raised in the same family environment, and see the degree to which they are similar.

Table 3.2 shows an example of the correlations of several personality traits across pairs of people with more or less genetic similarity. For example, the correlation for intelligence across identical twins is, at $r = .86$, far higher than it is for siblings of the same parents, at $r = .47$. This relationship would be expected if genes contributed to intelligence, because it indicates that people with 100 percent overlap (identical twins) are more similar in intelligence than siblings, who share only 50 percent overlap. In turn, intelligence between siblings is more related, at $r = .47$, than intelligence between cousins ($r = .15$) or between other individuals, for whom the correlation drops to about zero.

TABLE 3.2	Heritability Estimates for Several Traits across Twin Studies					
Trait	Monozygotic Twins Raised Together	Monozygotic Twins Raised Apart	Siblings Raised Together	Siblings Raised Apart	Cousins	Unrelated Pairs (Expected value)*
Intelligence	.86	.72	.47	.24	.15	.00
Extraversion	.54	.30	.06	.04	—	.00
Neuroticism	.41	.25	.24	.28	—	.00
Openness	.51	.43	.14	.23	—	.00

* Unrelated pairs have been tested in a few studies, and do, in fact correlate about $r = 00$ with one another. Given the obviousness of the prediction, and the expense of data collection, this group is often omitted.

Source: Intelligence figures are from Bouchard & McGue (1981); Extraversion figures are from Pedersen, Plomin, McClearn, & Friberg (1988); Openness figures are from Bergeman et al. (1993).

Some people have argued that identical twins might have more family resemblance simply because twins are probably treated more alike than other family members. Furthermore, twins experience the same family history (not to mention societal history), attend the same schools simultaneously, and are more likely to take part in the same activities, perhaps even, than non-twin siblings. Fortunately, there is a way to examine the influence of family environment on personality as well. We can examine sets of twins, both raised together and raised apart. To test this hypothesis we can examine the correlation for intelligence in pairs of identical twins raised apart (i.e., where one or both twins have been adopted). In this case we see that the relation for intelligence between identical twins drops from $r = .84$ for those raised together to $r = .72$ for those raised apart. That is, the relationship remains high, and is only slightly higher when the twins are raised in the same environment (Bouchard & McGue, 1981).

Other traits seem heritable as well—but at levels somewhat lower than intelligence. For example, neuroticism (emotional anxiety and mood swings) correlates $r = .41$ between identical twins and $r = .24$ between siblings. Although this plainly indicates a genetic component for neuroticism, environmental factors appear to affect such emotionality more dramatically than they do general intelligence (Pedersen et al., 1988).

From such analyses it is possible to generate a heritability quotient that indicates within a population how much variation in a trait is due to genetic influence and how much is due to other influences. Different methods and different studies render these estimates rather variable, however. For example, the range of heritability estimates for IQ is from $h = .30$ to $h = .70$, meaning that about 30 percent to 70 percent of the individual differences in IQ is determined genetically—a broad range for a heavily studied topic (Plomin, 1990, pp. 70–71). It is worth noting here that there is not one gene for IQ, or emotionality, or probably for most other traits. Rather, these traits are likely the products of many genes and their interactions.

Case Study

The Case of the Mathematician in the Guest Room

If you were a promising mathematician living in the 1960s, '70s or '80s, you might have been visited at some time by the mathematician Paul Erdos. You probably might even have put him up—willingly, or perhaps somewhat reluctantly—in your guest room. Paul Erdos had a rather remarkable personality and it probably requires a number of perspectives to understand it.

Erdos was dubbed "The man who loved only numbers" in his biography (Hoffman, 1998), although it might be added that Erdos loved a number of people throughout his life. Erdos was born in Budapest on March 26, 1913, the son of two high-school mathematics teachers. His two young sisters died of scarlet fever as he was growing up. When Erdos was eighteen months old, his father was captured during World War I by the Russians and sent to Siberia for six years. Erdos was raised by his mother and a German governess and began studying numbers by examining the calendar and calculating how many days it would be until his mother could stay home from work every day for the holidays (Hoffman, 1998, pp. 66–67).

At three he could multiply three-digit numbers in his head, and at four he discovered negative numbers. He recalled that he "discovered" death when he was on a shopping trip with his mother at age four. He suddenly realized that he would die and broke out crying. Throughout his career he would say to his collaborators, "We'll continue tomorrow if I live" (Hoffman, 1998, p. 11). At four he entertained himself by calculating imaginative things like how long it would take a train to travel to the sun. He also amused his parents' friends by asking them how old they were and then converting their answers from years into seconds.

Erdos had no home after his mother died, spending the rest of his life traveling from one mathematician's house to another. As one acquaintance put it, "He went around the world distributing his conjectures, his insights, to other mathematicians" (Hoffman, 1998, p. 41). He had a talent for posing mathematical problems that were just challenging enough to be interesting to the mathematician and just accessible enough to be solved. He collaborated with 485 coauthors, more than any other mathematician in history. Other mathematicians sometimes referred to themselves by their Erdos number: 1 if they had directly collaborated with him; 2 if they had collaborated with someone who had collaborated with him, and so forth.

Although he was a confident and commanding mathematician, he was nearly helpless in the outside world (Hoffman, 1998, pp. 15–17). He was said to have suffered from a medical condition that led him to remain celibate throughout his life. As soon as he received money Erdos gave it away, most often to homeless people and charities. At other times he set up prizes to challenge his colleagues to solve mathematical problems. Throughout his adult life, Erdos relied on his friend Ronald Graham, a mathematician and supervisor at AT&T Bell Labs, to manage his worldly affairs.

During the last twenty-five years of his life, Erdos worked nineteen hours a day. He would stay awake by taking combinations of Benzedrine and Ritalin, strong espresso, and caffeine tablets, often remarking, "A mathematician is a machine for turning coffee into theorems" (Hoffman, 1998, p. 7).

Paul Erdos and the Biological Perspective

Perspectives also can be applied to the analysis of an individual's personality. Applications of the biological perspective to a person's life typically cannot develop a full sense of the person. Such an application can, however, illuminate important specifics in a person's life. Consider the eminent mathematician Paul Erdos. He lived a very productive life, publishing widely and traveling the world to help other mathematicians develop their own work. At the same time, he was a bit unusual, in having no home during the latter part of his life and in relying on others to manage his affairs. His life is discussed in some detail in the Case Study box.

Psychoevolutionary theory has interesting things to say about traveling behavior in general. Perhaps Erdos's constant movement was an inheritance from our hunter–gatherer days, when changing locations was important to maintain one's livelihood. In addition, Erdos was renowned for visiting young mathematicians and posing challenging problems to them to encourage their thinking. The teaching component of Erdos's life may fit with the altruism that promotes the survival of our species.

Toward the latter part of his life, Erdos consumed huge quantities of coffee and amphetamines; at the same time, he published a large number of papers. The biopsychological theories would explain (as did Erdos himself) how the caffeine he took kept him awake and operating at a feverish pitch of productivity. In fact, as noted in the box, Erdos often remarked that "a mathematician is a machine for turning coffee into theorems." The intrapsychic and sociocultural perspectives will yield more ideas concerning Erdos's life.

What Is the Intrapsychic Perspective?

The biological bases of human behavior indicate that human beings are uniquely evolved to learn from and to modify their behavior depending upon the surrounding social environment. Intrapsychic perspectives, by contrast, emphasize the parts and organization of the mental system itself. They draw on both biological and learned social influences to explain what goes on inside the individual. Yet they focus most of all on mental mechanisms such as memory, learned mental models, and psychological tendencies called traits. In a sense they are most purely psychological approaches because they are centered on the operation of that personality system itself.

Trait psychologists look at the relatively consistent patterns in the operation of personality. Some theorists view traits as primarily biological (e.g., McCrae & Costa, 1999) and others emphasize their behavioral origins and expression (e.g., Allport, 1937). Today, many trait theorists view traits as defining the psychological operation of personality. By contrast, psychodynamic psychology looks at personality structure and the ever-changing dynamics that take place in the context of that personality structure.

The Trait Psychologist Views the Person

The trait perspective views personality as involving a group of relatively consistent patterns. These patterns, called **traits**, involve an individual's most persistent styles

Traits: Thematic regularities in personality—a person's most common styles of, and capacities for, feeling, thinking, and responding to situations.

of feeling, thinking, and responding to situations. The trait perspective leads to a view of the personality as largely defined by these long-term characteristics. Traits are not all there is, to be sure, but when a person says something like, "I don't enjoy large parties," the trait theorist views such a statement as a potential expression of a trait. Upon hearing a series of similar comments (e.g., "I like to be alone," "I like to read"), the trait theorist would conclude that the individual is somewhat "introverted" (preferring to be alone), along a continuum from being introverted, on the one hand, to being extraverted (wanting to be with other people), on the other. Other examples of traits include high-versus-low intelligence and emotional stability versus emotionality (neuroticism). Trait theory and research address such questions as what a trait is, the best way to measure traits, and how traits can be used to predict life outcomes.

The Nature of Traits and Their Role in Personality

One early advocate of trait research was Gordon Allport. For Allport, a trait existed when an observer could identify "by some acceptable method the *consistency* in a person's behavior" (Allport, 1961, p. 343). Allport wrote:

> Suppose you say that a certain friend of yours is *generous*. . . . And suppose I ask, "How do you know he is?" Your reply would surely be, "Well, I've known him quite a long time and in situations where other people's interest and welfare are concerned he usually does the big-hearted thing." (p. 340)

Allport emphasized both the neurobiological origins of traits, and their learned, behavioral manifestations. Studies of how behavior was learned were very active in Allport's time and Allport drew on such conceptions. Explaining how a trait might be learned, Allport described a man who "decorates his room in blue, is also unusually fond of blue in clothes, and plants many blue flowers in his garden." Where might this preference for blue have come from? One possible contribution to the trait of blue-preference is from **classical conditioning** (Allport, 1937, p. 152; Dollard & Miller, 1950; Pavlov, 1906; Skinner, 1953; 1974; Watson, 1925).

Classical conditioning: Learning based on the pairing of a stimulus to a natural, reflexive (unconditioned) response.

Classical conditioning addresses how an organism's natural responses to stimuli in the environment can become paired with other, originally neutral, stimuli. Allport suggested his readers think back to when the man was an infant. At that time, most infants would have an innate, strong, positive reaction to their mothers. The color blue, in contrast, would be initially neutral for the infant.

Unconditioned stimulus: A person, object, or symbol that naturally and automatically triggers a response.

Unconditioned response: An innate response to an unlearned stimulus, such as salivating in response to food.

Conditioned stimulus: An originally neutral stimulus that, having been paired with an unconditioned stimulus, now produces a response.

Conditioned response: The learned response to an originally neutral stimulus.

Further imagine that this infant's mother liked blue and kept many blue things around her, including blue pictures, flowers, glasses, and clothes. The blue, which was originally neutral for the child, would become paired with the pleasure of seeing his mother. Innate (or pre-learned) responses to stimuli are called "unconditioned." In the terminology of conditioning, the man's mother was an **unconditioned stimulus** and his positive emotions in response to her were an **unconditioned response**. As the color blue became paired with the infant's mother; the infant gradually learned a positive response to blue. Blue, although originally neutral, became a **conditioned stimulus**; that is, a new stimulus paired to the unconditioned stimulus (i.e., the mother). Pleasure in response to the color blue (which would likely be less than the pleasure in response to his mother herself) is referred to as the **conditioned response**. The conditioned response is the response that is elicited in reaction to the

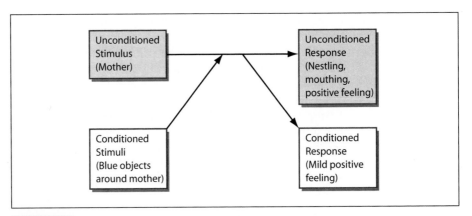

FIGURE 3.3   Conditioning of a Trait Preference for the Color Blue

Early personality psychologists such as Gordon Allport suspected that at least some traits emerged through classical conditioning.

Source: From Personality: A Psychological Interpretation 1st edition by Allport. © 1941. Reprinted with permission of Wadsworth, a division of Thomson Learning: www.thomsonrights.com. Fax 800 730-2215.

conditioned stimulus after learning (Pavlov, 1906). An outline of this relationship can be seen in Figure 3.3.

Another possible way a personality consistency can occur is through operant conditioning. **Operant conditioning,** in contrast to classical conditioning, emphasizes the consequences of behavior. It presupposes that many behaviors are learned and maintained because they are rewarded or punished at certain intervals. For example, a gambler gambles because every so often he or she wins. A person considering a life of crime might be persuaded to lead a law-abiding life, if convinced that at some time or another he or she will get caught. The rate at which one's behavior is reinforced positively (i.e., attaining a winning in gambling), or negatively (i.e., removing an unpleasant stimulus, such as reducing a debt owed), is referred to as a reinforcement schedule.

For example, the trait of extraversion—lively sociability—may begin with certain basic biological tendencies. Often-mentioned candidates include the desire for excitement, high energy, and a tendency toward positive feeling. Such an individual may find that attending nearly every single party he or she is invited to is positively reinforced by others' greetings and smiles. The consequence is that the person will attend many more parties than otherwise.

These tendencies will then promote certain more complex forms of learning. The frequent partygoer will better learn how to talk to people at parties and learn about the different kinds of parties that exist. Having learned this information, the person will be a more competent partygoer, and will enjoy them more than otherwise, in part because he or she understands parties so well. Thus, biology and learning weave together intrapsychically to support consistency of traits (Mayer, 1995b; 1998).

Operant conditioning: Learning as a consequence of the various rewards and punishments surrounding an individual.

Learn from others what to pursue and what to avoid, and let your teachers be the lives of others.

Dionysius Cato

TABLE 3.3	Hypothetical Changes in the Trait of Aggression over the Life Span
Age in Years	**Expression of Trait**
1 year old	pouting, biting, and screaming
2 years old	temper tantrums
7 years old	bullying others
18 years old	participating in more violent sports (e.g., wrestling, football)
25 years old	seeking occupations with aggressive aspects (e.g., criminal, butcher, courtroom lawyer)
30 years old	arguing vehemently at home and at work
35 years old	teaching one's own children to fight
45 years old	promoting violent solutions to problems for family members

In terms of development, traits are considered to be relatively consistent over long periods of time (e.g., years or decades of a person's life). It is important to note, however, that although a given high or low level of a trait may be consistent in a person throughout his or her life, the particular expression of the trait is likely to change as the person develops. For example, the expression of aggression will change considerably over the life span. Table 3.3 shows some different ways that aggression expresses itself at different ages. Whereas the aggressive one-year-old is apt to bite, that would be fairly unusual for a thirty-year-old, who might be more prone to arguments, road rage, or have successfully channeled the aggression into sports or occupational competition.

A Micro-Theory about Central Personality Traits

Trait theory has given rise to the micro-theory that there exist five super, or big traits, which collectively provide a good overview of human personality (Goldberg, 1993). That there exist "super" or "big" traits—global traits, where each one was made of smaller ones, was suggested early-on by the English psychologist Hans Eysenck (1972). The idea that there are five such traits is based on careful examinations of the English language (and now other languages) and collections of the language's major trait terms.

The trait adjectives that describe personality are then carefully collected and placed on personality tests. The tests typically employ a list of trait words as items, which the person is asked to endorse; for example, whether the test-taker is *punctual*. Other tests ask extended items getting at the same idea, such as, "I am usually on time wherever I go." Tens of thousands of people have answered such survey items. Through factor analysis, researchers find that the individual traits on such surveys fall into five groups (i.e., factors) corresponding to the five big traits. These traits, often called the Big Five (Goldberg, 1993), include extraversion-introversion, neuroticism–emotional stability, openness-closedness (sometimes called cultured-

> The most valuable thing I
> inherited was a temperament
> that does not revolt against
> Necessity and that is
> constantly renewed in Hope.
> Thornton Wilder

uncultured), friendliness-hostility, and conscientiousness-carelessness (which is measured by "punctual").

Each big factor, in turn, can be divided into more specific subcomponents. Extraversion can be divided into the more specific traits of impulsiveness, liveliness, and sociability. In one approach, each of the five big traits at the "top level" is broken down into six more specific traits (Costa & McCrae, 1985).

Criticisms of the Big Five do exist, of course, and also alternatives to it (Block, 1995; Buss & Craik, 1985; Loevinger, 1994; Mayer, 2003). Still, there is considerable consensus that these five traits provide an excellent way to describe personality. The issues surrounding the Big Five will be considered in more detail in Chapter 8 on Personality Structure.

Connecting Window   *Factor Analysis*

Recall from Chapter 2 that a central question of factor analysis is: How many things does a test measure? Factor analysis groups together test items that rise and fall together across people (correlate highly with one another). By using such techniques in certain contexts, psychologists have identified one possible division of traits into a "Big Five." Review Chapter 2, "Multiple Variables and Multivariate Techniques," for more on factor analysis.

Psychodynamic Theory Views the Person

The trait approach is a highly regarded approach to understanding the internal parts of the mind and how the mind's consistencies are expressed. It is in some ways surprising to find that it is possible to describe the internal workings of personality in an equally valid way that is utterly different from that of examining traits. This other way, called the *psychodynamic approach,* is not so much interested in the consistencies of behavior as it is in understanding the tensions, conflicts, and interactions among personality parts—often caused by conflicts between biological needs and the cultural demands that interfere with their expression.

Psychodynamic research began with the case studies and observational approaches employed by Sigmund Freud. He developed the idea that many psychiatric symptoms were formed as a consequence of early conflicts between the individual and society—often represented by parents. Or, alternatively, through traumatic early events caused by uncontrolled social forces. A number of colleagues were drawn to Freud's theorizing and developed theories of their own. For example, the theories of Alfred Adler, Carl Jung, Karen Horney, and others developed from this tradition.

Psychodynamic theories view the personality as a system caught between a desire to satisfy its basic biological yearnings, on the one hand, and social pressures to civilize those natural yearnings, on the other. A comparison of the trait and psychodynamic theories is shown in Table 3.4. From the psychodynamic perspective, a central part of the human equation is that people are animals—immensely bright and talented animals, to be sure—who experience lust and greed and the need to defend themselves and who behave aggressively at times. (Key instincts from the psychodynamic perspective include sexuality and aggression.) At the same time, the individual person is weak relative to the world in which he or she functions, and would not survive without the protections and institutions of human civilization. As a conse-

TABLE 3.4	The Intrapsychic Perspective: A Comparison of the Trait and Psychodynamic Theories	
	Trait	**Psychodynamic**
View of Personality	• Personality is a collection of long-term consistencies in behavior called traits. Traits arise due to biological and/or social influences. • Traits change only gradually, although their expression may vary.	• Personality must compromise between biological urges and the pressures of society to be civilized. • Consciousness is limited, and much of mental life takes place in the unconscious.
Central Issues	• How do people differ from one another? What are the central traits of personality?	• How do compromises between biological needs and the social order affect individuals? • Why is it so difficult to understand ourselves?
Typical Research Approach	• Develops tests and testing methodology; typically, data from large samples are collected and measured on various tests. The tests, in turn measure one or more personality states or traits.	• Early work was based entirely on case studies and observationism. • Since mid-century, correlational and experimental tests of hypotheses related to mental defense and other concepts have been employed.

quence, the individual must make compromises between his or her biological needs and the requirements of living in an organized society.

A chief way people compromise with civilization is by trying to suppress internal sexual and aggressive feelings and needs when they violate social norms. Because people are rewarded for doing so, they often lose touch with their own instinctual drives. Thus, self-knowledge is limited in most people, who lose track of their own motivations and reasons for doing things. A split occurs between what is conscious and what is actively blocked out of our consciousness—that which is blocked out is ultimately disowned as part of ourselves.

Defenses, Mental Models, and the Role of Dynamics

Perhaps the most influential depiction of the mind Freud developed was his **topographic model**. Topography most commonly refers to the drawing of maps and charts that describe a region of the world. Freud's first map of the mind divided it into the conscious, preconscious, and unconscious.

For Freud, consciousness was an internal sense organ—a sort of inner eye—that watched over the rest of the mind. It was the seat of rationality and the location of a person's innermost observing self. The preconscious consisted of relatively neutral information that could become conscious at a given point, but that, because of the limitations of consciousness, existed outside of awareness much of the time. Examples of preconscious contents would include the meanings of words, the

Topographic model: Freud's division of the mind into the conscious, preconscious, and unconscious.

multiplication tables, and who is related to whom in one's family. The unconscious, by contrast, was characterized as a seething cauldron of urges, fantasies, and their associated memories. It emerged from evolved instincts that helped define the individual. Some mental contents were said to come from instincts that originated from biological level processes. Some of these contents were so threatening that the person avoided thinking about them. This avoidance allows worrisome thoughts to recede into the background until they are no longer conscious.

Freud sometimes used the analogy of an office with a waiting room to describe consciousness and its defense against threat. In the innermost office was consciousness. If a mental content—an idea, or feeling—were to become conscious, it would need to get into the innermost office to gain access to consciousness. Outside the office stood a receptionist, who acted in the role of the mental defense mechanisms—blocking out painful thoughts. This receptionist, in other words, did not let everyone through. Some mental contents, such as relatively neutral thoughts in the preconscious, could come in any time they were needed. Other ideas and feelings, however, would be avoided or blocked out by the receptionist. Forbidden sexual attractions—to relatives, say—would be blocked out, told they were unwanted, and sent back to the unconscious. At the same time, they would not necessarily go away altogether. Rather, they might influence behavior by subtly sexualizing a relationship the individual wished to keep neutral. Watching cousins at a party, one might momentarily notice the very sexualized way one of them begins to treat the other, and even feel uncomfortable noticing. This was the sort of hidden sexual motive Freud thought provided a common undercurrent to daily life—and sometimes became visible to others, even as the person involved was unaware of the feelings coming through.

> I found in myself, and still find, an instinct toward a higher or, if it is named, spiritual life, as do most men, and another toward a primitive rank and savage one, and I reverence them both.
>
> Henry David Thoreau

Freud conducted a Psychological Wednesday Society beginning in 1902. This society consisted of a group of interested colleagues who met at his house each week to discuss the psychoanalytic method. These society members later formed a new generation of eminent personality theorists who were influenced by the psychodynamic tradition, including Carl Jung and Alfred Adler. From those meetings, and Freud's writings more generally, a number of psychodynamic perspectives branched out from Freud's seminal work. These perspectives changed over time, new theories have been introduced, many under the banner of *object relations theory,* and a number of key figures have been successful in translating the original theories and their descendents into contemporary psychological thought and research (Baumeister et al., 1998; Elliott, 1994; Erdelyi, 1984; Westen, 1990).

A Micro-Theory of Hidden Sexual Desire

Part of psychodynamic theory concerns how certain mental contents are kept out of consciousness—and this portion of the theory can be translated into a number of empirically tested micro-theories. For example, Wegner and colleagues (1990) became interested in the process of blocking out thoughts: whether it can be done, how it is done, and what happens when it is done. They studied the suppression of sexual thoughts. Thought **suppression** involves the attempt to stop thinking about something. Some participants in their studies were instructed not to think about sex, oth-

Suppression: The conscious blocking out of threatening material.

Surrealist painters such as Giorgio de Chirico created dream-like depictions of reality in order to suggest the mystery of the psychodynamic, unconscious mind. Although the painting seems solid at first, the unconcerned girl seems to be in an unstable environment, threatened by the shadows up ahead. This effect was heightened by employing different visual perspectives for the buildings and wagon that would be physically impossible in our real world (e.g., Arnheim, 1954/1974, pp. 300–301).

ers to not think about a variety of other topics, such as dancing. The participants who were told to suppress sexual thoughts had elevated skin conductance levels—a measure of physiological stress—compared to those who were instructed not to think about various other topics. The successful sexual suppressors often showed stronger skin conductance levels—increased sweating relative to others—when sexual material was brought up later. This suggested that blocking out thoughts creates greater responsiveness to them later on.

Along the same lines, Morokoff (1985) studied sexual guilt among women. Consistent with psychoanalytic theory, she viewed guilt as a powerful means of social control and wondered whether a person who felt guilty about sex might try to suppress certain thoughts about it. In her study, women were first administered a psychological test to assess their levels of sexual guilt, and divided into high- and low-guilt groups. Next, both groups watched erotic videos while their sexual arousal was monitored via blood flow in the genital area. The high sexual-guilt group self-reported feeling less sexual arousal while watching erotic videos relative to the low sexual-guilt group. At the same time, however, blood flow monitoring indicated that the high sexual-guilt group was actually experiencing more sexual arousal than the low-guilt group.

These findings seem broadly consistent with Freud's idea that sexual thoughts blocked from consciousness continue to be active in the mind. The avoidance of sexual thoughts led to more responsiveness to sexual ideas in Wegner's study and more sexual arousal in Morokoff's.

Sigmund Freud, in his study, in Vienna Austria, about 1930, examining a manuscript. Freud developed psychodynamic theory—a central, early, and extensive theory of personality.
Psychodynamic theory viewed the individual as caught between biological instincts and social control. Voluntary self-control was difficult but essential to the survival of humankind. Freud once remarked: "Civilization began the first time an angry person cast a word instead of a rock."

It is worth noting, finally, that psychoanalytic theory has elaborated many parts of personality. Freud was the first to suggest that a person did not interact with actual others, but rather with mental models of others. His ideas came about as he noticed that his patients repeatedly misperceived him, apparently viewing him as they had viewed their parents—searching for clues that he would behave as their parents did. From this, he suggested that individuals carried about stereotyped views of their parents or significant others that they mistakenly transferred to others (Freud, 1917, chapter 27). These models of significant others can be very powerful and today are frequently studied in social-cognitive theory under the name of "schemas" and "prototypes" (Westen, 1991; 1998).

The Intrapsychic Approach to Paul Erdos's Personality

How would the intrapsychic perspectives on personality view Paul Erdos, the mathematician? Well, the trait perspective would look for consistencies in his personality: his creativity, his industriousness, his love of learning and teaching, his concerns with death, and his bleak outlook on life. If we tried to translate these impressions into the Big-Five approach, we might say that he is high on openness/culture and appears high in both extraversion and neuroticism.

A psychodynamic analysis might focus on Erdos's single-minded pursuit of mathematics and interpret it, in part, as an attempt by Erdos to block out or avoid other thoughts. Certainly, working hard as a mathematician and constant traveling would not permit many distractions. The traveling started in earnest after Erdos's mother's death, and it may have been a defense against the loss of a person who was both his mother and his first mathematics teacher. The psychodynamic tradition also looks for the symbolic meaning of behavior. Perhaps Erdos's traveling was a means to see if he could withstand the arrest and exile his father experienced, as well as a means to be free of any single government's power, so as to avoid his father's fate.

What Is the Sociocultural Perspective?

The sociocultural perspective stresses the importance of the environment—what can be learned from it, and how it can be acted on—in the operation of personality. Two theoretical approaches to the sociocultural perspective will be examined here: the social-cognitive view and the cross-cultural approach.

The Social-Cognitive View of the Person

To the social-cognitive theorist, the individual's personality is constantly adjusting to external situations around it, both to society's demands and also to look for potential personal advantages. Social-cognitive theory is concerned with how a society influences the person, and how the person's behavior arises as consequence of those influences. As such, it views the individual as a sort of scientist, forming theories of the world, testing them out in various situations, and attempting to meet his or her needs as efficiently as possible in an uncertain world. Social-cognitive theory grew out of an earlier social learning theory, that more strongly emphasized how the individual learns at a basic, behavior level. Contemporary theory emphasizes learning and planning at higher, cognitive levels. Both older and contemporary versions share in common the idea that the person dynamically responds to the surrounding environment. The crux of social-cognitive theory is the interaction between the individual and the environment.

The Person and Environment in Interaction

Some of the richest theorizing in the social-cognitive theory emerged from the counseling center at Ohio State University in the years between 1935 and 1955. One of the pioneers who worked there was Julian Rotter. In a 1954 book entitled, "Social Learning and Clinical Psychology," Rotter laid out a series of principles that would define the burgeoning perspective. The first boldly proclaimed that "the unit of investigation for the study of personality is the interaction of the individual and his meaningful environment" (1954, p. 85). Rotter believed that the individual's behavior could be understood as a function of the individual's goals. The seventh principle of his theory stated that people's actions were a function of what they expected from the environment surrounding them.

In the late 1960s, Walter Mischel reviewed studies of the consistency of personality and concluded that human behavior was not terribly consistent, and that most of the individual variation was due not to traits at all, but to social influences. Mischel acknowledged high levels of consistency for intellectual traits. He also noted, however, that although the study of broad stable dispositions was historically justified, there turned out to be upper bounds on what such traits could predict, because people's behaviors are influenced by the situation. Today, reviews of the literature suggest an upper bound of about r = .40 for these predictions of single behaviors—although the figure can rise higher under certain conditions (Mischel, 1968, pp. 147–148; Nisbett, 1980).

Most people believe the others around them act with some consistency. To explain why we see so much consistency in behavior, Mischel and others suggested that much of the consistency is a cognitive illusion. For example, Shweder and his colleagues suggested that the reason people perceive a consistent "factor" of extraversion is because terms such as "outgoing" and "sociable" are near-synonyms to one another, and that creates a cognitive illusion in people's minds of relatedness among behaviors—relatedness that doesn't really exist. That is, consistency is "caused" by the language rather than by any consistency in a person's behavior (Shweder, 1975; Shweder & D'Andrade, 1979).

Schweder and D'Andrade's arguments about cognitive illusions are contradicted by the fact that traits predict both simultaneous and future life actions and outcomes for individuals. Moreover, we now know that predictions can be enhanced well over the boundaries Mischel set in the 1960s. This can be done, for example, by averaging a person's specific behavior, such as how on-time he or she is, or how talkative he or she is, over a series of situations, rather than employing just one observation (Epstein & O'Brien, 1985). Such approaches were unknown at the time Mischel wrote, however. In fact, they were developed in response to his critique.

The still-valid part of Mischel's point is that situations do determine a great deal of moment-to-moment behavior for an individual. The emphasis of the social-cognitive perspective remains, today, on the interaction of the individual and the social environment. For example, reciprocal determinism concerns the idea that the environment, behavior, and the person all influence one another. This view and others acknowledge that traits influence behavior. For example, tradition-minded people are more apt to follow traditions than others. Also, however, behavior is guided by the environment. For example, a person attending his or her family's traditional Thanksgiving dinner would think and behave more in accordance with tradition than at other times. Finally, people influence their environment, which can increase their level of a trait. For example, a tradition-minded person will attend more traditional observances where there are other tradition-minded people, and this will reinforce his or her traditional outlook on life (Bandura, 1978; 1984).

To be sure, social-cognitive theorists also have something to say about the internal parts of personality. For example, George Kelly (1955) depicted the individual as flexibly behaving so as to understand and react to the outside world. For Kelly, the individual, like a scientist, was always trying to anticipate events so that he or she could control the environment and meet cherished goals (Kelly, 1955a, p. 4). To do so, the individual develop a number of theories about the surrounding world that govern his or her behavior. A person's collective theories were contained in a **personal construct system,** a collection of beliefs and predictions that ultimately channeled behavior (Kelly, 1955a, p. 56).

Personal Construct System: A system of beliefs and predictions that help direct behavior.

Today, social-cognitive theories recognize many internal cognitive mechanisms for representing and interacting with the outside world. These include expectancies and beliefs about what may happen in the future, emotional reactions to outside events, and personal goals, as well as plans for self-regulation to ensure those goals are met (Cervone, 2005; Mischel & Shoda, 1995, p. 253).

A Micro-Theory of Conditional Aggression

If-Then or Conditional Traits: Traits that only occur when very specific situational cues are present.

Social-cognitive research attempts to understand how a person's behavior changes from one situation to another. One micro-theory empirically tested in this area concerns **conditional** or **if-then traits**—the idea that a person expresses a trait-related behavior in some situations but not others (Mischel, 1973, p. 258; Shoda & Leetiernan, 2002). **If-then traits** describe a sort of behavioral signature of an individual, which may predict personality outcomes more accurately than traits or simple learning alone. These conditional traits can be illustrated with data collected at a summer camp for children (Shoda, Mischel, & Wright, 1994).

At Camp Wediko, the activities included woodworking, cabin meetings, playground, and similar activities. In the psychological sense, however, whether a person views two situations as similar or not related more to such interpersonal interactions as power relationships, and whether what happened in the situation was positive or negative. Shoda and his colleagues first divided the campers' interpersonal interactions into those with peers and those with adult counselors. They further divided the situations into those that were positive, such as those that involved receiving praise from a peer or counselor, and those that were negative, such as those that involved teasing from peers or warnings and punishments from counselors.

Observers recorded the campers' behaviors in these various situations. For the purposes of the research report, the observers focused on aggressive verbal behavior (making threats, name-calling, and the like). The conditional trait perspective predicted the way the campers' verbal aggression varied across situations. For example, Figures 3.4 and 3.5 refer to two campers in the study, numbers 17 and 28. The zero point on the "Y" (vertical) axis represents the average level of verbal aggression, and the numbers above and below it represent standard deviations from the mean.

According to the social-cognitive perspective, a given trait may be exhibited more readily in some circumstances than in others. A child might be argumentative and defensive with adults, and yet play cooperatively with other children.

Child 17's Level of Verbal Aggression

This child was observed to be most verbally aggressive when being disciplined by an adult.

Source: After Shoda et al. (1994), Figure 1, reprinted with permission of American Psychological Association.

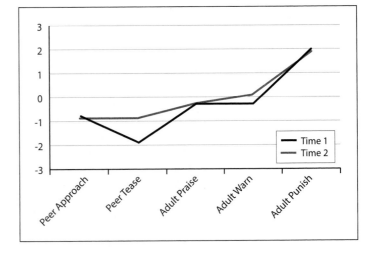

Child 28's Level of Verbal Aggression

This child was observed to be most verbally aggressive when other boys approached him.

Source: After Shoda et al. (1994), Figure 1, reprinted with permission of American Psychological Association.

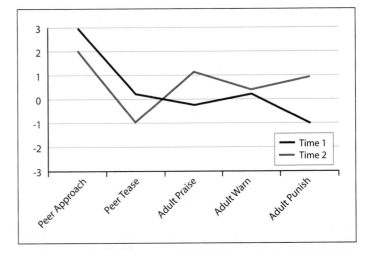

Camper 17 was usually not verbally aggressive—except when he was punished by an adult; then he said some angry things at well above average levels. Camper 28, by contrast, scored well above average in verbal aggression when around peers—even when peers were merely approaching him. On the other hand, he was roughly average in aggression when in the presence of an adult. Note that each child's graph has two lines. These lines represent two independent times of assessment. The profiles are highly similar (Camper 17's two measurements correlate $r = .96$; Camper 28's profile was less consistent, but still $r = .48$).

Such studies indicate that psychologists may be able to go beyond traits in understanding the stability of behavior. A person also behaves in a stable way in "micro situations"—according to his or her psychological perceptions of the situation, and dependent upon his or her goals and plans in each situation.

The Cross-Cultural View of the Person

The cross-cultural approach to personality goes further than the social-cognitive approach in emphasizing that an individual is a product of his or her learning. From this perspective, an individual is a carrier of cultural knowledge. His or her personality is evaluated in relation to that culture.

The cross-cultural differences that are apparent to Western scientific observers may be quite different than the cross-cultural differences observed by, say, a Japanese historian using traditional scholarship. So, a certain caution about the inherent biases of the Western scientific viewpoint is worthwhile (Marsella, Dubanoski, Hamada, & Morse, 2000). Nonetheless, the comparison of personality over cultures is critical to understanding the various forms that personality may take, not to mention the influence of culture on personality. A comparison of the social cognitive and cross-cultural theories can be found in Table 3.5.

A Micro-Theory of Collectivism versus Individualism

Collectivistic Cultures: Cultures that emphasize the interdependencies among people, families, and groups.

Individualist Cultures: Cultures that emphasize the individual's personal goals and needs.

Cross-cultural psychologists have developed a micro-theory that people in collectivist cultures have different personalities than those in individualist cultures. In **collectivist cultures**, people perceive themselves as interdependent within their families, tribes, nations, and other groups, and they focus on their relationships with others (Mills & Clark, 1982). In **individualist cultures**, people tend to focus on their personal goals more than on those of the group, to stress their personal attitudes, and to behave more in accordance with their own visions than on the basis of their

TABLE 3.5	The Sociocultural Perspective: A Comparison of the Social Cognitive and Cross-Cultural Theories	
	Social Cognitive	**Cross-Cultural**
View of Personality	• The individual is involved in a constant interaction with the environment. • The person attempts to anticipate and control the surrounding environment.	• The person is the way he or she is because of the culture in which the individual was raised. • The culture, from its language to practices, to its current events, shapes personality.
Central Issues	• How does the person see the world? • How do mental models influence behavior?	• How can cultures be classified? • How do cultures influence their members?
Typical Research Methods	• Experimental examinations of behavior change depending upon the situation. • Examination of how a person's expression of his or her traits varies according to the situation.	• Anthropological research and cultural studies are employed to examine cultures. • Cross-cultural survey research is employed to detect differences in people as a function of their culture.

relationships with others. People growing up in a collectivist culture will be exposed to stories, values, and life examples that stress the goals of the group; people who grow up in individualist cultures will be exposed to stories, values, and life examples that stress the contributions of individuals. Japan and China represent good examples of societies that stress a collectivist orientation. The United States is a good example of a society that stresses individualism, although perhaps it is not the most individualistic.

Collectivist and individualistic cultures emphasize different values and goals for the people within them; they teach different perspectives and ideas. People who live in collectivist societies and who follow a relatively collectivistic philosophy are known as **allocentrics**. People who live in individualist societies and subscribe to a relatively individualistic philosophy are known as **idiocentrics**. Although idiocentrics are more common in individualistic societies, some can be found in collectivist societies, where they often emphasize their own goals and find social rules confining and restrictive. Similarly, some allocentrics can be found in individualistic societies, where they focus on their relationships with others and the good of the groups to which they belong (Triandis, 2001, p. 910). These outlooks have different influences on personality.

Allocentrics tend to define themselves in relation to other people (e.g., "Other people think of me as nice"), whereas idiocentrics define themselves in relation to themselves (e.g., "I am nice"). Moreover, allocentrics see other people's behavior—particularly people in their own group—as stemming more from the influences of their relationships and their group than from any individual personality characteristics. Idiocentrics, on the other hand, view people's behaviors as more dependent upon their individual characteristics such as motives and traits (Triandis, 2001, p. 914). Whereas allocentrics feel more social support, their self-esteem may be lower; idiocentrics may feel more self-esteem, but be lonelier (Markus & Kitayama, 1991). In other words, the collectivism or idiocentrism of the culture is also reflected in the individual—and there exist important variations among individuals in a given culture.

> **Culture, the acquainting ourselves with the best that has been known and said in the world, and thus with the history of the human spirit.**
> Mathew Arnold

Allocentrics: People with collectivistic outlooks.

Idiocentrics: People with individualist outlooks.

Environmental Approaches and Paul Erdos

The sociocultural perspective directs us to aspects of Erdos's personality that are different than those of the earlier approaches. For example, Erdos exhibited many conditional traits; especially notable was his change in behavior when children were present. He was especially kind to children and often spontaneously gave them gifts, but nearly never behaved that way with adults. Erdos also hid many of his outspoken views in the presence of children and spoke to them in a loving, more conventional way. When he was with adults, by contrast, he was quite frank about his concerns about death and a hostile universe. The cross-cultural viewpoint might direct our attention to Erdos's concern with death and dying. These were common preoccupations in the then war-torn Hungary in which Erdos came of age. A Hungarian expression of the time could be loosely translated as "Burying people, that is something we understand well." In this sense, at least, Erdos's personality appears to reflect the outlook of his culture.

What Is the Temporal-Developmental Perspective?

The temporal-developmental perspective emphasizes personality viewed over the lifespan. As with all personality theories, the ones dealt with here are multifaceted and concern biological, intrapsychic, and social influences as well. Yet, psychosocial development theory, and humanistic theory and positive psychology, all seem focused on how personality develops—or optimally develops—over the life span.

A Psychosocial Stage Theory and Development

According to psychosocial theories of development, as the individual grows and matures, he or she interacts in definably different ways with the surrounding society. The person progresses through a sequence of psychological stages of life: infancy, toddlerhood, early childhood, and so on. These developmental stages are mirrored by specific social activities, rituals, observances, and institutions that are tailored, in part, to each phase of life. The social observances, institutions, and other structures and activities are designed to support and guide the person as he or she grows. For example, as a child becomes ready to read, he or she enters kindergarten and first grade where such skills are taught; as a young adult seeks independence he or she enters an institution such as a college or trade school or the armed forces or peace corps, where considerable independence is possible and yet there still exists the opportunity for adult guidance and supervision.

Erik Erikson developed an early theory of psychosocial growth from his experiences with psychodynamic theory. In Erikson's model, there were eight stages of development throughout the lifespan. Each of Erikson's eight stages were elaborately described. To get a flavor of the theory, consider the first, trust versus basic mistrust, stage.

In this stage, which corresponds roughly with the first year or two of life, the infant is first thrust into a social world of interaction with parents—agents of society. When the social environment is well constructed, the parents accept and love the infant, are attentive and can understand the developing needs of the infant, and can satisfy most of the needs that the infant has. They are responsive to the infant, encourage this new individual to explore the world, and provide security as needed. The infant develops a sense of basic trust in this environment. Sometimes the social environment is less well constructed, however. In such a case, the parents create an untrustworthy environment in which the infant it is not attended to—and the infant's actions are actively thwarted and discouraged.

Next, according to Erikson's theory, the child learns autonomy versus shame, and then moves through further stages. By adolescence, the individual must develop an identity or else be confused by what role to play in life. In adulthood, such issues are addressed as how to be intimate (versus isolated). And, in the final stage, if all has gone well, a person has developed a sense of integrity.

A great deal of compatible theorizing has grown up around such notions as Erikson's stages. Attachment models examine the early interaction between infant and parent and how those patterns of attachment persevere through youth and into adulthood (Ainsworth, et al., 1978; Bowlby, 1988; Meyer & Pilkonis, 2001). Vygotsky viewed the child as a social apprentice to older peers, learning how to operate among others in the older world (Emihovich & Lima, 1995). What ties each of these theoretical approaches together is a willingness to consider the interaction between the individual's psychological development and the age-sensitive social milieu.

A Micro-Theory of the Emergence of Traits

Mary Rothbart and her colleagues have found that, indeed, new psychological capacities emerge in the transition from infancy to toddlerhood. For example, both infants and toddlers' temperament can be described fairly well by two emotion-related factors: surgency (positive feelings) and negative affect (negative feelings). A third infant dimension involves how soothable, cuddly, and desirous of contact the infants are. This is an important dimension because cuddlier infants probably attract more positive attention from parents, on average (Gartstein & Rothbart, 2003).

By toddlerhood, however, cuddliness recedes in importance in how the child is perceived. By two or three years of age—according to their parents—the third major trait dimension now concerns the degree to which children can exert self-control (Rothbart & Putnam, 2002). Perhaps this change reflects Erikson's idea that infants and parents have made a transition to a new stage of interaction that emphasizes autonomy, during which a key developmental task becomes controlling general social interactions. Toddlers with superior effortful control may accrue a number of advantages later on, including being able to express more empathy and altruism to other children, and therefore enter later stages of development with greater peer respect (Kochanska, et al., 2000).

The Humanistic and Positive Psychology Views of the Person

A second theoretical perspective that has important developmental implications in regard to personality concerns the humanistic and positive psychology perspectives. Humanistic perspectives view the personality as a holistic, growing organism that strives toward fulfillment. Humanistic psychologists have elaborated a number of motives and traits that lead to the most positive developmental outcomes possible. These theories stress a concept called "actualization" which means that the individual personality becomes everything it is capable of being. Positive psychology represents a more recent approach that emphasizes cataloging important human strengths. The psychosocial development approach is compared with these humanistic and positive approaches in Table 3.6.

> The living self has one purpose only: to come into its own fullness of being.
> D. H. Lawrence

Humanism takes many of its ideas from "A Humanist Manifesto," a 1933 article that appeared in the philosophical magazine, *The New Humanist* (Wilson, 1995, chapter 13). The creators of the humanist manifesto viewed themselves as creating a new religion that considers "the complete realization of human personality to be the end of man's life and seeks its development and fulfillment in the here and now." It also aims to "foster the creative in man and to encourage achievements that add to the satisfactions of life." These ideas appear over and over in humanistic psychology's vision of the healthy personality (Wilson, 1995, chapter 13; quotes from propositions 8 and 12).

TABLE 3.6	The Temporal-Developmental Perspective: A Comparison of the Psychosocial and Humanistic and Positive Psychology Theories	
	Psychosocial Theories	**Humanistic and Positive Theories**
View of Personality	• As the person develops he or she faces a sequence of new social tasks; society creates practices and institutions relevant to each task. • The individual's personality can be understood as a function of the individual's age and stage of development.	• Humanistic approaches view the individual as a developing organism that attempts to maximize (actualize) its potential. • Positive psychology views the individual as possessing many potential strengths and positive qualities.
Central Issues	• What are the major tasks of development and how do they unfold? • What are the possible variations of the developmental sequence and what implications do they have for the individual?	• What are a person's potential strengths? • How can a person actualize those strengths?
Typical Research Methods	• Case study and observationism including biographical and autobiographical records of a person's life. • Cross-sectional and longitudinal studies of peoples' growth.	• Humanistic psychologists employ case study and observational methods; they also conduct therapy outcome studies. • Both humanistic and positive psychologists emphasize trait measures and correlational studies of positive human attributes.

The humanistic movement in psychology emerged in the 1950s and 1960s under the joint influence of Carl Rogers and Abraham Maslow. Rogers, then a young psychotherapist at the Rochester Guidance Clinic, employed a radically new therapeutic technique that called upon the therapist to adopt a warm, empathic tone with a client in order to create a safe environment in which that person could grow. Rogers's idea was that by supporting a client with compassion and openness, the therapist could encourage the individual to gradually discover the right path toward optimal psychological health. Using the therapist as a model, the client could cast off false selves—qualities that didn't really fit his or her innermost motives and feelings—and gradually progress to a healthier state.

Meanwhile, Abraham Maslow studied a number of individuals he identified as extremely healthy so as to characterize what an extremely healthy individual looked like. His aim was to capture a sense of what was best in human nature (Maslow, 1970). In the past few years, Seligman and Csikszentmihalyi (2000), among others, have renewed and updated the call for the study of the positive aspects of human nature. Today's positive psychologists have created a project to catalogue the positive traits they find in individuals. Members of the positive psychology movement distinguish themselves from humanists in their emphasis on empirical research into positive traits, into how those traits can be developed, and what those traits lead to (Seligman & Csikszentmihalyi, 2000; Snyder & Lopez, 2002).

A Micro-Theory of Empathy and Psychotherapy

The humanistic tradition encouraged and fostered research both in traits and in change processes (e.g., Hattie & Cooksey, 1984; Shostrom, 1964). Carl Rogers was one of the first therapists to openly encourage the recording of therapeutic sessions. He also conducted some of the first therapy outcome studies on the client-centered approach he pioneered. Remember that the humanistic tradition stresses the importance of a human-centered, encouraging environment in which people can grow and actualize themselves. If this viewpoint holds true, then individuals in such a positive environment should grow best. Rogers (1959) stated his theory of psychotherapy in a way that was clear enough to generate specific hypotheses—in what here is referred to as a micro-theory. He hypothesized that a therapist's empathy, genuineness, and positive regard toward the client were the most important factors in the client's personal growth. Of these three characteristics, **empathy** is perhaps most studied. Empathy refers to the ability of an individual to understand the feelings and thoughts of another person.

Empathy: The capacity to understand and feel what another person is experiencing.

Many studies indicate the importance of empathy in psychotherapy. For example, William Miller developed a system of "Motivational Interviewing," which is a brief, directive, client-centered approach to helping patients resolve conflicts over drinking. Rather than telling patients "You must stop drinking!" the interviewer elicits the client's own thoughts about the behavior, and reinforces his or her concerns about drinking and desires for change. The theory is that such a process will highlight a developmental goal: for the client to move toward adopting the practice of abstinence. In one study by Miller and Taylor (1980), the empathy ratings of the counselors conducting the therapy predicted a considerable degree of positive client outcomes at half-year, year, and two-year post-treatment intervals, at significant levels (r's = .50 to .85; Miller & Taylor, 1980). Another general study of the therapeutic process found that, among a group of psychotherapy trainees divided according to those who were more and less effective, the more effective ones scored higher in empathy (Lafferty, Beutler, & Crago, 1989). In general, empathy and related characteristics such as warmth and genuineness do not by themselves guarantee good therapeutic outcomes. When coupled with sound psychotherapeutic approaches, however, they appear to lead to a greater likelihood of positive change (Beutler, Crago, & Arezmendi, 1986, p. 279).

Developmental Perspectives on Paul Erdos

Erdos's amazing productivity and his ability to draw out the best in his fellow mathematicians reflect both his enormous gifts and his actualization of those gifts in the practice of mathematics. According to contemporary positive psychologists, his life and work expressed a number of positive qualities worth emphasizing in a person's life. These included a sense of conscious involvement in his work, termed *flow*, humor, and the pursuit of meaningfulness in life through his work in mathematics.

How Does One Cope with Multiple Theories?

Which Theory Is Right?

We now have considered the biological, sociocultural, intrapsychic, and temporal-developmental perspectives on personality. We examined some representative theoretical approaches in each, and some research each one inspired. This treatment is similar to the one you would experience with a semester-long course on personality perspectives or theories—albeit far more condensed. If you are like most people, you found at least one or two of these theories provided intriguing insight into the people around you—and perhaps you found one that agreed with some observations you had made about people. Also if you are like most people, you are now wondering of the theories: "Which one is best?" Or, "Which one should I use?" It is traditional to attempt some kind of answer to that question at the conclusion of most theory-focused textbooks.

The problem is that there is no easy answer to the question. Hall and Lindzey (1978), who first organized such theories in this way, concluded pessimistically that all the theories were wrong, and that learning them was, at best, a path toward finding better future theories. Salvatore Maddi (1993, p. 100), tended to agree. By teaching the theories and comparing them, however, he hoped that the better theories could be distinguished from the worst, and that the better ones would form a basis for future generations of theory writers. Maddi's comparison of theories was largely theoretical, though he drew on the limited research at the time.

• FACTS • AT • A • GLANCE •

What Personality Perspectives Do Clinical Psychologists Say They Use?

Theoretical Perspective, or General Integration, in This Book	Closest Perspective(s) Actually Surveyed	Percent of Clinical Psychologists who Employ It
Biological Perspective	Not surveyed	Not surveyed
Intrapsychic Perspective	Behavioral	2.6 %
	Cognitive	16.2 %
	Existential	1.3 %
	Gestalt	1.5 %
	Psychodynamic (including psychoanalytic)	28.8 %
Sociocultural	Interpersonal	3.0 %
	Systems/family systems	3.0 %
Temporal-Developmental	Rogerian/client-centered	1.7 %
	Humanistic	1.5 %
Systems Approach	Eclectic/Integrative	35.8 %

Source: Norcross, Hedges, & Castle (2002), Table 3, p. 99 with permission of American Psychological Association.

Smith and Glass's Comparison of Psychotherapies Based on Different Perspectives

How does one test the relative value of a perspective on personality? As this chapter indicates, most theoretical perspectives on personality are groups of ideas, often laid out by different individuals working in different places and even using different terminology. Even psychodynamic theory, so heavily identified with Freud, reflects Freud's own shifting viewpoints over the roughly forty years he worked on it. It also reflects the ideas of his followers and subsequent interpreters.

One possible way to consider the value of the various personality perspectives is to examine how they fare as tools in guiding psychotherapists. In the 1960s and 1970s, for example, psychotherapists often explicitly labeled themselves as using one of the grand personality theories. Therapists referred to themselves as "psychodynamic," "client-centered" (i.e., humanistic), "behavioral," and so on. The individual psychotherapist serves as an indicator of how well the theories can be translated into positive outcomes for clients.

The era of grand perspective building in personality psychology extended from roughly 1900 to 1970. Since then, it is probably fair to say, evolutionary psychology has been added to the roster of these major theories. Before 1970 most theories were represented as schools of psychotherapy.

Another milestone of the 1970s was the development of a new statistical technique called **meta-analysis**. Meta-analysis involves pooling the statistical results of many studies in order to draw general conclusions from them. The basic principle is that the result of a statistical test in a given study is converted into an "effect size"—a universalized measure of change. Then, the effect sizes are pooled with those from other studies and are weighted for the number of participants in the study. It is helpful to know that negative effect sizes, reflecting decreases in well-being, are considered detrimental. In the case of therapy outcome, effect sizes from .01 to .25 are considered small, from .26 to .50 low moderate, from .51 to .75 high moderate; and

Meta-analysis: A research technique for combining the results of smaller research studies into larger statistical analyses so as to be more certain of their collective meaning.

One empirical test that does pit the power of (some of) the respective theories against one another has been conducted. Many of the theories have given rise to schools of psychotherapy. One can create a loose test of such theories by comparing the power of various psychotherapies to bring about change. Smith and Glass examined such outcome studies and found that many of the theories had merit, particularly the social-learning and psychodynamic approaches (see the Research in Focus box). The problem is, one could have a perfectly good theory, such as trait theory, that lacks a therapeutic approach associated with it. It is also possible to have a good theory linked to a less-good therapy. So this does not definitively answer the question of which theory is best. Moreover, newer approaches, such as the biopsychological and psychoevolutionary approaches were not included.

One alternative to the multiple theories is the One Big Theory that explains everything and solves all the problems. Unfortunately, there is no One Big Theory today and, although I would like to be mistaken, I don't see one just around the cor-

.76 to 1.00 are considered large. The effect size range up from there, with psychotherapy outcomes occasionally reaching 1.5 and higher.

In one of the earliest and most well-known meta-analyses, Mary Smith and Gene Glass (1977) and Smith, Glass, and Miller (1980) of the University of Colorado reviewed all well-conducted studies of psychotherapy and compared the effectiveness of the various theoretical perspectives in treating clients. What did they find?

Even people in a no-treatment group improved, and those in a placebo group showed an effect size improvement of .56. Therapists employing a humanistic perspective were able to improve on that effect size, generating a .63 level of positive change in their clients. This is only somewhat better than the placebo. Psychodynamic therapists fared better, with those employing a purely psychodynamic approach effecting positive results at a level of .69, and those using psychodynamic approaches mixed with other techniques showing improvements of .89 among their patients. Clients treated with behavioral therapies did quite well, with effect sizes ranging from .77 to 1. Those employing cognitive-oriented therapies (including rational-emotive and cognitive-behavioral therapies) showed effect sizes of 1.13. In the past, trait perspectives have not lent themselves to psychotherapeutic schools. Perhaps this is because trait psychologists are interested in identifying relatively long-standing personality consistency rather than in addressing change. Whether the psychoevolutionary approach will lead to a school of psychotherapy in the future remains to be seen.

Taking the results of psychotherapy studies at face value, the effectiveness of cognitive approaches is best supported by research, followed by the behavioral and psychodynamic perspectives, with the humanistic perspective trailing behind. But now we must exercise some caution. First of all, the various schools of psychotherapy often specialize in treating particular kinds of patients with greater or lesser disturbances. This fact may account, in part, for their different levels of success. In addition, a given perspective might account for phenomena outside of psychotherapy better than it does for areas within psychotherapy.

ner that can answer everything we would like to know about personality either. So, although the one big theory approach is appealing, it doesn't appear possible at present (Hall & Lindzey, 1978; Funder, 2001, p. 5).

The Systems Approach

Another idea is that the multiple theories are complementary to one another because each one addresses a somewhat different set of research questions (Funder (2001, pp. *xxi,* 509). That is the approach used here. Using such an integrated approach assumes that all the competing perspectives can be translated into a consistent, more-or-less common language of personality psychology. Fortunately, forward-looking theorists within the discipline have spent considerable effort to develop a common terminology across perspectives. This allows us to use a common language in this book. For details, see the Inside the Field box on page 118.

Starting with the next chapter, personality's parts will be examined in sequence (and later, personality's organization and development). As a given topic is examined—say emotion—the discussion will draw on the most powerful theoretical and research ideas relevant to that area of study. Thus, the theories are employed where they can help with the understanding of a given topic.

For example, the four theoretical perspectives we just covered are listed in the left-most column in Table 3.7, each one at the head of its own row. The remaining three columns of the table represent forthcoming topics of the systems framework:

TABLE 3.7	Theoretical Perspectives and the Questions They Ask		
Perspectives on Personality	Questions about Personality Parts	Questions about Personality Organization	Questions about Personality Development
Biological	Evolutionary theories help examine the role of the emotion system and how it evolved to signal about relationships	Psychobiological theories inquire about whether separate brain structures coincide with different areas of personality function such as motivation, emotion, and cognition	Psychobiological theories examine how sexual maturation contributes to some of the issues of identity formation
Intrapsychic	Trait theory helps describe the different motives human beings experience	Psychodynamic theory examines how conscious attention may be diverted from unpleasant thoughts about oneself	Attachment theory (an extension of psychodynamic theory) examines the forms of infant-caregiver bonds
Sociocultural	Social cognitive theories examine how people form "schemas"—mental models of themselves and the world, and the consequences of such models	Social cognitive theories help explain how and why people seek feedback to direct their behavior	Cross-cultural research examines whether personalities develop differently, on average, in individualistic and collectivist cultures
Temporal-Developmental	The humanistic perspective is employed to describe a developmental hierarchy of motives	Social-developmental theory examines whether mental defenses such as denial and sublimation can be arranged in a hierarchy of maturity, with some mental defenses immature, and others more mature	Social development theory examines the ways in which people form or fail to form identities and fit into society; positive psychology examines how personality leads to good outcomes in living

Even in cultures that emphasize collective activities, people vary, and some people prefer to engage in their own individual activities more so than others.

personality's parts, organization, and development. The table illustrates how each section of the book draws on the theories connected to each perspective. For example, the "Personality Parts" section of the book (Part 2) will draw on theories from evolution to understand emotions, and theories from the trait perspective to understand the motives people experience. Part 3 draws on biopsychological theories to understand how the mind is divided into different processes such as motivation, emotion, and cognition, and it will draw on social-cognitive theories to understand how people seek feedback to direct their social lives. Further examples are provided for personality development. Thus, personality theories are an integral part of this book, because this book draws on the most relevant theories—and the micro-theories they have given rise to—in order to explain its topics. Although the perspectives are used and discussed, the focus of this book is using the theories to gain a better understanding of the personality system itself.

Inside the Field

Translating One Perspective into Another

Personality psychology was gradually unified in part by psychologists who translated the theories and concepts of one theory into the language of another. An early example of this was Dollard and Miller's (1950) groundbreaking book, *Personality and Psychotherapy*. It was intellectually daring, in that it promised to join together psychoanalysis and learning theory—two apparently opposing theoretical forces.

The two men who did this uncharacteristically spanned both viewpoints. Dollard was a sociologist who was dedicated to the unification of the social sciences. Miller was a behaviorist whose early research concerned the acquisition of drives, reinforcement, and related phenomena. From 1935 to 1936, however, Miller obtained a training analysis (an analysis so as to become a therapist) at the Vienna Institute of Psychoanalysis (Hall & Lindzey, 1978, pp. 568–71), while on a Social Science Research Council traveling fellowship to Europe.

To create "a psychological base for a general science of human behavior," they hoped to unite Freudian psychoanalysis, the classical conditioning of Pavlov and subsequent interpreters, and "the facts of culture" (Dollard & Miller, 1950, p. 3). To get a flavor of how Dollard and Miller translated Freudian ideas into learning theory, consider how they dealt with the psychoanalytic idea of suppression: that the mind rejects certain ideas that are threatening to it. They began with a day-to-day observation:

A group of people are engaged in pleasant conversation at a party. Somehow the topic of people who have recently had strokes or heart attacks is introduced. Quite a few cases are known by different members of the group. This is a painful subject; it raises the general level of anxiety of everyone present. Finally someone says, "How did we ever get on this gruesome subject? Let's talk about something else!"

Reviewing Chapter 3

The purpose of this chapter is to acquaint you with the idea of personality perspectives, theories, and microtheories. Four major perspectives covered included the biological, intrapsychic, sociocultural, and temporal-developmental. The chapter also examines the problem of conflicting perspectives and alternatives to studying personality in that way. Can you answer the following questions, organized within the major sections of the chapter?

What Is the Biopsychological Perspective?

1. What is the evolutionary perspective and what does it study?

The evolutionary perspective tries to understand the mental mechanisms that have evolved within personality to promote survival and reproduction. The pressures surrounding the person are divided into the forces of

The topic of conversation is changed and everyone feels relieved. (p. 199)

Freud would interpret the scene as representing a situation in which a person thinks to him or herself, "this is a painful thought—best to think of something else." Dollard and Miller translated the case into behavioral terms: people are driven to reduce excess anxiety; reducing anxiety therefore serves as a reinforcer. In this specific instance, the reduction in anxiety brought about when people change the subject serves to reinforce changing the topic of conversation away from illness. In this way, they translated Freud's description of thought suppression into behavioral language.

Dollard and Miller went on to describe how the same type of thought-stopping could occur unconsciously, again using the example of conversation at a party. Reminding their readers of the dread that occurred after the explosions of the first atomic bombs, they noted that in intellectual circles there was a lot of discussion about the atomic bomb, accompanied by much anxiety, and yet,

there seemed to be no practicable way to reduce this anxiety by making and following through any plan of action. Thus, the anxiety persisted until the topic of conversation was changed. Often the change occurred inadvertently, without any verbal statement or thought about the desirability of change. Nevertheless the reinforcing effect of the reduction in anxiety was automatic so that the change tended to occur sooner and sooner until the atomic bomb was crowded out of many people's conversations and thoughts. (p. 200)

Again, the anxiety-reduction causes the reinforcement, and people's discussion of the anxious topic ceases.

Through careful examples and translations such as these, Dollard and Miller translated much of Freudian theory in behavioral terms. Their accomplishment paved the way for later efforts at establishing a common language within the field (e.g., Erdelyi, 1984; Westen, 1991).

natural selection and sexual selection. Can you define those two terms? Can you describe surveys on helping others, and how their results are explained from the evolutionary perspective?

2. What are some of the studies on brain structure and function that tell us about the brain's relation to personality?
Different brain structures also influence personality. There are sometimes said to be three evolutionary "layers" of brain development: the reptilian brain, the old (paleo-) mammalian brain and the new mammalian brain. Do you know how each one's functions are characterized?

3. What are the similarities and differences between neurotransmitters, hormones, and the chemistry of immunity?

As anyone who has ever tried an alcoholic beverage or taken a painkiller knows, chemicals influence brain function. Several classes of chemicals are often studied in relation to the brain, including neurotransmitters, hormones, and chemicals of the immune system. Can you describe the differences among these classes? What important relations have been found between the neurotransmitter serotonin and behavior? What about dopamine?

4. What are twin studies?

Genes—units of heritability—are thought to underlie at least some psychological function. Studies of the inheritance of psychological traits have focused on examining people with different degrees of relatedness. Do you understand how monozygotic twins and other groups differ in their degrees of relatedness? What is the logic behind such studies?

What Is the Intrapsychic Perspective?

5. What are the ways that people learn?

One thing biology makes clear is that human beings are learning organisms. People learn according to a variety of principles. At a behavioral level, these include classical conditioning, operant conditioning, and modeling. Can you explain the basics of each of the three?

6. What is a trait and what do trait psychologists study?

This perspective emphasizes the identification of consistencies in mental and behavioral life, called traits. It is probably one of the oldest perspectives on character and personality. Some psychologists believe traits are mostly biological; others view them as primarily behavioral. There is also an integrated position. Can you describe the biological and learned portions of a trait such as extraversion? More recently, trait theorists have conceived of traits as arranged in a hierarchy. "Super" or "Big" traits are composed of smaller, more fine-grained traits. Do you know the psychologists involved in this debate?

7. What is the Big Five?

Today, personality is often said to be studied according to the Big Five, five big traits thought to encompass much of personality. Can you say what the Big Five traits are?

8. What is psychodynamic theory and what do dynamic psychologists study?

The psychodynamic perspective views the individual's mental life as working out compromises between biological needs and sociocultural expectations and requirements. The conflict set up by these two forces causes certain mental currents to go underground; that is, the individual suppresses and defends against certain mental contents, which become unconscious. What were two fundamental areas of threatening mental contents proposed by Freud? Freud also suggested a division of the mind into three areas related to levels of awareness,

according to his topographic model. Can you list and define them?

9. What is mental defense?

Mental defense involves the blocking out of certain ideas that are painful or threatening to think about. One initially conscious form of mental defense is thought suppression. Can you define suppression, and describe a study in suppression that represents some research from the area? One form society has of exerting social control is by making people feel guilty. How do women who experience higher levels of sex guilt react to erotic pictures; how does that compare to those low in sex guilt?

What Is the Social-Cognitive Perspective?

10. What is the social-cognitive perspective and what does it study?

The social-cognitive perspective views the person as a thinking, analyzing being who behaves in interaction with the environment. One of the founding principles of social cognition is that the individual exists in interaction with the environment. Can you identify its author? A contemporary view of this relationship between the person and the environment is called "reciprocal determinism." Do you know who described "reciprocal determinism," and can you describe how it operates?

11. What does it mean that the person interacts with the environment?

Walter Mischel noted that traits can only go so far in predicting behavior. In fact, across situations, there appear to be upper bounds on consistency. A person's trait will generally correlate only $r = .40$ with his or her single behaviors in a given situation (this is revised upward from Mischel's initial claim, and excludes intellectual traits, which predict at higher levels). This relationship is a modest one, and doesn't seem to reflect the consistency we perceive in others. How did Mischel and others explain the consistency we see in other people? What has the response been to Mischel's concern?

12. What is internally consistent from the social-cognitive perspective?

The social-cognitive view emphasizes stable parts of personality such as expectations and personal constructs. Can you define both the personal construct system and expectancies?

13. What are conditional traits?

One idea of social-cognitive theory is that some aspects of traits are "if-then," or conditional, that is, they are expressed under certain circumstances but not others. Can you describe a research study that examined conditional traits?

14. In what ways can culture influence personality?

There are many ways that culture influences personality and many different dimensions along which culture varies. One way culture varies is according to how much a culture emphasizes community and the commonality among people (communitarian cultures) and how much the individual is emphasized (individualistic cultures). Can you describe the difference? What differences are found in people in the two sorts of cultures?

What Is the Temporal-Developmental Perspective?

15. How is the individual viewed in relation to society in psychosocial theory?

Psychosocial theory views the individual's development as working in synchrony with practices and institutions provided by society. So, as a person matures, he or she engages with a sequence of institutions that are appropriate to the individual's age level. Can you provide an example of this? What is an example of a new trait that toddlers have that is not present in infants?

16. What are the humanistic and positive psychology perspectives?

The humanistic perspective emerged in the mid-twentieth century and applied principles of humanistic philosophy specifically to psychology. Can you identify some of those humanistic principles?

17. What is the positive psychology movement?

Abraham Maslow focused on the study of psychological health and the needs individuals face. Carl Rogers was a clinician who focused on the therapeutic conditions his clients needed to grow mentally healthy. More recently, since the mid-1990s positive psychologists have been active elaborating positive human qualities. What are some of those qualities?

18. What is some research in the humanistic tradition?

In the 1950s, Carl Rogers suggested that psychotherapists should adopt certain characteristics to facilitate their clients' growth. Can you name those characteristics? He and others researched the psychotherapeutic process and found that empathy was a contributor to positive client outcomes. How is empathy defined?

How Does One Cope with Multiple Theories?

19. Which theory is right?—and are there alternatives to asking?

Each of the just-described theories has attractive points, but which one is right? There really doesn't exist an answer to the question. Those who advocate learning about the theories often view the decision as to which one is best as an individual choice. Another alternative looks to developing one big theory that combines all the ones covered here. Has this been done? How does the systems framework approach used in this book integrate the theories?

Part 2
Parts of Personality

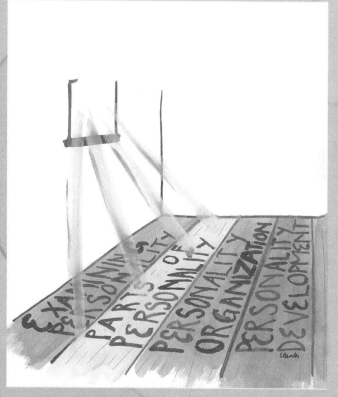

*P*art 2 continues the exploration of the personality system. Through the past century, psychologists have been developing and refining their understanding of the most important parts of personality. Part 2 guides us in an examination of personality's parts: of motives and emotions, of mental models of the self and the world, of intelligence and other mental abilities, and finally, of such fascinating—though less well understood—parts as the innermost self, consciousness, and free will. The definitions and measures of these will be discussed, as well as how people differ from one another in the personality parts they possess.

Chapter 4
Motivation and Emotion

Guided by theory, and using research tools such as psychological measurement and experimental design, psychologists have gradually begun to understand the specific parts of personality. This chapter begins our exploration of the parts of personality with a look at an individual's motives and emotions. Motives help direct our behavior—they guide us toward some aims and away from others. Emotions interact with motives, amplifying or subduing them. Emotions also tell us about our relationships with others and how to achieve our aims in a social context.

- ### What Are Motives and How Can They Be Measured?
  Motives, goals, and plans propel personality to do the things it does. To find out which motives and goals are most fundamental, psychologists have employed psychological tests to understand and organize people's personal directions.

- ### How Are Motives Expressed?
  Motives aren't just something a person feels internally—rather, they have real-life impact on the choices a person makes. For example, a person who values achievement will behave differently from someone who values power.

- ### What Are Emotions and Why Are They Important?
  Of course, we don't just follow our motives wherever they lead. Motives are expressed—or not—depending in part on how we (and others) feel about them; that is, according to how we respond to them emotionally. If we like a motive, the emotions can amplify our motivated behavior; if we feel guilty or ashamed about a motive, the emotions can subdue it. Emotions also signal us about our relationships with others.

- ### What Are Emotional Traits and How Are They Expressed?
  Many different emotions exist and some general dimensions can be used to organize the specific feelings they give rise to. People vary in the kinds of emotions they experience. Some people really are sadder than others; some really are happier.

- ### What Are Happy People Like?
  If people vary in how emotional they are, then what are the characteristics of, say, the very happiest people?

What Are Motives?

Motives, Instincts, and Needs

On March 10, 1996, Jon Krakauer, a reporter for *Outside* magazine, was riding aboard a Russian-built helicopter with other members of an expedition that would climb Mount Everest. The men and women had all paid steep fees—$65,000 a head—to be guided to the top by an experienced mountaineer. At the start of the expedition, Krakauer had wondered about his fellow climbers: Could he have confidence in them? His life would depend upon these expedition members during the climb (Krakauer, 1998, pp. 37–38). A number of mountaineering teams ascended the peak on the same day as Krakauer's team. An unexpected storm along with other mishaps took the lives of several people. Although Krakauer survived, many of those he climbed with did not, including the leader of the expedition.

In appreciating such an heroic and dangerous endeavor, we might ask, "Why were they there? Why did Krakauer and his fellow climbers spend two months away from their homes and families and strain themselves to the breaking point in order to climb the mountain?" Such questions involve the **study of motivation**. The study of motivation involves an examination of why people do the things they do.

Study of Motivation: The investigation of the reasons that people behave the way they do.

125

"Because it is there" was the famous reason George Leigh Mallory gave for climbing Mount Everest. Mallory had become irritated by the repeated questioning by a reporter when he provided the response. Was Everest's "there-ness" the real reason that Mallory, and later many others, like Krakauer, would risk their lives to climb it? Were there other aspects of their personalities that entered into the equation as well? The ascent is unquestionably dangerous; Mallory died while climbing it on June 8, 1924, as have one in four climbers since (Krakauer, 1998, pp. 18, 28). Krakauer's self-described motives included his childhood idolization of mountaineers. (See the Case Study box for more about Krakauer's personal motives.)

Case Study

Jon Krakauer and the Uneasy Fulfillment of a Boyhood Dream

Jon Krakauer was a reporter for *Outside* magazine who accompanied an ill-fated climbing expedition to the top of Mount Everest. He writes that when *Outside* offered him the assignment, he said yes with no hesitation, adding that "boyhood dreams die hard, and good sense be damned" (Krakauer, 1999, p. 28). Many people who attempt the peak die along the way, and Krakauer and several members of his expedition were caught in an unexpected storm during the ascent; some of them died and others were severely injured. Krakauer was physically spared, but deeply influenced by the events on the mountain.

Although he had decided to go on the assignment immediately, he experienced misgivings even as he left. Krakauer's wife had herself been a climber but had injured herself and had learned to make hard calculations about the inherent risks of climbing. She felt her husband's trip to Everest would be "stupid and pointless," and feared he would not return. Krakauer had, in fact, given up climbing temporarily when they got married. Yet, he noted, "I'd failed to appreciate the grip climbing had on my soul . . . or the purpose it lent to my otherwise rudderless life. I didn't anticipate the void that would loom in its absence," and within a year he had taken it back up. His wife

had begun to accept that she could not control this need of his, but the Everest trip was a terrible strain on their relationship. Why did he climb? To fill a void? But what does that mean?

As a child, Krakauer lived in Corvallis, Oregon. He explains how he idolized Willi Unsoeld, a mountain climber who lived in the same town, and whose son he played with. When Krakauer was nine, Unsoeld completed an especially challenging climb of Mt. Everest with his partner Tom Hornbein. A few months before the ascent, Krakauer had climbed his first mountain. While his friends idolized astronauts and great baseball and football players, he wrote, "my own heroes were Hornbein and Unsoeld" (Krakauer, 1999, p. 22).

Elsewhere in his account, Krakauer writes that he disobeyed his better judgment: "There were many fine reasons not to go, but attempting to climb Everest is an intrinsically irrational act—a triumph of desire over sensibility" (p. xvii). Indeed, he continued, "The plain truth is that I knew better but went to Everest anyway. And in doing so I was a party to the death of good people, which is something that is apt to remain on my conscience for a very long time" (p. xvii). Such is the power of the motives that psychologists attempt to understand.

A person can be motivated by a situation "because it is there [Mt. Everest]," or by identification with a hero. People also vary in how much excitement they seek. The brochure for the guided ascent Krakauer went on appealed to people's desire for thrills. It addressed the reader bluntly, opening with: "So you have a thirst for adventure!" (Krakauer, 1999, p. 37). Technically, individuals who thrive on excitement such as Krakauer and his fellow climbers are known as "sensation seekers," and often engage in extreme sports to satisfy their needs for adventure. But there are many other human motives including: eating, sex, affiliation, and power. Each such motive may have a different origin in the brain (or mind) and highlight different aims to which the person aspires.

Instincts, Motives, and Goals

Those who study motivation often distinguish between basic motives or needs, and specific goals that are learned or acquired from the social environment. Among basic motives and needs are a variety of biologically based desires including hunger, thirst, varieties of sexual behavior, and tendencies toward different sorts of social behavior as well. These basic motivations are often innate, although they can be modified through learning. In contrast, more specific goals might be to learn Spanish or to read the next Harry Potter book. This chapter's emphasis will be on the more basic motives that serve as the foundation for a person's more specific, learned, goals and strivings.

Originally, a given human motive was viewed as arising from an **instinct** (William James, 1890). By instinct is meant a biologically based urge, which can be satisfied by a specific action. At the beginning of the twentieth century, for example, William James saw expressions of sympathy, modesty, sociability, and love all as involving innate qualities. When Freud considered motives he began by tracing them from their biological origins in the brain to their psychological manifestations. For Freud, instincts were

> a borderland concept between the mental and the physical, being . . . the mental representative of the stimuli emanating from within the organism and penetrating to the mind. (Freud, 1915/1963a, p. 87)

For Freud, human behavior was largely directed by a sexual or life instinct. In the infant, this sexual instinct involved nearly any bodily pleasure; touching, eating, even defecating were all considered part of the sex, or pleasure, drive. Any impulse to join others was part of this broadly defined instinct, including many feelings of friendship and love. Freud even viewed curiosity as beginning with the sexual instinct because sexuality encourages people to explore their personal physical sensations on their own and with other people. Toward the end of his career, Freud (1937/1964) defined a second class of human urges stemming from a group of instincts related to aggression and death.

The concept of the instinct soon came under fire. Anthropologists' work suggested that wide cultural variations in people's behavior undercut any simple idea of inherited instincts (e.g., Benedict, 1959; Mead, 1939). Their observations indicated that a given motive might be expressed in different ways depending upon the culture. Psychologists gradually gave up speaking of universal instincts expressed in fixed

Instinct: A biologically preprogrammed fixed set of behaviors that, when triggered, is meant to accomplish a particular goal under certain circumstances.

Motives or Needs: Basic motives and urges involve a mostly innate part of personality that directs the individual toward a specific source of satisfaction.

ways and began to speak in terms of **motives**. Motives are defined as biologically based and or learned urges or tendencies to behave in a particular manner.

The term *motive* is often used interchangeably with the terms **needs,** *urges,* and *desires.* Whichever term is preferred, a motive directs us toward certain aims or goals that will satisfy it (Winter, John, Stewart, Klohnen, & Duncan, 1998). A motive such as thirst can be satisfied in a simple fashion by drinking some water, or in a more elaborate manner by sipping an *espresso Italia.* Different motives emerge from different areas of the brain, activate different plans, and work in different ways.

Take the comparison between hunger and sex, for example. Hunger arises from a combination of neurophysiological processes, such as the detection of sugar in the bloodstream and fat molecules in the blood, and also from environmental stimuli such as the presence of a good-smelling, attractive meal. Hunger aims to help a person maintain his or her energy level (Mook, 1996, pp. 72–73). When a person is prevented from eating, he or she fantasizes about food more frequently (Keys et al., 1950).

Sex with another person, on the other hand, does not serve to maintain any particular aspect of the individual's physiology. It bears no immediate relation to sugar or fats in the blood, or the maintenance of any other known chemical (Mook, 1996, p. 111). In addition, sex is socially complex. Eating alone is possible; sex takes two. Sexuality and sexual desire are regulated by their own set of hormones: particularly testosterone in men and estrogen in women. Adults with fewer sexual encounters fantasize about sex *less* frequently than do those with more sexual experience (Knafo & Jaffe, 1984). These examples serve to make the point that each motive is individually complex and each one may vary dramatically from another.

In the realm of personality, motives may be quite diverse, some may be quite well known to the particular individual, whereas others may be unobserved, unnoticed, and outside of awareness. Motives also interact with one another dynamically (a point that will be covered in the sections on personality dynamics). Some psychologists have even postulated a "master motive" concerning the need to become all that one can be, called self-actualization. That motive for growth will be examined in the chapters on personality development. This beginning will simply introduce the concept of a motive, and will examine a few basic examples, one at a time.

Projective Measures of Motives

Do you like to dominate and control other people? If you do, would you admit it on a psychological test? People may not only hide such motives from others, they may hide the urges from themselves, or even be unaware of them. The idea that many basic psychological motives are caused by biological mechanisms suggests that they may arise somewhat automatically and never reach consciousness. Moreover, even if the motives were momentarily conscious, people may avoid thinking about them to the extent that the urges conflict with social ideals. People, in other words, may often not know or accept their own motives. Based on such logic, psychologists sought ways to measure people's nonconscious motives.

Thematic (or Projective) Test: A test that uses ambiguous stimuli as its items. The test-taker must respond to each item by completing a sentence, or telling a story, or otherwise supplying a response.

Projective Testing and the Projective Hypothesis

The key element that defines a **thematic test** (or **projective test**), is the presence of an ambiguous stimulus to which an individual responds (Frank, 1939). The hope is

In projective tests such as the Thematic Appreciation Test, the test-taker looks at a picture and tells a story about what happened to lead up to the picture, what is happening in the picture, and what will happen next.

Thematic Apperception Test (TAT): A projective test developed by Henry Murray and Christiana Morgan consisting of pictures. The respondent must tell a story with a beginning, a middle, and an end to a given picture.

Need for Achievement: A broad need characterized by the desire to meet standards of excellence.

Need for Power: A broad need characterized by the desire to exert control over others.

Need for Affiliation: A broad need characterized by the desire to be friendly and cordial with other people.

that by examining the overall themes of a person's responses, their motives and other qualities may be understood (McClelland, Koestner, & Weinberger, 1992).

The **Thematic Apperception Test** (**TAT;** Morgan, 1995; Murray, 1938) is a projective test that is often employed to measure motives. It consists of a number of sketches and drawings, mostly of people alone or in interaction with one another. Probably the best known card shows a boy who is gazing into space, sitting at a desk on which rests a violin. The examiner presents a card of the TAT to the participant and says, "Tell me a story about this picture. Tell me how it began, what is going on now, and what will happen in the end?" The test-taker then composes a story in response to the instructions and the card. The respondent weaves together elements of the picture into a story as the examiner dutifully records what the respondent says.

The content of the test-taker's stories are then evaluated according to the themes and ideas the individual has expressed. (Note that the test-taker answers nothing directly about him- or herself.) The themes are hypothesized to reveal important concerns, or even preoccupations, of the individual. For example, a person who describes the boy with the violin as dreaming of a concert at Carnegie Hall might be judged to have a need to achieve. A person who discusses love and romance in various stories would be judged as needing other people.

Types of Motives

What Motives Are Found with Projective Measures?

Many of the needs measured by the TAT can be loosely divided into three broad groups: Those reflecting the **needs for achievement,** for **power,** and for **affiliation.** The needs are often abbreviated as *n achievement, n power,* and *n affiliation.* The *n* refers to the fact that the need is assessed as a theme on the TAT or similar instrument, rather than depending upon self-judgments. The three broad groups of needs

> **A man always has two reasons for the things he does—a good one and the real one.**
>
> J. P. Morgan

can be viewed as a somewhat loose confederation of more specific needs. For example, *n* achievement includes a need to meet standards of excellence, which is specifically called the *n* for achievement, as well as a need to be superior to others, known as *n* superiority, and the need to develop an independent perspective on the world, known as *n* autonomy. Similarly, *n* affiliation includes such other needs as the need to play, *n* play, the need to seek aid and protection, known as *n* succorance, and the need to seek others who can care for oneself, known as *n* nurturance. Murray's specific needs are shown in Table 4.1. One benefit of using the three broad motives rather than the more specific ones is that it is easier to develop a scoring system that accurately identifies each of the three needs, rather than trying to code for twenty-plus needs.

Disciplinary Crossroads

The Projective Hypothesis in Shakespeare

The idea that one's personality can be revealed through how one interprets ambiguous material was around well before projective tests. Sigmund Freud noted that Shakespeare had used the technique in the *Merchant of Venice* (Shakespeare, c. 1598/1936). In Freud's essay on, "The Theme of the Three Caskets," he analyzed the passage in question from a psychodynamic perspective (Freud, 1913/1989). The passage concerns Portia, a rich heiress whose father sets up a test to choose a suitor for her. To win Portia's hand in marriage, each suitor must choose from among three caskets: gold, silver, and lead. Each of the caskets contains an inscription on its back. These read:

GOLD: "Who chooseth me shall gain what many men desire."
SILVER: "Who chooseth me shall get as much as he deserves."
LEAD: "Who chooseth me must give and hazard all he hath."

These inscriptions are ambiguous, like the items on a projective test, in that each admits of more than one meaning. In the play, the caskets and their inscriptions serve collectively as something like a projective test so the audience can learn about the character of each of Portia's suitors. Those suitors are the princes of Arragon and Morocco, and the fair Bassanio.

The Prince of Morocco
The Prince of Morocco reads each inscription, ponders it, and then concludes his consideration in this way:

Is't lead that contains her? 'Twere damnation
To think so base a thought: it were too gross
To rib her cerecloth in the obscure grave.
Or shall I think in silver she's immured,
Being ten times undervalued to tried gold?
O sinful thought! Never so rich a gem
Was set in worse then gold. They have in
    England
A coin that bears the figure of an angel
Stamped in gold, but that's insculp'd upon;
But here an angel in a golden bed
Lies all within. Deliver me the key:
Here do I choose, and thrive I as I may!

And so he chooses the gold casket, but his reaction ("O hell!") alerts the audience with admirable directness that he made the wrong choice (Act II, Scene vii).

The Prince of Arragon
The Prince of Arragon had earlier rejected gold as appealing to the "fool multitude." He prefers

Self-Judgment of Motives

Standard Self-Judgment

Self-Judgment (or Self-Report) Items: Test items in which a person is asked a direct question about themselves, e.g.,"Do you like parties?"

Not all psychologists use projective methods to study motives; some prefer a more direct approach. These psychologists have developed tests of motivation that employ **self-judgment (or self-report) items**. Self-judgment items directly ask people questions about themselves. Such psychologists are willing to overlook possible concerns over a person's concealment of undesirable motives, or lack of self-knowledge about their motives.

For example, the self-report–based Motivation Analysis Test includes items such as, "I want to lie in bed in the mornings and have a very easy time in life," and "I want

a more considered choice. His reaction to the inscription on the silver casket in Act II, Scene ix, is as follows:

"Who chooseth me shall get as much as he
    deserves":
And well said too; for who shall go about
to cozen fortune, and be honourable
Without the stampe of merit? Let none pre-
    sume
To wear an undeserved dignity.
O, that estates, degrees and offices
Were not derived corruptly, and that clear
    honour
Were purchased by the merit of the wearer!

Arragon opens the silver casket and is silent. Portia remarks in an aside, "Too long a pause for that which you find there," foreshadowing that he has not found her portrait.

The Fair Bassanio

In Act III, Scene ii, it had been Bassanio who rejected appearances—gold and silver—and dared to choose lead:

So may the outward shows be least
    themselves:
The world is still deceived with ornament . . .
Therefore, thou gaudy gold,
Hard food for Midas, I will none of thee;

Nor none of thee, thou pale and common
    drudge
'Tween man and man: but thou, thou meagre
    lead,
Which rather threatenest than dost promise
    aught,
Thy paleness moves more than eloquence;
And here choose I: joy be the consequence!

Bassanio opens the casket and discovers he has won his "Fair Portia's" hand in marriage.

How would you describe the qualities of each of the three suitors' characters? What features of Bassanio's personality do you think attracted Portia to him? One issue with projective tests is that responses to them may be interpreted differently by different observers. Freud was intrigued by Shakespeare's choice of the lead casket to hold the prize. Arguing from an examination of the myths upon which Shakespeare based this drama-within-a-drama, Freud suggested that lead represents a fusion of both love and death. Only the person who could fully appreciate his own mortality and the glory of love within his allotted time of life would be courageous enough to choose lead. Bassanio's capacity to recognize both the threat and promise embodied in the lead casket revealed that he was such an individual.

TABLE 4.1	A Presentation of Murray's Needs

I. Needs Having to Do with Inanimate Objects*[*]

n Acquisition	To gain possessions and property. To grasp, snatch, or steal things
n Conservance	To collect, repair, clean, and preserve things
n Order	To arrange, organize, put away objects
n Retention	To retain possession of things, to refuse to give or lend . . . To be frugal, economical
n Construction	To organize and build

II. Actions That Express Ambition, Will-to-Power, Accomplishment, and Prestige

n Superiority	This was divided into the two following needs: The will to power over things, people, and ideas (n achievement), and the effort to gain approval and status (n recognition). The two subsidiary needs are defined as:
n Achievement	To overcome obstacles, exercise power, do something difficult well and quickly
n Recognition	To excite praise and commendation. To demand respect. To boast and exhibit one's accomplishments

III. Needs Complementary to Superiority, Involving the Defense of Status

n Inviolacy	Attempts to preserve self-respect, one's "good name," to be immune from criticism
n Infavoidance	To avoid failure, shame, humiliation, and ridicule
n Defendance	To defend oneself against blame or belittlement. To justify one's actions
n Counteraction	Proudly to overcome defeat by restriving and retaliating

IV. Needs Concerned with Human Power

n Dominance	To influence or control others. To persuade, prohibit, dictate. To lead and direct
n Deference	To admire and willingly follow a superior allied other
n Similance	To empathize. To imitate or emulate. To identify with others
n Autonomy	To resist influence or coercion. To defy an authority or seek freedom. To strive for independence
n Contrariance	To act different from others. To be unique. To hold unconventional views

V. The Sado-Masochistic Group of Needs

n Aggression	To assault or injure another. To murder. To belittle, harm, blame, accuse, or maliciously ridicule a person
n Abasement	To surrender. To comply and accept punishment. To apologize, confess, atone

VI. Needs Concerned with Human Affection

n Affiliation	To form friendships and associations. To greet, join, and live with others. To cooperate and converse sociably with others. To love
n Rejection	To snub, ignore, or exclude another
n Nurturance	To nourish, aid, or protect a helpless other
n Succorance	To seek aid, protection, or sympathy
n Play	To relax, amuse oneself, seek diversion and entertainment

[*]*Note:* Murray preceded each of his needs with an *n* to indicate he was measuring the need as expressed implicitly on a thematic measure of personality—not as a self-judgment.

Source: Quoted from the text, with some summarizations, from Murray (1938), pp. 80–83.

to enjoy fine foods, fine drinks, candies, and delicacies," to which people agree or disagree (Cattell, Horn, & Butcher, 1962). Jackson's (1974) Personality Research Form (PRF) includes questions for each of twenty needs identified by Murray. Jackson's test has been subjected to a number of factor analyses.

The results of one such factor analysis are shown in Table 4.2 (after Lei & Skinner, 1982). There, the twenty test scales from the Personality Research Form, each one reflecting a specific Murray need, along with a twenty-first scale measuring social desirability, are listed down the left-hand side. The obtained factors—identified with roman numerals of I through V—are listed across the top of Table 4.2. The numbers in the center of the table, called factor loadings, show the relation between the original scales of the Personality Research Form and the factors to which they relate.

Remember that the **factor** in **factor analysis** is a variable that summarizes the more specific observed variables. For example, Factor 1 represents a need for achievement, in that its highest loading specific scale is "Achievement," and its highest negative loading is with "Play." Lei and Skinner interpreted their Factor 2 as representing

Factor (in factor analysis): A factor is a hypothetical variable that can be used to summarize two or more specific, observed variables. Sometimes the factor is said to "underlie" (i.e., cause) the observed variables.

TABLE 4.2   A Factor Analysis of Self-Report Items Related to Murray's Needs

Test Scale	I	II	III	IV	V
1. Abasement	.00	−.26	−.10	−.52	.38
2. Achievement	.66	.00	−.20	.10	.64
3. Affiliation	.10	.63	.40	−.28	.00
4. Aggression	−.26	.00	.00	.58	.09
5. Autonomy	−.23	−.10	−.69	.00	.09
6. Change	.00	.14	−.18	.00	.37
7. Cognition	.79	.00	.11	.29	.27
8. Defendance	.00	.00	.00	.68	.00
9. Dominance	.38	.43	−.22	.20	.26
10. Endurance	.57	.00	−.28	.00	.59
11. Exhibition	.00	.75	.00	.00	.00
12. Harm avoidance	.09	−.08	.36	.00	−.44
13. Impulsivity	−.80	.00	.00	.00	.00
14. Nurturance	.26	.07	.26	−.20	.51
15. Order	.73	.00	.00	.13	.28
16. Play	−.63	.40	.13	−.13	−.23
17. Sentience	.00	.00	.00	.00	.49
18. Social Recognition	.08	.08	.39	.31	.11
19. Succorance	.00	.00	.71	.00	.00
20. Understanding	.37	.00	−.23	.00	.43
21. Desirability	.57	.35	.00	−.15	.00

Source: After Lei & Skinner (1982), Table 4.

a need for outgoing, social leadership. Factor 3 represents a need for dependence. Factor 4 represents self-protection, and Factor 5 represents aesthetic, intellectual achievement.

> **Connecting Window**　*Recalling Facts about Factor Analysis*
> Recall that factors are combinations of variables—subscales of the test, in this case. The numbers in the table, called factor loadings, indicate the correlation between the original test subscales and the obtained factors. For more, see Chapter 2, "Multiple Variables and Multivariate Techniques."

At first glance, Lei and Skinner's results seem quite different than the needs for achievement, power, and affiliation used with the TAT. Some experts, however, see at least a loose correspondence between these results and the three broad motives studied with the TAT. For example, the first factor seems reasonable to consider as assessing *n* achievement. The "outgoing, social leadership" factor could be related to *n* affiliation, and the "self-protective versus submissive orientation," might map onto *n* power. That leaves, however, two new clusters of motivations not addressed by projective testers. Other experts have wondered whether what looks like "outgoing, social leadership," might simply measure a more general trait such as extraversion (e.g., Ashton et al., 1998).

Aside from the similarity (or lack of it) in measuring motives across methods, some researchers have expressed skepticism over whether self-judgment items can assess a person's true motives. Consider the test item, "I want to see violent movies where many people are injured or slain." If a young person enjoyed watching such mayhem, would he or she really admit to it? Many young people might be concerned others would question their values if they made such an admission. For such reasons, modified self-judgment methods have been introduced.

Modified Self-Judgment (Self-Report): The Case of Forced-Choice Responding

Social Desirability (of a test item): The social desirability of a test item concerns the degree to which endorsing the item would be viewed as good by society.

Forced-Choice Items: Test items in which a person is forced to choose between two items that are paired such that they are equivalent in social desirability. That is, the two items might both be highly desirable, or highly undesirable. The item type is believed to force the participant to express a motive or preference independent of social pressure.

The willingness of a person to endorse a test item has to do in part with the **social desirability** of the test item. Social desirability concerns the value society places on a particular way of thinking or feeling. For example, the thought "For me, family comes first," represents a socially desirable attitude, whereas, "I care more about fine wine and fast cars than family," does not. Although there are people who care more about fast cars than family, at least some people who hold such attitudes may be justifiably cautious about expressing them.

To control for the impact of social desirability on test responding, psychologists have developed a form of self-report item called the **forced-choice item** (Edwards, 1957). A forced-choice item is one for which a person has to choose between two alternatives of roughly equal social desirability. In the Edwards Personal Preference Inventory test items were developed to measure fifteen of the specific Murray needs. Edwards hoped to overcome a person's tendency to select only socially desirable alternatives by carefully constructing items that forced a choice between alternatives of near-equal social desirability. For example, an item on Edward's test might ask people to commit to one or another undesirable alternative.

Which would you prefer:
a. To watch a sexy movie, or
b. To watch a violent movie.

The 225-item scale was employed in a great deal of research and correlates well with other tests intended to measure similar needs (Edwards & Abbott, 1973; Edwards, Abbott, & Klockars, 1972). The forced choice method does have some drawbacks, however. For example, to equalize the social desirability of items measuring the need for aggression and the need for autonomy, the aggressive-need item might be edited so that it is relatively mild whereas the autonomy item would be edited so that it is strong enough to be undesirable. Thus, in theory, at least, one could end up with a relatively mild aggression item such as, "I don't mind it when children play with toy guns," paired with a relatively negative autonomy item such as "I think a person's independence takes precedence over other people's needs.

Self-Judgment and Thematic Measures Compared

In those cases when thematic and self-judgment tests measure the same need, such as *n* achievement, they often don't correlate very highly. Conscious self-reports and thematically expressed motivations seem to reflect two different motivational qualities. McClelland (1992, p. 52) has argued that self-reported motivation indicates what a person thinks guides his or her behavior. So, if a person reports feeling motivated by achievement, he may choose to engage in an achievement-oriented activity (e.g., studying) rather than an affiliative or power-oriented activity. It is, however, the thematically measured trait, the "implicit motive," as McClelland refers to it, that is more likely to determine the individual's long-term planning and setting of goals. The idea is that the sorts of motivational preferences one consciously believes one possesses (e.g., preferring to work rather than go to a party) can predict one's immediate behavior, but it is the deeper, longer-term, more automatic ways of organizing the world—revealed by thematic (projective) tests—that in the end determine where one will go in life. Of course, tests such as the TAT have both their critics and defenders and a debate continues as to their validity for use in individual cases. Most critics acknowledge, however, that research with such tests indicates validity for some purposes (Garb, Wood, Lilienfeld, & Nezworski, 2002; Hibbard, 2003). In the next section we will examine what such scales tell us about different human motives and how they are expressed in a person's life.

How Are Motives Expressed?

The Achievement Motive and Its Relation to Personality

One picture-card on the TAT shows young people watching a surgeon in an operating room. A person high in achievement motivation told the following story in reaction to it:

A group of medical students are watching their instructor perform a simple operation on a cadaver. . . . In the last few months they have worked and studied. The skillful hands of the surgeon perform their work. The instructor tells his class *they must be able to work with speed and cannot make many mistakes.* When the operation is over, a smile comes over the group. Soon they will be leading men and women in the field. (McClelland et al., 1992, p. 160)

Achievement-oriented people are motivated to compete against standards of excellence, attain unique accomplishments, and commit themselves to pursue a goal over the long term (McClelland et al., 1992).

In a review of the literature on *n* achievement, McClelland (1992) concluded that people high in achievement motivation share several characteristics. First, they set challenging goals that keep them learning, improving, and approaching their standards of excellence. They avoid goals that are so easy as to be boring or that are impossibly difficult. In addition, they are more persistent than are others when their progress at various tasks is frustrated, and they are more future-oriented.

Students high in *n* achievement obtain their chief satisfactions primarily from tasks they perceive as relevant to their goals. Interestingly, *n* achievement does not predict overall school achievement (McClelland, 1992). Rather, students with high achievement motivation will get higher grades only in those courses they perceive to be relevant to their future goals. In work settings, high *n* achievement people are more interested and involved in their occupations and are more upwardly mobile. They tend to be highly entrepreneurial and enterprising and better at finding jobs when they are unemployed (McClelland, 1992).

The Power Motive and Personality

Westerners often feel uncomfortable acknowledging power motives—gaining power seems associated with controlling others and dictatorial styles. Yet it is an important motive for many people. The topic is regarded more positively and more openly discussed in many Asian cultures (Winter, 1992a, p. 301). The power motive involves direct and legitimate control over other people's behavior—that is, interpersonal power.

The power theme can be recognized when people evaluate and heighten their influence, impact, and control over others (Winter, 1992b, p. 312). For example, on TAT stories, a high-power person might tell stories in which characters directly express their power (e.g., "They plan to attack the enemy"), or try to influence, impress, or control other people (e.g., "She told him she went to Harvard."), or protect them. An example of a story with a power motive is the following response to a picture of an older man and a younger man together:

These two men are planning a break from the political party to which they both belong. The elder man is the instigator. Noticing the disapproval the young man has shown with the party policy, *he is convincing him to join with him. The elder man was pushed into the party.* At first, he thought it was a good idea. As he saw the workings of it he became more against it. . . . *The two will start a new opposition party.* (Veroff, 1992, p. 290)

Power-motivated people tend to enter professions in which they direct the behavior of other individuals and in which they can reward or punish others within the legitimate policies and procedures of organizations (Winter, 1992b). Such occupations include business executives and managers, psychologists and mental health workers, teachers, journalists, and members of the clergy. Occupations in which the

Disciplinary Crossroads

Achievement Motivation and Economic Progress

When a person tells a story in response to a picture from the Thematic Apperception Test the story can be coded for motivational themes. The coding systems developed for TAT stories sometimes are applied to other texts as well—to various works of literature, for example. Berlew (cited in McClelland, 1958), examined the relationship between *n* achievement and economic welfare in ancient Greece. Literature from the time was coded for achievement imagery. So, if an Athenian poet rhapsodized about the beauty of a runner who excelled and won a race, *n* achievement would be scored, whereas if the poet ruminated on love, an affiliative motive would be applied. Berlew found that achievement imagery declined over the eight-hundred-year period studied, along with the number of nations with which Greece traded. This suggested a connection between the Greeks' cultural emphasis on achievement and economic prosperity. These results were replicated for Spain during its economic decline (1200–1730; Cortés, 1960).

The stage was now set for more ambitious studies that could determine if *n* achievement causes economic development. One way to accomplish this is to show that *n* achievement *precedes* economic development. Bradburn and Berlew (1961) first accomplished this by illustrating how, from the 1400s to the 1830s in England, there were two waves of achievement imagery, in the late 1500s and the late 1700s, as measured in popular English plays, songs, and accounts of sea voyages. Each of these bursts of achievement imagery preceded periods of rapid economic expansion.

The most remarkable demonstration of this relation, however, was McClelland's analysis of second- through fourth-grade school readers, for twenty-three countries from 1920 to 1929 and for 140 countries worldwide from 1946 to 1950. The amount of achievement imagery in those readers was unrelated to previous economic growth but strongly predicted national economic growth for the years afterward. The correlation between achievement imagery and later economic growth was $r = .45$! This prediction held for a 15-year follow-up study of economic growth as well ($r = .40$; Winter, 1992, p. 112).

These results provide rich information about personality, culture, and economics. If it is true that school readers can influence the motivation of a generation of children, it suggests the profound effect that the cultural atmosphere can create among groups of people. Such widespread shifts in the constellation of personality attributes within a culture can, in turn, become central to determining the culture's future economic status. Although these results focus on achievement, it is likely that other personality-culture interactions also take place. For example, it has been suggested that high power and low affiliation motives in a culture may be a precursor to war, and that the reverse constellation may predict the end of war (Winter, 1992). Researchers in the future may find still more interesting correlations between culture-wide motivations and national action.

use of power is arguably more indirect, such as in law, science, or medicine (where the power is over someone's body), are less likely to attract those high in *n* power. Although you might guess that all politicians are high in *n* power, many politicians run for office because of their need to achieve or to be loved instead. Those politicians who are higher in *n* power are distinguished by being more likely to initiate their own

A man who lives, not by what he loves but what he hates, is a sick man.
Archibald MacLeish

candidacies for office. Among presidents of the United States, those highest in *n* power are, relative to other presidents, judged as greater figures by historians—but are also more likely to enter the country into war (Winter, 2005).

How do power-seeking individuals attain power? They seek visibility, sometimes by taking extreme positions or gambles. Student leaders high in *n* power may write letters with extreme opinions to campus newspapers. Other high *n* power students may acquire possessions that others may not be able to afford (such as big-screen TVs, cars, and nicer apartments). In addition, high *n* power students in general build alliances with others, particularly with those of lower status, and encourage them to participate in the organizations in which they are trying to attain power. People high in *n* power are not necessarily well liked, nor are they perceived as working hard or creating the best solutions for problems. In addition, such individuals may seek power to compensate for a fear of being controlled by others (Veroff, 1992).

The Affiliation Motive and Personality

The third area of motivation studied by Murray and his intellectual descendents was the need for affiliation. Evidence for affiliation requires expressions of companionship, mutual interest, and sympathetic understanding. The presence of a relationship is not enough. Rather, affiliative imagery is centered around maintaining or restoring a positive emotional relationship with a person (Heyns, Veroff, & Atkinson, 1992, p. 213). The following is an example of a response to the same picture of two men used above in the *n* power example:

> A younger man is approaching a man older than himself for help or advice on a problem. The younger man is *worried about his lack of acceptance in the new social group* he just became acquainted with. The young man seeks restoration of his confidence. He knows his problem. A short conversation will ensue in which the older man will restore the younger man's confidence. (p. 221)

People with higher affiliation needs spend more time with others, visit their friends more frequently, talk on the phone more frequently, and write more letters. In addition, these individuals appear more sympathetic and accommodating toward others, are interested in people-oriented careers, and have heightened desires to live in a peaceful world. Rather interestingly, however, these people end up being less popular than others. That result has led to the concern that affiliation imagery may indicate a more dependent, anxious social motivation than originally thought (Koestner & McClelland, 1992, p. 208). Among presidents of the United States, those high in affiliation were more likely to enter into relationships that resulted in scandals in their administrations (Winter, 2005).

Need for Intimacy: The need to share inner urges, feelings, and thoughts with others.

McAdams suggested that a new but related motive, the **need for intimacy**, might be more important in predicting success in relationships. Intimacy is defined as "the sharing of one's thoughts, feelings, and inner life with other human beings" (McAdams, 1992). Scoring intimacy themes on a thematic measure emphasizes the exchange of personal information between characters: "They enjoyed talking to each other," or "she had fun telling him a secret," or even, "they had a friendly argument about which movie was better." The measure of *n* intimacy correlates only modestly with *n* affiliation (*r* = .30 or so, Koestner & McClelland, 1992, p. 209).

Too much of a good thing is wonderful.
Mae West

This measure shows promise: intimacy motivation (but not affiliation) predicts general psychosocial adjustment, including better job satisfaction and marital satisfaction, as much as fifteen years after original measures were administered (McAdams, 1992a).

The Sex Drive and Related Motives

Beyond the three needs studied by Murray and his students there certainly exist others worth studying. For example, Freud viewed the sex drive (or instinct) as exerting important influences over a person's life. The first widespread surveys of sexual behavior in the United States were conducted by Alfred Kinsey in the 1940s and William Masters and Virginia Johnson in the 1960s (Kinsey, Pomeroy, & Martin, 1948; Kinsey, Pomeroy, Martin, & Gebhard, 1953; Masters & Johnson, 1966). And since that time, the techniques used to survey people about sex have been refined to promote better sampling, more accurate answers, and more ethical treatment of respondents.

For example, Laumann, Gagnon, Michael, and Michaels (1994) used a stratified random sample that was representative of the United States population. The experimenters targeted specific people drawn at random and did what they could to get them to participate. The survey further employed trained interviewers, so as to make it more certain that people understood the questions being asked. To ensure that the interviewers were not influencing results, participants could answer some sensitive questions anonymously, by placing written responses in a sealed envelope. The survey was not perfect—the question of subjects' sexual orientation was asked face-to-face. Consequently, some homosexuals might have been reluctant to answer the question honestly, and the survey is believed to have underestimated the number of homosexuals in the population.

This survey found that the average rate of sexual activity in the United States was rather conservative, with most married adults engaging in sex about once a week. One third of married couples reported experiencing little or no sexual activity over the prior year. In addition, most participants reported few sexual partners over the course of their lives. The survey also paints a picture of considerable difference in sexual activity among people, with wide variations in sexual frequency, number of partners, and sexual orientation.

Such differences are reflected in a scale of sexuality that included self-descriptors such as alluring, sexy, seductive, ravenous, and lusty. High-scoring college students on such sexuality scales are more likely to be single, have higher interest in dating, date for longer periods of time, and get over their last relationship more quickly to start dating again. Higher levels of sexuality also appear to predict having more partners and a more active dating life in early adulthood (Shafer, 2001). Getting married is another story—one covered in Chapter 12 on adult development.

Development and Personal Strivings

Classifying Motives according to Their Urgency

Arguments have been made that—to some degree—needs unfold in a hierarchy, according to their personal urgency (Alderfer, 1969, 1972; Murray, 1938). Maslow

(1943) suggested that people begin by ensuring their physiological needs are met—that they have enough air to breath, food to eat, and water to drink. Empirical studies indicate that physiological needs do come first for people (Wicker et al., 1993). According to Maslow's theory, they next seek to fulfill their safety needs by finding safe havens from violence, crime, and other threats to their physical selves. People who experience trauma are particularly focused on safety needs (Aronoff, 1967). Third come love and belongingness needs, which impel the individual to find others to be with and to share with. Fourth are the esteem needs; that is, a person hopes that others will respect who they are. Once these needs are all met, the individual can focus on further developing who they themselves are—a process called self-actualization, and one discussed in greater length in Chapter 12, on "Personality Development in Adulthood" (see Hagerty, 1999).

Personal Strivings

Personal Strivings: Activities people engage in so as to meet their goals. Many types of striving may be necessary in order to meet a single goal.

Whatever need a person is working on, the need is addressed through **personal strivings.** Personal strivings describe the class of things that a person does to attain his or her goals. Emmons (1986) writes:

> For instance, a person with a striving to be physically attractive may have separate goals about exercising, ways of dressing, or wearing his or her hair in a certain way. Thus, a striving may be satisfied via any one of a number of different concrete goals. (p. 1059)

Emmons found that people can reliably report the things for which they strive (e.g., staying in shape, doing well in school). How a person strives affects how a person feels. People who set realistic goals that require great effort tend to generate positive feelings and emotions for themselves. Holding goals that are unlikely to become true, however, leads to negative feelings. A person who holds a goal such as being charitable, that causes little conflict with others, is also likely to feel greater well-being. That is, specific motives interact with one's emotional status. These relations will be examined next.

Connecting Window   *How Do Motives Relate to Each Other?*
Maslow's division of motives into a hierarchy addresses one way motives unfold. Different needs can also conflict with one another—as when the need for love overpowers the need for respect or esteem. The dynamic interplay of motives is examined in Chapter 9, "Which Need Will Begin Action?"

What Are Emotions and Why Are They Important?

The Motivation-Emotion Connection

Correspondence between Motivations and Emotions

Motives and emotions interrelate in at least two broad ways. The first is that certain motives appear accompanied by specific emotions. For example, we can observe that aggression is usually accompanied by anger. The second relationship is that emotions can amplify those related emotions (Murray, 1938, pp. 90–91; Tomkins, 1984). If a person is aggressive and becomes angry, the anger will amplify the aggression,

**Maslow's Hierarchy
of Needs**
Abraham Maslow believed
that human needs could be
arranged in a hierarchy from
the more basic needs, such as
the physiological, to further
needs that would arise once
the more basic needs were
fulfilled.

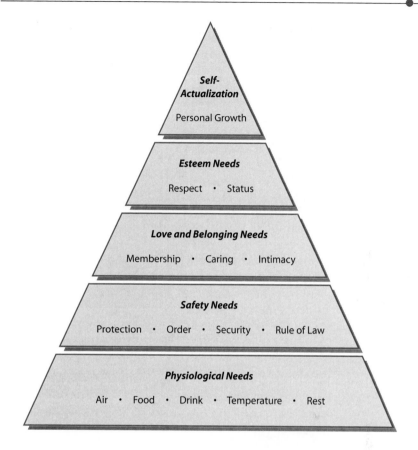

making its possible expression both closer to awareness and more likely to be acted upon. Similarly if a person is affiliative, the emotion of love will likely amplify the desire and need to be near others.

Plutchik (1984) identified eight basic motives such as self-protection and reproduction that were common to many animals and that were important to continuing the species. These motives (which he referred to as functions) can be seen in Table 4.3. Plutchik paired each function with a subjective experience—that is, an emotion. For example, the function of (self-) protection served to maintain the organism, and Plutchik believed it corresponded to fear. Destruction served to eliminate various threats, and Plutchik believed it corresponded to anger. Reproduction fostered mating and corresponded to joy, and so forth.

Are there really relationships between motives and emotions like those Plutchik proposed? Izard and his colleagues (1993) studied the relations between various motives (as measured by the Jackson Personality Research Form) and emotions. The list of motives was a bit different than that proposed by Plutchik, but they found results consistent with such thinking. For example, aggressive motives were highly related to anger; similarly, the motive for understanding/exploration was related to the emotion of interest. The complete emotional profiles of several motives (aggression,

TABLE 4.3	Plutick's Model of Emotions and Their Derivatives		
Emotion Language	**Behavioral Language**	**Functional Language**	**Trait Language**
Fear	Escape	Protection	Timid
Anger	Attack	Destruction	Quarrelsome
Joy	Mating	Reproduction	Sociable
Sadness	Cry (for help)	Reintegration	Gloomy
Acceptance	Bond	Incorporation	Trusting
Disgust	Vomit	Rejection	Hostile
Expectation	Map	Exploration	Demanding
Surprise	Stop	Orientation	Indecisive

Source: Adapted from Plutchik (1991), Table 2.1, p. 54. © John Wiley & Sons Limited. Reproduced with permission.

affiliation, and play) are shown in Table 4.4. As you can see, several of the motives are related to a number of different emotions. That is, they are defined by an emotional profile rather than by a single emotion.

Before we leave this topic, note too that emotions can depress motivation. Consider a person who is very depressed—devoid of feeling except for extreme sadness,

TABLE 4.4	Four Motives and Their Emotional Profiles			
	Sample Needs			
Emotion	**Aggression**	**Achievement**	**Affiliation**	**Play**
Interest	−.32*	.31*	.32*	.10
Joy	−.21	.17	.32*	.17
Surprise	−.07	.09	.13	.18
Sadness	.34*	.03	−.14	−.27*
Anger	.45**	−.11	−.06	−.05
Disgust	.45**	−.07	−.23	.01
Contempt	.48**	−.08	−.24	−.03
Fear	.28*	.04	−.21	−.15
Shame	.31*	.06	−.28*	−.19
Shyness	.18	−.07	−.29*	−.15
Guilt	.40**	−.02	−.06	−.19
Self-Hostility	.33*	−.17	−.20	−.26

Note: *Statistically significant at the $p < .05$ level; **Statistically significant at the $p < .01$ level.
Source: After Izard et al. (1993), Table 10, p. 856, reprinted with permission of the American Psychological Association.

> The passions are like fire, useful in a thousand ways and dangerous only in one, through their excess.
>
> Christian Nestell Bovee

and hostility toward the self. In Table 4.4, moderate levels of sadness, shame, and guilt reduce all motives but aggression. At extreme levels, depression acts as a global motivation dampener, reducing desires and needs until very little seems pleasurable and worth doing; depressed individuals often feel unmotivated and even useless (American Psychiatric Association, 1994, p. 345).

Emotions as an Evolved Signal System

From Motives and Emotions . . . to Cognitive Signals?

Do emotions signal meanings about a situation? Appraisal theorists study how emotions arise from specific kinds of situations. The Renaissance thinker Spinoza, for example, noted such relationships as that being threatened can make a person fearful, being denied justice often makes a person angry, and being cared for and loved by another makes a person happy (DeRivera, 1977; Mayer, Salovey, Gomberg-Kaufman, & Blainey, 1991; Roseman & Smith, 2001; Scherer, Schorr, & Johnstone, 2001; Plutchik, 1980). These connections between situations and emotions make sense, but how general are they? Could they be universal? To better understand them, we turn to emotional expressions in the face.

Facial Manifestations

If each specific emotion arises in response to a certain kind of situation, then emotions act as a kind of signal system about situations. Could this language of emotions

Charles Darwin first argued that emotional expressions are a signal system that evolved across mammals, and convey crucial messages from one animal to another. For example, anger signals a message that includes the potential for attack. In this woodcut of a dog from Darwin's book, he pointed out key features of anger: ears back, eyes forward and focused, mouth open, and teeth exposed.

An angry cheetah illustrates how the facial features of anger Darwin had identified in the dog and other mammals also are present in a wild cat.

have evolved? One of the major indicators of emotion is facial expression. Charles Darwin argued that such facial expressions of emotion had evolved exactly as such a signal system (Darwin, 1873/1965). According to Darwin, emotional expressions—especially facial expressions—serve the purpose of representing and signaling relationships and were biologically programmed via evolution. Particular expressions that are especially important to purposes of survival, such as anger, are especially similar across species. For example, the arched back of the cat, the way it bares its teeth, and its snarl and spit, are all readily recognizable and seem comparable to the growl of the dog, and the snarl of an angry person.

Darwin argued that human facial expressions were universal. He conducted several studies on the matter: For example, he solicited from his colleagues, who lived around the world, their meticulous observations of the facial expressions of the indigenous peoples in their area. "Mr. J. Scott of the Botanic Gardens, Calcutta," wrote Darwin,

> observed during some time, himself unseen, a very young Dhangar woman from Nagpore, the wife of one of the gardeners, nursing her baby who was at the point of death; and he distinctly saw the eyebrows raised at the inner corners, the eyelids drooping, the forehead wrinkled in the middle, the mouth slightly open, with the corners much depressed. He then came from behind a screen of plants and spoke to the poor woman, who startled, burst into a bitter flood of tears, and besought him to cure her baby. (1965, pp. 185, 186)

We do not know the fate of the mother and her ill child. We do know, however, that by the 1970s, researchers had demonstrated that much of what Darwin said about faces was correct.

Cross-Cultural Issues

Modern Studies of Cross-Cultural Facial Expression

Ekman and colleagues collected three thousand photographs of people's facial expressions and then selected those that were particularly pure representatives of basic emotions. In particular, Ekman focused on happiness, anger, fear, sadness, disgust/contempt, and surprise (see the photos on page 145). The **Facial Affect Coding System (FACS)** was developed to create a language of the face and its expressions. The FACS systems is a method of coding the muscular system of the face as it enters into various emotional expressions. His studies led to the identification of representative examples of basic emotional facial expressions.

Facial Affect Coding System (FACS): A method developed for coding emotions in the face according to the position of muscles in the face and facial features.

Ekman and his colleagues then showed these representative photographs to individuals in five literate but diverse cultures in Japan, Brazil, and elsewhere (see Table 4.5). Individuals were asked to identify which emotion each face displayed. Across cultures, individuals agreed that a given face showed a particular emotion more than 80 percent of the time.

Ekman and his colleagues next wanted to see whether this recognition of emotions would extend to remote preliterate cultures. They set off to Borneo, New Guinea (now in Indonesia), to test their hypothesis. Although members of the preliterate societies correctly identified many faces, they performed at levels far below those who participated from more developed nations. The Borneo participants were at a psychological disadvantage, however. Having no written language, they were unable to refer to the written list of emotion alternatives that those in literate societies had used. The Ekman team returned to the United States where they reconsidered their approach.

When they later returned to New Guinea, they employed a new procedure. Each participant was told a story (developed with help from people familiar with the culture) designed to elicit an emotion (e.g., happiness, anger, fear, etc.). At the same time, the examiners laid out the six face photographs. At the end of the story they asked the individual to choose the face that went with the story. The happiness story was simple: "Her friends have come and she is happy." The fear story was a bit more complex:

> She is sitting in her house all alone and there is no one else in the village; and there is no knife, ax, or bow and arrow in the house. A wild pig is standing in the door of the house and the woman is looking at the pig and is very afraid of it. The pig has been standing in the doorway for a few minutes and the person is looking at it very afraid and the pig won't move away from the door and she is afraid the pig will bite her. (Ekman, 1973, p. 211)

Using this procedure, agreement rose to mid-80 percent—about the same as that for literate societies. Why then, had anthropologists observed some differences in facial expressions across cultures?

Paul Ekman identified prototypical human facial expressions for each of six basic emotions (top row first): anger, fear, disgust, surprise, joy, and sadness.

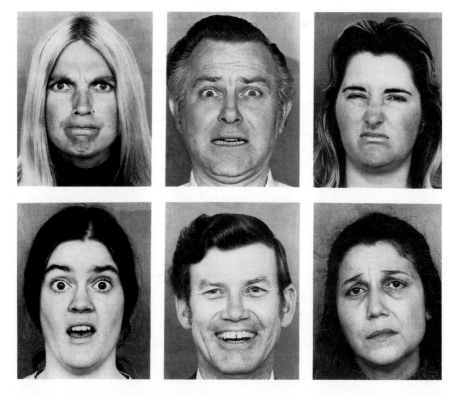

TABLE 4.5	Agreement as to Facial Expression Classification				
	Japan	Brazil	Chile	Argentina	U.S.
Happiness	87	97	90	94	97
Fear	71	77	78	68	88
Surprise	87	82	88	93	91
Anger	63	82	76	72	69
Disgust/Contempt	82	86	85	79	82
Sadness	74	82	90	85	73
N of raters	29	40	119	168	99

Source: Reprinted and revised from Ekman, Friesen, Ellsworth (1972), Table 13, p. 157, with permission from Elsevier.

Cultural Display Rules: The rules that people in a culture employ when expressing emotions, e.g., in some Western cultures, men are taught that they should not show fear.

Ekman suggested that there were **cultural display rules**, that is, rules by which people in a particular culture are taught to express their feelings. For example, men may be taught not to express fear, and women may be taught not to express anger. For some of Ekman's Borneo studies, for example, only women were used because men denied ever feeling fear.

Ekman wrote: "One hundred years after Darwin wrote his book on emotional expression, a conclusion is possible. There are some facial expressions of emotion that are universally characteristic of the human species" (Ekman, 1973, p. 219).

Emotional States, Moods, and Emotion-Related Traits

Emotion-Related Traits: A type of personality trait (e.g., long-term psychological quality) that describes a person's overall emotional quality (e.g., happy-go-lucky, sad).

So, the emotions system is a universally evolved signal system. It is extensive in its scope. It amplifies motives and signals specific situations. Certain emotions are universal in their meaning. At the same time, however, the emotions system is very personal in regard to how it works in the individual case. Some people are sad, some glad, and many in-between. To better understand this idea it helps to distinguish between emotional states, mood, and traits.

The emotions system responds to a situation in the short-term. Emotions can be considered transitory states—moments when the organism shifts into a particular configuration: afraid, or sad, or happy. Those states, however, are different from an individual's longer term emotional qualities, which are described by **emotion-related traits**. Emotion-related traits are long-term characteristics describing the individual's tendency to be fearful, sad, or happy, or otherwise.

State-Trait Scales: Scales that measure parts of personality, such as anxiety, in two different ways: once as a momentary state, and once as a trait.

States: Momentary feelings or internal qualities or activities.

Traits: Relatively long-term characteristics of the person, typically composed of thematically related features.

Spielberger drew a distinction between a momentary feeling, an emotional **state**, and a long-term likelihood of feeling a certain way, an emotion-related **trait**. Spielberger and his colleagues developed a set of scales called the **state-trait scales** of anxiety (e.g., Spielberger & DeNike, 1966). That is, a person could be in an anxious state—waiting for a medical test result—without being an anxious person. A generally anxious person—called a *trait-anxious* person—is more likely to be anxious in more situations more often than other people, but might not be anxious at a given time.

Inside the Field

Replicating Ekman's Results

Ekman's research on whether emotional facial expressions were universal came during a time of rapidly increasing globalization, with faster planes and more international travel, greater accessibility to remote, isolated areas, and the spread of communications. When Ekman and his colleague Friesen began to study emotional facial expressions with an eye to proving they were universal, they were able to borrow over 100,000 feet of film taken of two preliterate cultures in New Guinea (now Indonesia) in the late 1950s and early 1960s, at the moment of the cultures' first contact with the outside world. Although the people looked very exotic, Ekman noted, their facial expressions were totally familiar. After studying the films, he and his colleagues set out to explore the possibility of universal emotional expressions (Ekman, 1984, p. 320).

Part of Ekman's rationale for getting his cross-cultural research funded in the 1960s was that in just a few years, there would be no isolated people on earth left. In 1967, Ekman traveled to Papua, New Guinea, to study the South Fore people. These New Guineans had no written language and were visually isolated—having no televisions and living well before our present era of personal computers and the internet. Ekman and his team found that recognition of emotional faces in the South Fore was as good as it was among Westerners. Still this contradicted a great deal of anthropological opinion that culture determined how a person expressed emotion. Ekman proposed—and provided a first empirical demonstration with the South Fore people—that facial expressions were universal.

He introduced the concept of cultural display rules to explain that although emotional expressions were universal, they were often exhibited in different ways.

Karl Heider, an anthropologist who had conducted extensive research among the Dani people, also of Papua, New Guinea, didn't believe Ekman's findings. He and his colleagues collaborated in a research project designed to challenge what Ekman had found. Heider had been studying the Dani people of West Irian for many years. The Dani people were among the most isolated on earth. Heider knew that they lacked words for some of the six emotions Ekman had studied (i.e., happiness, sadness, anger, fear, surprise, and disgust). When Heider heard about Ekman's findings in Papua, New Guinea, he visited Ekman and learned his research techniques, and then traveled back to West Irian to prove Ekman and his team were wrong (Ekman, 1999, pp. 308–310; Heider, 1991, p. 88).

To their surprise, Heider and his colleagues were able to replicate Ekman's work with the Dani. They tested two Dani subcultures, one known for their placidness and peacefulness, and another group known for their emotionality, and found results supporting Ekman's work (as well as their own observations about the emotional differences between the groups) in both cases. As a consequence of this study and more recent studies of the brain physiology of the Minangkabau culture of West Sumatra (e.g., Levenson, Ekman, & Heider, 1992), the universality of emotional expressions has become widely accepted.

Some people use the term *mood* to indicate a mental state somewhere between a relatively quick emotional reaction and a long-term trait. If emotional states occur in seconds and minutes, moods are more on the order of hours and days, and traits reflect personality processes that extend for months, years, and decades.

Individual Differences in Emotionality

People vary along a number of emotional traits depending upon how happy or sad they usually are, and how variable their mood is, among other characteristics. In daily life we rely on people's statements about their emotional experiences to assess how they feel. Because those feelings are internal and hidden, a person's self-statements are the best and most obvious ways we have of knowing what emotional reactions a person is having. For those reasons, self-judgment techniques have been the measures of choice when examining emotions.

What Are Emotional Traits and How Are They Expressed?

The Two-Factor Approach to Measuring Emotion

Pleasant-Unpleasant Mood (or Affect) Factor: One member of a pair of two basic dimensions for describing the interrelation of specific emotions. The other pair-member is Activation-Deactivation. Each dimension is obtained through factor analysis of mood scales. Other factor solutions yield a second pair of dimensions.

Affect: A term used to encompass both moods and other related states such as alertness and tiredness.

Activated-Deactivated Mood (or Affect) Factor: One of a pair of two basic dimensions for describing the interrelation of specific emotions, based on how much the emotion conveys energy or action. The other pair member is Pleasant-Unpleasant Mood. This dimension is obtained through factor analysis of mood scales. Other factor solutions yield a second pair of dimensions.

As we begin to examine people's emotions and emotion-related traits, a key question is how many emotions there are. Recall that Ekman studied six. Strong cases have been made for as many as sixteen or as few as five, or even that the search for basic emotions is misguided altogether (e.g., Averill et al., 1994; Izard, 1992; Ortony & Turner, 1990).

The 1960s saw the introduction by drug companies of the first mood-altering pharmaceuticals. To understand how a drug affected a mood, pharmaceutical researchers needed good measures of how a person was feeling. To address this question, researchers such as Vincent Nowlis (1965) asked people to describe their present moods by checking off how much they felt each of a series of feelings. A sample version of such a scale is shown in Table 4.6., on page 150.

The test-taker was instructed to read through each mood-adjective and check off how he or she felt at the moment. When Nowlis (1965) first factor-analyzed a mood scale, he obtained a large number of factors, but they didn't seem very elegant. Perhaps, he concluded, there were about eight factors, beginning with "Surgency" (a blend of liveliness and dominance), and proceeding through other moods such as aggression, joy, and anxiety.

About fifteen years later, using newer approaches to factor analysis, Russell (1979) found a very elegant two-factor depiction of mood. The first factor represented a **Pleasant-Unpleasant Mood (or Affect) Factor.** The term **Affect** is often used in a slightly broader sense than mood, to include along with mood such states as alertness and tiredness. Russell's second factor reflected an **Activated-Deactivated Mood (or Affect) Factor.** Sometimes Activation-Deactivation is simply referred to as "Aroused-Calm." A schematic overview of this solution is shown in Figure 4.2.

Research by Deiner and Emmons (1984) and others (e.g., Zevon and Tellegen, 1982) generally supported Russell's findings and enlarged them by considering two alternative dimensions to explain the same phenomena. This well-known alternative solution redivides aspects of mood to yield two alternative dimensions of affect:

Test Yourself: What Is Your Current Mood?

When an area of personality is very well understood, as is mood, it is often possible to measure it well very quickly. The Affect Grid (Russell, Weiss, & Mendelssohn, 1987) is a tour de force of this sort of test—it is one item long. The actual instructions are long and have been abbreviated a bit here. The test is remarkably reliable and out-predicts many longer mood scales.

To take the test, you are told that each cell in the grid below represents a different sort of feeling. A check mark in the center of the 9 x 9 grid would represent a totally neutral feeling.

The vertical dimension represents arousal. The higher the arousal—and the higher the mark—the more awake, alert, or activated a person feels. The lower the arousal—and the lower the mark—the more sleepy, tired, and unactivated one would feel.

The horizontal dimension represents pleasantness and unpleasantness. The farther to the right, the more pleasant a person feels; the farther to the left, the more unpleasant. Now, choose the cell that best describes your current feeling.

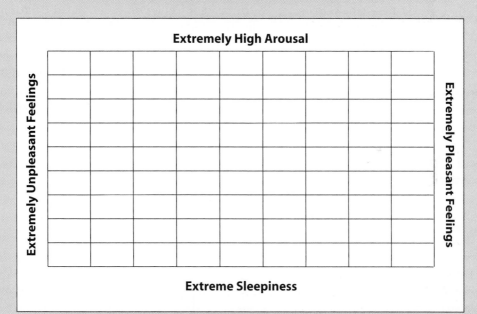

Scoring your answer The average student tested on the affect grid puts a check in the 6th box from the left, for pleasantness, and the 5th box from the bottom, for arousal. If you were upward and to the right of that, you felt happier and more alert than most; if you were downward and toward the left, you felt unhappier and sleepier than most. If you were upward and to the left, you felt more aggravated, agitated, or nervous than most. If you were downward and to the right, you were happier but sleepier than most.

Source: From Russell, Weiss, & Mendelssohn (1989), reprinted with permission of the American Psychological Association.

Positive Mood or Affect versus Tired Mood or Affect Factor: One of a pair of two basic dimensions for describing the interrelation of specific emotions. The other pair member is Negative-Relaxed Affect. This dimension is obtained through factor analysis of mood scales. Other factor solutions yield a second pair of dimensions.

Negative Mood or Affect versus Relaxed Mood or Affect: One of a pair of two basic dimensions for describing the interrelation of specific emotions, based on how much the emotion conveys energy or action. The other pair member is Positive-Tired Affect. This dimension is obtained through factor analysis of mood scales. Other factor solutions yield a second pair of dimensions.

TABLE 4.6	Sample of a Mood Checklist Similar to Those Employed in Emotions Research			
	Definitely Don't Feel	Somewhat Don't Feel	Somewhat Feel	Definitely Feel
Happy	YY	Y	X	XX
Sad	YY	Y	X	XX
Angry	YY	Y	X	XX
Afraid	YY	Y	X	XX
…	…	…	…	…

Positive Mood (or Affect) versus Tiredness, and **Negative Mood (or Affect) versus Relaxed.** These two alternative sets of dimensions are all part of the same picture—literally! In Figure 4.2, the Pleasant-Unpleasant and Aroused-Calm dimensions run vertically and horizontally. The Positive-Tired and Negative-Relaxed dimensions run at 45-degree angles to them. The specific, individual emotions such as fear, sadness, happiness, surprise, and so forth, are arranged within the sets of axes.

The two sets of axes represent directions like north-south, and east and west. In this case, however, there are no agreed-upon poles. Today both pairs of dimensions, Pleasant-Unpleasant/Aroused-Calm, and Positive-Tired/Negative-Relaxed, are com-

FIGURE 4.2

Two Dimensions of Mood

For at least a century, psychologists believed that many feeling terms could be represented according to two dimensions. In this specific example, the dimensions are labeled pleasant-unpleasant, and arousal-calm mood (e.g., Yik, Barrett & Russell, 1999; Watson & Tellegen, 1985).

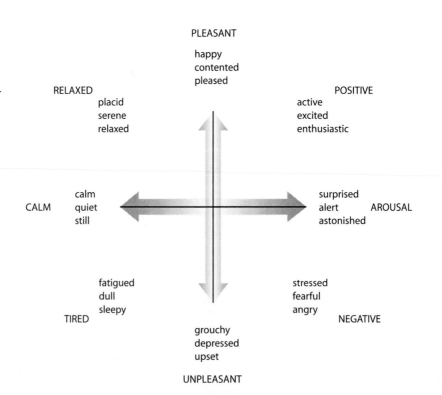

monly employed to organize specific emotional reactions, and there is an ongoing debate as to which is best (e.g., Green, Salovey, & Truax, 1999; Russell, 1999; Russell, & Barrett, 1999; Watson, Wiese, Vaidya, & Tellegen, 1999).

There are, of course, more dimensions of mood. For example, there is a Fear-Anger (or Submission-Dominance) subdimension that is of importance. Still, these two dimensions of positive and negative affect serve as a good first approximation of the dimensions along which specific emotions can be described.

Affect Intensity

Affect Intensity: A dimension indicating how intensely one experiences pleasant and unpleasant emotions.

Not only is mood pleasant or unpleasant, but it also differs in its **affect intensity** (e.g., Deiner, Larsen, Levine, & Emmons, 1985; Larsen & Deiner, 1987). Some people experience only mild instances of any positive or negative moods across time. These people experience low affect intensity. By contrast, others experience extremely positive and negative moods on a nearly daily basis, doing so more frequently and rapidly than others. These individuals exhibit high affect intensity.

High and low affect-intensity people can be identified either by studying their moods over several months, or, more simply, by seeing if they endorse more high-intensity statements such as, "My heart races at the anticipation of a happy event," relative to low-intensity statements such as, "'Calm and cool' could easily describe me" (e.g., Larsen, 1984, cited in Larsen & Buss, 2002, pp. 418–419).

> For every minute you are angry you lose sixty seconds of happiness.
>
> Ralph Waldo Emerson

High affect-intensity people experience both more pleasure *and* more pain. These individuals tend to be more energetic, vigorous, and outgoing in their lives than calmer individuals. High affect-intensity people often liven up a situation by playing jokes and seeking slightly dangerous activities; the worst thing is to be bored. One such individual described himself as an "intensity junkie"—hooked on emotional stimulation. Mood intensity is correlated with both Neuroticism and Extraversion (Larsen & Buss, 2002, p. 420); that is, people high in both neuroticism and extraversion are likely to have more intense emotions.

From Emotional States to Emotion-Related Traits

The Work of Hans Eysenck

Do emotional dimensions blend into personality dimensions? In the 1930s, Hans Eysenck became intrigued by the newly evolving techniques of developing personality measures. He wrote a scale that later became known as the Eysenck Personality Inventory, which included about 120 items similar to the following:

1. Do you enjoy going to parties on weekends?   YES   NO
2. Do you often worry?   YES   NO
3. Are you often happy or often sad for no obvious reason?   YES   NO

Neuroticism-Stability or Emotionality-Stability: A personality dimension (obtained through factor analysis) describing highly emotional individuals on the neurotic/emotional side, and people who are relatively emotionally stable on the stable end.

Eysenck employed the (then) newly emerging method of factor analysis to the scale and found that it measured two independent, uncorrelated factors. Eysenck called the first factor "**Neuroticism-Stability**" or, more tactfully, "Emotionality-Stability." This first factor was represented at the emotionality end by a group of items representing negative emotions, mood swings, anxiety, and uncertainty (e.g., "Do you worry?"—Yes), and at its stable end by calmness, mood stability, and security. The second factor was one of **Introversion-Extraversion**. People high on the extraversion end of the second dimension would answer "yes" to "Do you enjoy parties?" whereas more introverted individuals would be likely to endorse "Do you enjoy reading?"

Eysenck noted that you could locate a person within the dimensional space of common trait terms as reproduced in Figure 4.3. For example, a person high in emotional stability and extraversion would be located in the upper right of the two-dimensional space and be described by such terms as "easygoing" and "talkative," whereas an introverted, emotional individual would be located in the lower left and be described as "pessimistic" and "sober." Stable introverts (upper left) represented "peaceful and thoughtful" individuals, whereas extraverted neurotics (lower right) were "changeable and excitable." Eysenck was able to arrange a great number of personality trait terms in a highly organized way using the two dimensions.

You also may be wondering about the four terms, "phlegmatic," "sanguine," "melancholic," and "choleric" in the inner portion of the diagram. The ancient Greek physician, Hippocrates, had earlier classified personalities into four groups, as described in Chapter 1 ("Personality before Personality"). Eysenck believed that his two dimensions created four quadrants that closely corresponded to Hippocrates' ancient division. Thus, Eysenck's factor analysis integrated the ancient observations of Hippocrates with modern research measurements.

By 1980, there existed a two-dimensional model of mood and a two-dimensional model of personality. A number of personality researchers were intrigued by the similarity between these two models and wondered if they might be related in some way. Costa and McCrea (1980) suggested that a person described by an Eysenckian trait could be described by a parallel tendency to experience a particular type of mood. For

---

FIGURE 4.3

Eysenck's Two Dimensions of Personality

Hans Eysenck proposed that many personality traits could be described along the dimensions of Introversion-Extraversion, and Neuroticism-Stability. Here, many different personality traits are organized together in a circle described by those dimensions.

Source: Adapted from Eysenck & Eysenck (1963), Figure 1. Reproduced with permission from Psychology and Psychotherapy: Theory, Research and Practice © The British Psychological Society.

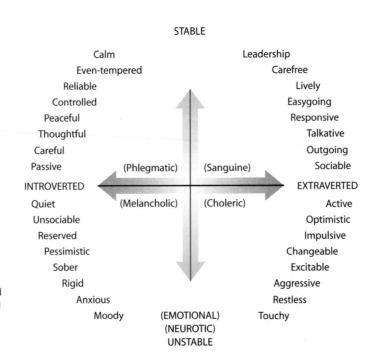

Research in Focus

Positioning the Emotional Dimensions of Inner Space

This chapter describes how researchers arrived at a two-factor solution to describe moods. This two-factor solution can be thought of, geometrically, as a two-dimensional space. When factors are interpreted as dimensions, they can be drawn according to certain geometrical rules depending upon their intercorrelations. Recall that correlation coefficients are numbers that express relationships between variables. These coefficients vary from −1.0 (a perfect negative relationship) to +1.0 (a perfect positive relationship) with a correlation of 0 indicating no relationship.

Correlation coefficients have a second interpretation as well. When one wants to create geometric or dimensional representation of factors and variables, the correlations among them can be interpreted as the *cosines of angles* (e.g., Gorsuch, 1983, p. 63). So, a correlation between factors of 1.0 corresponds to a cosine of 1.0, which defines an angle of 0 degrees between them: the dimensions are identical. A correlation—and cosine—of 0.0 corresponds to an angle of 90 degrees. This is the case with the Pleasant-Unpleasant Mood factor and the Arousal-Calm Mood factor. Most factor analyses are conducted to obtain independent, uncorrelated factors ($r = 0.0$).

If researchers find that Pleasant-Unpleasant Mood dimension correlates with the alternative Positive-Tired Affect dimension $r = .707$, the corresponding cosine would be .707, which corresponds to an angle of 45 degrees. In much early work with emotions and mood, the Pleasant-Unpleasant and Arousal-Calm Mood dimensions were the dimensions of choice. These were arranged north-south, east-west, to create a diagram including specific moods. Some researchers, however, prefer the Positive-Tired, Negative-Relaxed Mood dimensions. These correlate about .707 with the original mood dimensions. For that reason, they can be placed in the same two-dimensional space, but rotated 45 degrees from the originals. That is, they run northeast-southwest and southeast-northwest. That is how psychologists develop the sort of diagram as illustrated in Figure 4.2. The movement from the Pleasant-Unpleasant, Arousal-Calm dimensions 45 degrees to the right, to obtain the Positive-Tired and Negative-Relaxed dimensions, is sometimes referred to as "factor rotation."

example, highly neurotic people might typically feel negative moods, whereas extraverts might typically feel positive moods. If correct, then the two-dimensional personality trait structure would correspond to the two-dimensional mood structure, and they could be superimposed on one another in the same diagram. This has been done here in Figure 4.4; the major personality trait dimensions (e.g., Introverted, all capitalized) and words used to describe them form the main circle. Inside is the fourfold system of antiquity (e.g., Phlegmatic). In the outer circle are the mood dimensions placed so they correspond with the personalities most closely related to them—so, for example, relaxed moods correspond to emotional. Conceptually, they appear to correspond. Subsequent research supported Costa and McCrae's empirical findings that there were also day-to-day relations between mood and personality—for example, that introverted neurotics experienced more negative affect, and stable extraverts experienced more positive affect (Gross, Sutton, & Ketalaar, 1998; De Raad & Kokkonen, 2000).

FIGURE 4.4

Combining the Two Dimensions of Mood and Personality
Beginning in the early 1980s, researchers began to identify similarities in the two-dimensional representations of mood and personality. They wondered whether personality traits could, at a broad level, be a function of moods. Here, Eysenck's two dimensions of personality are shown with the moods that correspond to them.

Source: Adapted from Eysenck & Eysenck (1963), Figure 1, with mood markers added. Reproduced with permission from Psychology and Psychotherapy: Theory, Research and Practice © *The British Psychological Society.*

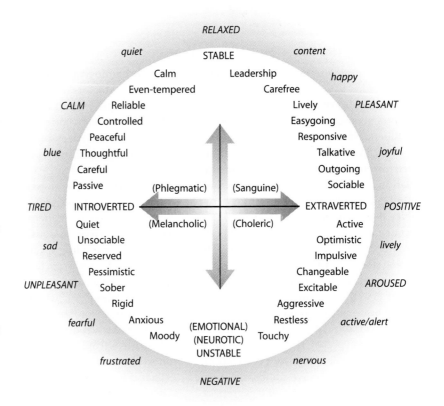

Causes of Emotional Traits

Today, biopsychologists and evolutionary psychologists have suggested the existence of two brain areas that relate to negative and positive emotional feelings. The **behavioral inhibition system (BIS)** has been described as a "stop, look, and listen" system to emphasize that it reduces behavior and increases attention (Gray, 1987). It helps the organism monitor surroundings, anticipate fear-provoking stimuli, and behave cautiously. This system is associated with negative emotions, particularly anxiety and sadness (Gray, 1987; Fowles, 1987; 1994).

Behavioral Inhibition System (BIS): A brain system that interrupts and suppresses behavior so that the individual can think and examine a situation.

Behavioral Facilitation System (BFS): A brain system that encourages and facilitates behaviors such as fighting or joining with others.

By contrast, the **behavioral facilitation system (BFS)** encourages the organism to engage with its outside surroundings, to explore, and to investigate (Depue et al., 1994; Watson, Wiese, Vaidya, & Tellegen, 1999). It is highly associated with positive emotions such as happiness and joy, although anger may also play a part in this behavioral system. There is some evidence for hemispheric differences in these two behavioral systems as well. Davidson, Tomarken, and their colleagues have found that happy, positive people have greater neural electrical activity in their left prefrontal cortex when resting. Dissatisfied, negative people show greater electrical activity in their right prefrontal cortex when resting (Davidson & Tomarken, 1989; Tomarken & Keener, 1998).

Why are there two largely independent systems—behavioral inhibition and behavioral facilitation—rather than one? Cacioppo, Gardner, and Berntson (1999, p. 847) have suggested that two systems permit the organism to be shaped through learning in more subtle ways than would be possible with one system. As a person experiences various events, the two systems learn to respond in partial independence of one another. Sometimes a person may be rewarded for inhibiting certain behaviors, sometimes for facilitating behaviors, and sometimes for both. Because there are two partially independent systems acquiring experience from the environment, more emotional configurations are possible—such as both pausing and watching some events (inhibition), and participating in others (facilitation) in reaction to a given situation.

Other biological models of Introversion-Extraversion and Neuroticism-Stability exist as well. Eysenck, for example, has suggested that introverts have higher physiological responsiveness to stimuli and a higher resting level of activation than do extraverts. For example, if you place a drop of lemon juice in the mouths of an introvert and an extravert, introverts will salivate more intensively than extraverts will (Von Knorring, Moernstad, & Forsgren, 1986). Introverts, in essence, strive to minimize the stimulation they experience so as to keep their activation level from rising even higher than its already high set point. Extraverts, on the other hand, go out and find stimulation so as to raise their initially too-low level of excitement (Eysenck, 1967; 1990, p. 248). All such explanations are at present little more than hypotheses, and their specific natures change as more research accumulates (Zuckerman, 1991, pp. 135–137).

Emotional reactivity is influenced by more than just one's biology, of course. People start learning emotional responses in infancy. For example, a toddler who receives a shot from a doctor may learn to associate the white coats of doctors with pain, and future doctors in white coats may elicit fear automatically as a conditioned reaction (Lewis, 2000). The child at eight months may exhibit only relatively simple fears such as those in response to shots or loud noises. By two years of age, however, a child may perceive more complex social relations—and feel apprehensive, for example, upon breaking her parents' favorite lamp (Lewis, 2000). Emotional learning proceeds based on early exposure to objects and people. A child who brushes his teeth with Willard's of Vermont Toothpaste, while standing next to his mother, may connect the brand to his mother and develop a basic positive reaction to it (Parkinson & Manstead, 1992).

Cultural factors come into play to further shape emotional learning: consider the case of anger and aggression. Among the !Kung bushmen of northwestern Botswana, if a small child has a tantrum he or she is typically allowed to frown, grimace, and cry, and also to throw objects at the mother and to hit her. Mothers behave in a serene fashion during such tantrums, brushing off the tiny blows, and laughing and talking to other adults while they take place. The children's aggression is later directed toward animals: they are free to kill small animals, and to chase and hit dogs and cows, in preparation for hunting. The !Kung children fight among themselves relatively infrequently.

In a Baltimore-area community in the United States, by contrast, mothers often teased their children and encouraged them to fight in order to learn to defend themselves against others. One mother described wrestling matches in which she encouraged her daughter to make a fist and hit her. When her daughter gave her a surprise punch, the mother reacted with pride and feelings of confidence that her daughter would be able to defend herself against others (Saarni, 2000, pp. 306–307). Such differences in emotional environment will certainly change how a person feels anger and aggression, its psychological meaning, and how it is expressed. Thus, both biological and sociocultural influences act upon the emotion system.

How Are Emotional Traits Expressed?

What Are Emotionally Stable and Unstable People Like?

Weissman and Ricks (1966, p. 195) described an extremely emotionally stable college student they studied—dubbed "Shield"—like this:

> Shield manifests no apparent nervous mannerisms and few expressive gestures. His features are regular and good-looking, though not striking. He is inconspicuously well groomed. His speech is quiet, soft, low, and gentle. He gives a sense of calm reserve and aloofness—polite but detached. No zest, no enthusiasms, no spontaneity ripples his urbane composure. He provides little warmth and appears to ask for none in return." (Weissman & Ricks, 1996, p. 195)

Compare this with their description of a more emotional student, dubbed "Swallow":

> Usually laughing and smiling, Swallow readily tosses puns and jokes into conversation, however inappropriate they may be. What he says is often colorful, spontaneous, and unguarded. On occasion there will be a slowness, or a plaintive clutch or sob in his voice that belies his humorous banter . . .
> He has periods of soaring enthusiasm when all the world is bright and promising and he is supremely self-confident. At other times he is despondent, melancholy, hopeless. (pp. 214–215)

Both Shield and Swallow were from divorced homes and it is interesting to compare their autobiographies in that regard. Weissman and Ricks note of Shield's autobiography that "the entire sequence of the family disruption, mother's death, and father's remarriage is recounted in barest outlines, entirely devoid of any account of Shield's personal emotions" (p. 200). An example: Shield says of his parents' divorce that, after his father fell ill, the "relations between my mother and father deteriorated and finally they were separated" (p. 200).

Sorrow makes men sincere.
Henry Ward Beecher

Swallow's narration, in contrast, was highly emotional: "When my parents were divorced, my mother, sister, and I came to live with my grandmother in the house that she owns. It's a real madhouse, everybody fighting with everybody else, really yelling . . ." (p. 219).

A study of mental and behavioral disorders among children further illustrates how emotional and stable development differ from one another (Eysenck & Rachman, 1972, p. 22). Emotionally stable children were relatively free of serious disorders in the study. In contrast, moderate levels of neuroticism in extraverted children led to egocentrism, rudeness, disobedience, fighting, and more serious conduct problems. Among introverted children, by contrast, neuroticism led to the appearance of laziness and daydreaming, mental conflict, nervousness, and, at still higher levels other more serious personality problems. Remember that this was a study of psychopathology and that emotionality can lead to many positive outcomes as well.

The emotion-related traits of emotionality-stability, and extraversion-introversion, can also be used to predict the career path an individual chooses later in life. In Figure 4.5, different psychiatric and professional groups are located according to their average scores on the two dimensions. For example, salespeople scored as very extraverted, and were emotionally average. American college students were equally extraverted but substancially more neurotic by comparison—though still within normal range. These relationships seem to agree in part with our intuitions about what people in those groups are really like (from Eysenck & Eysenck, 1968).

General Emotion Approaches: Contemporary Developments

Today, Eysenck's two dimensions are still studied both on their own and in the broader context of the Big Five personality traits. In Chapter 3 we discussed Big Five traits in some detail, which include Extraversion, Neuroticism, Openness, Agreeableness, and Conscientiousness. From model to model, the exact nature of a trait may

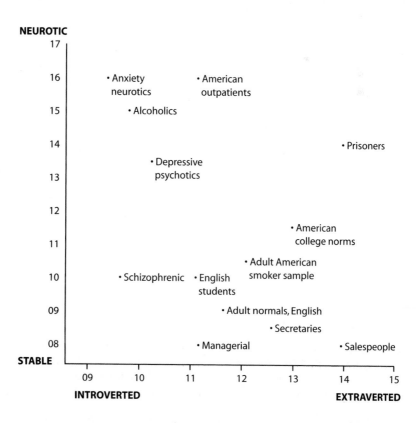

FIGURE 4.5

Groups Varying in Personality Traits
In the figure, various groups are positioned according to their neuroticism-stability and extraversion-introversion.
Source: Adapted from Eysenck & Eysenck (1968), Figure 2. Reproduced with permission. EPI Manual © 1968 EDITS Publishers.

change. For example, Neuroticism as measured in some of the Big Five models, emphasizes self-consciousness and emotional vulnerability rather than Eysenck's mood instability (e.g., Costa & McCrae, 1985). Others have suggested adding one of the Big Five traits—Agreeableness-Disagreeableness—to Eysenck's model to form a three-dimensional model "socio-emotional sphere" (Saucier, 1992). These dimensions form an intuitively appealing group that can be used to define and locate an even larger number of more specific traits than Eysenck had first organized.

What Are Happy People Like?

Natural Happiness

As we have just seen, some people are more prone to positive emotional styles; others to negativity; few possess the exact traits in the right amount to experience extreme happiness. What are such happy people like? From an emotions standpoint, happiness involves being low in neuroticism, somewhat high in extraversion, and having a general sense of well-being as well.

> **What do you take me for, an idiot?**
>
> General Charles de Gaulle, when asked if he was happy

The first thing to say about happiness is that some people seem to feel it rather naturally, whereas others do not (e.g., Watson, 2002). The great twentieth-century psychodiagnostician Paul Meehl (1975) wrote that some people seem to have more "happiness juice" than others. Some people, in other words, seem born happy, whereas others, according to one Wild West maxim, are born "three drinks behind" (Meehl, 1975, p. 299). Meehl describes those who lacked the ability to experience pleasure as often experiencing life as a struggle:

> Well, you know, I have to get up in the morning when I hear the alarm clock ring and go out and shovel the walk [Meehl worked in snowy Minnesota] and all that kind of junk, and what do I really get out of it? I mean, it strikes me that life is often pretty much a big pain in the neck—it just isn't worth it. (1975, p. 300)

Reading this description from today's perspective, incidentally, brings to mind the fact that seasonal decreases in sunlight (as might have been the case in Minnesota snowstorms) can also lead to rises in negative feelings.

The happy person, by contrast, is "born three drinks ahead" (p. 300). Such individuals are fun-loving and cherish their experiences. Indeed, research indicates a fair degree of heritability of positive emotions, with estimates at about $r = .40$ for both positive and negative emotions (measured on the Neuroticism-Extraversion-Openness (NEO) scale (Jang et al., 1998).

Demographic Influences

Neither age nor sex is correlated with happiness. Income is only weakly related to it. Between 1960 and 2000 in the United States, inflation-adjusted income more than doubled from roughly $7,000 to $16,000. Yet, over the same years, the percentage of people saying they were very happy remained surprisingly constant, hovering around

• FACTS • AT • A • GLANCE •			
What Are the World's Most Happy and Unhappy Nations?			
People Who Say They Are Happiest Are In ...	**Score (from 1 to 10)**	**People Who Say They Are Least Happy Are In ...**	**Score (from 1 to 10)**
Denmark	8.0	Italy	6.6
Sweden	8.0	Spain	6.6
Switzerland	7.9	Japan	6.4
Australia	7.9	Greece	5.8
Norway	7.8	Portugal	5.5

Source: From Inglehart (1990), cited in Myers & Deiner (1995), p. 13.

30 percent (Myers & Deiner, 1995, Fig. 4). Today in the United States the correlation between income and happiness is only $r = .13$. There is some indication in cross-national data, however, that extreme poverty does impact happiness negatively. For example, in a survey of forty-three nations completed in 1993, the then-poor nations of India and the Dominican Republic rated below average in happiness (Deiner & Deiner, 1996; Veenhooven, 1993; for reviews, see Argyle, 1987; Myers & Deiner, 1995, and Watson, 2002).

The Most Happy Students

Returning to happy people . . . what are they like? Deiner and Seligman (2002) examined 222 college students' emotions reported on a day-by-day basis over fifty-one days, their positive and negative thoughts, their general life satisfaction, and other similar measures. They then selected the twenty-four happiest students, judged against all the criteria. In certain respects, the happiest students were much like everyone else. They were identical to the depressed and normal students in their perception of how much money they had, their grades, how conscientious they were, their objective physical appearance (rated from photographs), and their time spent doing anything from watching TV to religious observances.

The happy students also were different from the other groups in some significant ways. They were highly satisfied with their lives, they nearly never thought about suicide, they could recall many more positive events than negative ones, and, almost every day, they reported many more happy emotions than unhappy ones (Deiner & Seligman, p. 82). These individuals had good-quality relationships in every area of their lives—with both family and friends. On the Minnesota Multiphasic Personality Inventory (MMPI)—a scale measuring various psychopathologies—they scored within the normal range in virtually every category, with one exception—six of the twenty-four scored a bit high on a scale measuring mania (the happy aspect of bipolar disorder).

> If only we wanted to be happy it would be easy; but we want to be happier than other people, which is almost always difficult, since we think them happier than they are.
>
> Montesquieu

Only 10 percent of us qualify for that most happy group. Another group of us are quite happy, without being among the happiest. Is there anything the person born without a tendency toward happiness can do? The psychodiagnostician Paul Meehl (1975) had foreseen advances in psychopharmacology when he wrote in the mid-1970s and believed that psychoactive drugs would someday offer the less-happy individual important support. In addition to such biological interventions, however, he believed that such individuals might improve by paying more attention to their emotional bookkeeping. To do so, individuals needed to "purchase" activities most carefully. He wrote that "it matters more to someone cursed with an inborn hedonic defect whether he is efficient and sagacious in selecting friends, jobs, cities, tasks, hobbies, and activities in general" (Meehl, 1975, p. 305). A second issue for such individuals was to free themselves somewhat from cultural pressures to interact and go to parties, given that that is not what they generally enjoy. As Meehl put it, "I have a strong clinical impression that, at least in American culture, many people develop a kind of secondary guilt or shame about it . . . not everybody gets a big 'kick' out of social interaction—there is no compelling reason why everybody has to be the same in this respect" (p. 305).

Subsequent research has obtained some encouraging findings concerning positive and negative affect. As a person ages, his or her happiness tends to increase—at least through age seventy (Mroczek, 2001). For men, being both extraverted and married further reinforces this trend (Mroczek & Kolarz, 1998). A variety of psychotherapies exist that are effective in teaching a person how to employ a more positive perspective on life. Such therapies are as effective as many drug therapies in improving a person's sense of well-being (Wampold, Minami, Baskin, & Tierney, 2002; Westen & Morrison, 2001). Additional benefits come from developing a sense of personal meaning (Mascaro & Rosen, 2005).

Recently, Fredrickson (2002a) has suggested that certain forms of coping with moods—particularly engaging in activities such as play and investigation, and tackling various problems with persistence, increases positive affect over time. Her idea is that, even when in negative moods, one can redirect thoughts and ideas more positively. This might involve practicing physical relaxation responses and attempting to engage in more positive, pleasant activities (Fredrickson, 2002b). Fredrickson's research may provide important alternatives to psycho-pharmacological approaches to increasing happiness, and by doing so, help better explain the nature of the emotion itself. These learned positive ways of thinking can make a person happier over the long term. The creation and influence of mental models of oneself, the world, and one's relationships is the topic of the next chapter, "Interior Selves, Interior Worlds."

Reviewing Chapter 4

The goals of this chapter are to introduce you to the motivational and emotional systems, and to discuss the role those systems play in allowing personality to function. In addition, the chapter examines key attributes of those systems, how they are measured, and how they are expressed. The chapter prepares you for the discussion, in upcoming chapters, of other parts of personality, its organization and its development.

What Are Motives and How Can They Be Measured?

1. What are motives, goals, projects, and plans?
The motivational system is made up of basic urges that drive the individual and the goals that satisfy such urges. To get from the motives (basic urges) to the goals, a person may work on projects and develop plans to achieve his or her goals over time. Can you describe and distinguish among motives, goals, projects, and plans?

2. What are projective measures of motives?
Projective measures of motives, such as the Thematic Apperception Test, were developed because researchers assumed that many people might not understand their own motives, or might be reluctant to speak openly about them. Can you describe how a projective test works and how it is scored?

3. What are some of the central motives of personality?
People are motivated by different desires and goals. Freud emphasized sex and aggression. Early in the century, Henry Murray laid out a list of between twenty and thirty motives. Since then, three larger areas of motivation—Achievement, Affiliation, and Power—have been examined, along with sexual motivation. Can you describe each of these?

4. What are self-judged motives?
Some psychologists believe that if you ask people to report their own motivations directly, you will obtain some useful answers. Sometimes to get such answers it is helpful to use "forced choice" formats. Can you describe the forced-choice method and any differences in findings between self-judgment and projective measures?

How Are Motives Expressed?

5. Personal Strivings and Goals.
Personal striving refers to some of the tasks people undertake to achieve their goals. Personal projects are the routes to which people hope to achieve those goals. Striving toward some goals will make a person feel better; other kinds of goals, however, may compromise a person's psychological well-being. Can you distinguish between the sorts of goals that will help and the ones that will not?

6. The Achievement Motive and Personality.
People with strong achievement motives often compare themselves to standards of excellence. They do well in entrepreneurial situations and on tasks they view as relevant to their performance. What else can be said about people high in this motive?

7. The Power Motive and Personality.
People with a high need for power tend to engage in power-motivated behavior, such as attempting to impress others. They may also be drawn to careers such as medicine, psychotherapy, or teaching. Can you say what attracts these people to such occupations?

8. The Affiliation Motive and Personality.
People with high needs for affiliation place greater value on—and more frequently engage in—relationships with others. They are not, however, necessarily well liked in their relationships. This has led psychologists to examine the need for intimacy. Do you know the difference between affiliation and intimacy? How are these two needs expressed?

9. The Sex Drive.
Very little is known about the sex drive in relation to personality beyond the facts that people vary substantially in their sexual interests and that women and men show different mating patterns. For example, men prefer women younger than themselves, and women prefer men of higher occupational status. Evolutionary psychologists have tried to account for some of those differences; can you explain how?

What Are Emotions and Why Are They Important?

10. The Motive-Emotion Connection.

Motives and emotions are intertwined with one another. For example, some emotions can be paired directly with corresponding motives: anger and aggression, fear and escape, love and altruism. Beyond such direct pairing, it appears that some emotions have amplifying effects on motives, whereas others dampen motives. Can you give an example of an emotion that amplifies motives and an emotion that would dampen them?

11. Emotions as an Evolved Signal System.

Emotions appear to have evolved in mammals to communicate social relations and intentions. Do you know who first proposed this idea?

12. Cross-Cultural Issues.

The idea that emotions are universal communications about relationships requires testing across cultures. Paul Ekman provided such tests, first among westernized nations, and then among relatively isolated communities in New Guinea and elsewhere. Do you know the general level of agreement across cultures over basic emotion expressions?

What Are Emotional Traits and How Are They Expressed?

13. The Two-Factor Approach to Measuring Emotions. Mood-adjective checklists are scales in which a person indicates how much of each of a number of feelings he or she is experiencing (e.g., happy, sad, angry, peaceful, etc.). Factor analysis can provide ways of summarizing these large numbers of feelings. One good solution from factor analysis indicates that mood can be represented according to two dimensions. There are, actually, two sets of two dimensions, depending upon how one wishes to label moods. One set describes mood as falling along Pleasant-Unpleasant and Arousal-Calm dimensions. Can you describe the other set?

14. Affect Intensity.

Another way of describing a person's moods is to examine how intensely he or she experiences them. Some people have relatively low-key experiences of feelings; for others, moods and emotions are intense. Can you describe any other differences between such individuals?

15. From Emotional States to Emotional Traits.
There is a two-dimensional representation of emotion suggested by several research teams, and Hans Eysenck earlier found a two-dimensional representation for personality that spanned emotional-stable and extraversion-introversion axes. This led to the idea that there might be a relation between the two dimensions. Do you know what it is?

16. How Are Emotional Traits Expressed?
Whatever one's emotional style, it has consequences in a number of areas, from how one appears to others to one's choice of occupation. Can you relate some of the more important consequences of emotion-related traits to everyday life?

What Are Happy People Like?

17. Natural Happiness.
Some people may be born happier than others; others are "three drinks behind." Can you name the eminent twentieth-century psychodiagnostician who proposed this?

18. Demographic Influences.
Happiness has been studied in relation to nationality, socioeconomic status, and other variables. Mostly, however, there is no relationship between happiness and these factors. Do you remember the one exception?

19. The Most Happy Students.
A recent study examined extremely happy students, selecting them according to a variety of different criteria. Can you say how they differed from the more typical student?

Chapter 5

Interior Selves, Interior Worlds

*I*n the last chapter, we examined how motives direct behavior and emotions assist in their expression. We now move to mental models—records in memory of what one's self and what the world are like. Such models are created as people strive to understand themselves and the world. These mental models address such questions as: Who am I? What am I like? and What is my relation to others? No one has perfectly accurate models of themselves or the world, of course, but everyone must have some such way of thinking about themselves and the world. These models serve as important guides to action, and for that reason, developing reasonably workable models is crucial to the adequate functioning of personality.

- ### What Are Mental Models?

  Mental models are structures in memory that describe the self, the world, and the self in the world. The group of such mental models has different forms; these are explored in this section.

- ### What Are Our Models of Ourselves?

  Each individual develops mental models of him or herself. These models include various models of the self, including the actual self and possible selves one might become. They further include our life stories and other self-models.

- ### What Are Our Models of the World?

  Models of the world concern how we look at and represent the world around us. They include formal learning we acquire at school, as well as more casual scripts we pick up for navigating social situations. Some important models concern how we understand other people.

- ### What Are Our Models of Relationships?

  We also learn about how we relate to others. This learning begins with our relationships with our parents and/or other significant caretakers. As we mature, we develop models for how to carry out more sophisticated social roles.

- ### How Good Are Our Mental Models?

  Some people are able to develop very accurate and constructive mental models of the world and others are not. This section examines what makes for a constructive model and what people are like who hold such constructive models.

What Are Mental Models?

Several weeks into the semester, a young woman was sitting in a college auditorium listening to a class lecture on personality psychology. The course had been going smoothly for her up that point. For that reason, she was surprised when, after class, the professor asked her to come to his office. She was even more dismayed when the professor said he had been distracted over the last few class periods by her behavior toward him. During the lectures, he said, she had begun rolling her eyes, and then looked alternately smug or disgusted. Her snickering had made him increasingly uncomfortable, and he asked her if she would stop. Although she was unaware of behaving in the way he described, she couldn't deny that she had an expressive face and was reacting a lot to the lectures. Mostly though, she told him, she had been enjoying the class.

Recognizing her surprise, the professor, Seymour Epstein, reevaluated the situation. Her snickering was something that was emerging from her unawares, habitually, and automatically. To his eyes, the student had a powerful, negative **mental model** of something occurring in the lecture that was triggering her feelings without her being fully aware of it. A mental model is an organized structure in memory that depicts the self, the world, or the self in the world. Such mental models often can trigger strong emotions. This particular model was likely triggering feelings of anger and

Mental Model: An organized structure in memory that depicts a coherent idea in the self or an object or quality of the world, for example, "the self concept" or (the idea of) "elephants."

165

insecurity that, in turn, were leading her to express her disgust and superiority (as represented by her eye-rolling and smirking).

To help the student understand her mental model—and to reduce his own discomfort—Epstein suggested she monitor her feelings during his next few lectures and check when unpleasant feelings arose. Then, she should see if those feelings might remind her of someone or something in the past that she felt particularly strongly about.

During the next few classes, the student had difficulty attending to her reactions (we can guess she might still have been uncomfortable from having been singled out by the professor). Gradually, however, she began to chart her feelings during the lecture. She found that her reactions were fairly positive during some of the class, but she began to feel uncomfortable and hostile whenever Epstein spoke about his own research. She noticed that Epstein's behavior reminded her of her father, a professional who also had been very wrapped up in his work. She had resented her father, who, she felt, had never had enough time for her.

She returned to Epstein's office two weeks later, excited about the connection she had made. She described how the image of her father—and her hurt feelings over his neglect of her—had come up in class. In her mental model, she wanted the attention of such a man, and he would often hurt her by paying more attention to his work. In response, she felt a welling up of resentment. Once the student recognized the source of her feelings, she realized that her snickering response didn't seem to fit the current situation, and her behavior stopped (Epstein, 1998, p. 73).

Mental models are essential to understanding the world around us. They guide us through the world around us, and help us understand it. Mental models provide clues about when something is about to happen and how to deal with a person's present circumstances. Usually, though, our predictions and reactions are only as good as the mental models on which they are based. What, though, is the nature of such mental models?

Mental Models and Their Structure

Schema: A cognitive structure in memory that organizes information about a specific topic or topics such as mothers, fathers, the self, or knowledge more generally of the world such as occupations or endangered species.

A mental model is not a free-floating idea, but rather, an organized structure in memory. A mental model, or **schema**, is basically a way of organizing related information about a topic in one's thoughts. It is usually learned and can serve as a preconceived way of fitting information together—a reality that a person expects to encounter. For example, a man may think that all men are supposed to act strong and all women are supposed to be caring. He will divide people according to their gender, and most observations he makes will be based on whether he is dealing with a woman or a man, and whether or not the individual fits into the schema he has for them. Such a simple schema sometimes may work, of course, but it will not work very well in accounting for all the real differences among individuals. For that, better models—more sophisticated schema—are required.

Mental models such as schemas can be distinguished according to their specific type. Schemas describe the broadest group, but there are also more specific types of memory structures such as prototypes, scripts, and life stories that are relevant to how we view the world. Table 5.1 provides an overview of such models and we will examine them next.

TABLE 5.1	Mental Models and Their Corresponding Mental Structures	
Knowledge Structure or Schema	**Brief Description**	**Specific Examples**
Schema	An organization of knowledge about a given topic that resides in memory and possesses a specific organization	Self-schemas consist of a group of characteristics that describe the self.
Prototype Structure	A list of prototypical features or characteristics that collectively indicate an object	Personality Prototypes consist of a group of characteristics that defines a particular type of person such as an extravert, or an emotional person.
Script-Based Structure	A prototypical sequence of actions that needs to take place in order to accomplish a goal	Scripts are memory structures that consist of a sequence of stereotyped actions that help one navigate the world. For example, a restaurant script is an outline of what one does to be seated and order food in a restaurant.
Life Story Structure	A specific sequence of events that tells a story of something that has happened to a person	Memory structures that contain the story of important events in one's life. Life stories are one's biographical self-description.
Relationship Structure	Attachments A style of relating to others	Secure attachment, Avoidant attachment.
Roles	A socially defined part that one plays in society	Persona.

Prototype: A type of schema consisting of a list of features that collectively define a concept or object. Typically, the most defining or common features are listed first, with progressively less-defining qualities coming later in the list.

Self-Concept: A mental model one constructs of one's self.

Self-Schema: A memory structure that holds information about the self.

A common form that schemas can take is that of a **prototype**. A prototype is a model of an object based on a list of its most typical or common features (Anderson, 1980, p. 133). In fact, if you are asked about your mental model of nearly anything, you are most apt to recall the most prototypical features first. For example, if you are asked to think of the characteristics of a moral person you are far more likely to produce such highly defining attributes as *honest, genuine, loving, respectful,* and *dependable,* and much less likely to produce the still relevant but less typical qualities such as *does not gossip, diligent,* and *modest* (Lapsley & Lasky, 2001).

Mental models can refer to the self, the world, or the part one plays in the world. Mental models of the self are the internal models that represent to ourselves who we are. For example, a person may say, "I am generous, thrifty, and kind." Another person may say, "I am often tired and sad, and have little energy." These descriptions of the self are sometimes referred to as one's **self-concept**, or as a **self-schema**. A

Self-Esteem: How positive or negatively one feels toward one's self.

Scripts: Stereotyped sequences of events and actions that describe how to do something.

Life Stories: Narrative descriptions of the highlights of a person's life that one uses to describe oneself.

Relationship Structures: Structures that contain procedural knowledge—knowledge about how to do something. Relationship structures contain information about how to act in a relationship.

self-concept (or schema) is a mental model of the self. The positivity or negativity of the self-schema is referred to as an individual's **self-esteem**. Models of the world, on the other hand, are representations of the outside world by which we navigate our surroundings. They tell us the rules by which the world operates. For example, some people think "love makes the world go 'round," whereas others focus on the exercise of power.

Another type of mental model is the script. **Scripts** are stereotyped sequences of events and actions ordered in time (Schank & Abelson, 1977; Tomkins, 1984). For example, most people who live in the world today know the script for a fast-food restaurant. You walk in, get in line (if there is one), and while in line, look at an overhead menu that is typically displayed behind the counter. You then wait for a staff member to say "next" or make eye contact with you, you place your order, and then you pay the cashier. A foreknowledge of such scripts help an individual navigate the outside world in an efficient manner.

The script concept can be applied to more open-ended interpersonal interactions as well. For example, a person in a relationship might envision him or herself as playing a particular character in a script, repeating the same interactions over and over again. Marriage partners often realize they repeat the same argument over and over and seek to change it. Berne (1957) divided the characters one often plays into a parent, an adult, or, a child. If one is a parent, of course, playing a parent is just right. Sometimes, however, a person may play the part of a parent when it is less appropriate, such as with a friend or coworker. In such instances, the interaction may go less smoothly.

A **life story**, another kind of mental model, is a narrative description of a sequence of events describing a central character (the protagonist) and other people. When we ask people about themselves, they often respond with a part of a life story calculated to make an impression on us. For example, a biographer began his book on the Australian art critic Robert Hughes this way:

> Robert Hughes and I were good friends for a few years in the 1950s. We met in 1956 at the University of Sidney . . . in the office of . . . *Honi Soit,* the undergraduate newspaper . . . it was, as I recall, a sunny, blustery autumn day. The door opened . . . I noticed a slim figure standing hesitantly on the step . . . Memory tells me that he was wearing a well-cut suit . . . but I am not sure how far that memory may be trusted. Nevertheless, I am certain of one thing: a sense of something that could only be described as style was unmistakable even before he had spoken. (Riemer, 2001, pp. 1–2)

The biographer's story suggests that he is impressed with Hughes and will write sympathetically of him. The story a person chooses to tell us will highlight some aspects of a life and deemphasize other aspects that might not fit into a particular purpose. Such stories are the means, in part, by which we define our identity for ourselves and for others.

Finally, a fourth class of mental model includes **relationship structures**. Relationship structures contain not only knowledge about the world, but also something called "procedural knowledge"—simply, the procedures for how to do something with others. For example, in his best-selling book, *How to Win Friends and Influence People,* Dale Carnegie (1936) taught millions of people how to make friends by following simple rules such as becoming genuinely interested in other people, smiling, and re-membering and using the other person's name. Models of relationships also include the roles we know how to carry out and play—the role of a student, a partygoer, a friend. We will examine many of these sorts of models of the self and world in this chapter.

Mental Models Are (Usually) Learned and Applied

Where Do Mental Models Come From?

Although mental models are typically learned, let us start with the observation that at least a few of them may have specific biological underpinnings. For example, human beings nearly universally appear able to recognize facial expressions for basic emotions such as anger, fear, and happiness. Evidence for a genetic contribution to such skills comes from the fact that domesticated dogs—but not the wolves from which they descended—appear to read human facial expressions as well (Bekoff & Goodall, 2003; Hare & Wrangham, 2002; Hecht, 2002).

Another kind of innate mental model involves "prepared fears." Human beings and their evolutionary cousins, chimpanzees, very readily develop phobias for spi-ders, lightning, and snakes—consistent dangers over thousands of years of evolu-tionary development. Human beings are far less likely to develop phobias of more recent—and far more injurious—present-day objects such as bicycles, cars, and knives. Relative to the threats persistently faced by our ancestors, there has been compara-tively little evolutionary time to evolve caution in respect to those newer objects (deSilva, Rachman, & Seligman, 1977; Mineka, David-son, Cook, & Keir, 1984; Poulton et al., 2001).

> But the idea of the nest in the bird's mind, where does it come from?
>
> Joseph Joubert

In a way, the chief form of prepared learning in human beings is their substantial capacity for general learning about the environment. That is, most of our mental models are flexibly constructed through our own experiences and education. Much of what children do all day long is to ac-quire knowledge structures with which they understand the world. Indeed, people can learn mental models very quickly (Haslam, 1994; Hess, Pullen, & McGee, 1996; Mayer & Bower, 1986).

Implicit Mental Models and Their Generalization and Overgeneralization

Implicit Knowledge: Knowledge that is acquired unintentionally in the course of doing or thinking about other things.

Something that is implicit is learned, understood, or conveyed without any direct consciousness of what is being communicated. **Implicit knowledge** is knowledge we learn without intentionally doing so; it is knowledge we acquire while doing other things. We often model our world without knowing we are doing so. Our mental models are so natural a part of us that we likely didn't notice when we acquired them, and typically fail to recognize their influence on our present thoughts. We are like fish that don't know they are swimming through water because they are totally sur-rounded by the liquid and they have never known anything else. Only rarely (if at all) do we intentionally sit down and say, "Now I am going to create a model with which to understand people." Rather, most of our models are learned gradually through ob-servation and through listening to others talk.

Given the implicit nature of mental models, we often use them without knowing we have them. Even if the model is consciously learned, we may feel invested in its being correct. Either such situation can lead to "model creep"—that is, we can overuse a model in places where it should not be applied. So, one of the critical aspects of world models is that they can be applied correctly and judiciously, but they can also be overgeneralized, as we will see.

Differences in Models across People

Another characteristic of mental models is that they differ dramatically from individual to individual. These differences determine, in part, the richly different ways human beings have of understanding and reacting to the same phenomenon. Consider Robert, a college student in a class studying mental models.

Robert described a recent encounter with his mother. His parents were getting divorced and blamed each other for the breakup. When Robert came home from school to pick up his winter clothes, he found his mother had locked all the doors—and changed the locks—so he couldn't come in. She yelled at him through an open window that he "didn't deserve to come in because . . . [he] sided with his father" in the divorce. Frustrated, and very angry, Robert called the police and was finally escorted into his home to collect his clothes (Epstein, 1998, pp. 27–29).

> O Memory! thou fond deceiver.
>
> Oliver Goldsmith

After Robert told his story, he learned that about two-thirds of the other students in the seminar agreed they would react just as he had. But he was surprised to find that about a third of the students said they would have reacted differently. One young woman would have been afraid that she had done something very bad for her mother to treat her that way. Another woman expressed fear that her mother might be going crazy. Yet another student said he'd be coolly detached, finding it amusing how a parent could behave so ridiculously. Their reactions vividly illustrate how mental models differ from person to person (pp. 27–29).

What Are Our Models of Ourselves?

The Self and Self-Models

Perhaps the most personal of all mental models is the model one holds of one's self. William James, a founder of American psychology, characterized the total self as consisting of both an "I" and a "me." He said, "The I watches the me." The "I" is the watching, aware consciousness. The "me" is the part of oneself that is watched. The "me" is the model one holds of oneself (James, 1920, p. 176).

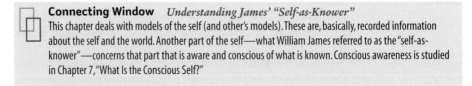

Connecting Window   *Understanding James' "Self-as-Knower"*
This chapter deals with models of the self (and other's models). These are, basically, recorded information about the self and the world. Another part of the self—what William James referred to as the "self-as-knower"—concerns that part that is aware and conscious of what is known. Conscious awareness is studied in Chapter 7, "What Is the Conscious Self?"

That me is the self-description. The following is a description given by an adolescent girl in response to the question, "Tell us about yourself."

Well, I am not very smart in some areas. I am not very pretty. I like almost all kinds of activities, especially summer sports. I like to have a good time at parties and get-togethers. I like dogs very much and horses. I do not have very many friends but the ones I have I like and get along with very well. I like to play my records while I am doing my homework and in my spare time I have a baby-sitting job. I am 14 and I have my problems too. (McGuire, 1984, p. 90)

At its simplest level, a model of the self (or self-schema) can be interpreted as a list of traits or features one notices and assigns to oneself. For example, Ivcevic and colleagues (2003) asked college students to write a brief essay describing their personalities. The descriptions were then coded into a number of content categories such as preferences (e.g., "I like good conversation") to descriptions of spontaneity ("I am flexible, impulsive, random"), to coping styles ("I can laugh at myself") and relationships ("My parents trust me").

The parts that make up a person's self-concept—as opposed to mental models of the world—possess a unique status. For example, people process self-related information faster and more efficiently than other information (e.g., Lewicki, 1984; Markus, 1977). In one study, for instance, forty-eight undergraduate women were divided into those who thought of themselves as dependent or independent, or did not think of themselves in either way. Later, participants rated trait words that were dependence-related, such as "conforming," and "submissive," on a screen as *Me* or *Not me.*" Those participants who thought of themselves as dependent endorsed dependence-related items far more quickly than they did independence-related adjectives such as "individualistic" and "assertive" (Markus, 1977). (See the Inside the Field box.)

Possible, Actual, and (Perhaps) Unconscious Selves

Actual Self: How a person thinks of his or her qualities, life experience, and interactions.

Possible Self: A mental model of what one's self might be like in the future if it were to change (or in the past, if one had been different).

Ideal Self: A model of oneself that one would like to become.

People employ more than one model of their selves. The **actual self** is a model of how a person thinks he or she is in reality. Note that a person's actual self may be very accurate, or may be quite different from how one is, objectively speaking. By contrast, **possible selves** form a broad class of alternative selves that one might anticipate becoming, given the right life circumstances (Markus, 1986).

One possible self is the **ideal self**—Freud's label for the self one would like to become (Freud, 1923/1960). A number of researchers have been interested in the concept of the ideal self because it can help a psychologist understand how a person might want to change. When the actual and ideal self are similar it is often thought to reflect psychological health. As the actual and ideal self diverge, it may create a sense of humility as one recognizes how far one falls short of the ideal; alternatively, such a discrepancy can cause an individual distress (Dewey, 1887; 1967; Freud, 1923/1960, p. 27; Higgins, 1987, p. 322; Rogers, 1951, pp. 510–513).

Ideal and Ought Selves

Ought Self: A self that sets a standard for what one should live up to.

Some theorists have distinguished an **ought self** from the ideal self. In this approach, the ideal self refers specifically to the ideas represented by one's own personal goals and aspirations. The ought self, by contrast, represents the standards of being and behavior expected by others around us. These selves can serve to guide us. The ought

Inside the Field

The International Society for Self and Identity (ISSI)

In 2000, a new scientific society was incorporated to study the self. Beginning in 1996, a preconference (a smaller conference before a more major conference) was held on the topic of "the self," just before the meeting of the Society of Social and Experimental Social Psychology. Soon afterward, the International Society for Self and Identity (ISSI) was formed.

Although a few personality psychologists were part of the early meetings, the new society at first was organizationally allied with experimental social psychologists. Interestingly, some of the early definitions of the self often sounded a great deal like definitions of personality. Tesser (2002, p. 185), for example, remarked that we can think of the self as "a collection of abilities, temperament, goals, values, and preferences that distinguish one individual from another." This led to the question of whether some members of the society might try to replace the concept of "personality" with the concept of "self."

The editors of the group's new journal, *Self and Identity,* have, however, clarified that the self is distinct from personality: "It is not useful to employ self as a synonym for person or personality, as these . . . encompass more than just a person's self subsystem," they have written and affirmed (Morf, 2005, p. 99; cf. Leary, 2004a, p. 2).

The self is plainly a key part of personality. So what can self researchers tell us about men-

tal models of the self, one of the topics of this chapter? Here are just a few key areas of theory and research on the self, as outlined by the founding editor of their journal (Leary, 2004b):

- We are almost always at least one step removed from the real world. In part, this is because we interpret the world through our own models of ourselves and the world.
- There is an "I'm better than average effect"—most people see themselves as more positive than they really are. One striking example: an average college student believes he or she is more likely to go to heaven than most others. Many students rank their chances of going to heaven higher than the average chances given to Mother Theresa!
- People evaluate things they own more favorably than those they don't. People even like the letters in their own name better than other letters of the alphabet.
- People think they understand others quite well, whereas they believe others don't understand them in return.

Leary concludes that all this leads people to underestimate how they might benefit from others and to overestimate what they as individuals might contribute. Note that when people are depressed they may lose these illusions, but sometimes at the cost of a sense of well-being.

Always remember that you are unique. Just like everyone else.

Unknown

self helps us steer clear of what others might find objectionable so as to protect us against feared negative outcomes. The ideal self focuses us on our goals and our ambitions and serves as a positive, promotional force in motivation (Higgins, Shah, & Friedman, 1997).

To understand these selves, Higgins (1987) asked his research participants for ten characteristics that define their ideal selves. In response, a participant might have replied in part: (1) always kind to others, (2) creative, and . . . (10) satisfied with life and happy. Higgins then asked participants to repeat the process for their ought self (the way others expect the person to be) and their actual self (the way the person is

The painting Mirror II *(1963) by the twentieth century American painter George Tooker, has an introspective quality about it. The painting relies on the near-universal human experience of self-reflection to bring about its effect on the viewer. An individual's self-concept arises in part from such reflections, as well as from feedback provided by others.*

now). The same participant's ought self characteristics might have included (1) being a good daughter, (2) doing well in school, and . . . (10) going out to bars less.

Higgins then compared the various selves a person described by calculating a discrepancy score between selves. An actual-ideal discrepancy of zero indicated that all ten characteristics of a person's actual self also appeared on their list for their ideal self. As you can imagine, discrepancies of zero are fairly rare. More commonly, people's actual selves have some incomplete overlap with their ideal and ought selves.

It makes a difference whether you are further from your ideal or from your ought self. People with big actual-ought discrepancies often imagine themselves failing to do what society says they should and are prone to feel anxious as a consequence. In contrast, people with big actual-ideal self discrepancies are not engaging in the sorts of activities they enjoy and that would make them feel good. These individuals tend to feel sad and depressed as a consequence (Higgins, 1987).

Feared and Desired Selves

Markus and Nurius (1986) focused on another group of possible selves that they labeled **feared** and **desired** selves. Desired selves are the extremely positive selves we hope we will become. A positive self might include an image of oneself as an intelligent, warm lawyer, enjoying love and acclaim, who is physically fit, can accurately read other people, goes to the theater, and is a gourmet cook. The feared possible self is an extreme negative self the individual envisions.

Feared Self: An extreme negative version of the self that the individual fears he or she will become.

Desired Self: An extremely attractive positive vision of the self that the individual desires to become.

Angela Nissel, a student at the University of Pennsylvania, faced serious financial pressures during her senior year. After being unable to pay bank penalties and insulting a bank clerk, she found herself unable to open further bank accounts in her city. She was forced to take her paycheck to a check-cashing service, where those too poor to have a bank account went. Unsettled and worried, Nissell experienced a feared possible self: herself as permanently poor. Her breezy commentary on the situation couldn't hide the worry: "I am really teetering on the edge of this temporarily broke/permanently poor dividing line because of this whole . . . episode. All I need is one push from the left and I might trip over that line and land smack-dab on Poor" (Nissel, 2001, p. 38).

Different groups exhibit powerfully different possible selves. Oyserman and Markus (1990) examined three groups of youth: Nondelinquent youth who were wards of the state due to general family problems; delinquent youth who were wards of the state due to criminal justice issues, and college students. The nondelinquent youth, who resided in a group home, had possible selves that included "on ADC, no job, poor housing, cannot pay bills" (see also Oyserman & Saltz, 1993). By contrast,

35 percent to 40 percent of the delinquent group possessed feared possible selves that were involved with criminal behavior, including "criminal, murderer, pusher, junkie, physical abuser of spouse or child." These possible selves existed within the delinquent group despite quite high reported levels of self-esteem.

By contrast, college students have many possible selves, both feared and desired, but they are generally positive. (See the Research in Focus box.) Writing about college students in the mid-1980s, Markus (1990) notes:

> Virtually all respondents thought it was possible for them to be rich, admired, successful, secure, important, a good parent, in good shape, and to travel the world. In contrast, almost none of our respondents thought it was possible that they could be a welfare recipient, a spouse or child abuser, a janitor, or a prison guard. (p. 958)

Such possible selves also appear to have an impact on a person's future well-being. Markus examined people shortly after they had experienced the death of a spouse. She then divided the group into those who believed they were adjusting poorly to the tragedy and those who believed they were adjusting well. She found that members of both groups viewed themselves as sad, lost, and helpless; their current selves were basically indistinguishable at the time of the tragedy. But people who were making a good recovery possessed positive future selves even at the time of the tragedy, compared with those who had made a poor recovery. They could distinguish a positive, healthy, optimistic self somewhere in the future, despite the terrible pain of the present.

Are there selves that are more integrated than these feared or desired possible selves? Showers (2002) has researched people who have "compartmentalized" selves—all good or all bad, versus those who have selves that are more integrated. Interestingly, college students who compartmentalize their failures—"I am a good student, but not in history"—tended to cope with stress better than others (Showers, 2002, p. 283; Showers, Abramson, & Hogan, 1998). Over the long term, however, she finds that people with integrated, positive selves who are able to add small doses of negative attributes to their selves may end up being the most healthy and able to adapt to change (Showers, 2002, p. 284; Showers & Ryff, 1996).

Unconscious Selves

Is it possible that a negative or threatening self-concept could be unconscious altogether? Carl Jung was an early twentieth-century psychodynamic theorist who emphasized the importance of opposites in psychic structures and other mental processes (Jung, 1956, p. 64; Friedman, 1966). Jung suggested that there existed both a conscious self and its opposite, an unconscious **shadow**. The shadow represented material or information about the self with which the person was unfamiliar, could not recognize, and often could not accept (Jung, 1968, pp. 21–24). The shadow part of the self often contains material that makes the individual feel quite uncomfortable and may be blocked from consciousness because it is painful to think about. A person who considers himself religious and upright may possess a shadow that is unfaithful and at times evil-seeming.

As another example, Jung suggested that men and women each contain within them aspects of the opposite sex that are repressed. For example, men have within

Shadow: An unconscious model of the self that contains the attributes and qualities that a person actually possesses, but rejects at the conscious level.

Research in Focus

Markus and Nurius on Possible Selves among College Students

Markus and Nurius (1986, p. 959) make the point that the possible self can be distinguished from the actual self. To demonstrate this difference clearly, they conducted a study in which researchers stated a positive characteristic and asked people two questions about it: (1) Does this describe you now? and (2) Have you ever considered this a possible self? Consider the differences in the responses obtained from 210 college students:

Positive and Negative Possible Selves of College Students

	Describes You Now?	Ever Considered a Possible Self?
Mostly Positive Possibilities		
Happy Personality	88%	100%
Confident Personality	84%	100%
Travel Widely	44%	94%
Have Lots of Friends	75%	91%
Be Physically Sexy	52%	74%
Be a Media Personality	2%	56%
Mostly Negative Possibilities		
Depressed Personality	40%	50%
Be Destitute	5%	20%
Have a Nervous Breakdown	11%	43%
Be Paralyzed	3%	45%
Be a Prison Guard	0%	4%

Source: Markus & Nurius (1986), p. 959, reprinted with permission of the American Psychological Association.

Anima: An unconscious portion of a man's mental models that includes feminine characteristics.

Animus: An unconscious portion of a woman's mental models that includes masculine characteristics.

them an **anima**—a female self—and women have an **animus**—a male self. Jung was writing at a time when sex roles were more restrictive than they are today. Thus, people often blocked out opposite-sex characteristics which were relegated to the shadow.

The Italian director Federico Fellini's semi-autobiographical movie, *8½*, depicts a film director who has repressed his feminine self. He behaves in a macho, sexist fashion that is depicted in the film. Not coincidentally, he also is blocked creatively and cannot figure out what movie to make. The shadow is not entirely negative for Jung. Rather, the shadow is a resource full of animal energy and, if it can be integrated with the conscious part of the individual, can often contribute to life energy. Indeed, for Jung, a person entirely cut off from his or her shadow would appear two-dimensional and lifeless (Jung, 1968, p. 23). The middle of Fellini's film features a mind reader who extracts an anagram for "anima" from the director's mind, and in so doing allows him to break through a mental block caused by his over-identification with his male qualities (Bondanella, 1998, pp. 102–104). When the director finally discovers his feminine self, he is able to bring the movie to completion. In real life, the film is considered a masterpiece. For most of us, filming a movie isn't on the horizon. Nonetheless, Jung would say, each year we have a sense of ourselves and yet the next year we learn something new about the way we are. What we have learned comes from the shadow portion—that part that normally lies in darkness (Jung, 1968, pp. 21–24).

The idea of the hidden shadow, dramatic though it is, has received little research attention beyond the case study approach. It is clear that many people have imperfect self-knowledge, and hidden sides, some of them shocking and even unspeakable, though most are more everyday. The topic of the shadow invites careful research study. Although the shadow has not been regularly studied, there does exist considerable research on mechanisms people use to avoid unpleasant parts of themselves. These will be covered in Chapter 10 on dynamics of the self.

Connecting Window   *The Totalitarian Ego*

A person's model of the self is often incomplete—focusing on the individual's own goodness and excluding anything discrepant (this positive perspective may fail when a person becomes depressed). Unpleasant information is simply avoided, or resides in many different memories that are too painful to observe. Such dynamics of the self are discussed in Chapter 10, "The Problem of the Egotistical Ego" and "Falling Short and Mental Defense."

Self-Esteem and Self-Efficacy

Self-Esteem: The overall positive or negative feeling one experiences toward one's self.

Are you pretty confident about yourself? Do you think you are easy to like? **Self-esteem** refers to the overall positive or negative evaluation one makes of oneself. People who like and value themselves are said to have high self-esteem, and those who devalue and dislike themselves are said to have low self-esteem. Self-esteem is generally measured by asking people to endorse statements such as "I can usually take care of myself," which reflects high self-esteem, versus, "I often feel as if I'm not good enough," which reflects low self-esteem (e.g., Rosenberg, 1965; Coopersmith, 1967; 1975; Robinson, Shaver, & Wrightsman, 1991; Wylie, 1974). Refer to the Test Yourself feature and take the self-esteem test.

Self-esteem has also been thought of as a more complex variable that includes not only attitudes such as, "I am easy to like," but also more complex relationships among schema, such as a close correspondence between one's actual and ideal selves (Marsh, 1993).

Beginning in 1986, a California task force spent three years and three-quarters of a million dollars on a study of whether increased self-esteem enhanced learning or helped resolve other school problems such as violence or drug use. They could find little evidence of any such relationships. Nonetheless, the notion that self-esteem is important is so pervasive in our culture that the task force went on to recommend programs to raise children's self-esteem. Self-esteem programs flooded the public

> **Ideas that we do not know we have, have us.**
>
> William Appleman Williams

Self-Efficacy: One's self-estimated ability to perform a specific task.

school systems, only to be judged failures several years later (Joachim, 1996; Leo, 1990). In fact, psychologists have often noted the potential dark side of self-esteem as well as the positive. For example, some forms of high self-esteem lead to a sense of entitlement and a willingness to exploit others that may contribute to violent or discriminatory behavior (e.g., Baumeister, 1997). Among the findings consistent with such a theory is the repeated finding that juvenile delinquents and similar groups have self-esteem equal to or higher than college students and others. The exact value of high self-esteem has remained elusive (McCrae & Costa, 1990).

A second dimension of self-evaluation—and one that has received more intensive research attention—is self-efficacy. **Self-efficacy** refers to one's self-judged ability to perform a certain task in life. For example, some students generally feel confident about taking an exam but are worried about writing a paper; other students may feel the reverse. Albert Bandura (1977, p. 79; 1999) introduced the concept of self-efficacy to describe such feelings when facing particular tasks in life. Bandura and others have found that when a person feels able to handle a specific task, he or she is more likely to carry it out well (Bandura, 1977; 1999). The advantage of self-efficacy over the somewhat related concept of self-esteem is that it is defined more specifically than the more general idea of self-esteem. That specific definition—one's belief about carrying out a task—has made it easier to research. For example, to examine a person's self-efficacy for learning to speak a foreign language, one asks specific questions on the order of, "How good are you at learning a foreign language?" (e.g., Bong, 1999; Pajares, 1996). Despite the apparent better focus of self-efficacy research, some have suggested that it is, in the end, best considered part of a broader concept of self-esteem. If so, perhaps the self-esteem literature can be helped by employing some of the practices of self-efficacy researchers (e.g., Judge, 2001).

Federico Fellini directed the movie, 8½, which was heavily influenced by Jungian theory. The movie revolved, in part, around the concepts of anima and animus. Anima was the feminine aspect of a man's personality; animus, the masculine aspect of a woman's personality. Jung believed that giving expression to both one's masculine and feminine sides would foster creativity and growth.

Test Yourself: Self-Esteem

	Strongly Agree	Agree	Disagree	Strongly Disagree
1. I feel that I am a person of worth, at least on an equal basis with others.				
2. I feel that I have a number of good qualities.				
3. All in all, I am inclined to feel that I am a failure.				
4. I am able to do things as well as most other people.				
5. I feel I do not have much to be proud of.				
6. I take a positive attitude toward myself.				
7. On the whole, I am satisfied with myself.				
8. I wish I could have more respect for myself.				
9. I certainly feel useless at times.				
10. At times I think I am no good at all.				

Scoring Instructions
Score items 1, 2, 4, 6, & 7 as follows:
    4 = Strongly Agree
    3 = Agree
    2 = Disagree
    1 = Strongly Disagree
Score items 3, 5, 8, 9, & 10 as follows:
    1 = Strongly Agree
    2 = Agree
    3 = Disagree
    4 = Strongly Disagree
A higher score means higher self-esteem.

Source: M. Rosenberg, 1969. *Society and the adolescent self-image.* Revised edition. Middletown, CT: Wesleyan University Press.

Stories of the Self

The final model of the self examined here is the person's self-constructed life story (e.g., Bruner, 1990; Cohler, 1982; Josselson, 1995; McAdams, 2001; Singer, 2001; Singer & Salovey, 1993). Storytelling is a fundamental way people communicate information about themselves and their worlds. Such life stories stress some events while they deemphasize or omit many others. Alfred Adler, an early psychologist with both psychodynamic and humanistic interests, was especially interested in studying a person's earliest memories. He felt that because they were the beginning of an individual's story, these earliest memories had particular significance (e.g., Adler, 1931; 1958), but little has come from such research (Watkins, 1992).

Contemporary perspectives take a more comprehensive approach to life stories. For example, Dan McAdams elicits life stories through structured interviews in which he asks research participants to divide their lives into parts like the chapters of a book, with chapters covering earliest memories, childhood, and adolescence, as well as chapters on low points, high points, and turning points (McAdams, 1993). Diana C. is a forty-nine-year-old teacher and mother who participated in one such study. In the early chapters of her life, she described herself as as "the first baby ever born" in a Methodist parsonage founded by her father, a minister. She enjoyed an exalted social status as a child, and later, when her family moved to a wealthier congregation in Chicago, associated with many famous people. Tragedy struck when she was eight, however, and her younger brother was killed by a car. At the same time, she had a second-grade teacher who ended up being institutionalized. But after that, she remarked, "things picked up." (McAdams et al., 1997, pp. 688–689). Although she could not become the son her father lost, she married a young man who became like a son to her father. Together, they raised a family, and she feels inspired by her job as a teacher.

Redemptive Sequence: A portion of a life story in which a person encounters a challenge or trauma and is then able to redeem the value of the experience.

Contamination Sequence: A portion of a life story in which a person encounters an ambivalent or negative event that is seen as negatively defining one's life.

McAdams and his colleagues coded features of this and other stories according to whether they possessed **redemptive** or **contamination sequences**. Redemptive sequences involve segments of life stories in which a person encounters a difficulty or trauma but is then able to redeem the value of the experience. Examples of redemptive sequences include responding to the death of a family member by understanding that it led to one's family becoming closer, or, after experiencing a bad year in school, experiencing success at a new school. Contamination sequences involve portions of life stories in which ambivalent or unfortunate events are interpreted as negatively defining one's life: for example, experiencing a wonderful marriage but then discovering one's spouse wants a divorce (McAdams & Bowman, 2001). As you might imagine, those who describe more redemption sequences in their lives are higher in well-being and lower in depression than are individuals who describe more contamination responses (McAdams et al., 2001).

What Are Our Models of the World?

Formal Models and Implicit Models

Formal Knowledge

Formal models of the world are carefully organized, well-worked-out descriptions of the world and how it works. Formal models are most typically developed, taught, and

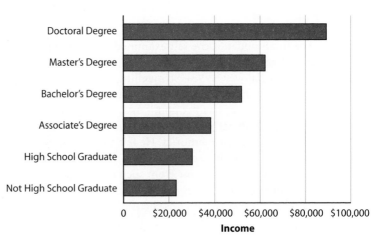

FIGURE 5.1

Average Earnings as a Function of Education
Our information-oriented societies increasingly reward people for their level of education. Education, in this case, is a proxy for the accuracy of the mental models a person has constructed of his or her world—or, at least, specialized parts of it.

Source: Modified from Cheeseman Day & Newburger (2002), Figure 1.

learned, in educational settings. They involve reasoned analyses, logical proofs, and empirical demonstrations. Higher education—and almost all schooling, in fact—assists people to create such carefully worked out models of the world around them.

Every course one takes and every degree one earns is valued precisely because it reflects the creation of more accurate models of the world, which is important given the growing complexity of society. Our society handsomely rewards such increases in accuracy of world models: the relation between schooling and income continues to grow in a dramatic fashion, as shown in Figure 5.1 (Cheeseman Day & Newburger, 2002).

But does the development of all mental models require formal education? Formal education, such as is carried out in schools, colleges, and universities, is only one way of learning. There is also the less formal learning that takes place in day-to-day observation of our situations—learning that depends on our street smarts and that is obtained in what used to be called the "school of hard knocks." Psychologists, too, have distinguished between the formal learning one receives in school and the more "vibe-driven," less formal learning that occurs throughout daily life.

Implicit Knowledge

Implicit Models: Models of the world that are learned incidental to, or as a consequence of, living, rather than learned in a formal, purposeful way.

Practical or Tacit Knowledge: A type of knowledge concerned with how the world actually works, as opposed to how it is said to work, or how teachers, instructors, and other experts say it works.

Tacit Knowledge

The learning of everyday life has been referred to variously as implicit, practical, and experiential as well as by other terms. **Implicit models** can be contrasted with formal models. Implicit models are gradually learned through living and watching what goes on rather than learned on purpose as, say, part of school curriculum (Epstein, 1998; Sternberg & Horvath, 1999; other terms include "episodic" [Tulving, 1972; 2002] and "narrative" [Bruner 1986; 1990]).

Sternberg and his colleagues call this general domain of knowledge **practical** or **tacit knowledge**. Such practical or tacit knowledge is focused on how things work in various social and institutional settings, and is of considerable use in understanding how to get along. Practical knowledge often goes unstated, is rarely stated, or re-

He said, "Who then are the true philosophers?" "Those," I said, "who are lovers of the vision of truth."

Plato

mains obscure in its statement. If your mother told you when you were a child to behave well at the house of someone you (and she) did not like, you may have realized that she attached some importance to the individual. Your sense that the person you visited was important in some way was tacit in that it was never explained (Sternberg & Horvath, 1999; Wagner, 1987; 2000).

As another example, every organization has stated rules for how things happen, but there are also the unstated rules that "everyone" knows (Sternberg et al., 2000). Spaeth (1999) pointed out that bar Associations require lawyers to practice with competence, and competence involves experience. Often, however, the methods a young lawyer can use to ensure that she or he practices with competence go unstated. The savvy beginning lawyer will apprentice herself to a more experienced colleague at first to learn the ropes and will consult with other experts in the specific area of law she or he is practicing. The individual who does not absorb these social practices will find it difficult to launch a career (Spaeth, 1999). Likewise, there is probably tacit knowledge about succeeding as a psychology major at your college or university. For example, it may, help to engage in extracurricular organizations or activities such as independent studies with particular professors. Do you know of such possibilities at your school?

Scripts for Navigating the World

Another example of practical everyday knowledge is the development of scripts. Scripts are relatively stereotyped sequences of actions that we follow day in and day out in order to accomplish goals (e.g., Anderson, 1983; Tomkins, 1987). If you were to read that John went into a restaurant and ordered lasagna, and later came out with a full stomach, you would know exactly what had happened inside the restaurant. That understanding comes from a long developmental sequence in which you have learned the restaurant script very well.

For example, here is a three-year-old's script for a restaurant:

INTERVIEWER: Tell me a story—what happens in a restaurant? What happens—you go inside the restaurant . . .
HANNAH: You sit down, and you uh, eat food.
I: How do you get the food?
H: From the waitress.
I: How does the waitress know what to give you?
H: If you ask for a hamburger, then she gives you a hamburger.
I: What happens if you ask for hotdog, do you get hamburger?
H: No you get hot dog.
I: And then what happens after she gives you the food?
H: She gives you dessert.
I: And then what happens?
H: And then you leave.
I: And then you leave? Just like that?
H: No, the waitress gives you some money and you pass some money to her and she gives you some money back to you and then you leave. (Schank & Abelson, 1977, p. 223)

Hanna's restaurant script is fairly impressive at three years of age, but it isn't completely developed. By a year later, it is much more comprehensive:

INTERVIEWER: Now, I want you to tell me what happens when you go to a restaurant.

H: OK.

I: What happens in a restaurant? Start at the beginning.

Disciplinary Crossroads

World Knowledge in the Field of Artificial Intelligence

Although personality psychologists such as George Kelly had discussed the critical nature of world knowledge as early as the 1950s, it was research in the field of artificial intelligence in the 1970s that helped to convince personality psychologists how important such knowledge truly is to people's comprehension of the world.

The 1960s were a time of great optimism for those who were attempting to teach computers to understand language. Many computer scientists thought that this breatkthrough was just around the corner. Indeed, computers of the time could, with some reliability, identify all the parts of speech in a sentence. Moreover, the computer could look up a dictionary meaning of each word. Yet it soon became clear that even with this kind of understanding the computer could not address the more complex facets of language understanding—and that scientists' hopes were premature. To understand the sort of problem that such artificial intelligence programs encountered, consider the following sentences:

The cat and mouse played together. "Squeak, squeak, meow, meow," they cried.

You will probably agree that any child could understand them. But these sentences would be incomprehensible to the artificial intelligence program just described. To understand why, try to find the place in the sentence that identifies

which animal said "squeak" and which said "meow." It simply isn't there—and even a computer that has a firm grasp of grammatical structure hasn't a clue. A three-year-old child, by contrast, knows who said what, because children know mice squeak and cats meow. We say, in this case, that the three-year-old child possesses world knowledge, which she brings to bear upon her understanding of language.

World knowledge is quite pervasive. We often speak in brief, telegraphic language that depends on well-worked-out knowledge. As another example, consider the question, "Gas?" which will have different meanings if asked by a gas station attendant, a nervous coal-miner deep under the earth's surface, or the diner sitting next to you at a banquet table!

To address this problem, artificial intelligence researchers had to teach computers about the world. They teamed up with psychologists in order to construct concepts of "knowledge structures" discussed in the text.

In their pioneering work, Schank and Abelson taught computers scripts for eating at restaurants. They began with a system that translated English sentences into a universal grammar. They assumed that there were only a limited number of concepts that people understand and that are expressed and re-expressed in a number of languages. For example, the verb PTRANS, meant physically transporting an object to another object. INGEST meant to eat, and so

H: You come in and you sit down at the table. And then the waitress comes. And she gives you a menu. And, then she takes it back and writes down your order. And, then you eat what she gave you. And, then you get up from the table. And you pay the money and then you walk out of the store. (p. 224)

Most people in developed parts of the world have a similar restaurant script, although it may vary somewhat from region to region. Computers have been taught

on. So John PTRANS John to the restaurant and INGEST frankfurter meant that after going to the restaurant, John ate a frankfurter.

One of the most impressive demonstrations of computer understanding involved first teaching the computer an extensive series of scripts about transportation and restaurants. Once the computer could integrate its vocabulary and grammar understanding with its script-based world knowledge, it could converse intelligently about fairly complex stories.

One famous example involved the story of a young man named John who takes a bus from New Haven to New York City. Arriving in New York, he takes the subway to a well-known restaurant called Mama Leone's to have dinner (Schank & Abelson, 1977, p. 178). The story "told" to the computer states:

On the subway his pocket was picked. He got off the train and entered Leone's. He had some lasagna. When the check came, he discovered he couldn't pay. The management told him he would have to wash dishes. When he left, he caught a bus to New Haven.

After reading the story, the computer elaborated each part of the story, filling in the details according to the various scripts it had learned. For example, whereas the story simply said John took the subway and had his pocket picked, the computer elaborated:

HE ENTERED A STATION. HE PUT A TOKEN INTO THE TURNSTILE. HE WENT TO THE PLATFORM. HE WAITED AT IT A FEW MINUTES. HE ENTERED A SUBWAY CAR . . . A THIEF WENT TO JOHN. THE THIEF PICKED JOHN'S POCKET. HE WENT AWAY FROM JOHN . . ."

And so on. In response to the restaurant script about Mama Leone's a researcher posed questions to the script-understanding device, and the device replied with various answers. Here are some examples that reveal the sophistication of the question and answer session:

Q3. Did anything unusual happen on the bus?
A3. I DON'T REMEMBER ANYTHING.
Q4. Did anything unusual happen on the subway?
A4. A THIEF PICKED JOHN'S POCKET.
Q5. What did John order?
A5. JOHN ORDERED LASAGNA.
Q6. Did anything unusual happen at the restaurant?
A6. JOHN DISCOVERED THAT HE COULDN'T PAY THE CHECK AND SO HE HAD TO WASH DISHES.

The script understanding mechanism goes on to answer more questions. It indicates that John couldn't pay because a thief had picked John's pocket, and even speculates that John got home to New Haven by bus because he had bought a round-trip ticket earlier. For more details about how the program performed these operations see Schank and Abelson (1977).

such restaurant scripts and use them to create better understanding of stories (see The Disciplinary Crossroads box). Some people may have only a limited number of scripts; for example, they may perceive every encounter as a competitive situation. Other more sophisticated people may employ a variety of social scripts. Do you have a friend, or are you a person, who is able to handle every social situation comfortably and who always knows how to do the right thing? Such a person could be said to have developed a number of carefully worked out scripts for how to engage in social situations.

Learning Personality Types

Part of our understanding of our world involves the ideas we formulate about other people and how they operate. People are exquisitely sensitive in discriminating among personality types. A laboratory demonstration begins our examination of how such learning is acquired. The researchers invented a new type of person description that people had never seen before. Each person was characterized by sixteen randomly selected features. The purpose of creating a new personality type was to minimize any influence of earlier-known real-life types on the learning that was to take place in the study. Each of sixteen characteristics that defined the new personality type seemed fairly unrelated—as you would guess, since they were chosen randomly. The sixteen features are underlined in the following sample person description:

> V. J. was a thoughtful child, raised in a close family by caring parents. He was brought up in a poor Midwestern suburb, and is now married. He is clumsy, unimaginative, and frivolous. Those who know him describe him as cold. He believes in gaining other's respect and also in being a leader. Physically, he is thin and good-looking. (Mayer & Bower, 1986)

After creating this prototype, the researchers generated sixty variations on it by changing the person's initials and systematically altering the underlined descriptive features. For example, M. L. might be an "active" child as opposed to a "thoughtful" one, and physically "tall" rather than "thin." If M. L. (or any other such person) possessed at least nine of the prototype's sixteen features, the person was a member of the group. Nonmembers possessed seven or fewer overlapping features. There were several billion possible members and nonmembers. Could people learn to identify the group member type?

The study procedure began with the experimenter instructing participants to read some descriptions of people and decide whether each person was a member of the group. After reading the first of the sixty descriptions, the participant was asked, "Is V. J." (or whoever) "a member of the group?" The typical participant then asked, "What group?" and was told that, knowing nothing about the group at the outset of the experiment, he or she would have to guess on the first description. After the guess, the experimenter told the participant whether or not V. J. had been a member (based on the nine-matches-or-more rule for membership). The participant then moved onto the second description, with only the knowledge that V. J. was (or was not) a member of the group. The process was then repeated for the third and fourth descriptions of A. R., P. B., and so on. Remarkably, after reading through twenty descriptions and receiving feedback about them, people began to discriminate members of the group (that is, the personality type) from nonmembers.

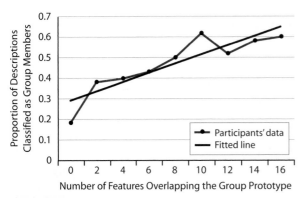

FIGURE 5.2

Probability of Classification of Person-Description as a Group Member People rapidly learn to identify newly described people as members of a particular group or not. This serves to increase accuracy—and stereotyping—in perceiving other people, for the two processes can be somewhat related.

Source: Mayer & Bower (1986), Figure 1, reprinted with permission of the American Psychological Association.

Figure 5.2 shows some typical results after participants had seen sixty descriptions with feedback. People were able to classify instances that had sixteen features as belonging to the group nearly 60 percent of the time. People also correctly classified individuals with no overlapping features as not belonging to the group 80 percent of the time. People were also fairly accurate for person descriptions with an in-between number of features.

Accurate and Inaccurate Perceptions of Others

Once a person identifies someone else as being a certain type—an extravert or an angry person, or a saint, or a random type as just seen—people may remember the person's characteristics as corresponding to the type more closely than in reality. When we come into contact with someone who is extraverted, we type her by guessing that she more-or-less fits with the prototype. Later, we may remember this new extraverted person talking constantly at a party, even though she may have been sitting quietly outside of our view for some of the time.

What happens once we have learned a given type and labeled a person with it? Cantor and Mischel (1978) identified traits that were unrelated, or moderately or highly related to extraversion. Then participants learned about Jane, a character they identified as an extravert because she was described by a number of moderately extraversion-related traits such as, "energetic," "entertaining," "impulsive," and "ambitious." Jane was also described by traits unrelated to extraversion, such as "punctual" and "neat." Table 5.2 provides an overview of the experimental procedure. Later, in a recognition memory test, participants were shown trait words for Jane that they had or had not seen before. The new, not-seen-before, trait words included some that were moderately or highly related to extraversion and some that were unrelated to extraversion. On average, the participants could readily identify extraverted trait characteristics that had been used before to describe Jane on the initial trait list. Of particular interest here, participants mistakenly recalled that they had seen new extraversion-related terms such as *spirited* and *exuberant* on the initial trait list. They did this at a greater rate than they misidentified the new extraversion-unrelated terms such as *thrifty* as having been on the initial list. That is, they showed a bias toward remembering the features that were associated with the extraverted type. The results are shown in Table 5.3. The same bias was found in the study of randomly created personality types described earlier. The results from laboratory research on mental models of other people indicate that people learn and use prototypes or schemata of personality types to understand others.

Do the results from these experimental studies generalize to real-life situations? David Funder and his colleagues have conducted research into how people perceive the real individuals around them. Funder's research indicates that people make accurate distinctions among different types of people. That said, he also finds that judges are more accurate in observing traits that are plainly visible. For example, traits such as extraversion and assertiveness are relatively easy to identify directly

TABLE 5.2	Overview of Experimental Procedure for Cantor and Mischel (1978)	
Pre-Experimental Work	**First Stage of Experiment: Acquisition Learning**	**Second Stage of Experiment: Recognition Memory**
Participants first rated trait words as to whether they were unrelated (U), moderately related (M), or highly related (H) to extraversion (or other prototypes used in other conditions of the experiment).	Instructions: Jane possesses the following traits. Please learn about Jane:	Instructions: Which traits that Jane said to possess?
	Acquisition Learning List: energetic (M) outgoing (H) thrifty (U) entertaining (M) sensible (U) impulsive (M) ambitious (M) punctual (U) neat (U) dominating (M) talkative (H) . . .	Recognition Memory List: *Items Drawn from Acquisition test:* dominating (M) energetic (M) neat (U) punctual (U) . . . *Unpresented Items (Distractors):* spirited (H) exuberant (H) thrifty (U) . . .

H: Highly related to Extraversion

M: Moderately related to Extraversion

U: Unrelated to Extraversion

TABLE 5.3	Summary of Key Findings from Cantor and Mischel (1978)	
	Trait Was in Acquisition List	**Trait Was Not in Acquisition List**
Trait was related to prototype	Moderately endorsed these (e.g., energetic) *(Accurate when endorsed)*	Moderately endorsed these (e.g., spirited) *(Inaccurate when endorsed)*
Trait was unrelated to prototype	Moderately endorsed these (e.g., neat) *(Accurate when endorsed)*	Did not endorse these *much* (e.g., neat) *(Inaccurate when endorsed)*

from the actions—talking, smiling—that take place between people. Other traits, however, such as emotionality and intelligence, remain more hidden, and judges are less good at assessing those (Funder & Dobroth, 1987; Funder & Colvin, 1988). As was revealed in Cantor and Mischel's (1978) study, observers also are likely to employ stereotypes at least initially. The use of stereotypes means that judges agree with one another about what a target person is like—but aren't necessarily accurate. As judgment time increases and more information is provided, judges increasingly focus on the information provided and, as they do so, they agree less with one another as some judges abandon the original stereotype and other judges do not. At the same time, the judges' overall accuracy about the person increases (Blackman & Funder, 1998; cf. Kolar, Funder, & Colvin, 1996).

Implicit Theories of Personality

Entity Theorists: Those who believe there are relatively fixed parts of personality. Almost everyone is an entity theorist in part.

Incremental Theorists: Those who believe that personality can change over time.

Sometimes our beliefs about people are centered on human nature in general rather than on typing a person as one sort or another. One of the central beliefs we come to hold about people concerns the degree to which we think they are capable of change. Dweck, Chiu, and Hong (1995) have suggested that those formal theories of personality mirror the implicit theories of nonpsychologists. They argue that some people are **entity theorists** of personality, whereas others are **incremental theorists**. They found that most everyone is an incremental theorist. If they ask a group of individuals, "Can people change?" everyone will agree. Some people qualify that notion, limiting the degree of change a person might be capable of undergoing. People who believe in change alone are called incremental theorists (Dweck et al., 1995). Those who believe in change amidst a healthy dose of stability, however, are called entity theorists. Such entity-theorist people might say, for example, "A person's moral character is something very basic and it can't be changed very much." Or, "Whether or not a person is responsible or sincere is deeply ingrained in his or her personality." People who are incremental theorists appear to perform better in response to challenges such as difficult courses because they believe in their own flexible responses to problems and capacity to learn (p. 269).

The Concept of the Archetype

Archetype: A schema that represents an imagined cultural icon, such as a hero or magician, that all people share.

As we have seen, people employ type-schemas to classify people into various categories such as extraverts and introverts. People may also use an **archetype,** a special type of schema which can be understood as a universal embodiment of a cultural icon (Jung, 1968). Archetypes include heroes and heroines, witches and devils, kings and queens, medicine healers, magicians and tricksters, and the like. According to the concept's originator, Carl Jung, many of the characters that appear in works of art or dreams arouse in us our knowledge and feelings about archetypes. Although the specifics of these figures change slightly from culture to culture, they share a common meaning to all of humanity. For example, "the good healer" may be a medicinal healer in Africa, an acupuncturist in China, an attending physician in a western-style hospital, or a saint who helps the sick in his or her particular church. When these figures play their part and cure us they elicit from us at a certain universal-appearing emotional reaction: trust, respect, gratitude, and maybe some awe.

Collective Unconscious: A part of unconscious that contains material that is more-or-less universal across people, such as emotional images of parents, kings, queens, and magicians.

Archetypes are said to be a part of a **collective unconscious**. The collective unconscious refers to a part of the unconscious that contains material that is largely the same from one member of a culture to another. The major evidence for the existence of archetypes (whatever their origins) comes from literary and cultural analyses that find the same sorts of symbols, myths, or dreams arising in culture after culture. The repetition of such images as heroes, devils, and magicians, suggests some sort of common process of recognizing certain culturally defined figures (Campbell, 1949; 1972).

Archetypal magicians share certain things in common. They wear robes, they are often aged and have beards, and they combine the light and the dark. We recognize these figures whether it is Obi-Wan (Ben) Kenobi in Star Wars, *or Dumbledore in* Harry Potter.

There is some experimental evidence that people do tend to associate certain qualities with certain archetypal symbols. For example, people more readily match femininity to the moon than to the sun; and health to the snake than to other symbols. The cause of such similarities in associations is unclear (Huston, Rosen, & Smith, 1999; Pietikainen, 1998; Rosen et al., 1991; Stevens, 2000).

George Lucas, director of the *Star Wars* films, consciously employed Jungian ideas in the construction of his films (Seabrook, 1999, p. 205). Lucas introduced his characters in the original *Star Wars* episode very quickly: the young hero, Luke Skywalker; the dark father, Darth Vader; and R2D2 and C-3PO, two robots who play the role of clowns, for example. Because Lucas based them on archetypes he hoped the audience would recognize and respond emotionally to them very quickly. Many other archetypes exist in the *Star Wars* movies as well.

What Are Our Models of Relationships?

Significant Other Models

Beyond models of the self and of the world, psychologists examine models of how the self exists in relation to the world and to the other people and objects in it. These models can be called models of relationships, as long as one remembers that relationships are formed not only between the individual and other people, but also between the individual and artworks, ideas, and cultures.

Relationship models found their origins in psychodynamic theory in the manifestation of what are now called models of **significant others**. Significant others are parents and caretakers to whom we are entrusted as children, or other adults who are very important to our lives and with whom we have spent appreciable time. Significant other models are the models we construct of those people and how they behave.

Sigmund Freud first observed the importance of significant-other schemes in his attempt to explain a fairly common but strange occurrence he observed in his practice

Significant Others: Internal representations of others, including parents and important relatives, friends, and teachers, who have played important roles in their lives.

In Jung's theory, a mandala—a symmetrical geometrical pattern drawn within a circular frame—is an archetypal symbol for psychological balance.

Transference: The idea that one will transfer what one has learned about a significant other to new people one meets. This term developed originally in the psychodynamic tradition but is now more generally used.

of psychodynamic therapy. His patients typically entered therapy in good spirits, but then, some sessions later, would often fall in love, or sometimes grow demanding and angry, with the therapist.

Where did these strong feelings come from? Freud believed that many of the patient's new perceptions of the therapist were formed in childhood. More specifically, Freud hypothesized that the patients were transferring feelings they had felt toward their parents onto their image of the therapist. Freud referred to this notion as **transference**. Transference involves the reemergence of a pattern of feeling that had originally been directed toward a significant person in one's life, and is now redirected—automatically and often incorrectly—to a new person. Even a small overlap between the new person and the original parent or significant other can trigger this transference of emotional patterns to the new relationship. In Freud's words:

the cause of the disturbance is that the patient has transferred on to the doctor intense feelings of affection which are justified neither by the doctor's behaviour nor by the situation that has developed during the treatment. (1920/1966, Lecture XXVII; pp. 440–441)

In one experimental study of transference, participants read descriptions of new people, some of whom possessed features that had been customized to overlap with the significant others that participant had earlier described. When the research participants learned about these partly overlapping new people, they perceived them to be more like their significant others than they actually were and had stronger emotional reactions to them (Andersen & Cole, 1990). Learning such significant-other schemas proceeds rapidly and can strongly bias interpersonal perception (Mayer, Rapp, & Williams, 1993).

Freud believed that such early mental models set the tone for our later relationships and that, in many circumstances, the individual would repeat these learned patterns of interaction over and over again. Freud referred to such patterns as "repetition compulsions" because the individual seemed compelled to repeat them over and over with new people.

Core Conflictual Relationship Themes

Can the specific relationship patterns that a person employs be identified in an objective way? The Core Conflictual Relationship Theme (CCRT) Method is a way of doing so (Luborsky, Crits-Christoph, & Mellon, 1986; Luborsky & Crits-Christoph, 1988). In it, trained clinicians look at the transcripts of psychotherapeutic sessions and examine them for repeated relationship patterns.

> **We don't see things as they are, we see things as we are.**
>
> Anais Nin

To do this, clinicians first tape or video-record sessions with their patients (with the patient's permission). These recordings can then be judged by additional therapists who are not involved in the treatment. Then, the agreement among the clinicians can be examined. Each of the patient's discussions of a specific interaction are called "relationship episodes." Based on Freud's theory of the repetition compulsion, researchers wondered whether the same themes would recur across various relationship episodes. Some examples of relationship episodes come from a patient who underwent psychotherapy in the early 1980s. In the course of discussing some recent events the patient reports a series of distinct relationship episodes (Gill & Hoffman, 1982a; 1982b, reprinted in Luborsky et al., 1986). In the first relationship episode, the young man is narrating what happened when a new acquaintance dropped by for a beer:

> I pretended to be enjoying it, enjoying him, you know, in the spirit of good fellowship and shit and stuff, but . . . [he] was keeping me from reading and that hassled me. I really fucking resented it a lot. You know among my friends, they're respecting and always have really respected my wanting to do my own thing . . . But you know, with a guy like this [clear throat], he's just in another world totally from that. And, you know, he wouldn't understand if I said that, you know, he would be insulted and that kind of shit. You know it was kind of a hassle. (Gill & Hoffman, 1982b, p. 151)

In the second relationship episode, the same young man discusses his reaction to coming to psychotherapy that morning, and the focus is shifted to his relationship with the therapist:

> This morning I, like didn't particularly feel like coming here, you know. Because like, I don't know, I felt some kind of, you know, I felt like I didn't need it. I guess I was just, you know, my spirits were a little raised. If only now I could get out of the bag of feeling that I have to. (p. 152)

In the third episode, the young man reveals his perception of the therapist's reaction to him. Would you trust his perceptions?

> Well, now I'm getting that same feeling that, you know, I'm sort of talking about worthless shit. Because, and you know, my basis for thinking that is the fact that you haven't said anything. Jeez, we go through this same nonsense every session, it's just amazing to me. I'm sort of ashamed that my mind isn't a little more creative, to think of different hassles. You know, it's sort of boring going through the same hassle four times a week, for what at this point seems like a timeless period. (p. 154)

The same model of a relationship may seem to you to be applied in all three passages, although it is different in its particulars. In the first episode, the young man wants to get away from his drop-in visitor and resents the intrusion. In the second episode, he doesn't want to see the therapist, and in the third he imagines that the therapist feels bored by his "nonsense," with the implication that the therapist feels intruded upon. In each of the relationship episodes, the young man is describing someone who wants to be free of someone else but feels resentful because it is difficult to get away. Indeed, therapist-judges listening to the three episodes agreed at levels far above chance that the central theme the young man presented was one of wanting to be free of someone but feeling resentful and compelled to suffer the other's presence. In one study, sixteen graduate student judges individually scored the above case and obtained an agreement level of $r = .88$.

Not only did these raters agree about what they saw, but they also indicated that, as Freud would have observed, the young man was reporting the same concern over and over again—to be free of obligation and imposition. Not only does the young man himself wish to be free of these burdens, but he attributes this desire to be free of others to others in his life as well (e.g., the therapist). It is interesting to note further that the young man generalized this pattern to his relationships with women. Consider another episode in which he is trying to make a date with a telephone operator:

> When I finally got through to her roommate yesterday and found out that she wasn't going to be in, like all the woman obligations just went off me. I knew that there was nothing I could do to find a woman and, you know, there was a kind of relief. (p. 153)

Raters again agreed that the young man feels obligated to date women and finds it a relief to be free of them.

More generally speaking, people vary in the relationship styles they exhibit. Some adults develop secure attachment styles; others are more worried about their relations. These can be measured by scales such as the Adult Attachment Inventory (AAI; Hesse, 1999; cf., Bowlby, 1988, p. 129). The **securely attached** pattern of relationships represents others as caring, reliable, and providing security. The **insecure/ dismissing attachment** pattern refers to a model of relationships that involves others as rejecting and thwarting of one's identity. The **insecure/preoccupied attachment** pattern refers to a relationship model that represents others in a rather confused mixture of love and hate, as giving rewards and taking away respect simultaneously, or providing respect, but taking away love.

Crowell and colleagues (2002) observed 157 engaged couples as they discussed a point of concern in their relationship for fifteen minutes. Each statement by the couples was coded for a variety of qualities, such as support, hostility, withdrawal, and the like. Secure couples, as measured by the AAI (Hesse, 1999), differed from those with insecure attachment models. The secure couples showed more direct proactive communication. They made straightforward communications that assumed the relationship could and should involve trust. For example, they might start a communication by saying something like, "Our relationship is supposed to help us each be better than we can be on our own," or direct requests for help such as, "It would help me if you could . . ." (Crowell et al., 2002, p. 7). Couples with more secure attachment styles reflected greater happiness, less verbal aggression and fewer threats to abandon one another. The development of attachment models has been studied extensively, and will be covered in greater depth in Chapter 11 on child development.

Secure Attachment Pattern: The healthiest of three relationship patterns commonly studied in attachment literature, in which the person feels unambivalent security with loved others.

Insecure/Dismissing Attachment Pattern: One of the three relationship patterns commonly studied in the attachment literature in which a child or adult feels frustrated or even rejected by others.

Insecure/Preoccupied Attachment Pattern: One of the three relationship patterns commonly studied in the attachment literature in which a child or adult feels ambivalent toward being intimate with others.

Roles and Role Playing

The Persona

Up to now, we have been talking about models of real, individual, people and their relationships. But society often requires people to behave not the way they actually feel

Persona: A mask, or social role, an individual uses so as to uphold social standards while carrying out tasks. Examples include "the concerned doctor," or "the strict professor," and so forth. Originally developed from the psychodynamic tradition, this term is now more widely understood.

or are, but according to a culturally defined role. Carl Jung said that people often assume a **persona** in the real world so as to inhabit such a role. The persona, a term which comes from the Greek word for mask, is a model that we "put on" in order to appear to be something in particular to those around us (Jung, 1934/1953, Chap. 3).

For example, in a lecture class, students often wear a "student" persona which consists of looking attentively toward the instructor, appearing to pay attention, taking notes, and so forth. But on certain days, even the best of students don't feel like this. Their minds are a million miles away on thoughts of romance, family issues, or simply what to eat for lunch. Meanwhile, they maintain the student persona: pen in hand, eyes on the professor, and the rest. The mask hides their daydreams and mental meanderings. Of course, professors sometimes employ a persona as well. They may be distracted by a personal concern, or simply want to be someplace else; still, they act out interest in their topic—so as to try to appear professional and to maintain their students' interest. Certain personas have clear developmental origins. In the United States, the cheery-person persona develops in response to our parents' requests of us to "please try to be pleasant!"

> **Two may walk together under the same roof for many years, yet never really meet; and two others at first speech are old friends.**
>
> Mary Catherwood

Case Study

Playing a Role While Playing Basketball?

In 1995 the Lady Hurricanes—the women's high school basketball team of Amherst, Massachusetts—won its state championship. It was in many ways an unusual event. Amherst is located in Massachusetts' historic Pioneer Valley. It is very much a college town, home to Amherst and Hampshire colleges, as well as the University of Massachusetts. It is not a place necessarily known for its high school sports.

Blais (1995) reported that singular season for the basketball team, including the personalities of the team players, of their coach, and of the town in general. Of particular interest here, she described how one of the team's most problematic players improved her game by adopting a new role—and maybe a new self.

The team's coach, Ron Moyer, had often made reference to his "Kathleen problem." Kathleen had been playing with her teammates in a tight-knit group for several years. She was a starter on the team, but as Blais put it, "the only thing she was fierce about was being gentle . . .

She constantly backed away from her opponents, she ran around screens; she played in an unconfident way" (Blais, 1995, p. 127). When she bumped into other players, she said, "I'm sorry."

Kathleen's parents had met at Duke University, and her father taught at Hampshire College. She had been born in Ithaca, New York, where her father had been in graduate school. She was a high achiever in school. Her kindness and lack of assertiveness came out in ways as well; for example, she didn't like to hurt animals and she was a vegetarian. Adding to the mix in complex ways, her parents had separated, and she lived on the Hampshire College campus with her father (Blais, 1995, pp. 75–77).

After Coach Moyer warned her never to use the words "I'm sorry" on the court again, Kathleen made the mistake of saying she was sorry to one of her teammates. The coach made an alarming announcement: Kathleen was no longer wanted on the team—she was to go home

Role Structure Theory

In Robert Hogan's (1983) *socioanalytic* theory of personality it is important that the person construct a series of social roles to portray the self in positive ways. The presence and use of roles occur even with very young children. Peekaboo games are one such example. By three years of age, children left in a playroom will initiate role-playing as a way to structure their play together:

> Nothing much happens [among young children] until at some point one child . . . says something like, "Pretend you were Batman and I was Robin." At that point, both children begin talking to one another, moving around, and gesticulating in a synchronous fashion—in short, interacting. (Hogan, 1983, p. 75)

> As another example, a four-year-old girl often plays with her father by saying, "Daddy, you pretend you're the teacher." If he agrees, she then points to stuffed animals and dolls, assigning each the role of a different member of her preschool class. Once the roles are assigned, a lengthy imaginative drama can take place. In other

immediately. The other team members stopped in mid-dribble to hear what was going on. The coach said he wanted a new person on the team. Staring at Kathleen, he said, "The new Hurricane . . . is named 'Skippy.' "

Later, Coach Moyer said that "Skippy" had simply popped into his mind, drawn from the name of the fictional evil twin of the first President Bush, as depicted in Gary B. Trudeau's "Doonesbury" comic strip. Moyer looked at Kathleen and said, "Okay, Skippy, put on your game face . . . Let's see Skippy take the ball to the basket."

After Kathleen realized she was being asked to try on a new identity, the idea appealed to her:

She grabbed the ball. She stormed forward, her face a seamless mask of concentration.

She bashed the ball in.

[Coach Moyer yelled:] "Skippy, I like that mean look. If there's a pick there,

knock it over. Let's stay in that frame of mind. Hold that."

This is great, he thought: *I can yell at Skippy . . .*

[And after practice, he commanded:] Don't forget, Kathleen, in this gym, you're Skippy." (pp. 127–128)

Kathleen's behavior also changed off the court. In the locker room, "Skippy" freely told jokes that would have been far too vulgar for Kathleen (p. 201). In the championship game, Kathleen (Skippy?) was involved in two plays that contributed to her team's victory. One of these involved a daring shot from the foul line that "was nothing but net" (p. 254).

We might wonder about the developmental impact of these events. When Kathleen first became Skippy, perhaps it was just a role—but did that role enlarge her understanding of her possible selves? Do roles and selves interact in potentially powerful ways?

words, by three or four years of age we have a pretty good idea about social roles and can act them out and manipulate them.

For Hogan, each social interaction involves some role-playing. When it does not, the social interaction falls apart and the relationship has failed. Hogan writes of encountering the distinguished British philosopher Gilbert Ryle on his college campus; he couldn't resist speaking to him, but had no adequate social role to play:

> I was walking to the computer center when I saw, coming down the sidewalk toward me, a man whom I thought was probably Ryle. Without thinking, I said, "Pardon me, sir, but aren't you Gilbert Ryle?" Ryle peered at me in the befuddled and mildly incompetent manner of an Oxford don and then allowed that he was indeed himself. Not knowing what to do next, I said, "Gee, it's just like meeting Robin Hood," and walked away. (p. 74)

For Hogan, this story illustrates how, when appropriate roles are not available, a person is left adrift socially and, occasionally, feeling sort of foolish.

According to Hogan, we carry out roles in order to create an image of ourselves among others. We carry out roles both to measure up to an esteemed group such as our relatives or teachers and to impress our friends and acquaintances. It is not always possible to please all groups at once. For example, a person who tries to satisfy one group of peers may be very popular but perceived as overly trendy or even theatrical by others. It is best to maintain a balance among such roles (p. 79).

Morals and Values

Earlier in this chapter, we encountered "ideal" and "ought" selves that describe one's possible selves and what they should be like. Relationship models elaborate on those ideas and concern ethical, moral, and ideological behavior. As a person relates to others and strives to reach particular goals, he or she must learn ethical and moral rules, as well as a philosophy by which to live in the world. Freud believed the conscience was developed in response to the child's fear of receiving punishment from the parent (Freud, 1923; 1960). Freud recognized, however, that mature men and women maintain their ethical or moral structure in part because of a voluntary social contract. The adult realizes that only when people follow ethical and moral rules—in effect, giving up some freedoms—can civilization meet the requirements of its citizens. A society in which people refused to work together or to respect those with legitimate authority could not create efficient organizations by which to feed its people and protect their safety (Freud, 1930; 1961).

One research approach is to examine how sophisticated one's moral reasoning is. Some people employ moral structures that seem relatively simplistic: all black-and-white, with few areas of grey. Others employ more complex sorts of moral reasoning. To investigate this, Kohlberg (1981) described a series of ethical/moral stages. At an early stage of development, one behaves morally out of a fear of receiving punishment from parents (as Freud proposed). As one develops further, one begins to tell right from wrong according to one's own analysis. Still later, one's ethical/moral standards may become relativistic, so that one can appreciate people who hold different sets of standards. Finally, one may become recommitted

• FACTS • AT • A • GLANCE •

Some Mental Models That Proved to Be Worth Revising

Models of the Self

- "When Upton Sinclair dies, he's dead; when I die, I'm immortal."—Author Benjamin De Casseres, American journalist and poet, speaking in 1932 of the lasting value of his writing. (p. 175)
- "The thought of being President frightens me. I do not think I want the job."—Ronald Reagan (in 1973, then-Governor of California. (p. 111)
- "It doesn't appear that the FBI is going to catch us anytime soon. The FBI is a joke"—The "Unabomber" (domestic terrorist) less than a year before being captured by the FBI. (p. 314)
- "And yet I told your Holiness that I was no painter"—Michelangelo, in a remark to Pope Julius II, who was complaining about the progress of the Sistine Chapel ceiling, 1508. (p. 310)

Models of the World

- "The world was created on 22 October, 4004 B.C. at 6 o'clock in the evening"—James Ussher, Archbiship of Armagh, 1581–1656. (p. 3)
- "Heaven and earth, centre and circumference, were created together in the same instant ... [T]his work took place and man was created by the trinity on the twenty-third of October, 4004 B.C., at nine o'clock in the morning."—Dr. John Lightfoot, 1859 (Vice Chancellor of the University of Cambridge), correcting by 15 hours the estimate of Archbishop Ussher two centuries earlier. (p. 3)
- "X-rays are a hoax."—Lord Kelvin, British physicist and former president of the British Royal Society, c. 1900. (p. 334)
- Benjamin Franklin "has very moderate abilities. He knows nothing of philosophy but his few experiments in electricity."—John Adams, diary entry, 1779. (p. 307)
- On Fred Astaire: "Can't act. Can't sing. Can dance a little."—MGM executive, reacting to Fred Astaire's screen test in 1928. (p. 191)

Models of Relationships

- "Nothing will ever separate us ... We'll probably be married another ten years."—Elizabeth Taylor describing her marriage to Richard Burton, June 21, 1974, five days before the announcement of their divorce. (p. 20)
- "We'll make it work. You can take it to the bank."—CBS News Anchor Dan Rather assuring skeptical reporters that he and his co-anchor Connie Chung would work well together. Two years later, with ratings their lowest ever, the anchors split. (p. 111)
- "I will never marry again."—Barbara Hutton: in 1941 after divorcing her second husband.
- "I will never marry again. You can't go on being a fool forever."—Hutton after divorcing her third husband, Cary Grant, in 1945.
- "This is positively my final marriage."—Barbara Hutton, in 1955, remarking on the sixth of her seven husbands. (p. 21)

Source: Drawn from Cerf & Navasky (1998).

to a particular ethical/moral standard even though one appreciates others' points of view.

Regardless of one's sophistication, people develop different types of values (e.g., Allport & Vernon, 1931; Rokeach, 1973). For example, some people envision a deity as setting the rules for human conduct and tend toward a conservative outlook. This

People are not moved by things but the views which they take of them.

Epictetus

view holds that there exists a reality apart from human beings and that humans must strive to meet the objective standards of that outside reality. Others see human beings as valuable in themselves and hold that any supreme being exists within each human being; thus, people set their own standards according to an inner authority (De St. Aubin, 1996; Tomkins, 1983).

People who believe in a deity who sets standards emphasize politeness and courtesy and deemphasize imaginativeness, whereas those who emphasize humanistic values emphasize broad-mindedness and love (de St. Aubin, 1996; Stone & Schaffner, 1988). Other research looks at extensions of such models such as people's perceptions of justice—which is remarkably similar across cultures but not necessarily across people (Cohn, White, & Sanders, 2000).

How Good Are Our Mental Models?

Developing Constructive Models

Constructive Thinking: Thinking that is productive for an individual and is based on the person's having accumulated accurate positive mental models and having avoided irrational, superstitious mental models.

Is there a global way to assess how good a person's models of him or herself and others really are? Probably no single way, but Epstein and his colleagues have developed a scale of **constructive thinking** that helps provide some insight into the question (Epstein & Meier, 1989). Constructive thinking is defined as the degree to which a person's implicitly learned mental models facilitate solving problems in everyday life at a minimum cost in stress (Epstein, 1998, p. 26). Epstein focuses on certain signs indicating that a person's models will be constructive rather than off-base. These signs

Rewarding good behavior helps the child learn models for standards of behavior.

include whether or not a person's models lead to constructive coping and avoid destructive and irrational lines of thought.

For example, when a person copes in an emotionally and behaviorally productive fashion, she is able to match her models to her own psychology and to the world. Epstein notes that a salesperson who copes poorly might conclude, "I failed to put across this deal, so I guess I'll never amount to anything." Someone better at coping would have a more realistic model, concluding that he lost only a single sale and that one can learn from experience (Epstein, 1998, p. 43). Similarly, behavioral coping involves a successful action-oriented approach. Behavioral coping involves such things as replacing a worry about a deadline with the action of actually meeting it. Epstein views coping as taking place when it can assist the mind "to obtain pleasure and avoid pain . . . to make sense of our experience . . . to have satisfying relationships with others; and . . . to think well of yourself" (pp. 83–84).

Avoiding Irrational Models

In addition to building mental models that facilitate active coping, constructive thinkers avoid models that are patently inaccurate. For example, people who are good at coping see the nuances of situations rather than dividing the world into dichotomies such as right and wrong, or into winning and losing sides. They also avoid models that involve esoteric beliefs, beliefs in the paranormal, good luck charms, bad luck omens, and the like. Whereas many people hold superstitious beliefs such as that bad events happen on the heels of good ones, the constructive coper emphasizes rational thinking.

Naïve Optimism: A set of especially unrealistic beliefs that emphasize that things will turn out well, and which one may hold so as to excuse oneself from taking responsibility for contributing to a given goal.

Finally, the person who is good at coping also avoids mental models that employ **naïve optimism**. Naïve optimism refers to unrealistic beliefs that things will turn out well. Such beliefs, although reassuring to the person who holds them, can sometimes be counterproductive. For example, a student who is a naïve optimist may fail to prepare for a test because he expects to do well without trying. Constructive thinking can be measured by a self-report inventory. Examples of the categories and descriptions of what is measured are shown in the Table 5.4 (after Epstein, 1998, pp. 39–41).

Expressing Better Mental Models

Do people who hold mental models that help them cope and that discourage irrational thinking do better in school and careers than others? Epstein studied constructive thinking among students in the classroom and on the job (most of his students worked part-time jobs of ten to twenty hours a week). Constructive thinking was related to job performance and success in student politics, although not to performance in the classroom. Students with high constructive thinking scores held more offices in clubs and organizations than did those with lower scores (Atwater, 1993; Epstein, 1998, p. 108–109). There is also evidence that those who score lower in constructive thinking may suffer from a greater incidence of drug use and abuse (Ammerman et al., 2001; Giancola, Shoal, & Mezzich, 2001).

Once students graduate, constructive thinking appears to help them in their chosen careers as well. Epstein compared fifty salespeople with national or international reputations and million-dollar-plus incomes to a group of two hundred highly

TABLE 5.4	Epstein and Colleagues' Concept of Constructive Thinking

Area of Constructive Thinking	What it is ...
Positive Indicators of Constructive Thinking	
Emotional coping	Managing emotions effectively, such as (mostly) avoiding worry about things you can't control
Behavioral coping	Acting to control those things one can, such as taking action to change situations for the better
Negative Indicators of Constructive Thinking	
Categorical thinking	Thinking in stark, stereotyped categories, such as thinking some people are all good or all bad
Personal superstitious thinking	Holding cultural beliefs for which there is little evidence, for example, believing in good and bad omens
Esoteric thinking	Paying attention to good-luck charms or other unusual beliefs
Naïve optimism	Maintaining positive attitudes that are, however, unrealistic and uninfluenced by experience, such as believing everyone should always love their parents

successful executives who worked in sales and marketing and who exhibited high but less than exceptional performance in their occupations. The exceptional achievers ranked higher than the successful executive group on many measures of success that were assessed. Although the two groups worked equal numbers of hours, the super-achievers had advanced more rapidly at work and reported higher job satisfaction. On the personal side, the super-achievers were more satisfied with their family lives and spent more time at home. They were happier and they experienced less anxiety, depression, and uncontrolled anger. Finally, the super-achievers also exhibited more constructive thinking on virtually every dimension measured. In emotional coping, their mental models revealed that they were relatively unconcerned with others' disapproval and were very action-oriented. They were also much less superstitious than members of their comparison group, they avoided esoteric thinking more easily, and they were less prone to naive optimism. In fact, members of both groups scored above average on this last measure (Epstein, 1998, pp. 102–105).

Constructive thinking may take a general "temperature" of the quality of peoples' models of the self and the world. Another way to do this is to examine a person's intellectual capacity—what their mental abilities are and how they are applied to the individual's life. Such issues will be dealt with next in the chapter on mental abilities.

Reviewing Chapter 5

The learning goal of this chapter is to introduce you to the significance and nature of mental models of the self, the world, and relationships. The chapter is intended to help you understand how these models can be assessed and how they are expressed in a person's life. Mental models share certain features in common, but the distinctions among them are worth exploring. Some of these are summarized below.

What Are Mental Models?

1. Models of the Self, World, and Relationships.
Models are often divided according to the contents they describe. It is convenient to divide such models into those that pertain to the self, to the world, and to relationships. Can you define models of relationships?

2. Mental Models Are Structured.
Mental models are memory "structures"—that is, they are not simply free-floating information, but rather, they exhibit certain characteristics that are a consequence of being stored in the memory in specific ways. For example, the most important attributes of a model are recalled first. Different kinds of mental models possess different structures. Can you describe the difference between a schema and a script?

3. Mental Models Are Learned and Applied.
Mental models are learned. We recall them when they seem useful in our attempts to interpret the world. There is room for error in our use of mental models. Can you identify one way mental models are often misapplied?

4. Differences in Models across People.
Mental models differ from one person to the next. How do those models affect our emotional or other reactions to events?

What Are Our Models of Ourselves?

5. Possible, Actual, and Unconscious Selves.
Models of oneself can be as simple as a list of traits, or as evocative as an imagined self that one is afraid to become (e.g., alcoholic, senile). The starting point among all these selves is the actual self—how one thinks one

actually is. Then, there are ought selves and ideal selves, feared and desired selves, and even an unconscious self called the shadow. Can you define these different selves?

6. Self-Esteem and Self-Efficacy.
It would be hard to feel completely neutral in regard to thoughts about oneself. More often, people feel good about themselves, or bad about themselves, or have some other emotional reaction to contemplating their own existence. Self-efficacy is more specific and action-oriented than self-esteem. It refers to the confidence people have in approaching a task. Research with self-efficacy has turned up some fairly reliable findings. Can you say what they are?

7. The Storied Self.
The broadest model of the self is a person's total life story. Life stories are not simply accounts of every single life event a person has faced. Rather, they are tales that weave together what strikes the person as significant. They reveal important elements of how the individual thinks about (and wants to communicate) what is going on in his or her life. What are some types of life stories—that is, how are life stories categorized and analyzed?

What Are Our Models of the World?

8. Formal Models and Implicit Knowledge.
Formal knowledge is the sort of knowledge we acquire in settings such as schools and universities. Implicit knowledge, on the other hand, is picked up more informally, by observing the events, objects, and people around us. Can you think of a way that formal knowledge affects a person's life?

9. Scripts for Navigating the World.
Scripts occupy an important place in the history of the study of mental models. They are important both to computers and to human beings in understanding how the world works. As children grow, for example, they need to learn many scripts, such as what happens at a restaurant and how to go to a birthday party. Can you define what a script is?

10. Implicit Theories of Personality.
People also create models of the people around them and how they behave. Perhaps it was inevitable that psychologists would discover some versions of their own views of human nature in people's everyday models of others. For example, people can be described as entity theorists or as incremental theorists. Although everyone believes in mental entities, only some people view others as being able to change incrementally. Can you define entity and incremental theories?

11. Learning Personality Types.
Beyond general theories of personality, people create models of particular personality types: e.g., the shy person, the extravert, and the significant others in their lives. Can you describe some research in this area and what it tells us?

12. The Concept of the Archetype.
One special kind of personality type is the archetype. Archetypes are models of iconic or mythic figures such as the magician, the hero, and the King and Queen. Can you name the psychodynamic theorist who proposed a theory of archetypes? One occupational group in particular makes a lot of use of the concept of archetypes. Can you say which group that is?

What Are Our Models of Relationships?

13. General Attachment Models.
In the aftermath of World War II, the psychodynamically oriented psychologist John Bowlby began to study infants in orphanages, and from his observations, suggested that young infants develop models for their attachments to their caregivers. From this work grew the general theory that people develop styles of attachment to others. Attachment theory specifies three types of attachment patterns. Can you name them and describe them?

14. Core Conflictual Relationship Themes.
Do people really repeat patterns of relationship over and over again? Will this show up in psychotherapy in

relation to the therapist? To examine this question, Luborksy, Crits-Cristoph and others recorded psychotherapy transcripts and then coded them for their relationship themes. How was their research then conducted and what were their major findings?

15. Adult Roles and Relationships.
So, there are a number of personal relationships one has with others. There are also, however, the less personal social roles one is supposed to play: the student, the employee, and the wedding singer. Can you define Jung's concept of the persona? Robert Hogan developed a socioanalytic theory of roles that made use of a series of roles. Why does he believe roles are important?

16. Moral and Values.
Another kind of model of relationships is the rules one will live by. What are some of the values and morals that people follow?

How Good Are Our Mental Models?

17. Developing Constructive Models.
Constructive thinking is a way of creating positive constructive models of the world about us. What are some characteristics of those constructive models?

18. Avoiding Irrational Models.
Constructive thinking also involves avoiding irrational models of one type or another. Can you list several kinds of irrational models about the world that people often hold?

19. Expressing Better Models.
If a person holds more constructive models of the surrounding world, does he or she experience any benefit from them, on average?

Chapter 6

Mental Abilities and Navigating the World

*I*ndividuals use mental models to understand themselves and the world. These mental models provide maps of the surrounding environment. The acquisition and modification of such models depends on an individual's mental processes and abilities. The individual's mental abilities: intelligences, cognitive styles, and creativities, are used in the analysis of what the outside world is like, the establishment of mental models, and the modification of those models. Other things being equal, high levels of mental abilities can contribute to a person's better understandings of the world, and promote innovative models.

- ### What Is a Mental Ability?
  Why is it that some people seem so able to solve problems that are insurmountable obstacles for others? What kinds of mental abilities do successful problem solvers employ?

- ### What Are Some Major Mental Abilities?
  To understand the mental abilities that people use, psychologists sought to investigate and identify what mental abilities there were. Among the earliest of the abilities they discovered was verbal-propositional intelligence. Other cognitive intelligences exist as well.

- ### Are There Additional Intelligences and Mental Abilities?
  Many psychologists, however, believed that there were mental abilities, including intelligences, that dealt with personally important information such as emotions and social life. These hot intelligences—so-called because they involve matters of immediate concern to our lives—have been a particular subject of study over the last several decades.

- ### What Is the Relation between Personality and Intelligence?
  Personality makes use of many mental abilities in its functioning. At the same time many personal qualities—including motives and emotions—seem independent of a person's abilities.

- ### How Does Personality Express Its Abilities?
  Psychologists have concluded that a person's success in school and on the job, as well as in relationships, depends on personality and the mental abilities on which it draws.

What Is a Mental Ability?

Questions about Mental Ability

Mental Ability: The capacity to perform mental tasks, such as solving problems, generating ideas, and similar challenges.

Intelligence: A specific type of mental ability involving the capacity to reason abstractly so as to arrive at the proper solution to a problem.

Personality could not function without a varied and extensive set of mental abilities. In general, an ability refers to the capacity to carry out a task: to lift fifty kilograms or to run five kilometers. A **mental ability**, more specifically, refers to the capacity to carry out a mental task—to work with information to obtain a desired answer. One type of mental ability is an **intelligence**. An intelligence is a specific kind of mental ability that involves the capacity to carry out abstract reasoning about a problem so as to find a correct solution. There are, however, other kinds of mental abilities (which some may consider intelligences, and others not). For example, creativity is a mental ability that involves coming up with new, novel, or unexpected, yet useful or meaningful, answers to problems. Or, in the case of practical knowledge, mental ability often involves knowing what is being said and left unsaid in a social situation. The more accurate a person's mental models of the surrounding world, the more in tune the person will be with what is going on and how to cope with it.

In the case of cognitive IQ, this involves heightened capacities to problem solve with verbal and mathematical problems. Marilyn vos Savant wanted to be a writer but she didn't want to be poor. Finding college unchallenging, she left after just two years to enter the worlds of finance and real estate. After five years, she had earned enough money to achieve financial security for the remainder of her life. She was now prepared to realize her dream of becoming a writer.

Before she got too far underway as a writer, however, *The Guinness Book of World Records* revealed her IQ score, which it had obtained from the Mega Society, then a group of the roughly thirty highest–IQ individuals in the world. Whereas the average IQ is about 100, and one in a hundred people score above 145, Savant's IQ was an extraordinary 228.

Vos Savant was a generally outgoing, fun-loving individual. She enjoyed the fame that her IQ score brought her. She went on the television talk shows and within a short time ended up moving to New York City and marrying Robert K. Jarvik, the surgeon who developed one of the first artificial hearts (Gale Research, 1988).

Vos Savant began writing a column for the *Sunday Parade* magazine, which she still writes, answering questions from readers. In 1991, she addressed a challenging statistical problem which, on its face, concerned a television game show named "Let's Make a Deal." Here is the situation:

> You are a contestant on the game show "Let's Make a Deal." Monty Hall, the host, describes a brand new sports car—the grand prize—that's yours if you can pick which of three doors it's behind. You pick door #2. Hall opens door #3, and behind it . . . is a live goat staring forlornly at you. Now, he asks you if, having seen the goat behind door #3, you want to change your choice from door #2 to door #1?

As a general principle, which strategy should work out best over time: To keep one's original choice or to switch? Vos Savant said you should change your choice to the other unopened door. For her troubles, she was resoundingly criticized by pro-

Marilyn Vos Savant's IQ is among the highest ever measured. It is reflected, in part, by her wide number of successful life pursuits.

You don't realize that you're intelligent until it gets you into trouble.

James Baldwin

fessors of statistics for getting the answer wrong. One professor wrote, "Our math department had a good, self-righteous laugh at your expense." Vos Savant stood her ground, however, and further explained her position. An enterprising *New York Times* reporter then consulted with the nation's best statisticians (and, for fun, with the game show host Monty Hall), and declared her correct (Tierney, 1991).

Today, vos Savant continues to write her column and has authored a growing number of books. Vos Savant's life and experience suggest that being high in the cognitive intelligences allows a person to accomplish her goals more readily, and to make many decisions better than others.

What part do mental abilities such as intelligence, creativity, and others play in vos Savant's—or anyone's—life? Both intelligence researchers and personality psychologists from Cattell to Wechsler agree that the intelligences form an inseparable part of personality (e.g., Cattell, 1965; Gardner, 1993; Guilford, 1967; Sternberg & Ruzgis, 1994; Wechsler, 1950). Each individual requires intelligence to think about how to conduct his or her life. Other mental abilities such as creativity help a person consider a broader range of life choices and paths. In part, for these reasons, mental abilities often are prized by society.

Case Study

Francis Galton's Own Intelligence

Sir Francis Galton himself likely would have earned a very high IQ on today's intelligence tests. As a child, Galton was tutored at the hands of his older sister, Adele. By age two and a half he was reading children's books and printing his name. He wrote letters by age three, and learned some Latin and French by age four. He wrote:

My dear Adele,
I am four years old and I can read any English book. I can say all the Latin Substantives and Adjectives and active verbs besides 52 lines of Latin poetry. I can cast up any Sum in addition and can multiply by 2, 3, 4, 5, 6, 7, 8 [and], 10 . . . I can also say the pence table. I read French a little and I know the Clock. (Cited in Fancher, 1985, p. 20)

Terman (1917) reported that when six years of age,

a visitor at the Galton home made Francis weary by cross-questionning him about points in Homer. Finally, the boy replied, "Pray, Mr. Horner, look at the last line in the twelfth book of the Odyssey" and then ran off. The line in question reads, "But why rehearse all this tale for even yesterday I told it to thee and to thy noble wife in thy house; and it liketh me not twice to tell a plaintold tale." (Terman, 1917, pp. 211–212)

By most objective criteria, Galton performed with excellence as a student in the most competitive English universities. Nonetheless, he so disappointed himself academically that he suffered a nervous breakdown. Shortly thereafter, he traveled to Africa as an explorer, making a highly regarded series of maps of a portion of that continent. When he returned to England, he was received well on account of his maps, and returned to his interests in intelligence.

Mental Abilities and Society

The English scientist Sir Francis Galton (1822–1911), for example, was a cousin to Sir Charles Darwin, and he was fascinated by his cousin's theory of evolution (see the box on Galton's life). Galton wondered whether good mental abilities—especially intelligence—would increase a person's evolutionary fitness and enhance his or her chances of survival. Looking at social success in England, he suggested that the English upper classes—those educated in the best schools—had higher intelligence than those found elsewhere. He also believed that people of great genius came from certain families more commonly than from others. In this way, society was structured so that those with higher IQ were more often found in the upper classes.

Galton's work supposed that people in the upper classes had greater amounts of mental abilities than others. Some reformers of the time argued that there were also many people in the lower and middle classes with high mental ability and they should be elevated across the artificial class barriers of inherited wealth and aristocracy.

Alfred Binet developed some of the first successful intelligence tests by examining the kinds of thinking that were required in school.

In the late 1800s, the French people and their government wanted to place nearly every child in school. Yet, they recognized that at least a few children did not have the ability to learn in school. The decision as to who had the ability to learn was a critical one: if a teacher misjudged a student, the decision could seriously compromise that child's future.

There was a great deal of public concern at the time that teachers would favor the children of the wealthy or the aristocracy over equal, but poorer, students. For that reason, the French sought a more impartial way of making the decision as to who could learn. In 1904 the French government appointed a commission to examine the state of mental subnormality in France. Alfred Binet (1857–1911) was a psychologist who became a founding member of the commission. He developed the first successful intelligence tests. These, in turn, provided the French government with a more impartial method of assessing one type of mental ability than relying on teachers' judgments.

Society values the intelligences studied by Galton and Binet, as well as the intelligences uncovered since their time. These mental abilities help to create better maps of the world as it is, as well as help to imagine better visions of possible futures.

The Range of Mental Abilities: Three Examples

Verbal Intelligence and the Binet Scales

A student is evaluating the merits of sending a manned mission to Mars by 2040. For her assignment, she must read several essays—both pro and con—about the goal, evaluate the logic of the arguments, and write her own opinion. To do this she must understand the words, sentences, and arguments of the essays, compare their similarities and differences, and form her own opinion based on which arguments she believes to be best.

Her ability to perform the task will depend heavily on a kind of intelligence called **verbal-propositional intelligence**. Verbal-propositional intelligence includes memory for and understanding of words (as in testing vocabulary), and understanding of logic and propositions. Verbal-propositional intelligence was the first intelligence to be uncovered and measured by intelligence testers.

Verbal-propositional intelligence is also the first of three examples of mental abilities we examine here before delving into mental abilities in greater detail. By the early 1900s, Alfred Binet had constructed his first intelligence scales for testing the capacity to learn in schools. He believed intelligence would be evident in such skills as memory, imagery, imagination, and comprehension. His tests evaluated how well students could remember short sentences, understand vocabulary, and recognize meanings. Note that understanding mathematical formulae also are considered logical, verbal propositions because they make statements about relations among numbers and symbols. Today's revised version of his original test—the Stanford Binet—is a thoroughly modern intelligence test that measures many things but continues to assess a "verbal reasoning" area that grew out of this original work (Thorndike, Hagen, & Sattler, 1986).

> **Verbal-Propositional Intelligence:** An intelligence that involves the capacity to reason validly with words and language, and to understand the meaning of words and language.

Words, Social Skills, and Hot Intelligences

Verbal-propositional intelligence is key to performance in school, but since Binet's time, other important intelligences have been uncovered. For example, although words can be analyzed as to their meanings and logic, they also can be used intelligently—or not—in a social context. When we meet someone, we might want to engage the person in conversation and to behave tactfully and kindly through our choice of words. As it turns out, using words in a social context to make conversation may draw upon a somewhat different sort of intelligence than verbal intelligence—social intelligence. Intelligences, such as social and emotional intelligences, that deal with matters of personal significance such as emotions, social life, and the practical aspects of life in general, are sometimes called hot intelligences. The hot intelligences form a second class of skills.

Verbal Fluency and Creativity

Finally, words can be used in a creative way, to write advertisements and poems, to weave pictures and analogies, and to create pleasing sounds. Whereas a test of cognitive intelligence might ask, "What is a bird?" a test of verbal fluency might ask, "What words rhyme with bird?" The person who can come up with many alternatives: "heard, nerd, assured, blurred, furred . . ." has an ability called *mental fluency*—the capacity to come up with many ideas, that may be a part of creativity. Whereas intelligence converges on a single, desired right answer or answers, creativity creates new alternatives that meet desired criteria.

The next sections outline some of the central cognitive, hot, and creative mental abilities. Then, the expression of these abilities in personality will be examined.

What Are Some Major Mental Abilities?

Verbal-Propositional Intelligence and Mental Development

Binet's Critical Insight

Earlier, we described verbal intelligence as the capacity to carry out reasoning with words and propositions. Verbal-propositional intelligence exhibits many of the crucial hallmarks of cognitive intelligence and mental abilities more generally.

The most central of these insights is that cognitive intelligence—especially raw intellectual power—increases with age until a person is about twenty years old (thereafter, intellectual power plateaus but learning continues). This is a relatively recent discovery. At the turn of the twentieth century, there was no recognition that intelligence grew with age. Although people of that time recognized that adults knew more than children, this was attributed solely to the fact that adults had lived longer. Because age was at first neglected as a factor in intelligence, the early attempts to measure it were not as successful as they might have been.

Inside the Field

Alfred Binet's Rough Start

There is no question that Binet had an inauspicious start to his professional life in general, and to psychology in particular. In general, Binet had difficulty selecting a career. Early on his father had near-forced him to touch a dead corpse so as to overcome his timidity, and this memory interfered with his later attempt at a medical education. On the other hand, after studying for the law he quit it in disgust, remarking that it was "the career of men who have not yet chosen a vocation" (Fancher, 1985, p. 50). After dropping out of medical school, Binet spent some time in the library, where he decided to become a psychologist.

Although he was now sure of his profession, his profession was not so sure of him. Binet published his first paper on two-point perception (when a person can distinguish between two simultaneous touches versus one). But soon after its publication, Joseph Delboeuf, a Belgian psychologist, wrote refuting much of his work and showing that he had published on the topic earlier and better. Binet had failed to acknowledge Delboeuf's work and was publically humiliated.

Still, Binet tried again. This time he moved on to study under the great French neurologist Charcot, who was studying hypnosis. (Binet and Sigmund Freud both studied with Charcot, overlapping briefly in their time with him.) With a fellow student, Binet studied a single hysteric patient, repeatedly hypnotizing her. As a result of these observations, Binet concluded that hypnosis occurred in three stages. Binet again rushed his work into print, and again attracted the attention of the Belgian psychologist Delboeuf, who not only found his claims unbelievable, but seeing Binet's name attached to them, decided to look into his work once again. After observing Binet at the Salpetriere (the hospital at which both Charcot and Binet worked), Delboeuf returned to Belgium where he conducted a series of carefully designed experiments that showed, once again, that Binet was in error. Binet grew from these experiences, becoming a more careful researcher.

Binet next moved from the Salpetriere to the Sorbonne, where he worked in the laboratory of Beaunis as a volunteer. Many years later, he

For example, Alfred Binet, the French psychologist who wrote the first IQ tests, developed a series of measures for important school skills such as memory, imagination, attention, and comprehension (see the Inside the Field box). He tested both mentally retarded and normal students of different ages. Although there were average differences between the normally developing and mentally retarded groups, there were always a few mentally retarded individuals who outperformed the normally developing children. At first this undermined any of his hopes to select those who could best learn in school (Fancher, 1985, p. 71). Then Binet realized that the age of children might affect their mental abilities. If he were right, it would be necessary to take age into consideration when comparing children who were mentally retarded with those who were not. He therefore began to build scales of mental abilities that were addressed to different age groups.

Binet determined the sorts of mental tasks that children at each age could carry out. For example, the average five-year-old was able to repeat a sentence of ten syllables, count four pennies, and copy a square. The average twelve-year-old, however, could repeat a sentence of twenty-six syllables, repeat seven figures, and interpret the

would take over its direction. Binet remained impressed with the value of the case study method from his earlier work in hypnosis. He studied his two daughters with great diligence as they grew up, examining their differences in personality from the time they first began to walk until they were in later life. From this he developed an impression of different styles of thinking people used. He characterized his daughter Madeleine as "the observer," and his daughter Alice as "the imaginer." Here are their quite different descriptions of a chestnut leaf:

Madeleine: The leaf I am looking at is a chestnut leaf gathered in the autumn, because the folioles are almost yellow except for two, and one is half green and yellow. This leaf is composed of several folioles joined at a center which ends at the stem called a petiole, which supports the leaf on the tree. The folioles are not the same size; out of the 7, 4 are much smaller than the 3 others. The chestnut tree is a dicotyledon, as one can tell by looking at the leaf, which has ramified nervures.

Alice: This is a chestnut tree leaf which has just fallen languidly in the autumn wind . . . Poor leaf, destined now to fly along the streets, then to rot, heaped up with the others. It is dead today, and it was alive yesterday! Yesterday, hanging from the branch it awaited the fatal flow of wind that would carry it off, like a dying person who awaits his final agony. But the leaf did not sense its danger, and it fell softly in the sun. (Fancher, 1985, p. 65)

Binet could observe and appreciate such differences in thinking, but the intelligence tests he developed, and other psychological thinking of the time, did not yet employ a language of personality suitable to reflect the different cognitive styles exhibited by each daughter. The first description is very scientifically oriented; the second, poetic. Today, one might say that such differences reflect the kinds of mental models people construct of the world around them, and, perhaps, the motives behind such ways of seeing.

meaning of a complex picture. Binet constructed scales for children of each chronological age.

The central idea was that scales at each age describe the average child. Some children could do much more than was average for their age; other children, far less. The level at which they performed was said to be their **mental age** or **MA**. Mental age refers to the highest age level at which a student could pass all the relevant mental ability items. For instance, a person with a mental age of thirteen would be thinking and solving problems at the level of the average thirteen-year-old. Binet found that people who did well at school had higher mental ages relative to their chronological ages; people who did poorly at school had lower mental ages relative to their chronological ages. In this way, Binet developed the first intelligence tests that were able to discriminate among those who could readily learn and those who had difficulty learning in school (Fancher, 1985).

Mental Age: The age that a person's mental functioning most resembles. If a child can solve problems that most six-year-olds can solve, for example, but fails most problems seven-year-olds can solve, the child is said to have a mental age of six.

Development

Binet's discovery that some children surpassed their peers whereas others lagged behind them reflected the idea that children developed their mental capacities at different rates. The **rate Intelligence Quotient**, or **rate IQ,** reflects this rate of growth (Stern, 1914). The rate IQ involves a ratio of mental age (MA) to chronological age (CA), which is then multiplied by 100 to yield the IQ; that is (MA/CA) × 100. The formula for the rate IQ is also in Table 6.1. When a child's mental age exceeds his or her chronological age, the intelligence quotient is greater than 100 and the child is mentally advanced; when the child's mental age is less than his or her chronological age, the quotient is less than 100 and the child is developing mental skills more slowly. A child with a mental age of five and a chronological age of five would be developing at an exactly average rate, and have an IQ of five divided by five times 100, or 100.

Intelligence Quotient: A score originally proposed as an index of a person's rate of mental (versus chronological) growth. The Intelligence Quotient, or IQ, has come to mean any score that reflects an individual's level of general intelligence.

Rate IQ: A measure of intelligence. The rate intelligence quotient (rate IQ) is calculated by taking a person's mental age, dividing it by the chronological age, and multiplying by 100 (Compare to Deviation IQ).

A different five-year-old with a mental age of four would have an intelligence quotient of 80 ((4 years/5 years) × 100). A rate IQ of above 100 means that a child's mental growth is progressing faster than the person's chronological age. If a five-year-old is able to perform tasks any average seven-year-old could perform, she would obtain an IQ of 140 ((7 years/5 years) × 100).

The Deviation IQ Concept

The rate IQ was essential to understanding the developmental nature of intelligences. It is, however, not in general use today because of two drawbacks. First, intelligence slows its dramatic increase at about age twenty. Therefore the calculation of a rate IQ in this way after age twenty is problematic. An average forty-year-old would score at about the same mental age of an eighteen-to-twenty-year-old. Using the rate IQ formula for an older adult (i.e., 20/40 × 100 = 50) would provide a gross underestimate of the average older adult's capacity, which would remain close to average.

Second, the same mental age may mean very different things for two different people. A five-year-old and a twenty-year-old, both with a mental age of ten, are quite different individuals. Although sharing the same mental age, the five-year-old will be seen as extremely clever and quick-witted, whereas the twenty-year-old's intellect will seem overtaxed.

> The folly of intelligent people, clear-headed and narrow-visioned, has precipitated many catastrophes.
> Alfred North Whitehead

| TABLE 6.1 | Comparison of Rate and Deviation IQ's |

Rate IQ	Deviation IQ
$IQ = \{MA/CA\} \times 100$	$IQ = \{RS - M_{RS}/S_{RS}\} \times 15 + 100$
MA = Mental Age CA = Chronological Age	RS = Raw Score (e.g., number correct) M_{RS} = Mean of the Raw Scores for the Sample S_{RS} = Standard Deviation of the Raw Scores
Comments: The Rate IQ is simply the ratio of mental age to chronological age, times 100.	*Comments:* The first part of the equation (in parentheses) transforms each of the raw scores (RS's) so that, as a group, they always have a mean of zero and a standard deviation of 1 (this is called a *z-score transformation*). The rest of the equation then transforms the z-scores of the test so that, like the rate IQ, they will have a mean of 100 and a standard deviation of 15.

Deviation IQ: A measure of intelligence. The deviation IQ is calculated by examining a person's distance or deviation from the average performance of all other people his or her age (compare to Rate IQ).

Standard Deviations: A measure of distance from a group mean. The standard deviation is a unit of measure. It is calculated by, first, summing the squared deviations from the mean of each person, second, obtaining the average of the summed squared deviations (referred to as the variance), and, finally, taking its square root.

The **deviation IQ** provides an alternative to the rate IQ (Wechsler, 1958). The deviation IQ is based on a person's standing compared to other people of the same age. A person at the mean (average) of the intelligence-score range would be given an IQ of 100 as with the rate IQ. Scores are then assigned above or below the mean depending upon how far a person's mental abilities are above or below the average of those the same age. Distances from the mean are measured in **standard deviation (SD)** units, which are set at 15 points. A standard deviation is a statistic that indicates the dispersion of an individual's scores around the mean. A person scoring one standard deviation above the mean relative to his or her peers would be given an IQ of 115. An IQ of 70 would indicate that an individual scored two standard deviations below the mean relative to his or her age peers (see Figure 6.1).

IQ scores are normally distributed (roughly speaking). For that reason it is possible to translate the scores into percentiles. When scores are normally distributed, 68 percent of the people will score plus-or-minus 1 SD from 100 (85–115), 95 percent plus-or-minus 2 SD (70–130), and 99.7 percent plus-or-minus 3 SD (55–145). In addition, one can calculate that a person with an IQ of 115 will have scored above 84 percent of other people, or at the 84th percentile. An IQ of 70 places the individual at the 5th percentile. The percentages of scores expected in each interval also are shown in Figure 6.1. (They are obtained by formulae taught in an introductory statistics course.)

IQ's calculated this way are near to those assigned by the original rate IQ's. Because so little was lost in the conversion, psychologists rapidly adopted the Wechsler deviation IQ, and today it is the more frequently employed measure of IQ.

Uncovering More Cognitive Intelligences

Perceptual-Organizational Intelligence and the Wechsler Scales

Almost from the start of intelligence testing, some theorists believed that more intelligences existed than verbal-propositional intelligence. For example, L. L. Thurstone

FIGURE 6.1

IQ Levels as a Function of Their Deviation from the Mean

The deviation IQ is calculated according to the number of standard deviations a person scores from the middle of the distribution (where IQ equals 100). A standard deviation is equal to 15 points. Because the distribution is normally distributed (i.e., shaped like a bell), the percentage of scores expected in each interval also can be estimated, as shown.

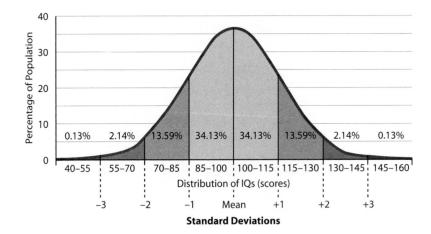

(1924; 1938) argued for the existence of eight mental abilities, including word fluency, memory, and reasoning. Nonetheless, verbal-propositional intelligence did such a good job of predicting school performance that there was little motivation to pursue other intelligences.

That changed when a major practical problem arose in the United States in the 1930s—assessing the mental ability of new immigrants to the country. Some of these immigrants appeared to have difficulty adjusting to their new country, and it was unclear why. Many could not take a traditional IQ test because they were unfamiliar with English, and intelligence tests were available only in a few languages at that time.

In those days, a staff member (and then director of psychology) at New York's Bellevue Hospital was a man named David Wechsler, who himself had immigrated to America from Romania. Many new immigrants who had difficulties finding housing, or holding a job, were brought to New York City's Bellevue Hospital for psychological testing. To address the language problem, Wechsler created a new intelligence test initially called the Wechsler-Belleview. Like earlier tests, it measured verbal-propositional intelligence. To do so, it employed six tasks. For the *vocabulary* task, people were asked to define words. On the *similarities* task, they identified what was similar about two concepts, such as light bulbs and fire. And, in the *comprehension* task, people were asked a number of questions concerning their understanding of the everyday world, such as, "What could you do if you became lost in a city?"

The second portion of the test, however, used measures that were relatively free of language requirements. It consisted of new scales that today are considered measures of **perceptual-organizational intelligence.** Perceptual-organizational intelligence is used when people perceive visual patterns, organize the perceptual information in them, and are able to divide the patterns into parts and to reconstruct them. This intelligence is important for many crucial tasks: creating patterns with fabric, or creating mechanical designs when drawing, or putting together pieces of a puzzle, or assembling mechanical objects such as a bicycle or engine (e.g., Kamphaus, Benson, Hutchinson, & Platt, 1994; Sattler, 1992; Tulsky & Ledbetter, 2000; Tulsky, Zhu, & Ledbetter, 1997).

Perceptual-Organization Intelligence: A type of intelligence that involves perceiving visual patterns, organizing the perceptual information in them, and being able to divide the patterns into parts and to reconstruct them.

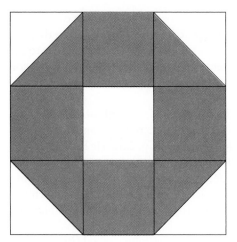

In the Wechsler Adult Intelligence Scales (WAISs), the Block Design task is a measure of perceptual-organizational intelligence, for which the individual must arrange two-toned blocks to form a pattern such as in the picture.*

A key measure of this intelligence is *block design.* In the block design task, a person examines blocks colored red, white, or both, on different sides. Next the person is shown a geometrical design and asked to recreate it by using four blocks (or nine, in harder problems). In another task, *picture completion,* the individual's job is to see what part of a drawing is missing. For example, a car might be missing one of its wheels. In *object assembly,* test takers are asked to assemble puzzle pieces, and in *picture arrangement,* people arrange pictures until they tell a coherent story. These tasks provided a better way to assess intelligence among people who were relatively unfamiliar with English. The Wechsler scales became a widespread success.

Spatial Intelligence

Still other intelligences were uncovered. Have you ever tried to create a mental image of the roads on which you were traveling and how the roads fit together? Did you check it against a road map, perhaps turning the map so that the roads were facing in the same direction that you were visualizing? If so, you were using **spatial intelligence**. Spatial intelligence refers to the capacity to reason about the movements of objects in space. The term *spatial intelligence* was used early in the twentieth century but the skill was not well measured until the work of Roger Shepard and his colleagues (e.g., Brigham, 1930; Coetsee, 1933; Kyllonen, Lohman, & Woltz, 1984; Lohman, 1988; Lohman, 2000, p. 319; Lohman & Kyllonen, 1983).

Shepard and his colleagues developed tasks in which people see a three-dimensional object. They are then asked to rotate the object in their minds, to see if they can identify which of several alternatives the rotated object might look like (e.g., Cooper & Shepard, 1984; Shepard & Metzler, 1971). Answering the question, "Is that an accurate picture of the rotated object?" may involve rotating the object in one's mind 45 degrees, or 90 degrees, or 135 degrees, or further. Shepard and his colleagues showed that people took longer to answer the question the further an object needed to be rotated mentally: for example, longer if they had to rotate it 90 degrees versus 45 degrees. (Talk about "turning something over" in your mind!) The intelligence to rotate such figures is measured by the spatial aptitude subscale of the Differential Aptitude Test and is somewhat distinct from perceptual-organizational intelligence (Bennett, Seashore, & Wesman, 1989). Individuals highest in this intelligence gravitate toward occupations that require spatial knowledge: architecture, engineering, mathematics, and the computer sciences (Shea, Lubinski, & Benbow, 2001).

Spatial Intelligence: A type of intelligence pertaining to understanding how objects move in space. Spatial intelligence is often measured by examining people's capacity to accurately rotate objects in their minds and identify what the rotated object would look like.

Are There Additional Intelligences and Mental Abilities?

Social Abilities and Related Intelligences

Intelligences such as the verbal, perceptual-organizational, and spatial can be considered "cool" intelligences as they concern matters of general reasoning that often

*Simulated items similar to those in the Wechsler Intelligence Scales for Children. Copyright © 1949, 1974, 1981, 1991, 1997, 1999, 2001 by Harcourt Assessment, Inc. Reproduced with permission. All rights reserved.

Hot Intelligences: A group of intelligences concerned with understanding and reasoning about information of direct personal, felt significance to the individual (for example, emotional intelligence).

Social Intelligence: A type of intelligence concerned with understanding social relations and how to carry out social tasks.

Personal Intelligence: A proposed intelligence that involves accurately understanding oneself and one's own mental processes and qualities.

Practical Intelligence: A type of intelligence involving the capacity to understand problems in everyday life that are often left undefined or poorly defined. Practical intelligence requires the problem solver to formulate the problem himself or herself, under conditions in which information necessary to a solution may be lacking. It is said to operate on tacit knowledge—that is, knowledge not often explicitly stated.

can be independent of one's personal concerns. Such cool intelligences can be contrasted with the "hot" intelligences. **Hot intelligences** are so-called because they operate on information that is of more immediate social and emotional relevance to the person's well being—whether it is feelings themselves, or one's personal or social status. The hot intelligences include the social and practical, personal, emotional, and others (Mayer & Mitchell, 1988).

E. L. Thorndike (1920) first proposed the existence of a **social intelligence**, and defined it as, "the ability to understand and manage men and women, boys and girls—to act wisely in human relations" (Thorndike, 1920, p. 228). He had concluded that the "cooler," academic sorts of intelligence were insufficient to fully describe how human beings thought. For college students, social information processing and social intelligence are required to figure out which friends to make, which dormitories or apartments to choose, and what activities to join (e.g., Cantor & Kihlstrom, 1987; Kihlstrom & Cantor, 2000).

One defining task of social intelligence involves describing a social situation and asking why it unfolds as it does (Moss & Hunt, 1927; Thorndike & Stein, 1937). For example, participants taking the *Social Insight Test* learned about a character named Mr. Asher. Mr Asher criticized a neighbor for buying too expensive a car, but then obtained a loan so as to purchase an equivalently expensive car. Why would Mr. Asher do such a thing? A test-taker could choose as an alternative that Mr. Asher criticized his neighbor because he felt envy at first, and later satisfied his envy by buying a similar car himself (Chapin, 1968).

Although social intelligence was at first difficult to distinguish from verbal-propositional intelligence (e.g., Cronbach, 1960), more recent studies indicate that it is more independent of verbal-propositonal intelligence than was once thought. Research in it continues at a modest rate (Jones & Day, 1997; Lee et al., 2000; O'Sullivan & Guilford, 1976).

A footnote to social intelligence research concerns **personal intelligence**. Personal intelligence involves an understanding of one's own mental processes and the ability to form a sophisticated identity that distinguishes oneself from others (Gardner, 1983; 1993, pp. 246–252). Few compelling scales of personal intelligence have been developed so far, although developing such a measure seems like a potentially rewarding research pursuit (McCallum & Piper, 1997). On the other hand, there is some burgeoning research on social skills and their use in various situations. The expression of mental abilities more generally will be examined later in this chapter.

Practical Intelligence

Another kind of hot intelligence is **practical intelligence** (e.g., Sternberg et al., 2000). Practical intelligence focuses on the capacity to identify and think about unstated, tacit knowledge, including social rules and obligations related to obtaining one's goals. Have you heard the expression, "It's not *what* you know, its *who* you know"? Well, even "who you know" requires a form of mental ability (as well as a lot of environmental influences such as family contacts, of course). Making contacts, knowing people, and the ways those connections can be used fall within practical intelligence. Such practical problems are characterized by having multiple solutions, each with different advantages and drawbacks, and there are multiple methods of obtaining a given solution. It includes knowing such things as "what to say to whom, knowing when to say it, and knowing how to say it for maximum effect (Sternberg et al., 2000, pp. xi, 204).

One of the first practical knowledge tests was conducted with beginning university professors at a prestigious university in the 1980s to see how well they understood how to become successful in their careers (Wagner, 1987; 2000, p. 381). A test item of the sort employed is illustrated in Table 6.2. Professors had to rate, on a 7-point scale, how actually important working on alternative projects would be for their future, "given the realities of the academic world as you know it." Scoring was matched against a sample of experts judges (e.g., highly competent, tenured professors). For example, grants and research were particularly important to the futures of these beginning professors. Not all of the hopeful professors, however, recognized that central truth.

As it turned out, the closer the assistant professors' ratings converged to the expert judges' ratings of the correct answers, the higher was the assistant professor's performance, as evaluated according to such objective criteria as how much their research was cited by others.

Emotional Intelligence

Emotional Intelligence: The ability to reason with emotions, and of emotions to enhance thought. Emotional intelligence involves the capacity to accurately perceive emotions, to use them in thinking, to understand emotions, and to manage emotional experience.

Just as one can reason about verbal information, or practical information, so can one reason about emotional information (Mayer & Salovey, 1997; Salovey & Mayer, 1990). Emotions are evolved signals about relationships (see Chapter 4). For example, happiness indicates the desire to join others; fear signals the need to escape, and anger signals the presence of threat. **Emotional intelligence** concerns the capacity

TABLE 6.2	An Item of the Sort Found on a Tacit Knowledge Test for Assistant Professors

It is your second year as an assistant professor. This past year you published two unrelated empirical articles. You don't, however, believe there is yet a research area that can be identified as your own. There is one graduate student who has chosen to work with you. Your teaching evaluations were about average. Your goals are to become a top person in your field and get tenure. Rate the importance of each of the following to obtaining your goal:

_____ Improve the quality of your teaching

_____ Write a grant proposal

_____ Begin several short-term research projects, each of which may lead to an empirical article

_____ Serve on a university-wide committee

_____ Serve on a departmental committee

_____ Recruit more graduate students

_____ Supervise honors undergraduates in research

. . .

Source: Adapted from Wagner & Sternberg (1985), pp. 440–441, reprinted with permission of the American Psychological Association.

• FACTS • AT • A • GLANCE •

Using Your Practical Intelligence at Work

Moran (1993) developed a list of more than 300 observations reflecting practical, on-the-job wisdom from his experience as a management consultant. Here are some examples:

6. Never take a problem to your boss without some solutions. You are getting paid to think, not to whine.

25. Never confuse a memo with reality ... most memos from the top are political fantasy.

32. Remember that the purpose of business is to make or do something and sell it. The closer you can get to those activities, the better.

36. Never go into a meeting without your calendar.

58. Learn to remember people's names. If your memory is poor, develop a system.

61. Don't hang your diplomas in your office unless you're an M.D.

216. Learn what finished work looks like and then deliver your own work only when it looks the same way.

228. Learn to recognize people who are bad medicine and stay away from them.

235. Graciousness always helps: when you have a visitor, make sure you offer soft drinks or coffee.

to reason about these emotional signals, and the capacity of emotion to facilitate reasoning (Mayer, Salovey, & Caruso, 2000). More specifically, emotional intelligence is said to involve four branches of skills: accuracy at emotional perception, understanding emotional meanings and concepts, and the self-management of emotion, as well as the capacity of emotion to facilitate thought (Mayer & Salovey, 1997). This four-part model is illustrated in Figure 6.2.

For example, what if some of your friends wanted to play a practical joke and you thought it was a bad idea? One high school student who scored very highly on an emotional intelligence scale faced just such a situation. Her friends wanted to paint someone they knew while he was asleep. She carefully monitored how her friends dared one another to do it, and how their emotions escalated around those dares. Instead of going along with the prank, though, she painted a picture for her friends of just how badly the sleeping person would feel when he woke up. By doing so, she put an end to the prank before it started (Mayer et al., 2000). Adolescents lower in emotional intelligence, however, often went through with dares from their friends despite the negative consequences.

> Intelligence alone, without wisdom and empathy for suffering, is hollow.
> John G. Stoessinger

Scales of emotional intelligence present people with emotional problems and ask them to provide the correct answer. For example, sample test items ask people to recognize emotions in faces, understand emotional vocabulary, and recognize the outcomes of different types of emotional communication between people (Mayer, Salovey, & Caruso, 2002). People who score high on such scales are more empathetic and connected with others. There also exist self-report scales of emotional intelli-

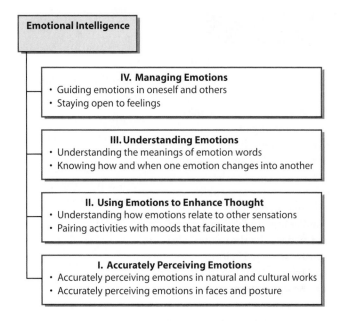

FIGURE 6.2

**Emotional
Intelligence: The
Four-Branch Model**
The Four-Branch model of
emotional intelligence
involves four areas of skills.
Ability scales of emotional
intelligence measure skills in
each area.

gence which largely grew out of a popularization of the concept and do not measure mental abilities per se (see Mayer, 2001, for a history; Brackett & Mayer, 2003; Mathews, Zeidner, & Roberts, 2002; Paulhus et al., 1998; Schutte, Malouff, & Simunek, 2002).

Measuring Creativity

Creativity: The capacity to generate multiple novel and appropriate solutions to problems.

Creativity involves the ability to come up with many new and novel solutions to problems (Brown, 1989; Sternberg & O'Hara, 2000). Creative people are often known for their unusual and unexpected solutions to important problems. Examples of such creative individuals include Albert Einstein, Pablo Picasso, Bach, Beethoven, and, Michelangelo, among many others.

Verbal Fluency: The capacity to generate a large number of appropriate words that fit a specified category (e.g., words that rhyme with "smell").

A variety of mental measures tap creativity. We have already mentioned **verbal fluency** as an example of creativity measures. Verbal fluency is the capacity to generate a large number of relevant words or concepts in response to a problem. Sample verbal fluency test items ask a participant to come up with all the words that rhyme with "bend," or all the names that rhyme with "Harry" (Cattell, 1971).

Alternate Uses: A task in which a participant tries to think of as many uses as possible for an everyday object, such as a desk or a pen.

Another key measure is the **alternate uses** task (Getzels & Jackson, 1962; Wallach & Kogan, 1965). Alternate uses tasks involve asking test respondents to list as many uses of an object as he or she can think of. In response to "book," a creative individual might respond, "It is useful for reading . . . You could use it for a paper weight. You could hollow it out and hide something in it . . . You could flatten a leaf inside it . . . You could balance it on your head to improve your posture." The think-

Research in Focus

Measuring Emotional Intelligence

Emotional intelligence can be defined as the capacity to accurately perceive, use, understand, and manage emotion. The measurement of emotional intelligence has developed and improved over more than a decade. In a first empirical test of whether such an ability existed, researchers asked whether the capacity to accurately perceive emotion was a skill that would generalize across perceptions of faces, abstract designs, and colors. In fact, one underlying factor seemed to describe the mental ability (Mayer, DiPaolo, & Salovey, 1990).

An issue in that early study of the intelligence, however, was how to determine the correct answer on the test. Since the researchers viewed emotions as universal signals of relationships, they used agreement with the group consensus as the correct criterion. So, if most of the group thought a picture of a face was angry, and so did the person being tested, then the person's score was marked as correct.

In 1996, a new study was carried out that asked participants to judge the emotions of targeted others. To set up the study, one group of participants first wrote down some emotional events they had experienced, and then filled out a mood scale for how they felt at the time. One participant wrote:

> My roommate has been kind of blowing off her boyfriend. She told him she did not want to see him until Spring Break. He is hurt because he thinks she does not like him anymore, and he wants to come up here to see her this weekend. I have been gone almost every weekend since school started, giving her plenty of opportunities to have him up here while I am gone, and now I'm finally getting to stay here for the weekend and he might be coming up. (Why can't she go visit him instead?!?!?) (Mayer & Geher, 1996, p. 98)

The job of the second group of participants was to guess how the people in the first group felt. If the new respondents agreed with the original target person about how he or she felt, they received points added to their scores. As it turned out, however, the target criterion appeared fairly poor, because participant-targets often inflated how positive they felt, reluctant to share negative emotions even anonymously. Using the original scoring method appeared best.

Divergent Thinking: The capacity to generate many alternative solutions to a specified problem. For example, to "What are all the things you can do with a water bottle?"

ing exhibited in such tasks is often referred to as **divergent thinking** in that it involves coming up with answers to questions that, although correct, diverge from the common way of looking at matters (Guilford, 1967).

Another such task is the Remote Associates Task (Mednick, 1962). For this task, people are given three words and must come up with another word that links them. For example, you might see: *jail, dog, out,* and be instructed to come up with another word that is related to all three. In this case, one remote associate would be *house,* because there are jail houses, dog houses, and out houses.

Just as there are multiple intelligences, so may there be multiple creativities. Averill and Thomas-Knowles (1991) developed an emotional creativity task called *emotional triads.* In emotional triads, the test-taker must create a story in which a person feels three different emotions. For example, in response to the triad "lonely/angry/joyful," one emotionally creative participant related the following.

In 1999, a new measure of emotional intelligence was introduced called the Multifactor Emotional Intelligence Scale (MEIS). It measured four areas of emotional intelligence and to do so contained twelve different ability measures (Mayer, Caruso, & Salovey, 1999). These included measures of perceiving emotions in pictures, faces, designs, and music, emotion vocabulary, understanding how emotions blend and change over time, and a number of other tasks.

The MEIS again was scored using a group-consensus criterion, for which it exhibited a great deal of reliability (r = .96). This was important because other researchers had bemoaned the difficulty or impossibility of creating reliable measures of ability in the area (Davies, Stankov, & Roberts, 1998). Issues concerning the correct answer still arose however. Some critics expressed concern that the consensus scoring might not agree with expert opinion as to correct answers (Roberts, Zeidner, & Mathews, 2001).

A newly revised emotional intelligence test called the Mayer-Salovey-Caruso Emotional Intelligence Test (MSCEIT; Mayer, Salovey, & Caruso, 2002) replaced the MEIS (it had the advantage of being much shorter). In order to address concerns over general consensus versus expert scoring, the MSCEIT was submitted to twenty-one emotions experts—members of the International Society of Research in Emotion (ISRE). Those experts answered the test in the ways they believed to be best and generated a new, expert, criterion for the scale. It turned out that the new expert criterion yielded much the same scores as did consensus scoring, with correlations above r = .98 for the two approaches on the overall test (Mayer, Caruso, Salovey, & Sitarenios, 2003). It appeared, at that point, that emotional intelligence had been established as a new intelligence with good measures that could be used to assess it.

Analyses of tests of emotional intelligence indicate that there exists a general, unitary factor of emotional intelligence. Those same analyses indicate that the tests' results also can be divided into four scores corresponding to the theory of emotional intelligence just described: that is, the capacity to perceive emotions accurately, to use emotions to enhance thought, to understand emotions, and to manage emotions (Day & Caroll, 2004; Mayer et al., 2003; Roberts et al., 2001).

At present, researchers have turned their attention to what emotional intelligence predicts. (See the text on "How Does Personality Express Its Abilities?" for more information.)

Driving on never to return—I wish. Another family fight, my typical reaction, get in the car and take off. Riding into the summer night air, mild and damp, makes me glad to be in motion. The breeze coming through the windows produces sensations of joy.—I'm angry as I was chased out of my own home . . . And I'm lonely as I drive alone with my broodings . . . that it is I who must go into the night . . . It's a lonely feeling yet so peaceful it brings its own joy—and so I run [until]. . . I yield to my weariness and head for home." (Averill & Thomas-Knowles, 1991, p. 292)

Creativity tasks correlate among themselves at moderate levels. This suggests that they define a distinct domain of mental ability. In addition, different types of creativity have been distinguished from one another; for example, emotional creativity differs from cognitive creativity. The creativities tend to be relatively independent of general intelligence (Ivcevic, Brackett, & Mayer, 2006; Wallach & Kogan, 1965). Nonetheless, their mental ability–like nature has led some people to consider them intelligences as well, and they have been included in recent hierarchical models of intelligence, to be discussed next (e.g., Carroll, 1993; cf., Sternberg, 2003).

The Theory of *g*

As the first cognitive intelligences were identified, one could calculate an IQ for each one. For example, Wechsler's scales produced two separate IQ's: One for verbal-propositional intelligence, and one for perceptual-organizational intelligence. Wechsler also combined the IQ's, however, to create one overall IQ score. The idea of an overall IQ suggested to some people that there might be just one intelligence that could summarize the rest. Is this possible?

General Intelligence (*g*): An overall index of a person's ability to solve problems accurately and quickly across all major areas of cognitive reasoning—verbal-propositional, perceptual, organizational, spatial, and others.

Charles Spearman (1927) first suggested there existed a **general intelligence**, or simply, **g**. General intelligence can be thought of as a general index of a person's overall intellectual functioning. Spearman's hypothesis included the idea that there existed a hierarchy of intelligences, with the most specific mental abilities at the bottom, large intelligences in the middle, and general intelligence on top. Although everyone acknowledges that there exist separate mental abilities, Spearman's theory included the idea that all measured mental abilities correlate together. If a person does well on one test, he or she tends to do well on other tests; if a person does poorly on one test, he or she tends to do poorly on them all. Hence the average skill level, or more technically, the person's level on the first factor of intelligence (from factor analysis), takes on a special significance.

This idea works fairly well for many cognitive measures. For example, in Table 6.3, you can see that diverse scales from the Wechsler Adult Intelligence Scale—including vocabulary, comprehension and arithmetic (all classified as verbal tests), as well as block design, picture completion, and object arrangement (all classified as measures of perceptual-organizational skill), correlate at roughly the same level. If one factor analyzes mental abilities, such as those in Table 6.3, for example, one would find a single factor that accounted for a great deal of variation among the orig-

TABLE 6.3	Intercorrelations among Selected Subscales of the WAIS					
WAIS Subscales	Comprehension	Arithmetic	Vocabulary	Picture Comp.	Block Design	Object Assembly
Comprehension	1.00					
Arithmetic	0.54	1.00				
Vocabulary	0.72	0.58	1.00			
Picture Complet.	0.54	0.46	0.57	1.00		
Block Design	0.45	0.48	0.46	0.61	1.00	
Object Assembly	0.38	0.37	0.40	0.51	0.59	1.00

Source: From J. E. Birren & D. F. Morrison, Table 2. Copyright © 1961, The Gerontological Society of America. Reproduced by permission of the publisher.

	Factor		
WAIS Subtest	I	II	III
Information	.84	−.20	−.15
Comprehension	.75	−.22	−.09
Arithmetic	.70	.03	−.03
Similarities	.75	.32	.01
Digit Span	.69	.62	−.10
Vocabulary	.86	−.27	−.22
Digit Symbol	.63	.05	.22
Picture Completion	.72	−.09	.28
Block Design	.66	−.02	.48
Picture Arrangement	.66	−.02	.26
Object Assembly	.55	−.05	.44

TABLE 6.4   **Factor Loadings on the WAIS**

Source: From Morrison (1976), p. 318.

inal measures. When you do so, you find out that all the scales correlate highly with a first factor (Table 6.4; Morrison, 1976). When you look at this first factor, you are looking straight at *g*. This is the mathematical evidence that Charles Spearman first saw for general intelligence. (Incidentally, for this data set, the second and third factors can be interpreted as representing a short-term memory and a perceptual-organizational factor, respectively.)

Recent Work on the Hierarchy and Spearman's g

Carroll (1993) reanalyzed 450 studies of mental abilities to create a new look at the data on the hierarchy of mental abilities. At the bottom-most level are individual tasks that might appear on some of the intelligence tests we discussed in this section: the individual subscales such as *vocabulary* on the Stanford-Binet, *block design* on the WAIS, and *mental rotation* on the Differential Aptitude Test. Carroll's findings included a number of unexpected new factors including, for example, abilities related specifically to auditory and visual perception. At the second level are specific intelligences such as verbal-propositional, spatial, and so forth. Finally, at the highest level, one finds the overarching general intelligence, or *g*. A simplified overview of the hierarchy examined by Carroll is shown in Figure 6.3. At the lowest level of the figure are individual measures of cognitive abilities. Above that are fairly broad intelligences such as verbal and spatial intelligence. Finally, general intelligence is at the top.

The right-most part of the diagram includes one "hot" mental ability not included by Carroll—emotional intelligence. The study of such hot intelligences is relatively new and it is unclear whether such hot intelligences also are a part of *g*. Although emotional intelligence appears to be an intelligence, it is remarkably independent of other kinds of intelligence, sharing only a modest overlap with cognitive intelligence, of about *r* = .35 (Mayer, Salovey, & Caruso, 2004). The implication of this

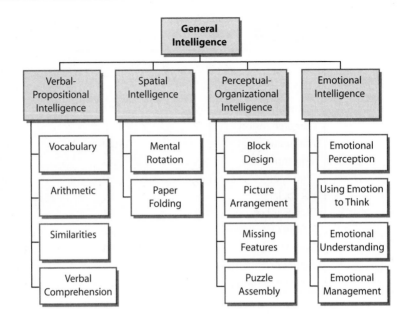

FIGURE 6.3

A Partial Overview of a Hierarchy of Intelligences: Tasks, Intelligences, and General Intelligence
Spearman and others have proposed that intelligences are related in a hierarchy, with specific mental abilities at the bottom, broader mental abilities in the middle, and general intelligence at the top.

low relationship is that ability tests of emotional intelligence appear to measure something beyond what has been measured before in the realm of personality or intelligence (Barchard, 2003; Ciarrochi et al., 2000; Mayer et al., 1999; Roberts et al., 2001).

> **Connecting Window**   *Addressing Theoretical Questions with Factor Analysis*
> Once again, the importance of correlational techniques to personality psychology—especially techniques such as factor analysis—is evident here. The empirical support for the hierarchy of intelligences is based on a theory—that of *g*—tested by empirical correlations. See Chapter 2, "Multiple Variables and Multivariate Techniques," to refresh your memory of factor analysis.

What Is the Relation between Personality and Intelligence?

Personality Calls on Abilities

Personality has at its command many mental abilities: cognitive IQ, emotional intelligence, creativity, and the like. When used properly these abilities and talents can lead to awe-inspiring heights of thought, creativity, and performance. These capacities of personality that include memory, abstract thinking, creativity, and the like, are a product of the large human brain—as well as the education and other social support it recieves.

You can't beat brains.

U.S. President John F. Kennedy

Generally speaking, intelligence-like behavior increases over animal species according to the size of the brain relative to the body (Jerison, 2000). Figure 6.4 indicates the relative sizes of chimpanzee and

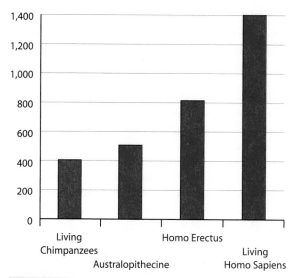

1,400
1,200
1,000
800
600
400
200
0

Living Chimpanzees

Australopithecine

Homo Erectus

Living Homo Sapiens

FIGURE 6.4   **Brain Size in Milliliters in Chimpanzees, Human Ancestors, and Humans Today**
Personality can draw on a wide range of mental abilities thanks, in part, to the rapidly expanding size of the brain over recent evolution.
Source: After Jerison (2000), pp. 232–234.

human brains (estimated from the size of their skull cases), with some human ancestors added for purposes of comparison.

Chimpanzees and human beings have the largest brain-body ratio of any animals, with the exception of dolphins. This larger brain and its greater processing capacity account in part for the greater range of intellectual performance of human beings when compared to other living organisms (Jerison, 2000). Although more controversial, there is evidence that brain size within human beings also relates to mental abilities such as intelligence. The most recent studies are done with MRI techniques (Flashman, Andreasen, Flaum, & Swayze, 1998; Pennington et al., 2000; Schretlen et al., 2000; but see Gould, 1981). Human beings may also have evolved an increased speed of mental processing due to the particular form of connections between neurons—and this may account for a portion of intellectual functioning as well (e.g., Bates & Eysenck, 1993; Jensen, 1987).

Unsurprisingly given these biological bases, genetics make a substantial contribution to an individual's potential range of mental performance, at least in the cognitive area, with estimates that as much as 50 percent to 70 percent of the variance of cognitive IQ may be due to genetic factors (McGue et al., 1993, p. 353). Such patterns may extend to the hot intelligences as well. For example, people high in emotional intelligence show brain patterns indicating that they can solve emotional problems with less effort than others (Jaušovec, Jaušovec, & Gerlic, 2001), though no direct evidence is available.

The Relations among Mental Ability Traits and Other Traits

Although the wide range of mental abilities begin with the brain, they interact—or not—with other dimensions of personality. Perhaps the most striking aspect of personality is how varied it can be and still draw on mental abilities. For example, extraverts, introverts, those high in achievement and those low in it, may all be high in intelligence (or low). There are only very minor relationships between most other personality traits and most mental abilities (e.g., Eysenck, 1994; Mayer, Caruso, Zigler, & Dreyden, 1989; Sternberg & Ruzgis, 1994; Zeidner & Mathews, 2000). There are often, however, a few more specific traits that do relate to areas of mental ability functioning and may possibly enhance or suppress it.

Intellectual Absorption: A trait related to intelligence that concerns the capacity to become involved in intellectual problems to the point of losing track of other activities.

Intelligence and Absorption

Intellectual absorption, for example, is the capacity to become absorbed in intellectual problems such that one may even forget what is going on around oneself. On the positive end, the intellectually gifted seem to become highly absorbed in their pursuits. Geniuses like Newton, Michelangelo, and others seemed to possess an absorbed, flowing involvement in their intellectual work. Newton's absorption in his work was so intense and complete, for example, that no one knew him well enough to record the rest of his life.

As another example, the mathematician Feigenbaum immersed himself in modeling irregular objects as he was developing chaos theory. He took a great number of plane trips, apparently partly motivated by watching the irregular cloud patterns up close. This so frustrated his employer, Los Alamos Laboratories, that they finally had to suspend his scientific travel privileges (Gleick, 1987, pp. 1–2). A study of highly intellectually gifted fourteen-year-olds indicated that they were higher in intellectual absorption than incoming first-year college students of the same mental age, and also higher in intellectual absorption than a same-age control group of other fourteen-year-olds of average intelligence (Mayer et al., 1989).

Emotional Intelligence and Empathy; Openness and Creativity

Perhaps unsurprisingly, self-judged empathy correlates most highly with emotional intelligence, at the r = .35 range. That makes sense because emotional intelligence measures the ability to, say, track the emotions of another person talking about feelings on a videotape (e.g., Geher, Warner, & Brown, 2001).

Creativity, in turn, is related to the personality trait Openness to experience, one of the Big Five traits introduced in Chapter 3. Openness to experience involves the willingness to appreciate and to try new things. People who score high on such scales endorse such items as, "I like to try new foods I haven't tried before."

Although creativity is a healthy psychological strength for many people, it also seems related to at least two specific traits associated with psychopathology. Some creative individuals, for example, experience alterations in conscious experience that are similar to those found in the milder forms of the schizophrenic-spectrum disorders. Both those who are creative, and those with a **schizotypal style** of thinking endorse test items that indicate unusual mental experiences, such as, "It has seemed at times as if my body was melting into my surroundings," and "I have felt there were messages for me in the way things were arranged, like in a store window." (Fisher et al., 2004, pp. 25–26). The schizotypal style involves unusual modes of thinking and is believed to be genetically related to schizophrenia. Such manifestations of a schizotypal mind-set have been associated with better performance on divergent thinking tasks. Moreover, the first-degree relatives and offspring of people with schizophrenia can be found in more creative occupations than others (Brod, 1997; Karlsson, 1984). The creative thinking style, however, can be found in otherwise healthy personalities and does not mean a person has or will develop a mental disorder.

A similar set of relationships exists for people who experience larger-than-average mood swings. People who experience such regular variations in mood appear to be more creative, perhaps benefiting from seeing problems from alternating optimistic and pessimistic perspectives (Jamison, 1993; 1996; Mayer et al., 1995). This variation in mood exists in many normal people but appears stronger in first-degree relatives of those with **bipolar disorder**. Bipolar disorder is a mental disorder marked by severe mood swings, often alternating between paralyzing depressions and out-of-control excited states called mania. First-degree relatives of those with bipolar disor-

Schizotypal Style: A cognitive style associated with a mental disorder involving very odd forms of thinking and perceiving, and behavioral eccentricities.

Bipolar Disorder: A mental disorder marked by severe swings in mood.

der who are otherwise normal also are found often in more creative occupations than others (Richards et al., 1988).

Personality, Mental Abilities, and the Construction of Mental Models

Mental Abilities and Learning

Personality development involves not only calling on its available mental abilities but also developing them for a particular context or project. That begins with understanding one's own culture. For example, as immigrant groups from poorer countries come to wealthier nations they may at first score lower on their chosen country's intelligence tests (Eysenck & Kamin, 1981). These same groups often show rises in intelligence to the average or to above average as they assimilate in the general culture (Ceci, 1996). Factors contributing to the rise include learning the host country's language, although such rises may also involve improved pre- and postnatal medical care, and better nutrition.

Social contexts are important; so too may be stereotyping of the immigrant group—or any group—which may contribute to lower test performance. Experimental studies have shown that when a person is stereotyped as less than intellectually adequate in a particular area, his or her performance on intellectual tasks will be temporarily lowered (Aronson, Lustina, & Good, 1999; Steele, 1998; Steele & Aronson, 1995).

People may develop particular mental abilities in response to an environment that fosters those abilities. Perhaps the most striking changes in human mental performance are due to public education. The fact that societies worldwide devote extensive time and effort to schooling their youth is testament to how crucial formal teaching practices are. During at least junior high school and high school instruction, each year of schooling may raise an individual's IQ as much as two points (Gustafsson, 2001). From one perspective, the fact that it requires full-time academic study for a year to create a two-point IQ difference seems a modest effect. On the other hand, it adds up to a substantial effect over several years.

In turn, some parental practices also may foster mental abilities. The humanistic psychologist Carl Rogers (1954) suggested that parents could foster creativity for their children by respecting their creative achievements when they were young. In one study, some parents endorsed creativity-fostering statements on a parental style questionnaire, such as, "I respect my child's opinions and encourage him to express them," and "I feel a child should have time to think, daydream, and even loaf," whereas other parents endorsed statements that seemed likely to suppress creativity, such as, "I try to keep my child away from children or families who have different ideas or values from our own." Parental child-rearing practices at age 4.5 were highly predictive of creativity in adolescence, with child-rearing practices predicting adolescent creativity with correlations in the mid r = .40's. (Harrington, Block, & Block, 1987).

In addition to pure mental abilities, creativity is enhanced by situational influences as well. When situations allow people to lower their competitive urges and focus on the intrinsic pleasure of a task, for example, it enhances creative processes and output (Amabile, 1996).

Water and ice suggest the differences between fluid and crystallized intelligence. Fluid intelligence addresses new problems in a flexible, flowing fashion. Crystallized intelligence draws on knowledge that gradually has been accumulated and fixed over time.

Crystallized Intelligence: Actual knowledge stored about the world that can be applied to the solutions of mental problems.

Fluid Intelligence: A type of ongoing mental capacity or ability to deal with novel, new problems.

Crystallized Intelligence and Mental Models

In Chapter 5, personality was said to be made up, in part, of mental models. Those mental models are constructed through intelligences and other mental abilities. In fact, intelligence researchers sometimes distinguish between two broad forms of intelligence: **crystallized intelligence** and **fluid intelligence**. Crystallized intelligence involves mental models developed of well-learned material that has been acquired through prior experience, such as vocabulary, mathematics, and knowledge of relationships (Carroll, 1993, p. 626; Cattell, 1963). Crystallized intelligence, as one example, might involve knowing about novels in general, Charles Dickens's life, English language literature, the different forms of literature (plays, novels, sonnets, and the like), as well as more generally about many forms of human relationships.

Fluid intelligence refers to the active, immediately occurring processes of intelligence that show up most clearly on new problems—for example, in identifying a theme in a book one is reading, or in solving a logical problem for the first time. Fluid intelligence, for example, might be used to draw upon the many parts of Charles Dickens's novel, *David Copperfield,* for recurring themes of relationships, so as to discover a significant theme that runs through the novel.

Fluid and crystallized intelligence operate together, of course. To identify themes in Dickens's novels (or any other novels) requires fluid intelligence, yet one also must compare what is written to what one already knows about words, sentences, and relationships, which requires crystallized intelligence.

The crystallized intelligence of the intelligence researcher overlaps to a considerable degree with the mental models of the personality psychologist discussed in the last chapter. Our personality is made up, in other words, of layers upon layers of mental models. The more accurate these are, the better one may be able to solve problems and navigate the world.

How Does Personality Express Its Abilities?

Intelligence in the Expression of Thought

Concrete and Abstract Reasoning

What parts of personality's expression are due to mental abilities? One fundamental type of reasoning that nearly everyone can carry out is called **concrete thinking**.

Concrete Thinking: Thinking that correctly holds symbols, ideas, and thoughts in memory, but without any comparisons or generalizations about those ideas.

Concrete thinking involves observing, recording, and the simple labeling of events and occurrences. Almost all people are capable of at least some concrete thinking.

Nigel Hunt suffered from mental retardation due to a genetic abnormality, Trisomy-21 (also known as Down syndrome). Tutored extensively by his parents, who were both teachers, Nigel learned to read and write and in his late teens produced a complete autobiography with only minimal help from others. "I am Nigel Hunt," he began:

> . . . and I live at 26 Church Avenue, Pinner, England with my parents. They are very nice indeed. I was born at Edgware in 1947. I have never been to America yet. The lady who advised me to write this was Mrs. Eileen J. Garrett and she says that I shall be very busy.
>
> So it's hallo! Welcome to my first good attempt in making this book and [his father] Douglas Hunt is assisting me. (Hunt, 1967, p. 46)

Nigel's autobiography is full of descriptions of his warm family life and his interests and activities. Here, he further describes his education at the Atholl School:

> Since my father was Headmaster I had joined the school at the age of eleven. I was very proud of my school. I had very good teachers, such as: Mrs C. Parry, Mr Warrington, And the school's old Headmaster, Mr J. H. Hale . . .
>
> The first time I went to school my father had left something behind; it was his handkerchief, and my mother told me to take it to him. When I got to school one of the boys came up to me and said, "Would you like to play cricket?" and do you know who the boy was? Michael Killick, who played well in the athletics match at Harrow Town.
>
> One day I was taught good English from Mr Hunt and then came the periods. Periods 1, 2, 3, 4, and so on; when I went there I became independent and polite to all the boys. Then we had two French teachers. One French master was Mr Piper. He was a very good person. (Hunt, 1967, pp. 105–106)

This passage contains a variety of accurate individual observations, facts, and feelings. Although it is easy to appreciate them, they seem unarranged and unorganized at times. Does more intelligent expression have a hallmark feature? Some people believe that it does, and that hallmark feature lies in abstract thinking.

Abstract Reasoning: The capacity to manipulate symbols, see relationships among concepts, and to integrate ideas in thought.

Abstract thinking is a second type of reasoning often crucial to high intelligence. Abstract thinking goes beyond concrete thinking to look at the relationships among individual observations and perceptions. Abstract thinking is the ability to hold concepts in mind and to compare their similarities and differences, to organize them, to generalize across concepts, and to synthesize ideas.

In 1921, a number of eminent psychologists participated in a symposium in which they were invited to submit definitions of intelligence (Thorndike, 1921). Abstract reasoning featured prominently the "ability to carry on abstract thinking" (Louis Terman), "ability to judge, understand, and reason well" (Alfred Binet), and the "apprehension of relevant relationships" (Wyatt).

Abstract thinking becomes more prevalent as one examines people of increasingly high intelligence levels. For example, Alexander Hamilton (1757–1804) was a close confidant of George Washington and an author of the Federalist Papers, which recommended ratification of the new United States constitution. As a young man, just before the U.S. War for Independence, he wrote a letter to a schoolmate in which he neatly balanced several concerns for his own future:

> To confess my weakness, Ned, my ambition is prevalent, so that I contemn the groveling condition of a clerk or the like, to which my fortune, etc., condemns me, and would willingly risk my life, though not my character, to exalt my station. I am confident, Ned, that my youth excludes me from any hopes of immediate preferment; nor do I desire it; but I mean to preface the way for futurity. I'm no philosopher, you see, and may justly be said to build castles in the air; my folly makes me ashamed, and I beg you'll conceal it; yet Neddy, we have seen such schemes successful when the projector is constant. (cited in Terman, 1926, p. 785)

Note how Hamilton draws a careful distinction between taking risks in general, versus risking one's character, and that he has noticed, as well, how plans can succeed for those who follow them (hold constant). Such abstract reasoning is a hallmark of intelligence. Hamilton composed and sent the letter when he was twelve years old.

Rapid Development

So, the personality of an individual with high intelligence can be characterized by abstract thinking thing and faster developing mental capacities. An extreme example can make this point. John Stuart Mill (1806–1873) learned Greek at age three and read Plato with understanding at seven. At eight he studied Latin. Also at eight (sec-

Here, ENIAC, one of the first computers, is pictured with two of its designers, Eckert and Mauchly (von Neuman was a third). The advent of computers meant that intelligence—as abstract reasoning—could now be studied as a property of machines as well as human beings.

ond or third grade), he covered geometry and algebra. At age nine he was familiar with the conic sections and spherics of geometry, and had begun calculus. As he learned math, his tutors remarked that "He performed all problems without the book and most of them without any help from the book" (Cox, 1926, p. 707). He began a history of Rome, the first paragraph of which was as follows:

John Stuart Mill, the philosopher, learned Greek and Latin as a young child, and, as a schoolchild, taught himself geometry and calculus with little help from the textbooks he studied. He once remarked, "I have learned to seek my happiness by limiting my desires, rather than in attempting to satisfy them."

> *First Alban Government: Roman conquest in Italy.* We know not any part, says Dionysius of Halicarnassus, of the History of Rome till the Sicilian invasions. Before that time, the country had not been entered by any foreign invader. After the expulsion of Sicilians . . . Aeneas, son of Venus and Anchises . . . succeeded Latinus in the government, and engaged in the wars of Italy. The Rutuli, a people living near the sea, and extending along the Numicius up to the Lavinium, opposed him. However, Turnus their king was defeated and killed by Aeneas. Aeneas was killed soon after this. The war continued to be carried on chiefly against the Rutuli, to the time of Romulus, the first king of Rome. By him it was that Rome was built. (Terman, 1926, p. 795)

Mill wrote this at age six and a half, by which time he had already developed a fully mature writing style (note the flair in the last sentence). The writing shows a good ability to communicate complex concepts as well as careful qualifications of generalizations (e.g., "The war continued to be carried on *chiefly* against the Rutuli." The example illustrates the nature of accelerated intellectual development, although only a few individuals will exhibit mental development this rapid. Mill's IQ has been estimated at about 200.

Adaptation

Such mental problem solving contributes to constructing mental models of the sort examined in Chapter 5. For that reason some people say that intelligence also involves successful adaptation (Gardner, 1983; 1993; Sternberg, 1997). Wechsler, for example, emphasized adjustment and adaptation when he described intelligence as involving the understanding of how to deal effectively with the environment, and providing the "resourcefulness to cope with its challenges" (Wechsler, 1975, p. 139).

Others are less sure about intelligence and adjustment, noting that well-adapted creatures—moths and ants, for example—don't require much individual intelligence. Also, at extremely high levels at least, intelligence may distance and even isolate people from others. John Stuart Mill, whose IQ was exceedingly high, suffered a nervous

TABLE 6.5	Average IQ at Different Grade Levels, and Correlations between IQ and Grades[*]	
School Level	**Avg. IQ**	**IQ and Grades**
Elementary/Middle	82	.65
Junior High	90	.61[**]
Some High School	96	.60[**]
High School	100	.58
Some college	108	.44
College graduate	116	.50

Note: [*]Average values are reported where multiple sources were available; [**]prorated from elementary and high school values.

Sources: Conry & Plant (1965); Matarazzo (1972); Matarazzo & Herman (1984); Reynolds et al. (1987).

Disciplinary Crossroads

Valued Qualities and Social Meritocracies

Mental abilities are plainly valued by society. People with high intelligence earn more partly because they have stayed in school longer and enter occupations of higher social prestige. This led psychologist Richard Herrnstein (1971; 1973), along with sociologist Charles Murray (Herrnstein & Murray, 1994), to ask whether society was arranging people from lowest to highest in mental abilities, and rewarding them, essentially, based on those qualities. Herrnstein and Murray's several arguments were presented in a book called, *The Bell Curve,* and discussed and critiqued in a series of rejoinders (e.g., Fraser, 1995). Kaus (1992, p. 25) summarized one central argument in this way:

1. If differences in mental abilities are partly inherited, and
2. If success requires those abilities, and
3. If earnings and prestige depend on success,
4. Then social standing (which reflects earnings and prestige) will be based to some

extent on inherited differences among people.

Kaus described the political reception such an argument typically receives:

There are two strongly held opinions about Herrnstein's thesis. The first is that he is, of course, wrong. The second, privately held by many of the same people who espouse the first view in public, is that he is of course right but we should act as if he's wrong.

Controversy surrounding intelligence tests makes for exciting news stories in part because people often express their opinions on the matter strongly and because social policy is concerned with promoting innovation, which requires intelligence and creativity. The period from the mid-1970s to the 1990s saw a wide variety of stories discussing intelligence tests in the media. Many of them reported on controversial and extreme positions (often approvingly)

breakdown as a young man, perhaps because he was so different from others (e.g., Mayer et al., 2001).

The Stability of IQ

For intelligence to be expressed over the course of a person's life, it must be somewhat stable. This is the case. When IQ is measured in a group of children at age three, for example it generally correlates $r = .83$ with those same children's scores at age four (Sontag, Baker, & Nelson, 1958). After a ten-year period, it correlates between $r = .72$ to .78 with the same children's scores, and still exhibits a relationship of about $r = .60$ level after a full twenty-five years (Bradway, Tompson, & Cravens, 1958; Harnqvist, 1968; Husen, 1951).

Intelligences at School

IQ and Educational Performance

The original intelligence tests were designed to predict school learning, and those original tests, as well as present-day intelligence tests do predict such learning. The average IQ levels at different levels of schooling are shown in Table 6.5 (cf., Reynolds, Chastain, Kaufman, & McLean, 1987).

---

such as that IQ tests were invalid or that there is no reasonable evidence that IQ has an inherited component (e.g., Kamin, 1974; Lewontin, Rose, & Kamin, 1984). Such stories often obscured a general scientific consensus: in one national survey, between 80 percent to 99 percent of psychologists (depending on the specific question) believed that intelligence was well defined (as abstract reasoning), adequately measured, and had substantial genetic contributions that determine its level. These same experts also acknowledge that IQ tests may at times express cultural bias and have other limitations that need to be addressed (Synderman & Rothman, 1987).

Why—if there is agreement among experts that IQ tests have demonstrated validity (and limitations)—and if there exist other mental abilities of importance, are some people so quick to dismiss them? The very notion of differences in mental qualities among people is profoundly disquieting to many, especially if some of those differences are inherited. The United States, France, and many other nations are founded on the idea that everyone is created equal. To the extent that important attributes of personality are heritable, there may well be invisible limits on the social mobility of many people in a meritocratic society. Even if present psychological testing cannot discover these limits, the limits are there all the same (Kaus, 1992, p. 25).

Do you find this troubling? Will advances in genetics lead to greater choices on behalf of our children? If so, would you trust parents to make such genetic choices?

Mental abilities such as intelligence are just one class of personality parts; others include motives, emotions, and mental models. Although mental abilities are unquestionably important, they are far from the only important talent or characteristic that people can possess. Perhaps there are dozens, or even hundreds of valuable personality characteristics that vary from person to person. This makes it likely that everyone possesses more than a few characteristics that society considers good and will reward. The story of those further attributes also is part of the story of personality psychology.

The left-hand side of Table 6.5 indicates that the average IQ's of elementary and middle school children in one study was 82, whereas that of college graduates was 116. IQ goes up with schooling because of the influence of education, and because people with lower IQ's drop out of the educational system as time goes by. For example, high school students with IQ's less than 85 have only a 14-percent chance of graduating; those with IQs between 84 and 94 have a 54-percent chance, and those with IQ's above 115 have nearly a 90-percent chance (Matarrazzo, 1972). Overall, there is a correlation between IQ and number of years of schooling of $r = .61$ (Bajema, 1968). Within a given sample of students, the correlation between IQ and grades is generally $r = .45$ to .50 in primary and secondary school, $r = .45$ to .50 in secondary school. It rises further to $r = .60$ in high school as the material becomes more advanced (Matarazzo, 1972).

The predictions of IQ decrease slightly in the first year of college. The relationship between IQ and freshman GPA is $r = .44$; and between IQ and attending graduate and professional school is $r = .50$ (Conry & Plant, 1965; Jensen, 1980, p. 329; Matarazzo, 1972, p. 284). The reason for this is because the range of intelligence levels gradually decreases as one moves to ever more demanding levels of education. That is, only those who can best learn and compete successfully are retained. Prediction becomes increasingly difficult as only the average or above IQ individuals are left and there is less and less difference in IQ among them.

Does Emotional Intelligence Matter in School?

Emotional intelligence does correlate with academic performance, but in doing so it appears mostly to duplicate measures of cognitive intelligence. Its predictions do not rise over the predictions of academic performance that one can obtain from SAT scores (Barchard, 2003; Boyce, 2002; Lam & Kirby, 2002). One exception may be in areas in which emotional knowledge is critical to performance. For example, Marsland and Likavec (2003) studied graduate students who were training to become clinical psychologists. The new psychotherapists were evaluated for their promise by their supervisors. Their capacity to be empathic—but not their academic performance—was predicted by ability scales of emotional intelligence. Others have found that higher emotional intelligence leads to better communication and smoother relationships on the job (Lopes, Salovey, Coté, & Beers, 2005).

On-Task Behavior

People with higher mental abilities often take longer to begin certain tasks. Laboratory studies of high IQ individuals have suggested that they spend more time understanding a problem than comparison groups with lower IQs, but then take a shorter period of time in actually executing a plan. For example, a brighter person might take longer in choosing a topic for a class paper, in researching the topic, and in outlining his or her remarks. Once writing gets underway, however, he or she may work faster than others (e.g., Larkin, McDermott, Simon, & Simon, 1980; Sternberg, 1981).

Intelligences and Other Mental Abilities at Work

Intelligence tests also predict some degree of occupational success. In one study, 18,000 soldiers' IQ scores were examined in relation to the forty-eight civilian occu-

TABLE 6.6	Relations between Occupation and IQ among U.S. Enlisted Men during World War II	
Occupation	**Average IQ**	**Range of IQ**
Accountant	128	94–157
Lawyer	128	96–157
Engineer	127	100–151
Reporter	125	100–157
Teacher	122	76–155
Purchasing agent	119	82–153
Electrician	109	64–149
Butcher	103	42–147
Painter, general	98	38–147
Cook and Baker	97	20–147
Farmhand	91	24–145
Miner	91	42–139

Source: Modified and selected from Harrell & Harrell (1945).

pations they had occupied. There was a strong relation between IQ and occupational prestige, with miners, teamsters, and undertakers having IQs that were, on average, relatively lower, and accountants, teachers, and judges having IQs that were, on average, relatively higher.

The findings for several occupations are shown in Table 6.6 (Harrell & Harrell, 1945; Stewart, 1947). These results replicate earlier studies done in World War I (see, for example, Tyler, 1965, pp. 330–364). On average, occupations requiring high education and possessing high prestige have people in them who possess higher cognitive intelligences. The correlation between the rated prestige of an occupation and the average IQ of the individual within the occupation is about $r = .80$ (see Table 6.6; Matarazzo, 1972, pp. 178–180; Morris & Levinson, 1995).

That said, there are high-IQ individuals in all occupations. Even very bright people may choose not to use their gifts—or may not have the opportunity to do so due

If you're so smart, how come you ain't rich?
American saying

to low socioeconomic status. Although nonintellectual occupations often have a few high-IQ individuals in them, more mentally demanding occupations often appear altogether to discourage those with lower IQs. In fact, occupations such as lawyers and reporters seem to demand IQ's of at least around 100—as indicated by the failure to find anyone in them with lower ability levels (see Table 6.6).

General and Specific Cognitive Intelligences

General cognitive intelligence is modestly related to predicting occupational success (Ree & Earles, 1992). Specific intelligences, too, also account for important outcomes. Those high in spatial intelligence, for example, may choose (and succeed) at certain occupations others do not, including certain branches of mathematics that can benefit from spatial thinking (e.g., geometry and calculus), architecture, and other areas (Lubinski, Webb, & Morelock, 2001; Shea, Lubinski, & Benbow, 2001).

Practical Intelligence at Work

With regard to practical intelligence, studies suggest that those highest in practical intelligence are more likely to be employed in a company with greater prestige and to have higher salaries. Within an organization, those higher in practical intelligence were also more likely to have attained higher positions, and higher salaries (when age is taken into account). Those in sales have sold more (Wagner, 2000). Subsequent studies of practical knowledge have been promising, although there is some controversy concerning how much it adds to the prediction of success over and above other intelligences (Gottfredson, 2003; Sternberg, 2003).

Creativity at Work

High school students who scored high on a battery of creative ability scales had distinctive life patterns twelve years later (Torrance, 1972; cf., Runco, 1986). They often experienced relevant but unusual detours in their training and occupational paths; the more creative participants also experienced a tendency to have their careers delayed by relevant work or educational experiences. On the other hand, they ended up in innovative, distinctive occupations: writers, entertainers, and artists, but also, dog trainers, centerfielders on baseball teams, and similar less usual pursuits. Sometimes the creativity was reflected in an unusual combination of training. For example, one creative individual had obtained advanced degrees in law, economics, and history, with a life experience in social action. The study-member ended up teaching American public policy and constitutional law (Torrance, 1972, p. 79). High scorers also created more publicly recognized creative productions (e.g., poems, dances, musical pieces, scientific publications) as adults—even when the follow-up is more than twenty-three years (Torrance, 1988, p. 61).

Intelligence and Creativity Interacting at Work

In biographical studies of the creative output of scientists and artists, it appears that an individual's highly creative output is directly related to the amount of overall output. That is, the more tries that a person makes to produce something—be it sculptures, scientific articles, or musical compositions—the more likely something will be creative. Moreover, even highly creative individuals do not seem to "hit" on something creative more often; rather, they are simply more productive, and because they create so many productions, generate more creative products. Happily, creative output can occur any time in life, and there is no one period of adult life to which such creations are most likely (Simonton, 1997; 2002). At the same time, however, the highly productive individuals in the studies are identified because they have met very high standards for the quality of their work, so overall quality of work also contributes to creativity.

Mental Abilities in Relationships

People with high emotional intelligence have different relationships than others. Such individuals engage in fewer problem behaviors than others: they have a lower

> **If you have a great work in your head, nothing else thrives near it; all other thoughts are repelled, and the pleasure of life itself is for the time lost.**
>
> Goethe

risk of excessive use of alcohol and drugs, keep fewer alcoholic beverages and drugs around the home, are less likely to smoke cigarettes, and are less likely to take illegal drugs with their parents. They also exhibit a lower tendency to get into fights with others (Brackett & Mayer, 2003; Brackett, Mayer, & Warner, 2004; Formica, 1998; Rubin, 1999).

A related line of research indicates that higher emotional intelligence predicts closer and smoother interpersonal relationships—that is, as emotional intelligence rises, relationships with others become more positive. Parents with higher emotional intelligence may foster better attachment styles in their children (Marsland & Likavec, 2003). In addition, people higher in emotional intelligence exhibit closer social networks and can rely on more assistance from others. More generally, they possess the ability to regulate their own and others' emotions to make relationships smoother, and in the workplace perform better in certain on-the-job situations (Lopes, Brackett, Nezlek, Schütz, Sellin, & Salovey, 2004).

Assortive Mating: The tendency for people to marry or otherwise mate with those people who are similar to themselves in particular dimensions or traits. People exhibit assertive mating for intelligence.

Cognitive IQ also affects relationships. It turns out that IQ is related to the choice of a mate or marriage partner. **Assortive mating** refers to the tendency of people to pick marriage partners who are similar to themselves on certain observable features. It turns out that assortive mating exists for intelligence. The correlation between IQ's in spouses is $r = .50$ (Jencks, 1972, p. 272). This indicates that people with high intelligence tend to marry one another, and people of average or lower intelligence tend to marry one another as well. Marriages between one person high and one person low in intelligence are fewer than would be expected by chance.

> **Connecting Window**   *Considering Intelligence in Relation to Other Personality Variables*
>
> Certain mental models, such as those about relationships, can be formed without much conscious thought or analysis. Indeed, something like falling in love seems to be the *opposite* of employing thought or analysis. And, as Chapter 5 suggested, as long as the models are good and healthy, that may be fine. For people who repeat bad relationships, though, awareness and intelligence may help them identify the pattern and analyze it so as to change it. For more, see Chapter 5, "Models of Relationships."

Personality and Mental Abilities: The Big Picture

Intelligence, Education, and Training

No matter how smart a person is, he or she can benefit from learning what others have learned or discovered. In fact, as many understand, a fine education often can compensate for a less-than-fine intellect. This is true not only for academic skills such as learning algebra or how to parse a sentence grammatically, but also for social and emotional skills.

For example, as important as social intelligence might be to social effectiveness, there are other social skills that are simple and can be taught. When meeting someone new, for instance, is it best to be ingratiating or to be self-promoting? It pays to be ingratiating. This is true not only of social situations but even of job interviews (e.g., Godfrey, Jones, & Lord, 1986; Higgins & Judge, 2004). How to be ingratiating? One skill that might help is called partner attention. Partner attention involves

Test Yourself: Remote Associates: A Mental Ability Related to Creativity

Some Problems Like Those on a Remote Associates Test

Problem

1	BED	GARDEN	ARRANGEMENT
2	GUEST	DOG	TREE
3	PHONE	MEMBRANE	TERRORIST
4	OVER	COMPUTER	CAREFULLY
5	MEDICAL	ADMINISTRATOR	YOURSELF
6	FISH	WEIGHT	CONVERSION

Answers: 1: flower; 2: house; 3: cell; 4: drive; 5: test; 6: scale

> **I not only use all the brains I have, but all I can borrow.**
> Woodrow Wilson

partner references, questions, and continuations of topics started by the other person. There is some belief that partner attention can reduce the loneliness experienced by those with few friends, although research results are still controversial (Bell, 1985; Vandeputte et al., 1999).

Moral education, too, can enhance a person's effectiveness. For example, the educational program, "Facing History and Ourselves," involves studying historical

Artistic creativity involves coming up with types of expression that are both novel and interesting to people. Vincente Paratore, shown here in 1996 with some of his works, first paints by drawing an outline in clay and then painting the clay cutouts. He developed this technique in part as an adaptation to having lost his sight in 1986.

racial, ethnic, and religious conflicts so as to enhance understanding across groups. A recent outcome study of the program studying 346 learners in fourteen classes, along with a comparison group, indicated that the program reduced school fights for all participants, as well as racist attitudes (for women only) and promoted maturity (Schultz, Barr, & Selman, 2001).

A Broader Approach to Mental Abilities

There is little question that creativity, various intelligences, and other mental abilities predict a number of important criteria. At the same time, the measures now in use may not work for everyone. The predictions between intelligence and various criteria are excellent, for example, but such relationships might come about even if the tests worked for only, say, 75 percent of the population. The tests might be less valid for some set of individuals who have a different approach to thinking not readily tapped by the tests. Those people might be either especially creative, or come from a different culture, or possess other idiosyncratic or as-of-yet unknown qualities.

Consistent with this idea, there has been a gradual broadening of the types of mental abilities studied. Whereas work early in the twentieth century focused on cognitive intelligence, now attention has turned to hot mental abilities of the social and emotional variety, as well as to creativity. Many mental abilities: those specifically related to music, art, and, perhaps, sports activities, and even spirituality were not dealt with here because the focus is on the best-understood abilities. It is likely that a better understanding of these other talents, as well as the discovery of further mental abilities, will continue into the future. Thus, some final broader accounting of intelligence and mental ability is still to be made. What is known already, however, is that the personality system can draw on many mental abilities to achieve its goals.

Reviewing Chapter 6

Mental abilities including the intelligences and creativities are important to personality. Such abilities contribute to planning, to understanding one's mental models of the self, world, and relationships (examined in the last chapter). Moreover, society values and rewards those who have certain mental abilities.

The aim of this chapter is to help you understand what mental abilities are, what kinds of mental abilities there are, how they are related, and what they predict. The kinds of intelligence vary from verbal-propositional intelligence to emotional intelligence. The concept of general intelligence, or g, comprises at least some of these abilities. Personality calls on those mental abilities in performing its tasks. Each intelligence predicts impor-tant life outcomes, from school performance and occupational prestige to better social relations.

What Is a Mental Ability?

1. Mental Ability Itself.
What is a mental ability and how does it differ from a motivational or emotional trait?

2. Mental Ability and Society.
Sir Frances Galton, in England, and Alfred Binet, in France, were both interested in studying intelligence. How were their approaches similar, and how were they different? What social pressures led to the study of mental abilities?

What Are Some Major Mental Abilities?

3. The Major Cognitive Intelligences.
The early Binet scale asked a lot of questions that depended upon a good understanding of the language, and often asked about words and language. What intelligence was it said to measure as a consequence? Wechsler was faced with an immigrant population in New York, not all of whom were fluent in English. What intelligence did he measure to correct for such difficulties in language? Another cognitive intelligence, spatial intelligence, was first proposed to exist early in the century. How did Roger Shepard and his colleagues measure it?

4. Mental Development and the IQ Score.
One of the key aspects of mental capacity is that it develops with age at least through childhood. Which intelligence researcher developed that insight—perhaps, in part, through observing his own daughters? How does rate IQ capture the idea of mental development? Deviation IQ's are not calculated according to rate of development, but do they reflect rate of development anyway? If so, how?

Are There Additional Intelligences and Mental Abilities?

5. Social Abilities.
In the 1920s, some psychologists began to study social intelligence. Unfortunately, it was difficult to distinguish from verbal intelligence and was heavily criticized; work in the area languished. What is the present status of this intelligence?

6. Practical Intelligence.
Another kind of intelligence is practical intelligence. What does that measure? It is based on implicit-tacit knowledge. Can you define what sort of knowledge that is?

7. Emotional Intelligence.
In the 1990s, other psychologists studied emotional intelligence. Considerable evidence has been obtained reflecting the existence of the ability. What are some sample tasks that measure emotional intelligence?

8. How Is Creativity Measured?
Creativity involves the capacity to come up with novel solutions to problems. One mental ability related to creativity involves verbal fluency—the ability to come up with words to fit a given requirement, such as rhymes to a word like "clang." What other ways are there of measuring creativity?

9. The Theory of g.
Charles Spearman suggested that there existed one general intelligence that contributed to all the other intelligences. His theory of g was based on what observation about the correlation among mental abilities?

What Is the Relation between Personality and Intelligence?

10. Personality Draws on Mental Abilities.
Personality draws on mental abilities to get its work done. These abilities seem to be greater in human beings than in other animals. Intellectual capacity seems to rise across animal species, with increases of brain size. This has led researchers to try to connect brain size and intelligence. Are there, in fact, any genetic bases for intelligence?

11. The Relations between Mental Ability Traits and Other Traits.
As it turns out, most motivational and emotional traits—such as extraversion and neuroticism—are unrelated to intellect-related traits. There are, however, some exceptions. For example, empathy is related to emotional intelligence. What traits relate to creativity, and what to cognitive intelligences? Creativity is also associated with alterations of consciousness and mood swings. Though creativity is itself a healthy process, what mental disorders may unusual conscious experiences and mood swings be related to?

12. Personality, Mental Abilities, and the Construction of Mental Models.
Evidence exists that there are environmental influences on intelligence. For example, what happened to immigrant groups after a few generations in the United States? Schooling influences intelligence as well. How does a year in school affect IQ? Fluid intelligence involves pure, abstract reasoning. What is crystallized intelligence and how does it relate to mental models?

How Does Personality Express Its Abilities?

13. Intelligence and the Expression of Thought. Nearly everyone carries out concrete thinking, recording times, objects, and events. A central characteristic of higher intelligence, however, is abstract reasoning. Can you say what abstract reasoning involves? What other characteristics of intelligence were commonly mentioned?

14. Intelligences at School. Cognitive intelligences are highly predictive of school performance. The relationships are expressed as correlations between intelligence tests and various criteria. What are some of the educational outcomes that intelligence predicts, and what are the general levels of those predictions?

15. Mental Abilities at Work. Although intelligence tests were not developed to measure occupational performance, such relationships do exist. One of the most striking concerns the relationship between the average IQ of people in an occupation, and the prestige of the occupation. Do you know what this relationship is? What are some other relationships between mental abilities and occupational status? How does practical intelligence relate to work performance? People with higher creativity produce more creative products—books, poems, and scientific studies. Creativity alters an individual's career path. Can you say how?

16. Mental Abilities in Relationships. Emotional intelligence predicts academic success, but often not much better than cognitive intelligence. When it comes to relationships, however, emotional intelligence appears to predict a variety of outcomes. What is the relationship between emotional intelligence and connectedness? What does it predict about problem behaviors?

17. The Scope of Mental Abilities. As the measures of mental abilities broaden, it is more likely that people's abilities will be measured and that the tests will become fairer. What other limitations or strengths of intelligence measurement are there?

Chapter 7

The Conscious Self

The conscious self is one of the most mysterious parts of personality. Sometimes equated with a soul or a "ghost in the machine," it is a considerable challenge to scientists. What is consciousness? Can a person exercise free will? Might there exist other, hidden, parts of personality that temporarily exert control over an individual? What does it mean to have an authentic conscious self?

- ### What Is the Conscious Self?
  What does it mean to say that a person is a conscious, willful being? What is the individual's innermost "I"? These ideas refer to a self that has both subjective awareness and the power to influence events.

- ### What Does It Mean for the Self to Be Conscious?
  What is the nature of consciousness? How is consciousness explained—and how do scientists try to deal with something they cannot fully explain?

- ### Does the Self Possess Free Will?
  Can a person decide to act entirely on his or her own, apart from prior influences and events? If so, does that contradict the basic tenets of science? What is the difference between a person's voluntary and involuntary action (if any) and how is that related to free will?

- ### Are There Alternatives to the Conscious Self?
  The conscious self can be considered part of a broader collection of personality "agencies." Agencies are sub-personalities that are hypothesized to act in place of the conscious self—such as the id and superego. But do such agencies as these really exist?

- ### How Is the Conscious Self Expressed?
  We will examine some individual differences in conscious selves regarding how consciousness is structured and levels of awareness.

What Is the Conscious Self?

The Appearance of the Conscious Self

The French artist Paul Gauguin (1848–1903) possessed what has been described as an independent and highly self-conscious personality (Rapetti, 1996, p. 187). He purposively cultivated an image as an untamed artist, a personal quality he attributed to his mother's influence. His mother had been characterized as egocentric and involved in ceaseless traveling.

Gauguin's family fled France for South America during political turmoil in 1848. His father died during the voyage, and the young painter's early years were spent in relative luxury at an uncle's estate in Lima, Peru. His mother and he then returned to France, where he took a job as a stockbroker. In 1873 he married Mette-Sophje Gad, a young Danish woman, and they had five children together.

During this time, Gauguin was increasingly attracted to the art world and began to paint. His paintings were attracting increasingly positive attention. The stock market crashed in 1882, and he lost his job at the brokerage. In a period of conscious self-reflection, he committed himself to "paint every day" (Gauguin, 1998, p. 147). He moved his family to Copenhagen but neither he nor his paintings were well received in Denmark. Struggles with his in-laws contributed to strains with his wife, and his marriage deteriorated. He returned to France alone except for one son. He now escalated his commitments, self-consciously determining to sacrifice everything for his art.

During the Autumn of 1890, despite poor health, Gauguin made one of the most important decisions of his life: he would sail to Tahiti, to learn from and to be inspired by the art forms there. True to his guiding lights, he left friends and remaining family contacts behind. He sold off his paintings to raise money for the voyage and arrived in Tahiti in 1891. This was followed by a second longer visit during which his favorite daughter died and he broke off communication decisively with his wife (Gowing, 1995, p. 236). Tahiti had proven to be a bit of a disappointment in terms of its nature and art, and so he had brought some native art forms from China, Japan, and elsewhere, to fill in the gaps. His paintings matured during this time. They become more colorful and more representative of an island paradise—a paradise, perhaps, more of his imagination than reality. These later paintings firmly established his international reputation as an artist through to the present. He died of illness at age fifty-five.

Reflecting the outline of Gauguin's life, we might wonder about the self-conscious series of decisions he made about his art: how and why did he decide, in young adulthood, to paint every day? We might further contemplate his similar decisions to leave his wife and several children in Copenhagen, to return first to France and, most famously, to travel to Tahiti to paint.

As psychologists interested in the self, some of the striking facets of Gauguin's life included his acutely conscious sense of his own life and of the role art played within it. His life decisions about painting illustrate what people often mean when they speak of free will. Here, it seems, is a person making his own decisions, almost regardless of the consequences. Moreover, Gauguin's decisions seem, at least, to be related to his growth as a person and an artist.

Philosophers have used Gauguin's life decisions as a jumping-off point to consider whether they represented a moral way to live—in the sense of creating the greater good for the greatest number of people (e.g., Williams, 1993; Statman, 1993). It is hard to draw a general rule from his decisions; did he commit to a life of art because he was convinced he was a great artist? In such a case, would any person with, perhaps, an inflated self-image feel entitled to decide similarly? Should Gauguin have consulted professors of art to see if his decision was warranted? (Williams, 1993, p. 39). Part of what the philosophers conclude is that Gauguin could not know how matters would turn out. In essence, he was rather lucky.

In this chapter we will examine the aware self, its consciousness, and its self-control. We will inquire as to the role that the conscious self plays in an individual's personality and broader life.

James's Self-as-Knower

Self-as-Knower: According to William James, a person's innermost aware identity. It watches with consciousness, and exerts will where useful.

The seat of conscious awareness in personality has been variously referred to simply as consciousness, or as the ego, or as a **self-as-knower**. The self-as-knower, according to William James, was that part of you that observed and had awareness of what was going on in the mind (James, 1892). To fully imagine it, James suggested a thought experiment. Imagine losing parts of your body, he said, your legs, your trunk, arms, and then imagine losing your hearing, your sight, all those parts of you that you could lose and still be yourself. Now imagine losing some memories, such as what you ate for breakfast this morning. The part that was left after everything else had

Consciousness is the perception of what passes in a man's own mind.

John Locke

been taken away was the self-as-knower. It is you—your awareness—in the purest sense.

This conscious self consists of the personal sense of observing and awareness. It is the innermost citadel of the person (James, 1892). It possesses a special, personal, familiar quality that no one else's consciousness has. The conscious self can be distinguished from the models of the self we discussed in Chapter 5. Whereas a model of oneself might contain a list of attributes, such as strong-willed, obstinate, introverted and conscientious, the conscious self is something inside that looks at that mental model, that is aware of what is going on inside. One might change one's model of oneself, deciding on a more downbeat day that one is more careless than conscientious, but one cannot change one's innermost awareness; it is always one's own.

James's self-as-knower had two central, internal qualities: consciousness and will. Both are controversial. What, after all, can we say about consciousness? Is there a way to break that down into its parts?

Freud's Concept of the Ego

Ego: That portion of the mind that includes a conscious sense of self and capable of rational thought and self-control. Although originally a psychodynamic concept, the term is now used in a number of theoretical orientations.

Freud, too, had an idea of a conscious self—although only partially conscious. Freud's name for it was the **ego**. The ego begins development near the body homunculus. This body homunculous is the brain area that controls the fingers, the legs, the arms, and so forth. It resides in the cerebral cortex, and from it project neural pathways to the rest of the body. Freud imagined his self as growing out of this brain representation of the outside, acting self—a not too far-fetched idea from an evolutionary standpoint. This is also why one of the central ideas of the ego was that it controlled access to the outside world. It did so by controlling the various parts of the body.

The ego is primarily able to judge and reason. It learns rationality and reasoning from its trial-and-error experience with the outside world. Of importance here as well, it contains consciousness, which Freud defines as a sense organ for the inside of the mind. As Freud put it:

> We have formed the idea that in each individual there is a coherent organization of mental processes; and we call this his *ego*. It is to this ego that consciousness is attached; the ego controls the approaches to motility—that is, to the discharge of excitations into the external world; it is the mental agency which supervises all its own consitutent processes, and which goes to sleep at night, though even then it exercises the censorship on dreams. (Freud, 1923/1960, p. 7)

Dialogical Self: A type of consciousness that switches between one's model of one's own self and mental models of other people. As the dialogical self switches its focus to models of oneself or others, it animates the given model, bringing it imaginatively to life as if the person were there, talking or acting.

Although the ego contains this conscious, acting self, some of its rationality and planning is also unconscious. Indeed, the ego helps enlarge the unconscious by repressing material that is unpleasant to it (Freud, 1923/1960, p. 7).

The Dialogical Self

A rather different perspective on the conscious self is Hermans and colleagues' recently-proposed **dialogical self**. This is a version of a normal person's self-as-agency, but instead of one stable, organized self, the dialogical self shifts around the person, inhabiting and breathing action and perspective into other fictional entities (Hermans, Kempen, & Van Loon, 1992). For example, if you have an imaginary conversation with your father, the dialogical self is first you, then your father, and then you again, and so on. This self-model provides a more flexible view of the traditional self-as-knower. The knower not only knows oneself, but also the imagined character of many others. In some ways, the dialogical self occupies a kind of gray area between the traditional self-as-knower and nonconscious parts of one's self that may also participate in controlling the mind.

To the modern theorist concerned with the self-as-knower, the exciting thing about the self is that it is the part of the person that can exert control over the rest of the person to change it according to its hopes and dreams. It is the part of personality that decides among careers of doctor, lawyer, or chief. Should some people be cast by disposition and environment into the dark boundary between mental health and madness, or between goodness and evil, it is the self which can at some point marshall itself to choose between the two (e.g., Epstein, 1972; James, 1892).

What Does It Mean for the Self to Be Conscious?

What Is Consciousness?

What Does the Word Consciousness *Mean?*

What does it mean for the self to be conscious? The origins of the word *consciousness* can provide some insight into what the term means. The term consciousness originates from the Latin *conscientia*, which refers to the mutual understanding or joint knowledge of a number of people who are engaged in a common goal or plan. For example, two people plotting a coup d'etat would share conscientia, as would two people plotting a surprise birthday party (Baruss, 1986–7; Natsoulas, 1986–7).

It is only a short jump from shared knowledge between people to shared knowledge within a person. Perhaps the idea of sharing knowledge with yourself seems odd, but what about when you talk to yourself? In such an instance, one part of the individual is sharing information with the other. Who is doing the talking? The listening? This interaction between two parts of the self seems quite a bit closer to the idea of consciousness because the listener must be aware of what the talker is saying, and such awareness seems close to consciousness (Hilgard, 1977).

What Is Consciousness?

Self-Awareness: A type of awareness, in which the topic, or subject, of awareness is awareness itself; that is, reflective awareness.

Access to Information: In the study of consciousness, the state in which conscious awareness can obtain information, retrieve it, or attend to it, as opposed to being blocked off from information.

Many philosophers of mind divide what we mean today by consciousness into three aspects: self-awareness, access to information, and subjective experience (Block, 1995; Jackendoff, 1987; Pinker, 1997, pp. 134–148). By **self-awareness** is meant reflective awareness rather than simple awareness—that is, awareness that reflects on itself. One psychologist describes self-awareness as involving a realization like: "Not only can I feel pain and see red, I can think to myself, 'Hey, here I am, Steve Pinker feeling pain and seeing red!' " (Pinker, 1997, p. 134).

A second sense of consciousness is to have **access to information**. For example, if you tell me what is on your mind right now it might include your current worries, your delights, and your plans for the day. It would not include the internal flows of your neurotransmitters, the patterns of neural firings in your brain, or even the relative activation of various concepts in memory. You have access to some material of the mind; but no access to neural-level activities (Dennett, 1978, pp. 150–160).

One aspect of this access to information is that consciousness puts some ideas under the spotlight of attention. One of the important adaptive features of consciousness is probably to focus attention selectively on important matters. Think of the mind as perpetually engaged in trade-offs in taking in and attending to the world. It can either do a lot of things poorly, or a few things very well. Consciousness provides a working area in which a few things can be thought about well—or at least as well as possible.

Consciousness seems critical to providing comprehensive information processing. When something is in our consciousness, we can think relatively clearly about it, define it in detail, and give it the thought it deserves. Matters outside consciousness, by contrast, will be unglued, floating, and in the periphery. It is peripheral processing that leads to common cognitive errors—seeing "World's Worst Coffee" on a sign, when in fact, it reads, "World's Best Coffee," or seeing "Brothel Hotel," instead of "Brother's Hotel" (Pinker, 1997, p. 142). When we are surprised by seeing such signs, we attend to them, and consciousness resolves the problem (Duncan & Humphreys, 1989; Marcel, 1983).

Many theorists of consciousness suggest that it serves an adaptive, evolutionary purpose. Its role in survival is to place the really hard problems in life on center stage and to subject them to scrutiny, so as to be able to respond in a flexible way to the issues those problems have raised (Baars & McGovern, 1994; Ornstein, 1986; 1991; Rozin, 1976). Consciousness, in other words, is the part of the self that operates so that, when your mental models fail and you need to revise them, you can gather your attention, caring, and thought to converge on the issue and come up with a better way of operating.

Sentience: A state of being someone, of possessing internal, subjective experience.

But the core essence of consciousness for Pinker (and others) is **sentience**. Sentience refers to the internal, subjective experience: that feeling of what it is like to be someone (Pinker, 1997). This feeling of consciousness includes an awareness of a rich field of sensation coupled with a direct sense of personal ownership of that field, in the midst of which is the spotlight of attention. Often accompanying consciousness is a sense of the possibility of being able to act on the things that are attended to.

Awareness of a rich field of sensation refers to the fact that consciousness links things together. It integrates together sounds, sights, and ideas, so that one sees a tree blowing in the wind rather than fragments of sensations. Moreover, consciousness moves from idea to idea, so that William James referred to it as like stream (James, 1892; Singer, 1975). One of the central things it integrates is a feeling of self-hood. There is something warm and personal about our own stream of consciousness, and something ultimately impersonal about the streams of consciousness of others. Our own stream of consciousness provides us with our own personal eyes on ourselves and the world. It is comfortable, cozy, and ours alone. True, when we go to sleep it goes away, but when we wake up, it always returns to us rather than to someone else (James, 1892).

Scientific Accounting for the Feeling of Consciousness

Consider the following thought experiment. You are seated in a chamber while your brain is being scanned. The experimenter presents you with cards of different colors.

Each time she shows you a blue-colored card a particular part of your brain, which is imaged on the computer monitor, lights up. That, she says, pointing to the illuminated part of your brain on the monitor, is your consciousness of the color blue. "But no," you say, "that is just a part of my brain being activated when my eyes register blue, it does not convey my conscious feeling of blue!" (Flanagan, 2002).

Where does this feeling of conscious subjective sentience come from? How can this internal subject "blueness" be explained? For the **subjective realist**, it comes from being hooked up to one's own neurons. **Subjective realism** provides a philosophical integration of the objective scientific understanding of consciousness as it exists thus far, and the subjective experience of consciousness. The perspective of subjective realism assumes that all mental events—including subjective states—are caused by some set of physical events or another. At the same time, many objectively real objects in the world also have a subjective, mental quality of feeling to them (Flanagan, 2002, p. 89).

Water would be H_2O whether a person was there to witness it or not; it objectively exists. The wetness of water, however, also has a subjective feel that can only be realized by experiencing it through being "hooked up" to the human nervous system, and touching water through it. Subjective realism states that people have certain subjective feelings—including consciousness—that reflect what it is like to be hooked up to a human nervous system operating in a particular fashion, such as being awake, alert, and perceiving something (Flanagan, 2002, p. 89). Some day science may develop a better language for how the subjective experience of blue emerges from being hooked up to the nervous system. For now, say the subjective realists, this is the best that can be said (p. 87).

Subjective Realism: A school of philosophy according to which the subjective experience of consciousness is real and is generated by the physical and mental organism that experiences consciousness.

Is Consciousness of Recent Origin?

It is not entirely clear when the concept of consciousness first emerged in the West. Early biblical and Greek writings appear to ignore the concept of consciousness. The fact that early records have so few mentions of consciousness has led some scholars to question whether or not consciousness, as we currently understand and perceive it, is of relatively recent origin in the evolution of the human mind. Julian Jaynes (1976) suggested the radical hypothesis that people were not fully conscious, in the modern sense of the word, until consciousness evolved some time between the eighth and second centuries BCE. Before that there was little sense of identity, and people often mistook their inner voices for other people, or even gods. He traces the emergence of consciousness in various literatures. For example, Amos is one of the earliest books of biblical literature, dating to the eighth century BCE. (Jaynes, 1976, p. 295). The book of Amos includes no mention of a mind, or of thinking or thoughts, or of feeling, or of understanding. Amos describes himself minimally, as a shepherd, a "gatherer of sycamore fruit." Nor, in a sense, does Amos even speak. He pronounces, and after each pronouncement announces, "Thus speaks the Lord!" (Jaynes, 1976, p. 296). Amaziah, the priest of Bethel, reported that Amos was raising a conspiracy against Israel. Amaziah tells Amos directly to leave the land: "Get out, you seer! Go back to the land of Judah." In response, Amos answers in the third person, saying he is acting on the basis of another's commands:

I was neither a prophet nor a prophet's son, but I was a shepherd, and I also took care of sycamore-fig trees. But the Lord took me from tending the flock and said to me, "Go, prophesy to my people Israel." Now then, hear the word of the LORD. (Amos 7:10–12)

There is little sense of personal awareness in this passage and others like it. By contrast, in the book of Ecclesiastes, dating from the second century BCE, we see personality in all of its introspective grandeur. The author of Ecclesiastes wants to share his knowledge and teach it to others (Kushner, 1986, p. 36):

> I thought to myself, "Look, I have grown and increased in wisdom more than anyone who has ruled over Jerusalem before me; I have experienced much of wisdom and knowledge." Then I applied myself to the understanding of wisdom, and also of madness and folly, but I learned that this, too, is a chasing after the wind. For with much wisdom comes much sorrow; the more knowledge, the more grief.
>   I thought in my heart, "Come now, I will test you with pleasure to find out what is good." But that also proved to be meaningless . . . I wanted to see what was worthwhile for men to do under heaven during the few days of their lives. (Ecclesiastes 2:1–3)

The contrast between the eighth-century BCE Amos and the second-century Ecclesiastes could not be more striking. Here, finally, is a modern-seeming personality talking to us. This same transition to consciousness appears in the literary works of the ancient Greeks, and of other peoples of the Middle East, the Mediterranean, and elsewhere (e.g., Jaynes, 1976, p. 74).

Since Jaynes's time, others have reported a waxing and waning of the sense of self. Some social psychologists have suggested, for example, that people's identities were so fixed in the middle ages that self-definition and self-conception was minimized. Identity only became an important problem with the onset of more modern social mobility in which people needed to make decisions (Baumeister, 1987).

The Brain and Consciousness

Bicameral Mind: A descriptor of the human mind, bicameral refers to the fact that the mind is dependent upon the right and left hemispheres of the brain, which do things in different ways and may not be fully integrated, even in the recent past. In the early bicameral mind, according to Julian Jaynes, before about 300 BCE, people did not realize that one part of the brain (speech production) can talk internally to the other (speech reception). As such, this internal speech was misinterpreted as coming from sources outside the individual, such as gods and apparitions.

Several theories have been proposed about how the brain generates conscious awareness. The bicameral theory of mind is one such idea. The **bicameral mind** refers to the fact that speech production and reception are split across the right and left hemispheres of the brain. It envisions a mind based on two working areas of the brain that may only sometimes be in communication with each other. Wernicke's area is a left-hemisphere structure responsible for understanding the meaning of speech. Some believe there evolved a parallel area in the right hemisphere which was responsible for hearing interior voices and understanding them. Jaynes, who proposed this theory, believes that sometime after 800 BCE, people began to understand that voices from the right hemisphere were their own thinking processes "talking to them." Before that, however, they had hallucinated the voices of gods. It was this interior talking that evolved into present-day consciousness (Jaynes, 1979, chap. 5). Although Jaynes's tracing of the change in perspective in literature is provocative, relatively little attention has been afforded his brain theory. Rather, contemporary psychobiologists have developed their own ideas.

Crick and Koch (1995), for example, have suggested that in looking for consciousness, one should seek areas of the brain that only operate when the organism is awake and alert. Beyond that, they suggest, one hallmark of consciousness is that

Neural transmissions just
seem like the wrong kind of
materials with which to bring
consciousness into the world.

Colin McGinn

it integrates material. Therefore, one should look for synchronized neural firing from many parts of the brain. Several neuropsychologists have suggested such holistic patterns for consciousness (e.g., Meade, 1999; Pribram, 1978). Kosslyn and Koenig (1992) use a simple and resonant metaphor, describing consciousness as a chord being struck by all the individual brain activities (individual notes) sounding at a given moment.

Brain scanning techniques have allowed for a few pieces of information about the brain and consciousness. First, the brain must be active for subjective reports of consciousness to be present. This is important because it establishes a brain-consciousness link. Second, areas of the cortex need to be active for consciousness, particularly the frontal lobes. Beyond that, the support system for consciousness seems to involve much of the nervous system, including, potentially, the limbic system, certain areas of the visual cortex, and even nerves from the skin, joints, and gut. This is not an integrated answer yet, but advances in this area are occurring so quickly that much more may be known in a few years (Carter, 2002, pp. 105–106; Gazzaniga & Heatherton, 2003, p. 269).

Consciousness involves more than just watching, of course, it also appears to exert will (Pinker, 1997, p. 135).

Does the Self Possess Free Will?

The Appearance of Will

One of the most important things we use consciousness for is to make decisions. To be sure, we make "decisions" every day that are not conscious. We may put on our socks without thinking, and turn toward the doorway to go outside with little conscious reflection at all. Important decisions, however, often require conscious attention. William James described several types of decisions, roughly according to the degree that **will** is involved. Will is the self-conscious exertion of mental effort to perform an act (James, 1892, pp. 429–433).

Will: That part of the mind
that exerts conscious,
intentional, control over
thoughts and actions.

In easy decisions requiring little will, we may recognize that one alternative is simply much better than the other according to one or more criteria. Choosing a job for which we know we can do the work, will be paid more, will receive more respect, will be convenient to travel to, and meets the needs of our family, requires little consideration. In a second kind of decision (according to James) outside pressures are present and we don't much mind, and go with whatever is desired. For example, if our friend strongly prefers to eat out, well . . . why not?

In another of James's decision types, however, the person's will is strongly experienced. In this type of decision, the alternatives are kept firmly in mind as we consider the possible outcomes. We recognize that we are having difficulty deciding, perhaps because we know that making the decision will require a price to pay, although "it may be better for the long run."

> . . . it is a desolate and acrid sort of act, an entrance into a lonesome moral wilderness . . . here both alternatives are steadily held in view, and in the very act of murdering the vanquished possibility the chooser realizes how much

John Calvin, a strict religious determinist, wrote, "God preordained, for his own glory and the display of His attributes of mercy and justice, a part of the human race, without any merit of their own, to eternal salvation, and another part, in just punishment of their sin, to eternal damnation." At least some psychologists share one aspect of this belief, called determinism: *that all behavior is causally determined by what has come before, and that the individual cannot and does not exercise free will.*

Free Will: The idea that people can exercise self-control in a fashion at least partly independent from any causal influences, and stemming from their own independent judgment.

Determinism: The belief that all action in the universe, including human action, has already been set in motion at the beginning of time, with each event caused by the events that have come before, and, as consequence, that all human behavior is preordained.

in that instant he is making himself lose . . . [T]he sense of inward effort with which the act is accompanied . . . makes of it an altogether peculiar sort of mental phenomenon. (James, 1892, p. 433)

James (1892) acknowledged that the existence of free will could not be proven, but the subjective experience of free will, he noted, certainly existed in those difficult decisions.

The Free Will–Determinism Debate

The idea of **free will** in its purest form says that there exists a part of mental life that is itself a "prime mover," entirely unconstrained and able to choose whatever seems best to itself (Flanagan, 2002, p. 103). The free will concept was stated clearly by the philosopher Descartes (1596–1650) who argued that there existed, in each person, a soul that belonged to a spiritual rather than material world, and that could cause the person to do things. This soul and its free will were independent of any pressures that the body (including the brain) might place on it. The will existed, instead, on a spiritual level (Descartes, 1641/1968, Fourth Meditation, p. 137).

The concept of **determinism** is often placed in contrast to the idea of free will. Strict determinism is the belief that everything in the universe is caused by something—or some set of things—that came before it. It, too, had religious origins. John Calvin was a sixteenth-century French theologian who believed that God is eternal and choses each human being's fate before the creation of the world. So, some Calvinists were saved and some not—from before the universe began, rather than by their own good deeds. The original Calvinists, it is often said, monitored their own behavior quite closely to find out what had been decided earlier.

The debate went on. Jacobus Arminius, a sixteenth-century Dutch theologian, disputed Calvin by arguing that people exercised free will and could determine their own salvation if they were sufficiently faithful to Christianity and its teachings. (More on the origins of the concept of free will in Western religious thought is found in the Disciplinary Crossroads box.)

Scientists in general, and personality psychologists in particular, are similarly split over free will versus determinism. Most scientists profess to believe in determinism, probably because this initially appeared more scientifically supportable. Both Sigmund Freud, the founder of psychodynamic theory, and Carl Rogers, an eminent humanistic psychologist, professed strict determinism (Freud, 1920; 1943, p. 27; Rogers, 1957; 1989, pp. 417–418). On the other hand, Henry Murray, who studied motives, not only believed in free will but viewed those scientists who wished to deny it as dangerously imperiling the future of humanity. The idea that one can "pull oneself up by the bootstraps" or "exercise independent judgment," or "better oneself" are traditional values that depend on the idea that people exercise some free will. See his strong-willed remarks in the Inside the Field box on page 255.

Disciplinary Crossroads

The Idea of Free Will: Origins in Western Religious Thought

The many religious and philosophical traditions of the world are split on the issue of whether free will exists. One example from a Western religious tradition can serve here. The original view of a human being in the Hebrew Bible was that he or she was a single, unified being. Spirit contributed life energy to the body and body and spirit function together as a single entity.

> The biblical conception . . . views the soul as part of the psychophysical unity of man, who, by his very nature, is composed of a body and a soul. As such, the Bible . . . sees in man only his tangible body and views the soul simply as that element that imparts to the body its vitality. (Elior, 1987, p. 889)

As religious thought evolved, however, a somewhat more complex view of human nature emerged. For one thing, humanity was created in the creator's image and in some instances, the creator seemed conflicted. Steinsaltz (1987) points out that the first incident of soul-searching took place on a grand scale by the creator, who experiences in turn regret, repentance, and an attempt at correcting a problem. That is, from Genesis 6:5–6:7:

> The Lord saw how great was man's wickedness on earth, and how every plan devised by his mind was nothing but evil all the time. And the Lord regretted that He had made man on earth, and His heart was saddened. The Lord said, "I will blot out from the earth the men whom I created . . . for I regret that I made them."

Over time, both the Jewish and Christian view of the soul was that it was full of conflict.

For one thing, there existed within the soul (according to many but not all branches of Jewish and Christian religion) a struggle between good and evil, reflecting, perhaps, the mysticism of the Gnostics (Elior, 1987, p. 895). The Gnostics were a group of early religionists who saw the world in the light of an eternal struggle between good and evil. This struggle took place in part in one's own soul.

By the time of the enlightenment, the discovery of hypnosis and of multiple personalities made the everyday populace sensitive to the fact that the mind was divided in multiple fashions. This belief was reinforced by the recognition that the mind could be divided in many parts. (Modern versions of such divisions are represented each time we divide one part of personality from another in the "Parts" section of this book. Such divisions are also treated in Chapter 8 dealing with personality structure.)

The idea of free will was generally assigned to consciousness, and most philosophies held that at least some of the outcome of an individual's personality was a product of free will.

One difference of opinion was represented in the doctrine of Calvinism. In Calvinism, a branch of Christianity, religious doctrine holds that people's fates—including whether they go to heaven or hell—are all determined before they are born. No one, including the individual person, knows how a given life will turn out ahead of time; only God knows that, and God made the choice for the individual before the world was created. Therefore, people learn whether or not they will end up in heaven, which is predetermined, by watching their own actions.

The Calvinists find allies in certain scientific circles in which strict determinism is professed. Other scientists, however, try to make room for free will.

Jacob Arminius, who believed in free will, argued against Calvin's doctrine. He contended that people could exercise independent judgment, and that those who chose well would be rewarded by God. Many psychologists, too, share an aspect of this belief, called free will: *that people can make their own choices and determine their futures independent of what has come before.*

Finally, in a manner calculated to spin philosophers in their graves, Abraham Maslow, a humanistic psychologist, viewed free will as an individual differences variable that some people possessed and others did not (Maslow, 1970, pp. 161–162).

Although the physical and biological sciences may have appeared to rely on strict determinism early in the twentieth century, by mid-century, matters were not so clear. In physics, Heisenberg's Uncertainty Principle states that you cannot measure a subatomic particle accurately enough to know both its position and velocity at the same time: they are, effectively, undetermined (Hawking, 1998). Biophysicists have suggested that there is a kind of "trickle up" of indeterminacy from the subatomic level to the level of consciousness and free will. (The Disciplinary Crosswords box on the biophysics of free will describes some of this thinking.)

With no easy solution to the free will–determinism debate in sight, some philosophers of psychology, and psychologists, have suggested it is posed in the wrong terms. These theorists suggest a switch to a more modest problem that is both closer to what the average person means by free will and easier to address as both a philosophical and empirical problem. Free will, as Descartes and others described it—as a prime mover of the person unmoved by one's own learning or genes—is viewed as a naïve statement of what people believe. What most people mean by free will is a much more limited form of free action. Free will versus determinism is replaced, in this approach, by a distinction between voluntary versus involuntary action. Voluntary action, it is argued, still permits us to have the opportunity to improve ourselves and our world, and to experience the sense of accomplishment and self-respect such improvements will bring. At the same time, it acknowledges that much about the universe and people is determined (Flanagan, 2002, p. 103).

Freedom from the Free Will Debate

According to this position, most people do not mean "free will"—in Descartes's sense—when they say they believe in free will. That is, most people don't claim to be prime causes, uninfluenced by anything in one's history or genes. Rather, what a person believes in when he or she claims to have free will is the possibility of voluntary action, and along with it, self-control, self-expression, individuality, and the ability to rationally deliberate and be morally accountable. These qualities are probably better called something like *voluntary action* rather than free will. A more meaningful distinction can be drawn between voluntary and involuntary action (Flanagan, 2002, pp. 143–144).

Voluntary Cause and Control

A voluntary movement can be said to take place when a person causes it. (Note, unlike the case of free will, the person causing the voluntary action may be prompted to

Disciplinary Crossroads

Is There a Biophysics of Free Will?

Many personality psychologists believe in free will, or at least voluntary action. If people have free will, then studying personality psychology can help people enhance their futures by making the right choices. But how could such a thing as free will exist? Scientists, after all, believe in control and prediction; they believe in a world that is at least in part like a machine, in which one part moves in response to the next. How do you build free will into such a system? Several answers have been given. Most of these identify free will with consciousness. This is because it is through consciousness that we have the experience of exerting control over ourselves.

Here is one account of how free will might operate:

First, consciousness (like much other thought) may depend on neuronal synapses that are so small that they may fit the physicist's definition of "undetermined." To understand this argument, one must have some idea of the Heisenberg uncertainty principle.

Physicists can plausibly argue for deterministic influences in machines that exist at everyday, readily observed levels: levers, motors, and gears, for example. Strict determinism, however, seems to break down at the subatomic level of observation. At this level, one can either know exactly where something is, or exactly where it is moving, but it is not possible to know both. Moreover, such limits to knowledge are not due to limitations in measurement, but are due to the physical system itself.

Returning to mental functioning, the gap between neurons—the synaptic gap—may be small enough, some argue, as to involve some features that are undetermined in Heisenberg's sense. Theorists like Pelletier (1985) believe that activities at the synaptic gap, because they are so small, may be influenced by subatomic influences. He believes that "these potentials can be influenced by infinitesimal amounts of energy on the order of quantum events" (p. 134).

This explanation might be taken to a further level. Perhaps, according to Sir John Eccles,

> **We are responsible human beings, not blind automatons; persons, not puppets. By endowing us with freedom, God relinquished a measure of his own sovereignty and imposed certain limitations upon himself.**
>
> Martin Luther King Jr.

do so from past cues.) If we watch the balls on a billiard table, for example, we say that one ball caused another to move. People generally identify a cause of a movement when three qualities are present: the cause precedes the movement, the cause is consistent with the movement, and the cause occurs in the absence of some competing explanation (Mischotte, 1963). We noticed the first ball strike the second before the second moved—that is, the first ball's hit of the second preceded its movement. We noticed that balls hitting one another often move, and we noticed no other events that would cause the second ball to move (e.g., no strong person lifted one end of the billiard table). So, if one billiard ball hits a second, and the second begins to roll, we say the first billiard ball caused the second to move. This same experience of cause and effect—looking at what happens first, then second, and so on—is often read into the voluntary actions a person takes (Presson & Benassi, 1996).

To illustrate this point, Wegner and colleagues (1999) created ambiguous situations in which participants believed they had voluntarily "willed" something—caused

there might exist something other than the physical universe—perhaps some sort of a "ghost" in the mind does exist—which operates things. In other words, mind and the body really are two different things. The mind's ghost can create fields of influence:

> These spatio-temporal fields of influence are exerted by the mind on the brain in willed action. If one uses the expressive terminology of Ryle (1949), the "ghost" operates a "machine," not of ropes and pulleys, valves and pipes, but of microscopic spatio-temporal patterns of activity in the neuronal net woven by the synaptic connections of ten thousand million neurons . . . It would appear that it is the sort of machine a "ghost" could operate, if by ghost we mean in the first place an "agent" whose action has escaped detection even by the most delicate physical instruments. (Eccles, 1970; cited in Pelletier, 1985, pp. 135–136)

Eccles was trying to explain the result of certain experiments in brain surgery in which the patient distinguished between electrical current leading to a movement versus the person making the movement:

> By stimulation of the motor-cortex (of the exposed brain of patients undergoing a brain operation) it is possible to evoke complex motor acts in a conscious human subject. The subject reports that the experience is quite different from that occurring when he "willed" a movement . . . there was the experience of having "willed" an action, which was missing in the other. (Eccles, 1953, cited in Pelletier, 1985, p. 138)

Although this mystery is intriguing, it may not provide a very satisfying answer as to whether free will exists, and if so, how it can be free. Perhaps we have to live with William James's assertion, that, for now, at least, "*The fact is that the question of free-will is insoluble on strictly psychologic grounds . . .*" (James, 1892, p. 456).

Experimental Confederate (or simply, Confederate): A research assistant who impersonates a research participant in front of other research participants, while actually following predetermined instructions of the experimenter.

Good resolutions are useless attempts to interfere with scientific laws. Their origin is pure vanity. Their result is absolutely nil.
Oscar Wilde

it—to happen. Before describing the experiment, it helps to remember that an **experimental confederate** is someone who appears to be a regular participant in an experiment, but who is actually allied with the experimenter and follows the experimenter's instructions.

In one of Wegner's studies, a research participant and confederate together controlled the action of a cursor on a computer screen. To do so, both students sat across from one another, holding onto respective sides of a floating board that controlled the computer mouse. As they moved the board together on the desk, the cursor would move across the screen in response to the board. Various objects were pictured on the computer screen, such as swans, dinosaurs, monkeys, and the like.

For a given trial, the real participant and confederate were told to allow the cursor to come to rest every thirty seconds or so on an object on the screen. The real participant heard background music and, at a given point, the name of an object on the computer screen was repeated over the headphones. The real participant probably assumed in

The strongest knowledge—
that of the total unfreedom of
the human will—is nonetheless
the poorest in successes, for it
always has the strongest
opponent: human vanity.

Nietzsche

most cases that the confederate was hearing exactly the same thing. In fact, however, the confederate was moving the board (or allowing the real participant to move the board) directly in response to prerecorded instructions left by the experimenter and played back on the headphones. During some trials, the confederate allowed the real participant to stop the board and cursor it controlled. During other trials, the confederate controlled the board, often so that the cursor stopped at the picture of an object the participant had heard named on the tape.

As soon as the board came to rest, the real participants rated how much they had controlled where the cursor stopped, from "I intended to make the stop" (rated as 100) to "I allowed the stop to happen" (rated at 0). As you have probably guessed by now, participants consistently believed they had caused the stop when it had actually been the confederate—following recorded instructions—who stopped the cursor. When the object's name was read over the headphones just a few seconds before the forced stop, the participants had an even stronger (and mistaken) sense of control. From such experiments, Wegner concludes that "the experience of will is the way our minds portray their operation to us, then, not their actual operation." The real causes of behavior, he argues, and others have shown, are often unconscious and automatic (e.g., Bargh, 1997; 1999; Wegner & Wheatley, 1999, p. 490).

If Wegner and colleagues' studies don't make you think twice about your experience of voluntary behavior, consider the mind-boggling finding that people's voluntary actions often begin before they are conscious of them. That is, people begin a movement before they are conscious that they are going to voluntarily make it. Libet (1985) took advantage of the finding that the brain exhibits a slow negative shift in electrical potential near the scalp about a second or more before the person emits a voluntary motor movement (Kornhuber & Deecke, 1965). Libet set up an experiment in which he started a clock and asked participants to notice when they became aware of deciding to move their finger. As it turned out, their brains emitted a negative electrical shift first, indicating that the move was about to take place. Only 300 to 400 milliseconds after that did participants become aware of deciding to move their fingers. That finding and others like it indicate that the brain moves a finger before the individual is conscious of "willing" it. The participants may have thought that they had willed the finger movement. In fact, however, the movement began automatically a few milliseconds before they became aware of the thought! These findings open up the possibility that a lot more is controlling voluntary action than the conscious self.

Are There Alternatives to the Conscious Self?

Agencies

The self, then, is conscious, and yet that consciousness is not unitary nor always accurate, particularly when voluntary self-control is being monitored. The self may overestimate the voluntary control it can exercise. If the self is not in control, then what is? Most commonly, nonconscious brain processes or environmental cues bring

Inside the Field

Some Personality Psychologists *Really* Don't Like the Denial of Free Will

There are many people of different backgrounds who believe that personality has no free will. In their view, everything about the personality is determined ahead of time, and whether or not people help themselves is determined by earlier biosocial influences. Because such people believe everything is determined, they are called *determinists*. Determinists (as well as those who believe in free will), can be found among the religious and the nonreligious, as well as among scientists and nonscientists. Many scientists believe that all physical behavior has a cause and, because there is a chain of causality working itself through from the beginning of time, everything in the future is determined. If only we understood the physical and psychological rules of the universe, we could predict everything that would occur. Most of these scientists admit that some things (notably at the subatomic level) are indeterminate, but argue that such indeterminacy does not apply to the level at which human beings live. (See the Disciplinary Crossroads box, "Is There a Biophysics of Free Will?" on page 252, for more on this.)

Such deterministic positions hold that everything a person does is determined by biological or environmental influences. Even a person's belief in free will arises because one is taught, or influenced, to believe in such a thing. According to this view, the person is a helpless spectator in his or her own life. But there are reasons to argue against such a position. Of course, if you don't believe in determinism, these theorists argue, it is simply because something is causing you to believe in something else, and not a matter of free will.

But some opponents of determinism have been offended and troubled by the approach. Henry Murray, a psychologist who helped identify a broad range of human motives, claimed that determinism in psychology promoted devilish outcomes. Murray (1962) wrote:

And here is where our psychology comes in with the bulk of its theories . . . and images of man, obviously in league with the nihilistic Satanic spirit. Man is a computer, an animal, an infant. His destiny is completely determined by genes, instincts, accidents, early conditionings and reinforcements, cultural and social forces. Love is a secondary drive based on hunger and oral sensation *or* a reaction formation to underlying hate . . . There are no provisions for creativity, no admitted margins of freedom . . . no fitting recognitions of the power of ideals, no bases for selfless action, no ground at all for any hope that the human race can save itself from the fatality that now confronts it. (Murray, 1962, p. 53)

about such behaviors. Simple motives can direct the individual toward some aim and away from others, with or without awareness. Such simpler parts exert more-or-less automatic influences on personality.

There is, however, a second possibility that has often been suggested by personality psychologists. This is the operation of a kind of organized "sub-personality" that knits together various functions and operates in partial autonomy from the rest. This class of personality parts have been called **agencies**—and the self is a special, conscious instance of one (e.g., Mayer, 1995; 1998). Agencies are parts of personality that are organized, central to the operation of personality, and that periodically take control of personality and govern its actions.

Agencies: Central parts of the mind distinguished by the fact that they are self-regulating, partly autonomous, and exert influences on the rest of personality.

Semi-Autonomous:
Operating partly on their own; partly following their own rules independently of other influences.

The most central feature of agencies is that they are **semi-autonomous** agents—parts of personality that act as if they possess "minds of their own." The agency is, in other words, a hypothetical subpart of personality large enough to include groups of motives, ways of thinking, and goals. An agency can be the "conscious self"—self-consciously deciding whether to study harder or to go to a party. Or, an agency may be a set of unconscious impulses, connected together and stealthily revealing alternative intentions.

Dissociative Disorders: A group of psychiatric disorders characterized by sudden alterations in identity and its history. Portions of identity may be lost or regained, or many identities may arise.

Some evidence for agencies come from observations of people with **dissociative disorders**. Dissociative disorders represent a class of psychiatric diagnoses in which the identity seems split into multiple parts, each of which has some control over the totality of the person, but each of which seems to operate on its own. Agencies began with the understanding that the memory system is made up of many associations between ideas. Just as ideas could become associated in memory, so can they become disassociated—that is, separated from one another—if some ideas are extremely painful to think of. If so, then whole aggregations of ideas might stay out of consciousness.

Such disassociated ideas, however, would not necessarily go away. Rather, these ideas could, in some cases, continue to operate within personality (Perry & Laurence, 1984, p. 28). Subconscious agencies are sometimes labeled "automatisms." These operate like a second self, cut off from the first. For example, the French neurologist Jean Janet, a contemporary of Freud, had a patient, Irene. She had been a caretaker of her ailing mother, who then died while under Irene's care. The trauma of her mother's death appeared to split Irene's mind into two states. When she awoke from sleeping after her mother's death, she could not remember that her mother had died and, indeed, behaved as if she was very much alive. In a hypnotic trance, however, she could remember everything that had happened surrounding her mother's death. Remarking on the mystery of her waking state, she noted,

> I know very well my mother is dead since I have been told so several times, since I see her no more, and since I am in mourning; but I really feel astonished at it. When did she die? (cited in Hilgard, 1977, p. 5)

Janet interpreted this as reflecting a divided, or a dissociated, mind.

Alters

Dissociative Identity Disorder (DID): This is a contemporary psychiatric diagnosis for what used to be called Multiple Personality Disorder. In it, a person may alternate among two or more personalities (or identities) over time, with no true central personality.

Alter: A contraction of "alternative personality"—the personalities that appear in Dissociative Identity Disorder.

Those with **dissociative identity disorders (DID)**—the current term for people with multiple personalities (American Psychiatric Association, 1994)—exhibit more than one identity. Each identity is called an **alter**. An "alter" is a contraction for alternative personality, and these, too, are examples of agencies, albeit unusual ones. People with Dissociative Identity Disorder exhibit different behaviors depending upon which identity (i.e., alter) is in control at the time. Each identity within a person may express distinct facial expressions, speech characteristics, gestures, styles of conversation and attitudes (Miller, 1989; Putnum, 1991; Rifkin et al., 1998). There also is some evidence for differences in brain patterns depending upon which alter is active (Cocker et al., 1994).

When Julie, a single mother, brought her son in for counseling because he was having trouble in school, the therapist saw little unusual about the case. During the sixth week of counseling, however, Julie told the therapist she would like to introduce him to someone. He expected to meet a teacher or friend in the waiting room. Instead, however, Julie closed her eyes, and when she opened them again, she spoke in a different voice: that of Jerrie, a gay business woman, who remarked, "I wish Julie would stop smoking." Still later in the session, a third personality, Jenny, emerged.

Once this was out in the open, Julie-Jenny-Jerrie's son, Adam, made great strides. He learned to accept his "two" mothers (Jenny stayed "inside" most the time), noting, "Mother is two people who keep going in and out, but both of them love me." Unfortunately, shortly thereafter, the various alters engaged in a pitched battle with one another, and as a consequence, Julie left town, unable to communicate further with the psychologist. In this case, each alter behaved as if it was acting autonomously (Davis & Osherson, 1977).

People with Dissociative Identity Disorder are very rare. One key contributing factor to the disorder may be an individual's general tendency toward dissociation that is reflected not only by the disorder itself, but also by extreme susceptibility to hypnosis (virtually all such patients are hypnotizable), and the presence of an early traumatic experience. Indeed, one model for the disorder is that children undergoing trauma may use self-hypnosis in order to enter into altered states and create alternative identities (Putnam & Carlson, 1998).

Id: An older psychodynamic concept referring to a collection of animal instincts, desires, and motives that operate in the mind.

Connecting Window   *Dissociation and Mental Control*

Personal control can be divided into conscious self-control—which includes conscious awareness and self direction—and nonconscious states and mechanisms that also exert control. Hypnosis provides a way to study the shifts between conscious and nonconscious control in some individuals, because in a hypnotic trance, control seems divided between the person and the instructions administered by the hypnotist. Such dynamics of self-control are elaborated in Chapter 10.

The Unconscious, Id, and Superego

Unconscious: That portion of the mind outside of a person's awareness. Social-cognitive theory emphasizes that it is evolutionarily adaptive for many processes to be outside of awareness. Psychodynamic theory emphasizes that some motivational and emotional processes are painful and threatening, and are purposively avoided by consciousness.

Conscious: Awareness, reflective observing of the inner mind (see text for further discussion).

Superego: A portion of the mind that grows out of the ego and contains both an ideal self and the conscience.

One of Freud's suggestions was that the normal personality, too, is split among agencies: the id, the ego, and the superego (Freud, 1923/1960).

For Freud, the **id** included animal-like motives and emotions, sensations of wishes, emotions related to those wishes, and nonverbal images. This id, according to Freud, "owns" all the mental energy when the person is born. It draws on unconscious energies. The **unconscious** is a cauldron of unacceptable but powerful unsocialized impulses—of sexual and aggressive motives (or instincts, as he called them) and related, uncontrolled emotions such as envy, jealousy, desire, and hatred. The id's energy derived from sexual needs to reproduce and aggressive needs used to protect its survival.

We have already discussed the ego earlier in this chapter. The ego is partly **conscious**. That is, it is the part containing (we would say today) the stream of consciousness, of which a person is aware. Large portions of the ego are also, however, unconscious. The ego controls bodily movement, among other functions. The ego thinks rationally and tries to satisfy id impulses best it can, given the constraints of outside reality—and its other master, the **superego**.

The superego grows out of the ego and is composed of two parts: the ego-ideal, which is what the ego aspires to be, and the conscience, which includes societal rules

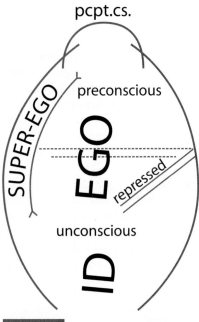

pcpt.cs.

SUPER-EGO

preconscious

EGO

repressed

unconscious

ID

that govern the ego. Collectively, the superego is responsible for the "shoulds" of personality—what the person should and should not do, should and should not be. The superego developed from learning within the family and identifying with the moral codes of parents (Freud, 1923/1960, p. 26).

Freud himself suggested a diagram of id, ego, and superego, superimposed on the conscious-unconscious mind, in his New Introductory Lectures on Psychoanalysis. His diagram is depicted in Figure 7.1.

For Freud, each of the entities could variously take over control of personality, and the possibility that some alternative mental structures might do so is worth contemplating in the context of considering the conscious self.

Are there really agencies? Contemporary psychologists don't find the split-personality metaphor of the id, ego, and superego entirely useful anymore. True, the metaphor to a split personality does get across certain ideas of conflict in the mind which are accurate enough. The id, ego, and superego, however, don't seem to be distinctly present and to act as true, organized, global agents as some had thought. Rather, the mind is made up of many conflicting parts. That said, it does make sense to divide personality into broad areas of functioning. Certain divisions of mind such as the id, ego, and superego may be somewhat outmoded, but other similar divisions may work fairly well. Today, there exist updated divisions of mind. Some of these will be examined in Chapter 8, "How the Parts of Personality Fit Together." Meanwhile, agencies remain one possible way to divide personality, and they may make sense to employ in such cases as dissociative disorders. Their usefulness in describing more common forms of personality is best interpreted as describing distinct areas of function rather than as sub-personalities.

Connecting Window   *The Id, Ego, and Superego as Divisions of Mind*
Here, Freud's division of mind into the id, ego, and superego are treated as Freud envisioned them—as interconnected yet independently acting agents. Chapter 8 offers a different perspective: on whether the dividing lines among the three entities are in the right place or whether there are better divisions.

How Is the Conscious Self Expressed?

Contents of Consciousness

People vary in the contents of the consciousness they experience, as they vary in other parts of their personalities. Three aspects of the conscious self are examined here: the contents of consciousness, the structured flow of consciousness, and levels of consciousness.

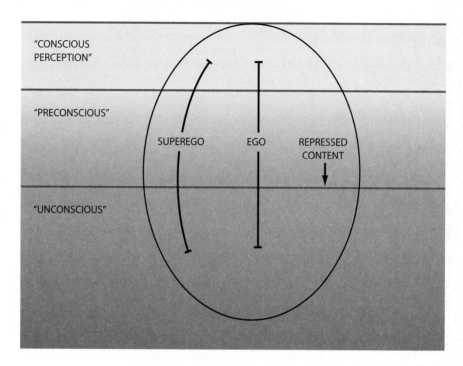

FIGURE 7.2

Rychlak's Interpretation of Freud's Depiction
This evolution of Freud's diagram by Rychlak adds in the all-important idea that much of the id, ego, and superego are unconscious, and that part of the ego is conscious.

Source: Joseph Rychlak, Introduction to Personality and Psychotherapy, Second Edition. Copyright © 1981 by Houghton Mifflin Company. Used with permission.

Qualia (*sing.* Quale): Elements, or an element, of consciousness—individual thoughts, feelings, and urges, or, images, tastes, and sounds.

Might there be something we can say about the contents of consciousness itself? The contents of conscious experiences are called **qualia** (singular, **quale**). Qualia are the sounds or sights, thoughts or urges, that pass through our conscious awareness. We all see a banana, for example, but whether we all register it the same way in consciousness is a matter of philosophical debate. Another question—perhaps easier to answer—is what we are aware of. The Facts at a Glance table shows the results of a beeper study in which people were paged and asked to record what they were conscious of at the moment. Consciousness involves a lot of talking to oneself, fragmentary sights and sounds, and equal parts emotions, and sensations such as pain, or simply the sensation of clothes. But what is the person actually thinking or feeling? What is the person talking to himself or herself about?

The most common contents of consciousness are current concerns. Current concerns are thoughts and feelings related to goals that an individual is seeking, is trying to meet, or is in the process of abandoning. For example, during the summer, a Boston Red Sox fan will have current concerns related to the baseball team's progress and will be interested in everything from the history of the team to its present coaching practices, and, of course, the players and opposition teams. Alternatively, a person who wants to get married will attend closely to tips on how to select an eligible partner, how to introduce the question of marriage, and what makes a good marriage. In one study, students were instructed to listen to two narratives, one presented to their right ear and one presented to their left ear, and to flip a switch back and forth to indicate which they were listening to. Students overwhelmingly chose to listen to

• FACTS • AT • A • GLANCE •

What Could We Have Been Thinking?

What are we conscious of? When undergraduates were beeped at random intervals, they recorded what was going on in their consciousness. Here are some things they were experiencing. Because more than one quality could occur at once, the total adds up to more than 100%.

Contents of Consciousness	Approximate Percent of Time
Unsymbolized thinking—thinking something, but without any clear words, images, or feelings	38%
Inner speech—the experience of talking to yourself in your own voice	32%
Sensory awareness—itches, pains, tickles, etc.	27%
Emotions and feelings—the experience of one or another distinct emotions (e.g., happiness, fear)	26%
Images—imagining something as seen that is not really there	23%
Just doing—just reading, just watching TV, just cooking, etc.	8%
Other—hearing someone else, thinking unspoken specific words	2%

Source: Percent of time is based on an average of high and low speech rate groups from Hulburt, Koch, & Heavey (2001, Table II, p. 128); several additional categories are not shown. With kind permission of Springer Science and Business Media.

narratives that were related to their own current concerns (e.g., the Red Sox), as opposed to someone else's (e.g., marriage; Klinger, 1978).

One form consciousness sometimes takes that has received considerable attention is the daydream. Daydreams appear to be a baseline quality of consciousness; they fill in the gaps not occupied by directed, working thoughts. Daydreams typically have clear beginnings and endings. They are composed of common behaviors the person typically carries out. Although daydreams are often directly or indirectly about a person's goals, they often lack a disciplined focus; that is, they lack any will to carry them out (Klinger, 1999; Singer, 1966; Varendonck, 1921).

At other times, consciousness may become filled with ruminations. Ruminations are repetitive thoughts associated with goals that appear to be blocked, or otherwise difficult to reach. Ruminations often involve feelings of anger, sadness, and fear, and may reflect a person trying to disengage from a goal. They are often associated with depression—although one notable exception is that people often ruminate when they are falling in love (Lyubomirsky & Nolen-Hoeksema, 1993; Martin & Tesser, 1996).

The Structure of Consciousness and Flow

The contents of consciousness can be diffuse—as in daydreams or ruminations—or structured. A scenario familiar to many adolescents is the sense of boredom and lack of structure they often experience, in which there is little around to challenge them.

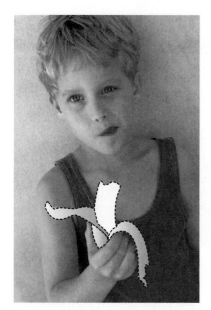

Qualia are the contents of consciousness. Does a banana's color look the same to each of us inside our minds?

Flow: A conscious state in which a person is highly involved in a task, such that time passes quickly, distractions recede, and the person is enjoyably engaged.

The teenager often comes home from school, say, drops his or her books in the bedroom, and after getting a snack, heads for the phone or goes out to be with friends. If nothing is going on, the student may sit and listen to the stereo or watch TV. These forms of entertainment are too easy, however, and his or her mind wanders to problems and worries, further sapping mental energy. By this time, if the teenager is tempted to choose a more challenging activity—reading a book or practicing a sport—his or her resolve is unlikely to last long.

Such states invite daydreaming and rumination—shadowy terrain that beckons to an unstructured mind. Teenagers are beset by various worries—about their appearance, social life, and future chances. The rumination increases the individual's negativity and further depresses any motivation, in a downward spiral of boredom and depression. At this point, the teen's further choices are limited: more TV or music, or talking to a friend one has just spoken to. Worse choices may involve drugs or destructive behavior (Csikszentmihalyi, 1990, pp. 171–172).

One way out of this dilemma is to structure consciousness through a **flow** experience (Csikszentmihalyi, 1990; 1997; Nakamura & Csikszentmihalyi, 2002). Flow states involve an alteration in consciousness that includes the simultaneous concentration on a task with a loss of self-consciousness, the merging of action and awareness, and an accompanying sense of timelessness. Different people will experience flow as they engage in different activities. But given the right person and right level of activity almost any pursuit can create flow.

Consider this example of flow from a dancer who describes how it feels when a performance is going well:

> Your concentration is very complete. Your mind isn't wandering, you are not thinking of something else; you are totally involved in what you are doing . . . Your energy is flowing very smoothly. You feel relaxed, comfortable, and energetic. (Csikszentmihalyi, 1990, p. 53)

This description of flow comes from the great hurdler, Edwin Moses:

> Your mind has to be absolutely clear. The fact that you have to cope with your opponent, jet lag, different foods, sleeping in hotels, and personal problems has to be erased from consciousness—as if they didn't exist. (p. 59)

A student studying may become engaged and engrossed in the material being learned—and forget altogether that she is studying. In each case notice that when the person is entirely involved in the task the sense of self is in the background. A person's concentration is focused on what is occurring, and the action and the self have merged.

One aspect that makes flow more easy to attain is the presence of clear goals or feedback for the task. For a beginner, this may involve working toward a standard laid out by a teacher. For a great artist or thinker, though, the standards may be entirely internal. An experienced painter who is painting, for example, will know after each brush stroke whether it works or not (p. 56). Flow also involves a sense of control. The following are one dancer's words.

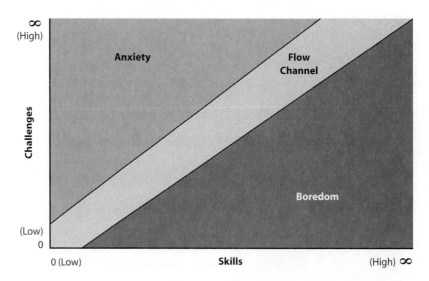

FIGURE 7.3

Flow

Flow states arise when an individual engages in a task of just the right difficulty. If the tasks are too easy, one will experience boredom; too hard, and anxiety will result.

A strong relaxation and calmness comes over me. I have no worries of failure. What a powerful and warm feeling it is! I want to expand, to hug the world. I feel enormous power to affect something of grace and beauty. (Csikszentmihalyi, 1990, p. 59)

Often, flow will be accompanied by a high sense of organization and coordination. Surgeons often say that during a difficult operation they experience their team as members of a carefully choreographed ballet operating together. That is, rather than a sense of control, per se, there is a feeling of harmony and power (Csikszentmihalyi, 1990, p. 65).

Finally, when a person is in the midst of flow, time is transformed. On the one hand, each moment can be appreciated, and on the other, the entire experience seems to be over in just a moment. A person becomes so aware of the details and of thinking about them that time seems entirely available and one proceeds through the task at just the right pace, without feeling rushed. In the end, much more time may have passed by than one has realized.

How to Enter into a Flow State

In the midst of a society pressuring one to behave in a particular fashion, the individual who has a structured consciousness can behave independently of momentary, and even long-term, pressures, in order to follow a path that one believes is right. From the preceding descriptions, it might seem as if flow states just happen unpredictably. But Csikszentmihalyi believes that the entry into flow states is under a person's control, that the flow state will occur when there is a match between an individual's level of skills and the difficulty of a task that is undertaken. When the individual is doing something too easy, he will feel bored; when he is doing something too hard, he will feel anxious. But when the individual chooses the right level of task difficulty, he will enter into the flow experience. Csikszentmihalyi represents this encounter with a task as illustrated in Figure 7.3.

Csikszentmihalyi (1990, p. 174) recounts the instance of Susan Butcher, a prize-winning Iditerod dog-sled racer. When she is not racing, she lives in isolation in a cabin twenty-five miles away from the nearest town. Within that isolation, however, she keeps her consciousness structured by setting tasks for herself in the caring of her 150 huskies. Most notably, she tries to get to know each dog by name and by its preferences and disposition. Of course, the tasks of everyday living in such isolation keep her engaged as well: in hunting and food gathering, and in keeping the dogs from predators. By setting herself such a routine, Butcher keeps her consciousness structured on manageable tasks and is able to attain flow, and hence, great satisfaction in her chosen pursuits.

Case Study

An Example of Flow in Adolescence

One impressive and amusing example of a flow experience is described by Mihalyi Csikszentmihalyi, who reports the case of Christopher, a high-school student, who sets himself a flow experience by deciding, quite intentionally, to transform himself from a shy person with few friends into a more popular person.

Christopher was a 15-year-old who was quiet, shy, wore glasses, and had few friends at his high school. Like most high schools, his had many cliques, but he wasn't a member of any of them. At the same time, he was quite capable of having relationships. Finally frustrated about his situation, he told his parents he had decided to become more popular and outlined a plan to them to do so. His parents listened, helped him develop his plan, and supported it.

Chris decided he would change from wearing glasses to contact lenses, buy only the trendy kinds of clothes the popular kids were wearing, learn about the latest hot music and fads of the moment, and dye his hair blond. He further decided to change his outward personality, and practiced a new, relaxed-looking posture, and a new, broad smile, in front of the mirror until he thought it would go over well with his classmates. According to Csikszentmihalyi, this approach, supported by his parents, worked extremely well:

> By the end of the year he was being invited into the best cliques, and the following year he won the part of Conrad Birdie in the school musical. Because he identified with the part of the rock star so well, he became the heartthrob of middle-school girls, who taped his picture inside their lockers. The senior yearbook showed him involved in all sorts of successful ventures, such as winning a prize in the "Sexy Legs" contest. He had indeed succeeded in changing his outward personality, and achieved control of the way his peers saw him. At the same time, the inner organization of his self remained the same: he continued to be a sensitive, generous young man who did not think less of his peers because he learned to manage their opinions or think too highly of himself for having succeeded at it. (1990, p. 187)

Levels of Consciousness

Another aspect of how people differ in consciousness concerns their levels of consciousness. Recall that consciousness is sometimes defined simply as attention or awareness. This might be called direct consciousness (e.g., seeing red). But consciousness also has levels. One can be aware of awareness. That is, "I am aware that I see the color red." Reflective consciousness is called higher order consciousness. In fact, some psychologists have argued that this capacity to reflect back on experience is both necessary for consciousness and explains what consciousness feels like (e.g., Rosenthal, 1993; 2002). These "higher order thoughts" of consciousness can be of multiple orders. "I see red" is zero-order; "I am aware I see red," first order; "I am aware I am aware I see red," second order, and so on.

Another use of the "levels of consciousness," metaphor, though, is to refer to developing a higher level of consciousness. Far from reflecting on reflections of awareness, this type of higher consciousness means getting rid of all the layers and layers and focusing instead on a pure experience of consciousness. One way to move in that direction is to take up focused meditation. Focused meditation involves clearing the mind of clutter and intrusions by focusing one's thoughts on a single action or perception, such as a current breath or a mantra—a calming vocal sound one makes as one exhales, such as "oohhmm."

Higher consciousness here refers to letting go of extraneous thoughts and distractions such that one can experience a state known as pure consciousness. This form of consciousness is called higher level because it is believed to reflect a truer understanding of nature and reality (Ornstein, 1986, pp. 191-194). Such ideas of consciousness are often spiritual and dualistic, with the idea that one leaves one's physical self behind and enters a plane of pure awareness (e.g., Wilbur, 1999). From a solely scientific perspective, however, legitimate interest has been expressed in the sort of brain states, internal phenomena, and behavioral correlates that relate to such higher levels (e.g., Ornstein, 1986). For example, the brain patterns of meditators who attain a level they describe as pure consciousness differs from those of others and may be able to tell us something more about what being conscious means, as well as about the different varieties of consciousness. (See the Research in Focus box for more.)

Self-Determination Theory

In addition to differences in the expression of consciousness, there are also differences in the expression of will. Self-determination theory is concerned with how much the self acts in accordance with its own desires—voluntary action in a broad sense—versus how much it acts in accordance with everyday outside pressures (Deci & Ryan, 2000; Sheldon & Kasser, 2001). This research takes a page from the humanistic psychology of Abraham Maslow who—recall—noted that some people had more free will than others.

Intrinsic Motivation: A type of motivation in which the process of carrying out an activity is rewarding to an individual in-and-of-itself, aside from any outside reward.

Generally speaking, a conscious self acting voluntarily and according to its own needs is considered to operate according to **intrinsic motivation**. Intrinsic motivation involves doing things that are viewed as rewarding to the individual in and of themselves. For example, a person genuinely interested in writing for magazines

In this painting, Salvador Dali indicates, by including himself in the painting (and by employing a mirror) that the painting process itself can be become the subject of a painting. The painter's reflection on the reflective process is itself considered a higher order or second-order consciousness.

Extrinsic Motivation: A type of motivation in which a person's activities are carried out in order to obtain an outside reward such as social recognition or money.

would be said to be intrinsically motivated to write. This might be contrasted with **extrinsic motivation**. Extrinsic motivation describes doing things in order to meet some form of outside expectations or rewards, such as to attend law school because one's parents regard it as a more practical and realistic life plan. There exist a number of types of extrinsic motivations, from those that are entirely brought about due to outside pressures (called the external subtype) to those that are more integrated with one's own needs. For example, identified extrinsic motivation is caused by outside pressures such as direction from parents, but in this case one has come to gradually accept these outside pressures as "for the best." Identified extrinsic motivation is closest to intrinsic motivation and is often grouped with it. These and more forms of specific motivation are defined in Table 7.1, page 267.

Intrinsic motivation and identified extrinsic motivation are perceived as volitional, self-chosen, and self-determined. Most other forms of extrinsic motivation are perceived as carried out due to outside pressure of one sort or another. Of course, one can also experience **amotivation**. Amotivation is the lack of any motivation at all. People are apt to feel amotivated when they lack any sense of being able to carry out a task successfully.

Amotivation: The lack of any type of motivation to carry out activities or tasks.

A close match between a person's intrinsic motives and the life tasks he or she must carry out, can add to the success and pleasure with which those tasks are accomplished. For example, Miserandino (1996) found that third- and fourth-grade students were happier, enjoyed school more, and performed better when they were self-motivated, that is, extrinsically identified or intrinsically motivated, than when they experienced other forms of extrinsic motivation. This was the case even after controlling statistically for ability levels among the students. Similarly, college students who are more voluntarily motivated to perform in organic chemistry enjoy the course

Research in Focus

Brain Correlates of Higher Consciousness

Newberg and colleagues (2001) studied eight highly skilled meditators of the Tibetan Buddhist school. They used Single Photon Emission Computed Tomography (SPECT), which tracks a radioactive substance that tags blood cells and can be traced through the brain. More active brain areas then draw the blood toward them and use the blood. SPECT allows researchers to see which areas of the brain are most active.

The researchers first implanted an IV into each meditator so the radioactive dye could be injected inobtrusively. Next, the meditator began his or her practice in a candle-lit room with incense burning. The meditator had a piece of string nearby and when he or she entered a higher state of consciousness, tugged on the string by prior arrangement. At that point, the radioactive trace was injected, and the meditator was quickly escorted to the brain scan machine.

The brains of these meditators were quite different from those of typical participants. As you might expect, they were calmer: many structures of the limbic system—the seat of emotion—were very quiet, including the amygdala and hypothalamic activity. There also was a startling decrease in the parietal lobe activity. The parietal lobe is responsible for the physical model of the self; this suggested that the meditators were shutting off any sensations of their bodies.

At the same time there was a great increase in prefrontal cortex activity, rising as much as 20 percent in some participants. The prefrontal cortex portion of the brain is responsible for the orienting response—that is, attending to something. Orienting is the "what is it?" response of the brain. In normal consciousness, orientation is constantly changing—from going to an appointment, to driving a car, to listening to a friend to remembering something we forgot to do. In concentrative meditation, by contrast, there is prolonged orienting to one object or event. The prefrontal cortex appears to participate in the meditation by "locking in" the object or event in concentration. Meditators report that they are aware of sensations but not affected by them. This seemed to be the case because the sensory regions of the brain continued to work at normal levels. The orienting response, however, kept the prefrontal cortex locked-in on the object of concentration. Although sensations came in, consciousness did not stray to them; rather it remained fixed and concentrated. The consciousness is dissociated from surrounding senses and bodies, and in this way approached the purity of awareness that those who meditate describe obtaining (Carter, 2002, pp. 284–288).

Studies such as these show how contemporary brain scanning techniques, coupled with meditative practices, can help us understand "where" in the brain conscious experience comes from. In the case of concentrative meditative experience, the internal sensations appear to be the result of some brain areas reducing activities, others remaining the same, and especially, alterations in the orienting response of the prefrontal cortex that may define the sense of pure consciousness.

more and obtain higher grades in it (Black & Deci, 2000). Students with greater self-motivation achieve more progress in school (even controlling for initial achievement levels), and when they attain their goals are happier than those who are at the more extrinsically motivated end of the spectrum (Sheldon & Kasser, 1998; 2001). Finally, patients in a weight-loss treatment program lost more weight and kept if off

TABLE 7.1	Motivations: From Least to Most Self-Determined
Type of Motivation	**Description**
Amotivation	The individual feels generally unable to carry out a task successfully.
Extrinsic Motivation External Subtype	The individual doesn't want to carry out the task, and doesn't believe it to be of importance, but does so to satisfy external demands.
Extrinsic Motivation Introjected Subtype	The individual doesn't want to carry out the task, but will do so anyway, in order to satisfy the perceived needs of others.
Extrinsic Motivation Identified Subtype	The individual genuinely wants to please others and will carry out a task to do so.
Extrinsic Motivation Integrated Subtype	The individual has integrated others' perceptions of a task's value as his or her own. As a consequence, the individual views the task to be carried out as having personal importance.
Intrinsic Motivation	The individual views a task as rewarding, pleasing, and consistent with his or her goals for its own sake.

Source: Summarized from Deci & Ryan (2000), pp. 235–237.

> How to gain, how to keep, how to recover happiness is in fact for most men at all times the secret motive of all they do, and of all they are willing to endure.
>
> William James

better nearly two years later when they were self-motivated, and self-motivated patients more generally better follow medical regimens (Williams, Freedman, & Deci, 1998; Williams et al., 1996).

Such findings indicate the importance of a *sense of voluntary control,* and that such voluntary control comes from successfully pairing one's own truly believed needs with the social environment around one. The sense of voluntary self-control is important to people and can amplify their abilities to carry out long-term, demanding requirements. To the extent that the conscious self is responsible for recognizing its own needs, for bringing them into the light of consciousness, and for fitting the self into the environment so that those needs can be met with a sense of self-determination, the conscious self may represent a critical core of personality.

Self-Control: A First Look

The concept of self-determination blends imperceptibly into the concept of self-control, for those with more intrinsic motivation are exercising a form of self-control. There is a considerable research literature on self-control, which will be examined later in Chapter 10 on the dynamics of self-control, and also in Chapter 11 on personality development in childhood. Meanwhile, it is worth considering here one issue of particular relevance to the expression of self-control: Is a person's apparent self-control a product of the fact that the person wants to do the right thing, or is it a matter of self-imposed will? Block and Block (1980) started out studying a concept

René Magritte's 1936 painting, The Key to the Fields, *encourages reflections on human awareness and consciousness. The broken window looking out on the field suggests a viewer's hope and intention to touch reality itself—even at the cost of breaking through established boundaries. And yet, personality is entrapped in the mind, and the mind brings its own perceptions to reality—just as the image of the field remains, shockingly, superimposed on the broken glass itself. Can we reach higher levels of awareness that allow us to see reality more clearly? Will we ever understand consciousness itself? Surely, many mysteries and surprises remain before finding the key.*

called "ego control." As the name suggests, the Blocks originally hypothesized that people who possessed personal control had a strong conscious self or ego. Those who lacked personal control lacked it due to a weak conscious self.

The Blocks found that it did make sense to divide the children they studied into under-controlled, flexible, and over-controlled groups, and even that that group membership was fairly stable over the lifespan. It turned out, however, that the main determinant of group membership seemed not to be any learned or acquired sense of self-control, as much as it might be the individual's possession of a set of particular motivations. Those who were sensation-seekers and had difficulty maintaining their attention ended up in the undercontrolled group. Those who were quite shy and introverted ended up in the over-controlled group. The rest of the sample ended up assigned to the flexible group. From this perspective, the concept of ego control was superfluous—it was all a consequence of a person's lower-level motivations and attentional style (e.g., Block, 2002; Van Lieshout, 2000).

It is interesting to consider how much the appearance of self-control might be due to some other part of personality. Returning to the example of Gauguin that began this chapter, for example, we might recall the major decisions he made in his life: to devote his life to painting, to leave his family, and to travel to Tahiti. We might wonder to what degree Gauguin truly made his own decisions, and to what degree he was compelled by other forces in his personality to do those things.

> **How ridiculous is Caesar and Bonaparte wandering from one extreme of civilization to the other to conquer men—himself, the while, unconquered, unexplored, almost wholly unsuspected to himself.**
> Ralph Waldo Emerson

With the conscious self and its alternatives, we come to the end of Part 2 of this book. We examined motives and emotions (Chapter 4), mental models of the self, world, and relationships (Chapter 5), mental abilities including intelligence and creativity (Chapter 6), and finally in this chapter, conscious and unconscious agencies. These are arguably the most important of personality's parts, as understood today. With the proliferation of parts it is important to understand how they fit together and influence one another. That is the topic of Part 3 of the book, on the organization of personality. Chapter 8, the first chapter of Part 3, begins with an examination of how the parts fit together.

Reviewing Chapter 7

The learning objectives of this chapter include to acquaint you with two fundamental issues in the study of psychology: the role of consciousness, on the one hand, and the issue of free will versus determinism, on the other. Those issues are then examined as they relate to agency parts of personality. Agencies such as the self-as-knower and the ego are examined, along with their characteristics and some thoughts about how they are expressed.

What Is the Conscious Self?

1. James's Self-as-Knower.
The conscious self was an important topic dealt with by William James, among others. What is the nature of the conscious self, as James described it?

2. Freud's Concept of the Ego.
Freud proposed the existence of three agencies that described personality—the id, ego, and superego. Of these, the ego is examined in some detail here. How is the ego similar, and how is it different, from James's concept of the conscious self, particularly in terms of how much is conscious?

3. The Dialogical Self.
The dialogical self is a recent view of the conscious self in which consciousness moves from enlivening not only one's own self, but also represents other internal characters. This is said to occur when one holds imaginary conversations with others. How is the dialogical self different from the conscious self? What does the notion of the dialogical self add to the conscious self?

What Does It Mean for the Self to Be Conscious?

4. What Is Consciousness?
How has consciousness been defined? What are some central attributes of consciousness?

5. Scientific Accounting for the Feeling of Consciousness.
What is subjective realism? How does it distinguish between consciousness as an objective quality and as a subjective quality?

6. Is Consciousness of Recent Origin?
Julian Jaynes suggested a radical hypothesis that consciousness has recently evolved. To when does he date the appearance of consciousness? How were people different before consciousness evolved?

7. The Brain and Consciousness.
Has consciousness been localized in the brain? If so, which part of the brain contains consciousness? If not, what explanations have been offered for how consciousness emerges?

Does the Self Possess Free Will?

8. The Appearance of Will.
The will is most purely a power that one exerts over oneself to try to control or cause oneself to behave in a particular way. What sorts of decisions did William James say most reflected the exercise of will?

9. The Free Will–Determinism Debate.
Is there a free will? Those who believe there isn't are called determinists. Religious determinism can be found in some religions; Calvinism is an example in the Protestant tradition. Such determinism can also be found in psychology. Both Sigmund Freud and B. F. Skinner were determinists. What does free will mean?

10. Freedom from the Free Will–Determinism Debate.
How is the discussion about voluntary versus automatic behavior different from free will versus determinism?

11. Voluntary Cause and Control.
A number of experimental studies suggest that people believe they are exercising free will when, in fact, they are not. Can you describe such a study? Does it prove the determinist position?

Are There Alternatives to the Conscious Self?

12. Agencies.
Consciousness itself is sometimes described as an agency. Although some agencies are conscious, others are unconscious. What are some qualities of agencies?

13. Agencies Are Semi-Autonomous.
Agencies are part of personality that are semi-autonomous from the other parts either in that they are self-regulating, or that they otherwise are the origin of some influence over the rest of personality. What do self-regulating and semi-autonomous mean?

14. Alters.
Multiple personalities present a fascinating instance of the agency at the extreme. Here are actual full-blown personalities alternating within a single individual. Each one is doing its own thing. In fact, one may trick another or even hijack the body someplace the other personality doesn't want to be. What are the alternative personalities called, and why are they considered agencies?

15. The Unconscious, Id, and Superego.
Early in his career, Freud divided the mind into the conscious, preconscious, and unconscious. Later in his career, Freud divided the mind into the id, ego, and superego. Are the unconscious, id, and superego unconscious

agencies? What characteristics of them did you use to decide the issue?

How Is the Conscious Self Expressed?

16. The Stream of Consciousness.
The various ideas and associations a person has during a day together form the individual's stream of consciousness. What does the stream of consciousness contain?

17. The Structure of Consciousness and Flow.
Flow experience results from an interaction between a person's skills and the challenges provided by a task at hand. The flow experience has a number of characteristics associated with it, including a quicker passage of time and an intense involvement. What other characteristics are there? What is it about the skills and tasks that brings flow about?

18. Levels of Consciousness.
The term, *levels of consciousness,* is generally used in two different senses. One sense refers to the amount of reflection involved in conscious awareness (e.g., I am watching myself watching myself) and is labeled according to how many reflections are involved, as first-, second-, and third-order consciousness. The other sense of levels of consciousness is quite different. Can you describe what it refers to?

19. Self-Determination Theory.
Self-determination theory distinguishes among amotivation, external motivation, and intrinsic motivation. Amotivatin refers to a lack of motivation of any sort. External motivation involves performing tasks for reasons external to oneself. Can you describe a few major types of such motivation? Internal motivation involves a person performing tasks because those tasks bring satisfaction to him or her, apart from any external pressures.

20. Ego Control.
Ego control is another word for self-control. It involves a balance between basic motives, on the one hand, and an individual's capacity for self-regulation, on the other. Children have been classified as belonging to three different ego-control groups: undercontrolled and overcontrolled are two of them. Can you name the third?

Part 3

Personality Organization

*P*art 3, Personality Organization builds on what has been learned up-to-now about personality and its parts. It examines how personality's parts are organized and how they work together. The parts that make up personality can be organized into larger and larger groups, and, ultimately, into global structures. Such structures form the relatively stable, defined areas of personality that carry out the system's functions. In addition to such structure, personality dynamics—one personality area's causal influences on another—also exist. Some dynamics motivate the person to take action in the social world. Other dynamics relate to self-control. This part of the book, Personality Organization, asks what the major structures and dynamics of personality are, examines how they can be identified within a person, and describes how they help the individual carry out the tasks of being an aware, active individual.

Chapter 8

How the Parts of Personality Fit Together

*A*central task of the personality psychologist is to integrate the many parts of personality and to examine how they work together. Personality's parts include many of those studied in previous chapters: specific motives, emotions, mental models, mental abilities, and the conscious self.

To examine the parts together, it is helpful to begin with personality structure. Personality structure refers to the long-term organization of personality and its parts. It refers to how personality is divided into major areas, and which parts belong in a given area. Understanding personality structure means developing a workable overview of personality itself, its major areas, and how its parts fit together. Structure, in other words, provides a big picture of personality and its parts.

- ### What Is Personality Structure?
  Personality structure refers to the relatively enduring aspects of personality: for example, areas of function that operate over the long term. Dividing personality into structural areas helps psychologists examine the whole system, and its specific parts, together.

- ### How Are Personality Traits Structured?
  Some approaches to personality structure take as their task to focus on organizing personality traits. Many traits can be arranged in hierarchies in which "big" or "super" traits are broken down into smaller traits.

- ### What Are Structural Models of Awareness?
  Another way to look at personality structure is to consider which parts of personality have channels of communication to conscious awareness, and which parts exist outside of awareness, in various nonconscious areas.

- ### Are There More General Approaches to Structural Divisions?
  Another way to divide personality is according to its different functions such as motivation, emotion, and motivation—in fact, that familiar trilogy marks one well-known structural of division of personality. There are other such divisions as well.

- ### What Are the Structural Connections from Personality to the Environment?
  Some further structural divisions specialize in how to connect a person's internal processes to the social environment. These are examined as well. Collectively, these divisions help connect various areas of personality with others, and to personality's surrounding environment.

What Is Personality Structure?

Personality Structure Described

Personality structure: The relatively enduring, distinct major areas of the personality system, and their interrelations and interconnections. These different areas of personality can be distinguished according to their different contents, functions, or other characteristics.

Personality structure is close to the core of what personality psychologists study. **Personality structure** refers to the relatively enduring, stable areas that are inside personality. Psychologists of all theoretical approaches have been concerned with structure (e.g., Block, 1995, p. 188; Cervone, 2005; Mayer, 2005; Rapaport, 1967, p. 803; Sanford, 1970, p. 45).

For the psychodynamic theorist Rapaport, they were the "abiding [continuing] patterns in the flux of processes." For the trait theorist, structure can take on a specifically mathematical meaning, referring to the "pattern of . . . a relatively small number of factors that represent the basic dimensions of personality." For the mid-twentieth-century integrator of personality theories, Nevitt Sanford, structure was the "organization or patterning" of personality's elements (McCrae & Costa, 1997, p. 509; Rapaport 1967, p. 803; Sanford, 1970, p. 46).

The term "structure" is often contrasted with the concept of personality dynamics. Structure speaks of the relatively enduring long-term qualities of the personality system, whereas personality dynamics speak of the relatively rapid, active processes and change within the personality system. All of these perspectives on structure share in common the idea that it consists of the "relations among parts [of personality] that are relatively static and unchanging" (Mayer, 1998, p. 130).

To further clarify the nature of personality structure, consider an analogy to a visible structure—the structure of a city. Imagine taking a flight by hot air balloon over, say, Boston, Massachusetts. A balloon ride is slow enough to allow us time to appreciate the change in perspective that takes place between being on the ground and examining the individual parts of the city, and being in the air and examining the city's more global structure. Say we lift off near a fountain in the Boston Commons. The Commons is one of the oldest parks in the United States, and occupies 55 acres in downtown Boston.

On the ground before our ascent, we might observe the fountain near our launch-site, several nearby park benches, a row of trees, and get to know the individual people who will help launch the balloon. We might observe others who are strolling through the park, talking, and enjoying the day. All these can be thought of as individual parts that make up the city.

As the balloon inflates, it rises, and we climb into the basket beneath it, in preparation for the ascent. As the balloon lifts off, we float upward and eastward toward the Atlantic Ocean, and our perspective begins to change. What has seemed to be individual trees merge together into clusters of trees. Individual people seem smaller, and we will notice if they are walking alone or standing in small groups. Benches and pieces of lawn combine to form the outline of a field. In fact, the perimeter of the Boston Commons, which could not be seen before, emerges as do the buildings at the park's periphery. This change of viewpoint is similar to the change we encounter when considering, first, the individual parts of personality, and then taking a

When a person focuses on a single object, such as this fountain in the Boston Common (a park in central Boston), the object itself fills one's attention. Analogously, when one focuses on a single part of personality such as, say, extraversion, that single part often becomes the center of one's attention.

As one's perspective broadens, however, by taking in more of the Boston Common, groups of parts become visible such as clusters of trees and walkways. Analogously, as one steps back from a single part of personality, regularities and areas of personality begin to define themselves.

A broader perspective still brings out heretofore unseen elements of the urban structure: the Boston Common as a whole park, the major streets surrounding it and their alignments, the financial district, and the harbor and its waterways. Analogously, as one considers all of personality, it becomes possible to define its major systems and how they work together.

broader, more global view of the entire personality system: The parts of personality, are numerous and small; we see broader structures when we consider them from a higher level.

As we float still higher above Boston, our view of the city shifts again to a yet more general level; we can appreciate a newly emerging sense of order from the latest position. Now, we can perceive larger aspects of the landscape: natural lines of demarcation and patterns. The individual trees, walkways, and lawns we saw as we went

> [Referring to the id, ego, and superego], viewing . . . structures, the psychic traveler felt he was in possession of superior maps of the mind and better able to navigate than his ancestors.
>
> Eugene Mahon

aloft merge into the greenery of the Boston Common. A group of older buildings on the hill before us surrounds a golden-domed building—the Statehouse in the Beacon Hill neighborhood. The tall buildings in front of us mark the Financial District, which extends down to the Fort Point Channel. As we continue further eastward, we will come upon Boston Harbor itself, and the Atlantic Ocean. In this way, the individual people, trees, buildings, and roadways have given way to a broader sense of the geographical areas of Boston—the parks, neighborhoods, and waterways—the visible structure of the city (Gleason, 1985, pp. vi, 7, 17).

Although we cannot fly over personality and see it as we can Boston, the human personality, too, has its boundaries, its regions, and its areas. As the analogy to a city suggests, one reason we are interested in personality structure is because it provides a way of dividing and organizing—obtaining an overview—of the system.

Why Is Personality Structure Important?

As we have learned, personality has a lot of parts. Personality textbooks such as this one typically mention about four hundred common parts (Mayer, 1995). There are hundreds more that psychologists study at a more advanced level. Structural divisions of personality provide a global organization and overview of those parts so that one can view them in meaningful groups rather than always being preoccupied with each one in detail; for example, rather than discuss every single emotion, we can talk of the emotion system.

To see how this operates in practice, consider the personality of Christopher Michael Langan (as far as we can based on several articles and websites). Let's say we divide his personality into the areas of motives, emotions, and cognition—a structural division called the "trilogy of mind" we will encounter later in this chapter.

Langan is motivated in a number of areas. At the age of twelve he began bodybuilding to protect himself from schoolyard bullies, won a lot of fights, and developed a reputation as a tough guy. He is now a tall, large, strong individual. Like most people, he is motivated to defend himself. He enjoys "a couple of beers" and "shooting bull," and riding his Harley Davidson motorcycle. This suggests he is sociable and (because of the motorcycle) may be motivated to seek thrills and excitement. During the 1980s and 1990s he lived in a cabin on Long Island with his Harley Davidson motorcycle and cat, and he worked as a bouncer in a nightclub, earning six thousand dollars a year. His relatively low earnings suggest he might not be motivated to earn money, but other possible explanations also exist (for example, he might enjoy the work a great deal, or be helping a friend who owns the club). He also organized a nonprofit organization and is involved in writing a book called, "Design for a Universe." (Quain, 2002). He likes to teach himself things. In other words, he appears to be curious and intellectually motivated.

He expresses few emotions with others (Quain, 2002; Sager, 1999). To the extent he does express feelings, the feelings appear to include a mix of happiness and enjoyment, but also some skepticism, doubt, and boredom. His mother told him his father died of a heart attack before he was born, but he says he sometimes doubts his mother was telling the truth. He says he often feels bored when listening to normal conversation (Quain, 2002). He found college boring and dropped out, in part because he felt that the faculty and administrators he met were unsympathetic toward him and the poverty he faced. During one point in his life, he said he maintained no respect toward academics and called them "acadummies." Others describe him has having a "bit of a chip on his shoulder" (Sager, 1999, p. 145). Part of his emotional distance may be reflected in his philosophical character. He notes, for example, that there are many people in the world, and many of them just get bad breaks, and he identifies with them based on his own experiences.

At this point, you might conclude that Michael Langan is a fairly ordinary person, who has suffered some disadvantages in life. Before you draw a picture of Langan too quickly, though, it is important to continue the overview of all the structural areas of his personality. In the area of intelligence, for example, Chris's IQ has been assessed at 195 (compared to the average of 100, or the college students' average IQ score of 120). That puts him somewhere in the area of Leonardo da Vinci, Ludwig Wittgenstein, and Rene Descartes. He skipped kindergarten through second grade. When he was a child working on a ranch he brought books by Bertrand Russell and Albert Einstein with him to read while he waited for the irrigation ditches to drain. He taught himself advanced math, physics, philosophy, Latin, and Greek. He is now married and helps run Mega-East Society, a nonprofit organization for the support of the "severely gifted." Most recently, he has begun publication of his theory in academic journals—highly unusual for someone who has dropped out of college. Moreover, his theory has been treated with considerable respect.

The structural overview of Langan's personality—superficial though it is—shows how examining parts together is an important complement to viewing parts in isolation. If you knew only the motivational and emotional side of Langan's personality, you might view him as a relatively unexceptional individual. If you knew only of his intelligence, you might imagine him as a highly cerebral individual. Only when a more global, or higher-level, perspective is employed to view all the parts, is it possible to more fully appreciate the individual who encompasses these qualities. To find out more about Langan's personality, you can examine the Case Study box on his life. The point of a structural approach is that by considering a few key areas together rather than in isolation we can better describe, predict, and change personality (Lubinski, 2000).

Multiple Personality Structures Exist

A little reflection will suggest that there is nearly always more than one good way to divide a complex system, and there exist multiple ways of dividing personality on a structural basis. To make this clearer, again consider the city of Boston and the multiple possibilities for dividing it up. An economist might divide the city according to its economic sectors, including its banking and financial services, its role as a seaport, its high-tech sectors, medical services sector, and its educational institutions. A real estate agent would divide it by neighborhood, examining Allston, Back Bay and Beacon Hill, through Mattapan and the North End, to Roslindale and West Roxbury. A geologist, by contrast, would divide the city by its landscape, including its urban areas, parks, waterfront, and islands, by its surface deposits and its bedrock geology, including granite and volcanic types, among others.

Case Study

More on Christopher Langan and His Life

It is difficult to assess personality even having close acquaintance with an individual, using psychological tests, and following the person for a while. Public figures, such as Christopher Michael Langan, present further difficulties in that media reports are fallible, and different people hold different perspectives on the person. Nonetheless, Langan's personal qualities provide a rich opportunity for seeing how the whole of personality is often different from any individual part of personality considered by itself.

The chapter opening introduces some of Langan's background: He is a man who faced challenging circumstances in his life, with a measured intelligence quotient of 195, which places him in the top .1 percent of people in terms of intelligence (i.e., the smartest person amidst a thousand people). But here we want to shift our focus away from individual parts of personality, such as IQ, to examine a more complete picture of a person. In this case, that would mean considering a (slightly) more developed picture of Langan's personality, and then

trying to organize it according to a structural division of personality.

During the late 1990s and early 2000s, Langan lived on Long Island, NY, in a trailer. He worked as a nightclub bouncer, sometimes as a bartender, and sometimes as a personal coach, showing celebrities how to work out. He had come to the attention of a journalist who was writing an article on people with very high IQ's and their lives.

Chris recounted some of his life story to the reporter. The reporter recounted that Langan learned from his mother that his biological father had died shortly after his birth—although Langan doesn't necessarily believe her, as she had often lied to him. Chris started talking at six months of age, skipped kindergarten through second grade, and began his schooling in third grade. His mother then remarried, to an alcoholic. His new stepfather expected the children to follow his commands—expecting the children, for example, to be lined up and ready for action early in the morning. He beat the children almost daily

Similarly, the different theoretical perspectives on personality psychology call for different kinds of structural divisions of the system. John Digman and other trait psychologists have equated the concept of personality structure to a group of large, important, relatively enduring traits (e.g., Deiner, Smith, & Fujita, 1995; Digman, 1990). Such structural models of traits often refer to "supertraits" or "big traits," and later in this chapter we'll encounter structural trait models such as the Big Three and the Big Five. Other trait theorists emphasize personality types that are based on combinations of trait dimensions (Weinberger, 1998, p. 1065).

Psychodynamic theorists are interested in consciousness and self-awareness and as a consequence emphasize what is conscious or not. The distinction between conscious and unconscious reflects another way that personality structures can be divided into a series of areas or parts—according to channels of communication with consciousness (Rapaport, 1960; 1967). Probably the most common way personality is divided is according to its major functions, such as those involving motivation, emotion, and cognition. Other important divisions tell us the relation of personality

in an attempt to control them. At school, Chris was smaller than the other children and yet knew much more than them. Chris responded to being picked on by focusing on lifting weights and developing his body. His mind didn't go to waste during this time either. Even while body-building to defend himself, he taught himself advanced mathematics, physics, philosophy, Latin and Greek.

Chris notes that he was highly self-controlled and well behaved—never speaking back to others. One morning, however, when he was lying in bed asleep, his stepfather punched him in the face, waking him. He lost his temper and threw his stepfather against a wall, and beat him. His stepfather told him to get out of the house and never come back. Chris left home for good.

Although he started college, Langan found that many of his professors and administrators were unsympathetic to his financial and family pressures. He reported, "to this day, I have no respect for academics. I call them acadummies. So I guess you could say that was the end of my formal education" (Sager, 1999).

Chris developed what is sometimes called a *dual life* strategy by those very high in IQ. On the

one hand, he seemed like a regular guy—a bouncer at a nightclub who drove a Harley motorcycle. On the other hand, however, he had ambitions to write a theory that integrated cognitive psychology and physics.

In the early 2000s, he married a woman with a high IQ, whom he met through running a website for the "severely gifted." An introduction to his now fully developed theory, "The Cognitive-Theoretic Theory of the Universe: A New Kind of Reality Theory," was recently published in the scientific web journal, *Progress in Complexity, Information, and Design,* where it was accorded considerable respect.

To integrate this material, it can help to try to organize aspects of it according to a structural division of personality. For example, one structural division discussed later in this chapter, the *systems set,* divides personality into an energy lattice (including motives and emotions), a knowledge area including thinking and identity, a social actor, and an executive consciousness that oversees the rest. Can some or all of this information be organized helpfully according to the system?

and its social behavior to the outside world (Mischel & Shoda, 1995). Finally, systems-oriented psychologists may look at ways of employing the different structural divisions in an integrated fashion (Mayer, 2001).

Personality Structure Provides Organization

Although there is more than one good way to divide up personality, not all such divisions are equally good. Four criteria in particular can help separate useful personality divisions from less useful ones. These criteria promote personality structures that are economical, useful, and scientifically valid (Mayer, 2001; 2005).

The first criterion is that a good structural model should divide personality into a few large, good areas (see Table 8.1). Using fewer than three divisions could threaten to oversimplify personality too much; using many more than seven would tend to undermine one of the points of a structural division, which is to employ a small number of areas.

TABLE 8.1	**Criteria for Good Structural Divisions of Personality**
Criteria	Rationale
Appropriateness of the Size of the Set	A desirable number of divisions is between three and ten. If the divisions are fewer than three, they may lack sufficient detail; if the divisions are greater than ten, they may begin to blend into individual parts of personality.
Adequate Empirical Basis	Each division should describe a scientifically plausible division of personality that is found in most or all personalities.
Distinctiveness	The divisions should describe areas of personality that are distinctly different from one another.
Comprehensiveness	The parts should comprehensively contain all the parts of personality.

Source: Based on Mayer (2001), Table 1.

The second criterion is that each division of personality possess an adequate scientific basis. That is, each area of personality should be reasonably recognized as occurring in every healthy personality. Describing an "emotions" area of personality, or a trait structure related to "sociability" or "extraversion" (as in the Big Five) have sound scientific bases: the phenomena exist, can be readily produced, and plainly have important effects. By contrast, describing an area that receives telepathic (i.e., paranormal) communication would be much more controversial, given the ongoing debate as to whether such phenomena in fact exist at all, and if they do, how to

Christopher Michael Langan's personality consists of far more than his high IQ. Knowing about the structure of personality helps integrate information about the individual's mental life to create a picture of the whole.

reliably produce such effects (e.g., Bem & Honorton, 1994; Milton & Wiseman, 1999; Storm & Ertel, 2001).

The third criterion is that the divisions of mind create distinct areas. If one divides the mind into motivation, emotion, and cognition—as is done in the trilogy of mind—it is necessary to be able to explain how one area differs from another. For example, basic motivations are often said to signal psychophysiological needs, and this distinguishes them from basic emotions, which signal aspects of changing relationships. A hypothetical division that separated an emotional area from a mood area would be less compelling because these phenomena are more closely interconnected, although they can be distinguished (moods outlast emotions, for example).

Fourth, a structural division of personality must be comprehensive in the sense that it covers the most important parts of personality. For example, a set that failed to include motives or failed to account for unconscious areas would be problematic because of the omission of these important areas. Even so, a structural model can be useful. For example, the first type of structure we will examine are structures for organizing traits. Although trait models are of undeniable importance, they have been criticized exactly because they provide only a partial coverage of the personality system and omit such important personality structures as the self and a conscience (Loevinger, 1994).

How Are Personality Traits Structured?

What if a global picture of personality could be provided by just a few global traits? If that were the case, then just taking one or two quick personality tests would provide an individual with a rich source of self-knowledge useful to explaining one's past and guiding one in the future. Identifying such key divisions is the aspiration of psychologists who try to divide personality into a few large traits.

Hierarchical Structure of Traits: This is a structural conception or theory about traits in which there are said to be big traits or super traits that can be divided into a larger number of lower-level, specific traits.

Psychologists generally agree that traits can be usefully represented in the form of **hierarchical structures of traits**, consisting of several levels. At the lowest level of the trait hierarchy are individual test items such as, "Are you an anxious person?" "Do people consider you nervous?" and "Do you have many fears?" Next, factor analysis is applied to the items and factors are extracted representing a second level of traits. The items just listed form a factor representing Anxiety. Other items might lead to related but distinct factors such as Emotional Sensitivity (e.g., "Are you sensitive to others' remarks about you?") or Moodiness (e.g., "Are you moody?"). Those mid-level traits (factors) may themselves be factor analyzed along with others. The result of such a second factor analysis usually results in obtaining a group of **big (or super) traits**. Big or super traits are broad traits such as Neuroticism that encompass the more specific traits. For example, Neuroticism is composed of mid-level traits including Anxiety, Emotional Sensitivity, and Moodiness.

Big or Super Traits: These are very general, broad, thematic expressions of mental life that are relatively consistent within the individual, and that can be subdivided into more specific traits.

A second example of such a big or super trait is that of Extraversion. Its measurement begins at the individual item level with questions such as, "Do you prefer parties to reading?" "Do you often search for thrills?" and "Are you a lively person?" Factor analyses of such items yield mid-level traits such as Sociability, Sensation-Seeking, and Liveliness, and a factor analysis of these yields Extraversion itself. These relationships can be portrayed in tree-like diagrams in which the largest factor

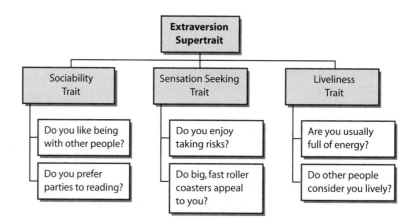

FIGURE 8.1

Test Items, Traits, and Supertraits
The diagram illustrates how the self-judgments reflected by individual test items combine together to form traits and then how traits, in turn, join together into supertraits.

structures are on top and the subfactors that make them up are in the middle, and the individual items are on the bottom. Figure 8.1 shows the division of extraversion into subtraits such as sociability, sensation-seeking, and liveliness.

You may recall from the chapter on intelligence that intelligences, too, were represented as a hierarchy that begins with individual mental abilities, includes a middle level of specific intelligences such as verbal and perceptual-organizational intelligences, and concludes with general intelligence at the top. This is yet another example of the hierarchical nature of traits. *Trait structure*, in the sense just described, refers to this hierarchical structure. The hierarchical structure, in turn, is based on the correlation of test items, the mid-level trait factors identified through factor analysis, and the big or superfactors, identified through a second round of factor analysis. The use of the term "structure" to refer to this statistical pattern of relationships is a usage with which virtually all psychologists would agree.

There exists, however, a second more controversial, sense in which the term trait structure is used. The second way in which trait structure is used is, essentially, synonymous with personality structure. In this sense, each trait is viewed as a bio-psycho-behavioral system that, in combination with other traits, describes much of personality (e.g., McCrae & Costa, 1999). In this sense, neuroticism refers not only to an intercorrelated pattern of psychological test items, but to a psychoneurological structure in the brain that leads to behavioral regularities. Viewed in this "strong" way, the structure of traits becomes synonymous with the structure of personality itself (e.g., Digman, 1990). On the other hand, many psychologists are reluctant to consider neuroticism as a structure per se. Rather, they say, neuroticism is best thought of as a description, or operating characteristic, of the emotion system (e.g., Averill, 1992; Block, 1995; Mayer, 2001).

Whichever viewpoint you subscribe to, a great deal of research has been conducted over the past fifty years to understand the structure of traits. It is only a slight simplification to say that the march of progress concerning traits has been almost entirely in one direction: more and more big traits are being found. We begin our coverage of trait structure with the Big Two and Three, move to the Big Five, and then briefly consider a Big Six and Big Seven. As we do you may want to ask yourself, "Is this or another set of traits enough to describe my whole personality?"

The Big Two and the Big Three

Sometimes important scientific ideas emerge from scientific debates. This was the case for the discovery of the hierarchical arrangement of personality traits. Hans Eysenck had proposed a two-dimensional model of personality traits made up of Extraversion-Introversion and Neuroticism-Emotional Stability—as you may recall from Chapter 4, "Motivation and Emotion." Raymond Cattell, another trait psychologist, challenged Eysenck by creating a test with very similar items that contained sixteen factors of personality rather than two. Many of Cattell's suggested traits appeared specific compared to Eysenck's. For example, whereas Eysenck focused on the broad dimension of Neuroticism—Emotional Stability, Cattell described more specific dimensions apparently related to Neuroticism, including Apprehensive—Self-Assured, Tense—Relaxed, and Reactive—Emotionally Stable. In all, he wrote of sixteen primary traits, along with several others (Cattell, 1965, pp. 95–97; IPAT, 1991).

Big Two Supertraits: This is a specific hierarchical structural model of traits, proposed by Hans Eysenck, in which two traits: Extraversion-Introversion and Neuroticism-Stability, are divisible into more specific traits. Collectively, the two supertraits and their subdivisions are said to describe much of personality.

Eysenck and Cattell debated whether a two- or a sixteen-factor depiction of personality traits was best. The debate was quite frustrating for those who witnessed it, leading two well-known textbook writers to wonder if factor analysis, "is so objective and rational, why is it that those who know most about it are least agreed as to just how the process should go?" (Hall & Lindzey, 1959, pp. 416–417).

Ultimately Eysenck and colleagues demonstrated that when Cattell's sixteen factors were treated as items on a test and factor-analyzed, they yielded a higher level of traits that corresponded reasonably well to Eysenck's two dimensions. These became known as the first two "big factors" or "superfactors" of today. Thus was born the hierarchical structure of traits (e.g., Adcock, Adcock, & Walkey, 1974; Cattell, 1956; Eysenck, 1972).

Big Three Supertraits: This is a later modification of the Big Two Supertrait model by Eysenck in which a third supertrait, Psychotocism-Tender Mindedness, was added.

Eysenck's Two-Factor model, Neuroticism-Stability, Extraversion-Introversion, thus became a "**Big Two**" model. It was, however, shortly followed by a "**Big Three**" model, in which Eysenck suggested a new broad supertrait he called "Psychoticism." Psychoticism referred to a tendency toward being solitary, being uncaring toward people, and being troublesome. In some individuals, this may be joined with insensitivity, inhumanity, and cruelty. People high in psychoticism experience alterations in consciousness and suffer many of the symptoms of people with mental disorders, including eccentricity, paranoia, and isolation. Unlike those with mental disorders, however, they do not appear to be at any higher risk for losing contact with reality (Chapman, Chapman, & Kwapil, 1994; Eysenck & Eysenck, 1975, p. 5).

Big Five Model: This is a hierarchical structural model of traits, developed by a number of researchers, in which five broad traits are used to describe personality. The five are: Neuroticism-Stability, Extraversion-Introversion, Openness-Closedness, Agreeableness-Disagreeableness, and Conscientiousness-Carelessness.

Eysenck's system was not the only Big Three, however. Auke Tellegen and his colleagues' Multidimensional Personality Questionnaire (Patrick, Curtin, & Tellegen, 2002) provided a second version of a set of three supertraits. The Big Three of this scale are Negative Affect (similar to Neuroticism), Positive Affect, and Control. Tellegen's Big Three can be conceived of as centering upon emotion and emotion-related self-control. This forms the core of infant and child temperament and is very useful in developmental studies (see Chapter 11).

The Big Five

More popular than any Big Three, however, is a competing solution known as the **Big Five Model**, a group of five traits. The powerful advantage of the Big Five over its

TABLE 8.2	The Big Five Personality Factors and Their Descriptions
Emotionality (or, Neuroticism)- Emotional Stability	This dimension is named identically to Eysenck's dimension of emotionality-stability and in fact essentially identical to it. The dimension reflects a high degree of (frequently) negative emotion on one end, and a generally stable, pleasant disposition on the other. This dimension can be broken down into facets. These tend to include such characteristics as anxiety, hostility, and depression, along with vulnerability, neediness, and self-consciousness.
Extraversion- Introversion	This dimension is named identically to Eysenck's dimension of extraversion-introversion and is in fact largely identical to it. The dimension reflects a motivation for and enjoyment of social contact on the extraversion side, and a motivation for and enjoyment of quietude and solitude on the introversion side. This dimension, too, has a number of subfactors, including warmth, assertiveness, activity, sensation-seeking, and positive emotionality.
Openness- Closedness	This dimension involves an openness and flexibility of thought on one end, and a closed rigidity on the other. Sometimes called "Culturedness," and even "Intelligence," this factor reflects facets in particular of aesthetics, feelings, and values. The open individual would be interested in aesthetics, even when they are novel or new, would be in contact with their feelings, and would value flexibility and give-and-take in their relationships with others.
Agreeableness- Disagreeableness	This dimension is sometimes also called Friendliness-Hostility. People high on the friendliness end tend to be trusting and straightforward, modest, and compliant. Those on the disagreeable end would be suspicious, oppositional, self-aggrandizing or hostile.
Conscientiousness- Carelessness	The final dimension describes a conscientious character in which the individual values and obeys order and duty, performs with competence, and, perhaps, values achievement.

Lexical Hypothesis: The hypothesis that the most important personality traits are those that can be found in the language people use to describe one another.

earlier competitors is that it employs a unique procedure for how to select items on a test. This procedure is defined by the **lexical hypothesis**, which states that the most important personality concepts can be found in people's everyday language. Identifying the personality traits that naturally occur in language should therefore direct psychologists to the most important traits that make up personality structure (Saucier & Goldberg, 2001, pp. 2–5). In practice, this means collecting and analyzing trait adjectives from dictionaries—words like "shy," "emotional," "prompt," and "cultured." By contrast, the earlier two- and three-factor tests of Hans Eysenck, and sixteen factors of Raymond Cattell, were based on test items written and selected by the researchers themselves.

To examine the traits embedded in English, Allport and Odbert (1936) listed approximately 4,500 trait adjectives related to personality from an unabridged dictionary. Cattell (1948) examined their list and, using factor analysis, suggested that there might exist about thirty-five bipolar dimensions represented by them. Shortly thereafter, Fiske (1949) reanalyzed some of Cattell's work and suggested that five factors might describe the themes encoded in the language. Others agreed, and this Big Five model, consisting of a five-factor solution, became the preferred one (Digman, 1990; Goldberg, 1993; John et al., 1988).

Although five factors are often treated as the preferred solution, the exact naming of the factors has been a matter of some controversy, as pointed out by John Digman (1990, pp. 422–424). For our purposes, the factors can be referred to as neuroticism, extraversion, openness, agreeableness, and conscientiousness. The first two factors should be familiar because they are essentially Eysenck's emotionality-stability and introversion-extraversion factors. These, along with the remaining three factors, are listed in Table 8.2. After each dimension is a brief description of what it is expected to measure. In addition to this are "facets"—smaller scales that occupy the mid-level of the hierarchy. The exact facet scales tend to vary from one Big Five model to another (see Costa & McCrae, 1985, for an example).

> [Referring to the Big Five]
> **Rapid progress has been made toward a consensus on personality structure.**
> Paul Costa & Robert McCrae

The widespread use of the Big Five trait approach has meant that results from many personality studies can be compared more easily because the researchers compared the same traits to see how they predict a given criterion (e.g., job success). The use of the Big Five and similar big sets has led to other interesting research as well. For example, Paunonen (1998) compared the use of big traits versus the more specific traits that make them up to see which level of the trait hierarchy would best predict such outcomes as students' grade-point averages, how many dates they went on over a month, whether they smoked, and (among students who drove), how many speeding tickets they had received. The result? The specific traits were often superior to using the broader, big traits. The drawback? One has many more traits to contend with and to understand.

Each of the Big Five personality traits can lead to fairly evaluative statements about people: *Disagreeable, Careless,* and *Neurotic,* for example (cf., Hare, 1952, p. 111). So what happens if you make the scales more descriptive and less evaluative? Saucier, Ostendorf, and Peabody (2001) created dimensions that were more neutral than judgmental-appearing dimensions such as *courageous* versus *cowardly*. For example, in their study, *courageous* versus *cowardly* became the more neutral *bold* versus *cautious*. Rather than five factors, they found just two fairly neutral dimensions. The first is a Tight-Loose dimension, and contrasts *orderly, organized,* and *economical* with *social, happy-go-lucky* and *impulsive*. The second is an Assertive-Unassertive dimension, and contrasts *confident, forceful,* and *aggressive*, with *uncompetitive, unaggressive,* and *naïve*. Interestingly, when people fill out more neutral—less evaluative—ratings, there may be higher inter-rater agreement as to what a person is like.

Beyond the Big Five

But wait a minute. If there is a Big Five, couldn't there be a Big Six, or a Big Seven as well? To examine this possibility, researchers have examined adjective clusters appearing in the English language that were not already part of the Big Five (Paunonen & Jackson, 2000; Saucier & Goldberg, 1998). There are apparently a number of potential big factors beyond the first five. Some of these are: Religious-Nonreligious, Deceptive-Honest, Sexy-Nonsexual, Thrifty-Spendthrift, Conservative-Radical, Masculine-Feminine, Conceited-Humble, and Humorous-Serious (Paunonen & Jackson, 2000).

Is the structure of traits the same thing as the structure of personality? There is considerable controversy about this in the field. Some say a good group of traits can

Inside the Field

Does the Big Five Count as a Personality Structure?

What counts as a personality structure? To create a model of personality structure requires dividing personality into broad areas that are distinct from one another, that comprehensively cover personality, and that are relatively stable. In practice, however, how far can this conception of structure be stretched? Inside the field, there is a debate as to whether trait structure is the same thing as personality structure. Some trait theorists believe that personality can be studied exclusively through its traits—with little attention to mental mechanisms such as motives or mental models such as schemas.

Researchers in the trait tradition identify a group of traits and show how smaller traits can be correlated together to make "big" or "super" traits (as with factor analysis, described in Chapter 2). A given superfactor represents traits that correlate among themselves, and not with other traits belonging to a different superfactor. Sets of traits such as the Big Three (Extraversion, Neuroticism, and Psychoticism) or the Big Five (Neuroticism, Extraversion, Openness, Agreeableness, and Conscientiousness) arise. Such sets are then said to count as—or to define—personality structure. It seems entirely legitimate to call these trait structures, but can they define personality structure? Those who

adopt the five-factor approach sometimes suggest that the Big Five Factors are all that is needed to assess personality (Goldberg, 1990; 1993; McCrae & Costa, 1990).

Not everyone agrees. Jack Block, for example, argued that the five-factor approach cannot be a personality structure. First, he argues, sets of traits are often selected according to empirical criteria. For example, the Big Five are selected because they represent common factors describing some trait terms in the English language. They cannot be a structural model because they are not theoretically based, and hence, cannot be explained according to any reasonable theory of how personality operates.

Block argued secondly, that traits such as the Big Five are identified by outside observation (e.g., through the language). Personality structure, on the other hand, lies within individuals. Block suggests that it makes sense to talk of a Five-Factor Variable Approach (FFA) to personality descriptions, but that it does not make sense to speak of a complete personality structure as described by five trait factors.

On different grounds, the argument has been made that personality structures ought to describe functional parts of personality as opposed to traits. For example, one such functional area, the emotion system, carries out

define personality structure. Many others, however, believe that the structure of traits, although essential to understanding personality, is something less than the structure of the whole personality itself. Structural models of traits do not cover interior selves and worlds, or the conscious self, or low-level mental mechanisms. For that reason, some have denied that they represent personality structure at all (e.g., Block, 1995). There is little question, though, that they at least represent one important approach to personality structure. That controversy is highlighted in the Inside the Field box. Before making up your mind about whether the trait structures are enough to describe a person, it is helpful to examine some alternatives.

a specific set of tasks (responding to social events with an organized set of feelings and thoughts, for example). Traits such as neuroticism describe how the emotion system functions (e.g., that it tends to be relatively negative) but such a trait description is different from the function it describes. The structure of traits, therefore, although describing an aspect of personality, is not a personality structure itself Mayer, 2001, p. 452).

Finally, Loevinger (1994) offered an important example of the difference between trait and structural approaches, by using the example of the Big Five trait of conscientiousness and comparing it to a fully developed personal conscience that is possible in a mature personality. In the Big Five, conformity and conscientiousness mean the same thing. Being conscientious means endorsing such ideas as being conventional and traditional; it means rejecting such ideas as being nonconforming, rebellious and unconventional (e.g., Goldberg, 1990). In real life, however, being truly conscientious involves understanding when to be conventional and when to rebel. For example, being conscientious in an unjust society would require fighting for justice, whereas the conformist is "just following orders." (Think about fighting for justice in the 1970s in apartheid South Africa, versus conforming to their political system of the time.) The conformist feels guilty for breaking rules; the conscientious person feels guilty when the consequences of his or her actions hurt others. The Big Five trait of consciousness blends these together, but they can be viewed—perhaps more meaningfully—as two different stages in the development of a functional area: the conscience.

For Loevinger, a person's moral models—his or her conscience—can be viewed as a functional area. Such areas may begin by viewing conformity as moral but develop into a higher more thoughtful approach to morality. Whereas the conformist tends to speak in simplistic terms such as following the rules, the person making the transition to a higher morality becomes aware that it is impossible to follow all the rules. There are qualifications to various rules, circumstances in which some rules don't apply, and when some rules must be broken. Such a realization, in turn, marks the emergence of new developmental structures (Loevinger, 1994, pp. 4–5).

In leveling her criticism at the Big Five, Loevinger has highlighted yet another feature of personality structures—that certain structures emerge through development. For Loevinger and others a person's mental structures change from stage to stage. "These stages," writes Loevinger (1994, p. 4) "are at bottom not merely behaviors, they are *structures;* they have implications for ways of perceiving, ways of knowing, and ways of acting and thinking."

What Are Structural Models of Awareness and Why Do They Matter?

Rationale for Structural Models of Awareness

Recall that any complex system, such as the mind, can be divided in more than one way. There is more than one way to divide most complex systems. A city, for example, can be divided into electoral districts, or into geological formations, and there will be little resemblance between the two models, although each is useful for its given purpose. Traits provide only one such division. We should not be surprised that there are other divisions useful for other purposes.

Structural models of awareness focus on the distinction between consciousness and unconsciousness. These models divide the contents of the mind according to what a person is and is not aware of. The given purpose of awareness models is to describe self-knowledge and its limits by understanding the flow of information in the mind, and specifically, the flow of information into awareness. Structural models of awareness tell us what a person can and cannot know about him or herself. For example, if people have conscious access to their emotions (i.e., their feelings) but they don't know why they behave the way they do, then asking a person about his or her emotions should be very informative, whereas asking questions about why the person did what he or she did will yield less reliable information.

Western philosophy is based partly on the belief that if one doesn't have good self-knowledge and doesn't know the limits of one's own self-awareness, one may be more likely to engage in foolish or reckless behavior. In Plato's ancient Greek meditation on self-knowledge, *Phaedrus,* Socrates exclaims that he cares only about knowing himself, every other pursuit being laughable so long as that self-knowledge is lacking (Griswold, 1986, p. 2).

The possibility that self-knowledge might be far more limited than acknowledged in classical philosophy became clearer in the eighteenth and nineteenth centuries. During that time, more and more evidence accumulated that important parts of the mind might be unconscious. A particularly striking example of this was the *post-hypnotic suggestion.* Here, a physician hypnotized a patient and suggested he or she perform some behavior upon awakening. After awakening from the hypnotic trance, the person often performed the act with no recollection of the suggestion. The increasing recognition of placebo cures in medicine—in which a harmless agent was presented to a patient as a cure and showed a discernable curative effect—was another example of how the mind could apparently fool itself (Ellenberger, 1981).

Structural models that divided consciousness from the unconscious were proposed in Austria by Sigmund Freud, and in France by Pierre Janet. Their models used terms such as the *preconscious,* the *unconscious,* and the *subconscious,* to describe areas that were not fully connected to conscious awareness (Perry & Laurence, 1984). Conscious awareness, and the unconscious regions of the mind that have been mapped out since the times of Freud and Janet, will be examined next (e.g., Bargh, 1997; Kihlstrom, 1990).

Consciousness and How Things Become Conscious

Consciousness: A subjective experience of attention and awareness, and the capacity to reflect on that awareness.

Structural models that separate the conscious from the unconscious typically treat consciousness as synonymous with awareness. In such models, **consciousness** simply refers to those things which are in our attentional spotlight and which we can describe. Freud likened consciousness to an internal sense organ, an inner eye, as it were. People can be asked to report what they are conscious of, and they are often willing to provide as accurate an answer as they can. The question therefore becomes, what can enter consciousness and what cannot?

Closely related to consciousness is the concept of memories—materials that could become conscious, or not. Freud suggested that there existed a class of mental thoughts that included all those materials in memory that could readily become conscious if needed—such as one's name, the sum of five plus five, or the meaning of the word "entertainment." In contemporary cognitive terms, Freud's idea is approximated by **declarative memory**. Declarative memory refers to information retrievable from memory that can be readily brought to mind (David, 2001; Eichenbaum, 1997; J. M. Ross, 2003). Freud referred to this same aspect of memory as the **preconscious**.

One model of declarative memory is that it consists of associations among concepts, through which activation spreads. Activation refers to a level of mental energy—perhaps the rate of neural firing—associated with a concept at a given moment. When activation rises over a threshold, a concept is retrieved (i.e., becomes conscious). If one wanted to remember the name of a red bird featured in a song, for example, one might try thinking of the color red, and of bird names, to retrieve the name of the type of bird one is seeking. Thinking of the color red and of bird names would raise the activation level of associated areas. For example, the concept "red" might spread activation to fire trucks, apples, and that elusive bird's name. The concept of "birds' names" might spread activation to pigeons, ostriches, and those elusive birds. When the two sources of activation intersect along such chains of association, the target concept itself—that red, red, *robin*—becomes further suffused with mental energy, raising the likelihood that finally it will come to mind (Collins & Loftus, 1975). So, concepts in declarative memory that are below the activation threshold are not conscious, but they may become conscious with the correct retrieval strategy.

Contrasting with consciousness and declarative memory are a number of **unconscious** areas—consisting of those mental processes that have no communication with consciousness.

Declarative Memory or Preconscious: Declarative memory includes all the information in memory that could be consciously retrieved if necessary. The preconscious was Freud's earlier term for this aspect of memory.

> The term psychic structure does not appear in the general index of Freud's writings. In fact no one seems to know who coined the term structural theory in the first place.
>
> Dale Boesky

Unconscious: A part of the mind that cannot or does not readily enter awareness.

The "No-Access" Unconscious, or Unconscious Proper

There is good reason to have an unconscious. If we were consciously aware of everything our minds did, we would be constantly distracted—and then we would have trouble concentrating on the really important things of life. Our consciousness is better put to use focusing on things of interest to us: our goals and values, and how to attain them. Perhaps for that reason, our mind seems to have evolved so that large areas of its activities are sealed off from consciousness and cannot disturb, or even communicate, with it. This sealed-off region goes by several names including the **no access unconscious** (which we shall use here) and the **unconscious proper** (Dennett, 1978, p. 150; Kihlstrom, 1990, p. 457). The no-access unconscious refers to all mental activities that simply lack any communication channel to consciousness.

The descriptor, "no access," comes from an essay by Daniel Dennett in which he draws an analogy to the operating system of a computer that reads the time from a separate clock in the computer hardware and displays the time on the corner of the screen for the user to see. The operating system displays the time without knowing how the clock works or what "time" is or how it is calculated. Similarly, for Dennett, our minds "display" to us pictures of the surrounding world, but we do not consciously track how the brain composes them—and we are unaware of how the brain composes them.

No-Access Unconscious or Unconscious Proper: Portions of neural activity that take place with no connection to consciousness, such as the firing of individual nerve pathways or the elementary processing of psychological information.

Research in Focus

If There Are Structural Areas, What Are the Boundaries between Them Like?

Each structural division of mind implies that there are boundaries between them. In the trilogy of mind, for example, if there is emotion, and if there is cognition, then presumably there is some line of demarcation, or at least a gradient, or neutral zone between them. Similarly for conscious and nonconscious effects. There are many interesting approaches to examining such boundaries.

The psychoanalyst Ernest Hartmann and his colleagues (Hartmann, Harrison, & Zborowski, 2001), for example, have examined whether some people have thin boundaries and others have thick boundaries. As Hartmann puts it:

> The basic underlying notion is a fairly obvious one. No matter how we think of the content of our minds—whether we think in everyday terms of thoughts, feelings, memories; in cognitive psychology terms of perceptual, semantic and memory processes (or "modules"); or perhaps in psychoanalytic terms of ego, id, superego, defenses, etc.—we are speaking of parts, or regions or processes, which in some sense can be considered separate from one another, and yet which are obviously connected. The boundaries between them are not absolute separations. The boundaries can be relatively thick or solid on the one hand, and relatively thin or permeable on the other hand.

In Hartmann's terms, a person with very thick boundaries would be someone who can easily keep matters in focus and block out distractions. The person is aware of either thinking or feeling, but would not do both at the same time. The individual is awake when awake, and asleep when asleep, and doesn't much experience in-between states. The individual has a very clear sense of boundaries, identity, and group identity as well ("I am a Republican and will always be one"). Many matters are black and white for this individual.

A person with very thin boundaries, by contrast, often has blending of sensory experiences (called synesthesia). The individual may see images in response to musical sounds, or hear notes in response to tastes. The individual will tend to be responsive to inputs from many different sources at once, and can be easily overwhelmed and confused by too much input. The thin-boundary person is often aware of feeling and thinking at the same time ("I always feel when I think") and often experiences half-asleep, half-awake states. Thin-boundary people may blend together different ages when think-

To some extent, parts of the mind form their own separate compartments, and those compartments often have little communication with one another (Fodor, 1985). This idea can be illustrated with the well-known Müller-Lyer illusion shown in Figure 8.2. We see two lines. It looks as if the bottom line is longer. But they are, in fact, the same length (Müller-Lyer, 1889). No matter how many times we see these two lines, one line looks longer than the other. We can study this illusion, delving into the principles of depth perception that are believed to bring it about, and yet the illusion will remain. In essence, the perceptual mechanisms for creating the illusion are compartmentalized. We have no conscious access to them, we cannot educate them, we cannot stop them from doing what they are doing. Nor can we understand what they are doing simply through "looking into our own minds" (Fodor, 1985; Nisbett & Wilson, 1977).

ing about themselves—seeing their inner child as adult, for example, and often think in terms of shades of grey.

Hartmann and colleagues have developed a scale to assess boundaries. People with thin boundaries endorse items such as, "When I awake in the morning, I am not sure whether I am really awake for a few minutes," "At times I have felt as if I were coming apart," and "Sometimes I don't know whether I am thinking or feeling." In contrast, people with thick boundaries endorse items such as "I keep my desk and work table neat and well organized," "I like heavy, solid clothing," and "A good relationship is one in which everything is clearly defined and worked out."

The Boundary Questionnaire is relatively independent of most other personality scales. Two exceptions are its high correlation with Tellegen's Absorption Scale (which is related to hypnotic susceptibility, and the Big Five scale: openness, with which it has been correlated $r = .73$). The Boundary Questionnaire, however, is conceptually different and perhaps more neutral in its formulation than is openness-closedness. That is, there are both advantages and drawbacks to scoring at either end of the thick-thin boundary continuum. Thick-boundary people refer to themselves as solid and reliable, and to thin scorers as flaky and far out. On the other hand, thin-boundary people refer to

themselves as exciting and innovative, whereas they refer to thick-boundary people as dull, rigid, and unimaginative.

High scorers on the BQ include art students, music students, adults with nightmares, frequent dream recallers, "lucid dreamers," models, people with unusual mystical experiences, and those with personality disorders in the odd and eccentric cluster (e.g., schizoid and schizotypal). Low scorers (those with thick boundaries) include naval officers, salespersons, lawyers, persons suffering from alexithymia (e.g., lack of emotional insight), and patients with sleep apnea.

A person might legitimately wonder whether self-perceived blending of mental processes really translates into thinner or fuzzier boundaries by some other measure. Interestingly, physiological recordings of brain activities indicate that those with thick boundaries have more clear-cut states of waking, NREM, and REM sleep. Those with thin boundaries have more blurred sleep physiology. For example, Phasic Integrating Potentials—a sign of REM sleep—occurs far more often outside of REM sleep for thin-boundary than for thick-boundary people. Similarly, musicians, who score as having thinner boundaries than other groups, have more massive connections between their left and right hemispheres than average (e.g., larger corpus callosums; Schlaug et al., 1995).

The Implicit or Automatic Unconscious

Implicit (automatic) Unconscious: A type of mental bias or process that can be determined from experimental measures of memory but of which the person is unaware.

False Fame Effect: An effect in which familiarity with a name leads a person to falsely believe the name is of a famous person.

A particular type of no-access unconscious directs our thoughts and judgments. The term **implicit** or **automatic unconscious** refers to cognitive processes that operate independently of consciousness and yet consistently direct a person's thoughts, judgments, and behaviors according to non-conscious rules and tricks (Bargh & Chartrand, 1999). One example of this involves the **false fame** effect (Jacoby, Woloshyn, & Kelley, 1989).

The false fame effect occurs when people misinterpret their familiarity with a name, as suggesting that the name belongs to a famous person. For example, is "John Digman" famous? If you have been reading along, you have encountered his name several times because of his research with the Big Five personality traits. He has made

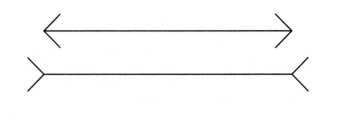

FIGURE 8.2

The Müller-Lyer Illusion
This visual illusion (like others) illustrates how one part of the mind can operate in partial independence of another. Even though people know the lines are the same length, one still looks longer.

important scientific contributions, but by most definitions he is not famous. If his name seemed famous, that sense of seeing his name before may be the reason.

In laboratory studies of the false fame effect, participants first read through a list of names. A day later, the participants are asked to review a new list of names and identify who in the list is famous. The list they see includes some names from the day before, some new names, and some names of genuinely famous people. Participants readily identify the non-famous names they had seen before as famous, along with the names of actually famous people.

This effect is both automatic and hard to make go away. When the experimenter tells participants that no name on the original list is famous, and asks participants to identify any name they recalled from the initial list, the false fame effect still occurs (Jacoby et al., 1989). In one dramatic study, the first list of names was presented to surgery patients while they were under general anesthesia. The patients then exhibited the false fame effect when tested during their recoveries (Jelicic et al., 1992). In the next chapter, we will see further examples of how simple exposure to ideas can promote certain actions taking place, all outside of conscious recognition (e.g., Bargh Chartrand, 1999).

Connecting Window   *Implicit Unconscious and Dynamics of Action*
A person's motivation can be unconscious to the individual. For example, repeatedly practiced behaviors can be carried out without thinking of them; unconscious desires can be acted on without the individual's knowledge. Such unconscious motivation and control are covered in Chapters 9, "Dynamics of Action," and 10, "Dynamics of Self-Control."

The Unnoticed Unconscious

Unnoticed Unconscious: A type of mental process that consists of influences that could be known if the person paid attention or if the person was taught about the influence, but that goes unnoticed for many or most people.

Yet another type of unconscious process is the **unnoticed unconscious**. The unnoticed unconscious consists of influences that go on in our mind that we could potentially know about if we paid attention to them, but that we often don't notice or understand (Bowers, 1984). For example, most shoppers unknowingly prefer merchandise that appears to their right. Nisbett and Wilson (1977) asked shoppers to select the best pair of nylon stockings from among four identical pairs. People in the study preferred the rightmost pair of identical stockings more often than the others.

When the experimenters asked the consumers why they chose the rightmost pair, most replied that the fabric was smoother, or that the stocking seemed better made. When the experimenters asked shoppers if they simply exhibited a right-side preference, participants often looked at them as if they were crazy.

This sort of unconscious process is particularly significant because a person can be educated to understand it, and to work around it if it is causing problems. But some among those who are directed to pay attention to the cause of their behavior may still miss the point. Bowers (1984, p. 245) conducted a study in which he socially reinforced students for choosing either a landscape or a portrait painting (depending upon the condition). In each trial, a participant viewed two postcards—one with a portrait painting and one with a landscape painting—and chose the one he or she preferred. During the first twenty experimental trials, the participants' baseline preferences of landscapes or portraits were assessed. During the next seventy trials, students in the experimental group were reinforced for choosing a class of paintings (portraits or landscapes) opposite from their initial preference. Students in the control group were reinforced for staying with their initial preferences. The experimenter smiled and said "good" after the desired choice so as to provide social reinforcement.

Although the reinforcement changed people's preferences in the experimental group, many participants failed to notice its influence on their behavior, or even denied it was possible. For example, one young woman had initially preferred portraits, and was reinforced to prefer landscapes. After the reinforcement phase, Bowers asked the young woman about her awareness of what was going on:

EXPERIMENTER: Did you notice whether I said anything during the course of the experiment?
SUBJECT: You said "good" whenever I picked landscapes.
EXPERIMENTER: Do you think your tendency to pick landscapes was influenced by my reinforcement of them?
SUBJECT: Of course not! I picked landscapes because I liked them better than the portraits. Besides, you only said "good" after I made my choice, so what you said couldn't possibly have influenced my selection of pictures. (Bowers, 1984, p. 245)

The woman failed to recognize that she was being reinforced for choosing landscapes as a general class of painting. Rather, she believed she received a smile for the choice of individual landscape paintings and that this had no bearing on her future choices. As a consequence, she failed to appreciate what was actually controlling her behavior even after it was pointed out to her. She suffered from unconsciousness due to the inability to notice and, in this case, an inability to understand.

The Dynamic Unconscious

Dynamic Unconscious: Material that is made unconscious, through the redirection of attention, because the material is too painful or unpleasant to think about or feel.

The **dynamic unconscious** refers to an unconscious in which mental contents are purposely banished from consciousness because the ideas contained are too threatening for the individual to face. This unconscious, elaborated by Sigmund Freud, holds many ideas that could be conscious but are conscious no longer. Consciousness has, in some fashion, turned away or moved its spotlight of attention in such a way as to avoid this threatening content. The dynamic unconscious is constructed

Defense Mechanisms:
Mental processes that divert attention from painful or unpleasant things to think about. Defense mechanisms help keep material dynamically unconscious.

through the action of defense mechanisms. **Defense mechanisms** are ways that consciousness has of defending itself from dangerous, painful thoughts. For this to occur, the threatening material must be quickly moved out of consciousness and forgotten before it can be recognized. Nonetheless, the banished material continues to exert an influence over conscious choices.

The discussion of defense and underlying motives is covered in detail in Chapter 10 on the dynamics of self-control. For now, one small example of how unconscious fear can change our reasoning will suffice. People exert considerable effort to keep thoughts of their own deaths out of consciousness (Solomon, Greenberg, & Pyszczynski, 1991).

Undergraduates in one condition of an experiment were asked to write an essay about their own deaths. Members of a comparison condition wrote about what dental pain felt like. In a second phase of the study, students read an essay that either argued that human beings were quite different than animals, or quite similar to animals. Those who had earlier written about their own deaths (compared to those who wrote about dental pain) far preferred the essay that argued humans and animals were quite different from one another (Goldenberg et al., 2001, Study 2).

The study results were explained in this way: Animals are a reminder of death threat in that they often live short, meaningless-seeming lives, and are frequently killed to be eaten, or are run over, or otherwise die unfortunate deaths (Becker, 1973). People who had participated in thinking about their own deaths were less willing than others to imagine themselves as similar to animals because they didn't want to further heighten their death concerns. The essay that drew the human-animal connection was therefore regarded as more problematic.

Can Identifying Key Functions of Mind Lead to Structural Divisions?

Functional Models:
Divisions of personality based on the idea that different parts of the system carry out different forms of work (e.g., meeting the organisms needs [motivation] versus solving complex problems [cognition]).

We have examined two different divisions of personality to this point. First, trait models divide personality into a hierarchy of traits. Second, awareness-based models divide personality according to what is conscious and various areas of the unconscious. A third way of dividing personality is according to the functional areas that carry out the different tasks of personality. **Functional models** divide personality into different parts based on the tasks those parts carry out. For example, dividing personality into motivational and cognitive areas would represent a functional area division. The motivation area ensures that the individual meets his or her biological needs. The cognitive area, by contrast, is more concerned with logic and thinking. Dividing personality according to its functions can help identify a comprehensive set of personality areas; these models are therefore helpful for making a statement about what personality does.

The Id, Ego, and Superego as a Functional Model

Freud employed several divisions of the mind. One we have examined already was a division of mind by levels-of-awareness into a conscious, preconscious (declarative memory), and unconscious area. Later in his career, Freud employed a functional

Id: Latin for the "it." One part of Freud's structural division of mind (the other parts are the ego and superego). The id contains sexual and aggressive instincts, and wishes and fantasies related to those instincts.

Ego: Latin for the "self," a part of Freud's structural division of mind that involves rational thought and the control of the person's actions in the world.

Superego: Latin for "above the self"; the superego is a part of Freud's structural division of the mind that involves internalized social rules of conduct and a sense of the ideal one would like to become.

division; he referred to the three areas as the **id, ego,** and **superego** (also see Chapter 7). Freud believed the three areas were ordered according to their evolutionary complexity.

The id's work was to ensure the fulfillment of the organism's animal instincts and needs by communicating those needs to the rest of personality. The id was first developing, and it contained an unconscious collection of sexual and aggressive urges common to lower animals. It operated according to primary, associationistic, imagistic processes common to those same lower animals.

The ego's work was to compromise between a human being's animal needs and the requirements of social reality. The ego contained portions of the mind that could think rationally. It allowed for reality contact and sensible behavior in the outside world, and ultimately for the intellectual processes unique to human beings.

The superego grew out of the ego and had as its purpose ensuring that the individual complied with the demands of society. It contained the learned commands of and influences of society, which a person employed to formulate an ideal self and a conscience.

Freud's division was a good one for its time. But some of the ways it was elaborated are now contradicted by contemporary research (Mayer, 2001). For example, Freud believed that, analogous to evolutionary development, each person's id developed first, and ego functions were added only later. That was a reasonable hypothesis in 1920, but extensive experimental studies since then indicate that infants engage in sophisticated perceptual understanding, some rational problem solving, and some rule-governed social behavior from the outset.

> The structural theory of personality, with its subdivision of the total mental organization into id, ego and superego, has been accepted by most psychoanalyists as a comprehensive theoretical model.
>
> —George Wiedeman

Another aspect of the id-ego-superego division is that it splits the associational, imagistic, qualities of the id from the rationality of the ego. Today, associational thinking is viewed as an integrated part of much rational thought. Rational thought, in turn, is viewed as less reliably logical than Freud and others of his time supposed it to be. So, Freud's division can still be applied but other divisions may provide better models of the mind (e.g., Epstein et al., 1996).

The Trilogy and Quaternity of Mind

A Trilogy of Mind

Trilogy of Mind: This structural model of personality divides the system into three different functional areas: conation (motivation), affect (emotion), and cognition (thought).

Probably the most continuously employed functional model of mental life is the **trilogy of mind** (Hilgard, 1980; Mayer, 2001). The trilogy of mind refers to a division of mind into areas of Motivation (or conation), Affect (emotion), and Cognition. The original trilogy of mind was introduced during the European Enlightenment by Moses Mendelssohn (1755). The trilogy of mind was developed further within a movement called **faculty psychology**. In this case, faculty refers to a mental faculty— that is, a mental capacity or quality. Two eminent Scottish psychologists elaborated the areas of the trilogy of mind by enumerating the individual capacities of the motivation area, the emotion area, and the cognitive area (Reid, 1785/1971; Stewart, 1833/1969). The system has since reappeared in the thinking of a variety of philosophers and psychologists (Hilgard, 1980).

Faculty Psychology: An eighteenth-century movement, predating modern personality psychology, to divide the mind into separate intellectual functions called faculties, which include such broad areas as motivation, emotion, and cognition. Each functional area is, in turn, divided into more specific functions. For example, cognition is subdivided into specific faculties of memory, judgment, evaluation, and the like.

There is now common agreement about what each area denotes. According to one contemporary summary, each functional area evolved to process different stimuli, in different ways, in different areas of the brain (see Table 8.3, first 3 columns; Mayer, Carlsmith, & Chabot, 1997). Motivation directs the organism to carry on basic acts in order to survive and otherwise enhance well-being. It arises in response to bodily states, precedes action, is very specific about what is needed, and seems related to multiple areas of the brain stem, thalamus, and limbic system. Emotion, by contrast, organizes response patterns that may occur in reaction to changes in relationships. Emotions identify interpersonal events that must be addressed, and are related to the amygdala and hypothalamic brain areas of the limbic system. Cognition concerns the capacity to acquire, store, and reason with knowledge. It arises in response to a broad variety of issues and is rather flexible in responding to problems. Its brain locus is the association cortex and cerebral cortex.

Quaternity of Mind: An expanded version of the trilogy of mind that adds consciousness to the traditional areas of motivation, emotion, and cognition.

Some recently have suggested turning the trilogy of mind into a **quaternity of mind**. The quaternity of mind refers to a modification of the trilogy in which consciousness is added as a fourth functional area (Mayer, Chabot, & Carlsmith, 1997). Consciousness, as depicted in Table 8.3, assigns focused mental awareness where needed. It arises as a response to novel or unusually intense events are called for, and it is plastic and creative in how it addresses issues (Ornstein, 1991). A variety of areas of the brain have been hypothesized to be associated with consciousness. When consciousness is added to the trilogy, the trilogy appears more complete in covering mental functions, as well as more comprehensive in organizing the traits of personality (Mayer, 2001).

A Brain to Match?

Triune Brain: A structural model of the human brain that divides its physical areas according to whether the structures resemble those found in reptiles, or whether the brain structures evolved at a later time and resemble those of early mammals, or of more recently evolved mammals.

One reason that the trilogy of mind may be so useful is its correspondence to a division of the brain called the **triune brain** (MacLean, 1977; 1993). The idea of the triune brain is that the brain has undergone three evolutionary bursts of development, each burst resulting in three rather different sets of neurological structures.

The Reptilian Brain

Reptilian Brain: The oldest part of the brain and the part of the "Triune Brain" structural model that includes such early-evolved, inner structures of the brain as the brain stem, pons, and the cerebellum, and portions of the thalamus and hypothalamus.

The first evolutionary burst occurred as animals left the sea for life on land and the brain's evolutionary development accommodated the behavior of reptiles. The newly enlarged **reptilian brain** helped reptiles defend territory on land, secure food, and reproduce; all qualities associated with basic motivations. This earliest evolved portion relied on instincts and stereotyped behavior; it is similar to the innermost core of the human brain.

The brain stem and portions of the thalamus and cerebellum correspond fairly closely to MacLean's reptilian brain (see Figure 8.3). Neurons enter the brain from the spinal cord through the brain stem. This structure is present in all vertebrates and is responsible for the regulation of internal states of the organism such as breathing and the beating of the heart. As they enter the brain, neurons from the right and left sides of the body cross at the medulla, so that the right brain controls the left side of the body, and the left brain controls the right. The reticular formation regulates alertness in the organism, keeping watch for threat and helping the organ-

TABLE 8.3	The Trilogy (and Quaternity) of Mind		
The Quaternity of Mind			
The Trilogy of Mind			
Motivation	**Emotion**	**Cognition**	**Consciousness**
What Is Its Function?			
Directs organism to carry out basic acts so as to satisfy survival and re-productive needs	Organizes a limited num-ber of basic responses to relationships quickly and adaptively	Capacity to acquire, store, and reason with in-formation	Assigns mental activity where needed
How Is It Initiated?			
In response to internal bodily states	In response to changing relationships	In response to internal or external issues	In response to novel or unusually intense events
What Is Its Temporal Course?			
Precede action; rise and fall rhythmically	Time course determined in part by specific feel-ing(s)	No set time line	No set time line
What Information Does It Provide?			
Specific as to what is lacking and what must be done	Identifies events that must be addressed; not specific as to how	Specific or general de-pending upon problem	Plastic and creative in how it addresses issues
In What Area of the Brain Might It Be Located?			
Limbic system, especially the hypothalamus	Limbic system, especially the amygdala and hypo-thalamus	Association and cerebral cortex	Reticular activating sys-tem, or emergent from whole brain

Source: After Mayer, Chabot, & Carlsmith (1997). Reprinted with permission from Elsevier.

ism wake and sleep. Portions of the cerebellum are responsible for posture, whole limb movements, and balance. The pons (Latin, for bridge) marks the entry of nerve signals from the body to higher brain structures. The thalamus, sitting above the pons, channels sensory information such as inputs from the ears and eyes (e.g., the optic chiasma) into the brain. MacLean observed that reptilian brains contain these structures, and also a partially developed thalamus and hypothalamus associated with feeding and sexual behavior, and with other reward and punishment centers (Zuckerman, 1991, pp. 159–164). (See Figures 8.4 and 8.5.)

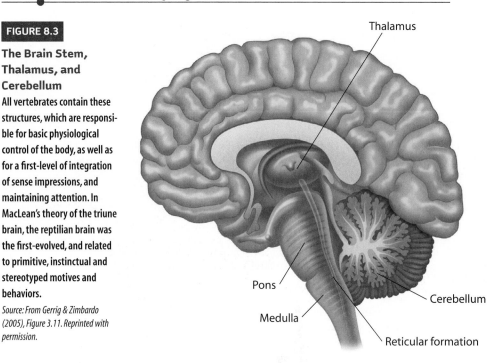

FIGURE 8.3

The Brain Stem, Thalamus, and Cerebellum

All vertebrates contain these structures, which are responsible for basic physiological control of the body, as well as for a first-level of integration of sense impressions, and maintaining attention. In MacLean's theory of the triune brain, the reptilian brain was the first-evolved, and related to primitive, instinctual and stereotyped motives and behaviors.

Source: From Gerrig & Zimbardo (2005), Figure 3.11. Reprinted with permission.

The Paleo-Mammalian Brain

The second evolutionary burst occurred as mammals evolved from reptiles. Mammals differ from reptiles in giving live birth to and rearing their young (as opposed to laying eggs and leaving them). Rearing the young and forming social groups requires more socio-emotional coordination than was necessary for the egg-laying, earlier-evolved reptiles. This required a second layer of brain structures that MacLean called the **paleo-mammalian brain**, and that corresponds to what, today, is referred to as the **limbic system** (see Figure 8.4). The limbic system consists of the hypothalamus, amygdala, and hippocampus. It organizes motivations, emotions, and memory structures at a basic level, along with key physiological functions underlying those states such as body temperature, blood pressure, and blood sugar. It supports the increased emotional and social complexities and requirements of mammalian life, including reproductive acts. In addition, it includes the corpus callosum, a structure that permits communication between the right and left hemispheres, and which may contribute to the integration of thought and feeling (Halpern, 1997, p. 1094).

Paleo (Old-) Mammalian Brain: A newer-evolved portion of the brain, shared in common among many mammals, that includes limbic system structures.

Limbic System: A group of brain structures including the hypothalamus, amygdala, and hippocampus, that together regulate motives, emotions, memory, and physiological processes.

FIGURE 8.4

The Limbic System
The limbic system is present only in mammals and functions to produce and regulate motives, emotions, and memories. In MacLean's theory of the triune brain, this portion of the brain, which he termed the old mammalian brain, evolved in mammals to regulate the emotions and social behavior necessary for raising young.

Source: From Gerrig & Zimbardo (2005), Figure 3.12. Reprinted with permission.

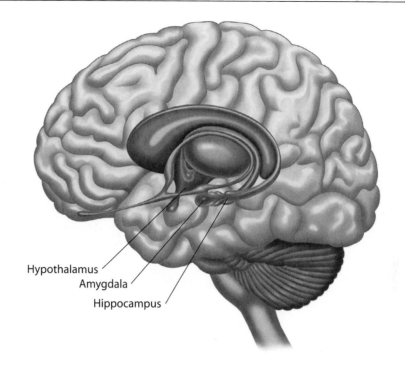

Hypothalamus
Amygdala
Hippocampus

The Neo-Mammalian Brain

Neo (New-) Mammalian Brain: The newest-evolved portion of the brain, shared in common among primates and including the thick outer layer of the cerebral cortex.

Finally, the cerebrum, a third, most sophisticated area of brain evolved among primates. MacLean referred to this as the **neo-mammalian brain,** (see Figure 8.5) because it occurred only among more recently developed mammals. The reason the cerebrum evolved over and above the old-mammalian brain is not fully understood, and yet, in humans, it dwarfs the rest of the brain. The most plausible explanation is that a growing capacity for pre-language communication and language itself provided an extraordinary evolutionary advantage to those who possessed it, and brought along with it the opportunity to better use flexible thinking (Deacon, 1997; Jerison, 2000).

Cerebral Cortex: The outer surface of the brain including massive inter-associations among neurons; most responsible for higher mental processes and reasoning.

The cerebral cortex (or neo-mammalian brain) surrounds the paleo-mammalian brain. It consists of a layer of tissue about 4 millimeters thick (1/10 of an inch) that is wrapped around the earlier-evolved brain structures. The **cerebral cortex** consists of massive inter-associations among neurons, set apart from direct sensory or motor connections. This association cortex permits planning, thinking, judging, communicating, and performing other sophisticated information-processing tasks. The neo-mammalian brain is divided into two hemispheres, right and left, and each hemisphere can be divided further into four lobes: the frontal, parietal, occipital, and temporal.

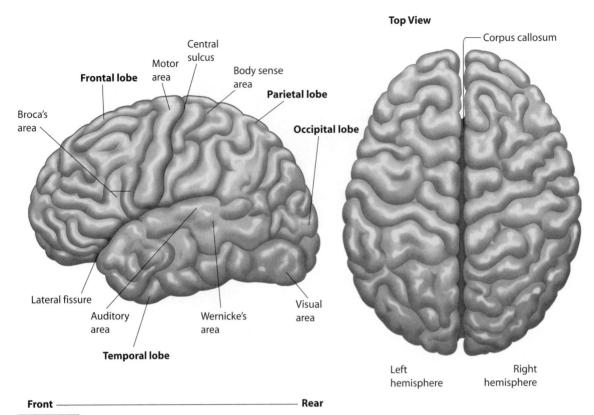

Top View

Corpus callosum

Central sulcus

Motor area

Frontal lobe

Body sense area

Parietal lobe

Broca's area

Occipital lobe

Lateral fissure

Visual area

Auditory area

Wernicke's area

Temporal lobe

Left hemisphere

Right hemisphere

Front ——————————————————————— **Rear**

FIGURE 8.5   **The Cerebral Cortex**

The cerebral cortex reached its pinnacle in primates, and especially homo sapiens. MacLean referred to the cerebral cortex as the new or neo-mammalian brain—which evolved as the seat of voluntary action, higher reasoning, and abstract thinking.

Source: From Gerrig & Zimbardo (2005), Figure 3.13. Reprinted with permission.

The frontal lobes (one in each hemisphere) appear important for complex voluntary actions, as well as the directed, sustained, thought involved in mental synthesis, coordination, and control (Zuckerman, 1991, pp. 148–149). The back area of the frontal lobe contains the *primary motor cortex*. Running parallel across from it, in the front most area of the parietal lobe is the adjoining somatosensory cortex. Together, these structures are sometimes called called the **body homunculus** (see Figure 8.6). Apart from MacLean's model, Freud placed the developing ego at the body homunculus so that it could control the person's actions according to its own rational judgments (Freud, 1923, p. 16). The temporal and occipital lobes are located further back and lower down in the brain.

Body Homunculus: A band of areas in the cerebral cortex, where each area corresponds to a part of the body, in order, such as toes, foot, lower leg, and so forth.

Summary of MacLean's Tri-Partite Division of the Brain

One of the points here is that the trilogy of mind corresponds to some degree to the threefold division of the triune brain, where motivation corresponds to the reptilian brain, emotion to the old-mammalian, and cognition to the neo-mammalian (Mayer,

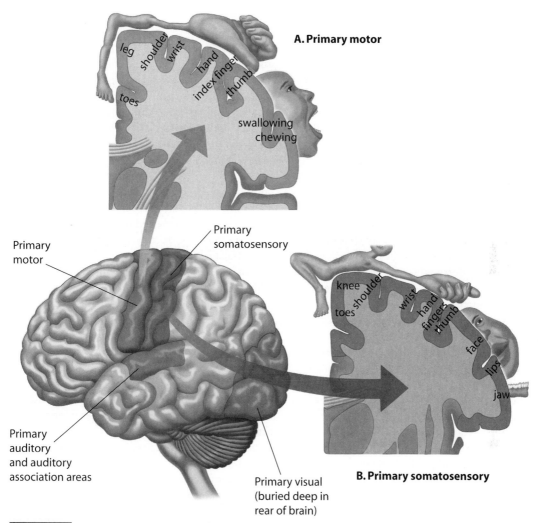

A. Primary motor

Primary
motor

Primary
somatosensory

Primary
auditory
and auditory
association areas

Primary visual
(buried deep in
rear of brain)

B. Primary somatosensory

FIGURE 8.6   **The Body Humunculus**

The body humunculous consists of the sensory and motor portions of the cortex. These portions control body movements themselves, and are arranged rather like the areas of the body itself. Freud suggested that the ego emerged from the motor humunculous—so as to control the person's actions.

Source: From Gerrig & Zimbardo (2005), Figure 3.14. Reprinted with permission.

Chabot, & Carlsmith, 1997). MacLean stressed that each of the three brains had its own means of operation and its own distinct design, and were not fully integrated. For example, the more emotional, lower limbic system in the paleo-mammalian mind might not fully understand or appreciate the cerebral cortex's impressive thought and judgment (Bailey, 1987). That said, it is also true that the brain is far more interconnected than the Maclean model might suggest (Isaacson, 1982). Some specific brain functions such as language, for example, integrate the three functions

Disciplinary Crossroads

Was That Octopus You Saw Last Night Shy?

Do animals have the same kind of personality structure as do human beings? If so, how closely does it resemble human personality? According to trait theorists, animals do possess some of the same trait structures as human beings—although it depends on the animal. Even the lowly octopus can exhibit some signs of shyness and boldness.

A first question is how personality can be assessed in animals. Recall that one method of personality assessment involves employing observer ratings. For example, observers of homo sapiens show good reliability at assessing other people's personalities along all five of the Big Five continua. This should come as relatively little surprise, since the Big Five represent linguistic terms we use in describing one another.

Similar rating scales can be used to assess personality structure in animals—assuming the trait is there to begin with, of course. Certain ratings seem reliable across raters and can often be translated into clear, unambiguous behaviors. Thus, extraversion in the monkey has been defined as "pulling limbs" (playful social contact), "grasping and poking" (relaxed social contact), and "gymnastics." Extraversion in the pig, by contrast, involves vocalizations, nose contacts, and location near other pigs in the pen (Gosling & John, 1999). Such rating scales show good convergence, even over time and situations (Capitanio, 1999).

When measures of the Big Five are examined across species, some traits seem near-universal. For example, a basic Three of extraversion, neuroticism, and agreeableness appear across many different animal species. Some have added confidence to those three dimensions to form a rhesus monkey Big Four (Capitanio & Widaman, 2005). Extraversion, neuroticism, and agreeableness (or close variants) can be found in pigs, dogs, rhesus monkeys, donkeys and others—where such behaviors are fairly consistent over time (Svartberg et al., 2005). Even the octopus appears to vary on a trait reasonably considered extraversion, although it seems to miss out on neuroticism and agreeableness. Introverted humans, of course, stay home, read a book, and avoid contact with others to unwind. The introverted octopus, by comparison, prefers to stay in its protective underwater den during feedings and is more likely than the extraverted octopus to hide itself by changing color or releasing ink into the water (Gosling & John, 1999, p. 70).

Gosling and John (1999, p. 70) argue that, in addition to extraversion, neuroticism, and agreeableness, openness, in the form of curiosity and playfulness, can be found in all forms of monkeys, including the rhesus and vervet, as well as in the chimpanzee. According to the authors you will not find conscientiousness anywhere other than in humans and chimpanzees. Although dogs can learn obedience, their behavior is rated as closer to learning ability and agreeableness than to conscientiousness itself. Chimpanzees, on the other hand, are sometimes judged to be truly dependable or not.

These studies make clear that personality structure—at least as it involves traits—has applicability in biology and zoology. Important evolutionary principles of mental development may reside in such studies. On a more pragmatic note, what kind of horse would you like to ride? For the beginner, agreeable horses might be preferred. As for cats and dogs, emotional stability could be a plus—so they don't tear up the couch while their human caretakers are out. One might also prefer that cat and dog be somewhat reserved so as to avoid any foolish or overintimate encounters with the neighbor's pets, as well as to be outgoing enough to say hello to human company, instead of hiding under the couch.

FIGURE 8.7

The Systems Set
One new way to divide personality is according to its major functions. The systems set begins with a comprehensive picture of the individual's major psychological systems. Each system has a sample subsystem or two beneath it. Systems that are most internal are to the left; those more external, to the right. Systems that are more molecular are toward the bottom; those that are more molar are toward the top. The dotted lines separate out the energy lattice (bottom), knowledge works (center), social actor (right), and conscious executive (top left).

Source: Mayer (2004). Reproduced with permission of John Wiley & Sons, Inc.

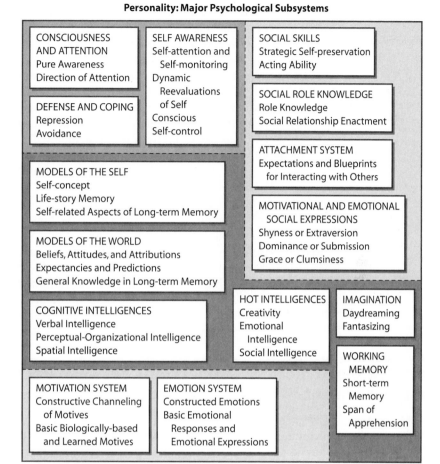

Personality: Major Psychological Subsystems

| CONSCIOUSNESS AND ATTENTION
Pure Awareness
Direction of Attention | SELF AWARENESS
Self-attention and Self-monitoring
Dynamic Reevaluations of Self
Conscious Self-control | SOCIAL SKILLS
Strategic Self-preservation
Acting Ability |

DEFENSE AND COPING
Repression
Avoidance

SOCIAL ROLE KNOWLEDGE
Role Knowledge
Social Relationship Enactment

MODELS OF THE SELF
Self-concept
Life-story Memory
Self-related Aspects of Long-term Memory

ATTACHMENT SYSTEM
Expectations and Blueprints for Interacting with Others

MODELS OF THE WORLD
Beliefs, Attitudes, and Attributions
Expectancies and Predictions
General Knowledge in Long-term Memory

MOTIVATIONAL AND EMOTIONAL SOCIAL EXPRESSIONS
Shyness or Extraversion
Dominance or Submission
Grace or Clumsiness

COGNITIVE INTELLIGENCES
Verbal Intelligence
Perceptual-Organizational Intelligence
Spatial Intelligence

HOT INTELLIGENCES
Creativity
Emotional Intelligence
Social Intelligence

IMAGINATION
Daydreaming
Fantasizing

MOTIVATION SYSTEM
Constructive Channeling of Motives
Basic Biologically-based and Learned Motives

EMOTION SYSTEM
Constructed Emotions
Basic Emotional Responses and Emotional Expressions

WORKING MEMORY
Short-term Memory
Span of Apprehension

of motivation, emotion, and cognition (Zuckerman, 1991). Nonetheless, the MacLean structural model remains a useful introduction to envisioning how the brain works.

Integration in the Systems Set

With the development of criteria for good structural divisions of the mind, and the collection of earlier models such as the trilogy of mind, Freud's divisions, and others, the opportunity arose to see if some more complete structural divisions of personality were possible. The systems set is one such model and is illustrated in Figure 8.7. To create the systems set model, a number of the major systems of personality first were arranged in a two-dimensional diagram. Each system has, beneath it, one or two examples of its own subsystems. The inner-related systems, such as motivational urges, are to the left, and more externally related systems, such as the attachment system, are to the right. In addition, those systems which are relatively more molecular, such as short-term memory, are toward the bottom; those that are more molar, such as the self-concept, are toward the top (Mayer, 2004; 2005).

Approximate though such a diagram might be, it is possible to pick out the major areas of personality we have discussed earlier in this chapter. The **systems set** is a structural division that marks out four general areas of personality functions, denoted by the dotted lines in the diagram. Briefly, the *energy lattice* includes motives and emotions (lower left). These can be distinguished from more cognitive-oriented systems, which extend vertically through the middle of the system. The *knowledge works* includes intelligence, mental abilities, and models of the self and world (extending vertically through the middle). The *social actor* includes the social roles a person knows and chooses to perform (right side). Finally, the *executive consciousness* involves awareness and self-regulation (top left).

Systems Set: A structural model of personality that emphasizes four functional areas: the energy lattice (motivation and emotion), the knowledge works (mental models and intelligence), the social actor (procedural knowledge for behavior), and the executive consciousness (self-awareness and control).

The systems set also includes a distinction between conscious and unconscious processes. The system is conscious to the extent that its functions and processes are accessible to consciousness, in the upper left of the diagram. Those functions that take place without connections to consciousness, however, cannot become aware. Moreover, additional processes may be blocked out of consciousness by various mechanisms of defense. Structural models that divide personality into areas based on what the areas do can also be used to organize traits (as will be seen in the concluding section of this chapter). When this is done, the systems set does a particularly good job of classifying and elaborating traits of importance to personality (Mayer, 2001a; 2001b; 2003).

What Are the Structural Connections between Personality and Environment?

Connective Structural Models: Models that illustrate the relationship between personality and its surrounding environment.

The last group of structural organizations we will examine connect personality to its surroundings. We know that personality influences how the individual survives and thrives in its surrounding world; **connective structural models** provide a framework for examining how personality is connected to the outside world. The first structural division is a specific one designed to highlight how personality makes sense of the environment and responds to it.

Structures of Social Interaction

Social-cognitive psychologists are interested in understanding how personality operates in the real world and how it makes sense of the social situations it encounters as it navigates its way through life. These models further concern how an individual behaves differently in different situations: quiet in a library, cheering at a football game, and lining up in a post office. Social cognitive psychologists have been particularly interested in such relationships (e.g., Cervone, 2005; Kammrath, Mendoza-Denton, & Mischel, 2005; Mischel & Shoda, 1995).

Cognitive-Affective Personality System (CAPS): A structural division of personality proposed by Walter Mischel and his colleagues which divides personality into cognitive structures such as expectancies and beliefs, and into affects (emotions).

For example, Walter Mischel and Yuichi Shoda have created a model of mental structures responsible for acting in the environment, called the **Cognitive-Affective Personality System** (CAPS). This model structurally divides the personality system into five parts (Mischel & Shoda, 1995). These are illustrated in Table 8.4.

The first structures, *encodings,* refer to the mental models people employ to understand the outside situations they face. Encodings consist of the perceptual mean-

TABLE 8.4	Mischel and Shoda's Cognitive-Affective Units in Personality
Encodings	Categories into which people, situations, and events are sorted
Expectancies	Outcomes that a person expects are possible in a given situation
Affects	Emotions and related feelings in response to people, situations, and their outcomes
Goals	Desirable outcomes the person hopes to achieve; and undesirable outcomes the person hopes to avoid
Self-Regulatory Plans	What the person hopes to do, based on a sense of his or her own competencies and beliefs about events, to bring about desired goals

Source: Adapted from Mischel & Shoda (1995), Table 1, p. 253. Reprinted with permission of the American Psychological Association.

ings people assign to the events and behaviors they observe. Imagine a sixth-grader walking down a school hallway. Just then, a bigger child who often bullies other children turns the corner and walks toward him. The sometimes-bully contorts his face as he passes by the child. The sixth-grader may encode the bully's face in several ways. He might guess that the bully is goofing around—pretending he is in mock-pain for some reason—or the sixth-grader might guess that the bully is making fun of him by contorting his face. These encodings will determine how the sixth-grader will react.

Expectancies and beliefs, the second set of structures, concern what the person expects and believes of the world around him. An individual who believes the world is an unsafe place and that many people don't like him or her, is more likely to perceive personal threats and insults in surrounding people. A child with such expectancies is likely to encode the larger child as making fun of him.

The third structure, *affects,* include emotions and other feelings (such as sleepiness or alertness) with which a person responds to the encodings and expectancies surrounding him or her. A happy child seeing the bigger child contorting his face may find it amusing and even laugh aloud. An anxious child may become frightened at what the larger child may do.

The first three structural areas, (1) encodings, (2) expectancies and beliefs, and (3) affects, tell us how the person interprets the surrounding world and how the individual feels about it. The fourth structural area, *goals and values,* direct what the person does with that understanding and feeling. If the person's goal is safety, he or she may attempt to avoid a larger child who behaves like a bully. If the child's goal is to impress others, however, a bully who is not too big and strong may serve as a perfect opportunity for a conversation, and even a challenge to a fight.

Finally, the ways in which one can act will be determined by the fifth sort of unit, *competencies and self-regulations.* If one is competent at poking friendly humor at others, a comment about the bully's contorted face might bring a laugh to everyone—the larger child included. A child would be ill-advised to try the same thing if his humor is more on the insulting side, and his capacities to run and/or fight are not so good.

These units operate in parallel with one another, sending messages through the system and collectively sorting out what a situation means and how to respond to it: Is that a bully? Is he attacking me? Do I have a good joke on hand? Will it work? How fast can I run if it doesn't? Understanding the status of each unit of a structural type can help predict how the person will behave in a given situation (Mischel & Shoda, 1995, pp. 253–254). The Mischel-Shoda model is a useful one for understanding the structures involved in coping with situations. Situations, however, are just one part of surrounding personal environment

Using Structural Dimensions to Fill in Personality

A more general structural model that connects personality to situations and to a broader life space can be drawn from the systems framework for personality. The framework's structural model is based on the idea that most personality theorists use a common structural language to describe how personality works and interacts with other systems.

First (you may recall from Chapter 1), personality is organized from smaller units beginning with smaller neuropsychological parts, and ranging up to larger, molar units such as the individual's major psychological subsystems—motives, emotions, and mental models. That is, personality and its parts exist along a molecular-molar dimension. Second, most theories of personality share a common view that personality is internal to the person and interacts with an external world. That is, it exists along an internal-external dimension (Mayer, 1995a).

Those two dimensions—a molecular-molar dimension, and an internal-external one—can be used to develop a two-dimensional diagram of personality and how its structure relates to the outside environment. That two-dimensional portrayal was shown in Chapter 1 and is reproduced here in greater detail in Figure 8.8 (Mayer, 2005). Recall that the vertical dimension represents molecular versus molar systems, and the horizontal dimension separates the internal from the external.

Personality and its major systems (see Figure 8.8) are in the middle. The interactive situation is at the psychological level, but to the right—outside the person. To be sure, it has an objective, physical reality—sound, movement, people—but what goes on in the situation is understood at the psychological level. Both personality and the situation emerge from smaller systems; in the case of personality, it emerges from the brain and other biological processes. The situation emerges from its components: its setting, props, and elements—rocks, wood, flesh and blood. The incorporative systems (on top) include the person, the interactive environment, and other smaller systems that make them up.

Extending Personality to the Life Space

Now consider how personality is positioned relative to the structure of the life space that lies around it. Surrounding personality are an underlying biological area (underneath), elements of the social situation (bottom, right), the interactive life space (to the right), which includes the ongoing situation, and at the top groups that include personality and the other people and situations with which it interacts (upper level). That provides a conceptual structure to the space.

Life Space: The systems, including biological underpinnings, social settings, interactive situations, and group memberships, which surround the individual and in which the individual operates.

In other words, there exists a **life space** in which the individual operates. This life space consists of multiple external environments surrounding personality. The neuropsychological level (below personality) is "external" to personality in the sense of underpinning it and functioning according to its own rules. The social settings concern matters such as the shape of a room and one's position in it as well as various social props such as furniture and cell phones. The interactive life space concerns the person or objects you are interacting with. Right now, for example, you are interacting with these words and this book, in some location. Finally, the incorporative life space includes groups to which the individual belongs, such as a member of the student body of a particular college or university.

Figure 8.8 shows one possible unified structural model, therefore, of the various internal regions of personality and the external life space with which it interacts. Other models are possible, of course, that will emphasize other aspects of personality. The model shown here has been chosen for its generality.

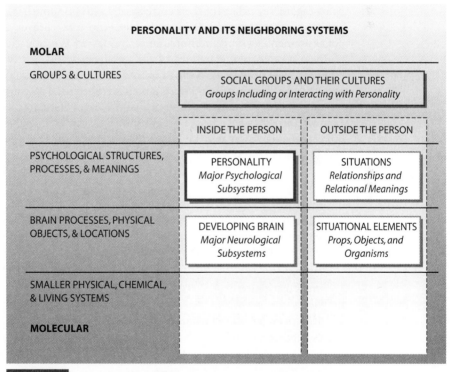

FIGURE 8.8   **Personality and Its Neighboring Systems**
The structural model of personality and its neighboring systems elaborates the model of personality first introduced in Chapter 1. This more detailed version again depicts personality at a psychological level, within the mind. The outside situation is at the same psychological level. The outside situation is psychological in the sense that, although it is physical and objective, it takes its meaning from the way it is understood by the individual. Below the psychological level are the person's brain and biological systems (within the person) and the situational elements (outside). Above personality and the situation are the incorporative, social environments.
Source: Mayer (2004; 2005). Reproduced with permission of John Wiley & Sons, Inc.

Do Structures Matter?

Revisiting the Organization of Traits

Structures matter for everything from organizing traits to relating personality to the environment, to ensuring that a given individual's personality is viewed in a balanced fashion.

To begin with, consider the issue of traits. Earlier in this chapter, various trait-based structures of personality were examined, such as the Big Two, the Big Three, and the Big Five and beyond. Functional divisions of mind, such as the trilogy of mind, the id, ego, and superego, and the systems set, also can be used to organize traits. In this case, traits are arranged not by their intercorrelation (as in stand-alone trait organizations), but rather, according to the functions of personality to which they are related.

For example, using the trilogy of mind, one can divide traits according to whether they describe the motivation area, the emotion area, or the cognitive area of personality (again, regardless of their correlations with one another). An example of such a sorting is shown in Table 8.5 (e.g., Buss & Finn, 1987; Mayer, 1995). There, the traits of excitement-seeking and nurturance are classed as motivations; empathy and fearfulness are emotion-related traits; and intelligence and creativity are cognitive traits. Raters generally agree as to which traits describe which areas. The systems set also has proven useful in organizing traits, and it has been used to arrange nearly seventy personality traits of interest. Table 8.6 summarizes the parts of the systems set and shows traits that have been organized by the system. Initial studies have suggested that the systems set may be better than earlier models in conceptually organizing traits (Mayer, 2003).

TABLE 8.5	**Using The Trilogy of Mind to Organize Traits**	
The Three Areas of the Trilogy of Mind		
Motivation	**Emotion**	**Cognition**
Urges that direct the individual's behavior	Organized feeling responses	Thinking, remembering, reasoning, and judging
Selected Traits Classified according the Three Areas		
Dominance-seeking	Emotionality-Neuroticism	Absorption
Excitement-seeking	Empathy	Creativity
Impulsivity	Fearfulness	Intelligence, *General*
Machiavellianism	Happiness	Intelligence, *Perceptual-Organizational*
N Achievement	Resentment	
Nurturance	Shame-Proneness	Intelligence, *Spatial*
Rebelliousness	Shyness	Intelligence, *Verbal*
Succorance		Locus of Control

Sources: For example, Buss & Finn (1987), Table 2, p. 435; Mayer (1995), Figure 2, p. 862; Figure 2, p. 394.

TABLE 8.6	Using the Systems Set to Organize Traits		

The Four Areas of the Systems Set

Energy Lattice	Knowledge Works	Executive Consciousness	Social Actor
An interweaving of motivation and emotion	Acquired models and the intelligence that acts on them	Conscious awareness, self-control, and voluntary behavior	Social plans that connect the person to outside roles and patterns of behaviors

Selected Traits Classified according to Those Areas

n Achievement	Creativity	Self-consciousness	Athletic
n Affiliation	Intelligence, *Verbal*	Absorption	Nonconforming
Neuroticism-Stability	Intelligence, *Spatial*	Will power	Artistic
Friendliness-Hostility	Intelligence, *Practical*		Machiavellian
	Locus of Control		

Source: Adapted from Mayer (2003). Reprinted with permission of the American Psychological Association.

Traits of the Life Space

A person's surrounding life space, too, has a structure and has traits as well. Recently, researchers have been exploring the question of what the traits of the life space are like. This research tries to bring a person's surrounding environment to life. In such studies, college students fill out surveys often containing hundreds of questions that ask about each area of their individual life space: biological, situational setting, social interactions, and group memberships (Brackett, Mayer, & Warner, 2004; Mayer, Carlsmith, & Chabot, 1997).

Biological life space questions, for example, ask everything from the color of a person's eyes to how many sit ups he or she can do, to any history of mental disorder the individual or his or her family members have experienced. Life space questions about the social setting include how many shoes, political posters, shot glasses, umbrellas, and jars of vitamins a person owns. Interaction questions include how many times a person has spoken with family members or gone to a movie over the past week. Finally, questions about groups memberships include questions about the sorts of clubs the individual belonged to in high school and now belong to in college, the courses he or she takes, the college major being considered, and the like.

When the items from such surveys are factor analyzed, some very interesting dimensions emerge. First is a cared-for, positive, social orientation that involves lots of healthy social interactions. Another is a sports dimension that involves participating in many sports activities, rooting for teams, and owning sports equipment. A third commonly found dimension involves a drug culture environment that includes

• FACTS • AT • A • GLANCE •

Historical Ideas Leading to the Personality Structures of Today

Originator	Brief Description
The Trilogy of Mind in the Middle Ages and More Recently . . .	
De Proprietatibus Rerun of Bartholomaeus Anglicus (thirteenth century)	The person was made of a soul and a body. The soul contained three parts: [updating the older English:] "the vegetable soul, that gives life, the sensitive soul, which adds feeling to life, and rational soul, which adds reason to feeling and life." (modified from Lewis, 1970, p. 153)
Upham (1869, Vol II, p. 130)	The mind can be divided into three parts: Intellect, Sensibilities, and Will. (Upham, 1869, II, 130, cited in Kosits, 2003, p. 412)
On the Disappearance of the Soul from Structures . . .	
William James, 1892	[In discussing whether the conscious self is a soul or a state:] It makes no difference in this connection whether this being be called Soul, Ego, or Spirit . . . If we had other grounds . . . for admitting the Soul into our psychology, then getting there on those grounds, she might turn out to be the [conscious] knower, too . . . (James, 1892, p. 200) . . . The logical conclusion seems then to be that *the states of consciousness are all that psychology needs to do her work with. Metaphysics or theology may prove the Soul to exist; but for psychology the hypothesis of such a substantial principle of unity is superfluous.* (James, 1892, p. 203)
Gilbert Ryle (1949), a philosopher of mind who argued that all mental events take place at the physical neural level	As views of people became more mechanistic, the concept of a soul—some immaterial life force connected to divine forces—shrank until it became a ghost haunting a machine. (Hampden-Turner, 1981, p. 30)
On Hierarchical Structure . . .	
Arthur Koestler (1949)	The mind is made up of holons. Each holon is a "subwhole" that organizes those parts beneath it and has considerable autonomy from the parts above it. The holons are arranged in a hierarchy called a holarchy. Each level of holons has its own rules and built in codes. (Summarized by Hampden-Turner, 1981, p. 162)
Meaning as a Structure That Links the Person to the Outside World . . .	
Existential philosophy including that by Kierkegaard and Camus (20th century)	People are unique in providing meaning to themselves and to otherwise meaningless objects in the outside world. We identify with universal objective systems such as culture, but are utterly lost in nothingness for ultimately we must separate from culture and die. (Hampden-Turner, 1981, p. 52)

It is the personality structure of an individual that, energized by motivations, dynamically organizes perceptions, cognitions, and behaviors so as to achieve certain "system" goals.

Jack Block

owning, taking, and perhaps abusing alcohol and drugs. Yet another life space dimension involves being highly interested and involved in the arts, and still another involves being involved in solitary intellectual pursuits. You probably can identify friends and others who would score high on one or another of these dimensions. As life space dimensions become increasingly worked out, one project will be to see which personality traits go together with which traits of the life space (Brackett, Mayer, & Warner, 2004; Mayer, Carlsmith, & Chabot, 1997).

There are many other structural approaches than those examined here. A few others of interest are shown in the Facts at a Glance.

Structure and the Description of the Person

Another point of structurally dividing personality is to ensure that psychologists provide a relatively complete overview of an individual's mental functioning. The use of Freud's id, ego, and superego, for example, would ensure a look at the animal instincts, rational powers, and the conscience of an individual, as well as links between defense mechanisms and consciousness. The trilogy of mind ensures an examination of an individual's motivation, emotion, and cognition. The systems set combines qualities of both earlier sets by examining a person's motives and emotions (the energy lattice), intelligence and knowledge (the knowledge works), social skills (the social actor), and the executive consciousness that overlooks the rest. This newer model allows one to discuss major areas of personality and also the communication channels involving, for example, defense mechanisms.

Once again, let us enlist structure to get an overall sense of an individual's personality; this time, United States president, Richard M. Nixon (1913–1994), for example. Without a consideration of personality structure, one could easily just focus on one part of Nixon's character. For example, some people believed that President Nixon possessed a devious character. Nixon was forced to resign his office in 1974, just after beginning his second term. During the preceding election, his campaign officials had arranged for an illegal break-in of a Democratic Party office, and the president himself became increasingly implicated in covering up the crime. The break-in at the Watergate Office Building in Washington, DC, became referred to, simply, as "Watergate" (Winter & Carlson, 1988). Those same people also might recall that President Nixon had been called "Tricky Dick" as a consequence of electioneering strategies he employed early in his career.

Such a focus on one part of Nixon's personality, however, would overlook many of his other qualities. A structural approach forces us to go beyond one attribute to examine the broader areas of a person's functioning. For example, in regard to the President's motives and emotions (energy lattice), his highest motive was to achieve. When he was ten years old, the former President announced to his mother his desire to be "a lawyer—an honest lawyer, who can't be bought by crooks." This is key because one of the frequent pitfalls of achievement-oriented people is their tendency to disregard rules in the pursuit of excellence. Nixon was also relatively high in the need for affiliation and sought others' companionship and approval. Nixon was an introvert in an extraverted profession, and he was relatively lacking in positive enjoyment. In law school at Duke University he earned the nickname "Gloomy Gus" (Mazlish,

1973, p. 55; Winter & Carlson, 1988). By contrast, Nixon was relatively low in the need for power, and some critics have used that to explain his hesitant and clumsy uses of power.

In regard to Nixon's knowledge, he possessed many mental models consistent with that of a high achiever. He believed that the southern California of his childhood was a time and place of almost unlimited opportunity for those willing to work hard, and also that to succeed one must accept the reality of the world as it is. His intellectual brilliance was rated as medium and his creativity high relative to other presidents (Nixon, 1978, p. 5; Simonton, 1986; 1988). Nixon's creativity may have been reflected in his political flexibility. He began his political career as a liberal, became a conservative, but then dined with Mao Tse-tung (Zedong) and reopened diplomatic contact with mainland China (Winter & Carlson, 1988). One ability in which he fell short was humor: his wit has been labeled as below average compared to other presidents.

The former president's social patterns and roles (the social actor) were somewhat limited. As an introvert, he far preferred meeting people in one-on-one situations, at which time he was often regarded as charming and warm, as opposed to operating in groups, where he was regarded as stiff and awkward. Beyond that, he often employed a self-deprecating style in which he introduced an accomplishment by starting with a personal limitation. For example, he drew attention to all the women's shoes he scuffed while learning to dance as a college student (Winter, 1996, p. 49). He was highly strategic and often manipulative in his political role. This suggests a high degree of self-consciousness and self-control on the part of his executive consciousness.

Indeed, Nixon often spoke in the third person and appeared to be analyzing, evaluating, and coaching his own behavior (Winter, 1996, p. 45). When his role in the Watergate break-in and its coverup was being investigated, he employed a variety of mental defenses, including blocking out the threat (called repression): "In the year 1972, I am afraid I was too busy . . . that I frankly paid too little attention to the campaign." He also employed denial: "The White House has had no involvement whatever in this particular incident [Watergate]." He further employed a defense called reaction formation—which in this instance meant trying to appear the good guy after causing the problem: "The action [Watergate] was wrong, the action was stupid . . . It should not have been covered up, and I have done the very best that I can over the past year to see that it is uncovered." (Remarks compiled by Winter, 1996, p. 84.)

This example, though brief, illustrates how describing a person according to structural divisions can ensure a more complete overview of some of the facets of the individual's personality, as opposed to a more haphazard attention to one part of personality or another. It is worth noting that President Nixon, who often had his intriguing personality analyzed by commentators—and often quite negatively—once remarked, "I always find it amusing when psycho-historians I have never met conclude that I have what they consider to be a warped personality." (Nixon, 1990, p. 79). Structural approaches to personality description can be used to ensure at least a minimum degree of balance, in that they help ensure that each area of personality gets its due.

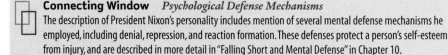

Connecting Window   *Psychological Defense Mechanisms*
The description of President Nixon's personality includes mention of several mental defense mechanisms he employed, including denial, repression, and reaction formation. These defenses protect a person's self-esteem from injury, and are described in more detail in "Falling Short and Mental Defense" in Chapter 10.

From Structures to Dynamics

The models covered in this chapter describe the trait structures, awareness structures, function-based structural divisions, and external-connective structures into which personality and its surroundings can be divided. Each of these structural models helps us understand the relatively stable aspects of personality organization.

Personality Dynamics: Broadly speaking, the influence of one part of personality on another.

Structure not only helps us organize personality's parts; just as importantly, it provides a context within which personality dynamics operate. **Personality dynamics**—the way one part of personality influences another—take place across the various areas of personality. For example, one chain of dynamics extends from the innermost working areas of personality—beginning with its motivational urges—and extends outward toward social action in the life space. This chain of dynamics could be said to begin motivationally, be amplified emotionally, and thought about cognitively. Finally, it goes on to be expressed in the outer world. This chain of dynamics will be examined in Chapter 9.

Reviewing Chapter 8

The purpose of this chapter is to acquaint you with the notion of personality structure and why it is important, and with some of the major structures that have been proposed for personality psychology. Basically, structure is important because it provides a relatively stable organizational scheme for defining parts of personality (which exist within a given structure or area of personality) and dynamics of personality, which cross structures.

It is possible to have more than one good structural system to describe personality. Much of this chapter is aimed at introducing different structures that stem from different perspectives: those based on traits, on levels of awareness, on functions, and on connecting personality to the outside world.

What Is Personality Structure?

1. Personality Structure Described.
What is personality structure and what does it let us do? What are some similarities and differences between personality structure and the structure of a city?

2. Why Is Personality Structure Important?
Several reasons are given for the importance of understanding personality structure. How can they help us understand the many parts of personality? How can they

help us make sure we have a comprehensive picture of an individual when studying a specific case?

3. Multiple Personality Structures.
The chapter outlines several valid types of personality structure. Personality, like other complex systems, can be divided in more than one way, and more than one division can be valid, even when they are quite unlike one another. Do you know the criteria for valid or good structural divisions?

How Are Personality Traits Structured?

4. The Big Two and the Big Three.
What were Eysenck's two factors, or Raymond Cattell's sixteen factors of personality and how do they relate? What is a superfactor or Big Factor. What are the Big Three?

5. The Big Five.
What is the lexical hypothesis, and how did it lead to the Big Five personality traits? What are the Big Five personality traits? *Suggestion:* the mnemonic, "OCEAN," can be helpful for learning the five factors: O=openness, C=conscientiousness … Can you fill in the rest? What argument could you provide that the Big Five personality traits are better than, say, the Big Two or Big Three.

6. The Big Six.
Although many psychologists are happy with the Big Five model of personality trait structures, others would like to add more dimensions. Why would they like to do so, and what are some suggested additional dimensions they would like to add?

What Are Structural Models of Awareness and Why Do They Matter?

7. Rationale for Structural Models of Awareness. Among the first structural models of personality was Freud's division of the mind into conscious and unconscious processes. Why have structural models that divide the consciousness from the unconscious been so interesting to psychologists?

8. The No-Access Unconscious (or Unconscious Proper). Most mental processing takes place in the no-access unconscious. For example, when we perceive depth, and visual illusions, or mentally construct any image, it occurs unconsciously. What are the defining characteristics of this no-access unconscious?

9. The Implicit or Automatic Unconscious. The implicit or automatic unconscious refers to memory events that often take place under the threshold of awareness, in the no-access unconscious. Automatic unconscious is often demonstrated with the use of memory priming—that is, showing stimuli and then covering them up. Can you describe an experimental demonstration of the operation of the implicit, automatic unconscious?

10. The Unnoticed Unconscious. Many mental functions would be accessible to us if only we noticed them. Can you give an example of an experimental phenomenon that illustrates that people don't notice what is actually influencing their behavior?

11. The Dynamic Unconscious. Freud's idea was that some material resides outside of awareness because it is too threatening to enter into consciousness. These motives and associated ideas nonetheless can influence our thinking, and they may be exhibited through dreams and errors in behavior, including slips of the tongue. Can you give an example of a study that demonstrates the action of the dynamic unconscious?

Can Identifying Key Functions of Mind Lead to Structural Divisions?

12. The Id, Ego, and Superego.
What work areas of personality did Freud's id, ego, and superego describe?

13. The Trilogy and Quaternity of Mind.
Long before modern psychology, many philosophers and faculty psychologists had begun to divide the mind into its basic functional areas. The trilogy of mind refers to three functions. Can you name them? When consciousness is added as a fourth area, the quaternity of mind is formed.

14. A Brain to Match?
Some brain scientists have suggested a rough division of the brain according to its evolution into the reptilian brain, paleo- (or old) mammalian brain, and neo-mammalian brain. The neo-mammalian brain corresponds to cognition. What functions of the trilogy do the reptilian and old-mammalian brain correspond to? What evolutionary pressures prompted the development of the old-mammalian brain?

15. The Systems Set.
As structural divisions are better understood, along with the criteria they must meet, it becomes more readily apparent how personality might be divided. One such new division is the systems set. Can you name its four areas?

What Are the Structural Connections between Personality and the Environment?

16. Structures of Social Interaction.
The social-cognitive perspective of the mind directly relates personality to its acts in the outside world. The mind is divided into areas particularly important to predicting such outside action. For example, a person's expectancies of reward are very important to what they do. What other divisions do social-cognitive psychologists employ?

17. Using Structural Divisions to Fill in Personality.
As we saw in Chapter 1, two dimensions—the molecular-molar and the internal-external—can be used to arrange

personality amidst its surrounding systems. These dimensions can also be employed to organize parts of personality. What parts are most molecular relative to personality? What parts are more molar?

18. Extending Personality to the Life Space.
Just as personality has a structure, so does the environment surrounding it. When people are asked questions about their environment, what sorts of dimensions of the surrounding environment are obtained?

Do Structures Matter?

19. Organizing Traits by Processing Area.
Psychologists have sought to organize traits according to the part of the trilogy (or quaternity) of mind they describe. Can you give examples of traits that would correspond to each of the three areas? What are the similarities and differences of this approach to the trait structures that are found from factor analysis? (*Hint:* factor analysis is based on the correlation among traits.)

Chapter 9

Dynamics of Action

*P*ersonality dynamics concern the influence of one part of personality on another, and how those influences are, in turn expressed in the person's environment. Personality dynamics take place against the background of the system's structural organization—discussed in the last chapter. The dynamic influences of motives can redirect a person's thoughts from, say, learning about music, to learning about medicine. Such dynamics guide how personality is expressed in the environment and how personality is changed by the environment in return. The central topic of this chapter is the progression from an individual's motivational urges to the coherent expression of those urges in the person's behavior.

- ## What Are Dynamics of Action?
  Personality dynamics are introduced and defined as chains of mental events that range from the small and local to those that take place across much of personality.

- ## Which Need Will Begin Action?
  A person has many needs at a given time. This section examines the competition among needs, how one need may serve another, and what happens when needs conflict.

- ## How Does Action Develop in the Mind?
  As needs develop they are often accompanied by emotions and thoughts about them. The likelihood of a plan being translated into action is discussed. Partial expressions such as slips of the tongue are discussed.

- ## How Are Acts Performed?
  Once a person has an intention to do something, it is ready to be expressed. The communication channels between the private personality and its expression in the social world are discussed. The sometimes double nature of acts is considered, as is the stagecraft of self-presentation. The interaction between the individual and situation is also considered.

What Are Dynamics of Action?

Approaching Dynamics

Personality Dynamics and Personality Structure

Personality dynamics concern the influence of one part of personality on another, as well as the mutual interaction between personality and its surroundings. The subject matter of personality is inherently dynamic (Vallacher, Read, & Nowak, 2002). You may have noticed earlier that Freud called his theory "Psychodynamic theory." This might seem strange. He could have called it "Unconscious theory," or "Theory of the Id, Ego, and Superego." Social-cognitive psychologists like to speak of dynamics as well, and trait psychologists sometimes speak of "dynamic" traits. So, what then, is so important to these psychologists as to lead to their emphasis on dynamics? A beginning answer to that question can be obtained by considering what the term "dynamic" refers to in this context more generally.

To understand the term *dynamics,* it is worth drawing an analogy to the dynamics of a city. Recall that we drew such an analogy between personality structure and city structure in Chapter 8. Whereas city structures involved the relatively stable areas of the city—its neighborhoods, parks, and waterways—city dynamics concern the "movement" or "moving parts" of the city. As with structure, many of the dynamics of a city are visible. This is particularly true of its daily rhythms. We can see the children head off for school, and people going to work in the morning: traffic circulating (or congested) on roads, and trains and mass transit in operation. We can see the children return home in the afternoon, and commuters return in the evening. When the weather permits, we can see public concerts and festivals in the parks. Throughout the day, we can see some results of the activities carried out by the city's citizens: people are fed, clothed, cared for, and they meet one another, plan activities, and build things.

Note that all this dynamic activity will potentially influence the city's structure. If the people are prosperous and well organized, they will build more homes, rebuild decaying parts of the city, and create prosperous new areas while preserving and enhancing the natural environment. The city may gradually expand by bringing more people, housing, business, and enterprise within its influence, while preserving its rivers, lakes, and parks. If the people are not prosperous, though, the city may fall into disrepair. Poorer sections, tent cities, and other impoverished areas may arise, and neighborhoods (structure) may decay and ultimately become abandoned. Dynamics, in other words, represent the action and change in a city. Dynamics determine what the system does and whether it prospers.

Dynamics as Critical Chains of Events

Personality dynamics concern the movements, interactions, and changes analogous in some ways to city dynamics—but within a person's psychology. Personality dynamics refer to a variety of phenomena such as the influence of motives on emotions, emotions on thoughts, self-regulation, and social action. These movements render such dynamics absolutely critical to understanding how personality works, and how it changes.

Loosely speaking, the sort of personality dynamics examined in this chapter involve a chain of events that begin with an urge or a desire in one part of personality, which then may be channeled into goals, and ultimately, may be carried out successfully. This progression from urge to expression is by no means assured. The exact dynamic that emerges will depend on the personality that an individual possesses. Even given a goal, urges are sometimes turned back, unexpressed. At other times, they are defeated by external obstacles. It is also true, however, that on occasion when an urge finds the right goal in the right environment, a person's energy can be released like an explosion.

For example, Homer H. Hickam Jr. was born in Coalwood, a rural, coal-mining town in West Virginia. His father was a manager at the mine who wanted his son to follow in his footsteps. Homer Junior was eleven years old in 1957, when the Soviet Union launched Sputnik, the first human-manned satellite. As it turned out, the Russian rocket, which threatened American technological esteem, passed right over southern West Virginia, and Homer and his neighbors went out to watch (Hickam, 1998, pp. 30–32).

Homer Jr. organized his friends to launch a rocket themselves—something Homer didn't have much of an idea of how to do. When he announced his plans at the dinner table, his mother told him not to blow himself up; his father ignored him, and his brother snickered (Hickam, 1998, p. 34). At Homer's instigation, his friends and he took the powder out of twelve fire crackers, loaded them into the body of a small plastic flashlight, added a fuse, and fit the whole apparatus into the body of a plastic model airplane.

The night of the launch, Homer and his friends attached the rocket to his mother's beloved rose garden fence, lit the fuse, and stood back. In a moment, there arose a considerable explosion that launched a sizeable portion of the fence into the air and set the still earth-bound portion of the fence on fire. Fortunately, the young boys survived unscathed (Hickam, 1998, pp. 39–40).

Case Study

The Mysterious Social Activities of Robert Leuci

Consider the case of Robert Leuci, a former Chicago police officer. His personality shows signs of emotional stability, sensation-seeking, and extraordinary social skill. But that doesn't quite tell us everything about the individual. Rather, we want to know how these components are integrated together dynamically. They are rather like beads: but what sort of a beaded necklace do we get: one that goes from red through the colors of the rainbow to violet? Or, one where all the colors are haphazardly intermixed? Dynamics address this issue. An emotionally stable, sensation-seeking, high-achieving, socially adroit police officer, for example, might decide, through good works, to seek a promotion and use his social skills to lead his own team of officers.

What if, however, the police officers around him were corrupt? He might move to a different force, or he might do what Leuci did. Leuci became an undercover informant—a police officer working for federal prosecutors to try to clean up the police force around him. He was up against criminal corruption among police officers and attorneys, which blended into an underworld of bail bondsmen, dope pushers, and members of organized crime.

He coupled his desire for excitement with his social adroitness in astonishing ways. For example, at one point he was starting a meeting with a suspected criminal named DeStefano. They were together in a bar and DeStefano was becoming increasingly wary of whether Leuci was an informant.

Leuci chose a daring way to deflect suspicion from himself. As they were choosing their seats, Leuci said:

> "Let's not sit next to the jukebox tonight, because I am not getting any kind of recording."
>
> "That's not funny," said DeStefano. Adding to the provocation, Leuci elaborated on his theme, bragging, and craftily insisting he was working for the government. He pointed to a barmaid across the room, and said his transmitter was stuffed in her private parts. As Leuci later recounted it, "They all laughed, but DeStefano's laugh was dry." (Daley, 1981, p. 101)

As the psychologist Paul Ekman observed:

> Leuci ridicules DeStefano by brazenly telling the truth—he really can't make a good recording near the jukebox, and he is working for the government. By admitting it so openly, and by joking about the waitress also wearing a concealed recorder . . . Leuci makes it difficult for DeStefano to pursue his suspicions without seeming foolish. (Ekman, 1985, p. 38)

The point to be made here about dynamics is that the parts of Leuci's personality really don't tell us about how he puts them together—the way he chooses to string together those qualities to perform his actions. Thus, at some point, it is useful to move beyond the discussion of individual parts alone, or even in combination, to begin to describe the individual's dynamics.

When Homer's parents rushed to the screen door to see what happened, Homer expected to be severely scolded by his mother. Instead, however, she came out, sat beside him, and asked, "Sonny, do you think you could build a real rocket?" He replied, "No ma'am . . . I don't know how." "I know you don't know how," his mother responded, "I'm asking you if you put your mind to it, could you do it?" If he remained in the coal town, she said, his future would be a dangerous and difficult one working in the mines. Rather, he badly needed to get out of Coalwood and go to college. To do that, however, he needed to demonstrate to his father he could succeed at something practical on his own. "Show him you can do something!" she challenged, "Build a rocket!" (Hickam, 1998, pp. 44–45).

Homer's somewhat disorganized, dreamy urge—a still unfocused interest and competitiveness—had led to something beyond casual play with firecrackers. His mother recognized the potential seriousness behind her son's act and helped him galvanize that urge. From there, he enlisted the help of more scientifically minded friends, machinists at the mine, and other townspeople and supporters. His project led to ever-larger and more successful rocket launches, regional fame, and finally, a dreamed-of career with the National Aeronautics and Space Administration.

> **Thought is a prelude to, and not an alternative to action.**
>
> Antony Jay

This chapter addresses dynamics from their initial urge through to their outward expression in successful behavior. First, though, we need to consider the nature of a dynamic in greater detail. We can better understand dynamics if we contrast micro, meso, and macrodynamics, examine how they change, and consider the existence of a special group of traits termed dynamic traits.

Dynamic Traits and Micro-Dynamics

Personality Dynamic: A motivated chain of interrelated psychological events that cross a set of major mental areas to bring about an outcome. Personality dynamics are potentially reversible or modifiable.

Micro-Dynamics: A smaller personality dynamic that involves one part of personality influencing another.

Dynamic Traits: A class of long-term stable mental patterns related to motives, including such examples as *n* achievement, sensation-seeking, and the like.

Earlier in the book we defined a **personality dynamic** as occurring when one part of personality influenced another. But this can happen on a relatively micro- or small scale, or on a larger scale. As it turns out, we have already discussed many sucy small-scale, or micro-dynamics. **Micro-dynamics** are causal connections that extend from one, smaller, specific part of personality to another. Examples of micro-dynamics include how guilt might interfere with love, or how spatial intelligence might influence reading a map, or how a given script of social interaction might influence how a person understands the world.

One kind of micro-dynamic is especially germane to global chains of action discussed in this chapter. Those are **dynamic traits**. Dynamic traits represent tendencies toward certain classes of needs and goals. These traits possess a particular capacity to propel a person, to initiate dynamics throughout an individual's personality. Cattell (1965, pp. 28, 165) defined dynamic traits as those concerned with "why and how [the person] is moved to do what he does . . . [and] the incentives to which he has learned to respond." The needs for achievement, power, and affiliation all are examples of dynamic traits (see Chapter 4). Another example might be a trait related to how motives are expressed, such as reflectiveness-impulsivness, which concerns the degree to which a person thinks over his or her actions before carrying them out. Similarly, those who study animal behavior frequently employ the term *dynamic trait* to refer to mating and other behaviors that relate one animal to another—for example, to summarize how a bird moves its feathers so as to attract mates (e.g., Rosenthal, Evans, & Miller, 1996).

"But wait a minute!" you might wonder, "Aren't all traits dynamic? Don't introversion and intelligence and emotionality all speak to how dynamic actions are carried out?" To some extent you would be right. There is no absolute boundary between traits that are dynamic and those that are not. Psychologists such as Raymond Cattell distinguished the dynamic-traits from emotion-related traits (which he called temperament traits) and traits of mental ability such as intelligence. The basis for this is one of degree: Dynamic (i.e., motivational) traits are directly related to personal, self-directed action. Emotional or ability traits modify or refine how the actions are carried out (Cattell, 1965, pp. 28, 165).

Mid-Level (Meso-) and Macro-Level Dynamics

Meso-Dynamics: A dynamic that crosses two or three major functional areas of personality.

Causal Attributions: Models of the self and world that are especially focused on what causes a particular behavior, event, or situation. Some people tend to see the world as caused by themselves, others tend to see the world as caused by other people or situations.

As dynamic traits propel personality they exert their influence on many different systems at one time. Dynamics that cross several systems are called mid-level or **meso-dynamics**. Meso-dynamics are dynamics that are larger in reach than microdynamics, while less grand than the far-reaching macro-dynamics of action or self-control. An example of such a meso-level dynamic is the **causal attribution**. Causal attributions concern an individual's beliefs about what determines events in the world. For example, if you think everything in the world is due to your own behavior, then you develop a strong sense of control over the world. Another person may see the same kinds of events occur but attribute them to the situation, to chance, or to fate (Weiner & Graham, 1999).

People who attribute events to their own stable, global, qualities have a higher sense of responsibility than others, but are also considered more prone to pessimism and depression (e.g., Abramson, Alloy, & Metalsky, 1995; Peterson, 1991). So, this mid-level dynamic—how a person attributes causes—can influence the sorts of actions a person engages in, as well as his or her mood. Some contemporary dynamic theorists have tried to build computer models of portions of the personality system involving such dynamic interactions (Read & Miller, 2002; Vallacher et al., 2002). To find out more about the reasons for this, see the Research in Focus box.

Macro-Level Dynamics: A larger dynamic that crosses all or almost all the many major functional areas or parts of personality.

Macro-level dynamics concern mental events that cross, or centrally influence, the entire personality system. The dynamics of action—the topic of this chapter—provide an example of a macro-dynamic that spans all of personality. For action to occur, it must begin someplace in the mind, be thought about (or not), cross from the mind to some external expression of the person (that is, be translated into behavior) and somehow influence the world. This chapter follows that chain of events from beginning to end.

Dynamics and Their Change

An important aspect of dynamics, and one thing that makes them so interesting, is that they can bring about change. Dynamic change occurs through learning, with experience, with education, and sometimes with counseling and psychotherapy. For example, Freud's psychotherapy began with the idea that dynamic changes could cure neurotics of their symptoms. In particular, Freud was interested in making unconscious processes conscious, and in learning about oneself in general (Paniagua, 2001; Weiner, 1975, pp. 40–44). Since Freud's time, therapies have continued their focus on

Research in Focus

Computer Models of Personality Dynamics

Variables influence one another in personality in ways that are sometimes very complex. As the number of parts interacting increases, it is often difficult to come up with adequate mathematical equations to describe them. Simple correlations simply won't do for complex, nonlinear relationships. For that reason, personality psychologists began to construct computer models of personality dynamics in the early 1960s (Loehlin, 1968), a practice that has continued to the present (e.g., Vallacher, Read, & Nowak, 2002).

A computer program can imitate the operation of any complex system. The model is something constructed in the computer through the use of a list of instructions called a computer program.

John Loehlin (1968) was one of the early advocates of computer models of personality. To introduce personality psychologists to the idea of computer modeling, Loehlin provided a very simple example of a computer model of a micro-dynamic in personality. The micro-dynamic combines two theories about anger. The first is the frustration-aggression hypothe-

sis, which states that frustration increases anger (Berkowitz, 1989; Dollard et al., 1939). The second theory is the theory of catharsis, which says that once a person has expressed anger, the individual's anger is reduced (see Bushman, 2002).

Loehlin's sample program is called "TEMPER." It is written in all capital letters because at the time Loehlin wrote it, computers mostly just read capital letters. TEMPER was written in the computer language FORTRAN in just eleven lines of code. Although FORTRAN is not much used any more, the program is so simple that people familiar with computer programs can understand it simply by looking at it. See if you can understand it by reading it. The complete program for TEMPER is reproduced. The lines of FORTRAN code are to the left, with an English language interpretation to the right.

Can you identify the line(s) of the program that represents the frustration-aggression dynamic? Can you identify the line(s) that represents the catharsis dynamic? (Answers follow.)

dynamic change. All share the idea that strategic alterations in the parts of personality and how they dynamically interact can lead to change.

Consider the relation between mental models and depression. People who dynamically respond to situations with persistently critical and negative interpretations of them are said to possess depressive schema (Segal, 1988). Such individuals are at greater risk for depression. If the depression lifts as a consequence of pharmacological (i.e., drug) therapy or simply due to the passage of time, the individual will still be at risk because the depressive schemas remain (e.g., Hedlund & Rude, 1995; Wenzlaff, Rude, & West, 2002).

On the other hand, one can make an effort to employ a more positive view of oneself, facilitated by thinking through one's positive attributes. Sometimes this process can be helped with psychotherapy designed to dynamically address and change depressive schemas. These therapies attempt to bring irrational, exaggerated negative views of the self into awareness, and then change them through learning. This dynamic change accounts, in part, for the success of such therapies. The re-

Original Fortran Code	English Language Description
1 PROGRAM TEMPER	Give the program a name, "TEMPER" to identify it.
2 ANGER = 0.0	Set up a variable named "ANGER" and set it equal to 0.0 as a starting value.
3 READ FRUSTR	Set up a second variable called FRUSTR (for frustration). Now read the value of FRUSTR from the input (at the time, this would have been a computer punch card in a card-reading machine).
4 ANGER = ANGER + FRUSTR	Now, the variable ANGER, which represents the level of anger and was 0.0, is going to be increased by the value of FRUSTR, by adding the two values together and setting ANGER equal to the new value.
5 IF (ANGER .GT. 1.0) 6, 8	If the new value of ANGER is greater than 1.0, go to statement 6, otherwise go to statement 8.
6 PRINT "BLOW TOP"	If the program is at Statement 6, then send instructions to the printer to print "BLOW TOP"—indicating that the individual exhibited a temper tantrum.
7 GO TO 2	The personality, having expressed its anger in Statement 6, now goes to statement 2, and starts all over again with ANGER set to 0.0.
8 ANGER = ANGER *0.5	If ANGER did not exceed 1.0, then over time it will dissipate, so it is set equal to half its former value (that is, multiplied by .5).
9 PRINT ANGER	Just to keep track of what is going on, send instructions to the printer to print the current value of the variable ANGER.
10 GO TO 3	Now return to Statement 3, and read in a new value of FRUSTR and continue over again.
11 END.	In FORTRAN, this statement marks the end of the program's instructions.

Could you recognize the parts of the program that represents the frustration-aggression hypothesis or the cathartic hypothesis? Here are the answers: Line 4 represents the frustration-aggression hypothesis. Line 6 followed by line 2 represent catharsis—that is, after anger is expressed, its value is reduced to nothing.

placement of depressive schemas with more positive schemas can lead to long-term changes in both mental models and emotion and better resistance to future depressions (Segal, Gemar, & Williams, 1999).

The contribution of dynamics to personal action and change make them crucial to understand. This chapter takes us step by step through a dynamic of action: from a motivated urge to its emotional and cognitive reverberations, to its translation into behavior, and finally, its social expression.

Which Need Will Begin Action?

Urges, Needs, and Presses

Urge: The conscious psychological awareness of a need.

People are often doing things, in motion, expressing themselves. Many of these actions begin with a set of **urges**. These urges may express one or more bodily needs: to

Need: A need refers to a state of tension within the individual that can be satisfied by a specific goal such as eating, or being sociable.

eat, drink, or sleep. They may include biosocial urges such as the needs for affiliation or for achievement. Each **need** is defined as a mental dynamic that guides personality so as to transform a lack of satisfaction into satisfaction. Needs often are focused such that they have specific aims (Murray, 1938). For example, the need for achievement might be represented in the aim of studying enough to get an "A" on a test. The urges may be triggered by the moment, or as a consequence of longer-term planning.

> **Connecting Window**   *Specific Examples of Murray's Needs*
> The needs Murray discussed related back to the list he and others developed, and that included, for example, the needs for achievement, affiliation, dominance, power, and the like. These were introduced in Chapter 4, "Projective Measures of Motives" and "How Are Motives Expressed?"

Press: Aspects of the environment that elicit needs in a person.

Needs also respond to environmental **presses** (Murray, 1938). An environmental press involves the incentives and disincentives of the surrounding situation, which can elicit some motives and suppress others. The environmental presses on a college student will often support studying, and be different than the presses faced by a high school friend who works locally as a carpenter, or an older sibling who is married with children. But, at some point, an action sequence is begun around one or more urges, or the hint of urges.

Needs and Their Relative Strengths

Murray's Model

For Henry Murray, an early twentieth-century personality psychologist, control of personality moved around from need to need. He suggested it was useful to monitor

The environment encourages some motives and suppresses others. A hot summer day, for example, may trigger the motive to sell lemonade—and maybe to drink some yourself.

Regnant Process: A process that is directing or ruling personality at a given point in time.

an individual's **regnant process**. Regnant has the same Latin root, *regnans,* as reign and ruler, and refers to governing. The regnant process is the one that exerts control over personality at a given point in time (Murray & Kluckhohn, 1956). Often the controlling agent is a particular need. Needs can be in conflict, however, and the question of which one is in control was a matter of how those needs interact. Here are some observations Murray had of how motives or needs influence one another (Murray, 1938, pp. 85–87; 1951, p. 452).

Prepotent Need: A need that would take over the actions of personality—that is, become a regnant process—more quickly than other needs; that is, a very important need.

Murray started with the idea that every person experienced a hierarchy of needs in which certain needs were more important, or **prepotent**, relative to others. A prepotent need is one that would take over the control of personality—become regnant—most quickly if it is not satisfied at a certain level. Basic needs such as pain avoidance and hunger are prepotent over others. If one is in great pain, or very hungry, these needs must be satisfied before later ones are. Or, as Bertolt Brecht put it in his *Three Penny Opera:* "First feed our stomachs, then talk politics."

Determinant Needs and Subsidiary Needs

Determinant Needs: Basic needs which may cause the establishment of secondary needs, as when a person's desire to be intimate with another person creates a need to behave well toward others as a means to impress the individual.

Subsidiary Needs: A state of needs in which one need serves another, as when a person tries to do well in school (need for achievement) so as to attain the ultimate goal of impressing others (need for esteem).

Determinant Needs are those basic needs which can motivate a person to do other seemingly less important things. **Subsidiary Needs** arise when a goal must be pursued to fulfill the determinant need. That is, the most determinant need sets the agenda; the other need is subsidiary to it. For example, a child might have a determinant need of being loved by his or her parents, and that might lead to a subsidiary to study hard so as to please them. Such a situation is illustrated in a study by Dowson and McInerney (2001), who interviewed 86 middle school children, to see why they wanted to achieve in school.

The interviews included questions such as, "Do you want to do well in school?" and "What reasons do you have for wanting to do well at school?" The researchers found that being together with friends was often a determinant need, and working hard and studying was a subsidiary need that helped the students remain with their friends who were performing well. As one student put it, "Me and my friends try to get the teacher to let us work together, but then we have to show her that we're doing the work, or she won't let us be together next time."

For another group of students, a desire to nurture others (or to look good oneself) was determinant; working hard was again subsidiary. These children felt concerned when they saw others having trouble, and good about themselves if they could help. They said things like, "If I know my work well, then I can help my friends if they need it. I like to help when I can"; and, "If my friends don't understand what they have to do, they ask me what to do because they know I like to help them" (Dowson & McInerney, 2001, p. 37).

Freud would not have be surprised by such comments as these. "Why would any child actually be interested in the hard work of learning entirely for its own sake?" he would ask. Rather, Freud, like Murray, believed that people have basic needs related to survival and reproduction which direct other, social needs. For Freud, each individual enters into a contract with society, carrying out responsibilities such as learning and working. In exchange, a good society fulfills the individual's basic needs and makes sure that he or she is taken care of as best as is possible (Freud, 1930). Freud would interpret studying with others as expressing the hopes to impress others, and to win a life partner in the future. For Freud, studying would set the stage for later romantic intimacy—and ultimately, for sexual reproduction.

Even if intellectual work begins for other reasons, some early theorists believed it could become **functionally autonomous**. A functionally autonomous motive is one that takes on an independent role of its own (e.g., Allport, 1968). Since Freud's time, however, other motivational theorists have been happy to accept intellectual interest as an innate motive in itself. For example, it may have evolved by leading people to learn more about their environment, others around them, and their culture, which would itself enhance chances of survival (e.g., De Waal, 2001, p. 24).

In the survey just discussed, the children didn't always want to study, of course. The young students sometimes felt bored, lazy, and angry. They made remarks such as, "I don't like subjects that are too hard. I'd rather be somewhere else," and "most of the time, I just try to do as little as possible" (Dowson & McInerney, 2001, p. 38). When a desire to achieve collides with a desire to do as little as possible, the result is called a need or goal conflict.

Functionally Autonomous: The state of a need or motive which, although originally caused by a biological urge, has taken on an independent life of its own.

Connecting Window   *Maslow's Hierachy of Needs*

Another way needs might be organized is according to a developmental progression such as Abraham Maslow proposed. Recall that Maslow had divided needs into those that were related to physiology, safety, belongingness, esteem, and self-actualization.

Needs and Need Conflicts

Each individual experiences a wide number of needs—many of which can come into conflict. Every person has both the need to be alone and to socialize, for example. In such cases, the prepotent—neediest—need typically wins out. Those people who have higher needs to socialize than to be alone will act sociable. Those who have higher needs to be alone than to socialize will remain solitary. Still, the conflict between the social and the solitary will be present to some degree in each person.

What effect do conflicts between needs have on the individual? Emmons and King (1988; 1989) reasoned that such conflicts would exert a negative overall influence on a person's emotional life. Emmons and King had previously studied **personal strivings** (see Chapter 4). Personal strivings are tasks a person is trying to carry out over the short or medium term in the course of meeting longer-term goals. Examples of personal strivings include the tasks of "appearing attractive," "seeking new and exciting experiences," and "avoiding being noticed by others." They proposed a model in which conflicts among needs would interfere with attaining certain goals. This, in turn, would cause individuals to dwell on missing their goals, returning their thoughts repeatedly to the problem—a state called rumination. The added stress would cause the person negative emotions and poorer health.

Emmons and King asked people to list their personal strivings (the average person in their study lists about fifteen), and then to identify any potential conflicts among them. The authors identified two different kinds of conflicts. The first is a **conflictual striving**, based on the direct conflict between one striving and another (cf., Heilizer, 1964). To identify conflictual striving, a given participant examines all pairs of their strivings and indicates those that are in conflict. For example, "to ap-

Personal Strivings: Specific activities a person is currently attempting to carry out in order to meet long term plans and goals.

Conflictual Striving: A personal striving or plan that meets one set of goals while frustrating another set of goals. This might happen, for example, when a person who is working hard in school so as to satisfy her needs to achieve, simultaneously thwarts her needs to have fun.

pear more intelligent than I am," is often rated as in conflict with "to always present myself in an honest light." (Emmons & King, 1988, p. 1042). Another conflicting pair was "to keep my relationships on a fifty-fifty basis" and "to dominate, control, and manipulate people and situations." A person's overall goal-conflict rating was the average of the conflict ratings they gave each striving pair.

Ambivalent Striving: A personal striving that involves a goal that is, itself, fraught with problems. For example, striving to be honest, although very desirable, entails many costs.

The second kind of conflict—called **ambivalent striving**—involves a striving that has its own conflict intrinsic in it. Meeting a certain goal, for example, can simply create conflict by itself. On top of the list of such ambivalent strivings (as rated by students in the same study) were: "to be all things to all people," "to be honest," and "to avoid being aggressive if I feel I've been wronged" (Emmons & King, 1988, p. 1042).

Emmons and King correlated the level of a person's conflictual and ambivalent striving with such criteria as the individual's well-being, the number of physical symptoms they experienced, and even the number of the trips they made to the student health service and the severity of the diagnosis for a medical problem they experienced after they arrived there.

Students with goal conflicts of any type reported thinking about them (ruminating) more and experiencing more stress on account of those thoughts. They had more negative feelings and a reduced sense of well-being. Those goal-conflicted people also reported more physical symptoms than others, and, more than a year later they reported more often to the student health service and were diagnosed with more severe health problems (Emmons & King, 1988, Study 3). Goal conflicts may be especially problematic for those who optimistically hope they can meet conflicting goals. Such naïve optimists appear susceptible to greater immune system dysfunction than those who accept they cannot achieve all their desires (Segerstrom, 2001; 2005).

Need Fusion

Need Fusion: A state or condition of several distinct needs that occurs when a person engages in an action or objective that satisfies all the needs simultaneously.

Finally, in fortunate cases, a person may experience **need fusion**. Need fusion occurs when a person's diverse needs are combined together to work toward a single aim. For example, when a person decides to go to college it may fuse a variety of needs: the need to be curious, through the opportunity to learn; the need for achievement, through mastering a subject areas; the need for status, through obtaining a college degree; and the need for affiliation, through the opportunity to make new friends, among others. When a goal is a good one, it creates a powerful positive motivation as the person's energy is fused and directed toward a single aim that will help him or her meet many needs together.

How Does Action Develop in the Mind?

Motivation, Emotion, and Mood-Congruent Thought

Mood Congruency and Feedback to Motivation

If motives guide and direct people toward goals, how are those guides then elaborated in thoughts and feelings? Chapter 4 described how sometimes emotions could amplify or suppress motivation. As motives arise, they are often accompanied by

Think before you act.

Pythagoras

emotional reactions to them and their aims. For example, a need for control may be accompanied by anger, which may lead a person to try to control others with threats. A desire to nurture someone may be accompanied by happiness, which will amplify the helping (see Chapter 4). These accompanying emotions, in turn, trigger mood-related thoughts.

From one cognitive perspective, memory is viewed as a network of nodes and their connections (Bower, 1981; Collins & Loftus, 1975). The nodes represent concepts, and the connections between the nodes represent the associations that exist between the concepts. Thus, the proposition "Jane wants to go to the circus" would be represented as a series of associations among the nodes *Jane,* the verb *to go,* and the place she went, the *circus.* Gordon Bower (1981) has suggested that in this memory network, there exist special nodes that represent moods such as *happiness, anger,* and *sadness.* The proposition that "Jane wants to go to the circus," might be associated with happiness because circus brings to mind happy thoughts for many people. When a person became happy, the "happy" node in memory would become activated—suffused with mental energy (e.g., the neuron would fire at a higher rate). That energy would then spread out from the "happy" concept node to related concepts such as circus, and the person would be primed to remember that Jane liked the circus, rather than a more neutral or negative thought such as that "Jane wants to avoid the dangerous part of town." Should a person enter a sad mood, however, the sadness would be more likely to activate Jane's desire to avoid the dangerous part of town, perhaps—rather than the circus.

That is, there exists a connection between moods and thoughts related to them. This is often referred to as a **mood-congruent cognition effect**. The "mood-congruence" of mood-congruent cognition refers to a match between the emotional quality of a person's mood and of his or her ideas. Thus, if a person is sad and thinking about war, the mood and the thoughts are mood-congruent because they are both unpleasant. Similarly, if a person is happy and thinking about winning the lottery, the person's mood and cognitions are congruent because they are both pleasant. However, a sad person who thinks about good weather is thinking in a mood-incongruent fashion.

Mood-congruent cognition has been studied a number of ways. **Mood-congruent judgment** refers more specifically to the tendency of judgment to shift congruently with mood. In a landmark study, Isen, Clark, Shalker, and Karp (1978) examined mood-congruent judgment in a local shopping mall. They stationed a first researcher at the beginning of an L-shaped portion of a shopping mall corridor, where she distributed small gifts of combs (to women) and pads of paper (to men) as the shoppers passed by. A pilot study had indicated such gifts made shoppers happy. The "interviewer" was around the corner, in the perpendicular section of the "L" where she could not see the gift giver at work. A third researcher was strategically placed in the bend of the "L" where she could see the other two, and could record which shoppers had received the positive-mood induction. By the time shoppers turned the corner of the "L" they had stashed their gifts away. The interviewer, blind to who was happier, stopped shoppers and asked them a series of questions concerning repairs to their vacuum cleaners, dishwashers, and so forth. The consumers who received the positive-mood induction recalled more positive features of their vacuum cleaners, dishwashers, and other appliances than did other consumers.

Mood-Congruent Cognition Effect: An effect in which ideas or concepts that match a mood in tone (e.g., pleasant thoughts; happy moods) seem more memorable, plausible, reasonable, and/or likely, than ideas or concepts that mismatch the individual's mood.

Mood-Congruent Judgment: A special case of the mood-congruent cognition effect concerning judgments of plausibility or likelihood. For example, in a happy mood, good weather seems more likely.

It isn't necessary to manipulate people's moods to find the effect. In one study, five hundred residents of the state of New Hampshire, randomly selected from the phonebook, were contacted for a telephone survey. Embedded in the survey were mood-congruent judgment questions (e.g., "What is the likelihood the economy of New Hampshire will improve in the next five years?"). At the end of the survey, which included many other questions concerning regional water quality, the state Department of Transportation, and statewide political figures, respondents were asked their mood. As predicted by the mood-congruent judgment hypothesis, the respondents' moods correlated with the positivity of their judgments in the survey (Mayer, Gaschke, Braverman, & Evans, 1992).

To determine whether such natural changes were really due to a mood effect, fraternity and sorority students were studied over a four-week period. Over that time, there was clear evidence that the individual Greek house members' moods and judgments shifted together over a four-week period, with greater changes taking place over longer periods of time (Mayer & Hanson, 1995). The findings concerning mood-congruency are quite extensive and cover many other such findings (e.g., Forgas, 2001). There are also similar findings concerning people who suffer from mood disorders. The causal direction can go either way. That is, bad thoughts can, in turn, enhance bad moods and lower motivation (e.g., Beck, 1967; Seligman, 1975).

The mind reverberates, in other words, around the particular urge or need. For example, a student deciding whether to study or take a break from studying will have many parts of her mind engaged in making that decision. This may be largely unconscious, or there may be an internal conversation about it. Either way, the striving to study brings up both feelings and thoughts that will contribute to the expression of any action.

The Dynamic Lattice

Ergs (Ergic): Another term for basic motives.

Sentiments: Emotional attachments to ideas or activities.

By now it will be clear that motives, emotions, and thoughts all interact with one another as one prepares for action. Is there a way to bring any clarity to these interactions so as to understand a person's dynamic structure of motives? Raymond Cattell suggested the use of a dynamic lattice to illustrate the relationship among motives and the emotional relationships and attitudes they brought about. Cattell used the term **ergs** (Greek for energy) to refer to basic motives of the sort Freud and Murray talked about. He believed that these basic ergs led to **sentiments**. Sentiments are emotional attachments to ideas or activities. Loving the flag, for example, would be a sentiment. Finally, the dynamic lattice ended at the specific attitude level. Connected to a love of the flag would be a specific attitude, such as, that displaying the flag is a good thing.

Cattell indicated what such a lattice might look like in a diagram reproduced in Figure 9.1. The man depicted exhibits an erg of curiosity. That curiosity might lead him to develop a hobby of photography (a sentiment). Finally, the hobby of photography might lead him to an appreciation of films because of their wonderful photography. You can see the diagram progress from motive to attitude, from right to left, in the Figure. As another example from the diagram, the man's ergic needs for sex, gregariousness, and protection lead to his feelings for his wife. These interrelations tell us something useful and personally significant about motivational

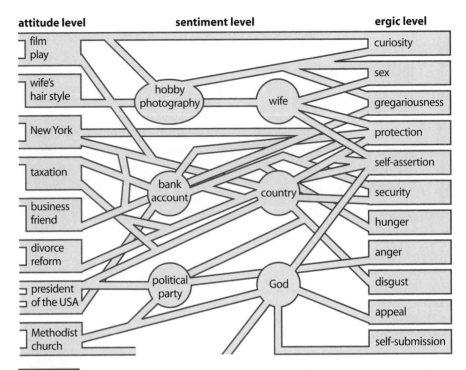

| attitude level | sentiment level | ergic level |

FIGURE 9.1   A Portion of a Dynamic Lattice, Showing Ergs, Sentiments, and Attitudes

Raymond Cattell drew this provocative picture of a dynamic lattice extending from *ergs* (his original term for basic mental energy), through sentiments (feelings), to social attitudes. The associations illustrate how motives begin (at the ergs) and gradually progress toward an external expression (not shown in the diagram). Note that the orientation of the progression is reversed (e.g., from right to left) from that usually employed in this book.

Source: From Cattell & Kline (1977), Figure 9.1. Reprinted with permission from Elsevier.

dynamics. Although the dynamic lattice has not been used frequently in personality research, it seems as if it might hold some promise as one way of organizing motives and their interactions with other mental contents such as emotions and attitudes.

From Thought to Action

Automatic Action

Ideomotor Action: A scientific label for the concept that simply thinking of a physical movement brings it about or increases the likelihood of bringing it about.

As needs and their associated emotions and thoughts are elaborated, how are they turned into action? We can talk about automatic tendencies toward action and considered action. Let's begin with automatic action tendencies. Carpenter (1874) popularized the notion of **ideomotor action**—the idea that simply thinking of an act will increase its likelihood of occurring (Bargh & Chartrand, 1999). Many have argued that ideas lead directly to action, and indeed there is consistent evidence for that proposition. The ideas need not be at the center of attention or even related to the task at hand.

It is somewhat provocative to understand that ideas that do not seem particularly important, or are far from the center of attention, can influence action. In one study, participants were told that they would be involved in two unrelated experiments. First, they were asked to solve word puzzles that included a number of neutral words, along with several experimentally manipulated target words. In the politeness condition, the target words were *respect, considerate,* and *polite;* in the rudeness condition, they were *rude, impolite,* and *obnoxious* (Bargh, Chen, & Burrows, 1996).

After solving the word puzzles, participants were then instructed to interrupt a conversation the experimenter was holding, so as to ask for the second experimental task. There actually was no second experiment. Rather, the measure of interest was how rude or polite the participant would be when interrupting the experimenter. Raters blind to the hypotheses judged that participants exposed to the rude words were far ruder than participants exposed to the politeness words (Bargh, Chen, & Burrows, 1996). Similarly, Carver and colleagues (1983) first exposed participants to aggressive words in a manner that led them to believe it was irrelevant to the main study. They then found that, in a second experiment, the participants exposed to the aggressive words gave longer shocks to learners.

Expectancies and the Likelihood of Action

The healthy individual expresses only some motives and urges. Some urges are insufficiently strong to merit expression. Even strong urges, however, may be held back due to social constraints. Sexual and aggressive ideas in particular might be held back from expression even when they preoccupy the individual. Only the more disturbed individuals in our society freely express such desires as to angrily tell off one's boss on every occasion, or to rub up against someone for a sexual thrill. Healthy people keep a good number of their motives and urges strictly to themselves.

Assuming an action is socially acceptable, how does one decide whether it is useful and ought to take place? Social cognitive theorists, such as Julian Rotter, developed motivational formulae to try to predict the likelihood someone would carry out an action. For Rotter (1954), action was a product of the **expectancy of reward** and its **reward value**. The expectancy of a reward concerned how likely a person's actions would be in securing the reward. For example, if there was no likelihood of getting the reward no matter what a person did, the expectancy would be zero. If, on the other hand, hard work would get a person the reward two out of three times, then the expectancy would be ⅔ or .67. The second part of the equation, the reward value, concerns how rewarding the individual would find attainting the desired goal. Some goals are relatively unrewarding, such as avoiding a parking ticket, and would have a low value (e.g., .1) whereas others are highly rewarding, such as meeting the love of your life, and would have a high value (e.g., .98).

To illustrate the expectancy of reward, and reward value concepts together, consider one of the scenarios outlined in Table 9.1 on page 334. A student enrolls in organic chemistry partly because he was thinking of going to medical school. By Rotter's formula, if we wanted to know the likelihood of the student obtaining an "A," we would want to know the student's expectation of reward, on the one hand, and how important it was to the student to get the "A" on the other. Let's say the student believes that if he studies hard enough, he is likely to get an "A" with a .9 probability. Even so, he may still not work hard if thoughts of medical school are only

Expectancy of Reward: The belief a person holds as to how likely it is he or she will or can succeed at gaining a particular, sought-after objective.

Reward Value: The assessment a person makes of how desirable or pleasurable a particular objective or goal is.

Inside the Field

Greenwald's Studies of Subliminal Perception and Motivation

Inside our field, Anthony Greenwald is among an elite corps of researchers whose work is characterized by meticulously developed methods, studies planned with remarkable care, and extraordinary patience and perseverance in examining key questions of the field. Through the years, Greenwald and his colleagues have examined many challenging issues. In many instances they have cleared up confusions that have plagued the field or have developed new techniques for measuring key aspects of personality. One area of Greenwald's work has been in subliminal perception.

In the early 1990s, Greenwald and his colleagues studied subliminal self-help audiotapes, of the sort one sees in a drugstore or superstore like Wal-Mart, or on the Web (Greenwald, Spangenberg, Pratkanis, & Eskenazi, 1991). *Subliminal* refers to the fact that information is passed to the individual below the threshold of conscious perception. The fact that there truly do exist unconscious influences on motivation raised the question of whether "subliminal audio" and similar measures could

really alter a person's dynamics of action for the better.

Greenwald and his colleagues bought two groups of audiotapes from commercial businesses. The first type of tape claimed to raise people's self-esteem. The second type of tape claimed to improve people's memory.

The researchers employed a double blind method in which neither they nor the participants knew what recording was on a given tape. The tapes were, however, relabeled and these labels were counterbalanced over what the tape supposedly influenced. That is, half the self-esteem tapes were labeled as raising self-esteem, and the other half of the self-esteem tapes were labeled as improving memory. The same was done to the memory tapes. Participants then listened to the recordings and, afterward, were asked whether their memory or self-esteem had improved. They were also given tests of memory and tests of self-esteem.

Participants who received self-esteem-labeled tapes believed that their self-esteem had grown, even though their self-esteem test performance

moderately appealing to him, say, .4 on a scale from 0 to 1. In a somewhat simplified approach to Rotter's formula, we could calculate the likelihood of the student working hard as his .9 expectancy of getting an "A" in the course multiplied times his .4 reward value, leading to a .36 likelihood of studying hard. If medical school seemed more desirable (e.g., and .8 on the 0 to 1 scale), his likelihood of hard work would rise to .72 (e.g., .9 × .8). Although people are not always quite this rational, there is experimental evidence that they do behave somewhat according to these logical rules (Champagne & Pervin, 1987; Eccles & Wigfield, 2002).

Regression (of an Idea):
The state of an idea or desire to act, when that desire is blocked from action. In such a case, the idea may further be considered and elaborated. It may, for example, be recast as an emotional fantasy.

What happens to motives and urges that don't make the cut? Say the student is in love with someone but the probability of gaining the loved-one's attention is near zero? In such cases, the motivations and urges associated with the aim are turned back from behavioral expression. In Freud's terms, the idea undergoes **regression**—it is blocked from behavioral action, and reenters the motivational, emotional, and planning sphere, where it may continue to be elaborated unconsciously or be elaborated in daydreams, or artworks, at night in dreamy wishes, or in other mental man-was unchanged and even though half of them received subliminal memory tapes. Participants who received memory-labeled tapes believed their memories had improved even though there was no actual change in memory. So, the labels on the tapes, but not the actual content, led participants to believe that their self-esteem or memory had improved. On the actual tests of memory and self-esteem, no improvement took place, even after tapes were sorted out for what they were actually supposed to do.

The authors of the study concluded that the participants experienced an "illusory placebo effect" (Greenwald et al., 1991, p. 121). It was a placebo effect because the participants perceived improvement in the direction of the tape's label, independent of the content of the tape. It was illusory because objective measures indicated no improvement took place at all.

In laboratory studies, the existence of subliminal perception has been demonstrated through examining the "direct" and "indirect" effects of a stimulus. For a subliminal effect to be demonstrated, the participant must have no direct awareness of what they saw or heard. If asked, "What did you just hear or see?" the participant should be unable to answer. The indirect effect, by contrast, involves a measurable change in motives, feelings or thoughts. Whatever went unseen or unheard should nonetheless bring about a detectable effect on this indirect part. Technically, subliminal perception can be defined as perception that shows no evidence of direct effects but which yields statistically significant indirect effects (Draine & Greenwald, 1998). Such effects are often obtained, but are not always easily replicable (Greenwald, Klinger, & Schuh, 1995; Reingold & Merikle, 1988). Recently, Draine and Greenwald (1998) developed a procedure that can be used to more reliably produce the effect. The technique examines the difference between direct and indirect effects under conditions of subliminal presentation. A variety of innovations ensures that this approach yields more consistent results than have been obtained in the past. So subliminal perception exists—but you probably wouldn't want to go out and buy any subliminal tapes on that basis.

> Twaddle, rubbish, and gossip is what people want, not action . . . The secret of life is to chatter freely about all one wishes to do and how one is always being prevented—and then do nothing.
>
> Soren Kierkegaard

ifestations of unfilled hopes and aspirations (Freud, 1900/1960, p. 541, e.g., Fig. 3). In Freud's early psychoanalytic theory, art works and writings, as well as dreams, were the consequence of unfulfilled wishes. As Freud (1962) put it—perhaps overstating the case—"Happy people never make fantasies, only unsatisfied ones do." Singer (1965, pp. 90–97), however, makes the important point that although fantasies may indeed serve drive-reducing functions, they also arise for other reasons; for example, as a means of distraction or, for that matter, out of a creative desire to muse over different possibilities.

Partial Expressions and Slips of the Tongue

Parapraxes: Mistaken behaviors or slips of the tongue that reveal something about a person's hidden motivations.

Finally, urges that "don't make the cut" may be partially or half expressed—sometimes in an embarrassing fashion. This often happens in **parapraxes**—mistaken behaviors that reveal hidden intentions. A common and heavily studied type of parapraxis is the slip-of-the-tongue, or "Freudian slip." For Freud, highly activated

Qualities of the Psychological Situation	Numerical Value
TABLE 9.1 **Two Examples of Rotter's Motivational Formula**	
Example 1: A student wants to get an "A" on an Organic Chemistry Exam to help his chances to go to medical school.	
Expectancy of Reward He believes with hard study he can almost certainly do it.	.9
This is coded numerically from 0 "Not Possible" to 1 "Definitely Happen."	
Reward Value He is increasingly uncertain about whether he really wants to go to medical school. This is coded numerically from 0 "Not Wanted" to 1 "Highly Desired."	.4
Likelihood of Act That Results	.36
Example 2: A student wants to get a "B" on a final so as to avoid failing a course.	
Expectancy of Reward She is uncertain, given her current pressures, whether she can get a grade as high as "B" on the final. This is coded numerically from 0 "Not Possible" to 1 "Definitely Happen."	.6
Reward Value She desperately wants to pass so that she can graduate on time. This is coded numerically from 0 "Not Wanted" to 1 "Highly Desired."	.9
Likelihood of Act That Results	.54

Source: Rotter (1954).

urges—sometimes hidden in the unconscious—might be mistakenly expressed when conscious self-control was weak, perhaps due to fatigue or stress. Freud referred to the unintended exposure of such urges as part of the "psychopathology of everyday life." Describing a German parliamentary session that was sure to become heated and factious, Freud recounted how the president of the Lower House had, "with his first words *closed* the sitting instead of opening it." Freud observed:

> we feel inclined, in view of our knowledge of the circumstances in which the slip of the tongue occurred, to recognize that the parapraxis had a sense.

Fantasies often represent suppressed actions. They remain inward imaginings precisely because their outer expression is often regarded as problematic or unacceptable.

Reprinted with special permission of King Features Syndicate.

SALLY FORTH   GREG HOWARD

Did the menu writer have some reservations about the Vegetable Crab Soup—or was its description on the sign an innocent mistake? Although it is hard to tell in an individual instance, experimental studies indicate that the expression of certain meanings can be motivated unconsciously.

The President expected nothing good of the sitting and would have been glad if he could have brought it to an immediate end . . . Or, once more, we are told that a lady who was well-known for her energy remarked on one occasion: "My husband asked his doctor what diet he ought to follow; but the doctor told him he had no need to diet: he could eat and drink *what I want.*" Here again the slip of the tongue has an unmistakable other side to it: it was giving expression to a consistently planned programme. (Freud, 1920, p. 35; italics added)

But are slips of the tongue really caused by underlying urges that ought not to be expressed? Research evidence supports the case. In one study, for example, male participants were asked to take two letter strings such as "od" and "ong" and insert the letter "l" before the first one and "n" before the second, and read them aloud. Thus, if a participant saw the strings: "od ong," "est in," and "ice egs," he was to say aloud, "lod nong, lest nin, and lice negs." Such a task is designed to produce involuntary slips of the tongue such as "nod long" for "lod nong" and "nice legs" for "lice negs." One group of men were administered the experiment under neutral conditions. In the other, the male participants were administered the experiment by an attractive woman in a short skirt. According to Freud, the presence of the woman could generate sexual ideas among the men that they would try to repress during the experiment. Indeed, the males who interacted with the short-skirted woman experimenter more frequently substituted "nice legs" for "lice negs" than in the other condition—and expressed considerable embarrassment when they did so. Similar findings have been found for the production of sexual innuendos (Motley, Camden, & Baars, 1983). (More examples of such slips are shown in the Facts at a Glance.) We might further ask: What are the ways that the inside of personality gets expressed?

How Are Acts Performed?

The Communication Channels

Motor Homunculus: A part of the brain, located on the surface of the rearmost area of the frontal lobe, that controls the movement of the body. The areas of this surface region are arrayed in sequences that mirror, in part, the arrangement of the external body.

The Motor Cortex

Recall that the brain has an area for motor control called the primary motor cortex. Located across the surface of the rearmost portion of the frontal lobe, its motor areas are arranged in sequences that mirror, in part, the arrangement of the external body. One such sequence, for example, extends from toes, foot, leg and knee, up through the eye, nose, face, lips, and tongue. Because it is arranged somewhat like the body itself, it is sometimes referred to as the **motor** (or body) **homunculus** (a homunculus is a little person).

• FACTS • AT • A • GLANCE

Three Examples of Real-World Freudian Slips

The Context	The Slip	The Interpretation
Example 1 Kimberly Bergalis, an early AIDS victim who had contracted the disease from her dentist, sought to require health professionals with AIDS from practicing certain forms of medicine that could spread the illness. After she died, her father, George Bergalis, promised to continue her crusade. In 1992, he testified in the New Hampshire Legislature. By then, however, it was increasingly apparent that few people were contracting AIDS from their healthcare professionals; his daughter had been a most tragic exception.	[Testifying in front of the New Hampshire Legislature, Wednesday, January 29th, 1992]: As we have learned over the past two years, this method of [AIDS] transmission [from Kimberly's dentist] was not a new revelation to our irresponsible public health officials. They were a rare—[correcting himself] They were aware—of this risk for years, but orchestrated, along with others, a masterful cover up in order to preserve tranquility and to protect certain interest groups and health professions.*	George Bergalis' loyal promise to his daughter to continue her crusade couldn't fully block out his growing awareness that his daughter's illness was not the product of a cover up, but was a tragic outcome of the practices of the dentist she had seen. Such instances of infection remain exceedingly rare. Mr. Bergalis, however, is not alone in his continuing concern about the issue. The *French Order of Doctors* concluded, for example, that doctors with AIDS should be reassigned from some positions, and the matter remains a topic of discussion among ethicists.
Example 2 Two colleagues were making an appointment while the second colleague was undergoing a divorce.	Colleague 1: We could do it February 14th, though it's a holiday. Colleague 2: Oh yes, good, that's on Veteran's day; oh, no, Valentine's day.	Love had turned to war for Colleague 2; for him, Valentine's day was Veteran's day; he was veteran of a failed marriage. The meeting date was so good because it would take Colleague 2's mind off his divorce.
Example 3 Graduation day at a high school in the Northeast, presided over by a highly respected, but also rather stern principal. The following occurred as he was making his closing remarks to the students and their parents.	And to the graduating class, I wish you much future sex…[correcting himself as the audience roared]—future *success*."	Freud said it all.

*Note: From a recorded transcript supplied to the author courtesy of Martin Murray, New Hampshire Public Radio.

Access to Motility: The capacity of a portion of the brain or mind to control and direct the individual's external movement, activity, and language.

That motor homunculus provides access to the individual's outward expressions of personality. Control of the motor homunculus is sometimes referred to as **access to motility** (or access to movement). Through the motor cortex, the personality system directs motor, vascular, and other organs and can express it itself through a diverse set of communication channels (Ekman, 1986). What began as urges and developed into intentions can be expressed, though the motor cortex, as social acts (Rosenbaum, 2005).

Human Communication Channels Considered

A person's communications and other acts are of many sorts, and involve language, emotional signals, and other nonverbal cues (Buck, 1984). Verbal communications use the vocal cords, mouth, lips, and tongue, and are sometimes accompanied by various physical gestures of the face, head and hands. Some aspects of language and communication appear to have co-evolved with discrete facial expressions. For example, each basic emotion has coupled to it a set of basic, often involuntary, facial expressions—such as sadness, anger, and genuine happiness and mirth (see Chapter 4). In addition, there are voluntary or controlled facial expressions including a "social smile," that is, a smile we produce on command when we greet others—even when we may not be feeling happy.

Language is often modified or amplified through specific bodily movements. **Emblems** are fairly precise gestures that have specific meanings in one's culture, such as shaking the head up-and-down to mean yes, or side-to-side to mean no. Another example is holding one's hand to one's ear to mean "can you speak up." **Illustrators** involve movements of the hands or other body parts to supplement the meanings of speech, as when a fisherman spreads his hands to indicate exactly how big the fish was that got away. Unlike an emblem, illustrators take on their meaning from the context. A small child may use the same gesture of holding her hands apart in order to ask for a hug (Ekman & Friesen, 1969). In literate cultures, language also is expressed through writing with the hands, and, with the advent of typewriters and computers, through keyboarding (Rosenbaum, 1991).

The whole body itself can be a communication device. Through posture, a person may express social dominance, reticence, extreme unease through rigidity, and the like. For example, a person's erect posture may indicate social confidence and dominance, whereas a bowed posture may convey socially lowered status and submissiveness. In Japan, people can indicate social status through exchanges of bowing, in which the degree to which one bows indicates one's assessment of one's own and the other's social status. Some bodily organs of communication are not entirely under our control such as the skin. We may sweat when experiencing social discomfort, or blush when we feel embarrassed. We may break out in acne or a rash over the course of a difficult week.

We can use **locomotion** to express our reactions to someone or some idea, moving closer to them to indicate greater intimacy, or leaving a room to indicate a desire for greater privacy. Of course, the body and hands also are also involved in complex tool use. We use our whole bodies to help move yard debris in a wheelbarrow. Our hands are involved in everything from the use of eating utensils at a meal to playing the keyboard of an organ. In such contexts, hands can communicate everything from anger and disgust (throwing down one's silverware) to the poetic subtleties of the music of a fugue.

With a subtle facial expression, and a small shift in posture, this woman seems to communicate considerable interest and attention.

Emblems: Fairly precise gestures that have specific meanings in one's culture, such as shaking the head up-and-down to mean "yes," or side-to-side to mean "no."

Illustrators: Movements of the hands or other body parts to supplement the meanings of speech, as when a person holds his hands close together to illustrate how small a child is.

Locomotion: Movement of the body or parts of the body for purposes of going someplace.

TABLE 9.2	Language-Related Communication Channels of the Body

The Vocal Cords, Mouth, Tongue, and Lips	
Words	People's greatest, and most unique, quality of communication involves the words they compose and speak. Human beings can communicate in any number of verbal forms from one word utterances, to sonnets, to song, to various types of oratory.
Language flow	There is a flow of words in addition to the words themselves: The flow concerns whether the words are interrupted or not, cover one another, are fragmentary, or whether they flow in a well-planned, well-fashioned, stream.
Voice expression	The voice also changes as means of expression, sometimes loud, sometimes soft, sometimes rising with anxiety or falling with calmness.
General Contributions of the Head and Hands to Language	
Emblems	Nonverbal gestures called emblems are very precise movements that have an approximate fairly or definite meaning to everyone in a given culture. Examples of emblems include vertical head nods to mean "yes," lateral head shakes for "no," and shrugs for "it doesn't matter," and the hand-to-ear "can you speak up" signal.
Illustrators	Illustrators primarily involve movements of the hands to clarify and emphasize speech, although sometimes raised eyebrows and other parts of the face may be employed. Examples of illustrators include moving the hands to indicate how small or big something is, indicating the points of arguments, and similar indications. In comparison to emblems, illustrators do not possess clear meaning apart from speech.
Specific Contributions of the Hands	
Sign language	Hands may be used more specifically in the service of speech, as in the case of sign language, baseball signals, and similar manual languages.
Keyboarding	Hands may express language through typing, as well as express musical language through playing a musical keyboard.

Conscious and Automatic Forms of Action

Automatized Actions: Physical movements that a person has performed over and over again until they are so over-learned the individual pays little or no attention to them. For example, leaning right and left to keep one's balance on a bicycle.

As motives and their elaborations travel from the inner mind to the outer world, the activities they unleash often communicate a meaning—and sometimes more than one. Moreover, external behaviors can be conscious or be unconscious just like the thoughts that control them. Human behavior can be conducted in an "unconscious" fashion because it often exists in automatized form. **Automatized actions** are those we perform over and over again until they are so automatic we need no longer pay attention to them. For example, when you first learned to tie your shoelaces, it required considerable concentration—and some luck—to carry out correctly. Nowadays, however, you probably don't pay much attention to tying your laces. You may remember how hard it was to first learn to ride a two-wheel bicycle whereas now it is second na-

TABLE 9.3	Other Communication Channels through the Body
Social Communication with the Whole Body	
Whole body posture	The nature of a person's overall posture can indicate aspects of their social status and intended action. For example, a stooped posture may indicate social submissiveness.
Locomotion	Similarly, moving toward someone can indicate interest or aggression; moving away can indicate termination of a relationship, rejection, or fear.
Emotion-Related Expression through the Face	
Involuntary facial expressions	A variety of automatic facial expresses are connected with emotions. Many of these are universal across human beings, and include joy, fear, anger, sadness, and disgust. These expressions are also quite close to those made by other primates.
Voluntary facial expressions	In addition, people learn to create voluntary facial expressions that mimic the automatic ones (to smile on command), or to alter facial expressions (to mask anger).
Other Emotional Expression	
Sweating	A person who sweats when others are feeling cool may communicate discomfort or stress.
Blushing	Some people who become embarrassed may find blood runs to their face and that they blush.

ture. You may even listen to the radio or exchange pleasantries with your roommate such that the activity is at the periphery of awareness, if in awareness at all.

Once behavior becomes automatized, it is possible to carry it out without hardly noticing it. Sometimes this is regrettable, as when a busy person eats her lunch at her desk while working, and hardly tastes it. Powerful examples of automatized behavior can take place as well—for example, a graduate student was being videotaped when she was severely criticized by her advisor. On the video, one hand rests on her knee, its middle finger extended in an obscene gesture toward her advisor. Fortunately, her advisor didn't notice. When asked about her hand gesture by the video-maker, she was utterly unaware of having made it (Ekman, 1985, pp. 100–101).

Latent versus Manifest Content

Manifest Content: The relatively direct and obvious meaning of a communication, as opposed to its more hidden or symbolic meanings (see for example, Latent Content).

Earlier in this chapter, we examined the fact that motives often conflicted with one another. Sometimes that conflict can be carried through into the public expressions of intentions. A person's single expressive act can convey two or more meanings, presumably both intended by the individual. Psychodynamic psychologists have worked out a language for separating out two meanings of the same message, distinguishing between the messages' manifest and latent content. **Manifest content** refers to what

The homeowner's manifest message is that this is a well-kept house and neatly trimmed garden. But might there be a latent content expressed as well?

Latent Content: Meanings of a communication that are symbolic, secondary or conveyed indirectly, but that still can be understood by a careful observer.

the words or actions of a particular communication are directly about. **Latent content** refers to a second, rather different, meaning that accompanies the first and that is equally conveyed by the words. The difference between manifest and latent content can be illustrated with a joke told by the comedian Groucho Marx. Marx was interviewing a contestant on a serialized, live-broadcast television show when he improvised the following:

> GROUCHO: How are you?
> MAN: Fine.
> GROUCHO: Well, tell me, are you married?
> MAN: Yes; I've been married for nine years.
> GROUCHO: Gee, that's swell! Do you have any kids?
> MAN: Yes, nine already and the tenth is on the way.
> GROUCHO: Wait a minute! Ten kids in nine years?!
> MAN: (sheepishly) Well, I happen to love my wife very much.
> GROUCHO: Well, I love my cigar too, but I take it out of my mouth once in a while. (Reprinted in Erdelyi, 1984, p. 93)

In this case, Groucho's comment is, at the manifest level, about his cigar. The joke, however, takes place at a latent level: the cigar's representation of something else. Latent messages can be powerful. Most television viewers probably got the joke. A few of them even called in to complain: so much so, that Groucho's show was temporarily removed from the air.

Identifying Manifest and Latent Content in Real Events

A divergence between manifest and latent content may take place in more serious contexts as well. The manifest content may communicate a socially acceptable message, whereas the latent content may express a communication that is more threatening to oneself or others. Erdelyi (1984, pp. 98–101) reported the case of a close friend who, after completing a brilliant year working at a prestigious university, had traveled abroad, and inexplicably returned home troubled and changed: anxious, experimenting with drugs, and drinking heavily. Soon thereafter, he lost a prestigious job and ended up working as a clerk.

Around that time, Erdelyi telephoned his friend to ask how he was. In response, the man answered, *"I have done it! I have flipped!"* Erdelyi asked him anxiously what was wrong. He replied, *"Right in front of my apartment. The sidewalk was a sheet of ice* [it was winter]. *I flipped full circle and broke my leg . . . My whole leg is in a cast."* Erdelyi wondered whether there was a second, latent, conversation taking place. His friend went on to say that at first he had minimized the problem but that he was *"only now coming to realize how ill* [he] *truly was."* He then began to talk about a visit to the United States by his brother, and that he would be unable to meet him. Raising his voice, he described how his mother and he had fought over whether he could pick up his brother at the airport. He bitterly said his brother could take care of himself and concluded, *"By God, [I have a broken leg and am] in no condition to go meeting anybody"* at an airport (Erdelyi, 1984, pp. 98–101).

Several weeks later, Erdelyi asked his friend whether there might have been a second meaning to the statement that he had "finally flipped," beyond that of turning over on the ice. Yet, his friend denied it, or was unaware of it (Erdelyi, 1985, p. 102). In real life conversations such as this (as opposed to laboratory-induced slips of the tongue, say), there is often no way to know for sure what has happened. Our experimental methods allow us only to know that such double meanings often arise. The exact moments when such double meanings actually take place are not always as clear as they are in Groucho Marx's joke.

Stagecraft and Self-Presentation

Tracing the dynamics of action makes clear that there is a boundary between the private personality that lies within, and the visible expression of personality outside (Henriques, 2003; Singer, 1984). The fact that personality processes are private allows a person to control and modify public expressions of that personality. It allows the person to engage in calculated self-presentation—the stagecraft of social life. This presentation may be for innocent reasons of entertainment and, perhaps, a bit of self-aggrandizement, or it may involve intentional deception designed to smooth social occasions—or calculated to bring about more nefarious ends.

The Emergence of Acting

Historians suggest that social acting may have begun before recorded history, perhaps around campfires when people recounted stories of their exploits, and realized it was easier to show than to tell. One person might narrate the action of the hunt, for example, by saying "I held the rock and threw it just like this . . . ." It would be impossible to mimic the action perfectly, and so there would be small deviations from the way it happened. Under such circumstances, it would be easy to falsify on the side of embellishing one's own stature (Duerr, 1962, pp. 5–7).

Documents indicate that ancient priests also engaged in a form of amateur acting as they narrated the creation and similar other religious stories for their

Each of us has certain social roles that we have learned. Knowing how to act in social situations helps us maintain social contact and carry out our goals.

congregations. In ancient Greece, the first professional actor took to the stage in about 534 BCE. His name was Thespis, and he wrote four plays. For each play, he donned a mask and portrayed a character other than himself. By so doing, he "invented" the actor. And this new creation, acting things out, very much appealed to the people who came to see him. Incidentally, early actors were called *hypocrites* in Greek, which meant, "answerers." From the same word we get "hypocrite"—someone who pretends to be virtuous while not being so. For some examples of deception in literature, see the Disciplinary Crossroads box.

Whereas Greek plays were so carefully crafted that the actors seemed nearly superfluous, the theater that spread to Rome required actors to more powerfully reach out and manipulate the audience. It was said that the Roman actors were able to preserve many inferior plays by enacting them in a lively, captivating way. Masks gave way to a direct view of the human actor's face (Duerr, 1962, p. 44).

Two broad approaches to acting are often taught. The first involves imagining a role to the fullest and "getting into the head" of the character one is preparing to portray. The great champion of this approach was Constantin Stanislovski (1948) who wrote, *An Actor Prepares.* In it, he recommended such techniques as empathizing with the tragedies faced by the character one is playing so as to cry on stage. If that didn't work, he suggested that the actor evoke a sad memory of his or her own. The major alternative to Stanislovki's techniques is called theatricalism. Theatricalism teaches how to move and act on a stage. One can move one's face into a perfectly emulated sad face, and manipulate one's muscles so as to appear to be crying while, with a sleight of hand, dropping tears down one's cheeks from an eye-dropper, as one appears to wipe them away. Some people believe that the best acting combines the psychological and the theatrical. Too much theatricality can bring a false, as-if quality to life. Too much psychological fit to the character can ignore the requirements of the stage.

Disciplinary Crossroads

Deception in Myth and Literature

Psychologists may draw on human myth, history, and literature for a more global understanding of the ways dynamic actions are carried out. Military histories and literature tell us that acting and deception have been a part of human existence and played a critical role in human history for centuries. One of the most dramatic examples of such stories is that of the Trojan horse in the battle between Greece and Troy. According to Homer in the *Iliad*, and supplemented by fragments of other epics, Troy was an ancient city with great walls, lofty gates, and fine towers. One of Troy's rulers, Paris, during travel to Greece, eloped with Helen, a relation to the most powerful king in Greece of that time, Agamemnon. Helen was reputed to be the most beautiful woman in the world. As Paris and Helen traveled back to Troy, the Greeks rounded up assistance and set off to reclaim her and sack Troy.

A series of inconclusive military engagements ensued for the next ten years. The Greeks patiently waited, because it had been foretold by a seer that their fortunes would change in the tenth year. In that year, the Greeks played a trick on the enemy. They built a hollow wooden horse, and placed within it several of their greatest warriors. They then burned their own camps at the outside of Troy, got in their ships, and set sail (but only out of eye-shot). When the Trojans found the horse, they interpreted it as a peace offering (along with the fact that the Greeks had left) and took the horse within their walled city and celebrated. At midnight, though, the warriors crept outside the horse, unleashed shots to signal the Greek fleet's return, and in the interim killed all the male firstborns in the city (Wood, 1985, pp. 21–26). For many years, Troy was thought to be a mythical place until an amateur archeologist, Heinrich Schliemann, finally unearthed it

(Wood, 1985). The course of the war, of course, is still told only by epics. Still, there exist no shortage of histories of actual wars played out with deception and surprise.

Individual deception was well known by Elizabethan England. One of the most beautiful juxtapositions of dramatic scenes occurs in Shakespeare's *Macbeth,* when King Duncan tells his son, Malcolm, about how he was betrayed by a follower. King Duncan instructs his son that he could not, nor could anyone, detect the follower's deceit until it was too late. He warns his son:

> There's no art
> To find the mind's construction in the face:
> He was a gentleman on whom I built
> An absolute trust. (Shakespeare, 1606/1936; Act I, Scene IV)

The lesson is apparently well taken. Shortly after, Malcolm awakes at Macbeth's Castle, hearing a commotion. King Duncan, his father, has been murdered. Macbeth and his wife express their shock at the news—fraudulent shock, as Macbeth is the murderer—and accuse the King's attendants of the deed. As Malcolm and his brother, Donaldbain, watch, the audience cannot help but recall the late King's words to his son. Will Malcolm have learned not to trust appearances? Indeed, Malcolm pauses contemplatively over the scene. He and his brother remark to themselves, ". . . there's daggers in men's smiles . . ." and off they proceed, separately, for safety, to England and Ireland (Shakespeare, 1606/1936, Act II, Scene III). Recognizing they are unable to see behind the others' smiles, they depart to make time to better understand what has transpired and plan how to counter it. Later they succeed reclaiming the throne for themselves.

When people portray social roles, they also act. A young man getting ready to ask a young woman on a date may rehearse his lines until they sound smooth and confident. Or, a person may rehearse asking for a raise at work. Students may rehearse the more important presentations they prepare for classes. There is a considerable stage-craft of everyday life (Goffman, 1959/2003, p. 131). People vary in how well they can enact various roles. Social acting appears to consist of six discrete dimensions or factors: (a) the ability to imitate, (b) to become involved in fantasy, (c) to remember others' mannerisms, (d) to fake convincingly, (e) to play unusual roles, and (f) to tell stories (Fletcher & Averill, 1984). Researchers have developed measures of the overall capacity to portray social roles. You can test yourself with one such measure in the Test Yourself feature.

Test Yourself: The Role-Playing Ability Scale

For each item below, indicate your level of agreement using the scale to the right.	1 = disagree 2 = disagree more than agre 3 = agree more than disagree 4 = agree	1	2	3	4
1. I am good at mimicking accents.					
2. I like to imitate the way people talk, move, gesture, and make facial expressions.					
3. I can imitate at least three different well-known people.					
4. I am good at playing the game of charades (acting out a concept in pantomime so that others can guess its meaning).					
5. I am sometimes able to get so absorbed in fantasy that I forget about my present self and become someone else in my imagination.					
6. I am able to exclude everything from my mind, construct a new, imaginary world, and feel for a time that it is real.					
7. I have had the experience of imagining something so hard that it became almost real for me.					
8. While watching a movie or show I sometimes become so involved that I feel myself participating in the action.					
9. I like to imagine myself as being various types of people.					
10. If I wish, I can imagine (or daydream) some things so vividly that they hold my attention in the way a good movie or story does.					
11. After acting in a play myself, or seeing a play or movie, I have felt partly as though I were one of the characters.					
12. I like to watch people for movements and mannerisms that set them apart from other people.					
*13. I do not have a good memory for the way people move, gesture, and make facial expressions.					

Test Yourself: *(Continued)*

	1	2	3	4
14. I have a good memory for voices and the way people talk.				
15. I often try to guess what people are thinking before they tell me.				
16. When I read a novel, I become very involved, experiencing what's going on, joining in with the action and characters.				
17. When I dance I often lose myself in the music and movement.				
18. I am good at faking things.				
19. I can make just about anybody believe anything I say or do.				
*20. People always seem to know when I'm telling the complete truth.				
21. If asked to play the part of an elderly person living alone in a big city, I could do so convincingly.				
22. If asked to play the part of a Russian peasant, I could do so convincingly.				
23. If asked to play the part of a tightrope walker with hiccups, I could do a convincing job of it.				
24. If asked to play the part of a "hillbilly" factory worker whom everyone makes fun of, I could do so sympathetically.				
25. I have a serious interest in creative activities such as painting, writing, designing, and the like.				
26. I have participated in a high school or college play or other amateur theater production.				
27. People tell me I am a good storyteller.				
28. When telling a story, I'm a good storyteller.				
29. When telling a story, I'm more interesting in presenting the facts than creating a mood.				
30. I can usually "put on a show" and liven things up without being self-conscious about it.				
31. I have had the experience of telling a story with elaborations to make it sound better and then having the elaborations seem as real to me as the actual experience.				
*32. When talking with people, I pay more attention to what they say than how they say it.				

To score: Add up your responses, subtracting your responses to the items with asterisks before them (item numbers 13, 20, and 32). The average score on the scale for college students is 81.5—but actors from a community theater group score an average of 103 on the scale.

Source: Fletcher & Averill (1984). Reprinted with permission from Elsevier.

Symbolic Interactionism and Social Alignment

Symbolic Interactionism:
A sociological perspective on social behavior which concentrates on how people represent themselves and each other in society.

People act to maintain interpersonal interactions in a smooth and mutually understood way. **Symbolic interactionism** is a branch of American sociology that attends to the self and its presentation in everyday life. It consists of several core ideas. First, individuals often think of themselves in the "third person"—as an objective being, in terms of their individual reputations or membership in a group. Second, individuals have the capacity to act in situations. Third, the way individuals are identified and act in situations can be analyzed according to the symbolic meanings they express (Hewitt, 2003, chap. 2).

Symbolic interactionism—and much social psychology—is concerned with the stagecraft of everyday life—the acts people use to present themselves to the world. For example, **disclaimers** are verbal devices people use to decrease the negative implications of something they are about to do. Examples of common disclaimers are, "I'm not prejudiced but I do believe . . ." or "I'm no psychologist but . . ." and "I don't mean this as a threat but . . ." (Stokes & Hewitt, 1976). People who use disclaimers can influence how others view them, making themselves seem less negative despite the concerns their comments raise for the listener (e.g., Shapiro & Bies, 1994).

Disclaimers: Statements people make to request a pardon or otherwise reduce the negativity of something they are about to say that they recognize may not meet the social ideals or expectations of the listener.

Accounts: Excuses or rationalizations people give of why they did or did not do something they should have done.

Accounts concern the excuses or justifications one provides for one's behavior, and provide a social lubricant so that problematic behavior can be put aside and interactions with another person can be continued. A person who uses justifications accepts responsibility but denies that the act was wrong or injurious—"I was late but it really didn't cause a problem" (Scott & Lyman, 1968). When a person employs an excuse, he or she acknowledges the act should not have been done but denies responsibility for the conduct. Excuses are a common form of interaction between students and professors. Anonymous surveys reveal that nearly half of all student excuses involving personal illness, family emergencies, alarm clock failures, and papers left in the dorm are fabricated. Such excuse-making involves considerable staging and enactment and take their toll in increased student nervousness and reduced happiness thereafter (Caron, Whitbourne, & Halgin, 1992).

Altercasting: The attempt to make other people look a certain way; for example, drawing attention to qualities that may make them seem more courageous or cowardly than otherwise.

Another social technique, **altercasting** involves presenting another person in a somewhat different manner than he or she is accustomed to. Politicians often altercast when they refer to their opponents as "tax and spend liberals" or "knee-jerk conservatives." On a more everyday level, people often altercast that someone is a closer or more intimate friend than is really the case, perhaps to obtain information or a special favor from them (e.g., Weinstein & Deutschberger, 1963).

Social acting isn't just for play. The ways one expresses oneself are critical for success. For example, one important kind of acting in social situations involves establishing control. Whether it is an experienced person waiting tables or a professor in a course, the establishment of control makes the job easier. Thus one teacher noted (privately):

> You can't ever let them [students] get the upper hand on you or you're through. So I start out tough. The first day I get a new class in, I let them know who's boss . . . then you can ease up as you go along. If you start out easy-going, when you try to get tough, they'll just look at you and laugh."
> (Goffman, 1959/2003, p. 134)

Or, as another example, consider the skills in working with diners at a restaurant. A person waiting tables

> may find that a new customer has seated himself before she could clear off the dirty dishes and change the cloth. He is now leaning on the table studying the menu. She greets him, says, "May I change the cover, please?" and, without waiting for an answer, takes his menu away from him so that he moves back from the table, and she goes about her work. The relationship is handled politely but firmly, and there is never any question as to who is in charge. (Whyte, 1946, pp. 132–133)

Even though we may not be intending to act, we may be cast in a role unwillingly, according to our ethnicity or gender. The sociologist Robin Kelley, who is of West Indies–African heritage, recounts a series of events that made him late for a movie—and that reveal some problems of self-presentation. It started when he had trouble convincing his four-year-old daughter to put her toys away. After some patient but ineffective cajoling, he threatened her by saying, "Okay, I'm going to tell Mommy!" (Kelley, 1995, pp. 356–357). Later, he ran through the theater lobby up to the ticket window to buy tickets for his family. The young woman who was selling tickets momentarily misinterpreted the young black man running toward her as signaling the beginning of a robbery.

[On acting in the movies:] I figured I needed a gimmick, so I dreamed up the drawl, the squint, and a way of moving which meant to suggest that I wasn't looking for trouble but would just as soon throw a bottle at your head as not.

John Wayne

Fortunately, she recognized her error almost immediately, became very embarrassed, and apologized to him. As he ruefully noted, due to the nature of racial stereotypes, members of minority groups, but particularly young American men of African ancestry, have been mistakenly arrested or worse under such circumstances. Note the contrasting dramas of self-presentation: On the home stage he had trouble intimidating his four-year-old daughter; cast in a different role by society, he had trouble innocently buying a movie ticket.

Social Cooperation and Deception

Machiavellian personality: A quality of the individual to be motivated and calculating so as to intentionally manipulate social situations for gain and power.

Is there a difference between someone who expresses himself or herself relatively directly and the social actor? Christie and Geis (1970) hypothesized that there might be a sort of person who intentionally manipulates social situations for gain and power. They labeled this individual the **Machiavellian personality**, after the Italian diplomat, Niccolo Machiavelli, who endorsed using any means necessary, including manipulation and deception, to ensure a safe, secure, and stable government (Machiavelli's work was published in 1513). Their test of Machiavellianism asks whether people agree with ideas such as, "Those who get ahead in the world often use a combination of deception and connection," and whether therefore, "It makes sense to tell people what they really want to hear to get them to do something." Unsurprisingly, people high on the Machiavellian scale follow an exploitative social strategy when compared to others.

Low scorers employ a more cooperative strategy based on reciprocity ("you scratch my back; I'll scratch yours"). It is true that many people likely carry out a Machiavellian act from time to time: a sample of ninety-three married couples indicated that between 25 percent and 29 percent admitted to performing a calculating

TABLE 9.4	Machiavellian or Calculating Acts as Identified by Judges	
Rank of prototypicality	Act	Percent of people who reported performing the act sometime during a 3-month period
1	I made a friend in order to obtain a favor.	12%
2	I asked "innocent" questions intending to use the information against someone.	13%
3	I pretended I was hurt to get someone to do me a favor.	17%
4	I tricked a friend into giving me personal information.	12%
5	I flattered a person in order to get ahead.	25%
6	I pretended to be sick at work, knowing I would not be there the next day.	12%
7	I made others feel guilty to get what I wanted.	29%

Source: From Buss & Craik, 1985, after Tables 1 and 3.

act at one time or another in their marriage (e.g., "I made others feel guilty to get what I wanted") (see Table 9.4, from Buss & Craik, 1985, Table 3, p. 942). It is nonetheless true that the vast majority of people are generally honest in their behavior most of the time: most prefer the rewards of honest cooperation, and prefer social respect and mutuality (e.g., Dubner & Levitt, 2004; Fiske, 1991).

People consistently high in Machiavellianism report more often than others that they engage in behaviors such as, "I made a friend in order to obtain a favor," "I flattered a person in order to get ahead," and "I asked 'innocent' questions, intending to use the information against someone" (see Table 9.4; Buss & Craik, 1985, p. 940). In experimental settings where their social behavior is carefully evaluated, higher Machiavellians are better liars than others, telling more convincing lies, making closer eye contact, and sticking to their story more consistently (Exline et al., 1970). Another study found that high Machiavellians generally fare best in loosely structured organizations that are only minimally constrained by rules (cutthroat stockbrokerages and automobile dealerships—perhaps similar in some respects to the emerging Italian city states of the Renaissance that Machiavelli lived amidst). They fare less well in more highly structured organizations (Wilson, Near, & Miller, 1996).

The Urge and the Situation

We are taught how to present ourselves from an early age. Parents begin to define different situations for their young children by asking them to use a quieter voice, to blow their noses, wash their hands, be kind to their siblings, and the like (Thomas, 1928/2003, p. 81). In this tug of war between the individual and the situation, who is more powerful, on average—the person or the situation? As discussed in Chapter 3 (in the section on social cognition), the typical prediction from a personality trait—such as a motive—to a single behavior is about $r = .40$ across many psychological studies. The typical correlation between various situations and behaviors are at a similar level; that is, about $r = .40$ (Bowers, 1973; Funder & Ozer, 1983). So, the individual's personality is in a constant give-and-take with the social situation in determining what will transpire.

> He who sees the inaction that is in action, and the action that is in inaction, is wise indeed.
>
> Bhagavad Gita

A closing example can illustrate some of the ways that personal urges and the environment interact, and also illustrate some of the concepts covered in this chapter. Considering a student in her dorm room trying to study for an exam. She expects that if she can just put in another hour or two studying, she might well get an "A," and that would make her very proud.

A pizza delivery is made to a nearby dorm room. The sweet scent of tomato sauce, cheese, and garlic are so scintillating that her hunger motive becomes uppermost. The scent of pizza cues memories of eating with friends that further stimulate her need for affiliation. The press of the situation, in other words, has interacted with her motives, strengthening some urges at the expense of others.

Without thinking, she gets up from her chair and walks across the hallway. By now, she realizes that she wants to go out to eat with someone. She pauses, realizing she is a bit low on cash. In a Machiavellian moment, she decides to invite one particularly well-off dorm-mate to go out for a pizza break with her. True, she doesn't want to be with this individual quite as much as with some others, but her friend is generous and might offer to pay for part of the meal. Her study session is at an end for now, as she and her friend head out for a break.

Will she go back to work later on? According to her expectancies for studying, it would be worth it to her. Whether or not she can really get back in time and study may depend on further events that intervene—will she become distracted by an interesting conversation? Will other friends stop by? Or, will a chance remark remind her of her longer-term professional goals and direct her back to her room? She may also choose to exercise some self-control because the goal of getting the "A," though not important in itself, is tied to larger dreams she holds of attending a professional school. The dynamics of self-control are examined in the next chapter.

Reviewing Chapter 9

The purpose of this chapter is to introduce you to the idea of personality dynamics—streams of mental action that cross parts of the mind. In addition, attention is directed to the issue that some action dynamics are conscious, whereas others are not.

The dynamic path specifically under consideration in this chapter begins with motivational urges and ends with the stagecraft of personal expression. Along the way, motives are filtered through the emotion system, and then emotions influence the possibility of behavior.

Behavior itself is not necessarily a direct expression of motives and emotions, but rather, may represent deception and false beliefs.

What Are Dynamics of Action?

1. Dynamic Traits and Local Dynamics.
Dynamics are processes by which one part of personality influences another. Local dynamics refer to processes in which one smaller part of personality influences another. Sometimes certain traits are referred to as dynamic. What kind of traits in particular are labeled as dynamic?

2. Mid-Level and Global Dynamics.
Mid-level dynamics involve the interaction of several different areas of personality. They are bigger than local dynamics, yet do not reach through the entire system. Can you give an example of a mid-level dynamic? The dynamics of action studied in this chapter are global dynamics in that they begin with motivational urges and end with social behavior. In doing so, they affect the whole system.

3. Dynamics and Their Change.
How are dynamics different than traits? If you can change a person's dynamic functioning, can you change what they do?

Which Need Will Begin Action?

4. Needs and Their Potency.
Within an individual, some needs are more important than others. Can you think of a technical term psychologists employ to identify the most important needs? If one need is stronger than another, will a person be most likely to express the stronger one? Would that be the case in any environment?

5. Determinant Needs and Subsidiary Needs.
According to Freud, the major determinant needs were sex and aggression. What would this mean in regard to subsidiary needs? Can you define determinant and subsidiary needs?

6. Need Conflicts.
Two sorts of conflicts arise around needs. One kind of conflict involves the case when two needs lead a person in different directions. What is the other kind of need conflict? When a person experiences many need conflicts, what can be expected in regard to the individual's well being?

7. Need Fusion.
Need fusion arises when a single aim satisfies many needs. How would this relate to need conflicts and the relation between determinant and subsidiary needs?

How Does Action Develop in the Mind?

8. Motivation, Emotion, and Mood-Congruent Thought.
Happy liveliness can work to enhance a person's overall motivation, whereas depression can be a global demotivator, undermining a person's energy and interest in doing things. Mood can also influence motivation-related thoughts through the mood-congruent cognition effects, influencing both memory and judgment. Can you give examples of each effect?

9. The Dynamic Lattice.
Cattell was interested in depicting how *ergs* were related to sentiments and attitudes. Can you define ergs and sentiments? Do you know which of the three starts off the dynamic lattice, and which concludes it?

10. Expectancies and the Likelihood of Action.
Julian Rotter introduced the idea of expectancies and the likelihood of action. In Rotter's conception, expectancies interacted with the reward value of an outcome. Can you define reward value and expectancy?

11. Partial Expressions and Slips of the Tongue.
Not all motives are ready for action, and some ideas and urges are turned back rather than expressed. What happens to these turned-back ideas? Sometimes the ideas may be expressed accidentally through slips of the tongue. Why are these called Freudian slips, and is there any research evidence to support their occurrence?

How Are Acts Performed?

12. The Communication Channels.
Communication begins at the motor cortex. Where is this and what is it like? People communicate through language and physical acts. What are some physical channels such as facial expressions through which people express themselves?

13. Conscious and Automatic Forms of Action.
Some behavior can be automatic, such as when acts are performed repeatedly. Why might it be adaptive for such repeated behaviors to become nonconscious?

14.   Latent versus Manifest Content.
Communication can be complex and can carry multiple meanings. One simple approach to deciphering it is to distinguish between a communication's simple, direct, obvious meaning and its underlying meaning. Sometimes this is referred to as a communication's manifest versus latent content. Do you know which is which?

15.   Stagecraft and Self-Presentation.
People manage their self-presentation in order to have desired influences on others; sometimes, however, their impact may be out of their control. Can you provide an example of an intended and unintended aspect of self-presentation?

16.   Symbolic Interactionism.
Symbolic interactionism is a school of social psychology that focuses on the symbolic analysis of interpersonal communication. In symbolic interactionism, a person attempts to conform his or her behavior to particular roles he or she desires. To maintain such roles, the individual may employ disclaimers, accounts, and altercasting. Can you define these and provide examples of each?

Chapter 10

Dynamics of Self-Control

*D*oes a person exert conscious self-control over his or her personality? Is it necessary? The conscious self provides a vantage point from which to pull together the various parts of personality and to direct the system in a well-considered manner. For that reason, people seek feedback as to what they are doing, and ways to improve their lives. At the same time, however, some self-control takes place at a nonconscious level. Some people have wondered whether the self might be improved, for example, by the effortful repetition of positive thoughts. Meanwhile, feedback can become painful at times and a person's mechanisms of defense may block worrisome messages—but how does this work? Self control is an intricate operation. Wouldn't the lack of self-control, however, be even more problematic?

- ### What Are Dynamics of Self-Control?
  The first section defines what the dynamics of self-control are. These are compared and contrasted with the dynamics of action, and the significance of self-control is considered. The section also examines the sorts of goals people set for themselves.

- ### How Does Self-Control Occur?
  For self-control to occur, the individual must have some kind of dynamic self-representation—that is, a sense of what he or she is doing at a given time. One important way of obtaining this information is through feedback. This section examines feedback loops, the role of feedback in self-control and the idea of feedback loops as a structure for describing personality dynamics.

- ### Is Self-Control Always Conscious?
  The third section looks at nonconscious personal control, using hypnosis as an example of unconscious states.

- ### How Do We Deal with the Pain of Falling Short?
  When we receive feedback about how we are doing, it isn't always positive. The personality system often makes use of defense mechanisms in order to cope with painful feedback.

- ### How Is Self-Control (or Its Absence) Expressed?
  The concluding section recounts some studies of those with higher versus lower levels of self-control.

What Are Dynamics of Self-Control?

How Dynamics of Self-Control Are Distinctive

Conscious Self, Conscious Executive, or Ego: The conscious, aware part of the self. *Note:* The "ego" was also used by Sigmund Freud as part of the id/ego/superego division of the mind. Freud's ego was defined differently than it is here.

This chapter focuses on a class of dynamics essential for the operation of personality: the dynamics of self-control. Many dynamics of self-control begin with the part of personality variously called the **conscious self**, **conscious executive**, or **ego**. These terms refer to that part of us which is aware; our innermost consciousness, that part of our self which seems most clearly aligned with our innermost core. The self-awareness of our own desires and their possible positive and negative ramifications motivates us to try to exert control over ourselves: to pick one thing to do, and reject another.

Sometimes a conscious executive is in control (or at least, it seems that way; Wegner, 2002). Although much of self-control and its influences are perceived as originating with the conscious self, some dynamics of control originate outside of awareness, in automatic personal self-regulation and control. In these instances, we might speak more generally of personal control. Personal control may involve various automatic feedback loops that take place outside of awareness, as well as other, intentionally guided control that is lacking in conscious awareness as well, despite the fact that it takes place at a high level of the system and, perhaps, *could* be conscious. Both self-control and more general, nonconscious personal control will be examined in this chapter.

In the last chapter, the dynamics of action were described as beginning with an urge, and extending to how the urge is felt and thought about, and ultimately expressed in the outer world. The self-control we are most concerned with here takes place in the context of gaining self-understanding and then using it to exert control over that chain of action, as well as over other processes such as our feelings and thoughts.

Connecting Window   *The Conscious Self*
The conscious self doing the self-regulation refers to the self-aware part of the person. Remember from Chapter 7 that there is some controversy as to whether the self really can act autonomously (on its own), independent of the rest of personality. How might that affect your interpretation of this chapter? See Chapter 7 on the conscious self.

One individual who exhibited considerable self-control though her life is Katherine Graham, publisher of the *Washington Post* for three decades (Graham, 1997, p. 611). She was a teenager when her father first bought the then-bankrupt newspaper. Graham was brought up in a wealthy family and felt, as a young woman, that she really hadn't learned how to manage much about her own life. After completing college, she went to work for her father at the *Washington Post* helping out on the editorial page. While doing so, she met Phil Graham, a young lawyer in Washington, D.C. They fell in love, married, and had four children. By 1941, her father had built the *Post* into what *Time* called, "The Capital's sole big-league newspaper" (p. 131). Katherine managed the household and gradually reduced her work at the *Post,* as her father and, increasingly, her husband, continued to build the newspaper. Her father transferred management of the *Washington Post* to her husband in 1947, and at the ages of thirty-three and thirty-one, she and her husband became the newspapers' owners (p. 182).

Although she enjoyed her home life, Ms. Graham felt increasingly insecure and shy. Her husband began treating her in a condescending, mean-spirited fashion. In the Fall of 1957, he descended into a deep depression. There followed increasingly rapid cycles of bipolar (manic-depressive) disorder, leading him from depression to mania and back again. During this time, Phil Graham took a reporter as a mistress, publicly humiliating his wife. Katherine continued to care for her husband, and threw a party with her mother to show that she was unbended by her difficult circumstances (Graham, 1997, p. 324; Halberstam, 1979).

As her husband's illness worsened, Katherine put into motion plans to preserve her ownership of the *Post* (Graham, 1997, p. 324). She wondered who would run it as her husband became increasingly incapacitated. A close friend remarked, "Don't be silly, dear. You can do it" (p. 319).

When Graham's husband committed suicide, she did indeed take over the company. She reported:

> I naively thought the whole business would just go on as it had while I learned by listening. I didn't realize that nothing stands still—issues arise every day . . . and they start coming at you. I didn't understand the immensity of what lay before me . . . and how many anxious hours and days I would spend for a long, long time. Nor did I realize how much I was eventually going to enjoy it all. (p. 340)

Her self-guidance created a network of caring friends around her. With their help, and her own talents and commitment—"I felt I *had* to make it work"—and some luck, she guided herself and the paper forward (p. 343). She was attentive to feedback about the paper, and actively addressed some of its problems such as its below-standard editorial quality (p. 379). Her self-image gradually shifted. She stopped comparing herself to her late husband; gradually she exerted her own form of self-control—and control over the paper, realizing, "...I could only do the job in whatever way *I* could do it" (p. 341). Ultimately, she built the Washington Post Company into a Fortune 500 company, and the *Washington Post* itself into an international newspaper. By doing so, she fulfilled her father's and her husband's dreams, as well as her own passionate devotion to the paper, which her father had viewed as a public trust (Graham, 1997, pp. 620–621; Halberstam, 1979).

The Need for Self-Control

Personality with and without Control

Self-control is carried out for the sake of fulfilling the person's physical, personal, and social needs and aims. These needs and aims include everything from nourishment and safety to desires for intimacy or power. Indeed, part of self-control involves integrating one's own conflicting goals, and then managing those goals along with the demands made by the surrounding bioenvironmental systems. The personality's awareness of its own goals and surrounding opportunities and obstacles require internal organization and planning so as to cope. This chapter focuses on how such organization takes place.

If the personality system no longer behaves under its own control—if it becomes destabilized, or if the conscious self can no longer govern the rest, the personality system degenerates into a disorganized collection of functions. The consequences of a lack of self-control are all too readily seen among the mentally ill and the criminally dyscontrolled. Those who have lost much of the capacity for self-monitoring and control engage in erratic behavior, are irrational and self-destructive, and, in the extremes of untreated mental illness, may stay in bed day after day, or shout at themselves, without a plan to follow. One also sees people with poor self-control in courts and prisons. Although there are many forms of criminal behavior, some crime results when individuals simply cannot or will not control their impulses and, instead, rob or assault someone out of their own poorly restrained greed or anger.

> There is only one corner of the universe you can be certain of improving and that's your own self.
>
> Aldous Huxley

Fortunately, most healthy human beings, as well as the majority of those suffering from various mental disorders, maintain large areas of successful self-control. Those dynamics that the self employs to organize the rest of the personality and its urges provide a reasonable first approximation of what is meant by dynamics of self-control. That is, the dynamics of self-control concern the maintenance of personality's coherent functioning and direct its long-term growth (a topic we'll examine in greater detail in the forthcoming chapters on development).

Aims of Self-Control

People exercise self control so as to meet their short- and long-term goals. When people are asked about their goals, certain patterns become visible across people. Some of these goals and their importance ratings appear in Table 10.1. Generally speaking, relationship goals, those that involve having a satisfying marriage and family life, seem most important. Next come pleasurable goals, such as having fun, having new and different experiences, and living an enjoyable lifestyle. After that, and at a distinctly lower level—but still very important—are a group of social and career-related goals. The social goals include helping and promoting the welfare of others in need. At roughly the same level are economic goals including having a career—especially one that makes one's family proud—and, to a lesser degree, possessing wealth.

Still important to many people—for most people, but at lower levels of importance—are a group of political, religious, and aesthetic goals. Political goals involve becoming a community leader or being influential in public affairs. Religious goals involve devoting oneself to spiritual matters and observance. Finally, aesthetic goals involve supporting or creating works of writing, art, and music (Roberts & Robins, 2000).

Not everyone ranks these goals in the same fashion. For example, a person's level on each of the Big Five personality traits is related to the goals he or she finds important. Extraverts find that goals involving pleasure (e.g., fun, exciting life) and a good career are much more important than others. People scoring high in openness, on the other hand, put a greater emphasis on aesthetic goals. Those high in neuroticism value goals concerning the welfare of others. Meeting life goals involves choosing the right aims for oneself and somehow finding one's place in the world. The goals reported by twelfth graders, for example, may well help shape their future (see the Facts at a Glance). Arguably, self-knowledge of these goals is important; to move toward them, however, also will require self control.

How Does Self-Control Occur?

The Self in Control

One defining characteristic of self-control is that it integrates a sense of oneself into plans for action. For example, say a person is aware he or she wants to be alone. To exert self-control is to say something on the order of, "I prefer to be alone, and therefore I am going to decline this invitation," or even, "I prefer to be alone. In this case, however, I am going to make an effort to enjoy this party because I know it is important to my friends." Another, different example, might be the thought, "I am not a vindictive person and therefore I am going to forgive this error." All these statements of self-control begin with a conscious sense of the self, and the knowledge of what one is like. This section, therefore begins with a consideration of the conscious self and its qualities.

The Problem of the Egotistical Ego

Totalitarian Ego:
Characterization of the ego as an entity that carefully controls information so as to promote its own positive image.

If accurate self-knowledge can contribute to effective self control, one of the issues involved is obtaining accurate self-knowledge. One of the central obstacles to this is the very nature of the conscious self in the first place. This conscious self—often referred to as the conscious ego—is, well, egocentric. The ego is naturally and normally self-centered in that the world revolves around its own perspective.

Greenwald (1980) characterized the typical conscious self as a **totalitarian ego**. By totalitarian ego, Greenwald meant that a person's conscious self typically behaves

TABLE 10.1	Mean Importance Ratings of Major Life Goals on a Five-Point Scale[*]		
		Mean Importance	
Goal	Total	Men	Women
Economic Goals Overall	3.5	3.6	3.5
Having a career	4.5	4.5	4.5
Make my parents proud	4.1	4.1	4.2
Aesthetic Goals Overall	2.5	2.5	2.4
Supporting artistic activities	3.1	3.0	3.1
Produce good artistic work	2.5	2.5	2.5
Social Goals Overall	3.7	3.4	3.9
Helping others in need	4.0	3.7	4.2
Promote welfare of others	3.8	3.5	3.9
Relationship Goals Overall	4.4	4.4	4.4
Having a satisfying marriage/relationship	4.8	4.8	4.8
Having harmonious relationships with my parents and siblings	4.4	4.4	4.5
Political Goals Overall	2.8	2.8	2.7
Be influential in public affairs	2.8	2.8	2.8
Becoming a community leader	2.7	2.8	2.7
Hedonic Goals Overall	4.3	4.3	4.2
Having fun	4.5	4.5	4.5
Having new and different experiences	4.3	4.3	4.3
Religious Goals Overall	2.7	2.6	2.8
Devoting attention to my spiritual life	3.0	2.9	3.1
Participating in religious activities	2.5	2.4	2.5
Personal Growth Goals Overall	4.6	4.4	4.7
Feeling a real purpose in life	4.6	4.4	4.7
Having a job that is personally satisfying even if it doesn't make me rich	4.1	3.8	4.3
Other Goals	–	–	–
Living in aesthetically pleasing surroundings	4.0	4.1	4.0
Having an easy life	3.1	3.0	3.3
Preparing myself for graduate school	4.1	4.1	4.1

Note: [*]Where 1 was "not important to me," and 5 was "very important to me."

Source: Abridged from Roberts & Robins (2000).

Egocentric: The quality of constructing mental models with one's own interests and perspective at their center.

like a dictator, in a self-preserving and often self-aggrandizing fashion. For example, the ego is naturally **egocentric**. Egocentrism means that the ego is at the center of things. In some sense this is true for all of us. Each person sees the world through his or her own eyes, and in particular, with himself or herself as at the center of that world. After all, how else can the person honestly perceive matters? The cognitive psychologist Donald Norman agrees, using an example of some of his own recollections.

• FACTS • AT • A • GLANCE •

Life Goals Rated as Important by U.S. Twelfth Graders

	1981		1991		2001	
	Male	Female	Male	Female	Male	Female
Being successful in my line of work	58%	57%	60%	64%	59%	66%
Having a good marriage and family life	71%	82%	71%	83%	72%	83%
Having lots of money	24%	13%	37%	19%	33%	19%
Making a contribution to society	19%	17%	20%	22%	21%	22%
Working to correct social and economic inequalities	9%	10%	11%	13%	10%	10%
Being a leader in my community	8%	7%	12%	10%	15%	14%

Source: U.S. Department of Health and Human Services (2002), pp. 193–194.

My memory for the University of Toronto campus in Canada . . . cannot be separated from my memory of my last visit to Toronto. Trying to recall how ones goes to the Psychology Department automatically recreates the last visit there—the snow, the heavy traffic, the various people I met, and the restaurants at which I ate. (Norman, 1976, p. 189, cited in Greenwald, 1980)

Because we remember so much in relation to ourselves, it is inevitable that our perception of events is self-centered. Because memory is so much a part of who we are, the ego cannot help but be egocentric in this regard.

Our thinking has built into it certain biases that often favor the conscious self and its role. **Beneffectance** refers to the tendency to take credit for the good things in one's life and to avoid responsibility for the bad. In regard to the good, athletes on sports teams tend to overestimate their effort, abilities and other contributions to team wins (e.g., Greenberg, Pyszczynski, & Solomon, 1982; Mullen & Riordan, 1988). In regard to the bad, those in automobile accidents, for example, tend to deny their responsibility. Consider two actual descriptions people reported to their insurance companies:

Beneffectance: In Greenwald's theory of the totalitarian ego, taking credit for causing good outcomes to happen while avoiding accepting blame for bad outcomes.

Confirmation Bias: The tendency of people to search for information that supports their point of view in preference to challenging information.

As I approached the intersection, a sign suddenly appeared in a place where a stop sign had never appeared before. I was unable to stop in time to avoid an accident.

Here's a second:

The telephone pole was approaching. I was attempting to swerve out of its way when it struck my front end. (*San Francisco Examiner and Chronicle,* April 22, 1979, p. 35, cited in Greenwald, 1980, p. 605)

People also suffer from a **confirmation bias** in which they seek to confirm ideas they already hold—often by ignoring contrary information (Nickerson, 1998). For example, if people believe someone they are about to interview is an introvert, they are likely to ask questions

> **The great deceivers of the world begin by deceiving themselves. They have to, or they wouldn't be so good at it.**
>
> Moliere

People often seek feedback to help them perform more effectively.

Feedback: Information about how closely an ongoing process is to meeting a standard.

Feedback Loop: A mechanism for controlling the action of a system that involves feedback as to whether or not it is meeting its goals.

Cybernetics: A field of study that focuses on communication and control in systems, particularly in relation to the system's self-governance.

Negative Feedback Loop: A mechanism for controlling the action of a system in which the discrepancy between a goal and its attainment is reduced (negated) through feedback.

Comparator: A portion of a feedback loop that judges the difference between the current state of affairs and the desired goal.

that are biased toward the introvert hypothesis (e.g., "Do you like to read books?") in order to confirm their beliefs (Snyder & Swann, 1978). Another example involves attitude research. People consistently tend to accept arguments that agree with their prior opinions and reject those that disagree with them (Sherif & Hovland, 1961).

The ego appears to be engineered to be a bit out-of-touch with its own fallibility. Some psychologists believe this is adaptive because it encourages the ego to keep going even when matters are tough (Taylor & Brown, 1988; 1994). This does not, however, tell the entire story. If the ego were totally self-centered and utterly out of contact with others' viewpoints, it would not be an effective self-manager. One way the ego has of better responding to the outside world is learning with feedback.

Feedback and the Feedback Loop

People's self-control is based at least in part on receiving accurate information about themselves and how they are doing. Accurate information about the self can be regarded as **feedback**. One such form can be nicely illustrated with the children's game "hot and cold." In one version of the game, a child searches for a hidden object as other players watch. The other players, who know where the object has been hidden, call out "hot" or "cold" or variations as the person gets closer or farther from the goal. The feedback from other players lets the child know how close he or she is from the goal and, in the case of "cool" or "ice cold," for example, to try another direction. As the child gets nearer the hiding place, the audience calls out "warmer" and "hot" and even, "sizzling" when the child is very close. The child's search is governed and directed by feedback.

A central building block of control in the hot-and-cold game is the **feedback loop**. A feedback loop involves a cycle that includes acting, receiving information about the success or failure of the act, and then acting again. The concept of a feedback loop comes from the field of **cybernetics** (Wiener, 1948). The field of cybernetics concerns itself with how systems are controlled and the flow of information within systems. To learn more about the relation between personality psychology and cybernetics, see the Disciplinary Crossroads box.

The most important feedback loop for psychological control is probably the **negative feedback loop**. It is called "negative" because it attempts to eliminate (negate) any discrepancy between a standard and an outcome. The hot-and-cold game can be analyzed in terms of a negative feedback loop. In it, the person tries to minimize the discrepancy between where he is searching and the object of his search. The standard is, ultimately, to have zero distance between one's hand and the object sought. So, the person plans a move, moves, and receives feedback from other players as to whether the direction was right. The person, in essence, "inputs" the feedback to a **comparator**. The comparator is so-called because it compares the feedback—"hot" or "cold"—in this case, with the aim "hot" or some variation of it. If the person hears "ice cold," a change in direction is called for. "Hot" encourages the

Disciplinary Crossroads

Cybernetics, Personality, and Robots

The idea that personality might be controlled through a hierarchy of feedback loops—or something like them—stems from the mid-twentieth-century field called cybernetics. The term *cybernetics* comes from the Greek word for *steersman*—a term Plato had used to indicate political governing. More generally, cybernetics is sometimes referred to as the study of organization.

The field of cybernetics was founded by Norbert Weiner (1949), a philosopher who studied and made important contributions to many subjects, including biology and physics and areas of mathematics such as time series analysis. During World War II, he applied his knowledge to how a gunner might track a target and plan to hit it. Using his powerful capacity for intuition and knowledge of the aforementioned fields, he developed a theory of information and control that he expanded into the science of cybernetics.

From Weiner's perspective, all governance relies in part on information. For example, if one wants to pick up a newspaper, communication must take place between one's visual system, as one's eyes spot the morning newspaper, and one's motor system, as one's arm reaches toward that newspaper. Wiener's idea was that the flow of communication and information can be analyzed. Information is "input," through the eyes, and as the information is processed, partial solutions for moving the hand nearer the newspaper are "output," and then the process continues. Terms such as *input, output,* and *feedback* were all drawn together and given their modern meanings in cybernetic theory.

It should be noted that "information" can be interpreted very broadly and includes emotional and motivational experiences, as well as thoughts (e.g., Mayer, Salovey, & Caruso, 2000). Weiner himself applied that field to such specific problems as those of brain disease, artificial limbs, and the social sciences more generally. For Weiner and subsequent theorists, the building blocks of control could be found in such structures as feedback loops, recursive loops and self-similarity.

Today, the relationship between cybernetics and personality is a two-way street, with psychologists employing concepts of feedback loops and self-control, and computer scientists borrowing discoveries concerning the emotions, for example, to build the emotional computers (e.g., Picard, 1997), and borrowing from studies of human self-control to create more lifelike robots (Ayers, Davis, & Rudolph, 2002).

person to proceed. That is how the loop works: the person is aiming in a direction and receives more-or-less continuous feedback as to how to orient himself. In this way, the person almost always finds the object. The principles of the hot-and-cold game are very fundamental and underlie many of our behaviors.

Personal Control as a Hierarchy of Feedback Loops

Levels of Feedback Loops

Some psychologists have viewed personality as consisting of a hierarchy of levels, with feedback loops at each level (e.g., Powers, 1973). At the more molecular level of the nervous system are feedback loops governing the autonomic nervous system, including heart rate and respiration.

At a somewhat higher level are simple negative feedback loops employed in motor control (e.g., Powers, 1973; Rosenbaum, 1991; Wiener, 1948). For example, if you are standing on the deck of a boat and the boat is swaying, you must adjust your legs constantly so as to remain in an upright, standing position. The feedback loop takes as its standard "standing up straight." As the boat tilts to the right, the comparator checks your position (you are tilting to the right) with the goal of standing up straight. Information about balance comes from neural circuits in the inner ear. Action is initiated to maintain yourself upright: you automatically bend your left leg to lower the left side of yourself and extend your right leg so as to raise your right. When the comparator sees that your position meets the standard, the action ceases. As the boat moves back toward center, however, the comparator now notes you are listing to the left. To compensate, you now begin to reverse your leg movements.

Powers suggests that the middle level of personality consists of feedback loops concerning simple goal-directed sequences of behavior such as finding one's glasses, buying some milk, and conducting certain aspects of interpersonal relationships (Powers, 1973, pp. 151–160). As an example, let's say you are trying to impress your cousin. To do so, you might e-mail her a story about a recent time you hit a home run in a baseball game and embellish it, describing your heroic levels of practice the week before the game and the pressure of the competition when you were at bat, so that it is very impressive. The sequence of psychological events and acts is illustrated in Figure 10.1. In actuality, of course, your story might not have the desired effect of impressing your cousin, but it would be the best you could do in the situation without any feedback.

> To avoid criticism, do nothing, say nothing, be nothing.
> Elbert Hubbard

Powers believed that it was far more typical to conduct such a social exchange with some considerable feedback. Consider the same situation with your cousin, but this time you are in the same room. As you begin to tell the story, your cousin reacts by emitting approving or disapproving facial expressions and you witness those reactions. If she likes your story (or appears to) you continue. If she expresses boredom or displeasure, however, you change your story, and then re-enter the loop. Of course, if she decides you are conceited, or laughs at you for trying to impress her, you will need to change loops altogether. This response is depicted in Figure 10.2.

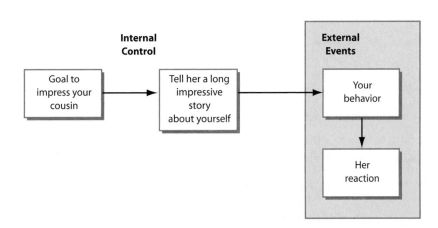

FIGURE 10.1

A Simple Method for Impressing Your Cousin
The flow chart shows a procedure for impressing someone—a cousin—in the absence of feedback.

Internal Control

External Events

Goal to impress your cousin → Tell her a long impressive story about yourself → Your behavior → Her reaction

FIGURE 10.2

A Feedback Loop for Impressing Your Cousin

The diagram depicts a feedback loop in which you start trying to impress your cousin by telling a story. Feedback from your cousin (see "External Events") can then be used to continue the story or change it.

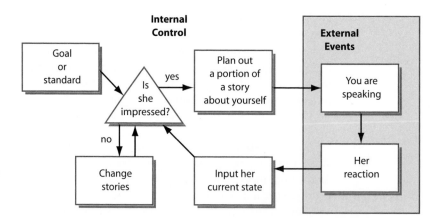

Here we have presented the feedback loop as a computer-like diagram. It is worth noting that neurons have the capacity to form negative feedback sequences, and people constantly behave in ways that are sensitive to feedback (Carver & Scheier, 1981; 1998; Powers, 1973a; 1973b, pp. 27–34).

The highest levels of feedback control begin with heuristics and brief intentions such as, "I'll help her" or, "Honesty is the best policy" (Powers, 1973, p. 168), and range up to the most general principles of control involving moral, factual, and abstract principles such as being loyal to a country, or adhering to the principles of democracy and free elections. The point of feedback at this level is for the person to maintain his or her behavior in line with these abstract principles (Powers, 1973, pp. 171–173).

Levels of Action and Behavioral Identification

People control themselves at different levels. At lower levels—such as maintaining one's balance on a boat—an individual may need to exert self-control at a detail-oriented, concrete level. At higher levels, a person is matching his or her own needs to more global, possible, personal goals. Vallacher and Wegner (1987) became interested in what level of control was most common for a person and why. In a series of research studies they found that, overall, people preferred to describe their actions at a more general, abstract, higher level. For example, when asked to describe what they were doing after a dinner at a friend's house, most people would prefer to reply, "helping a friend by washing the dishes" rather than "moving a sponge across the plate." That said, people do tend to employ concrete sensory-motor descriptions under some circumstances. The sponge-across-the-plate kind of response is preferred when tasks are unfamiliar, difficult and complex, when people believe they are doing poorly, or when their performance is disrupted (e.g., Vallacher & Wegner, 1987).

The Behavioral Identification Form (BIF; Vallacher & Wegner, 1989) measures the level at which people think about carrying out a sample of behaviors. The BIF consists of a number of behaviors such as "attending class," and "getting a job," and asks test-takers how they would identify the activity. For example, "attending class" can be identified as a specific task such as, "hearing the lecture," or at a higher level, as "getting an education."

High scorers on the test see their actions in relation to their causes and effects, their social meanings, and the goals they satisfy. Low scorers on the test perceive the world primarily at the level of detail and view their actions as carrying out mechanical activities. High scores are related to more proficiency at such tasks, and a wide range of task activity, including diverse hobbies and activities. Low scores on the BIF are correlated with individual reports of difficulty with carrying out tasks; low-scoring individuals also experience failure more often as they carry out activities.

Perhaps because high scores on the BIF reflect individual abilities to plan and understand their own actions, high BIF scorers are more reflective and less impulsive than low BIF scorers. Along those lines, in a sample of juvenile detainees, those with higher BIF scores were less likely to have a record of criminal offenses; lower scorers had higher offense records. Finally, the high BIF scorer may have a more developed self-concept than others, and may understand him or herself more often in relation to consistent traits and a consistent self-concept (Vallacher & Wegner, 1989, p. 666). These kinds of findings suggest that there may be something very useful in the concept of the hierarchical control concept. Before you go on, you may want to test yourself on the BIF (see the Test Yourself).

Kelly's Circumspection-Preemption-Control (C-P-C) Cycle

People's global self-control differs from the control of a mechanical feedback loop in many ways. For one, people's personalities are composed of many parts that are not always pulling in the same direction: feelings may conflict with thoughts, and thoughts may conflict with each other. In such a context, a person's choices and decision-making will be more complex than smoothly pursuing one clear goal.

A mid-twentieth-century personality psychologist named George Kelly (1955a) described a cycle of self-control he called the **Circumspection-Preemption-Control cycle**, or C-P-C cycle. The C-P-C cycle is a kind of feedback loop in a human context.

In the C-P-C cycle, circumspection enables the person to look at the elements of a decision in relation to his or her personality. For example, if a person were deciding on a career, circumspection might involve matching his or her own interests to the requirements of various careers. Some people don't think about such major decisions very much; these individuals impulsively make choices before really considering the alternatives. Most people, however, circumspect a great deal about major decisions.

One reason that circumspection can be so challenging is that a person's models and concepts of the world are fallible and changeable. Kelly's "Fundamental Postulate," in approaching personality, was that a person's thoughts were motivated so as to increase his or her control over the future (Kelly, 1955, p. 46). To do this, the individual developed a set of mental models that Kelly referred to as a "construct system." Kelly was struck by the fact that a person's construct system—their personal guides, principles, and beliefs—were far from logical and clear. People often believe incompatible things. As he put it: "A person may successively employ a variety of construction subsystems which are inferentially incompatible with each other" (p. 83). Under such conditions, a simple application of a feedback loop is going to run into problems. Rather, the feedback would have to be adjusted to fit the context of the person's own understandings.

Kelly used a rich, descriptive language for how a person's concepts could go right or wrong. For example, **dilated constructs** refer to concepts that are applied to too many areas of one's life. A child might believe that God will take care of her. If this idea becomes dilated—applied too generally—it might mean that, as an adult, the individual will always expect God to take care of everything in the person's life, and she

Circumspection-Preemption-Control Cycle: A mental process described by the social-cognitive psychologist George Kelly, in which a person thinks about a problem (circumspects), decides enough time has been spent on it (preemption), and makes a decision about how to act (control).

Dilated Constructs: In terms of social-cognitive theory, a concept or idea, such as trusting others, which is applied in too many cases or to too many situations.

Test Yourself: The Behavior Identification Form

Instructions: For each numbered task below, please identify the choice, from column A or B, that most closely identifies how you would describe your behavior. Please mark only one alternative for each pair. People differ in their preferences for the different behavior descriptions, and we are interested in your personal preferences. Be sure to mark your choice for each behavior. Remember, choose the description that you *personally believe* is more appropriate in each pair.

1. Making a list	a. Getting organized	b. Writing things down
2. Reading	a. Following lines of print	b. Gaining knowledge
3. Joining the army	a. Helping the nation's defense	b. Signing up
4. Washing clothes	a. Removing odors from clothes	b. Putting clothes into the machine
5. Picking an apple	a. Getting something to eat	b. Pulling an apple off a branch
6. Chopping down a tree	a. Wielding an axe	b. Getting firewood
7. Measuring a room for carpet	a. Getting ready to remodel	b. Using a yardstick
8. Cleaning the house	a. Showing one's cleanliness	b. Vacuuming the floor
9. Painting a room	a. Applying brushstrokes	b. Making the room look fresh
10. Paying the rent	a. Maintaining a place to live	b. Writing a check
11. Caring for houseplants	a. Watering plants	b. Making the room look nice
12. Locking a door	a. Putting a key in the lock	b. Securing the house
13. Voting	a. Influencing the election	b. Marking a ballot
14. Climbing a tree	a. Getting a good view	b. Holding on to branches
15. Filling out a personality test	a. Answering questions	b. Revealing what you're like
16. Toothbrushing	a. Preventing tooth decay	b. Moving a brush around in one's mouth
17. Taking a test	a. Answering questions	b. Showing one's knowledge
18. Greeting someone	a. Saying hello	b. Showing friendliness
19. Resisting temptation	a. Saying "no"	b. Showing moral courage
20. Eating	a. Getting nutrition	b. Chewing and swallowing
21. Growing a garden	a. Planting seeds	b. Getting fresh vegetables
22. Traveling by car	a. Following a map	b. Seeing the countryside
23. Having a cavity filled	a. Protecting your teeth	b. Going to the dentist
24. Talking to a child	a. Teaching a child something	b. Using simple words
25. Pushing a doorbell	a. Moving a finger	b. Seeing if someone's home

To score: Credit as one point: 1a, 2b, 3a, 4a, 5a, 6b, 7a, 8a, 9b, 10a, 11b, 12b, 13a, 14a, 15b, 16a, 17b, 18b, 19b, 20a, 21b, 22b, 23a, 24a, 25b. Typical sample means among undergraduates range from about 15.5 to 16.5, with standard deviations of about 5.5. So, if you scored above 20 you scored at a high level; below 10 represents a fairly low score.

Source: With modified instructions from Vallacher & Wegner (1989), Table 2, p. 644. Reprinted with permission of American Psychological Association.

Constricted Constructs: In terms of social-cognitive theory, a concept or idea, such as trusting others, which is applied in too many cases or to too many situations.

Tight Constructs: A type of mental model, in Kelly's theoretical system, that is rigid and is not easily changed.

Loose Constructs: A type of mental model, in George Kelly's theoretical system, that is like a "first draft," and may be readily revised in the future.

will show little personal initiative to take care of things on her own. **Constricted constructs**, on the other hand, involved limiting concepts to very small areas of one's life (Kelly, 1955a, p. 476). **Tight constructs** lead to unvarying predictions. Pretzels always taste good; potato chips, too greasy. **Loose constructs** are more like first drafts or sketches (e.g., I think I like Indonesian food; Kelly, 1955a, pp. 483–484).

When a person circumspects, the individual must match such conflicting and complex internal beliefs to his or her own models of the outside world. It is quite a task, and it is hard to know even when it is time to stop! Even people who spend considerable time circumspecting, however, eventually must choose.

At the *P*, or preemption, point of the C-P-C cycle the individual seeks to narrow down the alternative choices to just a few, and then to choose before important opportunities are lost. Perhaps the student reaches her or his senior year and it is time to apply for jobs, or to graduate school. At this point, the individual must no longer wait or hope for other possibilities, but rather, must preempt the process and choose what realistically is before her or him.

This brings the individual to the final *C* (control or choice) part of the cycle. The individual must choose one course of action and take it. Presumably the correct choice will help the person get closer to his or her goals. Kelly adds something that is very human to the high level feedback, though—the possibility of getting stuck in a loop, or having difficulty navigating it by, say, exiting too quickly. For example, perfectionists have a hard time completing things—including decisions about careers. They may return to the circumspection portion of the cycle and prolong it, choosing instead to be noncommittal, find a temporary or part time job, and continue taking courses (Leong & Chervinko, 1996; Kelly, 1955a, pp. 514–517; cf., Lounsbury et al., 2005). Little research work has been done on the C-P-C cycle though it seems compatible with research work, and it is intuitively compelling.

The Search for—and Effect of—Feedback

Seeking Feedback

Do people naturally seek feedback as they self-control? It seems they do in many diverse circumstances. For example, people are used to counteracting the effects of pain by taking over-the-counter pain-relievers such as aspirin and similar products. As the pain rises, they will employ the pain-reliever to reduce the pain. As the pain declines, they will stop taking the medicine.

The feedback cycle of taking medication when one has symptoms and stopping when one doesn't is so customary that it works against those with diseases that have hard-to-detect symptoms. The real symptoms of high blood pressure—emotional distress, dry mouth, and sleep disturbance—are only loosely tied to the disease and are sporadic. Unfortunately, many people who suffer from high blood pressure take their medication only when the real or imagined symptoms are present. Instead, they would be better off taking their medication constantly because the high blood pressure is there all the time. The absence of good feedback is, in this case, potentially quite lethal (Baumann & Leventhal, 1985; Meyer, Leventhal, & Gutmann, 1985).

Self-Monitoring: A state within a person, or a long-term trait, that describes a condition in which the individual closely observes his or her own mental processes or behaviors.

So people characteristically do seek and employ feedback, a process sometimes called **self-monitoring**. Self-monitoring is defined as the process of collecting feedback about the self and employing it to guide behavior. Carver and Scheier (1981;

1998) have suggested that people who employ self-directed attention use feedback more extensively to better adhere to their personal standards than do others. In Carver and Scheier's experiments, self-consciousness is heightened by placing participants in front of a mirror or a video camera. When people see themselves or know that others will see them under such conditions, it encourages them to think about themselves, to become self-conscious, and to attend to feedback.

In one experimental study of self-monitoring, students were asked about their attitudes concerning the use of punishment as a tool in education. Afterward, they were placed in the role of a teacher to see if they behaved in accord with their attitudes (Carver, 1975). In the teacher role, participants were asked to teach a confederate a word list, and to use mild electrical shock as a punishment for incorrect answers if they thought it might speed the learning.

Some students were randomly assigned to a mirror condition, in which they saw their reflections as they filled out the survey on educational practices and when they entered the role of the teacher; others were in a no-mirror condition. When participants were tested in front of a mirror (thereby inducing self-focus), their behavior agreed with their earlier-recorded attitudes about punishment in education. That is, those who believed punishment could be of value administered more shocks; those who believed punishment was out-of-place in an educational environment administered fewer shocks. By contrast, students tested without the mirror showed no correspondence between their attitudes and behaviors. This suggested that, when self-monitoring, people do indeed employ feedback loops to create consistency between their attitudes and behavior. People who score higher on scales of self-monitoring also show a closer match between their attitudes and behaviors than do others (Fenigstein, Scheier, & Buss, 1975).

Rigging the Feedback System

People often alter the feedback they receive to suit their purposes. They may, for example, seek to confirm their biases—that their decisions were correct and good, while ignoring evidence to the contrary. Sometimes, however, people focus on negative feedback so as to enhance their performance.

Defensive Pessimism: An adaptive type of pessimism in which a person imagines bad outcomes in order to motivate herself or himself toward higher achievement.

Norem and colleagues have studied **defensive pessimism.** When facing a challenge, defensive pessimists initially feel anxious and out-of-control and as if they are going to do poorly—despite evidence to the contrary. For example, a defensive pessimist facing an upcoming exam may think, "I'll do very badly at this one." These individuals endorse items such as, "I generally go into academic situations with low expectations, even though I know things usually turn out alright." (Norem & Illingworth, 1993, p. 825). The 25 percent of the sample who most strongly endorse such items are classified as defensive pessimists.

In essence, such individuals are "rigging" their feedback, pretending that all signs point to a poor outcome. Such a pretense solves two problems: first, it makes the defensive pessimists feel calmer by giving them permission to fail, but, paradoxically, it also motivates them because they believe that only by studying really hard can they avoid failure. As it turns out, defensive pessimists perform just as well as optimists on exams as well as on a broad variety of other tasks. In addition, defensive pessimists will perform worse if they are made less anxious or try to use other strategies (Norem & Illingworth, 1993).

Exiting the Feedback System

Of course, sometimes people don't always want feedback, and when they don't, they may engage in a variety of activities to avoid it, such as to get drunk. Alcohol appears to act by reducing self-awareness in those who drink. As self-awareness is lowered, people pay less attention to their standards of behavior, goals, and beliefs (Denton & Krebs, 1990; Hull & Reilly, 1986; Hull & Slone, 2004). For that reason, when people get drunk they often behave in an evermore disorganized fashion, participating in activities they would never take part in if sober, saying things they may later regret, and generally taking risks they would not otherwise take.

Bottom-up Control?

If personal control takes place at multiple levels, is there a particular level that exerts control over the others? Freud believed control over personality is exerted from the bottom up—that is, from biological urges and energy—rather than from the top down. To get an idea of what Freud meant, you might imagine yourself with no bodily desires and no social needs. What would you do? How would you behave? Why would you bother to behave?

Using the id to represent biological urges and the ego to refer to higher logical levels of control, Freud noted that the ego:

> in its relation to the id . . . is like a man on horseback, who has to hold in check the superior strength of the horse . . . The analogy may be carried a little further. Often a rider, if he is not to be parted from his horse, is obliged to guide it where it wants to go; so in the same way the ego is in the habit of transforming the id's will into action as if it were its own. (Freud, 1923/1960, p. 15)

Thus, our biological drives and needs determine our direction contingent upon our capacities. Freud says, in essence, look to the biological urges to find out where the person's trajectory in life will go.

Dynamic Self-Control

In all these examples, the self-view is a dynamic, changing entity. The person perceives his or her self as closer or farther from goals, and behaves so as to better attain those goals. Sometimes self-perception may shift from lower-level tasks, such as how to perform a task (e.g., impress a friend), to higher-level aims, such as establishing a relationship and getting married. Sometimes people may rig the system by viewing themselves as less prepared than they really are in order to help motivate themselves. These shifts in self-perception and self-evaluation create a picture of dynamic self-concept, one that varies to suit a particular purpose (Markus & Wurf, 1987).

Is Self-Control Always Conscious?

Automatic Control and Dissociation

The limitations of the conscious self are considerable. Working memory can handle only about seven chunks of information at any given moment. Attention can be directed toward one or two matters at a time. Conscious self-control, in other words, is a highly limited resource. We have already encountered the idea of a hierarchy of feedback loops that control personality. Surely, however, not all those feedback loops involve the self or consciousness.

Personal Control: High-level control exerted by the personality system in general, some of which involves conscious self-control, and other portions of which involve unconscious mechanisms.

For these reasons, it useful to think more broadly of **personal control**. Personal control involves the regulatory mechanisms of personality generally, some of which involve conscious self-control, and other portions of which involve nonconscious control more generally. It isn't surprising that personal control will commonly be carried out at automatic or subconscious levels as well as at conscious levels. In fact, self-control may be more efficient when behaviors that can be carried out automatically are shifted outside of conscious control, with some monitoring so as to be able to return them to consciousness if necessary.

Dissociated: A state in which concepts that are naturally associated in memory are divided from one another through the establishment of mental barriers and the ideas then operate independently of the ideas to which they had been related previously.

When thoughts and action programs are separated from consciousness temporarily, they are referred to as **dissociated.** Dissociated thoughts can be considered as divided off from consciousness. For instance, when a person performs two activities simultaneously, thoughts related to one activity may be conscious, while the unattended-to thoughts are unconscious (Hilgard, 1977; 1994).

One dissociation of this type that is familiar to many people is called highway hypnosis. Perhaps you have driven down a highway and then have begun to pay attention to the radio or to a conversation, and, suddenly, you arrive where you were going without much recollection of how you got there. Plainly, some part of you was driving while your own awareness was diverted elsewhere. In essence, the thought processes involved in driving can become divided from consciousness. Some people can barely remember details of their ride home (Lahey, 1989).

Tired college students preparing for examinations will often find themselves reading an assignment, turning the pages at the approximate rate at which they read, and suddenly realize they have no idea what they have seen for the past two or three pages (and sometimes more). Once again we may ask, "Who was reading?" or at least, "Who was turning the pages?" It may turn out that the answer was the subconscious part of the personality. (Don't rely on this subconscious part to get the exam questions right, though!)

Dissociation and the Unconscious

When certain portions of consciousness are divided off, or dissociated from the rest, the divided-off mental processes are said to be subconscious (Hilgard, 1994; James, 1892). The idea of divided, or a dissociated unconscious was first suggested by the French neurologist Jean Janet, a contemporary of Freud's. Janet believed that thoughts become conscious through their associations with prior thoughts. If so, then other ideas might also stay out of consciousness because they have become dissociated from conscious concepts. Sometimes this is just for mental efficiency—such as highway hypnosis. At other times, however, ideas may be dissociated because they are threatening or painful.

Such disassociated ideas, however, would not simply go away. Rather, they would continue to exert influence as an automatism (Perry & Laurence, 1984, p. 28). The subconsciousness automatism was not "lower" than conscious; it was more like a second part of the mind, cut off from the first. The automatism—the closely inter-associated ideas—acted independently of the person, but with some control over the person's beliefs, thoughts, and actions.

Hilgard's (1977) theory of **neo-dissociationism** preserves much of Janet's original conception but updates the conceptions to fit a more recent cognitive psychology. In Hilgard's (1974) approach, cognitive barriers are dynamically erected by an individual in his or her perceptual/memory system, so as to block out certain thoughts. For example, if a person feels pain, and dissociates it, he does it by erecting a second thought, "I feel no pain," and surrounds the feelings of painful sensation with a dynamic barrier, formed, perhaps by inattention, which blocks those feelings out. A diagram of how this works is shown in Figure 10.3. In the top of Figure 10.3, pain is readily accessible to communication systems for expression to the outside world. In the bottom of Figure 10.3, however, the individual has added a second thought, such as, "I am feeling no pain," and erected a cognitive barrier between that and thoughts of pain. A second barrier is erected between the thoughts of pain and their outside expression. Together these result in the appearance and sensation of pain analgesia—the experience of markedly reduced pain such as occurs, for example, in hypnosis.

Individual Differences in Dissociation

Not everyone seems equally able or likely to dissociate ideas in consciousness. One interesting trait related to dissociation is whether or not an individual experiences something called conscious absorption. The trait of absorption describes a person's ability to become lost in a stream of consciousness so intensely as to loose track of everything else. Paradoxically, absorption in one's own train of thoughts appears to

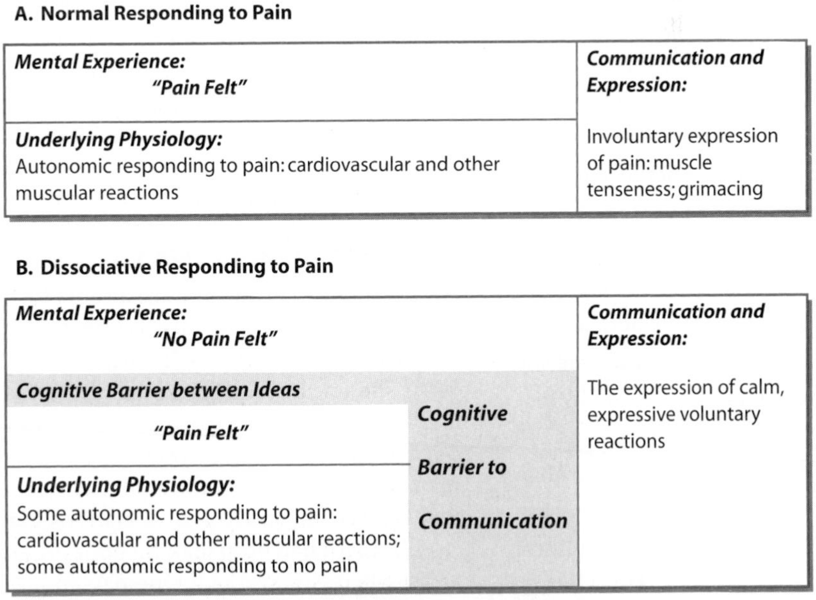

FIGURE 10.3

Responding to Painful Stimuli under Normal Conditions and under Dissociation
The top portion of the diagram depicts a standard response to pain. The lower portion depicts the same individual responding to pain, but this time with dissociative (cognitive) barriers in place to block both the painful experience and its expression.

Source: Adapted from Hilgard (1973). Reprinted with permission of American Psychological Association.

A. Normal Responding to Pain

Mental Experience: "Pain Felt"	*Communication and Expression:*
Underlying Physiology: Autonomic responding to pain: cardiovascular and other muscular reactions	Involuntary expression of pain: muscle tenseness; grimacing

B. Dissociative Responding to Pain

Mental Experience: "No Pain Felt"		*Communication and Expression:*
Cognitive Barrier between Ideas "Pain Felt"	**Cognitive Barrier to Communication**	The expression of calm, expressive voluntary reactions
Underlying Physiology: Some autonomic responding to pain: cardiovascular and other muscular reactions; some autonomic responding to no pain		

be related to more dissociation in general. The more intense one's conscious focus, it appears, the more may go on outside of consciousness, unattended to and unseen. For example, the correlation between absorption and the capacity to be hypnotized is about $r = .35$, so they are modestly related (Weitzenhoffer & Hilgard, 1962).

The Classic Suggestion Effect

Classic Suggestion Effect:
An introspective feeling that one has involuntarily responded to an instruction, such as hearing the direction to move one's head, and then having it move without willing it to do so.

Some people can "feel" or witness dissociation even as it is happening; this occurs in the classic suggestion effect. The **classic suggestion effect** occurs when someone suggests that you do something or feel something, and a part of you follows the suggestion but without the participation of the conscious self. For example, a person might be told to hold out his arms in front of him and feel how heavy his right hand feels. Some people will indeed feel their right hand is very heavy—and that the verbal suggestion itself caused this new feeling. For some people, that responsiveness to the suggestion seems to occur outside of their own conscious choice. Responsiveness to the classic suggestion effect is often used as a screening device to identify people more likely to enter a hypnotic state, with which it correlates about $r = .35$ (Bowers, 1982).

The Dissociative Experiences Scale indicates that there may exist two types of dissociation. One type, which is fairly common among healthy people, involves absorption and involvement in imagination and imagery. This is measured by items such as (does this describe you?): "Some people can get so involved in watching TV or a movie that they lose track of what is going on around them." There is also a more serious dissociation that involves more dramatic splits in self-regulation. This is measured by such items as, "Some people have the experience of finding new things among their belongings that they do not remember buying," and "Some people have the experience of finding themselves in a place and having no idea how they got there" (Waller, Putnum, & Carlson, 1996).

Severe dissociation is sometimes associated with trauma. A case of historical importance to the history of the field concerned soldiers who were caught in an intense aerial bombardment during World War I (one of the first such bombings in military history). Although the soldiers returned physically unharmed, they reported having lost their sight. In this case, the physicians hypothesized that they had witnessed events so horrible that they created a mental barrier against seeing. The use of hypnotherapy restored the sight of several soldiers (see Redlich & Bingham, 1960).

> Automatisms have an uncertain relationship to awareness . . . The "pure case" is an activity carried out with no awareness whatever that it is going on. An activity may be carried out in awareness, however, without any sense of control over it; compulsive acts or obsessive acts may be of this kind. Sometimes the processes are only mildly dissociated, such as the "doodling" that occurs while one is talking on the telephone or listening to a lecture.
> Ernest Hilgard

Evidence from Case Studies

A number of case studies of dissociated mental ideas exist. An everyday case of dissociation concerns "Elizabeth," a first-year graduate student in a psychology program (Erdelyi, 1984). Whenever Elizabeth became angry, she would break out in a specific, peculiar rash, that included pink blotches that turned to dark spots of red and scarlet, in response to her anger. Her rash, in other words, was an external signal that indicated her emotional condition. When her verbal reports contradicted such signals, unconscious dissociations were likely to be present.

Elizabeth had been making poor progress in the psychology laboratory where she worked. One day, in a lab meeting, Elizabeth presented a recent study she had conducted. A graduate student who had just joined the group was present. He soundly criticized her work, speaking in an overbearing, superior tone. During this encounter her rash appeared, and the professor put an end to the meeting. After the student left, the professor urged her not to be too angry. She responded, "But I wasn't angry!" The professor, overcome by his curiosity, said, "But Elizabeth, you have your famous rash all over your face and neck; you look like a pink leopard!"

"You are putting me on," she said. Quite a bit surprised, she whisked her compact from her pocketbook, and looked at herself in the mirror. "That's amazing," she said, and giggled with embarrassment. "I was completely unaware of it. A blush lit up her pale cheeks" (Erdelyi, 1984, pp. 75–76).

Case Study

An Example of Divided Consciousness

Dramatic examples of divided consciousness come from cases of abnormal psychology. In extreme cases, whole portions of a person's life may appear to be controlled by a sort of second self. For example, in 1919, a young man was brought to a psychologist after the police found him wandering the streets of Los Angeles. He had identification papers made out to Charles Poulting of Florida, as well as British and French war medals, and no idea who he was (cited in Hilgard, 1977). He had lost all memory of his life before February 1915, didn't know his name, and recalled only his recent life. He believed he may have come from Canada, and Michigan also seemed to figure importantly in his life—but he spoke with an Irish accent. Beyond that, he had no sense of his identity. After World War I, he had traveled widely trying to find some identity for himself. After some mostly failed treatment, the young man was released, which would have ended the story— except that he was again found wandering the streets of Los Angeles eleven years later in March 1930. The police, who recalled the earlier incident, brought him to the same psychologist as before (Dr. Franz, who chronicled his case).

This time the man was able to recall certain details from his earlier life but nothing of the recent years. From the two separate visits, Dr. Franz was able to understand what had happened to him. As a young man, the patient had joined the French Foreign Legion and had fought in Africa. During that time, he kept a pet monkey who had become his traveling companion. He had purchased the monkey in a bazaar, and over time had come to care about it very deeply. During his service in the foreign legion, Charles, his monkey, and a fellow soldier were traveling one day through leopard country. The first night in leopard country he had urged his companion to tie himself in the branches of a tree to avoid being attacked overnight. His companion scoffed at the idea and went to sleep at the tree's base. Charles tied the monkey to the base of the tree as well, and then climbed up the tree himself and tied himself in. Later that night, leopards arrived and attacked, killed, and ate both his companion and the monkey at the base of the tree. Charles apparently had not felt particularly badly about his companion because he had warned him about the leopards. But Charles felt traumatized about his monkey companion. Because Charles himself had tied the monkey to the base of tree, he felt responsible for the creature's death. This traumatic stress triggered a dissociative disorder that afflicted him during the years his case was followed.

Inside the Field

A Brief History of Hypnosis

Hypnosis was discovered by Franz Anton Mesmer (1734–1815) who grew up in a rural, densely forested part of Austrian countryside where beliefs in spirits and special powers were commonplace. In some respects, Mesmer was a transitional figure, blending together both superstition and science.

Mesmer studied at and graduated from the medical faculty of Vienna as a young man. The time was seventeen years before the last witch was executed in Europe, and twenty-seven years before Pinel's first reforms in the mental institutions of France. His medically approved dissertation, "The Influence of the Planets on the Human Body," was concerned with possible astrological influences on people's health and personality.

At that time in Europe word was spreading about magnetism, a new and fascinating force. Mesmer became interested in magnetism as a possible mechanism by which one object (such as a planet) might influence the human body. He therefore set out to find a magnet. In 1774 most magnets were in the universities, and many universities were administered by Jesuits, Catholic priests particularly responsible for education, and so it was from a Jesuit astronomer with the unlikely name of Maximillian Hell that Mesmer borrowed his magnet.

Securing his magnet, Mesmer brought it home to treat a woman who was employed part-time in his household and who had numerous physical complaints. As he waived the magnet over her body and suggested its forces would work on her, she felt "surging sensations," which Mesmer believed indicated that fluids were mov-ing through her. After the treatment, her complaints went away. Over a series of further experiments, Mesmer discovered the original iron magnet was not necessary. Believing he himself had become magnetized, he began to refer to himself as possessing "Animal Magnetism."

Mesmer moved to Paris where he set up a practice curing the ills of wealthy and noble patients, who he treated in unorthodox ways. He had his patients sit, for example in a large, covered wooden tub filled with bottles floating in water (all of this was in the service of enhancing the animal magnetism). He often wore a black cloak, and a sorcerer-like hat, and took to waving a wand that he believed carried magnetic forces.

After a time, Mesmer's unorthodox activities raised the suspicions of the authorities. In 1784, the King of France appointed a number of august scientists to investigate Mesmer. This group included the American, Benjamin Franklin, who was then serving as ambassador to France, as well as the famous chemist Lavoisier. The commission set to work. They invited Mesmer to demonstrate his activities. Mesmer refused on grounds of health, but his assistant did show up. Demonstrations ensued that were not entirely successful. As a result, the commission attributed hypnotic effects to peoples' imagination, concluding that "imagination without magnetism produces convulsions, and that magnetism without imagination produces nothing" (cited in Bowers, 1976, p. 8).

The conclusions of the commission cast grave doubts on the scientific validity of hypnosis, but such doubts were perhaps overstated.

Such extreme skepticism probably occurred because scientists were very concerned with distinguishing their work from the era's superstitions. It is interesting to note that shortly after this, a new commission was formed to study whether such a thing as meteorites existed. (The new commission included some of the same members.) The commission concluded that meteorites could not exist. Part of their reasoning was based on the argument that meteorites were heavenly bodies, and since there was no scientific proof that heaven existed, meteorites could not exist either. As a result, many of the great museums of Europe threw out their irreplaceable collections of meteors. Animal Magnetism, too, was thrown out too quickly.

The Rehabilitation of Animal Magnetism.
Not everyone gave up on Animal Magnetism as a scientific effect. Around 1850, a French physician named Braid coined the term *hypnosis,* which more accurately reflected that magnetism was not involved in the process.

The term *hypnosis* was neutral sounding, and also had the effect of toning down the sensationalistic images that surrounded animal magnetism, or Mesmerism, by which the effect had been known previously. In 1885, the eminent French neurologist, Jean Charcot, who was then at the peak of his professional career, began to use hypnosis with his patients. Charcot gave a number of public demonstrations of hypnosis—and was quite charismatic. A young neurologist who had travelled all the way from Austria to study with him described him thus:

> M. Charcot came in at ten o'clock, a tall man of fifty-eight, a silk hat on his head, with dark and curiously mild eyes (one of them expressionless and has an inward cast), with long hair held back by his ears, clean shaven, with very expressive features and full protruding lips: in short, like a worldly priest, of whom one expects much wit and that he understands how to live well. (Jones, 1955, V. 1. p. 185)

Charcot influenced his students tremendously. The same student wrote,

> I believe I am changing a great deal. Charcot, who is both one of the greatest physicians and a man whose common sense is the order of genius, simply demolishes my views and aims. Many a time after a lecture I go out as from Notre Dame, with new impressions to work over. But he engrosses me: when I go away from him I have no more wish to work at my own simple things. My brain is sated as after an evening at the theater. Whether the seed will ever bring forth fruit I do not know; but what I certainly know is that no other human being has ever affected me in such a way. (Jones, 1955, V. 1. p. 185)

The young neurology student who wrote the above was Sigmund Freud, who went on to develop many theories of his own regarding unconscious dynamics.

Charcot's name finally brought hypnosis some respectability. From that time on, a number of scientific investigations into hypnotism occurred. In the United States, Shor and Orne (1965) and Ernest Hilgard (1965) publish important research studies legitimizing the effect.

Nonconscious Personal Control: The Model of Hypnosis

To study nonconscious forms of personal control, psychologists have used the model of the hypnotic trance. Hypnosis provides an experimental condition in which a researcher can control portions of a person's mental processes, apart from the individual's consciousness. As a research tool, the hypnotic induction is valuable for suggesting possibilities of how nonconscious urges and commands can control the individual.

One limit of the use of hypnosis to understand mental control is that it may not be generalizable to everyone; only some people can be hypnotized. The individual differences in dissociation and in hypnotic ability are profound. About a third of all people are relatively unaffected by hypnosis. The other two-thirds are increasingly susceptible to its influence, up to a small group called **hypnotic virtuosos** who are able to enter into deep hypnotic states with ease, and to carry out profoundly difficult mental dissociations and alterations of consciousness once in the state (Hilgard, 1965).

Hypnotic ability is measured with scales such as the Stanford Scale of Hypnotic Susceptibility, Version C. It employs a graded set of mental challenges that a person attempts under hypnosis—such as imagining a bothersome insect where there is none. Only a few people can perform them all (Kurtz & Strube, 1996; Weitzenhoffer & Hilgard, 1959; Weitzenhoffer & Hilgard, 1962). Advances in understanding have laid the groundwork for a potential new generation of hypnotic scales as well (e.g., Kirsch, 1997; Kirsch & Lynn, 1995; Lynn & Rhue, 1988, Woody, 1997).

Hypnotic Virtuoso: A hypnotic participant who is especially able to enter into the trance state and is especially talented at carrying out mental tasks under hypnosis.

Background on Hypnosis

One interpretation of hypnosis is that an individual's conscious self-control is temporarily disabled, and that a part of the personality comes under the control of the

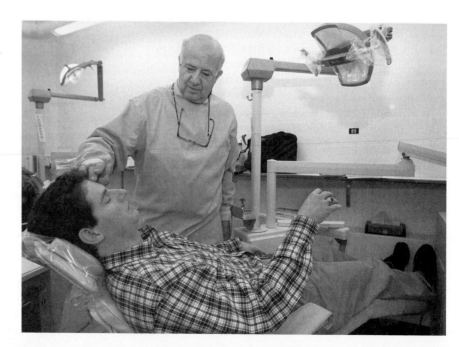

One form of self-control involved dissociating awareness from the rest of the conscious self. Some people can do this voluntarily under hypnosis. Here, a dentist hypnotizes a patient so as to numb his mouth in preparation for drilling a tooth. Hypnosis serves as a highly effective analgesic for some individuals.

TABLE 10.3 Characteristics of an Hypnotic State	
An individual in a hypnotic state . . .	**This is called . . .**
gives up control of planning to the hypnotist or other party.	Suppression of planning
can attend to certain parts of the environment and screen out other parts.	Redistribution of attention
recalls experiences from the past in a more emotionally and visually intense manner.	Enhanced availability of visual and emotional memories
is prepared to imagine and accept alternative realities, such as imaginary beings or creatures.	Reduction in reality testing
responds to suggestions such as "your arm is getting stiff," or "there is a fly on your nose."	Increased suggestibility
easily acts out unaccustomed or forgotten roles, such as an adult becoming her ten-year-old self.	Role behavior
forgets some or all of the hypnotic session afterward without being instructed to do so.	Spontaneous amnesia

Source: Summarized from Hilgard (1965).

hypnotist. In old movies, hypnotists induced a trance by saying, "you are under my control . . . you will hear only my voice, you will do as I say . . ." This is not a very good hypnotic induction. Actually, it would be so anxiety-provoking to many people as to keep them quite alert. But it does get across the idea of dissociation—that a part of one's self leaves one's own control and comes under the control of someone or something else. You can examine a colorful part of the history of personality psychology—the discovery of hypnosis—in the Inside the Field box.

Dissociation and the Unconscious

Indeed, perhaps the primary characteristic of a hypnotic state is the suppression of one's own planning and self-direction (Hilgard, 1965). Suppression of planning refers to rendering one's own goals and plans inactive, and to exist with someone else's goals. (See Table 10.3 for an overview of this and the other characteristics.) In one study, hypnotized students were given instructions to attend a holiday party going on in the building, and to pretend they were not hypnotized (Hilgard, 1965). Experimental observers followed each hypnotized student to study what he or she did, and for the participant's own safety.

At first, the hypnotized individuals behaved like everyone else at the party, chatting and helping themselves to the food. After a while, however, the hypnotized party-goers became a bit glassy-eyed, and many of them, after some time, found themselves a comfortable chair in which to relax, and stared blankly out into space. They remained there until finally rescued by the experimenters. Under hypnosis, the hypnotized participants seemed to have lost their own line of conscious intentions at least temporarily. Incidentally, you may wonder what might have happened if the participants had been left in their seats indefinitely. The vast majority of hypnotic participants would have awakened on their own after a time. (A few exceptional participants might not awaken until obtaining the proper attention.)

Perhaps related to this dissociation is the redistribution of attention. The person can (under instruction) block out awareness of certain parts of the environment. For example, a hypnotized person may not see someone else who is in the room with them, or the hypnotized person may feel no pain, if so instructed. "Make a stroke on paper or blackboard, and tell the subject it is not there . . ." remarked William James, with some amazement:

> . . . and he will see nothing but the clean paper or the board. Next, he not looking, surround the original stroke with other strokes exactly like it and ask him what he sees. He will point out one by one all the new strokes and omit the original one every time, no matter how numerous the new strokes may be, or in what order they are.
>
> Obviously, then, he is not blind to the kind of stroke in the least . . . and paradoxical as it may seem to say so, he must distinguish it with great accuracy from others like it, in order to remain blind to it . . . (James, 1890, II, pp. 607–608)

Also under hypnosis, people will accept realities that they wouldn't accept when awake. The hypnotic state involves the enhanced availability of visual and emotional memories. With less conscious monitoring, there is also the greater chance for more poorly directed behavior—and maybe more creative, associative thinking. For example, people under hypnosis exhibit increased suggestibility—the tendency to accept others' ideas under hypnosis. A simple suggestion, such as, "your right arm is getting stiff," may result in hypnotized people being unable to move their right arms. Of course, such a suggestion would have little effect on most people under normal circumstances.

The hypnotic trance involves a marked reduction in reality testing. For example, if instructed to do so, a hypnotized individual may believe that there is a third person in the room with him when there are only two, and the hypnotized participant may even see the imaginary person as if he or she were really there. In fact, there is always the possibility that people will add imagined events to what they recall under hypnosis—the reason the American Psychological Association cautions against employing hypnosis when interviewing witnesses to a crime (e.g., Scheflin, Spiegel, & Spiegel, 1998).

A most relevant and striking aspect of the trance in regard to nonconscious personal control is the post-hypnotic suggestion. For this, the hypnotist asks the participant to carry out a task—such as opening a window upon a signal (e.g., when the clock chimes the hour). The participant is also told he or she will remember nothing about the suggestion. The participant is then awakened, and will carry out the task of opening the window at the prescribed time, with no apparent knowledge of why he or she did it. Actually, the person will typically supply an incorrect explanation—such as that the room was stuffy. This has led some psychologists to argue, on the basis of the hypnotic model, that complex chains of behavior can and do take place in otherwise normal individuals without their awareness. And that moreover the individual will provide a false reason for doing so afterward.

Causes of Hypnotic Susceptibility

What leads a person to behave in a hypnotically susceptible way? There is some evidence that hypnotizability may be genetic (Morgan, 1973). Jean Hilgard (1979) concluded that hypnotic ability also arises in childhood among individuals who find pathways into the altered state. Some of the central pathways to hypnotic ability include the childhood experience of fantasy involvement in reading, drama, creative artwork and related activities such as religious imagination, among others.

In the case of reading, for example, hypnotizable adults reported that as children they didn't simply read, but entered in a new fantasy world. After putting down a book, a hypnotizable person might imagine herself talking or playing with the characters in the book for several days thereafter, as if they had become real people, in a real world of their own. Recent research has suggested that hypnotic susceptibility may also be related to everything from intense attachments to pets, to certain milder aspects of schizophrenic-spectrum disorders (Brown & Katcher, 2001; Jamieson, 2001).

Positive Affirmations

Hypnosis provides a dramatic example of shifting self-control to an automatized state. Can we also improve ourselves by making some helpful thoughts automatic? In the early 1900s, a French physician, Coué, suggested that people repeat to themselves over and over, *"Tous les jours, à tous les points de vue, je vais de mireux en mireux,"* or, in English, "Every day in every way, I am getting better and better" (cited in Paulhus, 1993). Coué argued that substantial repetition of this formula—twenty times upon waking up, going to bed, and several times during the day, if possible—would provide an automatic positive self-concept for people that could be helpful.

If Coué's phrases sound vague and simplistic to you, he argued that there was a sophisticated reason for it: people would be less inclined to automatically argue against it precisely because the statement was general. For example, if one attempted to repeat that one was a good friend, gradually, one would come to recognize exceptions to it and lose the motivation to repeat the statement. Coué's phrase was designed to illicit few specific rational objections. Of course, Coué was not the only one to suggest this. Yogananda Paramahansa, among the first California gurus, introduced such self-affirmations in the 1930s (Paulhus, 1993, p. 375).

Coué's method became the rage in France, and crossed the English Channel where it was similarly popular (in English form) in London. For some reason, the idea fared a bit less well in America, where one might imagine its optimistic message would be popular.

Arguing from the standpoint of contemporary psychology, Paulhus suggests that an automatic self-concept is important because attentional processes are limited. The automatic self-concept fills in the gaps when a person is focusing on other matters. In a series of studies Paulhus and his colleagues found that when people are distracted by white noise or through heightened exam anxiety, their self descriptions become more globally positive and less believable and accurate. They conclude that honest trait descriptions require attentional capacity (Paulhus & Lower, 1987; Paulhus & Lim, 1987, cited in Paulhus, 1993).

Consistent with these conclusions, Paulhus and his colleagues have found that repetition of general positive statements about the self do change the self-concept.

First, participants make optimally positive statements about themselves. Later, they are asked to endorse self-descriptive traits flashed on a computer screen under two conditions: an honesty condition in which they are asked to be as accurate as possible, and, second, a speeded condition in which they are asked to respond as quickly as they can. Results indicate that, particularly in the speeded condition, the repetition of positive statements biases their self-image positively for up to twenty-four-hour periods (the longest they have investigated thus far).

How Do We Deal with the Pain of Falling Short?

Falling Short and Mental Defense

No matter how much we can control ourselves, we are never adequate in relation to every possible yardstick. As human beings, we all share desires that cannot be met, possess social shortcomings, and fall short of moral commandments that few human beings are good enough to meet all the time. As if all that were not enough, we must contend with the fear of death, which greets everyone at the end no matter how well we act. We can—and do—try, try, again. And yet, we don't always make it. People often employ defense mechanisms to block out the pain that such thoughts inevitably raise.

Defense Mechanisms:
Mental processes that are in place to protect the conscious self (ego) from psychic pain.

One way that individuals maintain their self-esteem is through the action of such **defense mechanisms**. In Freud's original formulation, defense mechanisms protected consciousness from psychic pain caused by ideas related to threatening sexual and aggressive desires. These defenses were later systematized by the psychoanalyst Anna Freud (1937), Freud's daughter. Today, defense mechanisms are understood to protect the conscious self from threats to self-esteem and psychic pain more generally (Fenichel, 1945). The defenses do this by blocking out or modifying any information that would seriously threaten the individual's sense of security (e.g., Baumeister, Dale, & Sommer, 1998; Cooper, 1998).

Suppression

Suppression: A defense mechanism that involves the conscious blocking out or expelling thoughts that one wishes to avoid thinking about.

You are probably aware of saying something to yourself like, "I'm just not going to worry about this now," or "I need to distract myself from this problem." This is called **suppression**. Suppression involves the conscious blocking out of awareness of unpleasant thoughts (Wegner, 1989). For example, surveys indicate that when individuals feel an unpleasant emotion, they often urge themselves to "don't think about it," "fight the feeling," and "pretend everything is okay" (Mayer, Salovey, Gomberg-Kaufman, & Blainey, 1991).

In a series of experiments, Wegner (1989) had people try *not* to think about something. Participants in an experimental group were instructed to try not to think about a white bear for three minutes—to block any thought of white bears out of their mind. Whenever a white bear came into their mind, they signaled the mental intrusion by pressing a button, and then continued to attempt to block out the white bear thought. A comparison group spent three minutes actively thinking of white bears. Later, when members of each group were asked to think about anything they pleased, the group that had blocked out white bears thought a lot more about white bears than did members of the control group. When we suppress ideas they tend to return.

Suppressed feelings sometimes emerge as well. A patient, "Mary," had been hospitalized for depression when she sought a weekend pass to go home to visit her family. In reality, she was quite unhappy and had every intention of killing herself on the way home. She lied to her psychiatrist and the treatment team so successfully, however, that she received the pass. Fortunately, she had second thoughts about suicide before going home, and confessed them to the psychiatrist.

As it had turned out, the session with the psychiatrist had been videotaped. Was anything on the videotape that might reveal Mary's true feelings? In searching through the tape of Mary's conversation with the psychiatrist, Paul Ekman and his colleagues found a number of partial physical expressions such as shrugs related to depression. Moreover, as Ekman put it:

> using slow-motion repeated replay, we saw a complete sadness facial expression, but it was there only for an instant, quickly followed by a smiling appearance. (Ekman, 1985, *Telling Lies,* pp. 130–131).

Micro-Expressions: Full facial expressions of basic emotions that occur in roughly a quarter of a second or less and then disappear.

These were **micro-expressions**. A micro-expression is a complete, full-faced, emotional expression that takes place in a highly compressed period of time—in about 40 milliseconds, and that is invisible to the naked eye. Pure micro-expressions are fairly rare, but other emotions are suppressed all the time. Squelched expressions—expressions covered up by another one—frequently happen in social interactions. One may look angrily at someone but try to cover it quickly with a smile (Ekman, 1985, p. 131).

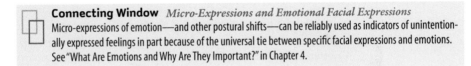

Connecting Window *Micro-Expressions and Emotional Facial Expressions*
Micro-expressions of emotion—and other postural shifts—can be reliably used as indicators of unintentionally expressed feelings in part because of the universal tie between specific facial expressions and emotions. See "What Are Emotions and Why Are They Important?" in Chapter 4.

Repression

Repression: The unconscious forgetting or blocking out of unpleasant or threatening ideas that one wishes to avoid thinking about.

It is not a giant leap from suppression to **repression**. Repression involves the motivated nonperception or forgetting of unpleasant material. For example, a student who doesn't want to study for examinations might forget about an upcoming exam entirely. It may begin as a suppression—a conscious ignoring of the idea—but then the suppression itself may become automatized, and both the feared exam and one's attempt to forget about it may gradually sink below consciousness altogether. Most defense mechanisms typically use repression, either alone, or in combination with other mental processes.

Weinberger, Schwartz, and Davidson (1979) studied repression in a group of male college students who were told that they would be receiving a painful electrical shock. The experimenters monitored the students' fear in two ways. First, they measured well-accepted physiological indicators of fear, including blood pressure and heart rate. Second, they asked the students if they were afraid. Most men responded to the threat of the shocks physiologically with increased heart rate and blood pressure, suggesting a fear reaction. Most also reported being afraid. A few men, however, were "physiologically" afraid (e.g., increased heart rate), but reported being entirely calm. This last group was labeled "repressors," because they apparently repressed their feelings. Subsequent studies have clarified that such individuals are doing more than impression management, and appear to lack access to internal experiences (Weinberger & Davidson, 1994). Weinberger and colleagues speculated that these men had learned early to please themselves and others by displaying little or no negative feeling. Interestingly, a decade of follow-up studies has suggested that such repressors show unusually high levels of health problems (Weinberger, 1995).

It is worth mentioning that some repression may be automatic and may never involve conscious awareness at all. Collins, McLeod, and Jacoby (1992) conducted experiments in which they asked participants two different kinds of questions—neutral and threatening—that were masked by a louder background noise. An example of a neutral question was, "Is Albany the capital of New York State?"; a threatening question asked, "Would it be upsetting if your parents stopped supporting you?"

The questions themselves were played at a level below the threshold of reliable hearing, and the participants' job was to judge the loudness of the background noise. The sentences and background noise were carefully controlled for clarity and loudness. Participants in the experiment judged background noise as much noisier when the threatening sentences played. This suggests that part of their minds were blocking out what other parts found fearful to hear—as Freud described repression. Additional studies indicated that this perception of loudness was nonconsciously controlled, and that participants could not overcome it (Jacoby et al., 1988).

Specific Defense Mechanisms

Anna Freud suggested that there was a developmental hierarchy of specific defense mechanisms, an idea investigated and supported by contemporary researchers (e.g., Cramer, 1991; Vaillant, 1971). Each of the defense mechanisms can be viewed as a dynamic of self-control specifically designed to avoid personal pain. One early developing defense is denial.

Denial

Denial: A defense mechanism in which the individual maintains a claim in the face of obvious information to the contrary.

Denial is a normal form of mental defense for children between the ages of three and 6 years, but its use decreases thereafter, making it among the earliest forms of defense that children learn to use. Denial can be defined as the outright rejection of something that is clearly true. For example, a small child might wave her hands and, while doing so, spill her glass of milk onto the floor. Her father might observe, "Oh, you spilled your milk because you were waving your arms." A child using denial will innocently respond, "*I* didn't do it." If asked *who* did it, the child is likely to shrug as if ignorant, or make up a story—"My teddy bear!".

Healthy adults employ denial only in times of extreme stress. Adults who lose a loved one might momentarily experience denial, but the use of denial becomes less frequent with age. Still, it can persist as a personality pattern. For example, students believe that tests are less valid and fair when they do poorly on them (e.g., Pyszczynski, Greenberg, & Holt, 1985; Schlenker, Weigold, & Hallam, 1990), particularly when their self-esteem is unstable (Kernis, Cornell, Sun, Berry, & Harlow, 1993). In addition, young adults who score high on projective measures of denial are more irresponsible, unpredictable, and rebellious; they are also less able to see the heart of a problem, and are less straightforward in their communications (Cramer, 2002).

Projection

Projection: A defense mechanism in which the individual sees his or her own unpleasant attributes in another person while being unable to see them in him or herself.

The mental defense of **projection** involves a confusion between one's own characteristics and the characteristics of others. Projection can be defined as denying a negative quality in oneself and yet falsely identifying it in others. So, for example, a businessman who spends much of his time cheating others might view most other business people as cheats. Such projection is sometimes used to explain bigotry in which a person's own negative impulses—say, laziness—are seen as characteristics of other ethnic or religious groups. Over time, the use of projection improves one's self-esteem but also increases one's anxiety, perhaps because disconfirming evidence of one's beliefs becomes harder to block out (Cramer & Tracy, 2005).

False Consensus Effect: A research finding that people often believe more others agree with them than is actually the case.

The most robust experimental finding related to projection is that people tend to see others as more like themselves than they really are (Ross, Greene, & House, 1977). This effect, called the **false consensus effect** also occurs more frequently in those with higher self-esteem (Crocker, Alloy, & Kayne, 1988). Still, the research evidence is less complete when it comes to finding evidence that the person then represses his or her own bad qualities (Baumeister et al., 1998).

Rationalization

Rationalization: A defense mechanism in which a person employs a plausible, but false, reason for explaining her or his behavior that covers up a real but more unpleasant or threatening reason.

Rationalization is a commonly used defense in which a person finds some false reason for doing (or not doing) something so as to cover up the real reason. For example, a person who is afraid of going on a date because she is painfully shy and ashamed of her body may find all sorts of reasons not to go on the date that have nothing to do with the real reason: "I have to prepare for an exam," "I don't have any clean clothes," or, "I'm not feeling well." In any single instance, these reasons may make sense. But if a person always finds a different excuse to avoid the same activity it becomes clearer over time that rationalization is being used. Kunda (1990) developed a theory of motivated reasoning, in which she finds that people do what they feel like, and find a reason for it afterward. For instance, a person may like a member of a different ethnic group he meets, and so recall a positive stereotype of the ethnic group to support the feeling (Kunda & Sinclair, 1999). If he doesn't like the person, he will recall negative stereotypes (cf. Tsang, 2002).

Reaction Formation

Reaction Formation: A defense mechanism in which someone acts opposite to their real inclinations in order to hide them—for example, is intentionally generous in order to mask feelings of stinginess.

The defense of **reaction formation** begins with a person denying an unwanted trait in himself or herself, and then acting in ways that are opposite to the covered-up characteristic in order to hide it. A woman might really feel superiority and hatred toward others, for example, but might try to cover it up from both herself and others by claiming to love them. For example, European American, nonprejudiced participants in a research study were told (depending upon their experimental condition) that their test results indicated they were racist. Such participants later gave a pan handler of African American heritage more money than they gave a similar European American pan handler, compared to others in a control condition (Dutton & Lake, 1973). In another study, male participants who exhibited higher blood flow to the

In the mental defense, reaction formation, *an individual may maintain a public moral position opposite to that of his or her private personal urges. The public position distracts from and covers up the private feelings. Congressman Gary Condit had campaigned and won an election on a family values platform, and then was discovered having had an affair with a Washington intern. When the intern was reported missing the scandal came to light. Journalists focused on the contradiction between the congressman's political ideals and his personal behavior. Condit himself attempted to keep the affair from the press. He also maintained his public position remarking, "I've been married for 34 years, and I intend to stay married to that woman as long as she'll have me."*

genital area (indicating sexual responsiveness) to a videotape of homosexual intercourse expressed the most homophobia on several attitude measures (Adams, Wright, & Lohr, 1996).

There also are striking examples of cases where an individual's hidden personal characteristics finally break through. Jim Bakker, with his wife Tammy, developed Praise the Lord (PTL) Ministries, an evangelical religious empire with a budget in the hundred of millions of dollars. The couple joined an elite group of evangelists on national television and based their mission on preaching love, purity, and wholesomeness before God. But in 1987, while preaching on television Bakker also was committing adultery with a church secretary and using ministry money to buy her silence. More significantly to the United States government, he had fraudulently oversold at least $158 million worth of lodging-partnerships to the members of his ministry—which amounted to the largest consumer mail fraud in the United States up to that time (Tidwell, 1993).

So, at the same time Bakker was preaching the importance of moral behavior, he was engaging in fraudulent behavior himself. Bakker was judged personally responsible for these and other transgressions, enough for him to be found guilty of the crime. Awareness is not an all-or-nothing matter, however. To the extent that Bakker's role as a minister helped him avoid paying attention to his own impulses toward deception and their consequences, we might conclude that the processes of reaction formation were at play.

Sublimation

Sublimation is among the healthiest of defenses. Here, the individual represses an unacceptable desire, but then finds a constructive social role that will let that desire express itself. By choosing to become a painter or sculptor, for example, a person can satisfy various sexual impulses in a socially approved way. Spreading paints or molding clay provide tactile experiences that can be similar to those involved in physical contact with a sexual partner. Moreover, artists often take human figures as their models, and this opportunity to look carefully at others' bodies is another way in which a sexual drive can be partially satisfied. Similarly, people who choose to become butchers, police officers, or surgeons may be sublimating an aggressive drive, and by doing so, turning their desire to act aggressively to the service of the community.

In a survey of research on defense mechanisms, Baumeister, Dale, and Sommer (1998) were unable to find research in the psychological literature that they considered relevant to the defense of sublimation. This raises the question of whether there is no evidence for the defense, or whether, because the defense is so much a part of healthy functioning, it has been ignored. Sublimation, then, is an understudied topic at present.

How Is Self-Control (or Its Absence) Expressed?

The Search for Self-Control

Self-control can direct a search for a better life. People control themselves in difficult circumstances, delay gratification, and make difficult but correct decisions to obtain gains in the long term. Early studies of mental control often divided people who were strong-willed and could control their impulses, from those who appeared relatively weak-willed and who were subject to the pressures of everyday life with little capacity to plan or adhere to those plans (Klausner, 1965; Wegner & Pennebaker, 1993). In the early 1920s, though, the eminent eductator John Dewey (1922) argued that the will could be educated and improved.

A cottage industry of self-help books that coach people about how to increase their self-control has long existed (Dornbush, 1965). These books advocate techniques such as employing more positive thinking, changing one's disruptive emotions, meditation, and more complex multi-step programs for personal enhancement and self-guidance. At the same time, there has been little research to refer to on the

In another case arguably illustrating reaction formation, Jim Bakker, a well-known televangelist, encouraged high moral standards among his followers. His calling provided an effective means of keeping his own more unsavory motives hidden—perhaps even to himself. At the height of his career, however, he cheated on his wife while defrauding the US government of millions of tax dollars.

> **The worst of all deceptions is self-deception.**
>
> Socrates

matter, so most such popular works have been speculative. More recently, psychologists have begun to examine the processes of self-control with an eye to what its outcomes might be, and how to improve self-control (Wegner & Pennebaker, 1993). Some fascinating findings already have emerged, including that self-control demands considerable effort and cost. For example, the control of thoughts elicits heightened physiological activity (e.g., Wegner et al., 1990; Gross & Levenson, 1997). Exerting self-control can also interfere with other cognitive activity because a person can only think (or not think) about a few things at once (Gilbert, 1991; Wegner & Pennebaker, 1993).

The varieties of self-control mean that the different ways in which it is expressed are potentially infinite. Here we will examine just a few examples of this important new research area.

Control versus Impulsiveness

In a now classic series of studies, Mischel and Ebbesen (1970) studied children's self-control. To do so, they first developed a method in which preschool children would be willing to wait in a room by themselves for at least a short time without becoming upset. The experimenter and child played a game in which the experimenter left the room and the child could immediately call the experimenter back by a simple signal. When summoned, the experimenter quickly darted back inside the room. This step was practiced thoroughly, until the child felt secure that her or his signal would be answered.

Next, the child was shown two food treats, one of which the child was known to prefer from pre-testing, and a second, less-preferred treat. Children were told that the experimenter was going to leave. If the child signaled for the experimenter, he or she could have the less-preferred treat right away. If the child could wait for the experimenter to return "by himself," however, he or she would get the preferred treat. That is, the longer they waited, the greater the reward. There were four conditions: one in which neither of the treats was visible, one in which both rewards were visible, one in which only the less-preferred (immediate) treat could be seen, and one in which the most-preferred (delayed) treat could be seen. Generally speaking, children waited far longer when no treat was present, and least well when both treats were present, as shown in Figure 10.4.

What made the study classic, however, was more related to the observation of the children who successfully waited. Those children created highly inventive strategies to distract themselves. They did nearly anything and everything. Rather than sit and stare at the less preferred treat, some children covered their eyes with their hands, or rested their heads in their hands. Some children invented elaborate tapping games with their hands and feet to create a rhythm to distract themselves. Some talked animatedly to themselves, other sang songs aloud. When all else failed, a few tried to go to sleep—and one child successfully did fall asleep during the wait! All these preschoolers surely deserved the treats they ultimately received.

Implications of Self-Control

As we will see in the coming chapters on personality development, individual differences in being able to wait—to postpone gratification—are highly predictive of life

Research in Focus

The New Research on Developing Self-Control

A new era of research concerns how to best use and develop self-control. This research has important applications. The research conveys a new idea: that the best form of self-control to use will depend upon the situation—and even on a person's age and other factors. Three brief examples are given here: of eating, of thinking positively, and of pain control.

In regard to eating, recent research indicates that optimal strategies may change from childhood to adulthood. Recall that children in Mischel's study on self-control were presented with a treat they hoped to resist. The most successful children in the original preschool study succeeded by distracting themselves from the treat. Studies on adults who diet, however, suggest that actually concentrating on food can assist those who are on a weight loss plan. For example, Polivy and her colleagues (Polivy, 1976; Polivy, Herman, Hackett, & Kuleshnyk, 1986) found that when people trying to diet distracted themselves from eating, they sometimes ate more than they otherwise would. On the other hand, having people self-monitor their eating—actually writing down everything they eat—serves to reduce the amount eaten (Herman & Polivy, 1993; Prokop et al., 1991).

Trying to think positively also benefits from focused attention—but the specific matter one focuses on is important as well. Wenzlaff and Bates (2000) wanted to help participants to think positively. They gave participants six scrambled words and asked them to make a five-word positive sentence out of them. For example, the scrambled words, "have life succeeded failed I at" could be unscrambled as, "I have succeeded at life," rather than the less desirable "I have failed at life." In one condition, participants were told to concentrate on composing only positive sentences. In another, they were told to avoid making any negative sentences. Later on, Wenzlaff and Bates discovered that those participants who concentrated on making pleasant sentences had far fewer intrusions of negative thoughts from the sentences, compared to the avoidance group and a control group.

But such focused concentration does not work the same way in pain relief. Fauerbach and colleagues (2002) divided hospital patients who were still in pain after receiving medication to try one of three strategies (in three experimental conditions): ignore the pain, imagine the pain as something positive, or distract themselves by listening to music. In such conditions, listening to music was by far the most effective method of self-control (Fauerbach et al., 2002).

As psychologists learn more about such methods of self control, the possibility arises that most of us or all of us will learn to feel, think, and act, more like we would wish to.

outcomes over time. The children in the Mischel study, for example, were followed up as adolescents. Those who were more controlled as preschoolers were described when they were adolescents by their parents (on California Q-Sorts) as more verbally fluent, better able to concentrate, good planners, and competent and skillful. Those who had had difficulty waiting, on the other hand, were described as easily rattled, and as going to pieces under stress (Mischel, Shoda, & Peake, 1988, Table 2).

Similarly, Smith (1967) rated a number of students on their impulsiveness prior to their entry to college. The higher the impulsiveness of the student, the lower the college GPA; with a substantial correlation of $r = -.47$. Similarly, Kipnis (1971) found

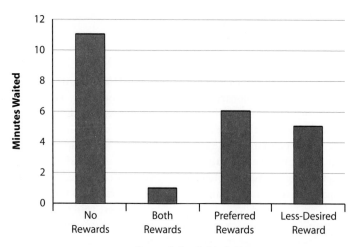

FIGURE 10.4

Waiting Time as a Function of the Presence of Reward In Mischel and Ebbesen's (1970) study, children waited longest when the rewards were not in sight, and least long when both rewards were present.

Source: After Mischel & Ebbesen (1970). Reprinted with permission of American Psychological Association.

> A little self-control at the right moment may prevent much subsequent compulsion at the hands of others.
>
> Arthur Schopenhauer

that students with self-reported impulsivity had lower average grade-point averages than did comparable students who were not impulsive. This effect held true only for high SAT–score students, suggesting either that higher SAT students knew better when they were impulsive, or that impulsiveness interferes more strongly with those high in intellectual ability. Biopsychologists have begun to trace the chemical roots of such impulsivity (Cools et al., 2005).

Increasing research also studies the best ways to exert self-control. The research is sufficiently recent that few conclusions can be drawn from it at present. One compelling conclusion, however, is that self-control is a limited resource, and if one tries to exert self-control in too many areas at once, the energy for self-control will become depleted (Muraven & Baumeister, 2000). Another finding is that the best form of self-control to employ may vary from challenge to challenge. For example, breaking certain habits is sometimes more easily done when changing one's circumstances—such as moving, or transferring to a different college (Wood, Tam, & Witt, 2005). A different strategy would be called for, though, to control one's eating, or to change one's negative thoughts. Some examples of such research are given in the Research in Focus box on developing self-control.

Self-control is critically important to us in everyday life, and also has implications for our futures. We will revisit this topic in the next chapters on personality development, where further evidence of the importance of personal self-control on future outcomes will be presented.

Reviewing Chapter 10

The purpose of this chapter is to examine how the conscious executive (the self) intervenes and controls the rest of personality—and the difficulties it has in doing so. We begin with an examination of why control is necessary. The conscious executive is by its nature somewhat egocentric. It governs the person and sees things its own way. It also seeks feedback, however, and acts on the basis of that feedback. It engages in feedback loops in an attempt to meet its goals. It may also be described as employing a circumspection-preemption-control (CPC) cycle.

Self-control is often distributed in the sense that some of it is automatic and unconscious. Conscious control can be divided or dissociated experimentally and studied through the use of hypnosis.

Mechanisms of defense form one way in which the executive consciousness prevents uncomfortable ideas and feelings from reaching consciousness. Sigmund Freud and his daughter, Anna Freud, provided good descriptions of these. Is there any evidence for them? Experimental evidence comes from studying hypnosis, facial expressions, and cognitive psychology.

Studies examining self-control show that individual differences in such control are already evident in children and have important consequences for later behavior.

The following questions should help you test your knowledge about this chapter.

What Are Dynamics of Self-Control?

1. How Dynamics of Self-Control Are Distinctive, and the Need for Self-Control.

The dynamics of self-control begin with a sense of wanting to do something and carrying through on it. What kinds of activities are enhanced by self-control. Can you describe what personality is like when the individual loses self-control?

2. Aims of Self-Control.

When people's goals are studied in surveys, certain goals appear again and again, and some of them are more important than others. Relationship goals, for example, are consistently among the most important in people's

estimations. What other goals are of importance? Do those high in extraversion order their goals differently than those high in neuroticism?

How Does Self-Control Occur?

3. The Self in Control.

From some standpoints, it is altogether normal to see the world in an egotistical fashion. People's memories, for example, naturally revolve around themselves as actors. Greenwald described the ego as experiencing three biases or qualities so as to maintain its positive self-regard, can you identify them and provide examples of each?

4. Personal Control as a Hierarchy of Feedback Loops.

Norbert Weiner, the founder of cybernetics, identified negative feedback loops as a central part of the self-control of systems. Can you identify the parts of a feedback loop? How can feedback loops be applied to self-control in personality? Do you understand where the hierarchy of feedback loops begins and ends, according to Powers?

5. The Search for—and Effect of—Feedback.

Do people actually seek feedback? There is a psychological dimension called "self-monitoring." People high in self-monitoring do seem more prone to seeking feedback. Can self-monitoring be induced? If so, how? What difference does it make if people conceive of their actions as relatively simple motor actions, versus involving high-level goals and plans? Do you know what "C," "P," and "C" stand for in Kelly's CPC cycle?

Is Self-Control Always Conscious?

6. Automatic Control and Dissociation.

Consciousness is limited, and for that reason, much control must be unconscious. What is dissociation?

7. Dissociation and the Unconscious.

Janet suggested that, in dissociation, people disassociate ideas from their consciousness. Then, those ideas might take on a life of their own. How did Hilgard apply his revised theory of dissociation (neodissociation theory) to pain control?

8. Individual Differences in Dissociation.

People dissociate in everyday life, and some people seem very responsive to suggestions. Can you give some examples of dissociation in everyday life? Describe the classic suggestion effect?

9. Nonconscious Personal Control: The Model of Hypnosis.

Hilgard enumerated several characteristics of people in hypnotic states, these ranged from the suppression of planning to enhanced role taking. What were some of the other characteristics? Some people dissociate more than others, and are higher in hypnotic suggestibility. According to studies by Jean Hilgard, these individuals found "paths" into hypnosis at an early age. Can you identify some of the paths?

10. Positive Affirmations.

Positive affirmations involve repeating general, simple, positive things about oneself over and over. Why are the affirmations repeated, and why have some argued that it is best for them to be simple and general? Are there any research findings that show such affirmations work?

How Do We Deal with the Pain of Falling Short?

11. Falling Short and Mental Defense.

It is human to fall short of important standards at one time or another. At such times, people use mental defense mechanisms. What do such mechanisms defend against?

12. Suppression.

One way people have of maintaining their positive self-regard is to avoid thinking of negative events or problems. What sorts of suppression do people use when experiencing a bad mood? What happens when people do successfully suppress material (hint: Do the suppressed thoughts come back?)?

13. Repression.

Repression involves the forgetting of unsetting material. How is the same and how is it different from suppres-

sion? What research evidence exists that repression takes place? For example, how do studies of listening to threatening comments and the noise that mask them provide evidence for the concept?

14. Specific Defense Mechanisms.

Specific defenses are sometimes said to form a rough developmental hierarchy from most primitive to most advanced. Can you state the most primitive of the specific defenses? If children employ that defense, does that mean they are having psychological problems? What is some of the evidence for and against projection? Can you name the remaining specific defenses covered here and say something about them?

How Is Self-Control (or Its Absence) Expressed?

15. The Search for Self-Control.

Early studies of self-control divided people into strong and weak-willed groups and examined their differences. The eminent educator, John Dewey, however, believed that self-control could be taught. How did Dewey's views set the stage for popular books on the topic, and for contemporary research on self-control?

16. Control versus Impulsiveness.

Research often looks at those who can exert conscious self-control versus those who seem overcome by impulsiveness. A classic study was conducted on children's ability to delay gratification. Who conducted the study and what strategies did the children use to get a valued treat?

17. Implications of Self-Control.

The study of children's delay of gratification found that when they distracted themselves they were able to delay their gratification best. Is that always the case? For example, when adults think of food, does that increase their eating? What sorts of strategies are useful in pain relief?

Part 4
Personality Development

*P*art 4, Personality Development, focuses on how the personality system grows and changes over time. Examining the growth and development of personality provides an important look at how the system integrates an individual's psychological functioning. Charting the growth of the parts of personality and their organization is part of the study of personality development, as is studying the increasing demands placed on the maturing system by biology and its surrounding society. Throughout the life span, an individual's personality will exhibit both continuity and change, and play a central role in helping the person survive and thrive.

Chapter 11

Personality Development in Childhood and Adolescence

How does personality begin? Do infants possess a sense of self? Personality development concerns the changes that personality undergoes over time. Infants vary from one another in their reactions, behaviors, and attachments to others. Family influences such as parenting style and family size may all impact the growing child. The child must also navigate the social world: forming friendships and developing a sense of what he or she can do. By adolescence, the young person is often attempting to establish an identity: a sense of who he or she is. These changes in personality from infancy forward are the departure point for the study of personality development.

- ## What Is Personality Development?

  Personality development is defined and several issues in its study are examined. The nature of research in personality development is compared to research in other areas of personality psychology. Personality can be viewed as developing according to stages or as developing more-or-less continuously.

- ## Do Infants Have a Personality?

  What kind of personality might an infant have? What are its limits? The section on infancy examines such issues as an infant's underlying physiological responsiveness (called temperament) and attachment to others.

- ## How Does the Young Child's Personality Develop?

  Early childhood is shaped in part by such environmental influences as the parents and their style of parenting, the individual's birth order, gender, and family size.

- ## What Are the Challenges of Middle Childhood?

  Personality in middle childhood is also influenced by—and influences—friends and peers.

- ## What Are Adolescents Doing?

  The final section of this chapter focuses on adolescent development. It examines the psychological aspects of puberty, and looks at the formation of identity and its influence on personality.

What Is Personality Development?

Questions of Personality Development

Each individual's development is the result of a wide range of unique influences—genes, parental practices, the social environment, and the individual's own reaction to these. Each individual's life is an "experiment of one" in the sense that influences are applied to a person's life in a way that can never be duplicated for someone else. Many children are reared in a good environment, but many are not.

In her memoir the writer Joelle Fraser describes her early upbringing in the counterculture of the 1960s. Her memoir is a carefully researched document based on her mother's diaries, her interviews with friends and relatives, and her own recollections. She took turns living with her mother's family on the Oregon coast, with her mother in the San Francisco Bay area, and with her father in Hawaii. Her father and mother had separated during her first year.

As an infant, Joelle lived in a commune-like environment, sometimes in disheveled apartments, sometimes in houseboats so rickety that their floors would cover with water at high tide. She experienced the 1960s drug culture as a toddler, taking hits of joints along with her parents' friends, drinking beer from a straw and wine from a plastic cup. Thereafter, her father's drinking intensified and she was surrounded by her mother's boyfriends and husbands. She writes: "Any man, every man, could be my father . . . I was loved. I had no bedtime. I fell asleep on laps and couches and on piles of coats, and sometimes a dog or another kid slept beside me. I was never alone" (Fraser, 2002, p. 20).

As she grew, her mother took various partners and husbands and she, in turn, experienced a series of fathers:

> My fathers, in chronological order: Ken, Michael, Mac, Tom, Brad, and Steve. That's how I keep track—I put them in order . . . Some fathers let me jump on the bed; others watched to make sure I made it properly. The older I got, the smarter I felt. I believed I was superior to the new man, that I knew something he didn't. I placed bets . . . on how long the guy would stick around." (Fraser, 2002, pp. 96–97)

She also developed an ability to withstand and thrive despite the fairly unique challenges she faced. She describes her capacity to cope in these words: "[B]y sixteen I'd become very good at taking reality and turning it just slightly so that it was seen at another, more pleasant angle—like a kaleidoscope. I could do this as long as I had to" (Fraser, 2002, p. 89). Describing a particularly difficult visit with her first (biological) father, who had just taken a lover not much older than herself, she noted, "That is how I got through those few days, by shifting the truth in my mind, by seeing what I wanted to see" (p. 89). Fraser's father died of liver failure, and she reread his one novel trying to understand him better. She grew up to become reconciled with her now more stable mother. She became acclaimed as a memoirist and successful essayist.

People who are able to withstand difficult upbringings possess a characteristic that psychologists call **resilience**. Resilience is the capacity to survive and thrive in response to tough circumstances (Rutter, 2000; Werner & Smith, 2001). Yet, like many of us, Frasier wonders about the effects of her early upbringing on who she is today. For example, she wonders if she keeps a greater distance from others because of it: "It became natural by the fourth or fifth father to withdraw a bit, keep my distance. This was wise because of the new rules and habits to adapt to" (Fraser, 2002, p. 89). Resilience appears to be more common than was once believed (Bonanno, Papa, & O'Neill, 2001).

Because each of us is a "case of one," understanding causes and effects in individual growth patterns is challenging and cannot necessarily be answered in a given instance. By examining and tracking the regularities in personality development across many people, however, consistent patterns can be identified and understood with greater certainty. Understanding these regularities in growth and development is what the science of personality development is about.

More formally, **personality development** refers to how the parts of personality and their organization grow and change throughout the lifespan. The study of personality development, like personality psychology more generally, emphasizes personality's major parts and their configurations. The developmental perspective focuses on how those major parts and their organization develop and change over time. For example, psychologists who study personality development examine broad trends in motivational and emotional responsiveness, called personality **temperament**, which many believe to be the building blocks of traits. For example, Joelle Fraser described her child-self as quiet and well-controlled (Fraser, 2002, p. 5). Such characteristics may be important in a person's ultimate capacity to thrive.

Resilience: The capacity of the individual child or adult to grow healthily and thrive in the context of negative social or environmental circumstances.

Personality Development: A sub-field of psychology concerned with how the parts of personality and their organization develop and change over time.

Temperament: Biobehavioral elements of the individual, such as tempo, activity level, and positive emotions that form building blocks of later traits and behavior.

Personality Types or Forms: A personality type (or form) representing a constellation of mental features such as traits or dynamics that occurs with enough frequency to form a category. Members of the group are different in their mental qualities from members of other groups.

Another way that developmental psychologists have examined personality growth is by dividing people into different groups based on their **personality types or forms** (Mayer, 1999). Throughout this book, we have examined dozens of parts and dynamics of personality. To now observe the development of each of these different parts and dynamics individually would require an entire second book at least. To simplify the research process, experts in personality development (as well as those in personality psychology more generally) have attempted instead to group people according to their different types of personalities (Caspi & Roberts, 1999). As we proceed in this chapter, some of those groupings will be examined.

To understand personality development, psychologists must take into account numerous influences on the system. They may study biological influences such as temperament, social setting concerns such as birth order and family size, social interactions such as friendship, and larger groups such as parents and peer groups. In Fraser's case, for example, she was influenced by the unique time period and culture in which she grew up—the 1960s youth rebellion and counterculture—as well as by a special family configuration of one mother but many fathers in succession, as well as by her unique constellation of friends and siblings. Figure 11.1 diagrams some of those influences in the by-now familiar systems framework structural model (e.g., Chapters 1, 2, and 8).

Dividing the Life Span

Another central point about personality development concerns the specific research approaches that are employed in the field. The single most distinguishing feature of research in personality development is that time is central to the research question. Time is reflected in such studies by intervals between testing, or by examining people

FIGURE 11.1

Personality Arranged among Its Developmental Influences
Here the familiar picture of personality amidst its surrounding systems is repeated. This time, developmental influences are displayed around the system.
Sources: After Mayer (1998); Peterson & Rollins (1987), Figure 3, p. 497.

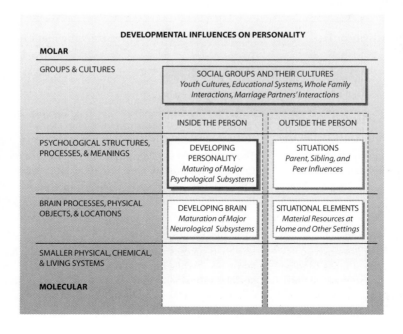

DEVELOPMENTAL INFLUENCES ON PERSONALITY

MOLAR

GROUPS & CULTURES	SOCIAL GROUPS AND THEIR CULTURES *Youth Cultures, Educational Systems, Whole Family Interactions, Marriage Partners' Interactions*	
	INSIDE THE PERSON	OUTSIDE THE PERSON
PSYCHOLOGICAL STRUCTURES, PROCESSES, & MEANINGS	DEVELOPING PERSONALITY *Maturing of Major Psychological Subsystems*	SITUATIONS *Parent, Sibling, and Peer Influences*
BRAIN PROCESSES, PHYSICAL OBJECTS, & LOCATIONS	DEVELOPING BRAIN *Maturation of Major Neurological Subsystems*	SITUATIONAL ELEMENTS *Material Resources at Home and Other Settings*
SMALLER PHYSICAL, CHEMICAL, & LIVING SYSTEMS		
MOLECULAR		

Developmental Stages: Periods of growth, arranged in a sequence, in which each period can be distinguished from the next according to a set of criteria.

at different ages, or different grade levels in school, or different historical periods. Whatever way time is involved, its importance distinguishes developmental research from other personality research in which measures are taken close together in time of people who are roughly the same age.

Developmental psychologists often divide the life span into time periods and discuss each time period in turn. Sometimes, such psychologists will speak of **developmental stages**—relatively fixed phases or units of development into which a person's growth can be divided. For example, Erik Erikson famously divided the human life span into eight "ages" or stages. There is probably no single best way of dividing personality development into stages. Moreover, some people might pass through a set of stages in a different order than others. That said, however, Erikson's outline provides a useful first overview of personal development.

Erikson's first five stages track the individual from infancy to adolescence. Each stage is associated with a view of the self or the world that is crucial for later development. In the stage approximately corresponding to infancy (I), for example, the development of trust is crucial—trust in one's parents, in other significant people, and in one's surroundings. This is followed in toddlerhood by the growth of a sense of autonomy; that is, the sense of being able to carry out activities independent of one's caretakers (stage II). In the next two stages of childhood (III and IV), Erikson saw the individual first developing a sense of initiative; that is, the capacity to carry out plans and goals in the context of learning social responsibilities, followed by developing a sense of industry; that is, the ability to accomplish things. In the transitional stage to adulthood (V), the young person enters adolescence and establishes a sense of identity—who one is, and how one relates to the world. See Table 11.1 for a synopsis of all

---

TABLE 11.1	**Erikson's Eight Stages of Development**	
Stage and Activity or Task	**Successful versus Problematic Resolutions**	
I. Infancy	**Trust versus ...**	**Mistrust**
The infant explores the world for the first time.	Parents provide a secure environment; the infant develops a sense of confidence and security.	Parents fail to support the exploring infant; the infant feels insecure and distrustful of the environment.
II. Toddlerhood/Early Childhood	**Autonomy versus ...**	**Shame**
The young person takes on responsibility in the family.	The child learns s/he can successfully control bodily functions (e.g., through toilet training) and social conduct.	The child develops an uncomfortable sense of being watched and judged negatively; she or he wishes to disappear before others' eyes.
III. Early Childhood	**Initiative versus ...**	**Guilt**
The young child develops goals and plans in the family, e.g., to entertain others, or diminish influence of a sibling.	The child successfully carries out some plans while being mindful of social responsibilities.	The child focuses on his or her shortcomings and inability to live up to social rules.

| TABLE 11.1 | (Continued) |
| | |

Stage and Activity or Task	Successful versus Problematic Resolutions	
IV. Middle/Late Childhood Aware of some day leaving the family, the child focuses on learning and developing skills for acting in the world.	**Industry versus . . .** The child develops a sense of industry and accomplishment—of competing successfully in the world beyond the family.	**Inferiority** The child may develop, when making such comparisons, a sense of inferiority—a felt inability to carry out the tasks and jobs that are required by parents, by schools, and by society at large.
V. Adolescence/Youth With the sexual and physical maturation of puberty, the child now looks much different, both to him or herself, and to others. The young person reevaluates who he or she is. To do this, the young person now looks for things with which to identify, with which to fall in love.	**Identity versus . . .** The youth must begin to understand and try out one or another social, occupational, political, and ethnic groups. To successfully traverse this stage, the individual must begin to understand the range of possibilities open to him or her.	**Role Diffusion** Other youths will experience an inability to develop an identity, and a conflicted, confused sense of who one is that results in a spreading of oneself over too many possibilities.
VI. Young Adulthood The young adult seeks intimacy and love with a partner. This love is based on the individual's capacity to be a productive member of society, and a sexually fulfilling companion to another person.	**Intimacy versus . . .** Members of the couple are able to discuss their roles and plans with one another, as well as their relationship with one another, and balance such needs against the needs and pressures of contemporary society.	**Isolation** The individual avoids contact and exists alone and in isolation from potential partners. Sometimes the individual has partners, but lives in isolation from the partner.
VII. Adulthood The healthy adult has created the opportunity for generativity—engaging with the world and adding to it so as to create a new, hopefully better generation.	**Generativity versus . . .** Generativity is most directly expressed through the creation of a new family. It can also be expressed through adding to society and enriching culture in many other ways, such as research, teaching, arts, and commerce.	**Stagnation** These individuals are stagnant, repeating their existence day by day with little growth and little giving, but rather, facing a more basic task or even ordeal to survive and just to get by.
VIII. Maturity The now-older person is able to understand his or her life in ways that were not possible before. Each life is only a specific, singular joining of life and history.	**Ego Integrity versus . . .** The individual develops a sense of self as a giving, productive person. It involves a love of the world that transcends the individual ego and extends to others in history, in the present, and in future generations.	**Despair** The individual fears death, and cannot accept his or her life. A thousand small disappointments create an apparent impossibility of starting over to an alternative route to integrity.

Source: Summarized from Erikson (1963).

of Erikson's eight stages of personality. Chapter 12, on adult development, will cover the portion of the life span relevant to Erikson's last three stages: the search for intimacy, for generativity, and for integrity.

Research Designs in Developmental Studies

Cross-Sectional Research Design: An approach to developmental research in which people of two or more different ages are compared in order to assess the influence of age on mental functioning.

Longitudinal Research Design: An approach to developmental research in which people are followed across time to see how they change or stay the same.

The empirical study of people's development across time can take one of two basic approaches. **Cross-sectional research designs** are those in which children (or adults) of two or more different ages are examined at a single point in time so as to compare and contrast their various personality characteristics. For example, preschoolers and fifth graders might be compared according to their understanding of friendship. Such a design tells us about relative differences in development at different ages. By contrast, **longitudinal research designs** follow the same people across a period of time—sometimes over a few years or even decades—examining the growth and maturation of the individuals within the group. Both methods are of substantial importance and value. Generally speaking, however, the longitudinal design is considered the gold standard in developmental research because it provides a researcher not only with a view of differences across different ages, but also with an understanding of how individuals or subgroups within the given longitudinal sample develop (Block & Block, 1980). Needless to say, longitudinal research is challenging, difficult, and requires great patience. Nonetheless, a great deal of it has been carried out and this chapter and the next are the richer for it. We can begin our studies of personality development with the infant personality.

Do Infants Have a Personality?

The Infant's Challenge

Does a newborn possess a personality? At the outset of this book, personality was described as the developing organization of the important parts of a person's psychology. But does the infant's mind possess enough organization—or even parts—for there to be a personality? William James, the founder of American psychology, described the infant's new world as "one great blooming buzzing confusion" (James, 1890/1950, p. 488). If James were correct and the newborn's mind were literally all confusion, the infant could legitimately be said to have no personality. Rather, the infant might be in a state of preparation for personality, or, perhaps, pre-personality.

Since James wrote, however, we have learned that the newborn brain and mind already possess substantial organization. At a minimum, that mind is prepared for social contact. Newborn infants presented with sets of faces and abstract patterns in the laboratory, for example, will gaze nearly twice as long at the face-like image than at similar nonface images (Umilta, Simion, & Valenza, 1996). Infants also prefer to look at objects that are about eight to twelve inches away—the approximate distance of the nursing infant's eyes to its mother's eyes (Maurer & Maurer, 1988).

Social Smile: A broad smile produced by six-month-old infants. Evolutionary psychologists believe the smile evolved to encourage parental attention.

Between six and ten weeks, the infant reliably produces a broad grin called the **social smile**, accompanied by cooing, both of which encourage parental care in return (Sroufe & Waters, 1976). Brief facial expressions of anger arise during the first

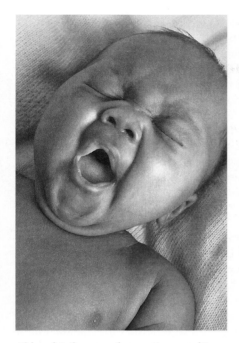

Although infants may be more interested in eating, sleeping, and cuddling than in psychology, certain building blocks of their personalities are already in place.

two months and can be elicited toward the end of the first year in response to frustrations, such as removing a sucking object from an infant's mouth; these brief angry responses increase in consistency in response to frustration over the first two years of life (Sternberg & Campos, 1990). By about eight months, the now crawling infant develops stranger anxiety. When the infant sees an unfamiliar face, he or she becomes distressed and seeks a familiar adult (Kagan, 1984). To be sure, much of what the infant does involves eating and sleeping. Yet, personality—in the form of preparedness for social interaction—is developing right from the beginning. Increasingly through this developmental time, the infant interacts with others, explores, and learns.

There is little evidence of much sense of self during the first year. Put a six-month-old in front of a mirror, for example, and the infant will reach and touch the image in the mirror as if it belonged to another child. Between fifteen months and eighteen months, however, the child recognizes the image in the mirror as his or her own. How do researchers know? When researchers covertly put rouge on the nose of the six-month-old, it goes unnoticed in the mirror. The fifteen-to-eighteen-month-old, however, will reach toward his or her own nose: there is both something expected about one's own face by that age, and a recognition of the alterations in it (Buttersworth, 1992; Gallup & Suarez, 1986). Such self-recognition requires considerable cognitive capacity. Across species, chimpanzees and orangutans are the only other animals that can do this. Reflecting the cognitive demands involved even for humans, infants who suffer from Trisomy 21 and its accompanying mental retardation are able to accomplish the same task, but not until they are three or four years of age (Mans, Cicchetti, & Sroufe, 1978).

To be sure, the two-year-old toddler possesses a limited view of the world in many respects. For months, the infant may not recognize that parts of its body are its own. More generally, when the infant loses sight of an object, it may believe that object has ceased to exist and stop looking for it. Is it also confused, then, about the continued disappearance and reappearance of its mother? The psychoanalyst Melanie Klein (1935/1975) suggested that the infant may imagine multiple mothers, some good, some bad, and some in between. Some have suggested that these multiple images of the mother may provide a developmental basis for the adult phenomenon of splitting, in which a person alternately idealizes and devalues a loved partner. In some forms of psychopathology this split image can become so extreme that it is as if the person is interacting with multiple partners (e.g., Siegel & Spellman, 2002). What keeps severe splitting out of most relationships, it is said, is that most healthy children later develop an integrated picture of the multiple images of the mother. It seems equally reasonable to suppose, however, that the infant simply accepts appearances and disappearances of the mother as normal without specially inquiring into their meaning beyond the temporary loss of security.

Babies are such a nice way to start people.

Don Herald

The infant must operate within a context in which there are frustrations, fears, failures to meet its needs, and, hopefully, lots of hugs, smiles, and kisses, to smooth the way toward a promising future. Recall that Erik Erikson believed that if the parents understood the infant, could meet its needs well enough, and kindly encouraged the infant to explore, then the infant would most likely end up with a sense of security. If, on the other hand, the parents neglected the infant and his or her emotional needs, then the infant would end up insecure in its environment.

Whereas secure infants will learn about the world around them and begin to form connections to the parents and others, the insecure infant will be more bound to the parent and less able to explore. Emerging parts of the personality will determine the nature of those interactions, explorations, and learning.

Infant Temperament

Temperament refers to the basic motivational and emotional building blocks that make up personality traits (as described earlier in this chapter). Temperament is often described according to a range of customary responses emitted by the developing infant. It may involve a child's activity level, physiological responsiveness, tempo, and emotional reactivity. There is a belief that the basic temperamental styles exhibited by the newborn will gradually differentiate into recognizable adult personality traits (Finch & Graziano, 2001). For example, the infant who responds to a toy with agitated motor movements and begins to cry may be less happy and more shy growing up than an infant who exhibits a different pattern (Kagan, 2003). Temperament researchers attend to a variety of cues as to an infant's growing personality (Mebert, 1991).

Three examples of temperament research can help illustrate some of the questions addressed in this area. The first instance involves the work of the physicians Thomas, Chess, and Birch (1970), who were interested in the challenges that parents faced with their children. Thomas and his colleagues suggested that infants varied along behavioral dimensions that fell into motor, cognitive, and emotional areas. Three dimensions included such specific areas as activity level, rhythmicity, distractibility, and adaptability. The characteristics shown in Table 11.2 formed the core of their measurement approach. This research has often been said to have begun modern temperament research.

The researchers then divided groups of children into "easy," "slow to warm up," and "difficult" based on such dimensions. Table 11.2 shows those three designations. For example, the easy children are very regular in their rhythms, very adaptable, and mildly reactive and positive in their moods. The difficult children are described as irregular in their rhythms, slowly adaptable, and intensely reactive and negative in their moods.

Thomas and colleagues (1970) took ratings of 141 children, drawn from 85 upper middle-class families of business people and professionals, and followed those children from birth, for over a decade. About 65 percent of the children could be classified into these three groups of easy, slow to warm up, and difficult. The remainder could not be reliably classified in that way. The researchers found considerable consistency as temperament gave way to personality traits—particularly when the temperament was extreme. For example, here Donald provides a possible example of a difficult child, due to his "extremely high activity level" from birth onward.

	The Easy Child Is ...	The Slow to Warm up Child Is ...	The Difficult Child Is ...
TABLE 11.2 **Three Temperament Styles**			
The Child's Characteristics			
Motor/Motivational · Activity · Rhythmicity · Approachability	somewhat to moderately high in activity, very regular in eating and sleeping, and approachable	typically low to moderate in activity, and varied in rhythmicity of cycles	variable in activity, very irregular in eating and sleeping cycles, and tends to withdraw
Cognitive · Distractibility · Attention	variable in how distractible or attentive s/he is.	variable in how distractible or attentive s/he is	variable in how distractible or attentive s/he is
Emotional · Reactivity · Mood	mild or moderate in reactions, and typically positive in mood	mildly reactive, and slightly negative in mood	intensely emotionally reactive, and negative in mood
Parenting Issues			
The Parents' Challenge	relatively easy to parent, and when mistakes are made, the child can adjust readily	somewhat easy to handle, but somewhat lacking in warmth in relationships	handling the child is an issue from the start; requires skillful handling and patience

Source: Adapted from Thomas, Chess, & Birch (1970).

At three months, his parents reported, he wriggled and moved about a great deal while asleep in his crib. At six months he "swam like a fish" while being bathed. At 12 months he still squirmed constantly while he was being dressed or washed. At 15 months he was "very fast and busy"; his parents found themselves "always chasing after him." At two years he was "constantly in motion, jumping and climbing." At three he would "climb like a monkey and run like an unleashed puppy." In kindergarten his teacher reported humorously that he would "hang from the walls and climb on the ceiling." By the time he was seven Donald was encountering difficulty in school because he was unable to sit still long enough to learn anything and disturbed the other children by moving rapidly about the classroom. (Thomas, Chess, & Birch, 1970, p. 104)

Such observations were important because they marked a first modern recognition of the importance of infant differences in responsiveness. These infants will be revisited later in this chapter.

A second example of temperament research reveals the rewards of an in-depth examination of infant responsiveness in temperament. Jerome Kagan, Nancy Snidman, and their colleagues (e.g., Kagan & Snidman, 1991) studied a number of children from infancy to middle childhood, taking dozens of physical, psychophysical, and behavioral measures potentially related to a dimension of shyness versus uninhibitedness.

Harry Harlow's infant monkeys preferred to cling to the comfort of a cloth mother, even while drawing milk from a wire-mesh mother. Such results convinced scientists that attachment itself was a powerful need, apart from such necessities as food and water.

In one series of studies, four-month-old infants were put through a series of tasks, such as having the mother look at the child in a soothing way but not speak, looking at novel toy objects that were sometimes fun but at other times mildly menacing (e.g., a robot face), or listening to nonsense syllables spoken at different volumes. The infants showed reliable individual differences in response to such situations. Some showed increased sucking or kicking in response to threat, and readiness to cry in response to threatening stimuli, whereas others were relatively unresponsive. Coders watched videos of the infants and rated their motoric restlessness and how often they cried. The overall fearfulness (e.g., high fretting and crying) at four months predicted the average number of fear responses at both nine and fourteen months, as they begin to differentiate into shy, average, and uninhibited groups (Kagan & Snidman, 1991). Among Caucasian infants (with which most of their research was conducted) about 25 percent were classified as uninhibited and sociable, about 10 percent of the group were inhibited, shy, and cautious, and the remainder fell in-between. This research is important because it provides experimental observations and measures of infant temperament. Kagan and Snidman's groups of children developed across time and will be examined later in this chapter.

A third example of temperament research is important because it allows for a connection between temperament measures and adult personality traits. Rothbart and her colleagues (e.g., Rothbart, 1981; Rothbart, Ahadi, & Evans, 2000; Rothbart & Mauro, 1990) examined three broad dimensions of temperament that they refer to as surgency, negative affect, and affliation. The first, Surgency dimension, describes infants with high activity level, smiling and laughing, high-intensity pleasure, and approach. The second, Negative affectivity dimension, includes distress in response to limits, fearfulness, sadness, and high reactivity to stimuli. The third, Affliliation dimension, involves orienting toward others, calmness, soothability, and cuddliness. We also will examine how these dimensions map on the Big Five personality traits later in this chapter. First, however, it is worth examining some other personality characteristics that arise in the infant and toddler.

Attachment Patterns

Infants and young children hold their parents close for comfort; when their parents aren't available, they may seek soft cuddly toys, blankets, and other objects to which they have become attached. There may be a direct bond between the way the infants cuddle with their parent(s) and the way infants comfort themselves with blankets and teddy bears. Soft, cuddly toys are particularly important in the West, where babies often sleep in a separate room from their parents at night; such cuddly toys are less common in the East, where infants and their parents often sleep in the same room (Hong & Townes, 1976; Morelli et al., 1992).

This drive for comfort from parents and from other objects of attachment is a fundamental one in human beings and in other primate species. In the 1970s, University of Wisconsin psychologist Harry Harlow had been following the standard practice of separating baby chimps early from their mothers for reasons of experimental control and sanitation. He noticed that these same separated chimps became closely attached to their blankets, perhaps, he reasoned, because they missed their mothers. Other scientists were skeptical. Many behaviorists of the day contended we were attached to our parents primarily because they fed us and cared for us, rather than due to any independent emotional bond.

To test which was the case, Harlow created two surrogate mothers: one made of terrycloth and the other made of wire. The wire mother had a milk bottle inside it, with a feeding tube that extended to the outside. When presented with the choice, infant monkeys clung to the terrycloth mothers, and, when they were hungry, reached their mouths awkwardly over to the bottles in the wire mothers so as to feed. They also returned to those terrycloth mothers when they became anxious. Harlow's work contradicted a common behavioral notion of the time, that the parental bond was a consequence of an association between parents and feeding. Other evidence contradicting the behavioral view included that many children become closely attached to their fathers and other close relatives who hadn't regularly fed them.

World War II saw a number of separations between children and their parents. The well-being of infants in orphanages also became a matter of concern. Various studies suggested that infants without steady caretakers to which they could attach were at a developmental disadvantage (e.g., Skodak & Skeels, 1949; Spitz, 1946). Even when children are with their parents, poor attachment bonds can impact their development. Although controversial, some researchers maintain that some instances of "failure to thrive" babies—infants who stop growing during infancy due to a reduced intake of food—are a consequence of poor parent-child attachment, including neglect and abuse (e.g., Ward, Lee, & Lipper, 2000). (A larger group of these infants, who are diagnosed with "Feeding Disorder in Infancy," have identified gastrointestinal problems.)

Attachment Theory: A theory proposed by John Bowlby that there exists a special mental system in infants responsible for establishing secure relationships with a caretaker, which continues to exert control over relationships as the indvidual matures.

John Bowlby (1958; 1988) examined orphans in England during and after World War II. He developed **attachment theory**, a theory about the existence of an **attachment system** in each person that is responsible for modulating the important relationship bonds the individual has with others around them (Bowlby, 1988). Bowlby suggested that the sometimes impaired development of children in orphanages, and in similar conditions, was due to the lack of a close emotional bond between the infant and the caretaker.

Attachment System: The system responsible for establishing an infant's secure relationship with a caretaker, which continues to exert control over relationships as the individual matures.

According to attachment theory, newborns begin developing characteristic relationships with their mothers or other significant caretaker almost immediately. Each infant has an attachment system that is programmed by these early relationships and has as its goal the establishment of a secure relationship with a caretaker. In order to become secure, the infant must have interactions with individuals who will care for it sufficiently. These relationships with (relatively) powerful primary caretakers are called **attachment patterns**. But not everyone develops the same patterns and Bowlby found that infants in orphanages faced particularly challenging circumstances in which to develop healthy attachments.

Attachment Pattern: A distinctive relationship an infant can form with its mother or other primary caretaker.

Attachment theory might have remained only a theory had it not been for a classic series of studies by Mary Ainsworth and her colleagues (Ainsworth et al., 1978). To

Strange Situation: An experimental situation in which attachment patterns are measured. A mother sits in a playroom and the infant is evaluated according to how far s/he will separate from her. The mother leaves briefly, a stranger comes in and leaves, and the other returns, while the infant's reactions are monitored.

identify attachment patterns, Ainsworth and her colleagues took recordings of infant-mother interactions in the home. From those naturalistic observations they then created a small drama called the **strange situation** that infants could undergo in a laboratory setting. Mother-child behavior at home and in the laboratory were similar (Bretherton & Waters, 1985, p. 15). The patterns of attachment Ainsworth and her colleagues observed in the first year are still largely present at the age of six, and may be somewhat stable through adulthood (Bretherton & Waters, 1985, p. 19; Hazan & Shaver, 1994). Ainsworth divided those attachments patterns into three types that a person might develop: secure attachment, anxious-avoidant, and anxious-resistant (Bowlby, 1988).

To understand the three patterns, it first helps to consider the general outline of the strange situation. Basically, it consists of a standard set of interaction episodes the infant experiences: an infant is placed in a playroom with its mother. After some time, a stranger enters the room and the mother leaves. Finally, the mother returns. During these and other stages, researchers observe the interaction between mother and child, focusing specifically on how the child responds to the reunion with its mother.

Secure Attachment: A relationship in which an individual has a reliable bond with another person that allows for safe separation and independence, coupled with comfortable, welcomed returns to the caretaker.

Secure attachment in the infant-mother pair has a distinctive, and desirable, quality. The mother consistently attends to the infant and responds to its feelings accurately and sympathetically. In addition, the mother attends to the infant's play and encourages it when it has difficulty. In the laboratory, such infants appear to tolerate their mothers' absence better than others do. And, when the mother returns, she and her child greet one another warmly and directly. More generally, secure attachment refers to a relationship pattern in which the individual feels that other people are comforting, important, and dependable.

Anxious-Resistant Attachment: A relationship in which an individual has an uncertain or nervous bond with another person that limits independence and is coupled with somewhat fretful, yet welcomed returns to the caretaker.

Anxious-resistant attachment in the infant-mother pairs present a mixed picture. Although the mothers here sometimes attend to their infants, they do not do so with consistency. Their infants, upon separation, are less able to tolerate being by themselves. They appear unsure about how they will next be treated by their mother. As a result, when the mother returns, the infants are very tentative about approaching her. It is as if they know they may be rejected. The quality of their attachment to their mothers is therefore fundamentally different from that of the more securely attached infants. More generally, anxious-resistant attachment refers to a relationship pattern in which the individual views others as important, but not always comforting, and somewhat unpredictable rather than dependable.

Anxious-Avoidant Attachment: A relationship in which an individual has an uncertain or nervous bond with another person that limits independence and is coupled with somewhat ambivalent, uncertain return to the caretaker.

In **anxious-avoidant attachment** in the infant-mother pairs, the mothers seem uninterested in their infants and seem to rebuff them consistently. As a consequence, the infant doesn't seek out the caretaker, but rather, seems to expect rejection. More generally, the anxious-avoidant attachment pattern describes an infant or growing person who perceives caretakers to be rejecting and nonnurturing. Anxious-avoidant-attached individuals attempt to deny the importance of others and avoid them; at the same time, the lack of a dependable other may render them anxious about those contacts with others that they do form.

The attachment pattern one develops with a parent seems somewhat independent of temperament. In one study, for example, one hundred temperamentally difficult infants were randomly assigned to one of two conditions. In the experimental condition, mothers were taught how to respond to their infant's needs in an empathic, responsive fash-

Children have never been very good at listening to their elders, but they have never failed to imitate them.
James Baldwin

ion. In the control condition, mothers received no such training. By the end of their first year of life, two-thirds of the infants with trained mothers were securely attached; compared to less than one third of the control group infants; moreover, differences between the groups were still observed at age 3 and a half (van den Boom, 1995).

Adult attachment patterns partly overlap childhood patterns for some people. If you would like to test your own attachment pattern, try the "Test Yourself" feature.

How Does the Young Child's Personality Develop?

The Young Child's Self-Concept

Beyond toddlerhood, during the period from roughly two-and-a-half to five years of age, the young child faces a new set of demands—and its personality and mental capacities will emerge in more powerful forms to address them. Freud characterized the young child as involved in a series of give-and-take interactions with the parent. The most central of these interactions involve issues of social versus self-control, for example, parent-child interactions surrounding toilet training (Freud, 1905, pp. 186–187). Similarly, the psychoanalyst Erik Erikson believed the child is expected to become more responsible for his or her actions more generally during this time. Among the child's growing responsibilities are the ability to control his or her own bodily functions, but also to control one's own behavior in regard to feelings and actions more generally, so as to develop a sense of autonomy and self-control. For Erikson, a sense of autonomy develops as the young child understands that he or she is successfully mastering the capacity for self-control and is able, gradually, to exercise such control independent of parental urgings. When self-control fails, shame may emerge in response to being watched and judged unsuccessfully.

Profound cognitive changes that help to bring about an explicit sense of a continuous self also take place between the ages of three and four. For one, children are able to develop permanent memories of life events for the first time. Events before about age three are part of what Freud called "infantile amnesia." The young child cannot remember what he or she was thinking or doing at an earlier age. For example, preschoolers at a daycare center were quickly ushered from the building one day after a fire alarm was sounded in response to a burning popcorn maker. Seven years later, those who had been four or five years of age could recall the fire alarm and what caused it. Those who were three years old at the time, however, could not remember the cause of the alarm and often mistakenly recalled being outside when the alarm rang (Pillemer, Picariello, & Pruett, 1995). One explanation of infantile amnesia is that the child's immature understanding of personal events may leave behind a confused toddler-eyed memory that is too different from more mature thinking to be retrieved. From this perspective, asking a four-year-old to recall early events is like expecting a new-generation computer to read from a disk formatted by an obsolete computer system (Loftus & Kaufman, 1992).

With a growing command of language and memory the child is able to describe himself or herself in some considerable detail. One child recounted:

> I'm 3 years old and I live in a big house with my mother and father and my brother, Jason, and my sister, Lisa. I have blue eyes and a kitty that is orange

Test Yourself: The Adult Attachment Style

This Adult Attachment Style scale sometimes is employed to classify a person's attachments as secure, avoidant, anxious/ambivalent, or disoriented/disorganized. Adult attachment may reflect childhood attachment styles,[*] but see below for caveats after you take the test.

Test Items	1 = Not at all characteristic 5 = Very characteristic	1	2	3	4	5
1. I do not often worry about being abandoned.						
2. I often worry that my partner does not really love me.						
3. I find others are reluctant to get as close as I would like.						
4. I often worry my partner will not want to stay with me.						
5. I want to merge completely with another person.						
6. My desire to merge sometimes scares people away.						
7. I find it relatively easy to get close to others.						
8. I do not often worry about someone getting too close to me.						
9. I am somewhat uncomfortable being close to others.						
10. I am nervous when anyone gets too close.						
11. I am comfortable having others depend on me.						
12. Often, love partners want me to be more intimate than I feel comfortable being.						

First reverse score item 1 and then add up items 1 through 6. That is your "Anxiety in Relationships" score. Next, reverse score 9 and 10 and add up items 7 through 12. That is your "Closeness in Relationships" score. The means of these scales are 16.2 and 21.2, respectively. Brennen, Clark, and Shaver (1998) suggest that the two dimensions of the Collins and Read scale can be used as a suggestion of a person's attachment styles. If you are below average in anxiety and above average in closeness, then you might be characterized in part by a "Secure Relationship" style. If you are above average in anxiety and above average in closeness, then your style might be characterized as an "Anxious/Ambivalent" attachment style. If you are low in closeness and low in anxiety then your style might be characterized as an "Avoidant" attachment style. If you are low in closeness and high in anxiety, then your style might be characterized as a "Disoriented/Disorganized" attachment style (a category developed by Brennan et al., 1998).

[*]This scale only measures self-reported attachment style. The norms are based on a small sample of college students, and adult attachment has only a modest relationship to infant and child attachment (and could be influenced, for example, by your mood at the moment). For those reasons, one's measured attachment style should be taken as one indication among many, rather than as a definite classification.

Sources: Collins & Read (1990), Table 2; Hazen & Shaver (1987). Reprinted with permission of the American Psychological Association.

and a television in my own room. I know all of my ABC's, listen: A, B, C, D, E, F, G, H, I, J, K, L, M, N, O, P, Q, R, S, T, U, V, W, X, Y, Z. I can run real fast. I like pizza and I have a nice teacher at preschool. I can count up to 100, want to hear me? I love my dog Skipper. I can climb to the top of the jungle gym, I'm not scared! I'm never scared! I'm always happy. I have brown hair and I go to preschool. I'm really strong. I can lift this chair, watch me!" (Harter, 1999, p. 37)

For more on a young child's sense of self, see the Case Study box.

Case Study

Jay's Self-Understanding

Jay is a firstborn young boy whose conversations were recorded between two and three years of age as part of a larger study of early development of the self in nine children from middle-income families (Wolf & Gardner, 1981). One focus of the study was the representation of self as it is revealed through conversation.

We first meet Jay just before he is about to turn two. His parents want him to show a guest how he can now count pennies. Jay, however, has mischief in mind and instead, he scatters the pennies his parents laid out for him with his hand. This happens a couple of times, and then, as he checks his parents' reaction, he takes his security blanket, which he calls "Ni ni" and puts it over his hand, and announces, "Ni ni did it." His parents laugh, and ask Ni ni to count the pennies, but Jay answers "Nooo" in his own voice (Wolf, 1990, p. 186). Such a simple exchange illustrates children's imagination, along with their attempts to manipulate the facts about a self—about who really is or is not making mischief.

By the middle of his second year, Jay has developed ideas about his present self and his earlier self, and compares the two and their abilities. For example, one afternoon he has brought home a new picture he has drawn, of "a Daddy man," and asks his mother to "Put it on a 'frigerator." Pointing to an older picture he drew, he says, "Take that one down. It's old. It's

yuck." His mother objects, "I like it. You just did it when you were little." But he replies, "I was little, yuck. Not now. Do the new one." (Wolf, 1990, p. 192).

By his third year, such a self also can convey important internal information about feelings. His father is recollecting how Jay fed the goats at the zoo. Together they recall how the goat put its mouth on Jay's hand to take food he was holding there. His father remarks, "You were a big boy, huh? Very brave." To which Jay responds, "Scary." (Wolf, 1990, p. 189).

By three years of age Jay's self reflects different roles. Sometimes he is himself, sometimes an observer, sometimes an imaginary character who comments on what he is doing. Jay was building with blocks, trying to construct an uneven wall of a building that might serve as stairs. He remarks, "I can't do it, I don't know how." Then, he turns the wall-like structure into a building. After some intervening play, he returns to the blocks, and tries to stack them. He takes a small toy figure and puts it at the top of the wall; he says in the figure's voice, "Hey, come on up here." He then has a second figure try to climb the wall. When the wall topples over, the second figure critiques the endeavor (and rather harshly!) "Hey, you dummy, that didn't work, you make dumb stairs" (Wolf, 1990, p. 198). The narration may serve to help clarify what is happening so that a child can learn for the next time.

Self-Control as a Part of Temperament

Recall that some temperament researchers describe infants in terms of their surgency (positive affect), negative affect, and social affiliation (cuddliness). Consistent with the idea that early childhood is a time in which self-control is important, parents now begin to regularly notice and reflect on their childrens' self-control as a new dimension of temperament (Miech, Essex, & Goldsmith, 2001; Rothbart & Putnam, 2002). By early childhood, self-control becomes central to coping with the child—and surpasses even affiliation (cuddliness) in its importance (Rothbart & Putnam, 2002). From the parent's perspective, the young child who is able to be calmed and soothed, and who can respond to parental control by augmenting it with self-control, is an easier child to cope with than a different child who is nonresponsive to social demands.

Parents and the Family Context

The family, and in particular, parents, continue to exert their influence on the young child. Their influence is, in part, a function of the family structure in which the child lives. A recent United States Census Bureau Survey indicated the wide variety of living arrangements that U.S. children experience (see Figure 11.2). There are 50.1 million children (71%) who live with both parents, 16.3 million (23%) who live with their mothers only, 1.8 million (3%) who live with their fathers only, and the remaining 2.6 million (3–4%) live in other arrangements. Among that last 3 to 4 percent, very roughly, 2 percent live with other relatives—chiefly grandparents—and the remaining 2 percent live with nonrelatives or in institutions. The living configuration and, chiefly, the impact of divorce (and other parental loss) can influence a child considerably. As can, simply, parenting styles.

As the infant grows the parent(s)' roles come into play as they set examples and control the child's behavior and environment. But what is it, exactly, that parents do?

FIGURE 11.2

Living Arrangements of Children in the United States (1996) Children live in many different family and nonfamily environments, which influence their development in different ways.

Source: Fields (2001).

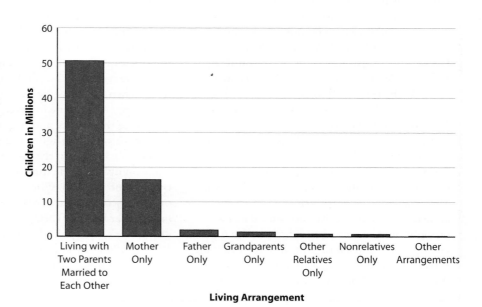

Disciplinary Crossroads

Cultural Influences on Child Personality

Recently, researchers have become interested in how the sense of self may vary in different cultures (e.g., Triandis, 2001). Twin studies indicate that children's beliefs in many instances are shaped by culture more than by genes (Segal, 1999). One contrast of importance is between Asian collectivist societies such as China and Korea, and more individualistic countries such as the United States (Han, Leichtman, & Wang, 1998; Wang & Leichtman, 2000; Wang, Leichtman, & Davies, 2000). Studying three-year-old children who spoke roughly comparable amounts across cultures, Leichtman, Wang, and their colleagues found some important differences.

Chinese mothers, when compared to Americans, made more comments and asked more questions regarding moral standards, social norms, and behavioral expectations. (Mom: "Tell Mom, when a Mom takes her child to cross the street, where should they look?" Child: "Look to their left and right. Look at the zebra lines.") American mothers, on the other hand, made more comments about personal needs and preferences, judgments or opinions. (Mom: "Is there anything else about camping that you really liked?" Child: "Swimming.")

Mirroring the mothers' talk, Chinese children spoke more about social standards whereas American children spoke more about independence. (Wang, Leichtman, & Davies, 2000, p. 170).

The increased social embeddedness of the child's self-concept in collectivist cultures is illustrated in the fictional stories six-year-old children from both cultures told about getting lost in a store. Both stories end with the children reuniting with their parents, but in ways that differ markedly in their sense of interdependence and autonomy. The American girl's story began with her getting lost and playing happily in the toy department of a store. It concludes with her journey from the department store:

> And then the little girl, she had a map in her pocket and she took it out and she found her way home. And she walked inside [home] and there was nobody there and she decided to stay anyway. And then her Mommy came home. And then they had dinner and they went to sleep. (Wang & Leichtman, 2000, p. 1340)

The Chinese girl describes the same moment of discovering she is lost in somewhat different terms, with her crying, and then being discovered:

> . . . an uncle policeman came and asked, "Little girl, what happened with you?" The little girl said, "My Mom and I got lost from each other." The policeman said, "What's the telephone number of your house?" She said, "Our number is 2929335876." Then the uncle policeman made a call. Five minutes later a taxi came. Mom said, "Where were you just now? Why didn't you follow mom?" The little girl felt very ashamed, said, "Sorry, Mom, I'll follow you next time." They thanked the uncle policeman, and they went home. (Wang & Leichtman, 2000, p. 1340)

Researches such as these suggest that character formation probably diverges across cultures in substantial ways at a very young age.

In a series of pioneering studies, Diana Baumrind (1971; 1973) observed preschool children at home with their parents, at school in interaction with their mothers, and at school on their own. Baumrind distinguished between two fundamental dimensions of parenting: **nurturance** and **control**. Nurturance concerned the degree to which the parents supported, cared for, and provided love for the child. Control concerned the degree to which the parents influenced the child, dictating what the child must do, and administering rewards and punishments. Depending on whether parents were low on both dimensions, high on them both, or high on one or the other, four parental types can be identified, as shown in Figure 11.3 (Maccoby & Martin, 1983).

Authoritative parents are both nurturing and controlling. These parents express care for their young children while at the same time guiding their behavior through gentle discipline and rule-setting. As their children grow, they guide through setting examples, reasoning, and continued setting of limits. **Authoritarian parents** are also controlling, but tend to exercise control through setting rules and enforcing them through discipline. These parents employ relatively little explanation or justification of their goals, and are lower in nurturance more generally. **Permissive (or Indulgent) parents** are highly nurturing, expressing love and caring, but generally fail to set limits or exercise control over their children. Finally, **Uninvolved (or Neglectful) parents** neither express caring for their children nor set limits or exercise discipline.

Parenting styles emerge as an interaction between parents and children, with the parenting influencing the child and vice versa. Certain types of parenting and types of children generally appear to go together. In general terms, authoritarian parents use more aggression and violence for control. In turn, they raise children who themselves are more violent, have poorer peer relations, and who are at risk for being bullied (Pettit et al., 1996). Children of authoritarian parents also suffer from lower self-esteem, less empathy for others, and poorer adjustment to school (e.g., Krevans & Gibbs, 1996). On average, children of permissive parents are similar to those of authoritarian parents in the sense of a relative lack of social responsibility and lack of independence (Baumrind, 1973).

The authoritative parent, by contrast, is more likely to raise children who are relatively friendly with peers and cooperative with adults. Such children tend to be better self-controlled, independent, and more achievement motivated (Baumrind, 1973). As children of authoritative parents reach adolescence, they exhibit greater academic performance, more prosocial behavior, and less involvement with substance abuse than others (Radziszewska et al., 1996).

Perhaps the most problematic parenting style of all is the uninvolved or neglectful parent (Maccoby & Martin, 1983). These individuals seem uninvolved with their role as parents and emotionally distant from their children. As their children grow, these parents tend to neglect them—having few conversations with their children, ignoring their activities, and knowing little about what is going on in their lives. Their children seem to be at greater risk of lower self-esteem, lower levels of some cognitive capacities, and at risk of higher levels of aggression, maladjustment, and drug abuse (Steinberg et al., 1994; Weiss & Schwartz, 1996).

Whatever parenting style they employ, parents are agents of cultural transmission. They communicate to their children what the culture is, the role of parents within it, and what is expected of the child. Cultural differences such as those between more individualistic Western and more collectivist Eastern societies can shape

FIGURE 11.3

Styles of Parenting
Parenting can be conceived of as varying on two dimensions: nurturance and control. Together these define four styles of parenting.

Source: Adapted from Maccoby & Martin (1983), Figure 2. Reproduced with permission of John Wiley & Sons, Inc.

		Nurturance	
		Responsive, Child Centered	Rejecting, Parent Centered
Control	Demanding, High on Control	Authoritative	Authoritarian
	Undemanding, Low on Control	Permissive	Uninvolved

> **How children survive being Brought Up amazes me.**
> Malcolm S. Forbes

how children develop. In many of the cultures of the West, children are encouraged to be independent and autonomous. In many of the collectivist cultures of the East, children are rather encouraged to be part of the family and larger social groups. Such teachings influence how children perceive social situations and how they act in those situations. An example of such differences in how a child responds to being lost is illustrated in the Disciplinary Crossroads box. Moreover, as cultures themselves change, so do the teachings that are conveyed by parents. For example, mother-child interactions within Native American cultures have changed as Western-style education is introduced to those cultures, reflecting how the cultural influences in regard to schooling, in turn, affect home life (Chavajay & Rogoff, 2002).

Developmental psychologists have generally assumed that parents exert strong influences on development. Not everyone agrees, however. Some of the controversies over this assumption are highlighted in the Inside the Field box.

Family Size and Birth Order

Family Size

Another aspect of the family context is the number of siblings a child has, and the birth order of a child. Does family size or birth order influence personality and later attainment? Sociologists have long noted that the larger the number of siblings, the lower the academic attainment of the children in a family, on average. In larger families, each child has available a smaller fraction of the overall family resources. As a consequence, parents may more often be forced into non-optimal parental styles such as taking authoritarian, permissive, or neglectful approaches, because of the greater demands on their time (Steelman et al., 2002). Children in such families perform with a slightly lower level of cognitive ability. Larger families in which there is greater spacing between siblings show less of the negative impact of family size. When children are spaced out, the parents may benefit from taking rests in-between, and the later-born children may benefit from the greater financial resources of the family at that time (Kidwell, 1981; Powell & Steelman, 1995).

Birth Order

Beyond number of siblings, there may be further effects of birth order on personality. In the 1800s, Sir Francis Galton, an individual-differences researcher with special interests in intelligence, argued for the relative eminence of the firstborn. The psychoanalytically oriented Alfred Adler (1931) mused about the firstborn's hostility over being "dethroned" by later-borns, and suggested that the middle child was psychologically healthiest. Yet, reliable findings in these areas have been hard to come by, and the matter pretty much rested there until the end of the twentieth century (Ersnt & Angst, 1983; Rodgers, 2001).

At the century's close, Frank Sulloway (1996) advanced a new theory that appeared to explain at least some psychological data. In Sulloway's view, siblings compete among one another for limited resources in the family. To do so, each individual must find a niche for him or herself. In this struggle, firstborns are at an advantage relative to later-borns as they are already known to their parents, have had access to resources first, and are larger and stronger than their newborn siblings. Sulloway points out that in some animal species, parents and firstborns may team up and punish, or even kill, later-borns as a means of preserving their precious resources (Sulloway, 1996, pp. 60–65).

In human families, firstborn children, because they are on the scene earliest, often identify more closely with their parents than with other siblings. As a consequence, such firstborns may be more comfortable with parental power relative to later children. As they grow, this comfort may lead them to become more conservative, to uphold society as it stands, and favor the status quo. Later-borns, on the other hand, question authority, and are open to alternative ideas and power structures. In Sulloway's terms, such later-borns are "born to rebel."

Sulloway was a historian of psychology who looked to history for evidence of his hypotheses. For example, Sulloway identified scientists who were contemporaries of Charles Darwin, and who had responded to Darwin's then-controversial theory of evolution. He then asked professional historians who had studied those scientists, but were blind to Sulloway's hypotheses, to rate the scientists' support of Darwin's theory. As Table 11.3 indicates, those scientists who argued for the scientific status quo and against Darwin's hypothesis were almost exclusively firstborn. Those who rebelled against the scientific status quo and supported Darwin were nearly exclusively later-borns.

In another analysis, Sulloway looked at eighty-three scientist siblings—brothers, sisters, or brothers and sisters—who were both on record responding to an innovative scientific theory. The firstborn members of the pairs supported innovations at a rate of 50 percent, whereas the later-borns supported innovation at a rate closer to 85 percent (Sulloway, 1996, p. 51).

Not everyone has found relations between birth order and rebellious social attitudes, suggesting that Sulloway's findings may hold true for a specific historical period (e.g., Freese, Powell, & Steelman, 1999). On the other hand, supportive evidence is found in the personality characteristics of contemporary siblings. Paulhus, Trapnell, and Chen (1999) examined the children in 1,022 families and compared the first to later-born children within each family. Note that this research design eliminates differences between families in socioeconomic status, ethnicity, and other variables. As Sulloway's theory predicted, firstborns were consistently nominated as more achieving and conscientious than later-borns, whereas later-borns were identified as more rebellious, liberal, and agreeable than firstborns. Another study found that

Inside the Field

Does What Parents Do Matter?

In her book *The Nurture Assumption: Why Children Turn Out the Way They Do,* the psychologist Judith Rich Harris (1998) argued that friends, peer groups, and schools are far more important to a child's development than are parental practices. For example, the children of immigrants adopt the language and ways of the dominant culture although the parents may have recreated the language and culture of their country of origin at home. Harris commented on a variety of social phenomena from this perspective, suggesting, for example, that given how little influence they had, parents perhaps ought not wait to raise children, but would rather have them and hand them over to a nanny, a daycare center, or even a boarding school (Gladwell, 1998).

In reviewing Harris's book for the American Psychological Association, another developmental psychologist wrote, "Unless you've been doing fieldwork in Antarctica, you have undoubtedly read at least a few of the media reports on Harris and her thesis that one's peers matter more than previously thought and parents matter less. From the cover of *Newsweek* to a BBC documentary, Harris has seized the popular press unlike any psychologist since the publication in 1995 of *The Bell Curve* by Herrnstein and Murray" (Williams, 1999, p. 267).

Dismissed from Harvard for failing to meet the standards of "what an experimental psy-

chologist should be," Harris never obtained her Ph.D., and went on to set up house in Middleton, New Jersey, where she raised a family and collaborated on two editions of a developmental textbook (Sleek, 1998).

In 1995 she submitted a review article to *Psychological Review,* the preeminent journal for theoretical papers in psychology. The quality of her submission overcame any lack of academic affiliation, and her article was accepted for publication by this most selective of the journals in psychology. Her article argued that the belief that parents' behaviors exert a major influence on their children's development had never been proven—and indeed, that the evidence for it was scant (Harris, 1995). The *Psychological Review* article went on to win the George A. Miller Award for the best article in General Psychology. Miller wrote her a personal letter of congratulation on the occasion of her winning the award.

Inside the field many applauded her scholarly efforts, arguing it was a wake-up call for the field, though noting her story in the media had become rather extreme (Sleek, 1998; Williams, 1999). Others argue that there is another side to the story that indicates parents do—or at least, in principle can—influence child development in important ways. Can you identify some of those studies in this chapter?

whereas firstborns tend to prefer products that others say are good, later-borns preferred more innovative newer products (Saad, Gill, & Nataraajan, 2005).

The Gendered World

Sex: The genetically designated reproductive role a person is biologically assigned.

Another influence on development is the child's **sex** and the cultural expectations as to how a person of that sex will behave. A person's sex denotes the genetically designated reproductive role the human being can carry out, and the biological charac-

TABLE 11.3	Examples of Scientific Position during the Darwinian Revolution (1859–1868)	
Rating of Support	**Interpetation**	**Birth Order of Individual Scientists (FB = First Born; LB = Later Born)**
Supporting the Status Quo		
1.0	**Extreme opposition** to new theory; often emotional in nature	Louis Agassiz (FB) Karl Friedrich Schimpter (FB) Adam Sedgwick (LB)
2.0	**Strong opposition** to new theory; generally reasoned	Léonce Élie de Beaumont (FB) John Herschel (FB) Roderick Murchison (FB) William Whewell (FB)
3.0	**Moderate opposition** to new theory; often respectful	James Dwight Dana (FB) John Stevens Henslow (FB) Fleeming Jenkin (FB) Richard Owen (LB)
Neither Supporting nor Opposing the Status Quo		
4.0	**Neutral or Ambivalent**	Charles Lyell (FB)
Rebelling against the Status Quo		
5.0	**Moderate support** of new theory but with qualifications	George Bentham (LB) William Carpenter (LB) Jeffries Wyman (LB)
6.0	**Strong support** of new theory with few qualifications	Asa Grey (FB) Joseph Dalton Hooker (LB) Thomas Henry Huxley (LB)
7.0	**Extreme support** of new theory bordering on zealousness	Charles Robert Darwin (LB) Ernst Haeckel (LB) Alfred Russel Wallace (LB) August Weismann (FB)

Based on ratings from ten historians of science; ratings have been rounded to the nearest whole number. Firstborns occur with great statistical frequency as supporters of the status quo.

Source: Adapted from BORN TO REBEL by Frank J. Sulloway, copyright © 1996 by Frank J. Sulloway. Table 1, p. 31. Used by permission of Pantheon Books, a division of Random House, Inc.

Gender role: The social behaviors and actions a person is expected to carry out in relation to his or her sex.

teristics associated with that role. A **gender role** defines the characteristic behaviors a person is expected to perform in relation to his or her sex. Some aspects of the gender role may be relatively easy for the growing child to fit into, and other aspects of the role may be more difficult depending upon the individual's personality system.

Sexual development diverges for the male and female fetus at about nine weeks after conception, when the ovaries and testes differentiate (Moore & Persaud, 1993). At birth, most infant girls and boys are identifiable as of one or the other sex, although there exist much rarer, genetically or chemically caused ambiguous sexes as well (Bender & Berch, 1987; Money & Lehne, 1999). The sexual development of the fetus into an infant girl or a boy will have continued influence on the individual's personality throughout life. Some of those influences will be due to different levels of sexual hormones and other sex-linked characteristics. Other influences will be due to social understandings of gender.

Children in thirty nations completed a survey about gender roles to study their understanding across cultures. In the survey, children read about various people, and their job was to assign the person a sex. One item read, for example, "One of these people is emotional. They cry when something good happens as well as when everything goes wrong. Which is the emotional person?" Children were then asked to point to a male or female figure to indicate their belief (Williams & Best, 1982, p. 33).

By five years of age, most children show some evidence of knowing the gender roles in their culture (Best et al., 1977; Williams & Best, 1982). By this time, children take care to play with toys and choose television programs preferred by other members of their sex (Luecke-Aleksa et al., 1995; Martin, Eisenbud, & Rose, 1995). Moreover, social play is segregated by sex, and will stay so through adulthood (Maccoby, 1990).

To jump just briefly to middle childhood, Figures 11.4 and 11.5 show that by eight years of age, children in most cultures identified gender-based stereotypes reliably. The figures also indicate some cross-cultural variations. For example, men in most countries are viewed as independent—but not in Japan, perhaps because of the greater emphasis on getting along with others.

Thus, at this age, boys and girls understand how they are expected to behave according to their sex and often are involved in gender-exclusive friendships. This influence continues until puberty, when sexual maturation introduces new changes in the relation between the sexes.

TABLE 11.4   Correlations of Temperament Dimensions with Big Five Personality Traits

Temperament	Big Five				
	Extraversion	Neuroticism	Openness/ Intellect	Conscientiousness	Agreeableness
Surgency: High intensity pleasure, sociability, pleasurable reactivity, high activity level	.59**	−.08	.40**	.10	.30**
Negative Affect: Fear, discomfort, reactive sadness, frustration	−.16*	.49**	−.17**	−.16*	.03
Orienting Sensitivity: Sensitivity to low level distractions, daydreaming, fantasy	.19**	.19**	.54**	.15*	.20**
Effortful Attention: Tracking information, paying attention	.08	−.34**	.21**	.43**	−.04

*Statistically significant at the $p < .05$ level; **Statistically significant at the $p < .01$ level.

Source: Modified from Rothbart, Ahadi, & Evans (2000), Table 2. Reprinted with permission of American Psychological Association.

FIGURE 11.4

Personality Qualities Rated as Characteristics of Men by Eight-Year-Olds from Four Countries

By age eight, most children are well-acquainted with male gender roles

Source: Data from Williams & Best (1983), Table 8.3a, p. 182. Reprinted with permission.

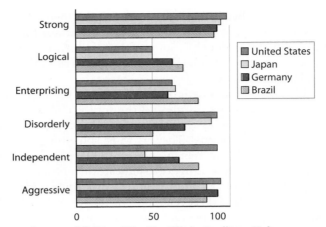

Percent of Children Who Identified a Quality as Male

FIGURE 11.5

Personality Qualities Rated as Characteristics of Women by Eight-Year-Olds from Four Countries

By age eight, most children are well-acquainted with female gender roles

Source: Data from Williams & Best (1983), Table 8.3b, p. 183. Reprinted with permission.

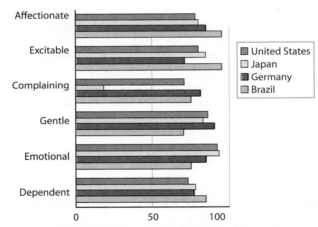

Percent of Children Who Identified a Quality as Female

What Are the Challenges of Middle Childhood?

Middle Childhood's Challenges and Self-Concept

In middle childhood, the growing person is dealing with the academic environment of school and the surrounding social world, and starting to more seriously think about adult relationships and occupations. Some of the child's tasks involve maintaining social relations and personal industry in school. If social relations fail, the child may become victim of others; if industry fails, the child may begin to develop feelings of inferiority. The self-conception continues to grow in complexity and so-phistication. One fourth-grade girl described herself as follows:

> I'm pretty popular, at least with the girls. That's because I'm nice to people and helpful and can keep secrets . . . I try to control my temper, but when I don't, I'm ashamed of myself. I'm usually happy when I'm with my friends, but I get sad if there is no one to do things with. At school, I'm feeling pretty smart in certain subjects like Language Arts and Social Studies. I got A's in these subjects . . . But I'm feeling pretty dumb in Math and Science . . . Even though I'm not doing well in those subjects, I still like myself as a person, because Math and Science just aren't that important to me . . . I also like myself because I know my parents like me and so do other kids. That helps you like yourself." (Harter, 1999, p. 48)

From Temperament to Traits

The Persistence of Temperament

Early temperament continues to exert influence on the child in middle childhood. Recall Chess, Thomas, and colleagues' first modern study of temperament. They had divided a sample of 141 infants into three groups based on whether they were easy, slow to warm up, or difficult. By the time the children were in middle childhood, 70 percent of the difficult children had developed behavioral problems that called for psychiatric attention, whereas only 18 percent of the easy children did so. For easy children nearly any parental style worked well. Greater efforts at parenting, however had been necessary to cope with the more difficult children. Thomas and colleagues observed that in the hands of more expert parents, the difficult children had been successfully guided toward psychological health.

A more nuanced understanding of the transition from underlying temperament to visible traits is provided by the research program of Jerome Kagan and his col-leagues on shy children. Recall that those researchers had sorted nine- and fourteen-month-old infants and toddlers into shy, normal, and uninhibited groups. The idea that biology underlies temperament was supported by the finding that, by middle childhood, certain physical differences were associated with the temperamental ones. As one example, in this mostly Caucasian sample, one child in four of the shy (high-reactive) children were small in size and had blue eyes, compared with only one in twenty in the disinhibited group (Kagan, 2003).

In Kagan's research, eleven-year-olds who had been classified as high-reactive (shy) or low-reactive (e.g., uninhibited) at four months of age were retested at eleven years of age. The high-reactive (shy) infants continued to exhibit higher-than-usual emotional activation in brain responsiveness as measured by greater EEG activation in certain brain locations, and brain stem responsiveness (Fox et al., 2005; McManis et al., 2002). Although this was the case, a small number of the high-reactive eleven-year-olds exhibited no evidence of being shy or subdued. Although these eleven-year-olds remained more physiologically reactive, they no longer exhibited the trait of shyness or negative affect (Kagan, 2003, p. 10). Kagan has speculated that parental coaching, coupled with other favorable environmental influences, permitted these children to compensate for their initially higher reactivity so as to become more sociable than they might otherwise have been.

Temperament-Trait Correlations

The multiple features of infant temperament gradually become organized, developing into the child's emerging personality traits. By preschool and middle childhood, children are able to complete personality scales on their own (and observers can also do this). By middle childhood, parents often perceive their children in part in terms of the Big Five personality traits: neuroticism, extraversion, openness, agreeableness, and conscientiousness (e.g., Kohnstamm et al., 1988; 1998). Earlier dimensions of temperament such as the threesome of surgency, negative affect, and self-control, studied by Rothbart and her colleagues, can be related to the Big Five (Rothbart, Ahadi, & Evans, 2000).

Temperament is regarded as representing building blocks of traits, and the nature of building blocks is that they can be assembled in different ways (Caspi, Roberts, & Shiner, 2005). For that reason, dimensions of temperament do not necessarily map directly onto the Big Five. Still, specific temperaments do appear to promote the development of certain traits. For example, surgency—energetic and active feeling states—seems to be a building block of Extraversion, correlating significantly with it. Similarly, negative affect—anxiety, depression, and frustration—correlates with Neuroticism. A third temperament dimension, termed *orienting sensitivity,* involves sensitivity to low-level distractions and day-dreaming. That dimension correlates with the Big Five trait of Openness. Effortful attention—self-control—relates to Conscientiousness. These relations are fairly substantial, and in the range from *r* = .40 to .60. The specific correlations for a sample of 207 children are shown in Table 11.5 (OR) the specific correlations for adult measures of temperament and the Big Five are shown in Table 11.4 (Rothbart, Ahadi, & Evans, 2000).

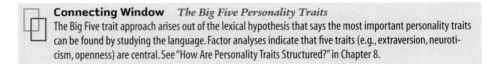

Connecting Window   *The Big Five Personality Traits*
The Big Five trait approach arises out of the lexical hypothesis that says the most important personality traits can be found by studying the language. Factor analyses indicate that five traits (e.g., extraversion, neuroticism, openness) are central. See "How Are Personality Traits Structured?" in Chapter 8.

Overcontrolled, Undercontrolled, and Flexible Children

By now you have noticed that different laboratories assess somewhat different features of temperament, employ different sets of traits, and classify children in somewhat different ways. An additional complication is that, as the years pass, those conducting longitudinal studies may need to change the personality measures they use to assess the participants in their studies, simply to keep up to date with the current advances in research. In addition, they must have a way to integrate changes in measurement techniques that occurred over time in order to still make sense of their study participants and their lives.

Jack and Jeanne Block were asked to analyze a longitudinal study that had employed a bewildering variety of measures over the first half of the twentieth century.

They developed an innovative approach to synthesizing large numbers of often-changing personality measures in longitudinal studies. The Blocks asked trained psychologists to go through all the data—interview, test, and observational—that had been collected on the children at each age. After forming as accurate an impression of the child as possible from the diverse records, the professional rated each child in the study on the **California Q-Sort**. The Q-Sort procedure involves sorting 100 statements concerning the child into eleven piles depending upon how well each statement described the person. For example, if "Gets along well with others," was highly descriptive of the child, it would be placed in the "most descriptive" pile; if "tends to avoid others" did not, it would be placed in one of the less descriptive piles. The Q-sort provided an integrative language into which trained psychologists interpreting earlier measures could translate their various findings.

Initial analyses of the Q-Sort technique suggested that two broad aspects of children's psychology were most obvious: **ego strength**, and **ego control**. Ego strength referred to the relative positivity of an individual's emotion system. So, high ego strength represented high positive affect and low negative affect. Children high in ego strength were also relatively extraverted and low in neuroticism. Ego control, on the other hand, referred to the type of control an individual exerts over his or her mental processes and behavior. At one extreme, an individual can be undercontrolled—impulsive, substance abusing, sexually promiscuous, and overtly risk-taking. At the other extreme, an individual may become overcontrolled—obsessive, rigid, and joyless. In between, a person's self-control is viewed as flexible (Block, 2002, p. 9).

When children are compared to one another on the California Q-Sort, by using statistical techniques that look for clusters of similar people, there often arise three primary forms or types of children this age: undercontrolled, well-adjusted, and overcontrolled children (Caspi, 2000; Eisenberg et al., 2000). As we have seen, variations of these groups have been studied by Kagan and others.

For example, Caspi and others (2000) analyzed data from an extensive longitudinal study in the fourth largest city in New Zealand, Dunedin. The Dunedin longitudinal study was begun in 1972–1973, and consisted of 1,037 individuals, or 91 percent of all those born in the city over those years. Based on a mathematical analysis of the temperament measures, of these now 21-year-olds, about 40 percent of the sample, was labeled "well adjusted," and consisted of children who were emotionally stable in the face of new situations, possessed self-confidence, and were capable of self-control when it was demanded of them. The second, "undercontrolled" type, about 10 percent of the sample, were emotionally reactive, negative, easily distracted, impulsive and restless. The third, "inhibited" type, another 10 percent of the sample, included children who were socially shy and easily upset by strangers.

These three types of children have now been found in longitudinal samples in Iceland, Netherlands, Germany, and the United States as well (Robins et al., 1996). Are there more types? There seem to be two smaller clusters of individuals, at least. There is evidence of a confident, impulsive group that is eager to explore but not negativistic, and that accounted for about 2 percent of the sample, and of a reserved yet not cautious or withdrawn group that made up 1.5 percent of the sample (Robins et al., 1998). In Chapter 12, we will examine what happens to these groups in adulthood.

California Q-Sort: A measurement technique in which a trained psychologist can integrate case and/or test material about a person by arranging 100 descriptions about an individual into 11 piles, according to those that best describe the individual.

Ego Strength: A trait describing the relatively stable, positive qualities of a person's ego system: his or her thoughts, feelings, and goal-directed behaviors.

Ego Control: A trait describing the relative capacity of an individual to respond flexibly to the environment in a fashion that is neither overcontrolled nor undercontrolled.

Friendship Patterns

By middle childhood, there is a great difference in the sorts of friendships different children maintain. Some children are well accepted, and others are rejected by nearly everyone. In one classroom, for example, a child had written a note that was being passed up and down the schoolroom, and read, "If you hate Graham, sign here." The note had been signed by virtually all the children in the class—and was headed to Graham's desk when the teacher intercepted it! (Asher & Rose, 1997, p. 196.)

Differences in social skills—and how they impact friendships—are vividly illustrated by watching a child trying to join others who are already at play. Some children do this very well; others lack the necessary skills. Black and Hazen (1990) asked children in a private setting who they most and least liked to play with in their preschool-room. On the basis of that interview, children in the classroom were divided into "liked," "disliked," "low-impact" (neither liked nor disliked), and "mixed" (liked by some, disliked by others) groups. The children were then divided into groups of three. Two children of each group were taken to a play area where they started playing, and the third child was introduced ten minutes later. How would the third child try to enter the dyad of children already playing?

Entering such a social situation successfully often involves indicating that one is willing to join those already at play, and to do what they are doing. For example, when one of the two already-playing children told the entry child, "We're being witches here, and I am the mean witch," a child with a good entry strategy replied, "Oh, hello witches, I am a witch, too." A poor entry strategy, on the other hand, would be to make an irrelevant comment such as, "My mom is taking me to get shoes today." Each entry-child's speech behavior was coded on a number of dimensions. Disliked children, relative to liked children, failed to direct their comments clearly to one or another dyad nearly twice as much as did liked children. The disliked children made irrelevant comments nearly three times as often.

Those who foster friendship gain valuable support. Even very young children will express concerns or fears in their play, and may find comfort in the caring of others. For example, in the following passage four-and-a-half-year-old Naomi, who is playing with a dinosaur, comforts her three-and-a-half-year-old best friend Eric, who is playing with a skeleton:

> NAOMI: I'm your friend the dinosaur.
> ERIC: Oh, hi dinosaur. You know, no one likes me.
> NAOMI: But I like you. I'm your friend.
> ERIC: But none of my other friends like me . . . They don't like my skeleton suit. It's really just me. They think I'm a dumb-dumb.
> NAOMI: I know what. He's a good skeleton.
> ERIC: I am not a dumb-dumb and that's so.
> NAOMI: I'm not calling you a dumb dumb. I'm calling you a friendly skeleton. (Asher & Rose, 1997, p. 202)

By middle school, third and fifth graders can speak clearly about friendships, noting the highs, such as, "Me and Lamar makes each other laugh and we play kick soccer," and intimacy, such as, "Yesterday me and Diana talked about how our parents got a divorce and how the world is going to end," and mutual responsibility, as

A friend is a second self.

Aristotle

in, "My friend is really nice. Once my nose was bleeding about a gallon every thirty minutes and he helped me" (Parker & Asher, 1993, pp. 270–271).

Both early attachment patterns and current relationships with parents can predict the quality of friendships among those in middle childhood. Ten-year-old children in forty-nine families, and their parents, were interviewed as part of the Northern German Longitudinal Study (Grossman et al., 1985). Secure attachment measured during infancy correlated with positive parent-child communication at age ten. Both infant attachment and current parent-child communication predicted the quality of the child's friendships at age ten (Freitag et al., 1996).

A child's own traits may also promote or impede friendship. Lower use of both verbal and physical aggression is associated both with better adjustment—as assessed by teachers' ratings of their students—and with better friendships. Teachers' ratings of their students' agreeableness also predicted less use of aggression and better friends—but for girls only. Self-rated agreeableness is unrelated to such qualities perhaps because children of that age may be unable to judge their own agreeableness (Jensen-Campbell & Graziano, 2001, p. 343).

Victimization and Friendship

Friendship is crucial to adjustment. An extreme example of how friendship can help a person is in the context of bullying. The type of child most likely to be bullied is characterized by submissive or nonassertive social behavior. This submissive style appears to be a consequence, perhaps, of temperament, maternal overprotectiveness, and general negativity in the home (Olweus, 1993; Schwartz et al., 1993). The second type of child at risk for bullying consists of aggressive victims whose angry responses may tend to provoke abusers. These victims often experience early home environments that include exposure to violence in the forms of spousal abuse, child abuse, or both (Schwartz et al., 1997).

Data analyses were conducted to examine the role of friendship in preventing bullying in two separate longitudinal studies: the Child Development Project, a multi-site study of children's social development and adjustment, and Fast Track, a multi-site study of schools in four geographic regions in the United States. Results from both longitudinal studies indicated that strong friendships reduced or prevented bullying for both at-risk boys and girls, and for both passive and aggressive-type victimized children (Schwartz et al., 2000).

What Are Adolescents Doing?

Puberty and the Changing Self-Concept

Puberty: A period of sexual maturation during which a child achieves the capacity to reproduce.

Having by now developed some experience in the world of relationships and skills, the child enters the world of adolescence. (In this chapter, we move along far more quickly than real life!) Adolescence begins as a series of physical changes that occur with **puberty**, a time of sexual maturation during which the child undergoes rapid sexual maturation and achieves the capacity to reproduce. These events include a growth spurt in the skeleton and the maturation of the primary sexual organs. In boys, testes and penis mature, and secondary sex characteristics mature as well: Their facial hair grows, their shoulders broaden, and childhood fat tissue changes to muscle. In girls, the vagina, uterus, and ovaries mature and **menarche**, the first menstrual period, occurs. Girls assume a more rounded appearance, and their breasts mature (Brooks-Gunn & Reiter, 1990).

Menarche: In girls, the time, often between ages eleven and thirteen, during which the ovary, uterus, and vagina mature and the first menstrual period occurs.

With rapid sexual and physical maturation, the child now looks much different, and often feels that all eyes are on her or him. The youth now becomes preoccupied with this outward appearance, and how to reconcile it with how he or she feels on the inside. At the same time, a new sense of identity must be worked out. The young person may carry out a series of experiments in identification. These include a search for things and people with which to identify or fall in love. These "fallings in love" may be with peer groups and with broader ideologies ranging from politics, to religion, to ethnic groups. In the social realm, the young person will feel yearnings and love toward other youths. From an adult vantage point, the love has not yet deepened to mature caring, but it seems overwhelmingly strong to the person feeling it (Erikson, 1963).

During this stage, the adolescent will begin to think about how to fit in with the world and try to experiment with some available social roles. These may start with the various groups to be found in school, but will set the stage for decisions about occupational, familial, political, religious, and ethnic identifications later on. Some psychologists believe that to successfully traverse this stage, the individual must begin to understand the range of possibilities open to him or her in each of these areas (Erikson, 1963; Marcia et al., 1993). Much adolescent exploration is healthy and provides important learning experiences. At other times, however, such explorations can become potentially risky and self-destructive. For example, some personality characteristics put the exploring young person at risk for the abuse of drugs. For more about this, see the Research in Focus box.

Some of the self-consciousness and self-exploration is illustrated in this self-description by a young woman in middle adolescence (fifteen years old):

> What am I like as a person? . . . I'm complicated! With my really *close* friends, I am very tolerant . . . but I can get pretty obnoxious and intolerant if I don't like how they're acting . . . At school, I'm serious, even studious every now and then, but on the other hand, I'm a goof-off too, because if you're *too* studious, you won't be popular . . . which means I don't do all that well in terms of my grades. But that causes problems at home . . . my parents . . . get pretty annoyed with me . . . I can switch so fast from being cheerful with my friends, then coming home and feeling anxious, and then getting frustrated and sarcastic with my parents. Which one is the *real* me? I have the same question when I'm around boys . . . I'll be a real extravert, fun-loving and even flirtatious . . . Then I get self-conscious and embarrassed and become radically introverted, and I don't know who I really am! . . . So I think a lot about who is the real me . . . (Harter, 1999, pp. 67–68)

The next section examines some of the identity issues surrounding sex and gender; then, adolescent identity is examined more broadly.

Research in Focus

Childhood Patterns and Experimentation with Drugs

Does seven-year-old personality affect drug use as an adolescent? Shedler and Block (1990) divided their eighteen-year-old longitudinal research participants into three non-overlapping groups: abstainers, who had never tried any illicit drug; experimenters, who had used marijuana with some frequency and had also tried other drugs, and frequent users, who used marijuana or other drugs more than once a week. Looking back into their sample, they discovered differences between groups already existed at age seven.

By age seven, abstainers already appeared more eager to please adults than the other children, were more neat and orderly, and more likely to think ahead. Such abstainers were also more anxious and fearful in response to risky behavior than were members of the other groups, more timid and constricted, less curious, and more likely to be immobilized under stress. By age eleven, the pattern of timidity, fearfulness, and fussiness continued. At age eighteen, the abstainers were described as proudly objective and rational but also as less accepted by others, more moralistic, unexpressive, anxious, and predictable, while also being less charming and less socially at ease (Shedler & Block, 1990, pp. 618–620).

By age seven, the later frequent drug users were described as unpopular, in part because they would not share or be fair with others. In fact, they had earlier been characterized as lacking moral concern. The later frequent drug users denied negative emotions and were likely to experience a relatively greater number of physical symptoms. They had few close relationships, little pride about their accomplishments, and reacted poorly to stress. They felt bad and unadmired. By age eleven, they were visibly deviant from peers, had difficulty concentrat-

ing, behaved in an overemotional fashion, were uncooperative, distrustful, and lacked both curiosity and standards for their own performance. By age eighteen, they were, "interpersonally alienated, emotionally withdrawn, and manifestly unhappy, [and they expressed their] maladjustment through . . . overtly antisocial behavior" (Shedler & Block, 1990, p. 617).

The drug experimenters-to-be presented a healthier picture than either the abstainers or frequent users. By age seven, they were socially outgoing and relaxed and neither over-orderly nor undercontrolled. They got along well with others, planned ahead, and were viewed as relatively trustworthy and dependable. They were socially skilled relative to the other groups, flexible, and well-regarded. They were also more self-confident than the other groups. These relations held at the eleven-year-old testing period, and by age eighteen, they were still regarded as dependable, productive, cooperative, able to constrain themselves, and sympathetic and considerate (e.g., Shedler & Block, 1990, p. 618).

Although the focus here is on drug use, can you detect the broad outline of the overcontrolled, normal, and undercontrolled groups often seen by developmental personality psychologists? If so, how would you relate them to problematic drug use? The authors note that throughout the years they had come to know each participant well and so it is likely most participants were very candid about their own drug use and patterns. In addition, they caution that the particular study of these 101 ethnically diverse participants grew up in a particular time and place (the 1980s, in the San Francisco Bay area of California) and may not be directly generalizable to other times and cultures.

Sexual and Sex-Role Development

With puberty comes a renewed focus on sex and gender in the growing person's self-concept. The sexes diverge dramatically in their desires regarding their sexual activity. Both women and men struggle with thoughts of sex, yet men experience the struggle more intensely. For example, male college students in the Netherlands more strongly agreed with such items as, "My desire for sex disturbs my daily life"; "I think about sex more than I would like"; and "My sexual behavior sometimes makes me not live up to my responsibilities" than did women (Vanwesenbeeck, Bekker, & van Lenning, 1998).

Peer groups exert increasing influence over the adolescents' behaviors. Men's peer groups often encourage them to experiment with and try sex. Men have far more positive attitudes toward casual sex, desiring upward of eighteen sexual partners during their lives, compared with an average ideal of four or five sexual partners reported by women (Buss & Schmitt, 1993; Oliver & Hyde, 1993). One survey of college students in California indicated greater extremes: that women ideally wished to have two or three sex partners over a lifetime; whereas men hoped for sixty-four (Miller & Fishkin, 1997).

At this age, women discuss their sexual behavior with their peers with some regularity. Women's peer groups, however, are different than men's. They are concerned with what their friends think of their sexual activity and try to restrain one another's sexual activity. For example, a group of college women friends may make a pact before going on spring break to refrain from sexual activity—and to help one another do so (Maticka-Tyndale, Herold, & Mewhinney, 1998).

Sex Differences in Traits

Specific but important differences exist between men and women in the motivational, emotional, and cognitive domains. In regard to aggression, men score more highly on aggression, relative to women on various measures: projective tests (e.g., the TAT), observer-ratings, and self-judgments (Hyde, 1986). Men are also far more aggressive behaviorally and commit far more violent crime than women; men are responsible for 90 percent of the homicides worldwide; women, 10 percent (Daly & Wilson, 1988). The largest difference on the Big Five inventory for women and men, is on the friendliness-unfriendliness dimension, which in part reflects aggression.

Adult women are more susceptible to depression than men. The two sexes start out with equal rates of depression in childhood. After puberty, however, the rates of depression in women relative to men rise to two or three times as high. These higher rates of depression relative to men occur in many different cultures and nations (Weissman & Olfson, 1995).

In regard to motivation more specifically, there is a pronounced difference between men and women on a dimension sometimes referred to as "people versus things." Women (relative to men) far prefer to be involved with other people, and, conversely, men (relative to women) far prefer to be involved with things. Interest in people manifests itself as interest in social planning, being with others, discussing relationships, and forming intimate connections with others. Interest in things concerns interests in objects such as chemicals, motors, gadgets, and computers, among many others. "Thing interest" includes understanding how things work, how they can be built, how to fix them and how to use them. The people-versus-thing dimension is relevant to occupational choice because certain occupations, such as management and human services, emphasize working with people whereas other occupations, such as engineering and the physical sciences, emphasize working with things (Lippa, 1998).

In the 1970s and 1980s, something similar to this people-versus-thing dimension was measured by scales that went under the names of **masculinity** and **femininity**. Masculinity referred to a person's correspondence to a uniquely male character. Femininity referred to a person's correspondence to a uniquely female character. In those earlier scales, masculinity was largely defined as interest in objects or things, and heightened assertiveness. Femininity was measured as interest in people. **Androgeny** was defined as having a more flexible character and being interested in both masculine and feminine interests. The idea was that androgeny would be the healthiest style because it was the most flexible (Bem, 1974; Spence, Helmreich, & Stapp, 1974). A schematic of that arrangement is indicated in Figure 11.6. The most problematic type, on the other hand, would be the undifferentiated, who represented characteristics of neither type. The scales are now viewed as tapping objects-versus-things research, and secondarily, assertiveness, rather than sex roles per se.

To understand sexual character more closely, Six and Eckes (1991) examined gender stereotypes for men and women. The stereotyped groups they uncovered may more closely approach what is meant by masculinity and femininity than did older approaches. Yet, the sexual stereotypes are certainly unflattering for both sexes. For men, the groups included, first, men who were soft, quiet, philanthropic or alternative and gay. Their second cluster included career men, managers and bureaucrats. The third was made up of middle-class egotists. The fourth included playboys and lady-killers, and the fifth and last group were macho and cool.

The women's first cluster included confident, intellectual, left-leaning feminists. The second cluster included conforming, maternal, housewives. The third cluster included (what they referred to as) sexual vamps and tarts. Smaller groups included "nasty pieces of work," and a group of spoiled young girls and society ladies.

Masculinity and femininity remain rich areas for future study, and, no doubt, the picture of these important dimensions will be clarified (and perhaps defined more positively) in the future.

Masculinity: Traits or other qualities typically associated with being male.

Femininity: Traits or other qualities typically associated with being female.

Androgyny: The quality of possessing traits or other qualities associated both with being male and with being female.

FIGURE 11.6

Bem's Conception of Sex Roles

Sandra Bem believed that those high in both masculinity and femininity could be characterized as possessing a more flexible pattern called androgyny.

Source: Bem (1974).

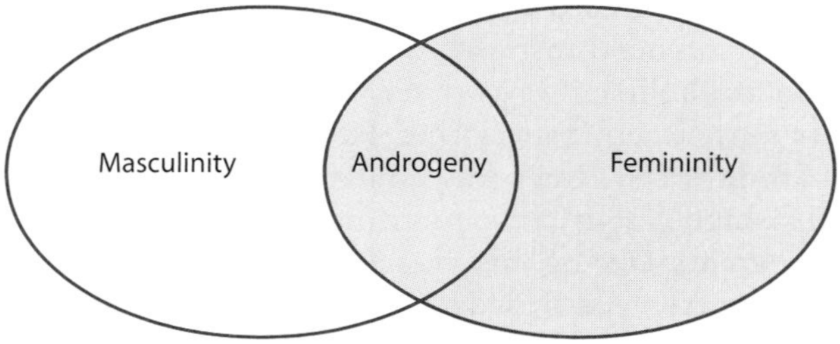

Establishing Identity in Adolescence

Identity: Identity refers to the model one creates of who one is in one's life. The term often suggests a specifically social emphasis, concerning in particular how one fits into or plans to fit into, the surrounding world.

Identity Crisis: A stage or period of time during which a person experiences frustration, concern, and worry about who he or she is in the social world and seeks to better understand how to fit in with the world.

Identity Exploration: A process during which an individual explores different identities, searching for the one that best fits his or her own being and outlook.

Identity Commitment: A process by which an individual gradually entrusts himself or herself to a particular social self-concept for fitting into society and the world more generally.

Identity Status: A classification of how a person views her or his occupational and social roles, based on whether the person has sufficiently explored those roles and committed to one.

Foreclosure Status: An identity status that involves committing oneself to a social and occupational role without having explored its alternatives.

Diffused Identity Status: An identity status that involves not recognizing that one needs to develop a coherent model of who one is. The individual experiencing this condition will often employ a series of partial or contradictory models of who he or she is.

Identity refers to who one is, the groups one belongs to, and the beliefs that guide one's life. The growing person needs to establish an identity in order to help navigate his or her many life choices. The psychological and physical growth spurts of adolescence directly encourage acute self-observation. When this is coupled with the looming decisions concerning one's education and occupational futures, the establishment of identity becomes a central task for the adolescent. People who successfully create an identity will be able to move forward in their lives with some success.

People who are unable to assemble such an identity suffer, either temporarily or for an extended time, from an **identity crisis**. The term originated with Erik H. Erikson, the psychodynamically-oriented psychologist whose rich description of this stage emerged in part from his own experiences. Erikson himself had dropped out of school in his adolescence and drifted across the beaches of southern Europe trying on the identity of a bohemian artist. He reflects that he was in the throes of a serious psychological crisis, occupying the borderland between anxious depression and loss of reality (Erikson, 1975, p. 26). Although in psychic pain, Erikson was involved in a valuable psychological process: **identity exploration**.

Identity exploration involves an adolescent's (or others') conscious self-exploration and self-understanding so as to form an identity. **Identity commitment**, in contrast, involves whether the individual could commit to one of the identities that were explored—to say, "I am this," and not something else. These two dimensions were employed by Marcia (e.g., 1964; 1966), who used them to divide adolescents into one of four possible identity-status categories (Figure 11.7). An **identity status** refers to the outcome of an identity-seeking process (Marcia, 2002).

At the lowest level was the individual with identity diffusion status. This individual has not yet conducted any self-exploration, and has made no commitments to an identity of one sort or another. At as nearly a low level is the individual with **foreclosure status**. This person has appeared to make a commitment but has done so with no self-exploration. Such a foreclosed adolescent often has agreed to carry out plans set for him or her by parents or other authority figures. This commitment is not viewed as mature, however, because it does not factor in any self-understanding achieved apart from the viewpoints of those others. The student whose father wants her to be a doctor and never questions the goal would be said to be in a foreclosed status.

Marcia discussed a psychotherapy patient named "Linda," who grew up in a rural town in northeastern Canada. Her mother was a homemaker, and her father was an alcoholic railway worker who, though in many ways absent, provided her with money to buy nice clothes. Her mother wanted her to attend nursing school, and Linda enrolled but was uninterested and ended up dropping out. She then tried fashion design at two more institutions but found herself unable to persist in the programs. During this time, Linda could be described as possessing a **diffused identity status**. A diffused identity status refers to the absence of a coherent sense of who one is in relation to the worlds of relationships and work. She neither explored identities on her own, nor made a commitment to anyone else's vision of her.

FIGURE 11.7

Marcia's Model of the Four Possibilities of Identity Status

The search for identity involves both exploration and commitment. Combinations of high and low levels of those lead to four identity statuses.

Source: From Marcia (1966).

		Commitment	
		Low	High
Self-Exploration	High	**Moratorium** involves the continued self-exploration that may potentially lead to identity commitment.	**Achievement** represents commitment to a given identity following exploration of that and other possibilities.
	Low	**Diffusion** involves the absence of any self-exploration, as well as the absence of any commitment.	**Foreclosure** represents a high degree of commitment but without any or much self-exploration leading up to it.

Moratorium Status: An identity status that involves postponing making a commitment to a social and occupational role until one has completed further exploration.

Achieved Identity Status: The highest level of identity status in which a person has adequately explored social and occupational roles and has committed to one that fairly represents her or his desires, needs, values, and goals.

Over the next years of her life, though, Linda's willing explorations marked the beginnings of a gradual transition to a higher level of identity status: **moratorium status**. The moratorium status reflects a person who is interested and engaged in self-exploration but is not yet ready to make a commitment. Linda spent the next decade of her life trying different life roles, but not staying with many of them for long.

In Linda's case, it took many years of further development (she was in her early forties) before she reached an **achieved identity status**. The achieved identity status reflects the individual who has engaged in self-exploration and does understand what he or she wants to do. At that time she enrolled in college, where she ended up doing quite well, in contrast to her earlier experiences, and was also better able to maintain mature relationships (Marcia, 1999, pp. 23–24).

In our increasingly multicultural society, one aspect of identity formation involves how an individual integrates a sense of ethnic, religious, or racial identity into the broader picture of selfhood. An eighteen-year-old female student described this recognition of her identity and ethnicity:

> When my family first migrated here, our parents separated us from the majority culture largely because they knew so little about it. Physical appearance for us was always a barrier, too. Our mother strictly forbade us girls ever to date a "European boy," and with us living at home, she was easily able to do this. But last year I left home for university . . . I was curious to discover what I was doing here, and who I really was . . . Questions like, "Where am I going?" and "Who will I become?" are still unanswered . . . I think feeling comfortable with my ethnic identity is a prerequisite to discovering my personal identity. (Kroger, 2000, p. 126)

Many researchers would agree that coming to terms with one's ethnic identity is a crucial aspect of forming a total personal identity. Growing up as an ethnic minority (which increasingly, everyone does), complicates identity formation by providing a set of possible identities different from those of the mainstream culture (Phinney, 1989; Phinney & Rosenthal, 1992). Somewhat parallel to Marcia's identity statuses, ethnic minority youth often progress through stages in which they first identify with the majority culture, then discover their own ethnicity, then immerse themselves in that ethnic culture, and, finally, internalize or integrate their own sense of ethnic identity with their own broader, personal identity (Cross, 1987). Bicultural identity also has come in for some analysis. Here, key variables include the degree to which the two cultures are perceived as overlapping or not, and the degree to which they are perceived as in harmony or in conflict (Benet-Martinez & Haritatos, 2005).

> **The conflict between the need to belong to a group and the need to be seen as unique and individual is the dominant struggle of adolescence.**
> Jeanne Elium and Don Elium

To classify an individual in one of Marcia's identity statuses, researchers use either clinical interviews or personality scales. Both approaches ask the adolescent about various areas of his or her life. Such areas as occupation, religion, politics, dating, sex roles, and recreation, for example, may be examined. From such information, an individual is coded according to the degree of identity exploration and identity commitment the individual has expressed (Adams, Shea, & Fitch, 1979; Grotevant & Adams, 1984; Marcia, 1966). From these two dimensions, participants are classified as belonging to one of the four identity statuses. Agreement between the clinical interview and self-report tests is moderately good—classifying 50 percent of the people in the same cateogory—or up to 80 percent using specially selected and trained raters (Berzonsky & Adams, 1999, p. 566).

Studies of adolescents and young adults in high school and college show that many individuals do follow a progression roughly from diffused identity states, to brief periods of foreclosure and moratorium, to an achieved identity. There are also, however, many who do not change at all, some who follow a different order toward identity achievement, and a substantial minority who appear to regress from moratorium, say, to foreclosure or diffuseness (Bezonsky & Adams, 1999; von Hoof, 1999, pp. 530–531; Waterman, 1999).

Several factors influence the development of identity status. For example, adolescents who exhibit less defensive patterns on the Thematic Apperception Test, were better able to advance toward identity achievement compared with more defensive students (Cramer, 1998). College students enrolled in academic departments that emphasize an expanding awareness of social issues such as national and world events may more readily reach identity achievement, compared to students in departments that place lower emphasis on such expanding awareness (Adams & Fitch, 1983). Having supportive student peers further increases one's capacity to question, and, in turn, helps promote achievement status (Berzonsky & Adams, 1999, p. 583).

Connecting Window   *The Thematic Apperception Test and Defensiveness*
Remember that Thematic Apperception Test consists of a series of ambiguous pictures. Test-takers tell stories about each picture, concerning what happened before, during, and after the scene depicted. The test was originally developed by Henry Murray to measure motives, but it also has scoring systems for measuring defenses. To learn more about the TAT see "What Are Motives?" in Chapter 4; to learn about defenses, see "How Do We Deal with the Pain of Falling Short?" in Chapter 10.

Another series of findings suggest that people who go through identity exploration—that is, are classified either as in moratorium or identity achievement status—

have richer and more differentiated self-concepts. Those who have reached identity achievement status appear better able to compare themselves with others in an integrated fashion; those who have not, often describe themselves along numerous, unintegrated dimensions (e.g., Berzonsky & Neimeyer, 1988). Students asked to create photo essays of themselves create richer, more integrative and individualistic descriptions when they are higher in self-exploration (Dollinger & Dollinger, 1997).

A reasonable assumption behind the identity formation research is that self-exploration and the establishment of an achieved identity status will provide a secure foundation for further growth and development. As fascinating as this research line is, it is particularly unfortunate that little is known about the outcome of identity formation later in life. One notable exception to this is a longitudinal study by Josselson (1996) who found that among thirty women, those classified as identity achievers in their senior year of college were able to move ahead with their lives in their thirties and forties in a more a clear and deliberate fashion than the other groups, and with a sense of meaning concerning what they were doing. Although they encountered obstacles and dead ends in their lives, they were better able to continue in the face of such setbacks.

Concluding Note

With the establishment of identity in adolescence, we come to a close of our consideration of personality development in childhood and adolescence. The stage has now been set for the growth of the individual's personality, and the development of the individual's life in adulthood. That will be the subject of Chapter 12 on adult development.

Reviewing Chapter 11

The learning goals of this chapter are to help you begin to understand how personality grows to meet the challenges of the individual. The chapter opens with a brief consideration of developmental stages and research approaches. Personality was then examined in infancy, childhood, and adolescence. The focus on childhood examined influences of infant temperament on later development, and also the influence of birth order. The chapter concluded with an examination of identity formation in adolescence.

What Is Personality Development?

1. Questions of Personality Development.

What is Personality Development? Each individual is born into a different time and place—an "experiment of one." Infants can develop well—sometimes even under demanding circumstances. What do psychologists call the quality that enables them to do so?

2. Dividing the Life Span.
A key element of developmental studies is that they include time as a central feature of their study. In thinking about development over the lifespan, it is often convenient to divide growth into stages. What are Erikson's stages from birth through adolescence?

3. Research Designs in Developmental Studies.
How is time included in developmental research, and what is the difference between longitudinal and cross-sectional research designs?

Do Infants Have a Personality?

4. The Infant's Challenge.
The newborn infant already has some organized perception of the surrounding environment. Can you distinguish a few examples of what is *not* a "blooming, buzzing, confusion" in the infant's mind?

5. Infant Temperament.
Temperamental qualities are described as the building blocks of traits. What were some of the original dimensions of temperament studied by Chess, Thomas, and their colleagues? How were these simplified by later researchers?

6. Attachment Patterns.
Infants develop models of other people in their lives. The models for intimate relationships are sometimes called attachment patterns. What are the major attachment patterns?

How Does the Young Child's Personality Develop?

7. The Young Child's Self-Concept.
The young child begins to develop a sense of autonomy and to exert will. What is the young child's sense of self like? How does this compare to the infant's sense of self?

8. Self-Control as a Part of Temperament.
What sorts of activities during young childhood reveal levels of self-control? Why is this important to parents and how is it reflected in temperament?

9. Parents and the Family Context.
The growing child is dependent upon, and greatly influenced by, parents and the family constellation. Two dimensions of parenting are nurturance and control. How do these combine to form parenting styles?

10. Family Size and Birth Order.
Children from larger families often obtain less education; what variable can eliminate that negative effect? Sulloway studied birth order effects on scientists and their acceptance of scientific and political revolutions. What characteristics distinguished first- from later-born children?

11. The Gendered World.
Girls and boys learn about their culturally assigned gender roles as they grow. How similar are some of the perceived differences between males and females across cultures? Is there something different about the case of Japan?

What Are the Challenges of Middle Childhood?

12. Middle Childhood's Challenges and Self-Concept.
In middle childhood the developing person is facing academic and social demands in school and beginning to ask about how they fit into the world.

13. From Temperament to Traits.
Features of temperament are thought to underlie traits. In middle childhood, children can begin to fill out personality questionnaires. How would you characterize the relationship between temperament and traits such as the Big Five?

14. Overcontrolled, Undercontrolled, and Flexible Children.
Undercontrolled children have difficulties with controlling their impulses, overcontrolled children are often shy. Some children change groups over time; why might this be?

15. Friendship Patterns.
Children have a very accurate understanding of the importance of friendship to support, intimacy, and having fun. At the same time, not all children benefit from friendship. Who is likely to be bullied in childhood; who is likely to bully? How can the existence of a friend affect bullying?

What Are Adolescents Doing?

16. Puberty and the Changing Self-Concept.
Puberty represents the stage in which children mature sexually. During this time, they often feel as if all eyes are on them, and become particularly self-conscious. What are some of the tasks of adolescence?

17. Sexual and Sex-Role Development.
What are some of the differences that arise between girls, boys, and their peer groups at this time?

18. Establishing Identity in Adolescence.
Identity is often said to involve the exploration of possible roles for oneself, coupled with the making of a commitment to one particular role. These two dimensions—exploration and commitment—have been said to describe four types of identity status. What is identity status and what are the four statuses that might arise? How does ethnic identity factor in?

Chapter 12

Personality Development in Adulthood

*D*oes a child's personality remain constant into adulthood? Will the emerging adult have a chance to change his or her personality? Adult development involves both consistency and change. The growing individual faces new life tasks, including, for many, finding a partner and choosing a career. Accomplishing these tasks means taking into consideration the qualities of one's own personality—one's preferences, styles, skills, and desires. How do various personality characteristics influence finding a mate? Do people with different personalities seek different occupations? What is the optimal personality like?

- **What Is the Nature of Adult Development?**
  Adult development addresses the consistency and changes in personality from young adulthood to the final stages of life. The continuity of personality from childhood to early adulthood is examined, and some of the challenges of adulthood are described in this first section.

- **What Are Young Adults Like?**
  One of the major tasks of the young adult is to find intimacy by choosing a mate and creating a positive and intimate relationship with that partner; different people do that differently. A second task is to match one's own interests and abilities to an occupation that one is happy with, and to develop one's skills at work.

- **How Does the Individual Traverse Middle Adulthood?**
  With relationships and careers begun, the mid-life adult often has the freedom to focus on maintaining important relationships and achieving success in an occupation. The ways in which personality contributes to such processes, and also to physical health, are examined. In addition, personality change is examined with an eye to who changes and who stays the same.

- **Where Is Personality Headed in the Concluding Parts of Life?**
  Personality develops up to the end of the life. The last stages of life often involve making meaning, developing a sense of one's life, and coming to terms with one's death.

What Is the Nature of Adult Development?

Questions of Adult Development

Mohandis Karamchand Gandhi (1869–1948) was born to a merchant family in Porbandar, Kathiawar, in India. He was an unremarkable student, leaving behind no brilliant record as a scholar or as an athlete; yet, in a premonition of the future, his teachers often gave him certificates of good character (Gandhi, 1942, p. 284). India was then a British colony, and as a young man Gandhi traveled to England to study law after his father's death. It was in England that he was first exposed to religious writings, including the Hindu *Bhagavad-Gita,* as well those from other religious traditions. These caught his attention and initiated the religious pursuits that would occupy him throughout his life.

After completing his legal training, Gandhi traveled to South Africa to establish a law practice there. He personally experienced the discrimination leveled against the Indian population of that nation. In response, he put his spirituality into practice, experimenting with methods of political influence through editorial writing and noncooperation with the South African authorities. At the request of his fellow Indian citizens, he remained in the country to fight discrimination rather than return to India as he had planned. Like many adults, Gandhi began to employ his own psychological gifts—in his case, spiritual and political skills—in an attempt to make a better world. This process of using one's own assets to care for the next generation is what the psychologist Erik Erikson referred to as generativity.

Mahatma Gandhi said, "Always aim at complete harmony of thought and word and deed. Always aim at purifying your thoughts and everything will be well." Gandhi has often been regarded as a paragon of psychological health by psychologists. At another time, he remarked, "Happiness is when what you think, what you say, and what you do are in harmony."

In 1914, at forty-five years of age, he returned to India, where he staged a series of peaceful political struggles to foster the well-being of Indian workers. He respected both sides of a confrontation, and he frequently left good will behind him after engaging in a conflict. His opponents often also felt relief when he shifted his focus to other political matters, for his advocacy could be formidable. After his successes on behalf of Indian workers, he set his sights on promoting Indian independence from Great Britain.

Gandhi used the term "self rule," or *Swaraj,* to refer to Indian independence. *Swaraj* has two meanings. Politically, it denoted India's liberation from England. Its second meaning, however, was no less significant and referred to an individual's spiritual self-management. *Swaraj* in this sense refers to freedom from illusion and ignorance. The Hindu text, the *Bhagavad-Gita,* saw the liberated individual as one who acts without craving and without possessiveness, and who can find peace in awareness of the infinite spirit. For Gandhi and his followers, *swaraj* represented not only a political movement but a personal journey to self-knowledge and mastery (Dalton, 1993, p. 2). The search for self-awareness is sought by many adults in both secular and religious traditions.

Gandhi was a charismatic leader at a time of many significant twentieth-century charismatic leaders. He became known as Mahatma Gandhi (Mahatma is an honorific referring to a particularly wise teacher). No individual can be a role model to all, of course, given the extent to which people differ from one another. In Gandhi's case, his spirituality and nonviolence led to his making choices that most people would choose not to emulate—even those who respected him (Erikson, 1969, p. 417). He had made a commitment to celibacy and poverty, whereas most adults will seek marriage and a successful career. His leadership sometimes failed, his empathy did not extend in all directions, and, toward the end of his life, his personal behavior raised questions of sexual propriety (Dutton, 1993, p. 136; Erikson, 1969, pp. 404–406). Nonetheless, he helped usher in Indian political independence, coupled with peace and democracy. Moreover, he expressed a commitment to love and to nonviolence, and a caring for excluded groups that was rare for his time and for our own. These are objectives to which many aspire but only a few meet so fully.

Psychologists have described Gandhi's greatness as having been achieved through the very highest levels of moral thought (Simonton, 1994, pp. 262–264), through generativity and caring for the next generation (Erikson, 1965), and as a potent expression of both the personal and social intelligences (Gardner, 1993, pp. 239, 252). Others have simply remarked that he could love well beyond the capabilities of most (Rokeach, 1960, p. 392). The fact that he was far from perfect also represents an inescapable feature of adult development.

How does one develop such greatness? Or, more prosaically, how does one become a better version of oneself? Although the study of personality development cannot answer the question directly, it does speak to the tasks one will face in one's psychological growth, and the common paths for meeting the challenges those tasks pose.

The Transition to Adulthood

The issue of developing well as an adult is an important one, especially given the length that adulthood can now extend. Longevity nearly doubled between 1850 and 1995, from forty years, on average, to seventy-seven years. The added years increase the importance of adulthood as a time of life (Stillion & McDowell, 2001–2002). Simply expecting to have more years of life ahead increases one's sense of control over one's life (e.g., Lewis, Ross, & Mirwosky, 1999; Mirowsky, 1997). In addition, the contemporary young person has more time to express his or her personality in adulthood—and to be subject to the troubles and rewards that various features of character can bring.

> **I get a standing ovation just standing.**
>
> The comedian, George Burns, performing in his nineties

Moreover, there exist an extraordinarily broad ranges of adult choices. An individual could be single, married, or divorced. He or she could be employed in an office, work at home or be unemployed, be sedentary or fit, have a large family or none. To be sure, social factors play a crucial role in one's future. The individual, also, however, contributes greatly to his or her adult life.

Personality development at the threshold of adulthood follows on what has come before. Emerging adults build their occupational and social progress on their identities defined previously in adolescence. For most adults, that still-developing identity will help them choose a life partner and an occupation. Of Erikson's eight stages of development, three pertained directly to adulthood and concerned growth during which the individual finds a partner and experiences intimacy (intimacy versus isolation), experiences a sense of generativity by contributing to society (generativity versus stagnation), and experiences a sense of integrity by reflecting and finding the meaning in his or her life (integrity versus despair).

> **Connecting Window**   *Erik Erikson's Eight Stages of Growth*
> Many experts have found Erikson's eight stages of growth helpful. For Erikson, the young adult attempted to develop intimacy (rather than isolation), generativity (rather than stagnation), and integrity (rather than despair). For the earlier stages see Chapter 11: What Is Personality Development?

Alternative stage models to Erikson's offer further insights into this period. Levinson (1976) studied the life stages of forty men from different occupations and social strata in depth. He divided up early adult life, basically, into a period of stability in one's twenties as the adult tests and develops marital and occupational relationships, with a readjustment period around age thirty, and then a period of stability in one's thirties and a readjustment period in one's early forties. Levinson's stages are outlined in Table 12.1.

Temperament and Traits: From Childhood through Adulthood

Does the child's personality give rise to his or her adult personality?. . . "How did the person get this way?" (Funder et al., 1993, p. 3). Some adult qualities can be

TABLE 12.1	Levinson's Adult Men's Stages, with a Focus on Middle Adulthood

Approximate Age and Stage	Brief Description
Earlier Stages in Brief	
17–22: The Early Adult Transition	During this transitional stage, emerging adults question their place in the world and try out their initial choices for adult living. To accomplish this, they must end many pre-adulthood relationships and begin early adult ones.
22–28: First Adult Life Structure	During this first stage of adulthood, the individual tries to connect the most valued parts of himself to adult society. To do so, he makes initial choices regarding what occupation to enter, choices in relationships, and regarding values and life style. He then lives with those choices, such as a job and a marriage, for an extended time.
The Age 30 Transition in Greater Detail	
28–33: The Age Thirty Transition	For Levinson, the Age 30 transition represents a time during which adult life becomes "more restrictive, serious, and 'for real'" (Levinson, 1977, p. 104). In response, men often feel pressured to institute changes in their lives before it is too late.
	• For some, the transition is relatively smooth, involving a reaffirmation of what has come before. There may be only modest changes to an already fairly well-developed adulthood.
	• For the larger majority, significant changes may seem necessary. Life may at times seem intolerable, and yet the means to attain a better life may seem difficult to figure out, or beyond reach.
	• Still other men find themselves in a low-point unlike any they have experienced during the period and must choose an altogether new path.
	During the Age 30 transition, marital difficulties and divorce seemed more common among the men studied. There were often shifts in occupation: Some men settled down from a time of trying out many jobs; others chose new careers. Men sought psychotherapy with a higher frequency than at other times.
The 40s and the Mid-Life Transition	
32–40: Settling Down	The Settling Down stage represents a time for the person to continue the newly revised life structure formed over the several years leading up to it, during the Age 30 transition. During this Settling time, the person hopes to climb the occupational ladder, establish his niche, and work at "making it" in terms of his valued goals.
40–45: Mid-Life Transition	Much like the Age 30 transition, the mid-life transition is a potentially tumultuous time of reflection and reevaluation, this time centered on questions such as: "What have I done with my life?" and "What has happened to my childhood dreams?"
	In Levinson's sample, most men again experienced a considerable struggle during this time. At its conclusion, some men were able to reattach to the people in their lives and the work environments around them, others made new choices, and still others entered into a decline.
The Later Stages in Brief	
40–65; 60–85; and 80+: Middle; Late; and Late, Late Adulthood	These three later stages of adulthood marked the outgrowth of the stages that came before. Although there remained time for further reevaluation and change during these stages, the bases of one's life had by now been established. Based on one's earlier choices and other life circumstances, the rest unfolded.

Source: Summarized from Levinson (1977).

predicted in part from childhood. For example, three-year-olds who had an emotionally negative temperament—prone to distress and impulsivity—were more likely to be aggressive, conflict-prone, and poorly-controlled as twenty-one-year-olds (Newman et al., 1997). Moreover, such undercontrolled young adults developed into less self-controlled middle-aged adults as well.

Traits: Set Like Plaster?

During adulthood itself, an individual's traits are relatively stable. For example, people generally maintain their relative standings on the Big Five personality dimensions throughout adulthood (e.g., Costa & McCrae, 1988; Costa et al., 1986; Douglas & Arenberg, 1978; Siegler, George, & Okun, 1979). At the same time, the average level of traits shifts over the lifespan. Between the ages of twenty and eighty, Neuroticism, Extraversion, and Openness can be expected to decline roughly one half of a standard deviation in the population. Agreeableness and Conscientiousness, on the other hand, either stay stable, or rise slightly (Costa & McCrae, 2002). These changes can be detected in the relatively brief four-year span of college. For example, 270 college students who were followed across their college years exhibited the expected decline in Extraversion and Neuroticism, as well as the expected rise in Agreeableness and Conscientiousness. Perhaps in response to the educational process, however, openness rose slightly for these students during college, in contrast to its gradual decline in adulthood (Robins et al., 2001).

Models of the Self and World

Another area of continuity concerns the person's mental models of the self and world. The development of the self, which is so central to the young child's personal identity, remains a lens through which the adult sees the world. Young adults, like adolescents, possess considerable self-consciousness, and often overemphasize the degree to which others notice them. In one experiment, college students at Cornell University were asked to wear a slightly embarrassing tee-shirt into a room of their normally dressed peers. The tee-shirt had a picture of a pop-singer on it who was considered to reflect generally poor musical taste at the time (Barry Manilow). Those wearing the tee-shirts imagined that about half of the students in the room would notice their Manilow tee-shirts when in fact only about a quarter did (Gilovich & Savitsky, 1999).

By early adulthood the self has integrated within it a long line of significant personal memories, personal traits, and formulations of identity (Pillemer, 2000; 2001; Singer & Bluck, 2001; Singer & Salovey, 1993). Thorne and Klohnen (1990), for example, studied ninety-five ethnically diverse twenty-three-year-olds who had been followed since they were three years old (Block & Block, 1980). These investigators asked the then-twenty-three-year-olds to recall ten specific memories that were personally important or represented problematic encounters from their childhoods.

The researchers found continuities between undercontrolled behavior in childhood and the adult's personally important memories of childhood. One of their participants, Edith Fay (a pseudonym), was consistently identified as undercontrolled through the years by various interviewers. Now, as a twenty-three-year-old, she recalled five early memories—all about failing to receive help. Her memories included being left to cry after her

Vanity plays lurid tricks with our memory.
Joseph Conrad

older sister stuck her with a pin while diapering her, and her father's telling her to go to sleep without her favorite teddy bear after it had fallen on the floor, rather than helping her retrieve it (Thorne & Klohnen, 1993, p. 248). Her difficulties in life now had become a part of her life story and broader identity.

The environment that a person experiences or creates for him or herself also may exert control on personality and cause it to change. For example, ongoing family conflict can make first-year adjustment to college more challenging (e.g., Feenstra, Banyard, Rines, & Hopkins, 2001). Looking ahead a bit, the emerging adult can exert some control over the environment in regard to marital choice. Caspi and Herbener

Case Study

How Consistent Is Stephen Reid's Personality?

In the 1970s, Stephen Reid led a notorious gang of bank robbers in a number of highly publicized bank robberies across the United States and Canada. The gang robbed over one hundred banks and stole a reported 11 to 19 million dollars during that time, including completing the largest bank robbery in California's history. Before Reid's capture, he and the other two members of the "Stopwatch" gang lived in a modern home in the Arizona hills, and they explained their prolonged absences to neighbors as due to their work as concert promoters. The personality development section focuses on issues of personality consistency and change. What does the life of Stephen Reid say about such issues?

Reid was born and brought up in northern Ontario, Canada (Nickerson, 1999). Despite his aptitude as a student, he became involved with drugs and petty crime. He quit school at the tenth grade to hitchhike west, and began his career as a bank robber. The notorious Stopwatch gang, which he led, was named by reporters after a security camera photograph showed Reid wearing a stopwatch on a cord around his neck during one of their series of precisely timed robberies. The gang had a large following, perhaps because though the gang was always heavily armed, most of its robberies were nonviolent. Reid was captured by the FBI

in 1980 and began a series of prison sentences, punctuated by three successful escapes. He led a daredevil criminal life and appeared to be utterly incorrigible.

Then Susan Musgrave, a poet and novelist as well as past-president of the Writers Union of Canada, read a manuscript Reid wrote in prison. Musgrave acknowledged she was a woman attracted to dangerous men. She edited the manuscript, an autobiographical novel based on his life in crime called, *Jackrabbit Parole*. After Musgrave wrote Reid a passionate love letter, the two met and were married on prison grounds in a 1986 ceremony. At its conclusion, Musgrave flung her garter onto the barbed-wire fence.

Reid won parole in 1987. His *Jackrabbit Parole* became a Canadian bestseller, and he announced his conversion to the path of the law abiding citizen. His success as a writer and teacher of writing, his marriage to Musgrave, and his role as father to Musgrave's child by an earlier marriage as well as to a child of their own, appeared to ensure his continued success and law-abiding behavior.

"My life is now Susan," he told the *Toronto Star* in 1987, "We lead quiet, work-filled lives. I would never put that at risk." He taught at a local college, became a handyman around the house, and even performed as an actor, portraying a bank guard in the film *Four Days*.

(1990), for example, divided married couples into those who had married others most similar to them, from those who had married people relatively different from themselves. Personality was assessed according to the California Q-Sort, which, recall, is a list of statements arranged according to the degree that they apply to the individual. The researchers found that those who married people most similar to themselves appeared to choose situations similar to each other, expected to change each other less, and, as a consequence, possessed personalities that remained relatively unchanged across adulthood. By comparison, those who married people more different from themselves changed more over the eleven-year period than others.

Reid was a well-known figure in British Columbia's arts scene, and an example to many that true rehabilitation was possible. He often began interviews by saying, "My criminal career ended on the day I took up writing." He had numerous friends in the art scene, and loved ones. William Deverell, a novelist who lived nearby, described him as "an exemplary character. He'd become a pillar of the community, one of the most gentlemanly figures in all Canada" (p. A5). Apparently, however, he also missed the exhilaration of his bank robbing days.

The city of Victoria is the mostly law-abiding capital of British Columbia. Situated on the harbor, its Beacon Hill Park is full of tourists. On June 9, 1999, Reid robbed a bank, but the job was botched. He and his fellow robbers led a reckless, careening, car chase—and later foot chase—around and through Beacon Hill Park. After a six-hour armed standoff, he and the others were arrested for bank robbery, along with hostage taking and attempted murder. At the age of forty-nine, Reid had returned to a life of crime.

Toward the end of Reid's domestic life, he had become addicted to heroin (although upon capture, he claimed to have gone straight). He was sentenced to eighteen years in jail by the judge in the case and is now serving out his time. Hana Gartner (September 8, 1999) of the Canadian Broadcasting Corporation, tried to explore why Reid reverted to a life of crime:

GARTNER: Can you help us understand a little bit?

REID: You know I wish I could. I wish I could say, you know, oh, I did heroin or I went crazy. Or you know I was the poster boy and I just fell apart and these pressures did this to me. Or you know: you know I served 14-and-a-half years, therefore I am damaged in a way that I can't. You know, whatever. You know I wish I could point to something. Or I am morally inferior to the rest of the population. Whatever. I am sure there are pieces of all of those that are true. You know but, I did some—I made some bad moves in there. You know I made some bad choices and I didn't do some things. And I think it's the absence of things that we do.

GARTNER: But it's more than that. It's clearly actively self-destructive.

REID: I think in the end, the last, you know the last actions that we're talking about, I think, you know, for sure that way.

GARTNER: Could you put me in your head at that time? What led up to it?

REID: You don't want to go there Hana. You don't want to go in my head at that time.

Frustratingly, Reid ends the interview that way. The case of Stephen Reid raises many questions. In relation to the consistency of personality, Reid's transition from criminal to community leader to criminal can be read in a variety of ways.

What Are Young Adults Like?

The Tasks of Young Adulthood

Developmental psychologists generally recognize a period that marks a transition to adulthood, termed the Early Adult Transition or, Emerging Adulthood (Arnett, 2000; Levinson, 1977). This period involves a sort of rehearsal for later life in which one begins to put into practice one's plans for adulthood. During this period, occupations are chosen, adult relationships are commenced (or continued), and the young person begins "climbing the steps" of a ladder toward greater accomplishments. During this period, the young person typically tries to keep some options open, because he or she is neither certain about the career or the relationships that are best. There is great diversity of possible living arrangements and life pursuits possible during the beginnings of the stage, relative to many other times of life (Arnett, 2000). As time goes on, however, the young person gradually increases his or her commitments. The tale is told that Sigmund Freud was once asked what he thought a normal person should be able to do well. He replied, quite briefly, "to love and to work"—and those are indeed, central tasks of this time as well as of later adulthood ("Lieben und arbeiten"; Erikson, 1963, pp. 164–165).

Finding a Desirable Partner

In Search of Intimacy

In terms of personal relationships, both men and women often share the desire to marry someone who is kind and understanding and who has an exciting personality. Beyond that, however, lie some sex differences. In survey research crossing dozens of cultures, men tend to favor physical appearance attributes more than do women, whereas women seek men with financial status and ambition that may lead to their higher status.

Such differences have both evolutionary and social explanations—which at times appear not so different. The general idea is that, in seeking physical attractiveness, men have developed the notion that physical attractiveness in a mate is likely to correspond to health and fertility. In seeking financial resources in men, women have developed the idea that, since men in many cultures exert more control over money, if they want good resources, that is an important part of choosing a spouse. Some psychologists believe that such ideas may be developed as a way of maximizing opportunities for survival and reproduction; others argue that the culture simply taught these ideas apart from their possible evolutionary advantages (Buss & Barnes, 1986).

These attitudes filter into how a person presents him or herself to the opposite sex. Consider the personal advertisements men and women place in newspapers and circulars to meet one another. Women's ads more often describe their physical attributes, emphasizing their own attractiveness; on average, they seek men older than themselves. Men's ads more often stress their financial resources and occupational status; they seek women younger than themselves (Kenrick & Keefe, 1992).

Another such difference is that young men report preferring far more sexual partners than women do (see Chapter 11). To see whether this preference operated in actual behavior, Clark and Hatfield (1989) studied male or female students who were walking alone across campus during the day. When they spotted a student, they sent an attractive individual of the other sex to the student walking alone. This person—called an experimental confederate—was actually working with the experimenter but hid this information. The confederate addressed the student, saying, "I've been noticing you around campus. I find you very attractive." Depending upon the randomly selected condition, the confederate then went on to ask one of three questions: "Would you go out with me tonight?"; "Would you come over to my apartment tonight?"; or "Would you go to bed with me tonight?"

In the three separate times this study was conducted, in 1978, 1982, and 1990, the results were much the same. Both men and women were willing to go on a date with the confederate at least 50 percent of the time (Men, 60% to 70%; Women, 50%). This makes some sense because of the developmental need during this time to find a partner. On the other hand, men were far more willing to go to an apartment with a woman than the other way around (50% to 70% for men versus 1% to 10% for women, across studies). Most dramatically, about 70 percent of the men expressed willingness to go to bed with the women after a three sentence invitation; among women, not one accepted the invitation over three studies over three decades. Women typically responded, "You've got to be kidding!" or "What's wrong with you?" Men, on the other hand, felt a need to make excuses if they *didn't* accept the invitation to go to bed. This sex difference has been explained both in terms of the evolutionary pressures for women to exert greater care over their choice of partner, as well as social considerations of the proper standards of behavior, their reputations, and concerns over their safety (Clark, 1990).

Connecting Window   *Experimental Designs and the Connections between Personality and Social Psychology*
The social situation often can be experimentally manipulated to see how the average personality responds to different situations. This is an instance in which experimental designs are very useful to the study of personality. See also, in Chapter 2:"What Research Designs Are Used in Personality?"

In more natural settings, men and women use a variety of strategies to meet one another. Much of what men and women do is similar (Buss, 1988). They often try to be around members of the opposite sex. They act nicely, they both take opportunities to touch the other, to display their sophistication—and sometimes, to lie a little. A list of some of the most effectively rated tactics men and women employ to form a relationship is shown in Table 12.2, rank ordered according to their importance (Buss, 1988, p. 624). Table 12.3 shows tactics that men and women used differently from one another. For example, men are more apt than women to discuss the money they expect to make and the prestige they will obtain. Women are more apt than men to enhance their appearance by wearing makeup and altering their appearance more generally. Buss (1988), who works from an evolutionary perspective, has explained such findings by suggesting that over history, men attracted mates through possessing resources, and women attracted mates through appearing healthy and able to bear and rear children. An alternative account for the differences is that they arise out of social teachings.

General physiological arousal heightens sexual attraction to a potential sexual partner. For example, male participants in one study sat next to a very attractive

---

TABLE 12.2 **Certain Tactics in Dating and Partnering Are Important and Effective for Both Sexes**

Tactics for Dating and Partnering	Mean Ratings	
	For Men	For Women
1. displayed a good sense of humor	6.38	6.41
2. was sympathetic to her/his troubles	6.07	6.15
3. showed good manners	5.93	6.07
4. made an effort to spend a lot of time with the individual	5.83	5.59
5. offered to help him/her	5.76	5.48
6. kept physically fit to create a healthy appearance	5.76	5.85
7. showered daily	5.76	6.04
8. wore attractive outfits	5.45	5.48
9. smiled a lot at women/men	5.14	5.30
10. participated in extracurricular activities	5.04	5.41

Source: Buss (1988), selections from Tables 5 and 6. Reprinted with permission of the American Psychological Association.

TABLE 12.3 **Examples of the Tactics Undergraduate Men and Women Use Differently in Dating and Partnering**

Used More by Men	Used More by Women
1. He lifted weights.	She was sympathetic to his troubles.
2. He gave encouraging glances to girls.	She wore facial makeup.
3. He bought a woman dinner at a nice restaurant.	She went on a diet to improve her figure.
4. He had sex on the first date.	She wore stylish, fashionable clothes.
5. He went to parties to meet girls.	She played hard to get.
6. He looked at a woman repeatedly.	She learned how to apply cosmetics.
7. He talked about how good he was at sports.	She wore a necklace.
8. He drove an expensive car.	She smiled a lot at men.
9. He pretended he was easy—he teased her.	She kept herself well-groomed.
10. He flashed a lot of money to impress her.	She got a new, interesting hairstyle.

Source: Buss (1988), selections from Tables 2 and 3. Reprinted with permission of the American Psychological Association.

female participant—actually, an experimental confederate—in a laboratory. The identified experimenter told the young man and woman that they would be receiving either mild or painful shocks. The young male participant and female confederate were then told to go into separate rooms to complete a questionnaire, during which the shock equipment would be readied. First, though, the attractive woman stood up, stepped directly in front of the man and searched for a pencil in her coat, so as to attract the young man's attention. On average, men who were expecting to receive stronger shocks reported on their questionnaires that they were more attracted to the woman than those expecting milder shocks (Dutton & Aron, 1974, Experiment 3). In other studies, women who have gone through a very upsetting experience have been found similarly to find an attractive man more romantically appealing than in other circumstances. The effects are found even when experimenters point out the arousing nature of the threat, so that participants know they are aroused by something other than someone else's attractiveness (Allen et al., 1989).

Powerful individual differences exist in sexuality as well. Recall from Chapter 4 that Shafer (2001) had developed a scale of sexuality that included self-descriptors such as alluring, sexy, seductive, ravenous, and lusty. These and other sexual terms are distinct enough from the Big Five traits to have been proposed as different dimensions, although some argue that they might fall into a Big Five–like pattern (e.g., Schmitt & Buss, 2000). People who score high on such sexuality scales are more likely to be single, have a higher interest in dating, date for longer periods of time, and more readily get over their last relationship to start dating again (Shafer, 2001). So, higher levels of sexuality may well predict having more partners and a more active dating life in early adulthood.

Falling in Love

Passionate Love: A strong feeling for a potential or actual life partner involving intense arousal and longing for joining with the other.

Companionate Love: A caring and desire for another person with whom our lives intertwine. It emphasizes intimacy and concern for the other.

Assortive Mating: The tendency to find a mate who is similar to oneself in one or more dimensions.

Complementary Selection: The tendency to find a mate who is different from oneself on one or more dimensions.

The degree to which someone is attracted to another may also be determined by their preferred romantic style. Several models have been proposed to describe individual differences in romance and love. Perhaps the most common distinction among such theories is between **passionate love** and **companionate love**. Passionate love involves intense arousal and longing for joining with another. It feels powerful, full of desire, and difficult to ignore on a moment-by-moment basis. By contrast, companionate love refers to the caring and desire we feel for another person with whom our lives intertwine. It emphasizes tenderness, intimacy, and concern (Hatfield, 1988; Hendrick & Hendrick, 2003). Beyond that, classifications of love include possessive love, in which a partner wants to bind together and control the other, altruistic love, in which a person is willing to suffer and sacrifice to protect the other, and erotic love, in which there is a great deal of physical and sexual excitement (e.g., Hendrick, & Hendrick, 1986; Sternberg, 1987; 1997). Exactly what causes people to fall in love is, you will not be surprised to hear, not yet entirely understood.

Similarity in Mate Selection

Two competing hypotheses concerning choosing a partner are the **assortive mating** hypothesis: that one chooses someone similar to oneself, and the **complementary**

selection hypothesis: that opposites attract. Of these two hypotheses, it is now well-established that people engage in assortive mating, choosing others who are like themselves. A number of mechanisms contribute to the preference for a similar partner. Freud's (1927) idea was that parents serve as a child's first love, and that later romantic attraction will be triggered by finding characteristics in a new person in common with one's parents. Evolutionary biologists have concurred that selection according to similarity both to oneself and to one's parents may favor finding someone with a similar genetic background (e.g., Epstein & Guttman, 1984). The parent of the opposite sex may influence such selection more strongly although both parents may exert such influences (Daly & Wilson, 1990; Epstein & Guttman, 1984; Geher, 2003; Jedlicka, 1984).

Empirical findings support matches both to oneself and to one's parents (Geher, 2003). Five-hundred undergraduates, their romantic partners, and their parents all described themselves on the Big Five personality traits. The prediction of similarity between the parent and the chosen partner was confirmed even after the student's

Research in Focus

Identical Twins Reared Apart

A focus on research doesn't always mean experimental design and statistics. Sometimes the core of a great research project is people who care about what—and who—they are studying. In her book *Entwined Lives: Twins and What They Tell Us about Human Behavior,* Nancy Segal provides readers with a personal view of the Minnesota Study of Twins Reared Apart. Segal, who herself has a fraternal twin sister, found working at the Minnesota study a "dream job" that complemented her doctoral research on twins (Segal, 1999, p. 120).

In the 1970s and 1980s when the Minnesota studies began, most people were unaware that twins were still being separated (Segal, 1999, p. 116). Separating twins at birth (or shortly thereafter) strikes most people as unfair and unkind—if not tragic. The separated twins in the Minnesota studies were mostly separated several decades before to hide the then-serious stigma of their illegitimate births. Others were separated due to the death or divorce of parents, because the adoption agency could not find suitable parents who could adopt two children at once, wartime crises, and even a "switching" at birth.

After one twin set, the "Jim twins," were separated, Jim Springer's adoptive parents were told by the adoption agency that his twin had died at birth. When he was thirty-nine, he contacted the adoption agency to find out more about his background and was surprised to learn that his twin was still alive. He called his twin and they were reunited several weeks later.

Other twins have been reunited through mistaken identity. When reared-apart fraternal twin Kerry Keyser moved to Burlington, Vermont at age twenty-five, people kept approaching her and referring to her as "Amy." Curious, she learned that they thought she was Amy Jackson. When she tracked down Amy they discovered they were twins reared apart. The late John Stroud, a British social service official who developed a unique specialty of reuniting twins, reunited the famous "Giggle Twins," Barbara Herbert and Daphne Goodship. Each twin sets off prolonged laughter in the other, and those outside the pair often cannot understand why (Segal, 1999, pp. 127–128).

The discovery of separated twins often came to the attention of the researchers at

own self-rated profile (which resembled both the parent and the romantic partner) was statistically controlled for.

Despite the overall evidence for assortive mating, there are some intriguing exceptions. Under strict assurances of confidentiality, Lykken and Tellegen (1993) asked identical twins whether they were attracted to their co-twin's spouse. They found there was no more attraction to one's twin's spouse for identical twins than there was for fraternal, dizygotic twins. Indeed, many twins disliked their co-twin's spouse. The same held true for the spouses of identical twins when evaluating the other twin. The researchers tentatively raised the question of whether people who are similar simply spend more time together, for example, because people attending the same college are likely to be somewhat similar in skills, or because people who share the same religion may meet one another while worshipping. If various social contexts bring together similar people, romantic love might operate in such contexts as a rather random phenomenon. To find out more about research with adult twins, including those twins reared apart, see the Research in Focus box.

Minnesota through a newspaper article, a report on the radio, or a phone call. Segal tracked down one set of twins—Iris Johns and Aro Campbell—after she found them listed in the Guinness Book of World Records as being the world's longest separated twins, reunited at age seventy-five. Iris and Aro were soon flown to Minnesota and added to the study (Segal, 1999, p. 123).

When separated twins are brought to Minnesota, they receive royal treatment, and are also put to work. A member of the research team picks them up at the airport. They are brought (usually together) to the University and interviewed and studied in depth—taking dozens of tests and even having their eye, dental, and other medical records compared.

When the "Jim" twins were brought to Minnesota for study, their remarkable similarities stretched people's imaginations about what genetics might account for. As children, both had dogs named "Toy." The twins each married a "Linda," divorced her, and then married a "Betty." One twin had a son named James Allen; the other had a son named James Alen. Both visited the same three-block stretch of a Florida beach for vacation, each one driving a blue Chevrolet. Both worked part-time as sheriffs, smoked Salems, and enjoyed Miller Lite beer. Both bit their fingernails, suffered from the same type of headache, and spread love-notes to their wives around the house. They did, however, wear their hair differently, express their thoughts rather differently, and one twin had been divorced a second time (Segal, 1999, p. 118).

When the Minnesota Twins baseball team were close to capturing the World Series in 1987, sports reporter Ira Berkow ended up in Segal's office—having been sent there by a departmental assistant who (mis)connected the (Minnesota) Twins and twins. Segal was on the way to the airport to attend a party thrown by her recently married sister when Berlow knocked on her door. Her interview, a comedy of errors about twins and the Twins, made it into the local sports pages. After mentioning that she liked Frank Viola, the Twins' pitcher, because of his intensity, Berkow asked her if Viola was her favorite twin. She answered, "No, my sister Anne is"—a comment that later greatly entertained her sister and the other party guests (Segal, 1999, pp. 208–209).

How similar are the members of a couple? Modestly so. Across pairs of couples, physical size and shape correlate between $r = .10$ and $.30$, physical attractiveness is higher at $r = .52$ (Murstein, 1972; Plomin, DeFries, & Roberts, 1977; White, 1980). IQ and educational attainment correlate between $r = .35$ and $.46$ (Bouchard & McGue, 1981; Plomin et al., 1977). The coefficients for self-reported personality traits range from about $r = .15$ to $.35$. The similarity for religious belief may range as high as $r = .60$ (Buss, 1984; Caspi, Herbener, & Ozer, 1992; Lykken & Tellegen, 1993).

In Search of Good Work

Realistic Occupations: Those jobs or careers dealing with work that must respond to definite requirements of land or objects (e.g., farmer, mechanic).

Investigative Occupations: Those jobs or careers involving the investigation of information, or exploration of new ideas or possibilities.

Artistic Occupations: Those jobs or careers stressing communication, creativity, art, and entertainment.

Social Occupations: Those jobs or careers involving working with people, including social workers, managers, and therapists.

Enterprising Occupations: Those jobs or careers involving the influencing of others, including salespeople, politicians, and entrepreneurs.

Conventional Occupations: Those jobs or careers involving work with numbers and letters, including secretaries, bookkeepers, accountants, and engineers.

As a young person tries to find the proper partner, he or she also will search for a match with an occupation. Every occupation, like every person, has its own character. One widely employed classification of occupations divides them into six broad categories: **realistic**, **investigative**, **artistic**, **social**, **enterprising**, and **conventional** occupations—described by the acronym RIASEC (Holland, 1997). Realistic occupations include farmers, surveyors, mechanics, and carpenters who must respond to the definite requirements of the land, of raw materials and of manufactured objects. Investigative occupations include biologists, chemists, and anthropologists, who undertake scientific research. Artistic occupations include writers, actors, art directors, and interior decorators, who must employ creativity and shape communication.

These occupations can be arranged in a hexagram to portray relationships among them (see Figure 12.1). Those types that are opposite one another have little overlap in interests or aptitudes. For example, the realism of the mechanic or carpenter shares relatively little overlap with the social occupations, including social workers, teachers, therapists, and clergy, who enjoy working with people.

On the other hand, occupations next to each other are more closely related, such as the Enterprising and Conventional. Enterprising occupations include salespeople, politicians, and television reporters, who are interested in influencing others. Conventional occupations include bookkeepers, accountants, industrial engineers, who enjoy working with numbers, letters, and words. The enterprising reporter must be concerned with words, just as the conventional accountant hopes to influence the salesperson.

Looking for an occupation that fits one's interests is important to finding a career match, just as looking for someone similar to oneself is important in finding a romantic match. Many of the occupational interest tests designed today are intended to help match a person to others with similar interests. The basic assumption here is that if a person has interests and abilities necessary to perform the job, then the person will be relatively happy in the job. For example, 345 paying-and-receiving bank tellers were studied at a major bank from the time they were hired to a follow up four months later. Expected satisfaction with their job was an excellent predictor of actual job satisfaction four months later, at $r = .67$ (Gottfredson & Holland, 1989).

Next, each of the beginning tellers' test profiles on a vocational interest survey was compared to the ideal profile of the profession. Bank tellers tend to score high on the conventional, enterprising, and social scales of occupational inventories relative to other scales (e.g., Holland, 1987). After statistically controlling for satisfaction, the interest-to-occupation match predicted job satisfaction and involvement, with an $r =$

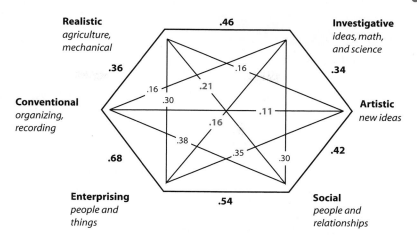

FIGURE 12.1

Psychological Types of Occupations
The Holland Occupational Hexagram divides occupations into six groups that correspond to different psychological interests and aptitudes. Higher correlations refer to greater similarities between occupational groups.
Source: Holland et al. (1969), Figure 1, p. 4.

.36. So, matching exists, and it is important. It does, however, operate secondarily to an individual's general sense of satisfaction (Gottfredson & Holland, 1990).

Occupations contribute to the individual's sense of meaning and purpose in life. They provide a means of generating support for one's family and of supporting society more generally. Such occupations also provide for the economic and general well-being of the next generation. A group of scholars called futurists study and prepare for the future. Some future thinking in regard to personality psychology is illustrated in the accompanying Disciplinary Crossroads box.

How Does the Individual Traverse Middle Adulthood?

Some people experience middle adulthood as a time of calm progress in their family and occupational spheres. Others are less satisfied and may confront the need for major change. For many individuals, the ages of thirty, forty, and fifty are considered landmark ages in that each refers to the end of an old decade and beginning of a new. As people traverse such landmark years, they are often prompted to consider how things have gone and might be expected to go in the future. Many people experience love and growth at home, and experience promotions and other signs of appreciation at work (Levinson, 1978).

Other people will lead less enviable lives. Some will obviously fail, being denied promotion or advancement, or losing jobs regularly. They will experience marital discord and risk divorce. Others, although maintaining the outward trappings of success, will suffer inwardly because they failed to adequately connect their interests to their activities earlier on; they now fail to feel their part, as it were, and experience a sense of alienation from their lives (Levinson, 1978). Some may try to stay the course while others find continuing up the ladder to be intolerable, and attempt to break out. This may be successful sometimes, but a new start can be costly, for it often takes eight to ten years to restabilize in another setting. That is, one must not only break out of where one is, but break in somewhere else, at a disadvantage relative to others who have gotten there many years before. In this section we will examine success in marriage, at work, in health—and mid-course corrections.

Disciplinary Crossroads

Personality and the Future

Just as individuals can be generative, helping to lay the groundwork for the next generation, so whole fields can be generative, by helping to improve humanity. But where will personality psychology contribute next? Futurists are people who form a discipline that attempts to plan for and predict the future. What sorts of visions do they see for human personality? Here are a few of their speculations. Although some sound as much like science fiction as science, they can help us imagine what might be possible—and whether or not we would like it.

- Computers with personality: People will order up computers that possess the personality of a favorite individual. The David Letterman personality would make your computer sound—and make jokes—like David Letterman. The Tom Brokaw or Peter Jennings personalities would keep you up-to-date on the world's latest news (Frey & Frey, 1998).
- Tests for alcoholism *before it develops*. Some alcoholics are anxious, rigid, and overcontrolled. They are hypersensitive to stress and their brains may release too much cortisol in response to stress. They drink to relax and feel normal. A second type of alcoholism involves impulsiveness, thrill-seeking, and antisocial qualities. Such individuals possess a unique EEG brain wave pattern that, ultimately, may be linked to the gene that causes

it. These alcoholics drink and take drugs to slow themselves down. It may be possible to identify both types of alcoholic disorders in children before the individual becomes an alcoholic and to treat them in order to prevent the disease (Stocker, 2002).
- Your brain could be connected to a computer that helps it think. During brain surgery, an extremely thin electronic probe designed to monitor a neural network could be inserted across the corpus callosum. Recall that the corpus callosum is the brain structure that connects the right and left hemispheres. The electronic probe would monitor messages passing from one hemisphere to the other, and transmit them to a helmet worn on the individual's head. The helmet would contain another computer that gradually interprets the messages. From there, well, the computer might insert auxiliary memories that might be helpful, record one's own memories so that they wouldn't be lost, or simply take over personality functions for a dying brain (Pohl & Moravec, 1993).
- Robots will gradually become so sophisticated that they take over human thought and develop sophisticated personalities themselves. They would create mental models of themselves and be able to act autonomously. Human personality would then become "transhuman"—that is, present in robots and other mechanisms as well (Moravec, 2000).

Staying Married

Success in marriage involves both being satisfied with one's marriage, and avoiding divorce. Divorce has been a regularly studied outcome as it provides a usually certain indication of a failed marriage. A number of factors predict marital satisfaction and divorce, including factors related to society, personality, and development. Among the social factors contributing to divorce, economic hardship looms large (Conger et al., 1990). A number of studies indicate that divorce rates rise during times of economic turbulence and dislocation such as occurred, for example, during the Great Depression in the 1930s and the lesser economic pressures of the 1980s in the United States (Bakke, 1940; Dooley & Catalano, 1988; Elder, 1974). Mounting economic pressures on families generally bring budgetary concerns into focus, creating a sense of frustration, irritability, and anger in the couple (Liker & Elder, 1983). In regard to parental influences, having nurturing, involved parents leads to greater social competence and relationship satisfaction—even controlling for personality traits (Donnellan, Larsen-Rife, & Conger, 2005). But what are the specific personality traits related to marriage and divorce?

Kelly and Conley (1987) followed three hundred couples from their engagement in the 1930s through their lives at age sixty-eight. The personalities of the members of the couples were rated by acquaintances on a number of personality dimensions at the time of their engagement. The authors found that three variables were predictive of marital satisfaction and continued stability of the marriage: the emotional calmness of the husband, the emotional calmness of the wife, and the lack of impulsivity in the husband. The researchers found that early-life ratings on impulsivity were related to the likelihood the husband would have an extramarital affair—one of the major listed causes of divorce in the sample. Indeed, impulsivity in the husband, and negative emotionality in the husband and wife together accounted for nearly 50 percent of the variance in whether the couple would be among the roughly one in six who divorced in the study—a very high rate of prediction.

Other studies have obtained similar findings for negative emotion (Eysenck, 1980), and for poor self-control (e.g., Loeb, 1966). Still other personality factors—like extraversion—appear to enhance the social opportunities for promiscuity (Bentler & Newcomb, 1978; Eysenck, 1980; Kelly & Conley 1987). Twin studies, too, have found some evidence for a genetic basis of mental life that leads to divorce, with estimates ranging from 25 percent to 50 percent contributions of personality to divorce (McGue & Lykken, 1992).

In a study of nearly two thousand couples, Jockin, McGue, and Lykken (1996) found that a number of personality traits are related to maintaining a marriage. They employed the traits measured by the Multidimensional Personality Questionnaire. At the broadest level, these include Positive Affect, Negative Affect, and Personal Constraint. The researchers found that negative emotionality predicted a greater likelihood of divorce, whereas more positive emotionality *also* predicts divorce. The reasons for negative emotionality are fairly clear—such emotions trigger frustration, hostility, and anger in the couple over time. Positive emotion's contribution probably entails a willingness to consider alternative partners. A third superfactor, Personal Constraint (the reverse of Impulsiveness), is related more highly to maintaining a marriage.

These general patterns are elucidated more clearly at the level of more specific traits that their test also measures. Among those specific factors, traits such as social potency contributed to higher likelihoods of divorce. Social potency involves forcefulness, decisiveness, dominance, and leading—which are likely to attract other potential partners and, perhaps, make dissatisfied partners even more unhappy. Alienation, a feeling of being mistreated or victimized, also predicts divorce. Absorption—that is, a certain capacity to become lost in thought, to be hypnotizeable, and to exhibit absentmindedness, also negatively impacts a marriage. Reactivity to stress—for husbands only—increases the likelihood of divorce as well.

TABLE 12.4	Correlations of Personality Traits with Staying Married (Two Levels)		
	Measures	**Men**	**Women**
Higher Order Scales	Positive emotion	−.07[*]	−.15[**]
	Negative emotion	−.13[**]	−.12[**]
	Constraint	.11[**]	.15[**]
Primary Scales	Well-being	.06[*]	.04[*]
	Social potency	−.14[**]	−.20[**]
	Achievement	−.03	−.16[*]
	Social closeness	.02	.05[*]
	Reactivity to Stress	−.10[**]	.04
	Alienation	−.08[**]	−.02
	Control	.05	.11[**]
	Harm Avoidance	.07[*]	.12[**]
	Traditionalism	.20[**]	.24[**]
	Absorption	−.11[**]	−.17[**]

[*]Statistically significant at the $p < .05$ level; [**] Statistically significant at the $p < .01$ level.

Source: Adapted from full sample results Jockin, McGue, & Lykken (1996), p. 293. Reprinted with permission of American Psychological Association.

Among factors that maintain a marriage, a higher desire for control—among wives only—serves as a positive factor. In addition, as a desire for traditionalism rises in either or both spouses, the marriage is more likely to be maintained. The same is true for a desire to avoid personal harm. The more one is self-protective, the more likely it is for a marriage to be maintained.

How important are these effects? The predictions account for about 14 percent of the variance of marriage maintenance in women and 8 percent in men, or about a quarter of the variance in divorce risk for a couple together, which is substantial when considering other social, economic, and chance factors (Jockin, McGue, & Lykken, 1996, p. 296).

Finally, in keeping with our developmental perspective, it is worth noting the effect of divorce on the next generation. The children of divorce are known to suffer relative to children of intact marriages (Amato & Keith, 1991; Hetherington, Bridges, & Insabella, 1998). Is that due to a genetic predisposition toward troubled traits on the part of children, or due to the negative impact of the divorce itself? A novel answer to this question was provided by O'Connor and colleagues (2000) who studied the biological and adopted children of parents who divorced. Those researchers found that all children reacted to divorce with elevated psychological problems, including increased substance abuse. This was true even though the adopted children shared little genetic relation to their parents. On the other hand, the biological children of divorced parents—but not the adopted children—exhibited lower achievement and poorer social skills, suggesting that lower mental skills in the parents led both to a greater likelihood of divorce and produced a negative genetic impact on their biological childrens' academic and social skills. These are average, relative, effects for the children of divorce; even given such findings, many of the children can be expected to go on to thrive in the future.

Finding Occupational Success

General Factors

Career success can be measured in relation to two general criteria. The first includes one's own sense of personal satisfaction and achievement. The second includes such objective measures as level of responsibility, prestige of position, and salary. Personality qualities influence each area. In cross-sectional studies, researchers examine correlations between various personality traits and career outcomes at one point in time (Judge et al., 1999). Concerning objective measures, by far the most pervasive findings are that general intelligence and conscientiousness lead to greater objective success across occupations (Barrick & Mount, 1991; Judge et al., 1999; Ree, 1991). Conscientious workers are rewarded with higher salaries, particularly those beginning on their career paths. Emotionally stable workers also earn more (Nyhus & Pons, 2005).

> Work is an extension of personality. It is achievement. It is one of the ways in which a person defines himself, measures his worth, and his humanity.
>
> Peter Drucker

Judge and others (1999) studied occupational success by analyzing data from three longitudinal studies, involving 354 individuals. Following such a set of individuals over time allows researchers to draw generalizations concerning how a person's beginning personality influences his or her later life outcomes. In this study, the single greatest contribution to objective career success was mental ability, with a correlation of slightly above $r = .50$. The Big Five factor of conscientiousness predicted objective success at a still very respectable level of $r = .40$. Figure 12.2 shows the relationships of several further personality attributes and

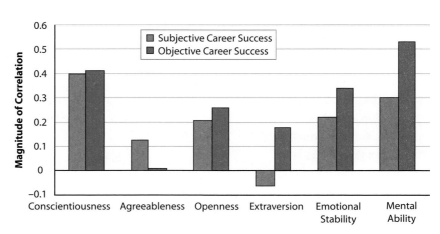

FIGURE 12.2

Personality Attributes and Their Correlations with Career Success

The bar graph represents the strength of correlations between personality traits and abilities, and success at various careers.

Source: Based on Judge et al. (1999).

ultimate career success in middle age. The contributions to subjective career success (e.g., career satisfaction) were similar, but with conscientiousness and intelligence reversed in importance. These individuals have learned that effort counts, and they appear to factor it into their own success. Next after these two influences, emotional stability (that is, low Neuroticism) contributes considerably to the picture, followed by Openness. Judge and colleagues' findings also indicate that job satisfaction and objective qualities of one's job are somewhat related.

Positivity and Job Satisfaction over the Lifespan

A second longitudinal study of careers placed more emphasis on studying motivation- and emotion-related traits and their influences. The sample was the approximately 1,037 children born during the year beginning April 1, 1972, in Dunedin, New Zealand (Roberts, Caspi, & Moffitt, 2003). For this study, the participants' personality was assessed at the age of eighteen, and then their occupational status and personality were examined again eight years later at the age of twenty-six.

The four broad traits studied included (a) negative affect, including aggression, alienation, and stress reactions, (b) positive communitarian emotions, including well-being and social closeness, (c) positive agentic emotions, including the need for achievement and social potency, and (d) personal constraint, including traditionalism and harm avoidance. Negative affect predicted lower occupational attainment, lower pay, and less work satisfaction. Positive communitarian emotions, positive agentic emotion, and personal constraint each individually predicted higher occupational and financial attainment.

Interestingly, young people with negative affect who nonetheless managed to obtain higher status occupations at age eighteen became more positive and self-controlled at age twenty-six—approaching in satisfaction those who were already more positive. There appears, therefore, to be a mutually positive interaction between positive communitarian traits, and high status positions (Roberts, Caspi, & Moffit, 2003).

Having a Temper

Undercontrolled childhood personality—especially evidenced by severe temper tantrums—may still exert problematic influences later in life. Caspi, Elder, and Bem (1987) obtained developmental data on a number of men and women over a forty-year period. Many of the children in the study had been rated by their mothers on their temper tantrums at the ages of eight, nine, and eleven. The researchers formed two groups: the first contained about 40 percent of the boys and 30 percent of the girls who had been rated as having particularly frequent and severe temper tantrums. The comparison group consisted of their calmer peers.

In the military (which 70% of the boys had entered), those with explosive tempers as children had achieved lower rank, on average, than their calmer peers. As they neared fifty, there were clear occupational differences between this temper tantrum group and the other children. The boys who had experienced explosive temper tantrums as children were less occupationally successful than the other boys. This appeared related to their shifting jobs more frequently and their longer periods of unemploy-

> Mathematicians tell the following joke: A certain individual had a personality that was so negative, that when he walked into a party, people would ask, "who left?"
>
> Paul Hoffman

ment. In fact, those with high tempers from a middle-class upbringing had been downwardly mobile and could now no longer be distinguished from their working-class counterparts. Finally, the men in the explosive temper group were divorced at nearly double the rate of their calmer peers (40% versus 22%).

Biological underpinnings may affect success in some occupations. Dabbs (1992) was interested in the paradoxical effects of testosterone on male status. Within animals, testosterone is associated with aggression that serves to achieve status (Svare, 1983). Among contemporary men, however, aggression is not highly prized, and greater aggressiveness may be problematic. Dabbs found that among more than four thousand men who were tested in the armed services, those with the highest testoterone later were more likely to be unemployed or in industrial occupations such as welders, ironworkers, and miners. Those with the lower testosterone were more likely to work as professionals and managers (farmers were also a lower testosterone group). Among women, however, testosterone may increase the likelihood of attaining career status. For example, women with high testosterone were more likely to become professional or technical workers relative to clerical workers or homemakers (Purifoy & Koopmans, 1979).

The Positivity Factor Further Considered

Positive emotionality is particularly important in areas that involve selling an idea or concept, or in selling oneself—as in an election. Indeed, one of the most important psychological variables in winning elections seems to be the optimism of the candidates who are running. The optimist holds the advantage. An extreme example of this was the Eisenhower–Stevenson presidential election of 1952. In Eisenhower's acceptance of the nomination, he announced, "Ladies and gentlemen, you have summoned me on behalf of millions of your fellow Americans to lead a great crusade—for freedom in America and freedom in the world." His opponent, Adlai Stevenson, by contrast, expressed considerable conflict over his own nomination: "That my heart has been troubled, that I have not sought the nomination, that I could not seek it in good conscience, that I would not seek it in honest self-appraisal, is not to say I value it the less" (Simonton, 1994, p. 253). Eisenhower won. Candidates who employed an optimistic style in their campaigning won in eighteen of twenty-two presidential elections from 1900 to 1984. Athletics is another domain in which optimism is important, where the belief one has about being able to win is related to winning (Simonton, 1994, p. 253).

Toward Greatness

Lotka-Price Law: A law of productivity of the members of a given field that states that the square root of the total will account for half the productivity.

If one wants to be more successful in a field, one especially key factor appears to be effort. The **Lotka-Price Law** (Price, 1963; 1986, chap. 3) states that, given k people active in a discipline, the square root of k identifies the number of people responsible for half the contributions. For example, there are about 250 classical composers whose music is still played actively. These range from the well-known, such as Mozart and Beethoven, to the relatively obscure, such as Busoni, Dukas, and Ponchielli. The square root of 250 is 15.8 = 16. By the Lotka-Price law, we split the 250 classical composers into two groups: 16 top composers and the remaining 234 composers. The top ten among these sixteen include Mozart, Beethoven, Bach, Wagner, Brahms, Schubert, Handel, Tchaikovsky, Verdi, and Haydn. These and the remaining top sixteen

• FACTS • AT • A • GLANCE •

Accomplishments at Older Ages

Name	Brief Description	Age of Accomplishment
James Earl Carter	U.S. President. After presidency brokered four-month cease fire between Bosnian Muslims and Serbs and secured pledges to resume peace negotiations	70
Agatha Christie	Prolific mystery novelist and playwright; wrote the novel, *Curtain* one year before death	84
Cecil B. De Mille	Produced and directed the movie, *The Ten Commandments*	74
Benjamin Franklin	Helped to draft the United States Declaration of Independence	81
Betty Friedan	At age 42 wrote, *The Feminine Mystique,* which helped launch the women's movement; recently wrote a memoir entitled, *Life So Far*	79
John H. Glenn, Jr.	First American to orbit the earth, later, a U.S. senator. Then, blasted off as payload specialist on the space shuttle *Discovery*.	77
Vladimir Horowitz	Concert pianist who continued performing in concert until his death	85
Akira Kurosawa	Director of many well-known films; directed the movie, *Dreams*	80
Duncan Maclean	Athlete who ran 200 meters in forty seconds	90
Nelson Mandela	After release from life sentence in prison, won presidential election against F. W. de Klerk in South Africa, and led nation to a new peaceful era.	75
Giuseppe Verdi	Wrote the opera *Falstaff*	79
Frank Lloyd Wright	Architect who designed and completed the Guggenheim Museum	91

Sources: From Papalia et al. (2002), pp. 223–224; Wallechinsky & Wallace (1995).

composers account for 50 percent of all pieces played and recorded. The remaining 234 account for the rest (Moles, 1958/1966, pp. 28–29).

In psychology, Sigmund Freud's bibliography lists 330 articles and books. Among inventors, Thomas Edison obtained 1,093 patents—still the record at the United States Patent Office (Simonton, 1994, p. 139). Effort may be the key to membership in the top group. Even in the eighteenth century, Sir Joshua Reynolds's lectures to art students emphasized the idea that well-directed, hard work would suffice for a great career. Those who lacked natural genius could make up for it through hard work; natural genius would benefit even more with such work (Reynolds, 1769–1790/1966, p. 37).

Type A personality describes people who are extremely competitive and hostile, work extremely hard, urgently, and have little time for their families—or anyone else.

Senator John Glenn with other astronauts preparing for his launch into space. Although an astronaut for a second time when he was 77, Glenn once remarked, "There is still no cure for the common birthday."

Type A's are expected to do more by their mothers. Type A's exhibit better academic success than Type B students and later in life exhibit higher career success (Mathews, Glass, Rosenman, & Bortner, 1977; Mathews, Helmreich, Beane, & Lucker, G. 1980). As will be seen below, Type A behavioral research also includes attempts to link the pattern to heart disease.

Although great accomplishments are more common earlier than later in adulthood, many accomplishments are brought about by those who have started late but persevered. The Facts-at-a-Glance illustrates some accomplishments that began, or continued, into people's eighties and nineties.

Personality and Health

A substantial body of research has focused on the relation between personality and health. The brief treatment here can only hint at the richness of research in this area. Many reviews suggest that negative, depressed people are not much different in objective measures of health than more positive people (Almada et al., 1991; Wiebe & Smith, 1997). There are some differences, however. First, people with high negative affect report many more health symptoms and problems than do people without such negative affect. Second, both clinical studies of humans and experimental studies with animals suggest that general depression can lead to heart disease, or affect it adversely once it has begun (Grippo & Johnson, 2002); this finding, however, remains controversial (Wiebe & Smith, 1997). One specific type of negative affect that has been shown to have a negative impact on heart disease is hostility.

The negative influences of hostility on heart disease were originally identified as part of a **Type A personality** (Friedman & Rosenman, 1959). The Type A pattern

Type A Personality: A personality type that emphasizes time pressure, competitiveness, achievement striving, impatience, and hostility, and that has been related to heart disease and high professional attainment.

The mystery writer, Agatha Christie, who wrote the novel Curtain *at 84, once remarked, "I live now on borrowed time, waiting in the anteroom for the summons that will inevitably come. And then I go onto the next thing, whatever it is. One doesn't luckily have to bother about that."*

involved competitiveness, hostility, impatience, achievement striving, job involvement, and loud, explosive speech. These characteristics—when identified by a trained interviewer—are indeed predictive of heart disease in samples of patients without other indicators for coronary risk (Mathews, 1988; Miller et al., 1991). Since then, hostility—measured either in an interview or on tests of psychopathology—has been identified as the most potent among the Type A contributors to heart disease (Wiebe & Smith, 1997). Consistent with such findings, when a person's need for power and control is repeatedly blocked and thwarted, it also will lead to increased health risks for the individual (Jemmott, et al., 1990; Wiebe & Smith, 1997).

Coping with stress—or failing to do so—also impacts health. People who are stressed are more susceptible to transient illnesses such as colds, and the depressed may give up—and die—sooner, upon contracting a chronic or fatal disease (e.g., Burton et al., 1986; Carney, Rich, & Freedland, 1988; Frasure-Smith, Lesperance, & Talajic, 1993; Salovey, Rothman, Detweiler, & Steward, 2000). Positive emotionality may buffer the influence of negative emotionality (Salovey et al., 2000).

Asked what his doctor thought of his cigar smoking, George Burns, the comedian who lived to be 100, replied, "My doctor's dead."

Individual differences in the ability to cope can be learned and represent a stable individual differences variable in people—and sometimes in animals as well—that may reduce illness and its effects (e.g., Drugan, et al., 1989; Snyder, 1995). Successful coping can increase the release of natural tranquilizers in the brain and mitigate other harmful health effects (Drugan et al., 1994; Snyder, 1995). Learning to control stress appears to be a promising means of enhancing health in the context of chronic medical conditions (e.g., Tennen, Affleck, Armeli, & Carney, 2000).

Who Adjusts Course?

Many people enjoy considerable social and occupational success, good health, and general satisfaction in middle adulthood; many others will be less fortunate. This means, too, that while some people will stay on the same course, others will feel the need for change. There are many reasons a person may choose to change. Block (1971) studied changers and nonchangers among children growing up in the Berkeley, California, area, who were part of the Berkeley Guidance and Oakland Growth Studies. His focus was on individuals whose personalities remained stable over a fifteen-year span from adolescence to adulthood, versus those who changed over the same period. Personality was assessed with the California Q-Sort. Recall that the technique employs about one hundred statements about a person, which are ranked from most to least applicable to a person. Sorts were completed at adolescence and at adulthood.

Block found that stable individuals of both sexes were more intellectually, emotionally, and socially successful as adolescents than the changers, and also better adjusted. It seems as if consistent individuals stay the same in part because they have good ego control, and that permits them to traverse society's requirements in productive ways.

In contrast, changers change for a variety of reasons (Caspi & Bem, 1990, p. 557). Some changers may appear to change simply because they were more immature to begin with, and their change was a reflection of undergoing more maturation than the rest of the (presumably more mature) sample. That is, they may have needed more time to build up a better-controlled, better-adjusted personality.

A second reason people may change is the pressure of social norms. Many of the changers in the Block study had personalities that, according to various measures, were rather unpleasant to be around. It seems likely that those around such unpleasant individuals put pressure on them over time to change in a more socially desirable direction. On the other hand, that cannot explain all the change, because many changers remained rather unpleasant, if different, as adults.

A third reason people may appear to change is that, although they are actually mostly the same, society views them differently. For example, some women who changed in Block's study became adults between 1945 and 1960, when they were rated by others around them as rebellious and poorly adjusted. The women's movement intervened in the late 1960s, and by later adulthood they were considered better adjusted, although still unconventional and rebellious. It is quite possible that these rebels may have been better adjusted later because society had changed the definition of a well-adjusted woman. Indeed, it seems likely that these women were the ones who participated in the women's movement and changed how society treated women.

No Regrets?

If you are in mid-life and things aren't going well, should you make some changes in your life, or try to stick it out? Stewart and Vandewater (1999) examined a group of two hundred women from the University of Michigan and seventy-six women from Radcliffe College (of Harvard University). The women were first tested when they were college students or recent graduates in the late 1960s, with follow-ups when they were forty-seven (Michigan) or forty-eight (Radcliffe). In the Michigan sample, at the age of forty-seven, roughly 90 percent were married or living with a partner.

Combinations of Growth and Mastery
Helson and Srivastava viewed developing adults as focused on either growth or mastery, neither or both. Four groups result from these possibilities.
Source: From Helson & Srivastava (2001). Reprinted with permission of the American Psychological Association.

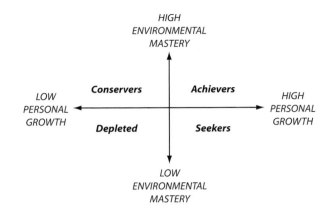

The remainder were evenly split among those who were single, divorced, or otherwise living alone. Roughly 90 percent were mothers.

The women's regrets were measured by the question, "In retrospect, are there any things you would have done differently?" Of the eighty-three women who had complete data in the Michigan sample, fifty-one expressed some regrets involving pursuing traditional roles. Of these 44 percent reflected wanting more education, 38 percent reflected wanting to engage in a different career. Only 15 percent concerned regrets about marriage, and 3 percent regrets about parenting. Levels of regret were similar but lower in the Radcliffe sample.

As it turned out, among those with regrets over their traditional lives, only some had made intentional, directed, mid-life corrections at age thirty-six. Those women with regrets who did make changes around age thirty-six experienced far more well-being at age forty-seven, as indicated by lower depression, better physical well-being, and better adult adjustment. Those who did make changes appeared to be more instrumental (e.g., thing-oriented) and experienced less rumination.

On the face of it, then, making a mid-course correction in adulthood would appear to be a healthy necessity for some people. Additional data analyses, however, raised the further possibility that those who didn't change were more dissatisfied and ruminative to begin with, and that the personality quality of rumination and, perhaps, depression, accounted for their lower well-being later on, as opposed to the lack of actual change itself.

Helson's Typology of Growth

Adaptive Functioning: The degree to which one can solve the practical, pragmatic problems of life.

Personal Growth: The degree to which one can attain inner understanding and wisdom apart from the social norms of success and failure.

People continue to grow psychologically, whether they stay on a consistent path or make changes in their lives. Two dimensions along which this growth may occur are in people's **adaptive functioning** and in their **personal growth** (Helson & Wink, 1987). Adaptive functioning concerns the sense of working well on practical, pragmatic aspects of life, with a focus on achieving in life. Personal growth involves a more internal development that may occur apart from social norms of success and failure.

One can classify people into four groups according to whether they are above or below average in the pursuit of adaptive functioning and personal growth (Ryff,

TABLE 12.5	Levels* of Life Satisfaction and Related Measures for Achiever, Conserver, Seeker, and Depleted Groups			
	Achievers	**Conservers**	**Seekers**	**Depleted**
Life Satisfaction	.11	.41	.09	−.61
Conventional Social Adjustment	−.53	.45	.19	−.11
Political Liberalism	−.04	−.58	.74	−.12
Occupational Creativity	.22	−.58	.52	−.16
Satisfaction with Job Security and Benefits	.34	.20	−.46	−.08

*Mean levels are reported such that the overall average is 0, and the sample standard deviation is 1 (i.e., standard scores).

Source: Abridged and adapted from Helson & Srivastava (2001), Table 5, p. 1005. Reprinted with permission of the American Psychological Association.

Achievers: Adults interested in both practical attainments and personal improvement.

Conservers: Adults interested in practical attainment.

Seekers: Adults interested in personal and spiritual self-development.

Depleteds: Adults who are no longer seeking further goals in life.

1989). Depending upon the level at which one pursues each objective, one would be classified as an **achiever**, **conserver**, **seeker**, or **depleted**. This two-by-two designation is shown in Figure 12.3. Achievers want it all: they want to be high in both the visible signs of success and to be high in inward psychological growth. Conservers, on the other hand, are happy to have the visible signs of success without necessarily seeking personal growth. Seekers desire high personal growth, but do not necessarily seek high mastery of the environment. Finally, Depleteds have stopped searching for growth of any type and are drifting along.

Helson and Srivastava (2001) studied 111 1958 and 1960 graduates of Mills College, a private women's college in Oakland, California. Most of the women were white, reflecting the ethnic makeup of the college at the time, most had fathers in the professions and mothers who were homemakers. The women were divided into the four groups based on the results of psychological testing employing the Ryff well-being scale.

The four groups were examined on a variety of measures including the California Q-sort, measures of maturity, emotionality, and social and intellectual competence. The results were expressed in positive or negative deviations from a zero point and are shown in Table 12.5. Achievers are occupationally creative and successful at work, while unconventional in their social adjustment. Conservers are by contrast far more conventional and less creative. Seekers are highly creative and liberal, but rather unsatisfied by their jobs. The Depleted group's most noticeable characteristic is their overall low life satisfaction. Some flavor of those differences is indicated by a summary of three life paths of such individuals described in Table 12.6.

Where Is Personality Headed in the Concluding Parts of Life?

The last developmental period to examine extends roughly from late middle age to the end of life. Increasingly, thanks to modern medicine and healthier life styles, this

TABLE 12.6	Life Course Examples of a Conserver, Seeker, and Achiever	
Cathy: Conserver	**Sarah: Seeker**	**Andrea: Achiever**
• Married young to a man approved by her family	• Described by interviewer as unusually perceptive, but with tendency to disengage abruptly	• Did not want to marry or have children
• Supported his career problems by going to work in people-oriented job	• Dropped out of graduate school when unexpectedly became pregnant	• Went straight to professional school from college
• Quit after 20 years of high competence because people were disrespectful to her	• Worked at becoming more sociable	• Continued career progress but began to drink heavily
• Much sought out by church and community groups	• In helping profession, where must work around bureaucracy	• Overcame drinking with great determination at age 40
	• Hopes to write great American novel	• Married a charming and successful man, created good relations with his children
		• Retired, and had second career as volunteer

Source: Drawn from Helson & Srivastava (2001), pp. 1005–1006.

can itself be a long period during which a person may begin a new career, get married or remarried, and enjoy many activities. To treat it as a single stage is, therefore, merely a reflection of this book, rather than a true indication of what these years can mean.

That said, the later years of a person's life can be a time of thinking and reflecting about one's self and what one has accomplished, and one's relation to the world. It involves asking many questions about what has become of one's childhood dreams, what one is contributing to the world, and what one is getting from it in return. For some, the answers are worked through and they are able to maintain their enthusiasm and hope. A second group will commit again to some old choices, but also will need to make some changes to continue. A third group has, by now, become so defeated and overwhelmed, that there may appear to be few opportunities to go on in a satisfied way (Levinson, 1977).

> How far you go in life depends upon your being tender with the young, compassionate with the aged, sympathetic with the striving and tolerant of the weak and strong. Because someday in your life you will have been all of these.
>
> George Washington Carver

Many of the individual and social bases that a person has laid down earlier in life continue to positively (or negatively) affect the aging individual. This period is one that is often marked by loss of others—of relatives and friends one's own age and those older and younger as well. Those who have established good coping skills, personal senses of well-being, and more positive social support networks will be able to face such losses with greater equanimity than others (e.g., Bonanno, Wortman, & Lehman, 2002; Wallace, Bisconti, & Bergeman, 2001). For example, in a prospective study of the elderly, those who were more psychologically healthy in the sense of experiencing positive affect and higher well-being before the loss of a spouse, recovered from the loss more quickly. Interestingly, those who were in difficult marriages before the loss of the spouse also improved after the loss. Those who showed poor adjustment before the loss, however, continued in that state afterward (Bonanno, Wortman, & Lehman, 2002).

Optimal Personality and Values

If we believe that the individual can become better, or even enter into an optimal state, what would that state be like? What would the now mature person like to look back on during these concluding years? Throughout the ages, philosophers and theologians have recommended ways for people to develop their personalities. In the present time, too, psychologists have made various suggestions. Today's psychological recommendations are, of course, value-laden as were those of the earlier philosophers and theologians. Most people accept and seek some shared values in their lives, however. They believe in such values as truth, beauty, respect for others, love, and mercy—and they would not entertain recommendations for a good life that did not take such values into account.

Good Functioning

Diagnostic and Statistical Manual (DSM): A manual of psychiatric diagnoses published by the American Psychiatric Association and providing the descriptions of mental disorders recognized by law in the United States.

The functional perspective views an individual as psychologically healthy if he or she is able to perform basic tasks necessary to a productive life. That is, a person should possess certain personality characteristics—emotional stability, the capacity for at least average coping, freedom from too much egocentrism—that are basics for good interpersonal relations. The **Diagnostic and Statistical Manual of the American Psychiatric Association (DSM)** is the reference work that assigns legal psychiatric diagnoses in the United States. According to the DSM, unhealthy individuals typically suffer from "dysfunction in social or occupational functioning." Presumably by contrast, healthy people are able to function in both social and work spheres: to love and to work, as Freud put it. This view of personal mental health as freedom from illness may seem rather minimalist. On the other hand, one of the advantages of this kind of approach is that, so long as one is free from a disorder, a person can be any sort of a positive person he or she wants to be.

Idealized (and Devalued) Views

Another set of positions concerning the healthy individual are those expressed in folk conceptions. Folk conceptions may involve such ideas as "always courageous" or "always rational" or "always generous." Such conduct, however, isn't very likely—and may not always be desirable. Most people do engage in repeated mistakes of one type or another, weaknesses in one area or another, or foolishness. As one investigator of very healthy individuals put it, "we could not use perfection as a basis for selection, since no subject was perfect" (Maslow, 1970, p. 151). Take the example of "thinking rationally." On the one hand, much of our educational folk wisdom says that a good person must reason carefully through problems. On the other hand, research in cognition and other areas of psychology tells us persuasively that people often think heuristically—that is, according to tricks and simplifications—rather than rationally. With the assistance of education and training, it seems reasonable to expect a healthy person to think rationally in certain circumstances when she or he desires to; but to expect consistent rational thought of anyone would be unrealistic.

Adding Strengths: Positive Psychology

Positive Psychology: A scientific movement to identify the positive strengths in individuals' personalities.

Rather than examine the mere absence of psychopathology or meeting unrealistic goals, some psychologists have sought to identify specific positive strengths that a person can develop, and so have created a new field, called **positive psychology**. Positive psychology is a term for the study of the positive aspects of human nature. Among its pursuits are a taxonomy of human strengths and an understanding of how to enhance those strengths and what those strengths lead to (e.g., Seligman & Csikszentmihalyi, 2001).

We have examined a number of these positive attributes throughout this textbook—positive affect, optimism, and self-control, for example—and there are indeed positive things to say about each. One of the issues, however, is the sheer number of positive possibilities. For example, a recent handbook of positive psychology included over fifty-five chapters—with forty-three chapters devoted to specific individual positive strengths. These included authenticity, benefit-finding, compassion, creativity, flow, gratitude, goal-setting, hope, humility . . . and so on through uniqueness-seeking and wisdom (e.g., Snyder & Lopez, 2002, pp. xii-xiii). A few examples of these strengths are described in Table 12.7.

TABLE 12.7	**Six (of Dozens) of Strengths Studied by Positive Psychologists**
Emotional Strengths	
Subjective Well-Being	A person's positive emotional and intellectual evaluation that he or she is experiencing a good life, that he or she is likable, and that the life he or she lives is satisfying. (Deiner, Lucas, & Oishi, 2002, p. 63)
Resilience	A person's capacity to adjust and adapt positively in the face of significant challenges, bad luck, and risk. (Masten & Reed, 2002, p. 74)
Cognitive Strengths	
Flow	A person's complete and total absorption in life projects and the things one does. (Nakamura & Csikszentmihalyi, 2002, p. 89)
Creativity	A person's independent, nonconformist perspective, coupled with wide interests and openness to new experiences, and cognitive flexibility. (Simonton, 2002, p. 192)
Strengths Related to the Self	
Authenticity	A competent sense of knowing and being oneself that stabilizes one's sense of self in social interactions. (Swann & Pelham, 2002, p. 366)
Humility	A person's ability to accurately assess his or her strengths and weaknesses, to acknowledge his or her limitations in social contexts, and to de-emphasize her or himself in social settings. (Tangney, 2002, p. 411)
Social Role Strengths	
Empathy and Altruism	Empathy is an emotional response directed at another person which leads one to want to help the other. Altruism leads to actions that benefit the other. (Batson et al., 2002, p. 485)
Morality	A true concern with the well-being of others leading to the development of principles of good behavior and one's identification with moral groups. (Schulman, 2002, pp. 449–450)

Perhaps we should simply be thankful there exist so many human strengths. The number of strengths does raise the question, however, of which strengths one should focus on. To complicate matters a bit, when the strengths are examined one at a time, they might not always act as strengths.

Strengths in Context

A central positive trait in this pantheon of strengths is optimism (e.g., Norem & Chang, 2002; Peterson & Seligman, 1987; Scheier & Carver, 1985). Certainly, an optimistic attitude can be helpful in many circumstances, such as for people trying to make sales or win elections, and for some people facing illness. At the same time, some have criticized psychologists—and Americans in general—as creating a tyranny of positivity in which positive qualities such as optimism are recklessly elevated to levels they do not deserve and anything negative is uninvited (Held, 2002, pp. 966, 974).

The reflexive labeling of optimism as a strength may be misguided unless one knows something about the type of optimism, the individual's personality, and the sorts of challenges a person faces. Among coronary heart patients, for example, optimism considered as a whole has no effect on exercise. But if one distinguishes between optimism as realistic hope versus naïve, unrealistic optimism, then far more interesting effects are obtained. Naïve optimists are already optimistic about their future health. For that reason, they have *less* motivation to engage in an exercise program, which, however, can actually make the positive outcome in their health more likely (Davidson & Prkachin, 1997). Naïve optimism, in this case, can endanger a person's health, as well as cause a person considerable difficulties in other areas as well (Epstein & Meier, 1989).

In other circumstances, something that looks like a drawback may, in some personalities, serve as a strength. We saw in Chapter 10, for example, that defensive pessimists calm themselves—and improve their performance—by beginning with the expectation that they will perform poorly at a task.

Optimal Types

The idea that one must deal with strengths and weakness in context has given rise to the notion that a more powerful way to understand positive people is to understand them as a complete type so as to take into account the interaction of strengths and weaknesses within the individual. Abraham Maslow sought to understand very healthy individuals. This was a considerable innovation in the 1950s when he began his work, for at that time psychology was heavily focused on the pathological and disease models of personality. If you would like to test your psychological health as conceived of by Maslow, first take the accompanying test; then read on.

Maslow first tried to study healthy people by combing literature and drama for examples, but could find few fictional characters who seemed healthy enough. In contrast, various descriptions of psychological health in folk wisdom appeared too demanding for real people to follow. He next examined students of his but found that they were too young to be considered fully developed. For these reasons, he ended up studying a diverse group of people including a number selected from among personal acquaintances and friends, and from among public and historical figures (Maslow, 1954/1970, chap. 11).

Among the public and historical figures he found were Abraham Lincoln in his later years, Thomas Jefferson, Albert Einstein, Eleanor Roosevelt, Jane Addams, William James, and Spinoza. He also included sixteen younger people who "seemed to be developing" in the direction of self-actualization, including G. W. Carver, Eugene V. Debs, Albert Schweitzer, and Goethe. In addition were included certain among Maslow's friends and acquaintances. Maslow labeled these individuals **self-actualized**. By self-actualized, Maslow meant that these individuals had managed to develop their own inner selves in a true and healthy fashion. Maslow concluded that these especially healthy individuals possessed certain core characteristics in common, summarized in Table 12.8.

According to Maslow, the self-actualized individual is governed most of all by an intense appreciation of and connection to reality. These individuals correctly and accurately perceive and understand many aspects of the human condition—including the painful ones. They are better able to distinguish between people who are real versus those who present false selves. They are also better able to distinguish real from faked or exploitative feeling in the arts and music.

Self-Actualized: The state of a person who is able to develop his or her innermost self in a healthy fashion that represents, expresses, and satisfies his or her true needs and characteristics.

TABLE 12.8   Maslow's View of the Self-Actualized Person

Characteristic Possessed	Further Description
Efficient reality perception	They are in intimate contact with reality.
Acceptance	They accept even those things many find unacceptable.
Spontaneity	They can do things at the spur of the moment, have fun.
Problem centering	They center their lives around fulfilling important tasks.
Detachment	They deal well with solitude, they view things independently of what others believe.
Autonomy	They are independent of others.
Freshness of appreciation	They can appreciate simple beauties as if they had never seen them before.
Peak experiences	They experience intense, mystical moments of appreciation for the world.
Gemeinschaftsgefühl	They are interested in helping the world.
Special relationships	They have relationships so intimate that they are like those among children.
Democratic character	They appreciate others for who they are (their personalities) not what they are (race, religion, etc.).
Means-ends	They value both means and ends to a problem.
Unhostile sense of humor	Their sense of humor is philosophical, rather than involving putting others down.
Creativity	They are creative in all areas of life, including social relations.
A few faults	They may be too trusting or tolerant of others, or seem harsh when they decide others do not warrant their attentions.

Source: Summary of Maslow (1970), chap. 11. Reprinted with permission of the American Psychological Association.

Test Yourself: Self-Actualization

The Items:	The Response Scale: 1. Definitely does not describe me. 2. Neither describes nor does not describe me. 3. Somewhat describes me. 4. Definitely describes me.	1	2	3	4
1. I do not feel ashamed of any of my emotions.					
2. I feel I must do what others expect me to do.					
3. I believe that people are essentially good and can be trusted.					
4. I feel free to be angry at those I love.					
5. It is always necessary that others approve of what I do.					
6. I don't accept my own weaknesses.					
7. I can like people without having to approve of them.					
8. I fear failure.					
9. I avoid attempts to analyze and simplify complex domains.					
10. It is better to be yourself than to be popular.					
11. I have no mission in life to which I feel particularly dedicated.					
12. I can express my feelings even when they may result in undesirable consequences.					
13. I do not feel responsible to help anyone.					
14. I am bothered by fears of being inadequate.					
15. I am loved because I give love.					

To Score...
1. Add up items 1, 3, 4, 7, 10, 12, and 15.
2. Reverse score items 2, 5, 6, 8, 9, 11, 13, and 14. That is, make: 4 = 1; 3 = 2; 2 = 3; 1 = 4.
3. Add up reverse scored items 2, 5, 6, 8, 9, 11, 13, and 14.
4. Add up the two totals from 1 and 3.
5. Compare to original sample average of 45.6.

Source: From Jones & Crandall (1986), reproduced with permission.

Reality, of course, can often be painful and uncertain. The self-actualized person can accept the unpleasant motivations of people, the realities of nature, and their own limitations. When they themselves have done something wrong, they seek to do better next time, and, if necessary, to make amends, rather than succumbing to crippling guilt or shame. They also accept aspects of themselves, such as sexual needs or

---

Inside the Field

Abraham Maslow's Early Life and His Theory of Self-Actualization

This chapter features a model of the self-actualized person developed by Abraham Maslow (1908–1970). We can better understand how the idea of psychological health and self-actualization evolved in psychology through examining Maslow's early life and psychological training.

Abraham Maslow's father had so strongly desired to emigrate from Russia to America that, as a boy of fourteen, he had walked and hitchhiked across Russia and through Western Europe to escape persecution there. Maslow himself was born in 1908 in Brooklyn, New York, and reared in a Jewish neighborhood. Nonetheless, he felt himself to be an outsider and lonely for much of his early life. His home life was unhappy and he felt unloved by his mother. He found solace in the local library. To get there from his neighborhood, however, he needed to cross ethnic lines, and was often subject to attack by gangs. Most days, he did make it to the library and once there, began to educate himself on a variety of topics.

After time at the City University of New York and at Cornell, he became interested in psychology. His decision to study psychology came after reading a book about behaviorism by John Watson, the founder of American behaviorism. He was particularly attracted to the behaviorist's plan to use psychology to help society to eliminate racism, superstition, and ignorance (Hoffman, 1999, pp. 30–31). Maslow decided to enroll at the University of Wisconsin, which then had a number of up and coming psychologists. There he married his fiancée, Bertha Goodman, at age twenty.

At the University of Wisconsin he became acquainted with several professors, who viewed him as a quite promising student and who helped him out in various ways. William H. Sheldon, for example, who later became famous for a theory connecting personality to body type, put his keen knowledge of physique to use by helping Maslow buy his first suit (Hoffman, 1999, p. 36). And there, Maslow and his wife had their first child. Maslow remarked:

> That was the thunderclap that settled things . . . I was stunned by the mystery and by the sense of not really being in control. I felt small and weak and feeble before all this. I'd say anyone who had a baby couldn't be a behaviorist. (Hall, 1967/1977, p. 36)

But the strongest intellectual connection that arose for Maslow on campus was with his Ph.D. advisor, a young professor named Harry W. Harlow. Harlow was an outspoken rebel against behaviorism in American psychology. He was—controversially at the time—thinking about love. When a behaviorist visiting his lab instructed Harlow to speak about proximity between animals rather than love, Harlow replied, "Perhaps all you've known in life is proximity . . . I thank God I've known more" (Blum, 2002, p. 2).

At that time, Harlow became interested in working with monkeys and he invited Maslow, now his first graduate student, to watch the monkeys with him at the Henry Vilas Zoo in

lusts, as part of being human. Such individuals are therefore low in defensiveness and artificiality. Their lack of defensiveness, in turn, allows them to frequently feel spontaneous. Although they often appear to follow social rules, they follow them more so as to not offend others, than out of a genuine conviction.

These individuals are centered on a particular problem or life task which they try

Madison. Every day they became more impressed by what the monkeys could do, and by the monkeys' relationships. Over time, they noticed that they themselves were forming complex relationships with the primates they observed. Harlow decided that, rather than run rats, he would open a primate laboratory. These sophisticated primates became their "animal model" of choice.

Maslow's dissertation was an extensive observational study of the dominance hierarchies among primates. Maslow detected a clear sense of winners and losers in this hierarchy. The dominant monkeys had it their way—gaining food, bullying others, and initiating fights as they pleased. The losers were defensive and challenged. Maslow carefully studied the monkeys' extraordinary social skills, and was startled to see how savvy they were with one another. The monkeys seemed to know when they needed cooperation, when to communicate, and when to get out of the way. Maslow concluded that for people too, social skills and knowing how to get along with others might be essential to a good and happy life (Blum, 2001, pp. 81–82). Harlow was extraordinarily proud of Maslow's work, which he considered the definitive study of primate dominance for decades (Blum, 2001, p. 82). Harlow went on to demonstrate the extraordinary importance of the love between infant and mother (critical to attachment theory) and this was work Maslow was keenly aware of.

After graduating, Maslow moved on to Brooklyn College as a professor where he and his wife set up household and created a far more positive family environment than the one he

had grown up with. This was during the Depression years, and, as a teacher, Maslow was one of the few members of his family with a steady job. One by one, many of his relatives came to live with him. This turned out to be a very happy time, with all the family members working together to keep the household running. Even Maslow's youngest daughter was assigned a job: to go around and wake everyone in the morning. When giving his friend, the early personality psychologist Gardner Murphy, a tour around the apartment, he showed off various appliances they had purchased on layaway programs. When he reached a daughter who was passing by, he happily swooped her up in his arms and said, "And this one we own outright" (Hoffman, 1999, p. 135).

One day, shortly after the United States had entered World War II, Maslow was driving home when his progress was blocked by a parade of veterans and Boy Scouts. As he sat in his car, he reports, tears streamed down his face, and he had a vision of a peace table with people sitting around it talking about war and peace and brotherhood. He wrote: "It was at that moment that I realized that the rest of my life must be devoted to discovering a psychology for the peace table. That moment changed my whole life" (Hoffman, 1999, p. 137).

Thereafter he began to more seriously examine the self-actualized. He began observing people he believed to be especially healthy among his friends and acquaintances. Later, he developed the theory of self-actualization presented in this chapter. Do you think Maslow's theory fulfilled his dream of contributing to a psychology of peace?

Many stories tell a narrative of searching, self-discovery, and personal growth across the life span. Psychologists have speculated that the success of such films as the Wizard of Oz is a consequence of how well they reflect such growth. Each one of Dorothy's new-found friends was looking for a psychological quality—a heart, a brain, courage—that would make them whole—or in psychological terms, self-actualized (e.g., Pancer & Pancer, 1988; Payne, 1989).

to fulfill. For example, the great twentieth-century physicist, Albert Einstein, was singularly focused on understanding the laws of the universe. When he was offered a highly expensive psychotherapy at no cost—so as to reveal the workings of his mind for the scientific community—he respectfully declined, noting that he was so committed to his pursuits in physics that he had never much thought about himself.

Because such individuals see things so much more clearly than those around them, they have a sense of being apart from others. Fortunately, they are well able to tolerate being alone. What stops their autonomous pursuits from becoming unpleasant is their ability to continuously perceive things with freshness. In nature, every sunset is as lovely as the first they saw; every moon as awe-inspiring. They have a particularly intense relationship with sexual experience, which may feel almost like a religious experience to them.

Often, in fact, their internal conscious experience becomes so intense and disorganized that they feel themselves merge with a sort of cosmic consciousness. In this **peak experience**, they feel one with all of life. Like most people who experience this feeling, it may last for just a little while. But perhaps because of the self-actualized individual's lack of defensiveness, they may enter into peak experiences as many as five or six times a day—as opposed to, perhaps, once every few months or few years for the average person.

Self-actualized people can be identified in part by their philosophical, unhostile sense of humor and their creativity. Hostile humor includes insult humor and violent humor and puts oneself or another person down. **Philosophical humor**, on the other hand, draws attention to some oddity of being human, without putting it

Peak Experience: An altered state of consciousness in which one's awareness appears to merge with a cosmic consciousness, and an individual feels at one with the surrounding environment or universe.

Philosophical Humor: A type of humor employed by the self-actualized that gently pokes fun at the oddities and commonalities of the human experience.

down. The comedian Steven Wright often draws humor from such oddities in brief observations delivered in a very plain tone, as in, "A lot of people are afraid of heights. Not me—I'm afraid of widths," and, "I have a large seashell collection, which I keep scattered on beaches all over the world," and, "I bought some batteries but they weren't included so I had to buy them again" (recounted in Brown, 1998, pp. 144, 255). Jerry Seinfeld is philosophical, as well, as he observes and comments on human nature:

> Candy is the only reason you want to live when you're a kid. And you have your favorite candies that you love. Kids actually believe they can distinguish between twenty-one versions of pure sugar. When I was kid, I could taste the difference between different color M&M's. I thought the red was heartier, more of a main course M&M. And the light brown was a mellower, kind of after-dinner M. (Jerry Seinfeld, quoted in Brown, 1998, p. 39)

Gemeinschaftsgefühl: An attitude of caring concern for the rest of humanity that leads to a desire to help others in one's life projects. Considered to be a quality of the self-actualized person.

To philosophical humor is also added a capacity for creativity, along with a sense of **Gemeinschaftsgefühl** (social feeling). These individuals have a strong identification and sympathy with humanity that leads them to care for and try to help others.

If this seems too good to be true, Maslow listed a few faults of the self-actualized as well. These individuals may often seem aloof and even cold because they are not interested in daily conversation or party-going. In addition, they can be ruthless if they find someone isn't living up to important standards. One self-actualized person quickly cut himself off from a business partner who he found out was dishonest. He refused to have any further contact with the man, even though the two had known each other for many years.

Carol Gilligan's Critique

Maslow examined self-actualized women and men. But he stressed autonomy almost to the exclusion of interconnectedness. Carol Gilligan has enriched depictions of healthy individuals with an eye to the unique ways that women attain psychological health. As she puts it, "women bring to the life cycle a different point of view and order human experience in terms of different priorities" (Gilligan, 1982, p. 22). Gilligan studied healthy professional women and found that they more often described themselves in terms of relationships than did men. For example, a doctor in training recounted:

What a wonderful life I've had! I only wish I'd realized it sooner.
Sidonie-Cabrielle Colette

> I see myself in a nurturing role, maybe not right now, but . . . as a physician, as a mother . . . It's hard for me to think of myself without thinking about other people around me that I'm giving to. (Gilligan, 1982, pp. 158–159)

Another woman described her hardworking and responsible professional life, and then went on to recount that:

> The other very important aspect of my life is my husband and trying to make his life easier and trying to help him out. (Gilligan, 1982, pp. 158–159)

Such remarks and commentaries help Gilligan illustrate the point that for both women and men, self-actualization may involve autonomy at times, but also interconnectedness and intimate relations with others.

A Final Life Review

Erik Erikson brings his discussion of the various ages of a human being to a close with a discussion of the final passage of personality development: the stage of ego integrity versus ego despair. Despair can be a consequence of a person's bad decisions, or, sometimes, a consequence of good decisions that have been thwarted by an impervious or hostile environment. A person with past regrets, who has not come to terms with them, tends to have lower well-being at this time of life (Torges, Stewart, & Miner-Rubino, 2005).

The more vibrant, hopeful, end of life, however, involves something Erikson called ego integrity. The person with ego integrity has mostly come to terms with his or her regrets, and goes far beyond this: He or she possesses a deep acceptance of life. The individual's personal integrity permits a transcendence of the self that reaches out to all humanity. Although this end stage is full of self-respect and self-love, it is no longer as self-centered as before:

> It is a post-narcissistic love of the human ego—not of the self—as an experience which conveys some world order and spiritual sense, no matter how dearly paid for. It is the acceptance of one's one and only life cycle as something that had to be and that, by necessity, permitted of no substitutions: it thus means a new, a different love of one's parents. It is a comradeship with the ordering ways of distant times and different pursuits . . . the possessor of integrity is ready to defend the dignity of his own life style . . . he knows that an individual life is the accidental coincidence of but one life cycle with but one segment of history; and that for him all human integrity stands or falls with the one style of integrity of which he partakes . . . In such final consolidation, death loses its sting. (Erikson, 1950/1963, p. 168)

Reviewing Chapter 12

Chapter 12 takes us through a person's development from young adulthood to the end of life. First considered is the legacy of childhood upon the life of the developing young adult. Many attributes, particularly traits and the degree to which a person is undercontrolled, controlled, or overcontrolled, carry over into adult life, although there is room for change. During young and middle adulthood, the growing person attempts to find intimacy in relationships, and ultimately a stable home life. The person also seeks out a good occupational fit, and, ultimately, work success. Such searches may continue into later adulthood, or begin anew.

At the same time, later adulthood is a time for reflection and renewed meaning-making in one's life.

Throughout the lifespan, many individuals aim toward a healthier or optimal version of themselves. This involves freeing themselves of psychopathology to the greatest extent possible, adding strengths, and creating an overall personality that is the best possible for the individual.

What Is the Nature of Adult Development?

1. Questions of Adult Development and the Transition to Adulthood.

Mahatma Gandhi represents one image of adult development. In what ways is his life typical? In what ways is it exceptional? According to Erikson and others, what are the main issues faced by the young adult? The extended lifespan influences adult personality development by making it more critical. How does increased longevity influence a person's sense of control?

2. Is the Child Parent to the Adult?
A great deal of personality growth and development has taken place in childhood, including the coalescence of temperament into traits, and the development of substantial models of the self and the world. What would this lead you to expect about childhood bases of personality?

3. Childhood Influences on Temperament and Traits; Models of the Self and World.
Given that childhood personality carries over to adulthood, in specific, what can you say about the influence of childhood personality traits on adulthood? What about mental models developed in childhood?

4. Traits: Set Like Plaster?
Findings in the middle 1970s indicated that personality traits are relatively set for the individual by young adulthood. There are, however, individual changes, as well as group changes in the overall level of traits. How do the Big Five personality traits, for example, change over adulthood.

What Are Young Adults Like?

5. In Search of Intimacy.
One of the tasks of young adulthood is to find a partner with whom to be intimate. What are some of the ways young adults do this? How are men's and women's strategies for impressing their potential partners the same or different? To whom are they attracted?

6. In Search of Good Work.
Another task of young adulthood is finding a good occupation. What are some of the criteria people use for finding a good job? What variables contribute to occupational satisfaction?

How Does the Individual Traverse Middle Adulthood?

7. Finding Occupational Success.
Some people find more occupational success than others. What are some of the personality variables that lead to success across occupations. How does positivity enter into job success? What is necessary for high levels of achievement?

8. Staying Married.
For those people who have been able to partner, the task of middle adulthood is to maintain the relationship. Here, too, personality traits and other variables can contribute. What are some of the personality traits that tend to preserve marriages? Which traits might place marriages in danger?

9. Personality and Health.
It turns out that although people with high negative affect (e.g., Neuroticism) complain more about their health, there are few objective health differences between such individuals and more positive people. Personality traits do, however, enter into the health equation. What findings in particular stand out?

10. Who Adjusts Course? Helson's Typology of Change; No Regrets?
People who have trouble early in their lives are more inclined to change than others. Helson argued that there were two dimensions, of personal mastery and personal growth, that people changed along. What four groups of changers does that create?

Where Is Personality Headed in the Concluding Parts of Life?

11. Good Functioning.
One approach to psychological health is to identify what is required for good functioning. Do you know how Freud referred to the capacity to function well? It also means being free of mental illness.

12. Adding Strengths; Strengths in Context.
Another approach to psychological health is to identify a number of potential strengths personality can take on—for example, acceptance, caring, compassion, and optimism have all been identified as strengths. Are there other such strengths you can identify? When is optimism not a strength? When is its opposite—pessimism—a strength?

13. Optimal Types; Optimal Types in Context.
Maslow suggested that the self-actualized person represented an optimal type. This individual had excellent reality perception, acceptance of the reality of the world, and freshness of perception. What other attributes did the self-actualized individual possess? What did Carol Gilligan believe was an alternative strength to Maslow's idea of autonomy?

Postscript

Personality development in adulthood—the topic of the final chapter in this book—seems like a fitting topic with which to conclude. Nonetheless, it leaves a few matters hanging: some personal and some more general. At a personal level, some students may wonder if they can, will, or should end up in the way described by Abraham Maslow and Carol Gilligan, or by Erik H. Erikson. A few personal words represent my own viewpoint on the matter.

When I was a college student, I learned Maslow's description of the self-actualized individual, and hoped I would achieve that sort of psychological health by the time I was middle-aged. Although I have been fortunate enough to reach middle age, I have not yet met Maslow's criteria for self-actualization. I suppose, for better or for worse, my personality is a bit too "complicated" or idiosyncratic to fully achieve that sort of psychological health. Perhaps Maslow's criteria are too stringent. I don't know. But even though I never quite made it to self-actualization, I found that his description (along with some of the modifications suggested by Carol Gilligan), provided a good objective toward which to aim. In my experience, most young (and older) adults do not—and cannot, really—fit the ideal patterns of development. Life for most has been, or will be, challenging and demanding, not to mention full of events that are a bit unexpected. Nonetheless, as Erikson reminds us, there are many ways to reach ego integrity.

It is the purpose of education to help a person by providing a way of thinking about a subject, rather than, necessarily, by providing cookbook answers about how to do something. Nowhere is this more the case than in developing oneself and in living a life, where simple rules of development and living simply won't do. I hope, instead, that along with the many things you already know, and enriched by the knowledge in this textbook, you will have a greater understanding of who you are and what you will face in your life. No one has a perfect understanding of himself or herself, and, needless to say, no one knows everything about anyone else either. In my estimation, at least, centuries of thought, and a century of empirical research in personality psychology, does provide some real understanding that may be of use in thinking about life, however superficial our knowledge today may seem to future generations.

I wish you the best of luck as you go on from here, and hope the knowledge conveyed in this book will have touched you and serve you in your future endeavors.

References

Abramson, L. Y., Alloy, L. B., & Metalsky, G. I. (1995). Hopelessness depression. In G. Buchanan & M. Seligman (Eds.). *Explanatory style* (pp. 113–134). Hillsdale, NJ: Erlbaum.

Adams, G. R., & Fitch, S. A. (1983). Psychological environments of university departments: Effects on college students' identity status and ego-stage development. *Journal of Personality and Social Psychology, 44,* 1266–1275.

Adams, G. R., Shea, J., & Fitch, S. A. (1979). Toward the development of an objective assessment of ego-identity status. *Journal of Youth and Adolescence, 8,* 223–237.

Adams, H. E., Wright, L. W., & Lohr, B. A. (1996). Is homophobia associated with homosexual arousal? *Journal of Abnormal Psychology, 105,* 440–445.

Adcock, N. V., Adcock, C. J., & Walkey, F. H. (1974). Basic dimensions of personality. *International Review of Applied Psychology, 23,* 131–137.

Adler, A. (1930). Individual psychology. In C. Murchison (Ed.), *Psychologies of 1930* (pp. 395–405). Worcester, MA: Clark University Press.

Adler, A. ([1931]1958). *What life should mean to you.* New York: G. P. Putnam's Sons.

Aiken, L. R. (2003). *Psychological testing and assessment* (11th ed.). Boston: Allyn & Bacon.

Ainsworth, M. D. S. (1989). Attachments beyond infancy. *American Psychologist, 44,* 709–716.

Ainsworth, M. D. S., Blehar, M. C., Waters, E., & Wall, S. (1978). *Patterns of attachment: A psychological study of the strange situation.* Hillsdale, NJ: Lawrence Erlbaum.

Alderfer, C. P. (1969). An empirical test of a new theory of human needs. *Organizational Behavior and Human Performance, 4,* 142–175.

Alderfer, C. (1972). *Existence, relatedness, and growth.* New York: Free Press.

Alexander, F. (1942). *Our age of unreason.* Philadelphia: Lippincott.

Allen, J. B., Kenrick, D. T., & Linder, D. E. (1989). Arousal and attraction: A response-facilitation alternative to misattribution and negative-reinforcement models. *Journal of Personality and Social Psychology, 57,* 261–270.

Allen, M. J., & Yen, W. M. (1979). *Introduction to measurement theory.* Monterey, CA: Brooks/Cole.

Allport, G. W. (1937). *Personality: A psychological interpretation.* New York: Holt, Rinehart, & Winston.

Allport, G. W. (1968). *The person in psychology: Selected essays by Gordon W. Allport.* Boston: Beacon Press.

Allport, G. W., & Odbert, H. S. (1936). Trait names: A psycho-lexical study. *Psychological Monographs, 47,* No. 211.

Allport, G. W., & Vernon, P. E. (1931). A test for personal values. *Journal of Abnormal and Social Psychology, 26,* 231–248.

Almada, S. G., Zonderman, A. B., Shekelle, R. B., Dyer, A. R., Daviglus, M. L., Costa, P. T., & Stamler, J. (1991). Neuroticism and cynicism and risk of death in middle-aged men: The Western Electric Study. *Psychosomatic Medicine, 53,* 165–175.

Amabile, T. M. (1996). *Creativity in context.* Boulder, CO: Westview.

Amato, P. R., & Keith, B. (1991). Parental divorce and the well-being of children: A meta-analysis. *Psychological Bulletin, 110,* 26–46.

American Psychiatric Association (1994). *Diagnostic and statistical manual of mental disorders* (4th ed.). Washington, DC: American Psychiatric Association.

Ammerman, R. T., Lynch, K. G., Donovan, J. E., Martin, C. S., & Maisto, S. A. (2001). Constructive thinking in adolescents with substance abuse disorders. *Psychology of Addictive Behaviors, 15,* 89–96.

Andersen, S. M., & Cole, S. W. (1990). "Do I know you?" The role of significant others in general social perception. *Journal of Personality and Social Psychology, 59,* 384–399.

Anderson, C. A. (1983). Imagination and expectation: The effect of imagining behavioral scripts on personal influences. *Journal of Personality and Social Psychology, 45,* 293–305.

Anderson, D. D., Rosenfeld, P., & Cruikschank, L. (1994). An exercise for explicating and critiquing students' implicit personality theories. *Teaching of Psychology, 21,* 174–177.

Anderson, J. R. (1980). *Cognitive psychology and its implications.* San Francisco: Freeman.

Andreasen, N. C., Flaum, M., Swayze, V. W., & O'Leary, D. S. (1993). Intelligence and brain structure in normal individuals. *American Journal of Psychiatry, 150,* 130–134.

Anshel, M. H., Williams, L. R. T., & Williams, S. M. (2000). Coping style following acute stress in competitive sport. *Journal of Social Psychology, 140,* 751–773.

Argyle, M. (1987). *The psychology of happiness.* New York: Methuen.

Arnett, J. J. (2000). Emerging adulthood. A theory of development from the late teens through the twenties. *American Psychologist, 55,* 469–480.

Arnheim, R. (1974). *Art and visual perception: A psychology of the creative eye (the new version).* Berkeley: The University of California Press.

Aronoff, J. (1967). *Psychological needs and cultural systems: A case study.* Princeton, NJ: Van Nostrand.

Aronson, J., Lustina, M. J., & Good, C. (1999). When White men can't do math: Necessary and sufficient factors in stereotype threat. *Journal of Experimental Social Psychology, 35,* 29–46.

Asher, S. R., & Rose, A. J. (1997). Promoting children's social-emotional adjustment with peers. In P. Salovey & D. J.

Sluyter (Eds.), *Emotional development and emotional intelligence.* New York: Basic Books.

Ashton, M. C., Jackson, D. N., Helmes, E., & Paunonen, S. V. (1998). *Joint factor analysis of the Personality Research Form and the Jackson Personality Inventory: Comparisons with the Big Five, 32,* 243–250.

Atwater, L. E. (1992). Beyond cognitive ability: Improving the prediction of performance. *Journal of Business and Psychology, 7,* 27–44.

Austin, E. J., Deary, I. J., & Willock, J. (2001). Personality and intelligence as predictors of economic behaviour in Scottish farmers. *European Journal of Personality, 15,* Supp. 1, pp. S123–S137.

Averill, J. R. (1992). The structural bases of emotional behavior: A metatheoretical analysis. *Review of Personality and Social Psychology, 13,* 1–24.

Averill, J. R., Ekman, P., Panksepp, J., Scherer, K. R., Schweder, R. A., & Davidson, R. J. (1994). Are there *basic emotions?* In P. Ekman & R. J. Davison (Eds.), *The nature of emotion: Fundamental questions.* New York: Oxford University Press.

Averill, J. R., & Thomas-Knowles, C. (1991). Emotional creativity. In K. T. Strongman (Ed.), *International review of studies on emotion* (Vol. 1, pp. 269–299). London: Wiley.

Ax, A. F. (1953). The physiological differentiation between fear and anger in humans. *Psychosomatic Medicine, 15,* 433–442.

Ayers, J., Davis, J. L., & Rudolph, A. (2002). *Biotechnology for biomimetic robots.* Cambridge, MA: MIT Press.

Baars, B. J., & McGovern, K. (1994). Consciousness. *Encyclopaedia of Human Behavior, 1,* 687–699.

Bacon, F. ([1861] 2001). *The advancement of learning* (G. W. Kitchin, Ed.). Philadelphia, PA: Paul Dry Books.

Bailey, K. G. (1987). *Human paleopsychology applications to aggression.* Hillsdale, NJ: Erlbaum.

Bajema, C. J. (1968). A note on the interrelations among intellectual ability, educational attainment, and occupational achievement: A follow-up study of a male Kalamazoo public school population. *Sociology of Education, 41,* 317–319.

Bakke, E. W. (1940). *Citizens without work.* New Haven, CT: Yale University Press.

Balmary, M. (1979). *Psychoanalyzing psychoanalysis: Freud and the hidden fault of the father.* Baltimore: Johns Hopkins Press.

Banaji, M., & Greenwald, A. G. (1994). Implicit stereotyping and prejudice. In M. P. Zanna & J. M. Olson (Eds.). *The psychology of prejudice: The Ontario symposium, 7,* 55–76. Hillsdale, NJ, England: Lawrence Erlbaum Associates.

Bandura, A. (1977). *Social learning theory.* Englewood Cliffs, NJ: Prentice Hall.

Bandura, A. (1978). The self system in reciprocal determinism. *American Psychologist, 33,* 344–358.

Bandura, A. (1984). Representing personal determinants in causal structures. *Psychological Review, 91,* 508–511.

Bandura, A. (1986). *Social foundations of thought and action.* Englewood Cliffs, NJ: Prentice-Hall.

Bandura, A. (1999). Self-efficacy: Toward a unifying theory of behavioral change. In R. F. Baumeister (Ed.), *The self in social psychology: Key readings in social psychology* (pp. 285–298). Philadelphia, PA: Psychology Press.

Bandura, A., & Walters, R. H. (1963). *Social learning and personality development.* New York: Holt, Rinehart, & Winston.

Barchard, K. A. (2003). Does emotional intelligence assist in the prediction of academic success? *Educational and Psychological Measurement, 63,* 840–858.

Bargh, J. A. (1997). The automaticity of everyday life. In R. S. Wyer, Jr. (Ed.), *Advances in social cognition* (Vol. 10, pp. 1–61). Mahwah, NJ: Erlbaum.

Bargh, J. A., & Chartrand, T. L. (1999). The unbearable automaticity of being. *American Psychologist, 54,* 462–479.

Bargh, J., Chen, M., & Burrows, L. (1996). Automaticity of social behavior: Direct effects of trait construct and stereotype activation on action. *Journal of Personality and Social Psychology, 71,* 230–244.

Barrick, M. R., & Mount, M. K. (1991). The Big Five personality dimensions and job performance: A meta-analysis. *Personnel Psychology, 44,* 1–26.

Bartlett, F .C. (1932). *Remembering: An experimental and social study.* Cambridge: Cambridge University Press.

Baruss, I. (1986-7) Metaanalysis of definitions of consciousness. *Imagination, Cognition, and Personality, 6,* 321–329.

Bates, T. C., & Eysenck, H. J. (1993). Intelligence, inspection time, and decision time. *Intelligence, 17,* 523–531.

Bateson, G. (1975). Logical categories of learning and communication. In *Steps to an Ecology of Mind.* New York: Ballantine.

Batson, C. D., Ahmad, N., Lishner, D. A., & Tsang, J-A. (2002). Empathy and altruism. In C. R. Snyder & S. J. Lopez (Eds.), *Handbook of positive psychology* (pp. 485–498). New York: Oxford University Press.

Baumann, L. J., & Leventhal, H. (1985). "I can tell when my blood pressure is up, can't I?" *Healthy Psychology, 4,* 203–218.

Baumeister, R. F. (1987). How the self became a historical problem: A psychological review of historical research. *Journal of Personality and Social Psychology, 52,* 163–176.

Baumeister, R. F. (1997). *Evil: Inside human violence and cruelty.* New York: W. H. Freeman and Company.

Baumeister, R. F., & Tice, D. (1994). Editorial. *Dialogue: Society for Personality and Social Psychology, 9,* p. 10.

Baumeister, R. F., Dale, K., & Sommer, K. L. (1998). Freudian defense mechanisms and empirical findings in modern social psychology: Reaction formation, projection, displacement, undoing, isolation, sublimation, and denial. *Journal of Personality, 66,* 1081–1124.

Baumrind, D. (1971). Current patterns of parental authority. *Developmental Psychology Monographs, 4*(1, Pt. 2).

Baumrind, D. (1973). The development of instrumental competence through socialization. In A. D. Pick (Ed.), *Minnesota symposia on child development* (Vol. 7). Minneapolis: University of Minnesota Press.

Beattie, M. (1987). *Codependent no more.* San Francisco: Harper and Row.

Bechger, T. M., Maris, G., Verstralen, H. H., & Beguin, A. A. (2003). Using classical test theory in combination with item response theory. *Applied Psychological Measurement, 27,* 319–334.

Beck, A. T. (1967). *Depression: Clinical experimental and theoretical aspects.* New York: Harper & Row.

Becker, E. (1973). *The denial of death.* New York: Free Press.

Bekoff, M., & Goodall, J. (2002). *Minding animals: Awareness, emotions, and heart.* Oxford: Oxford University Press.

Bell, R. A. (1985). Conversational involvement and loneliness. *Communication Monographs, 52,* 217–235.

Bem, D. J., & Honorton, C. (1994). Does psi exist? Replicable evidence for an anomalous process of information transfer. *Psychological Bulletin, 115,* 4–18.

Bem, S. L. (1974). The measurement of psychological androgyny. *Journal of Clinical and Consulting Psychology, 42,* 153–162.

Benassi, V. A., & Fernald, P. S. (1993). Preparing tomorrow's psychologists for careers in academe. *Teaching of Psychology, 20,* 149–155.

Bender, B. G., & Berch, D. B. (1987). Sex chromosome abnormalities: Studies of genetic influences on behavior. *Integrative Psychiatry, 5,* 171–176.

Benedict, R. (1959). *Patterns of culture.* Boston: Houghton Mifflin.

Benet-Martínez, V., & Haritatos, J. (2005). Bicultural Identity Integration (BII): Components and Psychosocial Antecedents. *Journal of Personality, 73,* 1015–1050.

Bennett, G. K., Seashore, H. G., & Wesman, A. G. (1989). *Differential Aptitude Test (DAT)—Form W (Personnel).* San Antonio, TX: The Psychological Corporation.

Bentler, P. M. (2000). *EQS-6 Structural equation program manual.* Encino, CA: Multivariate Software.

Bentler, P. M., & Newcomb, M. D. (1978). Longitudinal study of marital success and failure. *Journal of Consulting and Clinical Psychology, 46,* 1053–1070.

Bergeman, C. S., Chipuer, H. M., Plomin, R., Pedersen, N. L., McClearn, G. E., Nesselroade, J.R., Costa, P., Jr., & McCrae, R. R. (1993). Genetic and environmental effects on openness to experience, agreeableness, and conscientiousness: An adoption/twin study. *Journal of Personality, 61,* 159–179.

Berkowitz, L. (1989). Frustration-aggression hypothesis: Examination and reformulation. *Psychological Bulletin, 108,* 59–73.

Berne, E. (1957). Ego states in psychotherapy. *American Journal of Psychotherapy, 11,* 293–309.

Berscheid, E., & Walster, E. (1974). *Interpersonal attraction.* Reading, MA: Addison-Wesley.

Berzonsky, M. D., & Adams, G. R. (1999). Reevaluating the identity status paradigm: Still useful after 35 years. *Developmental Review, 19,* 557–590.

Berzonsky, M. D., & Neimeyer, G. I. (1988). Identity status and personal construct systems. *Journal of Adolescence, 11,* 195–204.

Berzonsky, M. D., Rice, K. G., & Neimeyer, G. J. (1990). Identity status and self-construct systems: Process X structure interactions. *Journal of Adolescence, 13,* 251–263.

Best, D. L., Williams, J. E., Cloud, J. M., Davis, S. W., Robertson, L. S., Edwards, J. R., Giles, H., & Fowles, J. (1977). Development of sex-trait stereotypes among young children in the United States, England, and Ireland. *Child Development, 48,* 1375–1384.

Beutler, L. E., Crago, M., & Arezmendi, T. G. (1986). Research on therapist variables in psychotherapy. In S. L. Garfield, & A. R. Bergen (Eds.), *Handbook of psychotherapy and behavior change* (3rd ed.). New York: Wiley.

Bigler, E. D., Johnson, S. C., & Blatter, D. D. (1999). Head trauma and intellectual status: Relation to quantitative magnetic resonance imaging findings. *Applied Neuropsychology, 6,* 217–225.

Birren, J. E., & Morrison, D. F. (1961). Analysis of the WAIS subtests in relation to age and education. *Journal of Gerontology, 16,* 363–369.

Black, A. E., & Deci, E. L. (2000). The effects of instructors' autonomy support and students' autonomous motivation on learning organic chemistry: A self-determination theory perspective. *Science Education, 84,* 740–756.

Black, B., & Hazen, N. L. (1990). Social status and patterns of communication in acquainted and unacquainted preschool children. *Developmental Psychology, 26,* 379–387.

Black, J. (2000). Police testing and police selection: Utility of the "Big Five." *New Zealand Journal of Psychology, 29,* 2–9.

Blackman, M. C., & Funder, D. C. (1998). The effect of information on consensus and accuracy in personality judgment. *Journal of Experimental Social Psychology, 34,* 164–181.

Blais, M. (1995). *In these girls, hope is a muscle.* New York: The Atlantic Monthly Press.

Block, J. (1971). *Lives through time.* Berkeley, CA: Bancroft.

Block, J. (1995). A contrarian view of the five-factor approach to personality description. *Psychological Bulletin, 117,* 187–215.

Block, J. (2002). *Personality as an affect-processing system.* Mahwah, NJ: Erlbaum.

Block, J. H., & Block, J. (1980). The role of ego-control and ego-resiliency in the organization of behavior. In W. A. Collins (Ed.), *Development of cognition, affect, and social relations: The Minnesota symposia on child psychology,* (Vol. 13, pp. 40–101). Hillsdale, NJ: Erlbaum.

Block, N. (1995). On a confusion about the function of consciousness. *Behavioral and Brain Sciences, 18,* 227–287.

Blum, D. (2002). *Love at Goon Park. Harry Harlow and the science of affection.* Cambridge, MA: Perseus Books Group.

Boesky, D. (1994). Dialogue on the Brenner Paper between Charles Brenner, M. D., & Dale Boesky, M. D. *Journal of Clinical Psychoanalysis, 3,* 509–540.

Bonanno, G. A., Papa, A., & O'Neill, K. (2002). Loss and human resilience. *Applied and Preventive Psychology, 10,* 193–206.

Bonanno, G. A., Wortman, C. B., & Lehman, D. R. (2001). Resilience to loss and chronic grief: A prospective study from preloss to 18-months postloss. *Journal of Personality and Social Psychology, 83,* 1150–1164.

Bondanella, P. (1998). *The films of Federico Fellini.* Cambridge: Cambridge University Press.

Bong, M. (1999). Comparison between self-concept and self-efficacy in academic motivation research. *Educational Psychologist, 34,* 139–153.

Bonwell, C. G., & Eison, J. A. (1991). *Active learning: Creating excitement in the classroom.* Washington, DC: ERIC Clearinghouse on Higher Education.

Bouchard, T. J., & McGue, M. (1981). Family studies of intelligence: A review. *Science, 212,* 1055–1059.

Boushka, B. (2000). *Do ask; do tell: Gay conservative lashes back: Individualism, identity, personal rights, responsibility and community in a Libertaria.* New York: iUniverse.

Bower, G. H. (1981). Mood and memory. *American Psychologist, 36,* 129–148.

Bowers, K. S. (1973). Situationism in psychology: An analysis and critique. *Psychological Review, 80,* 307–336.

Bowers, K. S. (1976). *Hypnosis for the seriously curious.* New York: W. W. Norton.

Bowers, K. S. (1984). On being unconsciously influenced and informed. In K. S. Bowers & Meichenbaum, D. (Eds.), *The unconscious reconsidered* (pp. 227–272). New York: Wiley.

Bowers, P. (1982). The classic suggestion effect: Relationships with scales of hypnotizability, effortless experiencing, and imagery vividness. *International Journal of Clinical and Experimental Hypnosis, 30,* 270–279.

Bowlby, J. (1958). The nature of the child's tie to his mother. *International Journal of Psychoanalysis, 39,* 350–373.

Bowlby, J. (1988). *A secure base: Parent-child attachment and healthy human development.* New York: Basic Books/Harper Collins.

Bowman, M. L. (1989). Testing individual differences in ancient China. *American Psychologist, 44,* 576–578.

Boyce, D. A. (2002) The correlation of emotional intelligence, academic success, and cognitive ability in master's level physical therapy students. [Abstract]. *Dissertation Abstracts International: Section B: The Sciences & Engineering, 62(12–B),* 5677.

Brackett, M. A., & Mayer, J. D. (2003). Convergent, discriminant, and incremental validity of competing measures of emotional intelligence. *Personality and Social Psychology Bulletin, 29,* 1147–1158.

Brackett, M. A., Mayer, J. D., & Warner, R. M. (2004). Emotional intelligence and its relation to everyday behavior. *Personality and Individual Differences, 36,* 1387–1402.

Bradburn, N. M., & Berlew, D. E. (1961). Need for achievement and English economic growth. *Economic Development and Cultural Change, 10,* 8–20.

Bradway, K. P., & Robinson, N. M. (1961). Significant IQ changes in twenty-five years: A follow-up. *Journal of Educational Psychology, 52,* 74–79.

Bradway, K. P., Thompson, C. W., & Cravens, R. B. (1958). Preschool IQ's after twenty-five years. *Journal of Educational Psychology, 49,* 278–281.

Brennan, K. A., Clark, C. L., & Shaver, P. R. (1998). Self-report measurement of close relationships. In J. A. Simpson & W. S. Rholes (Eds.), *Attachment theory and close relationships* (pp. 46–76). New York: Guilford.

Bretherton, I., & Waters, E. (1985). Attachment theory: Retrospect and prospect. In I. Bretherton & E. Waters (Eds.) *Growing Points of Attachment Theory and Research/ Monographs of the Society for Reseach in Child Development, 50*(1-2) [Serial no. 209].

Brigham, C. C. (1930). Intelligence tests of immigrant groups. *Psychological Review, 37,* 158–165.

Brod, J. H. (1997). Creativity and schizotypy. In G. S. Claridge (Ed.), *Schizotypy: Implications for illness and health* (pp. 276–298). Oxford: Oxford University Press.

Brooks-Gunn, J., & Reiter, E. O. (1990). The role of pubertal processes. In S. S. Feldman & G. R. Elliott (Eds.), *At the threshold.* Cambridge, MA: Harvard University Press.

Brown, J. (1998). *Joke soup.* Kansas City: Andrews McMeel.

Brown, R. T. (1989). Creativity: What are we to measure? In J. A. Glover, R. R. Ronning, & C. R. Reynolds (Eds.), *Handbook of creativity* (pp. 3–32). New York: Plenum.

Brown, S., & Katcher, A. H. (2001). Pet attachment and dissociation. *Society and Animals, 9,* 25–41.

Bruner, J. S., & Tagiuri, R. (1954). The perception of people. In G. Lindzey (Ed.), *Handbook of social psychology* (pp. 634–654). Cambridge, MA: Addison-Wesley.

Bruner, J. S. (1986). *Actual minds, possible worlds.* Cambridge, MA: Harvard University Press.

Bruner, J. S. (1990). *Acts of meaning.* Cambridge, MA: Harvard University Press.

Buck, R. (1984). *The communication of emotion.* New York: Guilford.

Burger, J. (1990). *Personality* (2nd ed.). Belmont, CA: Wadsworth.

Burnstein, E., Crandall, C., & Kitayama, S. (1994). Some neo-Darwinian decision rules for altruism: Weighing cues for inclusive fitness as a function of the biological importance of the decision. *Journal of Personality and Social Psychology, 67*(5), 773–789.

Burton, H. J., Kline, S. A., Lindsay, R. M., & Heidenheim, A. P. (1986). The relationship of depression to survival in chronic renal failure. *Psychosomatic Medicine, 48,* 261–269.

Bushman, B. (2002). Does venting anger feed or extinguish the flame? Catharsis, rumination, distraction, anger and aggressive responding. *Personality and Social Psychology Bulletin, 28,* 724–731.

Buske-Kirschbaum, A., Kirschbaum, C., Stierle, H., Jabaij, L., & Hellhammer, D. (1994). Conditioned manipulation of natural killer (NK) cells in humans using a discriminative learning protocol. *Biological Psychology, 38,* 143–155.

Buss, A. H., & Durkee, A. (1957). An inventory for assessing different kinds of hostility. *Journal of Consulting Psychology, 21,* 343–349.

Buss, A. H., & Finn, S. E. (1987). Classification of personality traits. *Journal of Personality and Social Psychology, 52,* 432–444.

Buss, D. M. (1984). Marital assortment for personality dispositions: Assessment with three different data systems. *Behavior Genetics, 14,* 111–123.

Buss, D. M. (1988a). The evolution of human intrasexual competition: Tactics of mate attraction. *Journal of Personality and Social Psychology, 54,* 616–628.

Buss, D. M. (1988b). Love acts: The evolutionary biology of love. In R. J. Sternberg & M. L. Barnes (Eds.), *The psychology of love* (pp. 100–108). New Haven, CT: Yale University Press.

Buss, D. M. (1988c). Biography. *American Psychologist, 44,* 636–637.

Buss, D. M. (1989). Sex differences in human mate preferences: Evolutionary hypotheses tested in 37 cultures. *Behavioral and Brain Sciences, 12,* 1–49.

Buss, D. M. (1991). Evolutionary personality psychology. *Annual Review of Psychology, 42,* 459–492.

Buss, D. M., & Barnes, M. L. (1986). Preferences in human mate selection. *Journal of Personality and Social Psychology, 50,* 559–570.

Buss, D. M., & Craik, K. H. (1985). Why not measure that trait? Alternative criteria for identifying important dispositions. *Journal of Personality and Social Psychology, 48,* 934–946.

Buss, D. M., Larsen, R. J., Westen, D., & Semmelroth, J. (1992). Sex differences in jealousy: Evolution, physiology, and psychology. *Psychological Science, 3,* 251–255. [Reprinted in H. S. Friedman, & M. W. Schustack (Eds), *Readings in personality: Classic theories and modern research* (pp. 93–100). Boston: Allyn & Bacon.]

Buss, D. M, & Schmitt, D. P. (1993). Sexual strategies theory: An evolutionary perspective on human mating. *Psychological Review, 100,* 204–232.

Butcher, J. N. (1995). Clinical personality assessment: An overview. In *Clinical personality assessment: Practical approaches.* New York: Oxford University Press.

Buttersworth, G. (1992). Origins of self-perception in infancy. *Psychological Inquiry, 3,* 103–111.

Buunk, B., Angleitner, A., Oubaid, V., & Buss, D. M. (1996). Sexual and cultural differences in jealousy: Tests from the Netherlands, Germany, and the United States. *Psychological Science, 7,* 359–363.

Cacioppo, J. T., Gardner, W. L., & Berntson, G. G. (1999). The affect system has parallel and integrative processing components: Form follows function. *Journal of Personality and Social Psychology, 76,* 839–855.

Campbell, J. (1949). *The hero with a thousand faces.* New York: Bollingen Foundation.

Campbell, J. (1972). *Myths to live by.* New York: Viking.

Cantor, N. (1986). Biography. *American Psychologist, 41,* 366–367.

Cantor, N., & Kihlstrom, J. F. (1987). *Personality and social intelligence.* Englewood Cliffs, NJ: Prentice Hall.

Cantor, N., & Mischel, W. (1977). Traits as prototypes: Effects on recognition memory. *Journal of Personality and Social Psychology, 35,* 38–48.

Capitanio, J. P. (1999). Personality dimensions in adult male rhesus macaques: Prediction of behaviors across time and situation. *American Journal of Primatology, 47,* 299–320.

Capitanio, J. P., & Widaman, K. F. (2005). Confirmatory factor analysis of personality structure in adult male rhesus monkeys (Macaca mulatta). *American Journal of Primatology, 65,* 289–294.

Carnegie, D. (1936/1998). *How to win friends and influence people.* New York: Pocket Books.

Carney, R. M., Rich, M. W., & Freedland, K. E. (1988). Major depressive disorder predicts cardiac events in patients with coronary-artery disease. *Psychosomatic Medicine, 50,* 627–633.

Caron, M. D., Whitbourne, S. K., & Halgin, R. P. (1992). Fraudulent excuse making among college students. *Teaching of Psychology, 19,* 90–93.

Carpenter, W. B. (1874). *Principles of mental physiology.* New York: Appleton.

Carroll, J. B. (1993). *Human cognitive abilities: A survey of factor-analytic studies.* New York: Cambridge University Press.

Carter, J. (1982). *Keeping faith.* New York: Bantam Books.

Carter, R. (2002). *Exploring consciousness.* Berkeley: University of California Press.

Carver, C. S. (1975). Physical aggression as a function of objective self-awareness and attitudes toward punishment. *Journal of Experimental Social Psychology, 11,* 510–519.

Carver, C. S., Ganellen, R. J., Froming, W. J., & Chambers, W. (1983). Modeling: An analysis in terms of category accessibility. *Journal of Experimental Social Psychology, 19,* 403–421.

Carver, C. S., & Scheier, M. F. (1981). *Attention and self-regulation: A control theory approach to human behavior.* New York: Springer-Verlag.

Carver, C. S., & Scheier, M. F. (1998). *On the self-regulation of behavior.* New York: Cambridge University Press.

Carver, C. S. & Scheier, M. F. (2000). *Perspectives on personality* (4th ed). Boston: Allyn & Bacon.

Carter, T. J. (1998). Psychological factors associated with anabolic steroid use in male body builders. *Dissertation Abstracts International: Section B: The Sciences & Engineering, Vol. 58 (8-B),* pp. 4439 [Abstract].

Casey, M. B., Pezaris, E., Benbow, C. P., & Nuttall, R. (1995). The influence of spatial ability on gender differences in mathematics college entrance test scores across diverse samples. *Developmental Psychology, 31,* 697–705.

Caspi, A. (2000). The child is father of the man: Personality continuities from childhood to adulthood. *Journal of Personality and Social Psychology, 78,* 158–172.

Caspi, A., & Bem, D. J. (1990). Personality continuity and change across the life course. In L. Pervin (Ed.), *Handbook of personality: Theory and research* (pp. 549–575). New York: Guilford.

Caspi, A., Elder, G. H., & Bem, D. J. (1987). Moving against the world: Life-course patterns of explosive children. *Developmental Psychology, 23,* 308–313.

Caspi, A., & Herbener, E. S. (1990). Continuity and change: Assortative mating and the consistency of personality in adulthood. *Journal of Personality and Social Psychology, 58,* 250–258.

Caspi, A., Herbener, E. S., & Ozer, D. J. (1992). Shared experiences and the similarities of personalities: A longitudinal study of married couples. *Journal of Personality and Social Psychology, 62,* 281–291.

Caspi, A., & Moffitt, T. E. (1992). When do individual differences matter? A paradoxical theory of personality coherence. *Psychological Inquiry, 4,* 247–271.

Caspi, A., & Roberts, B. W. (1999). Personality continuity and change across the life course. In L. A. Pervin & O. P. John (Eds.), *Handbook of personality: Theory and research* (pp. 300–326). New York: Guilford.

Caspi, A., Roberts, B. W., & Shiner, R. L. (2005). Personality development: Stability and change. *Annual Review of Psychology, 56,* 453–484.

Cattell, R. B. (1947). Confirmation and clarification of primary personality factors. *Psychometrika, 12,* 197–220.

Cattell, R. B. (1956). Second-order personality factors in the questionnaire realm. *Journal of Consulting Psychology, 20,* 411–418.

Cattell, R. B. (1963). The theory of fluid and crystalized intelligence: A critical experiment. *Journal of Educational Psychology, 54,* 1–22.

Cattell, R. B. (1965). *The scientific analysis of personality.* Chicago: Aldine.

Cattell, R. B. (1969). *16PF (Form C, 1969 Edition R).* Champaign, IL: Institute for Personality and Ability Testing (IPAT).

Cattell, R. B. (1971). *Abilities: Their structure, growth, and action.* Boston: Houghton Mifflin.

Cattell, R. B., & Butcher, H. J. (1968). *The prediction of achievement and creativity.* Indianapolis, IN: Bobbs-Merrill.

Cattell, R. B., Horn, J., & Butcher, H. J. (1962). The dynamic structure of attitudes in adults: A description of some established factors and of their measurement by the motivational analysis test. *British Journal of Psychology, 53,* 57–69.

Caughey, J. L. (1980). Personality identity and social organization. *Ethos, 8,* 173–203. [Selections reproduced with permission in D. C. Funder & D. J. Ozer, *Pieces of the personality puzzle* (pp. 378–382).] New York: W. W. Norton.

Ceci, S. J. (1996). *On intelligence.* Cambridge, MA: Harvard University Press.

Cerf, C., & Navasky, V. (1998). *The experts speak: The definitive compendium of authoritative misinformation.* New York: Villard.

Cervone, D. (2004). The architecture of personality. *Psychological Review, 111,* 183–204.

Cervone, D. (2005). Personality architecture: Within-person structures and processes. *Annual Review of Psychology, 56,* 423–452.

Cervone, D., Shadel, W. G., & Jencius, S. (2001). A social-cognitive theory of personality assessment. *Personality and Social Psychology Review, 5,* 33–51.

Champagne, B., & Pervin, L. A. (1987). The relation of perceived situation similarity to perceived behavior similarity: Implications for social learning theory. *European Journal of Personality, 1,* 79–92.

Chapin, F. S. (1968). *The social insight test.* Palo Alto, CA: Consulting Psychologists Press.

Chapman, J. P., Chapman, L. J., & Kwapil, T. R. (1994). Does the Eysenck Psychoticism Scale predict psychosis? A ten year longitudinal study. *Personality and Individual Differences, 17,* 369–375.

Chapman, M. (1997). French embrace common sense on surgeons with AIDS virus. *Human Events, 53,* 6.

Chavajay, P., & Rogoff, B. (2002). Schooling and traditional collaborative social organization of problem solving by Mayan mothers and children. *Developmental Psychology, 38,* 55–66.

Cheeseman Day, J., & Newburger, E. C. (2002). The big payoff: Educational attainment and synthetic estimates of work-life earnings. U.S. Bureau of the Census, Special Reports [P23-210], Washington, DC: U.S. Government Printing Office.

Christiansen, N. D., Wolcott-Burnam, S., & Janovics, J. E. (2005). The good judge revisited: individual differences in the accuracy of personality judgments. *Human Performance, 18,* 123–149.

Christie, R., & Geis, F. L. (1970). *Studies in Machiavellianism.* New York: Academic Press.

Ciarrochi, J. V., Chan, A. Y., & Caputi, P. (2000). A critical evaluation of the emotional intelligence concept. *Personality and Individual Differences, 28,* 539–561.

Claridge, G. S., Canter, S., & Hume, W. I. (1973). *Personality differences and biological variations: A study of twins.* Oxford: Pergamon.

Clark, R. D. (1990). The impact of AIDS on gender differences in willingness to engage in casual sex. *Journal of Applied Social Psychology, 20,* 771–782.

Clark, R. D., & Hatfield, E. (1989). Gender differences in receptivity to sexual offers. *Journal of Psychology and Human Sexuality, 2,* 39–55.

Cloninger, S. C. (2000). *Theories of personality* (3rd ed.). Upper Saddle River, NJ: Prentice Hall.

Cobb, C., & Mayer, J. D. (2000). Emotional intelligence: What the research says. *Educational Leadership, 58,* 14–18.

Cocker, K. L., Edwards, G. A., Anderson, J. W., & Meares, R. A. (1994). Electrophysiological changes under hypnosis in multiple personality disorder: A two-case exploratory study. *Australian Journal of Clinical and Experimental Hypnosis, 22,* 165–176.

Coetsee, A. S. J. (1933). The comprehension of spatial relations (among primary school children) by the elaboration of two-dimensional visual stimuli. *South African Journal of Psychology & Education, 1.2,* 25–33.

Cohen, D., & Strayer, J. (1996). Empathy in conduct-disordered and comparison youth. *Developmental Psychology, 32,* 988–998.

Cohen, S, Frank, E., & Doyle, W. J. (1998). Types of stressors that increase susceptibility to the common cold in healthy adults. *Health Psychology, 17,* 214–223.

Cohen, S., Tyrrell, D. A., & Smith, A. P. (1991). Psychological stress and susceptibility to the common cold. *New England Journal of Medicine, 325,* 606–612.

Cohler, B. J. (1982). Personal narrative and the life course. In P. Baltes & O. G. Brim (Eds.), *Life span development and behavior* (Vol. 4, pp. 205–241). New York: Academic Press.

Cohn, E. S., White, S. O., & Sanders, J. (2000). Distributive and procedural justice in seven nations. *Law and Human Behavior, 24,* 553–579.

Collins, A. M., & Loftus, E. F. (1975). A spreading-activation theory of semantic processing. *Psychological Review, 82,* 407–428.

Collins, J. C., McLeod, D., & Jacoby, L. L. (1992). When a hush falls over the room: An indirect measure of emotionality. Unpublished manuscript.

Collins, N. L., & Read, S. J. (1990). Adult attachment, working models, and relationship quality in dating couples. *Journal of Personality and Social Psychology 58,* 644–663.

Combs, A. W. (1947). A comparative study of motivation as revealed in thematic apperception stories and autobiographies. *Journal of Clinical Psychology, 3,* 65–75.

Committee on Scientific Awards (1986). Nancy E. Cantor. *American Psychologist, 41,* 365–368.

Committee on Scientific Awards (1989). David M. Buss. *American Psychologist, 44,* 636–638.

Conger, R. D., Elder, G. H., Lorenz, F. O., Conger, K. J., Simons, R. L., Huck, S., & Melby, J. N. (1990). Linking economic hardship to marital quality and instability. *Journal of Marriage and the Family, 52,* 643–656.

Conry, R., & Plant, W. T. (1965). WAIS and group test predictions of an academic success criterion: high school and college. *Educational and Psychological Measurement, 25,* 493–500.

Cook, J. (1997). *The book of positive quotations.* Minneapolis: Fairview.

Cooley, C. H. (1902). *Human nature and the social order.* New York: Scribner.

Cools, R., Blackwell, A., Clark, L., Menzies, L., Cox, S., & Robbins, T. (2005). Tryptophan depletion disrupts the motivational guidance of goal-directed behavior as a function of trait impulsivity. *Neuropsychopharmacology, 30,* 1362–1373.

Cooper, L. A., & Shepard, R. N. (1984). Turning something over in the mind. *Scientific American, 251,* 106–114.

Cooper, S. H. (1998). Changing notions of defense within psychoanalytic theory. *Journal of Personality, 66,* 947–964.

Coopersmith, S. (1967). *The antecedents of self-esteem.* San Francisco: W. H. Freeman.

Coopersmith, S. (1975). Self-concept, race, and education. In C. K. Verna & C. Bagley (Eds.), *Race and education across cultures.* London: Heinemann.

Cortés, J. B. (1960). The achievement motive in the Spanish economy between the 13th and 18th centuries. *Economic Development and Cultural Change, 9,* 144–163.

Cortina, J. M., Doherty, M. L., Schmitt, N., Kaufman, G., & Smith, R. G. (1992). The "Big Five" personality factors in the IPI and MMPI: Predictors of police performance. *Personnel Psychology, 45,* 119–140.

Costa, P. T., & McCrae, R. R. (1980). Influence of extraversion and neuroticism on subjective well-being: happy and unhappy people. *Journal of Personality and Social Psychology, 38,* 668–678.

Costa, P. T., Jr., & McCrae, R. R. (1985). *Revised NEO Personality Inventory (NEO PI-R) and NEO Five-Factor Inventory (NEO-FFI): Professional manual.* Odessa, FL: Psychological Assessment Resources, Inc.

Costa, P. T., Jr., & McCrae, R. R. (1988). Personality in adulthood: A six-year longitudinal study of self-reports and spouse ratings on the NEO Personality Inventory. *Journal of Personality and Social Psychology, 54,* 853–863.

Costa, P. T., Jr., & McCrae, R. R. (2002). Looking backward: Changes in the mean levels of personality traits from 80 to 12. In D. Cervone & W. Mischel (Eds.), *Advances in Personality Science* (pp. 219–237). New York: Guilford.

Costa, P. T., Jr., McCrae, R. R., Zonderman, A. B., Barbano, H. E., Lebowitz, B., & Larson, D. M. (1986). Cross-sectional studies of personality in a national sample: 2. Stability in neuroticism, extraversion, and openness. *Psychology and Aging, 1,* 144–149.

Cox, C. M. (1926). *Genetic studies of genius: Volume II: The early mental traits of three hundred geniuses.* Stanford, CA: Stanford University Press.

Craik, K. H. (1993). The 1937 Allport and Stagner texts in personality psychology. In K. H. Craik, R. Hogan, & R. N. Wolfe (Eds.), *Fifty years of personality psychology* (pp. 3–20). New York: Plenum.

Craik, K. H. (1998). Personality systems concepts and their implications. *Psychological Inquiry, 9,* 145–148.

Cramer, P. (1991). *The development of defense mechanisms: Theory, research, and assessment.* New York: Springer-Verlag.

Cramer, P. (1998). Freshman to senior year: A follow-up study of identity, narcissism, and defense mechanisms. *Journal of Research in Personality, 32,* 156–172.

Cramer, P. (2002). Defense mechanisms, behavior, and affect in young adulthood. *Journal of Personality, 70,* 103–126.

Cramer, P., & Tracy, A. (2005). The pathway from child personality to adult adjustment: The road is not straight. *Journal of Research in Personality, 39,* 369–374.

Crick, F., & Koch, C. (1995). Are we aware of neural activity in primary visual cortex? *Nature, 375,* 121–123.

Crocker, J., Alloy, L. B., & Kayne, N. T. (1988). Attributional style, depression, and perceptions of consensus for events. *Journal of Personality and Social Psychology, 54,* 540–546.

Cronbach, L. J. (1960). *Essentials of psychological testing* (2nd ed.). New York: Harper & Row.

Cronbach, L. J., & Meehl, P. E. (1955). Construct validity in psychological tests. *Psychological Bulletin, 52,* 281–302.

Cronbach, L. J., Rajaratnam, N., & Gleser, G. C. (1965). Theory of generalizeability: A liberalization of reliability theory. *The British Journal of Statistical Psychology, 16,* 137–163.

Cross, W. E. (1987). A two-factor theory of Black identity: Implications for the study of identity development in minority children. In J. S. Phinney & M. J. Rotheram (Eds.), *Children's ethnic socialization.* Newbury Park, CA: Sage.

Crowell, J. A., Treboux, D., Gao, Y., Fyffe, C., Pan, H., & Waters, E. (2002). Assessing secure base behavior in adulthood: Development of a measure, links to adult attachment representations, and relations to couples' communication and reports of relationships. *Developmental Psychology, 38,* 679–693.

Csikszentmihalyi, M. (1990). *Flow: The psychology of optimal experience.* New York: Harper Collins.

Csikszentmihalyi, M. (1997). *Finding flow: The psychology of engagement with everyday life.* New York: Basic Books.

Dabbs, J. M. (1992). Testosterone and occupational achievement. *Social Forces, 70,* 813–824.

Dabbs, J. M., Jr., Carr, T. S., Frady, R. L., & Riad, J. K. (1995). Testosterone, crime, and misbehavior among 692 male prison inmates. *Personality and Individual Differences, 18,* 627–633.

Dahlstrom, W. G., Welsh, G. S., & Dahlstrom, L. E. (1972). *An MMPI handbook.* Minneapolis: University of Minnesota Press.

Daley, R. (1981). *The prince of the city.* New York: Berkley Books.

Daly, M., & Wilson, M. (1988). *Homocide.* New York: Aldine de Gruyter.

Daly, M., & Wilson, M. (1990). Is parent-offspring conflict sex-linked? Freudian and Darwinian models. *Journal of Personality, 58,* 163–189.

Dalton, D. (1993). *Mahatma Gandhi: Nonviolent power in action.* New York: Columbia University Press.

Darley, J. M., & Latane, B. (1968). Bystander intervention in emergencies. Diffusion of responsibility. *Journal of Personality and Social Psychology, 27,* 100–108.

Darwin, C. (1965). *The expression of the emotions in man and animals.* Chicago: The University of Chicago Press. [Original work published 1873.]

David, T. J. (2001). Revising psychoanalytic interpretations of the past: An examination of declarative and non-declarative memory processes. *International Journal of Psychoanalysis, 82,* 449–462.

Davidson, K., & Prkachin, K. (1997). Optimism and unrealistic optimism have an interacting impact on health-promoting behavior and knowledge changes. *Personality and Social Psychology Bulletin, 23,* 617–625.

Davidson, R. J., & Tomarken, A. J. (1989). Laterality and emotion: An electrophysiological approach. In F. Boller & J. Grafman (Eds.), *Handbook of Neurology* (pp. 419–441). Amsterdam: Elsevier.

Davies, M., Stankov, L., & Roberts, R. D. (1998). Emotional intelligence: In search of an elusive construct. *Journal of Personality and Social Psychology, 75,* 989–1015.

Davis, P. H., & Osherson, A. (1977). The current treatment of a multiple-personality woman and her son. *American Journal of Psychotherapy, 31,* 504–515.

Day, A. L., & Carroll, S. A. (2004). Using an ability-based measure of emotional intelligence to predict individual performance, group performance, and group citizenship behaviours. *Personality and Individual Differences, 36,* 1443–1458.

Dayan, K., Kasten, R., & Fox, S. (2002). Entry-level police candidate assessment center: An efficient tool or a hammer to kill a fly? *Personnel Psychology, 55,* 827–849.

De St. Aubin, E. (1996). Personality ideology polarity: Its emotional foundation and its manifestation in individual value systems, religiosity, political orientation, and assumptions concerning human nature. *Journal of Personality and Social Psychology, 71,* 152–165.

De Raad, B., & Kokkonen, M. (2000). Traits and emotions: A review of their structure and management. *European Journal of Personality, 14,* 477–496.

De Waal, F. (2001). *The ape and the sushi master: Cultural reflections of a primatologist.* New York: Basic Books.

Deacon, T. W. (1997). *The symbolic species: The co-evolution of language and the brain.* New York: W. W. Norton.

Deci, E. L., & Ryan, R. M. (2000). The "what" and "why" of goal pursuits: Human needs and the self-determination of behavior. *Psychological Inquiry, 11,* 227–268.

Deikman, A. J. (1966). De-automatization and the mystic experience. *Psychiatry: Journal for the Study of Interpersonal Processes, 29,* 324–338.

Deikman, A. J. (1973). Deautomatization and the mystic experience. In R. E. Ornstein (Ed.), *The nature of human consciousness* (pp. 216–233). New York: W. H. Freeman. [Reprinted from (1966) *Psychiatry, 29,* 324–338.]

Deiner, E., & Deiner, C. (1996). Most people are happy. *Psychological Science, 7,* 181–185.

Deiner, E., Lucas, R. E., & Oishi, S. (2002). Subjective well-being: The science of happiness and life satisfaction. In C. R. Snyder & S. J. Lopez (Eds.), *Handbook of positive psychology* (pp. 63–73). New York: Oxford University Press.

Deiner, E., & Seligman, M. E. P. (2002). Very happy people. *Psychological Science, 13,* 81–83.

Deiner, E., Smith, H., & Fujita, F. (1995). The personality structure of affect. *Journal of Personality and Social Psychology, 69,* 130–141.

Deinier, E., & Emmons, R. A. (1984). The independence of positive and negative affect. *Journal of Personality and Social Psychology, 47,* 1105–1117.

Deinier, E., Larsen, R. J., Levine, S., & Emmons, R. A. (1985). Intensity and frequency: Dimensions underlying positive and negative affect. *Journal of Personality and Social Psychology, 48,* 1253–1265.

Dennett, D. C. (1978). *Brainstorms.* Cambridge, MA: MIT Press.

Denton, K., & Krebs, D. (1990). From the scene to the crime: The effect of alcohol and social context on moral judgment. *Journal of Personality and Social Psychology, 59,* 242–248.

Depue, R. A., Luciana, M., Arbisi, P., Collins, P., & Leon, A. (1994). Dopamine and the structure of personality: Relation of agonist-induced dopamine activity to positive emotionality. *Journal of Personality and Social Psychology, 67,* 485–498.

DeRivera, J. (1977). A structural theory of the emotions. *Psychological Issues, 40,* 9–179.

Descartes (1641/1968). *Discourse on method and the meditations.* New York: Penguin Books.

deSilva, P., Rachman, S., Seligman, M. E. (1977). Prepared phobias and obsessions: Therapeutic outcome. *Behaviour Research and Therapy, 15,* 65–77.

Deutsch, A. (1983). Psychiatric perspectives on an eastern-style cult. In D. A. Halperin (Ed.), *Psychodynamic perspectives on religion, sect, and cult* (pp. 113–129). Boston: John Wright PSG.

Dewey, J. (1922/1892). Human nature and conduct. New York: Holt.

Dewey, J. (1967). Psychology. In *John Dewey: The early works. 1882–1898, Vol 2: 1887.* Carbondale: Southern Illinois University Press. (Original work published 1887.)

Digman, J. M. (1990). Personality structure: Emergence of the five-factor model. *Annual Review of Psychology, 41,* 417–440.

Dodge, K., & Frame, C. (1982). Social cognitive biases and deficits in aggressive boys. *Child Development, 53,* 629–635.

Dollard, J., Doob, J., Miller, N., Mowrer, O., & Sears, R. (1939). *Frustration and aggression.* New Haven, CT: Yale University Press.

Dollard, J., & Miller, N. (1950). *Personality and psychotherapy.* New York: McGraw Hill.

Dollinger, S. J., & Dollinger, S. M. C. (1997). Individuality and identity exploration: An autophotographic study. *Journal of Research in Personality, 31,* 337–354.

Dooley, D., & Catalano, R. (Eds.). (1988). Special issue on: Psychological effects of unemployment. *Journal of Social Issues, 44,* 1–191.

Donnellan, M. B., Larsen-Rife, D., & Conger, R. D. (2005). Personality, family history, and competence in early adult romantic relationships. *Journal of Personality and Social Psychology, 88,* 562–576.

Dornbusch, S. M. (1965). Popular psychology: A content analysis of contemporary inspirational nonreligious books. In S. Z. Klausner (Ed.), *The quest for self-control* (pp. 126–140). New York: Free Press.

Douglas, K., & Arenberg, D. (1978). Age changes, cohort differences, and cultural change on the Guilford-Zimmerman Temperament Survey. *Journal of Gerontology, 33,* 737–747.

Dowson, M., & McInerney, D. M. (2001). Psychological parameters of students' social and work avoidance goals: A qualitative investigation. *Journal of Educational Psychology, 93,* 35–42.

Doyle, K. O., Jr. (1974). Theory and practice of ability testing in ancient Greece. *Journal of the History of the Behavioral Sciences, 10,* 202–212.

Draine, S. C., & Greenwald, A. G. (1998). Replicable unconscious semantic priming. *Journal of Experimental Psychology: General, 127,* 286–303.

Drugan, R. C., Basile, A. S., Ha, J-H., & Ferland, R. J. (1994). The protective effects of stress control may be mediated by increased brain levels of benzodiazepine receptor agonists. *Brain Research, 661,* 127–136.

Drugan, R. C., Skolnick, P., Paul, S. M., & Crawley, J. N. (1989). A pretest procedure reliably predicts performance in two animal models of inescapable stress. *Pharmacology Biochemistry and Behavior 33,* 649–654.

Dubner, S. J., & Levitt, S. D. (June 6, 2004). What the bagel man saw. *New York Times Magazine, 153,* 62–66.

Duerr, E. (1962). *The length and depth of acting.* New York: Holt, Rinehart, & Winston.

Duncan, J., & Humphries, G. W. (1989). Visual search and stimulus similarity. *Psychological Review, 96,* 433–548.

Dunn, A. J. (1989). Psychoneuroimmunology for the psychoneuroendocrinologist: A review of animal studies of nervous system—immune system interactions. *Psychoneuroendocrinology, 14,* 251–274.

Dunning, D. (2005). *Self-insight: Roadblocks and detours on the path to knowing thyself.* New York: Psychology Press.

Dutton, D. G., & Aron, A. P. (1974). Some evidence for heightened sexual attraction under conditions of high anxiety. *Journal of Personality and Social Psychology, 30,* 510–517.

Dutton, D. G., & Aron, A. (1989). Romantic attraction and generalized liking for others who are sources of conflict-based arousal. *Canadian Journal of Behavioral Science, 21,* 246–257.

Dutton, D. G., & Lake, R. A. (1973). Threat of prejudice and reverse discrimination in interracial situations. *Journal of Personality and Social Psychology, 28,* 94–100.

Dweck, C. S., Chiu, C-y., & Hong, Y.-y (1995). Implicit theories: Elaboration and extension of the model. *Psychological Inquiry, 6,* 322–333.

Dyer, M. G. (1983). The role of affect in narratives. *Cognitive Science, 20,* 211–242.

Eccles, J. C. (1953). *The neurophysiological basis of mind: The principles of neurophysiology.* Oxford: Clarendon.

Eccles, J. S., & Wigfield, A. (2002). Motivational beliefs, values, and goals. *Annual Review of Psychology, 53,* 109–132.

Edwards, A. L. (1942). The retention of affective experiences—A criticism and restatement of the problem. *Psychological Review, 49,* 43–53.

Edwards, A. L. (1957). *Manual for the Edwards Personal Preference Schedule.* New York: The Psychological Corporation.

Edwards, A. L., & Abbott, R. D. (1973). Relationships among the Edwards Personality Inventory Scales, the Edwards Personality Preference Schedule, and the Personality Research Form Scales. *Journal of Consulting and Clinical Psychology, 30,* 27–32.

Edwards, A. L., Abbott, R. D., & Klockars, A. J. (1972). A factor analysis of the EPPS and PRF personality inventories. *Educational and Psychological Measurement, 32,* 23–29.

Ehrlich, E., & De Bruhl, M. (1996). *The international thesaurus of quotations (Revised and updated).* New York: HarperCollins.

Eich, E. (1995). Searching for mood dependent memory. *Psychological Science, 6,* 67–75.

Eichenbaum, H. (1997). Declarative memory: Insights from cognitive neurobiology. *Annual Review of Psychology, 48,* 547–572.

Eisenberg, N., Cumberland, A., & Spinrad, T. L. (1998). Parental socialization of emotion. In *Psychological Inquiry, 9,* 241–273.

Eisenberg, N., Fabes, R. A., Guthrie, I. K., & Reiser, M. (2000). Dispositional emotionality and regulation: Their role in predicting quality of social functioning. *Journal of Personality and Social Psychology, 71,* 136–157.

Eisenberg, N., Fabes, R. A., Schaller, M., Miller, P. A., Carlo, G., Poulin, R., Shea, C., & Shell, R. (1991). Personality and socialization correlates of vicarious emotional responding. *Journal of Personality and Social Psychology, 61,* 459–471.

Eisenberg, N., Schaller, M., Fabes, R. A., Bustamante, D., Mathy, R., Shell, R., & Rhodes, K. (1988). The differentiation of personal distress and sympathy in children and adults. *Developmental Psychology, 24,* 766–775.

Ekman, P. (1973). Cross-cultural studies of facial expression. In P. Ekman (Ed.), *Darwin and facial expression* (pp. 169–222). Oxford: Academic Press.

Ekman, P. (1984). Expression and the nature of emotion. In K. R. Scherer & P. Ekman (Eds.), *Approaches to emotion* (pp. 319–343). Hillsdale, NJ: Lawrence Erlbaum.

Ekman, P. (1985). *Telling lies: Clues to deceit in the marketplace, politics, and marriage.* New York: W. W. Norton.

Ekman, P. (1999). Facial expressions. In T. Dalgleish & M. Power (Eds.), *Handbook of cognition and emotion* (pp. 301–320). New York: John Wiley & Sons.

Ekman, P., & Friesen, W. V. (1969). The repertoire of nonverbal behavior. Categories, origins, usage, and coding. *Semiotica, 1,* 49–98.

Ekman, P., & Friesen, W. V. (1975). *Unmasking the face.* Englewood Cliffs, NJ: Prentice-Hall.

Ekman, P., Friesen, W. V., & Ellsworth, P. (1972). *Emotion in the human face: Guidelines for research and an integration of findings.* New York: Pergamon.

Elder, G. H. (1974). *Children of the great depression: Social change in life experiences.* Chicago: University of Chicago Press.

Elior, R. (1987). Soul. In A. A. Cohen & P. Mendes-Flohr (Eds.), *Contemporary Jewish religious thought* (pp. 887–896). New York: The Free Press.

Ellenberger, H. F. (1981). *The discovery of the unconscious: The history and evolution of dynamic psychiatry.* New York: Basic Books.

Elliott, A. (1994). *Psychoanalytic theory: An introduction.* Cambridge, MA: Blackwell.

Emde, R. N., & Sorce, J. E. (1983). The rewards of infancy: Emotional availability and social referencing. In J. D. Call, E. Galenson, & R. Tyson (Eds.), *Frontiers of infant psychiatry* (Vol. 1). (pp. 17–30). New York: Basic Books.

Emihovich, C., & Lima, E. S. (1995). The many facets of Vygotsky: A cultural historical voice from the future. *Anthropology and Education Quarterly, 26,* 375–383.

Emmons, R. A. (1986). Personal strivings: An approach to personality and subjective well-being. *Journal of Personality and Social Psychology, 51,* 1058–1068.

Emmons, R. A. (1998). A systems framework or systems frameworks? *Psychological Inquiry, 9,* 148–150.

Emmons, R. A. (2000). Spirituality and intelligence: Problems and prospects. *International Journal for the Psychology of Religion, 10,* 57–64.

Emmons, R. A., & King, L. A. (1988). Conflict among personal strivings: Immediate and long-term implications for psychological and physical well-being. *Journal of Personality and Social Psychology, 54,* 1040–1048.

Emmons, R. A., & King, L A. (1989). Personal striving differentiation and affective reactivity. *Journal of Personality and Social Psychology, 56,* 478–484.

Epstein, E., & Guttman, R. (1984). Mate selection in man: Evidence, theory, and outcome. *Social Biology, 31,* 243–278.

Epstein, S. (1973). The self-concept revisited, or a theory of a theory. *American Psychologist, 28,* 404–416.

Epstein, S. (1979). The stability of behavior: I. On predicting most of the people much of the time. *Journal of Personality and Social Psychology, 37,* 1097–1126.

Epstein, S. (1997). This I have learned from over 40 years of personality research. *Journal of Personality, 65,* 3–32.

Epstein, S. (1998). *Constructive thinking: The key to emotional intelligence.* Westport, CT: Praeger.

Epstein, S., & Meier, P. (1989). Constructive thinking: A broad coping variable with specific components. *Journal of Personality and Social Psychology, 57,* 332–350.

Epstein, S., & O'Brien, E. J. (1985). The person-situation debate in historical and current perspective. *Psychological Bulletin, 98,* 513–537.

Epstein, S., Pacini, R., Denes-Raj, V., & Heier, H. (1996). Individual differences in intuitive-experiential and analytical-rational thinking styles. *Journal of Personality and Social Psychology, 71,* 390–405.

Erdelyi, M. H. (1984). *Psychoanalysis: Freud's cognitive psychology.* New York: W.H. Freeman and Company.

Erikson, E. H. (1958). The nature of clinical evidence. *Daedalus, 87,* 65–87.

Erikson, E. H. (1963). *Childhood and society* (2nd ed.). New York: W. W. Norton.

Erikson, E. H. (1965). Psychoanalysis and ongoing history: Problems of identity, hatred, and nonviolence. *The American Journal of Psychiatry, 122,* 241–250.

Erikson, E. H. (1969). *Gandhi's truth.* New York: W. W. Norton.

Erikson, E. H. (1975). *Life history and the historical moment.* New York: W. W. Norton & Company.

Ernst, C., & Angst, J. (1983). *Birth order: Its influence on personality.* Berlin: Springer-Verlag.

Exline, R. V., Thiabaut, J., Hickey, C. B., & Gumpart, P. (1970). Visual interactions in relation to expectations, and situational preferences: Personality influences on the decision to participate in volunteer helping behaviors. *Journal of Personality, 67,* 470–503.

Eysenck, H. J. (1967). *The biological basis of personality.* Springfield, IL: Charles C. Thomas.

Eysenck, H. J. (1972). Primaries or second-order factors: A critical consideration of Cattell's 16 PF Battery. *British Journal of Social & Clinical Psychology, 11,* 265–269.

Eysenck, H. J. (1980). Personality, marital satisfaction, and divorce. *Psychological Reports, 47,* 1235–1238.

Eysenck, H. J. (1982). *A model of intelligence.* New York: Springer.

Eysenck, H. J. (1990). Biological dimensions of personality. In L.A. Pervin (Ed.), *Handbook of personality* (pp. 244–270). New York: Guilford.

Eysenck, H. J. (1994). Personality and intelligence: Psychometric and experimental approaches. In P. Ruzgis & R. J. Sternberg (Eds.), *Personality and intelligence.* Cambridge: Cambridge University Press.

Eysenck, H. J., & Eysenck, S. B. G. (1968). *Manual: Eysenck Personality Inventory: Manual.* San Diego, CA: Educational and Testing Service [EDITS].

Eysenck, H. J., & Eysenck, S. B. G. (1975). *Manual: Eysenck Personality Questionnaire.* San Diego, CA: EDITS/Educational and Industrial Testing Service.

Eysenck, H. J., & Gudjonsson, G. (1989). *Causes and cures of delinquency.* New York: Plenum Press.

Eysenck, H. J., & Kamin, L. (1981). *The intelligence controversy.* New York: John Wiley & Sons.

Eysenck, H. J., & Rachman, S. (1972). *The causes and cures of neurosis.* San Diego, CA: Robert R. Knapp.

Eysenck, S. B. G., & Eysenck, H. J. (1963). The validity of questionnaire and rating assessments of extraversion and neuroticism, and their factorial stability. *British Journal of Psychology, 54,* 51–62.

Fagan, J. F. (1992). Intelligence: A theoretical viewpoint. *Current Directions in Psychological Science, 1,* 82–86.

Farber, B. A., & Golden, V. (1997). Psychological mindedness in psychotherapists. In M. McCallum & W. E. Piper (Eds.), *Psychological mindedness: A contemporary understanding* (pp. 211–235). Mahwah, NJ: Lawrence Erlbaum.

Fancher, R. E. (1985). *The intelligence men: Makers of the IQ controversy.* New York: W. W. Norton.

Fauerbach, J. A., Lawrence, J. W., Hathomthwaite, J. A., & Richter, L. (2002). Coping with the stress of a painful medical procedure. *Behaviour Research and Theory, 40,* 1003–1015.

Faulkner, W. (1929/1956). *The sound and the fury.* New York: Random House.

Feenstra, J. S., Banyard, V. L., Rines, E., & Hopkins, K. R. (2001). First-year students' adaptation to college: The role of family variables and individual coping. *Journal of College Student Development, 42,* 106–113.

Fenichel, O. (1945). *The psychoanalytic theory of neurosis.* New York: W. W. Norton.

Fenigstein, A., Scheier, F. M., & Buss, A. H. (1975). Public and private self-consciousness: Assessment and theory. *Journal of Consulting and Clinical Psychology, 43,* 522–527.

Fields, J. (2001). Living arrangements of Children. *Current Population Reports.* Washington, DC: U.S. Census Bureau.

Fieve, R. R. (1975). *Mood swing.* New York: Morrow.

Finch, J. F., & Graziano, W. G. (2001). Predicting depression from temperament, personality, and patterns of social relations. *Journal of Personality, 69,* 27–54.

Fisher, J. E., Mohanty, A., Herrington, J. D., Koven, N. S., Miller, G. A., & Heller, W. (2004). Neuropsychological evidence for dimensional schizotypy: Implications for creativity and psychopathology. *Journal of Research in Personality, 38,* 24–31.

Fiske, A. P. (1991). The cultural relativity of selfish individualism: Anthropological evidence that humans are inherently sociable. In M. S. Clark (Ed.), *Prosocial behavior* (pp. 176–214). Thousand Oaks, CA: Sage.

Fiske, D. W. (1949). Consistency of the factorial structures of personality ratings from different sources. *Journal of Abnormal and Social Psychology, 44,* 107–112.

Flanagan, O. J. (2002). *The problem of the soul: Two visions of mind and how to reconcile them.* New York: Basic Books.

Flashman, L. A., Andreasen, N. C., Flaum, M., & Swayze, V. W. (1998). Intelligence and regional brain volumes in normal controls. *Intelligence, 25,* 149–160.

Fletcher, K. E., & Averill, J. R. (1984). A scale for the measurement of role-playing ability. *Journal of Research in Personality, 18,* 131–149.

Fodor, J. A. (1985). Pieces of "The Modularity of Mind." *The Behavioral and Brain Sciences, 8,* 1–42.

Folkman, S., & Lazarus, R. S. (1980). An analysis of coping in a middle-aged community sample. *Journal of Health & Social Behavior, 21,* 219–239.

Folkman, S., & Lazarus, R. S. (1985). If it changes it must be a process: Study of emotion and coping during three stages of a college examination. *Journal of Personality and Social Psychology, 48,* 150–170.

Folkman, S., & Lazarus, R. S. (1988). *Ways of coping questionnaire manual.* Menlo Park, CA: Mind Garden.

Folkman, S., Lazarus, R. S., Dunkel-Schetter, C., DeLongis, A., & Gruen, R. J. (1986). The dynamics of a stressful encounter. *Journal of Personality and Social Psychology, 50,* 992–1003.

Foos, P. W. (2001). A self-reference exercise for teaching life expectancy. *Teaching of Psychology, 28,* 199–201.

Forgas, J. P. (Ed.). (2001). *Handbook of affect and social cognition.* Mahwah, NJ: Lawrence Erlbaum.

Formica, S. (1998). *Description of the socio-emotional life space: Life qualities and activities related to emotional intelligence.* Unpublished honors thesis, University of New Hampshire, Durham, NH.

Fowles, D. C. (1987). Application of a behavioral theory of motivation to the concepts of anxiety and impulsivity. *Journal of Research in Personality, 21,* 417–435.

Fowles, D. C. (1994). A motivational theory of psychopathology. In W. Spaulding (Ed.), *Nebraska Symposium on Motivation: Integrated views of motivation, cognition, and emotion* (Vol. 41, pp. 181–238). Lincoln: University of Nebraska Press.

Fox, N. A. (1991). If it's not left, it's right. *American Psychologist, 46,* 863–872.

Fox, N. A., Henderson, H. A., Marshall, P. J., Nichols, K. E., & Ghera, M. M. (2005). Behavioral inhibition: Linking biology and behavior within a developmental framework. *Annual Review of Psychology, 56,* 235–262,

Frank, L. K. (1939). Projective methods for the study of personality. *Journal of Personality, 8,* 343–389.

Frank, L. R. (2001). *Quotationary.* New York: Random House.

Fraser, S. (1995). *The bell curve wars.* Basic Books.

Fraser, J. (2003). *The territory of men: A memoir.* New York: Random House.

Frasure-Smith, N., Lesperance, F., & Talajic, M. (1993). Depression following myocardial infarction: Impact on six-month survival. *JAMA: Journal of the American Medical Association, 270,* 1819–1825.

Fredrickson, B. L. (2002a). Positive emotions trigger upward spirals toward emotional well-being. *Psychological Science, 13,* 172–175.

Fredrickson, B. L. (2002b). Positive emotions. In C. R. Snyder & S. J. Lopez (Eds.), *Handbook of positive psychology.* New York: Oxford University Press.

Freese, J., Powell, B., & Steelman, L. C. (1999). Rebel without a cause or effect: Birth order and social attitudes. *American Sociological Review, 64,* 207–231.

Freitag, M. K., Belsky, J., Grossmann, K., Grossmann, K. E., & Scheuerer-Englisch, H. (1996). Continuity in parent-child relationships from infancy to middle childhood and relations with friendship competence. *Child Development, 67,* 1437–1454.

Freud, S. (1927). Some psychological consequences of the anatomical distinction between the sexes. In J. Strachey (Ed. and Trans.), *The standard edition of the complete psychological works of Sigmund Freud* (Vol. 8, pp. 133–142). London: Hogarth.

Freud, S. (1943). *A general introduction to psychoanalysis* (J. Riviere, Trans.). Garden City, NY: Garden City. [Original work published 1920.]

Freud, S. (1953). Three contributions to the theory of sex: II. Infantile sexuality. In J. Strachey (Ed. and Trans.), *The standard edition of the complete psychological works of Sigmund Freud* (Vol. 7, pp. 135–243). London: Hogarth. [Original work published 1905.]

Freud, S. (1958). The dynamics of transference. In J. Strachey (Ed. and Trans.), *The standard edition of the complete psychological works of Sigmund Freud* (Vol. 12, pp. 99–108). London: Hogarth. [Original work published 1912.]

Freud, S. (1958). Remembering, repeating, and working through. In *The standard edition of the complete psychological works of Sigmund Freud* (Vol. 12, pp. 145–156). London: Hogarth. [Original work published 1914.]

Freud, S. (1960). *The ego and the id* (J. Riviere, Trans., and J. Strachey, Ed.). New York: W. W. Norton. [Original work published 1923.]

Freud, S. (1960). *The interpretation of dreams* (J. Strachey, Ed.). New York: Basic Books. [Original work published 1900.]

Freud, S. (1961). *Civilization and its discontents* (J. Strachey, Trans.). New York: W. W. Norton. [Original work published 1930.]

Freud, S. (1962). Creative writers and daydreaming. In J. Strachey (Ed.), *The standard edition of the complete psychological works of Sigmund Freud* (Vol. 9). London: Hogarth.

Freud, S. (1963). The unconscious. In P. Rieff (Ed.) and C. M. Baines (Trans.), *General psychological theory: Papers on metapsychology* (pp. 83–103). New York: Macmillan. [Original work published 1915.]

Freud, S. (1964). Analysis terminable and interminable. In J. Strachey (Ed. and Trans.), *The standard edition of the complete psychological works of Sigmund Freud* (Vol. 23, pp. 209–253). London: Hogarth. [Original work published 1937.]

Freud, S. (1965). *New introductory lectures on psychoanalysis* (J. Strachey, Trans.). New York: W. W. Norton. [Original work published 1933.]

Freud, S. (1966). *The ego and the mechanisms of defense* (rev. ed.) (C. Bains, Trans.). New York: International Universities Press, Inc. [Original work published 1937.]

Freud, S. (1966). *Introductory lectures on psychoanalysis* (J. Strachey, Ed. and Trans). New York: W. W. Norton. [Original work published 1917.]

Freud, S. (1989). The theme of the three caskets. In P. Gay (Ed.), *The Freud reader* (pp. 514–522). New York: W. W. Norton. [Original work published 1913.]

Freud, S., & Breuer, J. (1966). *Studies on hysteria.* New York: Avon. [Original work published 1893.]

Frey, T. J., & Frey, D. L. (August-September, 1998). Inventing the future. *The Futurist, 32,* 47–49.

Friedman, H. S., & Schustack, M. W. (2003). *Personality: Classic theories and modern research.* Boston: Allyn & Bacon.

Friedman, M. (1966). Jung's image of psychological man. *Psychoanalytic Review, 53,* 95–108.

Friedman, M., & Rosenman, R. H. (1959). Association of a specific overt behavior pattern with increases in blood cholesterol, blood clotting time, incidence of arcus senilis and clinical coronary artery disease. *JAMA, Journal of the American Medical Association, 169,* 1286–1296.

Funder, D. C. (1995). On the accuracy of personality judgment: A realistic approach. *Psychological Review, 102,* 652–670.

Funder, D. C. (1998). Why does personality theory exist? *Psychological Inquiry, 9,* 150–152.

Funder, D. C. (1999). *Personality judgment: A realistic approach to person perception.* San Diego, CA: Academic Press.

Funder, D. C. (2000). Personality. *Annual Review of Psychology, 52,* 172–221.

Funder, D. C. (2001). *The personality puzzle* (2d ed.). New York: W. W. Norton.

Funder, D. (2004). *The personality puzzle* (3rd ed.). New York: W. W. Norton.

Funder, D. C., & Colvin, C. R. (1988). Friends and strangers: Acquaintanceship, agreement, and the accuracy of personality judgment. *Journal of Personality and Social Psychology, 55,* 149–158.

Funder, D. C., & Colvin, C. R. (1991). Explorations in behavioral consistency: Properties of persons, situations, and behaviors. *Journal of Personality and Social Psychology, 60,* 773–794.

Funder, D. C., & Dobroth K. M. (1987). Differences between traits: Properties associated with inter-judge agreement. *Journal of Personality and Social Psychology, 52,* 409–418.

Funder, D. C., & Ozer, D. J. (1983). Behavior as a function of the situation. *Journal of Personality and Social Psychology, 44,* 107–112.

Gale Research (1988). "Marilyn Vos Savant." *Newsmakers, Issue Cumulation. Reproduced in Biography Resource Center.* Farmington Hills, MI: The Gale Group, 2003; www.galenet.com/servlet/BioRc.

Gallup, G. G., & Suarez, S. D. (1986). Self awareness and the emergence of mind in humans and other primates. In J. Suls & A. G. Greenwald (Eds.), *Psychological perspectives on the self* (Vol. 3). Hillsdale, NJ: Erlbaum.

Galvin, J. (February/March, 2002) Poet's Sample: Emily Wilson. *Boston Review.* Boston, MA.

Garb, H. N., Wood, J. M., Lilienfeld, S., & Nezworski, M. T. (2003). Effective use of projective techniques in clinical practice: Let the data help with selection and interpretation. *Professional Psychology: Research and Practice, 33,* 454–463.

Gardner, H. (1983). *Frames of mind.* New York: Basic Books.

Gardner, H. (1993). *Frames of mind: The theory of multiple intelligences* (10th anniv. ed.). New York: Basic Books.

Gardner, H. (2000). A case against spiritual intelligence. *International Journal for the Psychology of Religion, 10,* 27–34.

Gartner, H. (September 8, 1999). *The Magazine.* Canadian Broadcasting Corporation (http://cbc.ca/news/indepth/stopwatch/magazine.html).

Gartstein, M. A., & Rothbart, M. K. (2003). Studying infant temperament via the Revised Infant Behavior Questionnaire. *Infant Behavior and Development, 26,* 64–86.

Garza, D. L., & Feltz, D. L. (1998). Effects of selected mental practice on performance, self-efficacy, and competition confidence of figure skaters. *The Sports Psychologist, 12,* 1–15.

Gasking, D. A. T. (1946–1947). Types of questions. *Melbourne University Magazine,* pp. 4–6.

Gauguin, P. (1998). Entry in *The New Encyclopaedia Britannica* (Vol. 5; pp. 147–148). Chicago: Encyclopaedia Britannica, Inc.

Gay, P. (1988). *Freud: A life for our times.* New York: W. W. Norton.

Gazzaniga, M. S., & Heatherton, T. F. (2003). *Psychological science.* New York: W. W. Norton.

Geher, G. (2003). Perceived and actual characteristics of parents and partners: A test of a Freudian model of mate selection. In N. J. Pallone (Ed.), *Love, romance, sexual interaction* (pp. 75–102). New Brunswick, NJ: Transaction.

Geher, G., Warner, R. M., & Brown, A. S. (2001). Predictive validity of the Emotional Accuracy Research Scale. *Intelligence, 29,* 373–388.

Getzels, J. W., & Jackson, P. W. (1962). *Creativity and intelligence; explorations with gifted students.* New York: Wiley.

Ghandi, Mohandas (Karamchand). (1942). In M. Block (Ed.), E. M. Trow (Managing Ed.) *Current Biography 1942.* New York: H. W. Wilson Company.

Giancola, P. R., Shoal, G. D., & Mezzich, A. C. (2001). Constructive thinking, executive functioning, antisocial behavior, and drug use involvement in adolescent females with a substance use disorder. *Experimental and Clinical Psychopharmacology, 9,* 215–227.

Gilbert, D. T. (1991). How mental systems believe. *American Psychologist, 46,* 107–119.

Gill, M., & Hoffman, I (1982a). Analysis of transference: Studies of nine audio-recorded psychoanalytic sessions. *Psychological Issues, Monograph 54,* 1–229.

Gill, M., & Hoffman, I. (1982b). A method for studying the analysis of aspects of the patient's experience of the relationship in psychoanalysis and psychotherapy. *Journal of the American Psychoanalytic Association, 25,* 471–490.

Gilligan, C. (1982). *In a different voice.* Cambridge, MA: Harvard University Press.

Gilovich, T., & Savitsky, K. (1999). The spotlight effect and the illusion of transparency: Egocentric assessments of how we are seen by others. *Current Directions in Psychological Science, 8,* 165–168.

Gladwell, M. (1998, August 17). Do parents matter? *The New Yorker,* 55–64.

Gleason, D. K. (1985). *Over Boston: Aerial photographs by David King Gleason.* Baton Rouge and London: Louisiana State University Press.

Gleick, J. (1987). *Chaos: Making a new science.* New York: Wiley.

Goddard, H. H. (1917). Mental tests and immigrants. *Journal of Delinquency, 2,* 243–277.

Godfrey, D. K., Jones, E. E., & Lord, C. G. (1986). Self-promotion is not ingratiating. *Journal of Personality and Social Psychology, 50,* 106–115.

Goffman, E. (2003). The presentation of self. In J. A. Holstein & J. F. Gubrium (Eds.), *Inner lives and social worlds* (pp. 130–139). New York: Oxford University Press. [Original work published 1959.]

Goldberg, C. (1983). Courage and fanaticism: The charismatic leader and modern religious cults. In D. A. Halperin (Ed.), *Psychodynamic perspectives on religion, sect, and cult* (pp. 163–185). Boston: John Wright PSG.

Goldberg, L. R. (1990). An alternative "description of personality": The Big-Five factor structure. *Journal of Personality and Social Psychology, 59,* 1216–1229.

Goldberg, L. R. (1993). The structure of phenotypic personality traits. *American Psychologist, 48,* 26–34.

Goldberg, L. R., & Rosolack, T. K. (1994). The Big Five factor structure as an integrative framework: An empirical comparison with Eysenck's P-E-N model. In C. F. Halverson, G. A. Kohnstamm & R. P. Martin (Eds.), *The developing structure of temperament and personality from infancy to adulthood* (pp. 7–35). Hillsdale, NJ: Lawrence Erlbaum.

Goldenberg, J. L., Pyszczynski, T., Greenberg, J., Solomon, S., Kluck, B., & Cornwell, R. (2001). I am *not* an animal: Mortality salience, disgust, and the denial of human creatureliness. *Journal of Experimental Psychology: General, 130,* 427–435.

Gollwitzer, P. M. (1999). Implementation intentions: Strong effects of simple plans. *American Psychologist, 54,* 493–503.

Goodenough, F. L. (1949). *Mental testing: Its history, principles, and applications.* New York: Rinehart.

Gorsuch, R. L. (1983). *Factor analysis* (2nd ed.). Hillsdale, NJ: Lawrence Erlbaum.

Gosling, S. D., Ko, S. J., Mannarelli, T., & Morris, M. E. (2002). A room with a cue: Personality judgments based on offices and bedrooms. *Journal of Personality and Social Psychology, 82,* 379–398.

Gosling, S. D., & John, O. P. (1999). Personality dimension in nonhuman animals: A cross-species review. *Current Directions in Psychological Science, 8,* 69–75.

Gottfredson, G. D., & Holland, J. L. (1990). A longitudinal test of the influence of congruence: Job satisfaction, competency utilization, and counterproductive behavior. *Journal of Counseling Psychology, 27,* 389–398.

Gottfredson, G. D., & Holland, J. L. (1989). *Dictionary of Holland Occupational Codes* (2nd ed.). Odessa, FL: Psychological Assessment Resources.

Gottfredson, L. S. (2003). Dissecting practical intelligence theory: Its claims and evidence. *Intelligence, 31,* 343–397.

Gottman, J. M., Katz, L. F., & Hooven, C., (1996). Parental meta-emotion philosophy and the emotional life of families: Theoretical models and preliminary data. *Journal of Family Psychology, 10,* 243–268.

Gottman, J. M., & Silver, N. (1999). *The seven principles for making marriage work.* New York: Three Rivers Press.

Gough, M. G., McKee, G., & Yandell, R. J. (1955). Adjective check list analyses of a number of selected psychometric and assessment variables. Officer Education Research Laboratory, Technical Memorandum, OERL-TM-55-10. [Cited in Dahlstrom, Welsh, & Dahlstrom, 1972, 49].

Gould, D., Dieffenbach, K., & Moffett, A. (2002). Psychological characteristics and their development in Olympic champions. *Journal of Applied Sport Psychology, 14,* 72–204.

Gould, S. J. (1981). *The mismeasure of man.* New York: W. W. Norton.

Gould, S. J. (1991). Exaptation: A crucial tool for an evolutionary psychology. *Journal of Social Issues, 47,* 43–65.

Gowing, L. (1995). *A biographical dictionary of artists.* New York: Facts on File.

Graham, J. R. (1990). *MMPI-2: Assessing personality and psychopathology.* New York: Oxford University Press.

Gray, J. A. (1987a). Perspectives on anxiety and impulsivity: A commentary. *Journal of Research in Personality, 21,* 493–509.

Gray, J. A. (1987b). The neuropsychology of emotion and personality. In S. M. Stahl, S. D. Iversen, & E. C. Goodman (Eds.), *Cognitive neurochemistry* (pp. 171–190). Oxford: Oxford University Press.

Green, D. P., Salovey, P., & Truax, K. (1999). Static, dynamic, and causative bipolarity of affect. *Journal of Personality and Social Psychology, 76,* 856–867.

Greenberg, G. (1994). *The self on the shelf: Recovery books and the good life.* Albany: State University of New York Press.

Greenberg, J., Pyszczynski, T. A. & Solomon, S. (1982). The self-serving attributional bias: Beyond self-presentation. *Journal of Experimental Social Psychology¨ 18,* 56–67.

Greenbie, M. B. (1932). *Personality and the divers methods by which some men and here and there a woman have achieved it.* New York: The Macmillan Company.

Greenlaw, L. (1999). *The hungry ocean: A swordboat captain's journey.* New York: Hyperion.

Greenwald, A. (1980). The totalitarian ego. *American Psychologist, 35,* 603–618.

Greenwald, A. G., Klinger, M. R., & Schuh, E. S. (1995). Activation by marginally perceptible ("subliminal") stimuli: Dissociation of unconscious from conscious cognition. *Journal of Experimental Psychology: General, 124,* 22–42.

Greenwald, A. G., Spangenberg, E. R., Pratkanis, A. R., & Eskenazi, J. (1991). Double-blind tests of subliminal self-help audiotapes. *Psychological Science, 2,* 119–225.

Grigorenko, E. L. (2002). In search of the genetic engram of personality. In D. Cervone & W. Mischel (Eds.), *Advances in personality science* (pp. 29–82). New York: Guilford.

Grippo, A. J., & Johnson, A. K. (2002). Biological mechanisms in the relationship between depression and heart disease. *Neuroscience and Biobehavioral Reviews, 26,* 941–962.

Griswold, C. L. (1986). *Self-knowledge in Plato's* Phaedrus. New Haven, CT: Yale University Press.

Gross, J. J., & Levenson, R W. (1997). Hiding feelings: The acute effects of inhibiting negative and positive emotion. *Journal of Abnormal Psychology,106,* 95–103.

Gross, J. J., Sutton, S. K., & Ketelaar, T. (1998). Relations between affect and personality: Support for the affect-level and affective reactivity views. *Personality and Social Psychology Bulletin, 24,* 279–288.

Grossmann, K., Grossmann, K. E., Spangler, G., Suess, G., & Unzner, L. (1985). Maternal sensitivity and newborns' orientation responses as related to quality of attachment in northern Germany. In I. Bretherton, & E. Waters (Eds.), *Growing points in attachment theory and research* (pp. 233–257). *Monographs of the Society for Research in Child Development, 50,* (1–2, Serial No. 209).

Grotevant, H. D., & Adams, G. R. (1984). Development of an objective measure to assess ego identity in adolescence: Validation and replication. *Journal of Youth and Adolescence, 10,* 419–438.

Grunbaum, A. (1986). Précis of *The foundations of psychoanalysis: A philosophical critique. Behavioral and Brain Sciences, 9,* 217–284.

Guilford, J. P. (1959). *Personality.* New York: McGraw Hill.

Guilford, J. P. (1967). *The nature of human intelligence.* New York: McGraw-Hill.

Gustafsson, J-E. (2001). Schooling and intelligence: Effects of track of study on level and profile of cognitive abilities. Paper presented to the 3rd Annual Spearman Conference. Sydney, Australia.

Guyton, A. C. (1991). *Textbook of medical physiology* (8th ed.). Philadelphia, PA: Saunders.

Hagerty, M. R. (1999). Testing Maslow's hierarchy of needs: National quality-of-life across time. *Social Indicators Research, 46,* 249–271.

Haier, R. J., Siegel, B. V., Nuechterlein, K. H., Hazlett, E., Wu, J. C., Pack, J., Browning, H. L., & Buchsbaum, M. S. (1988). Cortical glucose metabolic rate correlates of abstract reasoning and attention studied with positron emission tomography. *Intelligence, 12,* 199–217.

Haier, M. S., Siegel, B., Tanc, C., Abel, L., & Buchsbaum, M. S. (1992). Intelligence and changes in regional cerebral glucose metabolic rate following learning. *Intelligence, 16,* 415–426.

Halberstam, D. (1979). *The powers that be.* New York: Knopf.

Hall, C. S., & Lindzey, G. L. (1957). *Theories of personality.* New York: John Wiley & Sons.

Hall, C. S., & Lindzey, G. L. (1978). *Theories of personality* (3rd ed.). New York: John Wiley & Sons.

Hall, M. H. (July, 1968). The psychology of universality (an interview with the president of the American Psychological Associations, Abraham H. Maslow. *Psychology Today, 2,* 35–39; 54–57.

Halpern, D. (1997). Sex differences in intelligence. *American Psychologist, 52,* 1091–1102.

Hamblin, C. L. (1967). "Questions" in Edwards, P. (Editor and Chief), *The encyclopedia of philosophy* (Vol. 7, pp. 49–53). New York: Macmillan/Free Press.

Hamilton, R. J. (1985). A framework for the evaluation of the effectiveness of adjunct questions and objectives. *Review of Educational Research, 55,* 47–85.

Hamilton, W. D. (1964). The evolution of social behavior. *Journal of Theoretical Biology, 7,* 1–52.

Hampden-Turner, C. (1981). *Maps of the mind.* New York: MacMillan.

Han, J. J., Leichtman, M. D., & Wang, Q. (1998). Autobiographical memory in Korean, Chinese, and American children. *Developmental Psychology, 34,* 701–713.

Hare, B., & Wrangham, R. (2002). Integrating two evolutionary models for the study of social cognition. In M. Bekoff, C. Allen, & G. Burghardt (Eds.), *The cognitive animal: Empirical and theoretical perspectives on animal cognition* (pp. 363–369). Cambridge, MA: MIT Press.

Hare, R. M. (1952). *The language of morals.* Oxford, England: Clarendon.

Hargrave, G. E., & Hiatt, D. (1989). Use of the California Psychological Inventory in law enforcement officer selection. *Journal of Personality Assessment, 53,* 267–277.

Harnqvist, K. (1968). Relative change in intelligence from 13 to 18. *Scandinavian Journal of Psychology, 9,* 50–82.

Harrell, T. W., & Harrell, M. S. (1945). Army General Classification Tests scores for civilian occupations. *Educational and psychological measurement, 5,* 229–239.

Harrington, D. M., Block, J. H., & Block, J. (1987). Testing aspects of Carl Rogers's theory of creative environments: Child-rearing antecedents of creative potential in young adolescents. *Journal of Personality and Social Psychology, 52,* 851–856.

Harris, J. R. (1995). Where is the child's environment? A group socialization theory of development. *Psychological Review, 102,* 458–489.

Harris, J. R. (1998). *The nurture assumption: Why children turn out the way they do.* New York: Free Press.

Harter, S. (1999). *The construction of the self: A developmental perspective.* New York: Guilford.

Hartmann, E. L. (1973). *The functions of sleep.* New Haven, CT: Yale University Press.

Hartmann, E., Harrison, R., & Zborowski, M. (2001). Boundaries in the mind: Past research and future directions. *North American Journal of Psychology, 3,* 347–368.

Haslam, N. (1994). Categories of social relationship. *Cognition, 53,* 59–90.

Haslam, N., & Baron, J. (1994). Intelligence, personality, and prudence. In P. Ruzgis & R. J. Sternberg (Eds.), *Intelligence and personality* (pp. 32–58). New York: Cambridge University Press.

Hatfield, E. (1988). Passionate and companionate love. In R. Sternberg & M. L. Barnes (Eds.), *The psychology of love.* New Haven, CT: Yale University Press.

Hathaway, S. R., & Meehl, P. E. (1952). Adjective check list correlates of MMPI scores. Unpublished materials. [Cited in Dahlstrom, Welsh, & Dahlstrom, 1972.]

Hattie, J., & Cooksey, R. W. (1984). Procedures for assessing the validities of tests using the "known-groups" method. *Applied Psychological Measurement, 8,* 295–305.

Hawking, S. W. (1998). *A brief history of time.* New York: Bantam Books.

Hazan, C., & Shaver, P. R. (1987). Romantic love conceptualized as an attachment process. *Journal of Personality and Social Psychology, 52,* 511–524.

Hazan, C., & Shaver, P. R. (1994). Attachment as an organizational framework for research on close relationships. *Psychological Inquiry, 5,* 1–22.

Hecht, J. (2002). When did dogs become our best friends? *New Scientist, 176,* 16.

Heckhausen, H. (1969). *The anatomy of achievement motivation.* New York: Academic Press.

Heider, K. (1991). *Grand valley Dani: Peaceful warriors* (2nd ed.). Fort Worth, TX: Holt, Rinehart, & Winston.

Hedlund, S., & Rude, S. S. (1995). Evidence of latent depressive schemas in formerly depressed individuals. *Journal of Abnormal Psychology, 104,* 517–525.

Heilizer, F. (1964). Conjunctive and disjunctive conflict: A theory of need conflict. *Journal of Abnormal and Social Psychology, 68,* 21–37.

Held, B. S. (2002). The tyranny of the positive attitude in America: Observation and speculation. *Journal of Clinical Psychology, 58,* 965–992.

Helson, R., & Srivastava, S. (2001). Three paths of adult development: Conservers, seekers, and achievers. *Journal of Personality and Social Psychology, 80,* 995–1100.

Helson, R., & Wink, P. (1987). Two conceptions of maturity examined in the findings of a longitudinal study. *Journal of Personality and Social Psychology, 53,* 531–541.

Hendrick, C., & Hendrick, S. (1986). A theory and method of love. *Journal of Personality and Social Psychology, 50,* 392–402.

Hendrick, C., & Hendrick, S. S. (2003). Romantic love: Measuring cupid's arrow. In S. J. Lopez & C. R. Snyder (Eds.), *Positive psychological assessment: A handbook of models and measures* (pp. 235–249). Washington, DC: American Psychological Association.

Henriques, G. (2003). The tree of knowledge system and the theoretical unification of psychology. *Review of General Psychology, 7,* 150–182.

Herman, C. P., & Polivy, J. (1993). Mental control of eating: Excitatory and inhibitory food thoughts. In D. M. Wegner & J. W. Pennebaker (Eds.), *Handbook of mental control* (pp. 491–505). Englewood Cliffs, NJ: Prentice Hall.

Hermans, H. J. M., Kempen, H. J. G., & van Loon, R. J. P. (1992). The dialogical self: Beyond individualism and rationalism. *American Psychologist, 47,* 23–33.

Herrnstein, R. J. (1971). I.Q. *Atlantic Monthly, 228,* 43–64.

Herrnstein, R. J. (1973). *IQ in the meritocracy.* Boston: Little, Brown.

Herrnstein, R. J., & Murray, C. A. (1994). *The bell curve.* New York: Free Press.

Heschel, A. J. (1965). *Who is man?* Stanford: Stanford University Press.

Hess, T. M., Pullen, S. M., McGee, K. A. (1996). Acquisition of prototype-based information about social groups in adulthood. *Psychology and Aging, 11,* 179–190.

Hesse, E. (1999). The adult attachment interview: Historical and current perspectives. In J. Cassidy & P. R. Shaver (Eds.), *Handbook of attachment: Theory, research, and clinical applications* (pp. 395–433). New York: Guilford.

Hetherington, E. M., Bridges, M., & Insabella, G. M. (1998). What matters? What does not? Five perspectives on the association between marital transitions and children's adjustment. *American Psychologist, 53,* 167–184.

Heyns, R. W., Veroff, J., & Atkinson, J. W. (1992). A scoring manual for the affiliative motive. In C. P. Smith (Ed.), *Motivation and personality: Handbook of thematic content analysis* (pp. 211–223). New York: Cambridge University Press.

Hewitt, J. P. (2003). *Self and society* (9th ed.). Boston: Allyn & Bacon.

Hibbard, S. (2003). A critique of Lilienfeld et al.'s (2000) "The scientific status of projective techniques." *Journal of Personality Assessment, 80,* 260–271.

Hickam, H. H. (1998). *Rocket boys: A memoir.* New York: Delacorte.

Higgins, C. A., & Judge, T. A. (2004). The effect of applicant influence tactics on recruiter perceptions of fit and hiring recommendations: A field study. *Journal of Applied Psychology, 89,* 622–632.

Higgins, E. T. (1987). Self-discrepancy theory: A theory relating self and affect. *Psychological Review, 94,* 319–340.

Higgins, E. T., Shah, J., & Friedman, R. (1997). Emotional responses to goal attainment: Strength of regulatory focus as moderator. *Journal of Personality and Social Psychology, 72,* 515–525.

Hilgard, E. R. (1965). *Hypnotic susceptibility.* New York: Harcourt, Brace, & World.

Hilgard, E. R. (1973). A neodissociation interpretation of pain reduction in hypnosis. *Psychological Review, 80,* 403–419.

Hilgard, E. R. (1974). Toward a neo-dissociation theory: Multiple cognitive controls in human functioning. *Perspectives in Biology and Medicine, 17,* 301–316.

Hilgard, E. R. (1977). *Divided consciousness: Multiple controls in human thought and action.* New York: Wiley.

Hilgard, E. R. (1979). *Personality and hypnosis: A study of imaginative involvement* (2nd ed.). Chicago: University of Chicago Press.

Hilgard, E. R. (1980). The trilogy of mind: Cognition, affection, and conation. *Journal of the History of the Behavioral Sciences, 16,* 107–117.

Hilgard, E. R. (1994). Neodissociation theory. In S. J. Lynn & J. Rhue (Eds.), *Dissociation: Clinical and theoretical perspectives* (pp. 32–51). New York: Guilford.

Hoffman, E. (1999). *The right to be human.* New York: McGraw Hill.

Hoffman, P. (1998). *The man who loved only numbers.* New York: Hyperion.

Hogan, R. (1983). A socioanalytic theory of personality. In M. M. Page (Ed.), *Personality, current theory and research. Nebraska symposium on motivation 1982* (pp. 55–90). Lincoln: University of Nebraska Press.

Hogan, R. (1998). What is personality psychology? *Psychological Inquiry, 9,* 152–153.

Holland, J. L. (1985). *Professional manual for the Self-Directed Search.* Odessa, FL: Psychological Assessment Resources.

Holland, J. L. (1987). *Manual supplement for the Self-Directed Search.* Odessa, FL: Psychological Assessment Resources.

Holland, J. L. (1997). *Making vocational choices: A theory of vocational personalities and work environments* (3rd ed.). Odessa, FL: Psychological Assessment Resources.

Holland, J. L., Whitney, D. R., Cole, N. S., & Richards, J. M. (April, 1969). An empirical occupational classification derived from a theory of personality and intended for practice and research. *ACT Research Report 29,* 1–22. Iowa City, IA: American College Testing Program.

Holmes, D. S. (1974). Investigations of repression: Differential recall of material experimentally or naturally associated with ego threat. *Psychological Bulletin, 81,* 632–651.

Holmes, D. S., & Shallow, J. R. (1969). Reduced recall after ego threat: Repression or response competition? *Journal of Personality and Social Psychology, 13,* 145–152.

Home, J. A., & Osberg, O. (1976). A self-assessment questionnaire to determine morningness-eveningness in human circadian rhyhms. *International Journal of Chronobiology, 4,* 97–110.

Hong, K., & Townes, B. (1976). Infants' attachment to inanimate objects. *Journal of the Academy of Child Psychiatry, 15,* 49–61.

Horner, M. S. (1972). Toward an understanding of achievement-related conflicts in women. *Journal of Social Issues, 28,* 157–176.

Horner, M. S. (1992). The motive to avoid success. In C. P. Smith (Ed.), *Motivation and personality: Handbook of thematic content analysis.* Cambridge: Cambridge University Press.

Horney, K. (1945). *Our inner conflicts: A constructive theory of neurosis.* New York: W. W. Norton.

Hovey, H. B. (1953). MMPI profiles and personality characteristics. *Journal of Consulting Psychology, 17,* 142–146.

Hoyenga, K. B., & Hoyenga, K. T. (1993). *Gender-related differences: Origins and outcomes.* Boston: Allyn & Bacon.

Hull, J. G., & Reilly, N. P. (1986). Information processing approach to alcohol use and its consequences. In R. E. Ingram (Ed.), *Information processing approaches to clinical psychology* (pp. 151–167). San Diego, CA: Academic Press.

Hull, J. G., & Slone, L. B. (2004). Alcohol and self-regulation. In R. F. Baumeister & K. D. Vohs (Eds.), *Handbook of self-regulation: Research, theory, and applications* (pp. 466–491). New York: Guilford.

Hunt, N. (1967). *The world of Nigel Hunt: The diary of a mongoloid youth.* New York: Garrett.

Hurlburt, R., Koch, M., & Heavey, C. L. (2001). Descriptive experience sampling demonstrates the connection of thinking to externally observable behavior. *Cognitive Therapy and Research, 26,* 117–134.

Hurley, J. R. (1955). The Iowa Picture Interpretation Test: A multiple-choice variation for the TAT. *Journal of Consulting Psychology, 19,* 372–376.

Husen, T. (1951). The influence of schooling upon IQ. *Theoria, 17,* 61–88.

Huston, H. L., Rosen, D. H., & Smith, S. M. (1999). Evolutionary memory. In D. Rosen & M. Luebbert (Eds.), *The evolution of the psyche* (pp. 139–149). Westport, CT: Praeger.

Hyde, J. S. (1986). Gender differences in aggression. In J. S. Hyde & M. C. Linn (Eds.). *The psychology of gender: Advances through meta-analysis.* Baltimore: Johns Hopkins University Press.

Isaacson, R. L. (1982). *The limbic system* (2nd ed.). New York: Plenum.

IPAT Staff (1991). *Administrator's manual for the Sixteen Personality Factor Questionnaire.* Champaign, IL: Institute for Personality and Ability Testing.

Isen, A. M., Shalker, T. E., Clark, M., & Karp, L. (1978). Affect, accessibility of material in memory, and behavior: A cognitive loop? *Journal of Personality and Social Psychology, 36,* 1–12.

Ivcevic, Z., Mayer, J. D., & Brackett, M. A. (2003). Exploring personality the natural way: An inquiry into open-ended self-descriptions. *Imagination, Cognition, and Personality, 22,* 211–238.

Izard, C. E. (1992). Basic emotions, relations among emotions, and emotion-cognition relations. *Psychological Review, 99,* 561–565.

Izard, C. E., Libero, D. Z., Putnam, P., & Haynes, O. M. (1993). Stability of emotion experiences and their relations to traits of personality. *Journal of Personality and Social Psychology, 64,* 847–860.

Jackendoff, R. (1987). *Consciousness and the computational mind.* Cambridge, MA: MIT Press.

Jackson, D. N. (1974). *Personality Research Form Manual.* Goshen, NY: Research Psychologists Press.

Jackson, F. (1982). Epiphenomenal Qualia. *Philosophical Quarterly, 32,* 127–136.

Jacobs, W. J., & Nadel, L. (1985). Stress-induced recovery of fears and phobias. *Psychological Review, 92,* 512–531.

Jacoby, L. L., Lindsay, S., & Toth, J.P. (1992). Unconscious influences revealed: Attention, awareness, and control. *American Psychologist, 47,* 802–809.

Jacoby, L. L., Woloshyn, V., & Kelley, C. M. (1989). Becoming famous without being recognized: Unconscious influences of memory produced by dividing attention. *Journal of Experimental Psychology: General, 118,* 115–125.

Jacoby, L. L., Allan, L. G., Collins, J. C., & Larwill, L. K. (1988). Memory influences subjective experience: Noise judgments. *Journal of Experimental Psychology: Learning, Memory, and Cognition, 14,* 240–247.

James, W. (1950). *The principles of psychology (Vol. 1).* New York: Henry Holt. [Original work published 1890.]

James, W. (1892). *Psychology.* New York: Henry Holt.

James, W. (1920). *Psychology: The briefer course.* New York: Holt.

Jamieson, G. A. (2001). Hypnotic susceptibility is positively related to a subset of schizotypy items. *Contemporary Hypnosis, 18,* 32–37.

Jamison, K. R. (1993). *Touched with fire: Manic-depressive illness and the artistic temperament.* New York: Free Press.

Jamison, K. R. (1996). Mood disorders, creativity and the artistic temperament. In J. Schildkraut & O. Aurora (Eds.), *Depression and the spiritual in modern art: Homage to Miro* (pp. 15–32). Oxford: John Wiley & Sons.

Jang, K. L., McCrae, R. R., Angleitner, A., Riemann, R., & Livesley, W. J. (1998). Heritability of facet-level traits in a cross-cultural twin sample: Support for a hierarchical model of personality. *Journal of Personality and Social Psychology, 74,* 1556–1565.

Jausovec, N., Jausovec, K., & Gerlic, I. (2001). Differences in event-related and induced electroencephalography patterns in the theta and alpha frequency bands related to human emotional intelligence. *Neuroscience Letters, 311,* 93–96.

Jaynes, J. (1976). *The origin of consciousness in the breakdown of the bicameral mind.* Boston: Houghton Mifflin.

Jedlicka, D. (1984). Indirect parental influence on mate choice: A test of the psychoanalytic theory. *Journal of Marriage and the Family, 46,* 65–70.

Jelicic, M., Bonke, B., & De Roode, A. (1993). Implicit learning during anaesthesia. In P. S. Sebel, B. Bonke, & E. Winograd (Eds.), *Memory and awareness in anesthesia: III* (pp. 81–84). New York: Prentice Hall Professional Technical Reference.

Jelicic, M., De Roode, A., Bovill, J. G., & Bonke, B. (1992). Unconscious learning established under anaesthesia. *Anaesthesia, 47,* 835–837.

Jemmott, J. B. III, Hellman, C., McClelland, D. C., Locke, S. E., Kraus, L., Williams, R. M., & Valeri, C. R. (1990).

Motivational syndromes associated with natural killer cell activity. *Journal of Behavioral Medicine, 13,* 53–73.

Jencks, C. (1972). *Inequality: A reassessment of the effect of family and schooling in America.* New York: Basic Books.

Jensen, A. (1980). *Bias in mental testing.* New York: Free Press.

Jensen, A. (1987). Psychometric *g* as a focus of concerted research effort. *Intelligence, 11,* 193–198.

Jensen, A., & Johnson, F. W. (1994). Race and sex differences in head size and IQ. *Intelligence, 18,* 341.

Jensen-Campbell, L. A., & Graziano, W. G. (2001). Agreeableness as a moderator of conflict. *Journal of Personality, 69,* 324–362.

Jerison, H. J. (2000). The evolution of intelligence. In R. J. Sternberg (Ed.), *Handbook of intelligence* (pp. 216–244). Cambridge: Cambridge University Press.

Joachim, K. (1996). The politics of self esteem. *American Educational Research Journal, 33,* 3–22.

Jockin, V., McGue, M., & Lykken, D. (1996). Personality and divorce: A genetic analysis. *Journal of Personality and Social Psychology, 71,* 288–299.

John, O. P., Angleitner, A., & Ostendorf, F. (1988). The lexical approach to personality: A historical review of trait taxonomic research. *European Journal of Personality, 2,* 171–205.

Johnson, W. G., Wildman, H. E., Downey, C., & Bell, S. (1980). Personality: Trends in theory and research. *Social Behavior and Personality, 8,* 209–211.

Jones, A., & Crandall, R. (1986). Validation of a short index of self-actualization. *Personality and Social Psychology Bulletin, 12,* 63–73.

Jones, E. (1955). *The life and work of Sigmund Freud (Vols. 1 and 2).* New York: Basic Books.

Jones, K., & Day, J. D. (1997). Discrimination of two aspects of cognitive-social intelligence from academic intelligence. *Journal of Educational Psychology, 89,* 486–497.

Jones, L. V. (1971). The nature of measurement. In R. L. Thornkike (Ed), *Educational measurement* (pp. 335–355). Washington, DC: American Council on Education.

Jopling, D. A. (2000). *Self-knowledge and the self.* New York: Routledge.

Jöreskog, K. G., & Sörbom, D. (1999). *LISREL8.30: User's reference guide.* Chicago: Scientific Software.

Josselson, R. (1995). Narrative and psychological understanding. *Psychiatry, 58,* 330–343.

Josselson, R. (1996). *Revising herself: The story of women's identity from college to midlife.* New York: Oxford University Press.

Judge, T. A. (2001). A rose by any other name: Are self-esteem, generalized self-efficacy, neuroticism, and locus of control indicators of a common construct? In B. W. Roberts, & R. Hogan (Eds.), *Personality psychology in the workplace: Decade of behavior* (pp. 93–118). Washington, DC: American Psychological Association.

Judge, T. A., Higgins, C. A., Thoresen, C. J., & Barrick, M. R. (1999). The big five personality traits, general mental ability, and career success across the life span. *Personnel Psychology, 52,* 621–652.

Jung, C. (1953). The relations between ego and the unconscious. In R. F. C. Hull (Ed. & Trans.), *Two essays on analytic psychology* (pp. 131–253). Cleveland, OH: World Publishing. (Original work published 1934.)

Jung, C. (1968). *Analytical psychology: Its theory and practice; The Tavistock Lectures.* [With a foreword by E. A. Bennet.] New York: Random House.

Kagan, J. (1984). *The nature of the child.* New York: Basic Books.

Kagan, J., & Snidman, N (1991). Infant predictors of inhibited and uninhibited profiles. *Psychological Science, 2,* 40–44.

Kagan, J. (2003). Biology, context, and developmental inquiry. *Annual Review of Psychology, 54,* 1–23.

Kamin, L. (1974). *The science and politics of I.Q.* New York: Erlbaum.

Kaminer, W. (1992). *I'm dysfunctional, you're dysfunctional: The recovery movement and other self-help fashions.* Reading, MA: Addison-Wesley.

Kammrath, L. K., Mendoza-Denton, R., & Mischel, W. (2005). Incorporating if . . . then . . . personality signatures in person perception: Beyond the person-situation dichotomy. *Journal of Personality and Social Psychology, 88,* 605–618.

Kamphaus, R. W., Benson, J., Hutchinson, S., & Platt, L. O. (1994). Identification of factor models for the WISC-III. *Educational and Psychological Measurement, 54,* 174–186.

Karlsson, J. L. (1984). Creative intelligence in relatives of mental patients. *Hereditas, 100,* 83–86.

Karni, A., Meyer, G., Adams, M., Turner, R., & Ungerleider, L. G. (1994). The acquisition and retention of a motor skill: A functional MRI study of long-term motor cortex plasticity. *Abstracts of the Society for Neuroscience, 20,* 1291.

Kaus, M. (June 22, 1992). The end of equality. *New Republic, 206*(25), pp. 21–27.

Kelley, R. D. G. (2003). Confessions of a nice Negro, or why I shaved my head. In J. A. Holstein & J. F. Gubrium (Eds.). *Inner lives and social worlds* (pp. 356–361). New York: Oxford University Press. (Original work published 1995.)

Kelly, E. L., & Conley, J. J. (1987). Personality and compatibility: A prospective analysis of marital stability and marital satisfaction. *Journal of Personality and Social Psychology, 52,* 27–40.

Kelly, G. A. (1955a). *The psychology of personal constructs. Volume One: A theory of personality.* New York: W. W. Norton.

Kelly, G. A. (1955b). *The psychology of personal constructs: Volume Two: Clinical diagnosis and psychotherapy.* New York: W. W. Norton.

Kenny, D. A., Albright, L., & Malloy, T. E., & Kashy, D. A. (1994). Consensus in interpersonal perception: Acquaintance and the Big Five. *Psychological Bulletin, 116,* 245–258.

Kenrick, D. T., & Keefe, R. C. (1992). Age preferences in mates reflect sex differences in reproductive strategies. *Behavioral and Brain Sciences, 15,* 75–91.

Kernis, M. H., Cornell, D. P., Sun, C-R., Berry, A., & Harlow, T. (1993). There's more to self-esteem than whether it's high or low: The importance of stability of self-esteem. *Journal of Personality and Social Psychology, 65,* 1190–1204.

Keynes, J. M. (1936). *The general theory of employment, interest, and money*. New York: Harcourt Brace.

Keys, A., Brozek, J., Henschel, A., Mickelsen, O., & Taylor, H. L. (1950). *The biology of human starvation*. Minneapolis: University of Minnesota Press.

Kidwell, J. S. (1981). Number of siblings, sibling spacing, sex, and birth order: their effects on perceived parent-child relationships. *Journal of Marriage and Family, 78,* 763–766.

Kihlstrom, J. F. (1990). The psychological unconscious. In L. A. Pervin (Ed.), *Handbook of personality* (pp. 445–464). New York: Guilford.

Kihlstrom, J. F., & Cantor, N. (2000). Social intelligence. In. R. J. Sternberg (Ed.). *Handbook of intelligence* (pp. 359–379). Cambridge: Cambridge University Press.

Kipnis, D. (1971). *Character structure and impulsiveness*. New York: Academic Press.

Kinsey, A. C., Pomeroy, W. B., & Martin, C. E. (1948). *Sexual behavior in the human male*. Philadelphia: Saunders.

Kinsey, A. C., Pomeroy, W. B., Martin, C. E., & Gebhard, P. H. (1953). *Sexual behavior in the human female*. Philadelphia: Saunders.

Kirsch, I. (1997). Suggestibility or hypnosis: What do our scales really measure? *International Journal of Clinical and Experimental Hypnosis, 45,* 212–225.

Kirsch, I., & Lynn, S. J. (1995). The altered state of hypnosis: Changes in the theoretical landscape. *American Psychologist, 50,* 846–858.

Klausner, S. Z. (1965). *The quest for self-control*. New York: Free Press.

Klein, J., Moon, Y., & Picard, R. W. (2002). This computer responds to user frustration: Theory, design, and results. *Interacting with Computers, 14,* 119–140.

Klein, M. (1975). A contribution to the psychogenesis of manic-depressive states. In R. E. Money-Kyrle (Ed.), *The writings of Melanie Klein* (Vol. 1, pp. 262–289). New York: Free Press. (Original work published 1935.)

Kleinmuntz, B. (1982). *Personality and psychological assessment*. New York: St. Martin's.

Klinger, E. (1978). Modes of normal conscious flow. In K. S. Pope & J. L. Singer (Eds.), *The stream of consciousness: Scientific investigations into the flow of human experience* (pp. 225–258). New York: Plenum.

Klinger, E. (1999). Thought flow: Properties and mechanisms underlying shifts in content. In J. A. Singer & P. Salovey (Eds.), *At play in the fields of consciousness: Essays in honor of Jerome L. Singer*. Mahwah, NJ: Lawrence Erlbaum.

Kluckhohn, C. K. M., & Murray, H. A. (1953). Personality formation: The determinants. In C. K. M. Kluckhorn, H. A. Murray, & D. Schneider (Eds.), *Personality in nature, culture, and society* (pp. 53–67). New York: Knopf.

Knafo, D., & Jaffe, Y. (1984). Sexual fantasizing in males and females. *Journal of Research in Personality, 18,* 451–462.

Kobasa, S. C. O. (1985). Personality and health: Specifying and strengthening the conceptual links. In P. Shaver (Ed.), *Review of Personality and Social Psychology, 6,* 291–311. Beverly Hills: Sage.

Kochanska, G., Murray, K. T., & Harlan, E. T. (2000). Effortful control in early childhood: Continuity and change, antecedents, and implications for social development. *Developmental Psychology, 36,* 220–232.

Koestner, R., & McClelland, D. C. (1992). The affiliation motive. In C. P. Smith (Ed.), *Motivation and personality: Handbook of thematic content analysis* (pp. 205–210). New York: Cambridge University Press.

Kohnstamm, G., Halverson, C. F., Mervielde, I., & Havill, V. L. (1998). *Parental descriptions of child personality: Antecedents of the Big Five?* Mahwah, NJ: Lawrence Erlbaum.

Kolar, D. W., Funder, D. C., & Colvin, C. R. (1996). Comparing the accuracy of personality judgments by the self and knowledgeable others. *Journal of Personality, 64,* 311–317.

Kong, D. (March 23, 1998). Prozac-like drug use for healthy stirs debate. *Boston Globe,* pp. C1, C4.

Kosslyn, S. M. (1992). *Wet mind*. New York: Macmillan.

Kosslyn, S. M., & Koenig, O. (1992). *Wet mind: The new cognitive neuroscience*. New York: Free Press.

Krakauer, J. (1999). *Into thin air (with a new afterword)*. New York: Anchor Books.

Kramer, P. D. (1994). *Listening to Prozac: A psychiatrist explores anti-depressant drugs and the remaking of the self*. New York: Viking Penguin.

Krevans, J., & Gibbs, J. C. (1996). Parents' use of inductive discipline: Relations to children's empathy and prosocial behavior. *Child Development, 67,* 3263–3277.

Kroger, J. (2000). *Identity development: Adolescence through adulthood*. Newbury Park, CA: Sage.

Kubie, L. S. (1939). The experimental induction of neurotic reactions in man. *Yale Journal of Biology and Medicine, 11,* 541–545.

Kunda, Z. (1990). The case for motivated reasoning. *Psychological Bulletin, 108,* 480–498.

Kunda, Z., & Sinclair, L. (1999). Motivated reasoning with stereotypes: Activation, application, and inhibition. *Psychological Inquiry, 10,* 12–22.

Kurtz, R. M., & Strube, M. J. (1996). Multiple susceptibility testing: Is it helpful? *American Journal of Clinical Hypnosis, 38,* 172–184.

Kushner, H. (1986). *When all you've ever wanted isn't enough*. New York: Pocket Books.

Kushner, L. (1991). *God was in this place and I did not know*. Woodstock, VT: Jewish Lights Publishing.

Kyllonen, P. C., Lohman, D. F., & Woltz, D. J. (1984). Componential modeling of alternative strategies for performing spatial tasks. *Journal of Educational Psychology, 76,* 1325–1345.

La Coste-Messelière, P. (1950). *The treasures of Delphi*. Paris: Éditions du Chêne.

Lafferty, P., Beutler, L. E., & Crago, M. (1989). Differences between more and less effective psychotherapists: A study of select therapist variables. *Journal of Consulting and Clinical Psychology, 57,* 76–80.

Lahey, B. B. (1989). *Psychology: An introduction* (3rd ed.). Dubuque, IA: Wm. C. Brown.

Lam, L. T., & Kirby, S. L. (2002). Is emotional intelligence an advantage? An exploration of the impact of emotional and general intelligence on individual performance. *Journal of Social Psychology, 142,* 133–143.

Landy, F. J. (1986). Stamp collecting versus science: Validation as hypothesis testing. *American Psychologist, 41,* 1183–1192.

Lang, A. J., Craske, M. G., Brown, M., & Ghaneian, A. (2001). Fear-related state dependent memory. *Cognition and Emotion, 15,* 695–703.

Langer, W. (1972). *The mind of Adolph Hitler: The secret wartime report.* New York: Basic Books.

Lapsley, D. K., & Lasky, B. (2001). Prototypic moral character. *Identity: An International Journal of Theory and Research, 1,* 345–363.

Larkin, J. H., McDermott, J., Simon, D. P., & Simon, H. A. (1980). Expert and novice performance in solving physics problems. *Science, 208,* 1335–1342.

Larsen, R. J., & Buss, D. M. (2002). *Personality psychology: Domains of knowledge about human nature.* Boston: McGraw Hill.

Larsen, R. J., & Deiner, E. (1987). Affect intensity as an individual difference characteristic: A review. *Journal of Research in Personality, 21,* 1–39.

Larsen, R. J., & Kasimatis, M. (1990). Individual differences in the entrainment of mood to the weekly calendar. *Journal of Personality and Social Psychology, 58,* 164–171.

Laszlo, E. (1975). The meaning and significance of general system theory. *Behavioral Science, 20,* 9–24.

Laumann, E. O., Gagnon, J. H., Michael, R. T., & Michaels, S. (1994). *The social organization of sexuality: Sexual practices in the United States.* Chicago: University of Chicago Press.

Lawrence, J. (May, 2000). What's your fitness personality? *Vegetarian Times,* pp. 64–72.

Leary, M. R. (2004a). Editorial: What is the self? A plea for clarity. *Self and Identity, 3,* 1–3.

Leary, M. R. (July/August, 2004b). Get over yourself! *Psychology Today,* 62–65.

Lee, J-E., Wong, C. M. T., Day, J. D., Maxwell, S. E., & Thorpe, P. (2000). Social and academic intelligence: A multi-trait-multimethod study of their crystallized and fluid characteristics. *Personality and Individual Differences, 29,* 539–553.

Lei, H., & Skinner, H. A. (1982). What difference does language make: Structural analysis of the personality research form. *Multivariate Behavioral Research, 17,* 33–46.

Leo, J. (April 2, 1990). The trouble with self-esteem. *U.S. News and World Report, 108,* 16.

Leong, F. T. L., & Chervinko, S. (1996). Construct validity of career indecision: Negative personality traits as predictors of career indecision. *Journal of Career Assessment, 4,* 315–329.

Lerner, B. (1980). The war on testing: David, Goliath, & Gallup. *Public Interest, 60,* 119–147.

Lerner, B. (1981). Representative democracy, "men of zeal," and testing legislation. *American Psychologist, 36,* 270–275.

Levenson, R. W., Ekman, P, & Heider, K. (1992). Emotion and autonomic nervous system activity in the Minangkabau of West Sumatra. *Journal of Personality and Social Psychology, 62,* 972–988.

Levenson, R., & Ruef, A. (1992). Empathy: A physiological substrate. *Journal of Personality and Social Psychology, 63,* 234–246.

Levinson, D. J. (1977). The mid-life transition: A period in adult psychosocial development. *Psychiatry, 40,* 99–112.

Levy, L. H. (1970). *Conceptions of personality.* New York: Random House.

Lewicki, P. (1984). Self-schemata and social information processing. *Journal of Personality and Social Psychology, 47,* 1177–1190.

Lewin, K. (1935). *A dynamic theory of personality: Selected papers* (D. K. Adams & K. E. Zener, Trans.). New York: McGraw-Hill.

Lewis, C. S. (1970). *The discarded image.* Cambridge: Cambridge University Press.

Lewis, M. (2000). The emergence of human emotions. In M. Lewis & J. M. Haviland-Jones (Eds.), *Handbook of Emotions* (2nd ed.) (pp. 265–280). New York: Guilford.

Lewis, S. K., Ross, C. E., & Mirowsky, J. (1999). Establishing a sense of personal control in the transition to adulthood. *Social Forces, 77,* 1573–1599.

Lewontin, R. C., Rose, S., & Kamin, L. J. (1984). *Not in our genes.* New York: Pantheon.

Libet, B. (1985). Unconscious cerebral initiative and the role of conscious will in voluntary action. *Behavioral and Brain Sciences, 8,* 529–566.

Liker, J. K., & Elder, G. H. (1983). Economic hardship and marital relations in the 1930's. *American Sociological Review, 48,* 342–359.

Lippa, R. (1998). Gender-related individual differences and the structure of vocational interests: The importance of the people-things dimension. *Journal of Personality and Social Psychology, 74,* 996–1009.

Little, B. R. (2005). Personality science and personal projects: Six impossible things before breakfast. *Journal of Research and Personality, 39,* 4–21.

Littwin, S. (1986). *The postponed generation: Why America's grown-up kids are growing up later.* New York: William Morrow.

Loeb, J. (1966). The personality factor in divorce. *Journal of Consulting Psychology, 30,* 562.

Loehlin, J. C. (1968). *Computer models of personality.* New York: Random House.

Loehlin, J. C. (2002). Group differences in intelligence. In R. J. Sternberg (Ed.), *Handbook of intelligence.* Cambridge: Cambridge University Press.

Loevinger, J. (1967). Objective tests as instruments of psychological theory. In D. N. Jackson, & S. Messick (Eds.), *Problems in human assessment* (pp. 78–123). New York: McGraw-Hill. [Reprinted from *Psychological Reports, 1957, Monograph Supplement 9.*]

Loevinger, J. (1994). Has psychology lost its conscience? *Journal of Personality Assessment, 62,* 2–8.

Loftus, E. F., & Kaufman, L. (1992). Why do traumatic experiences sometimes produce good memory (flashbulbs) and sometimes no memory (repression)? In E. Winograd &

U. Neisser (Eds.), *Affect and accuracy in recall: Studies of "flash-bulb" memories.* New York: Cambridge University Press.

Lohman, D. F. (1988). Spatial abilities as traits, processes, and knowledge. In R. J. Sternberg (Ed.), *Advances in the psychology of human intelligence* (Vol. 4, pp. 181–248). Hillsdale, NJ: Erlbaum.

Lohman, D. F. (2000). Complex information processing and intelligence. In R. J. Sternberg (Ed.), *Handbook of intelligence* (pp. 285–340). Cambridge: Cambridge University Press.

Lohman, D. F., & Kyllonen, P. C. (1983). Individual differences in solution strategy on spatial tasks. In R. F. Dillon & R. Schmeck (Eds.), *Individual differences in cognition* (Vol. 1, pp. 105–135). New York: Academic Press.

Lounsbury, J. W., Hutchens, & T., Loveland, J.M. (2005). An investigation of big five personality traits and career decidedness among early and middle adolescents. *Journal of Career Assessment, 13,* 25–39.

Lopes, P. N., Salovey, P., Coté, S., & Beers, M. (2005). Emotional regulation ability and the quality of social interaction. *Emotion, 5,* 113–118.

Lopes, P. N., Brackett, M. A., Nezlek, J. B., Schütz, A., Sellin, I., & Salovey, P. (2004). Emotional intelligence and social interaction. *Personality and Social Psychology Bulletin, 30,* 1018–1034.

Lubinski, D. (2000). Scientific and social significance of assessing individual differences: "Sinking shafts at a few critical points." *Annual Review of Psychology, 51,* 405–444.

Lubinski, D, Webb, R. M., & Morelock, M. J. (2001). Top 1 in 10,000: A 10-year follow-up of the profoundly gifted. *Journal of Applied Psychology, 86,* 718–729.

Luborsky, L., & Crits-Christoph (1988). Measures of psychoanalytic concepts—The last decade of research from "the Penn Studies". *International Journal of Psychoanalysis, 69,* 75–85.

Luborsky, L., Crits-Christoph, P., & Mellon, J. (1986). Advent of objective measures of the transference concept. *Journal of Consulting and Clinical Psychology, 54,* 39–47.

Luecke-Aleksa, D., Anderson, D. R., Collins, P. A., & Schmitt, K. L. (1995). Gender constancy and television viewing. *Developmental Psychology, 31,* 773–780.

Luria, A. R. (1932). *The nature of human conflicts, or emotion, conflict and will, an objective study of disorganization and control of human behavior* (W. Horsley Gantt, Trans.). New York: Liveright Publications.

Lykken, D. T., & Tellegen, A. (1993). Is human mating adventitious or the result of lawful choice? A twin study of mate selection. *Journal of Personality and Social Psychology, 65,* 56–68.

Lynn, S. J., & Rhue, J. W. (1988). Fantasy proneness: Hypnosis, developmental antecedents, and psychopathology. *American Psychologist, 43,* 35–44.

Lyubomirsky, S., & Nolen-Hoeksema, S (1993). Self-perpetuating properties of dysphoric rumination. *Journal of Personality and Social Psychology, 65,* 339–349.

Maccoby, E. E. (1990). Gender and relationships: A developmental account. *American Psychologist, 45,* 513–520.

Maccoby, E. E., & Martin, J. A. (1983). Socialization in the context of the family: Parent-child interaction. In E. M. Hetherington (Ed.), *Handbook of child psychology: Vol. IV. Socialization, personality, and social development.* New York: Wiley.

MacLean, P. D. (1977). The triune brain in conflict. *Psychotherapy and Psychosomatics, 28 (1-sup-4),* 207–220.

MacLean, P. D. (1993). On the evolution of three mentalities. In J. B. Ashbrook, (Ed.), *Brain, culture, & the human spirit: Essays from an emergent evolutionary perspective* (pp. 15–44). Lanham, MD: University Press of America.

Maddi, S. R. (1972). *Personality theories: A comparative analysis.* Homewood, IL: Dorsey Press.

Maddi, S. R. (1993). The continuing relevance of personality theory. In K. H. Craik, R. Hogan, & R. N. Wolfe (Eds.), *Fifty years of personality psychology* (pp. 85–101). New York: Plenum.

Mans, L., Cicchetti, D., & Sroufe, L. A. (1978). Mirror reactions of Down's syndrome infants and toddlers: Cognitive underpinnings of self-recognition. *Child Development, 49,* 1247–1250.

Marcel, A. J. (1983). Conscious and unconscious perception: An approach to the relation between phenomenal experience and perceptual processes. *Cognitive Psychology, 15,* 238–300.

Marcia, J. E. (1964). Determination and validation of ego identity status. Unpublished doctoral dissertation. Ohio State University: Columbus, Ohio.

Marcia, J. E. (1966). Development and validation of ego identity status. *Journal of Personality and Social Psychology, 3,* 551–558.

Marcia, J. E. (2002). Identity and psychosocial development in adulthood. *Identity: An International Journal of Theory and Research, 2,* 7–28.

Marcia, J. E., Waterman, A. S., Matteson, D. R., Archer, S. L., & Orlofsky, J. L. (1993). *Ego identity: A handbook for psychosocial research. New* York: Springer-Verlag.

Marinoff, L. (1999). *Plato not Prozac!* New York: HarperCollins.

Markus, H. (1977). Self-schemata and processing information about the self. *Journal of Personality and Social Psychology, 35,* 63–78.

Markus, H., & Kitayama, S. (1991). Culture and self: Implications for cognition, emotion, and motivation. *Psychological Review, 98,* 224–253.

Markus, H., & Nurius, P. (1986). Possible selves. *American Psychologist, 41,* 954–969.

Markus, H., & Wurf, E. (1987). The dynamic self-concept: A social psychological perspective. *Annual Review of Psychology, 38,* 299–337.

Marsella, A. J., Dubanoski, J., Hamada, W. C., & Morse, H. (2000). The measurement of personality across cultures: Historical, conceptual, and methodological considerations. *American Behavioral Scientist, 44,* 41–62.

Marsh, H. W. (1993). Relations between global and specific domains of self: The importance of individual importance, certainty and ideals. *Journal of Personality and Social Psychology, 65,* 975–992.

Marsland, K. W., & Likavec, S. C. (2003, June). *Maternal emotional intelligence, infant attachment and child socio-emotional competence.* Poster presented at the annual meeting of the American Psychological Society, Atlanta, GA.

Martin, C. L., Eisenbud, L., & Rose, H. (1995). Children's gender-based reasoning about toys. *Child Development, 66,* 1453–1471.

Martin, L. L., & Tesser, A. (1996). Some ruminative thoughts. In R. S. Wyer, Jr. (Ed.), *Advances in social cognition* (Vol. 9, pp. 1–48). Hillsdale, NJ: Lawrence Erlbaum.

Maruyama, G. M. (1998). *Basics of structural equation modeling.* Thousand Oaks, CA: Sage.

Mascaro, N., & Rosen, D. H. (2005). Existential meaning's role in the enhancement of hope and prevention of depressive symptoms. *Journal of Personality, 73,* 985–114.

Maslow, A. H. (1943). A theory of human motivation. *Psychological Review, 50,* 370–396.

Maslow, A. H. (1970). *Motivation and Personality* (2nd ed.). New York: Harper and Row.

Masten, A. S., & Reed, M-G. J. (2002). Resilience in development. In C. R. Snyder & S. J. Lopez (Eds.), *Handbook of positive psychology* (pp. 74–88). New York: Oxford University Press.

Masters, W. H., & Johnson, V. E. (1966). *Human sexual response.* Boston: Little, Brown.

Matarazzo, J.D. (1972). *Wechsler's measurement and appraisal of adult intelligence* (5th and enlarged ed). Baltimore: Williams & Wilkins.

Matarazzo, J. D. (1992). Biological and physiological correlates of intelligence. *Intelligence, 16,* 257–258.

Matarazzo, J. D., & Herman, D. O. (1984). Relationship of education and IQ in the WAIS-R standardization sample. *Journal of Consulting and Clinical Psychology, 52,* 631–634.

Matheny, A. P. (1989). Children's behavioral inhibition over age and across situations: Genetic similarity for a trait during change. *Journal of Personality, 57,* 215–235.

Mathews, K. A. (1988). CHD and Type A behavior: Update on and alternative to the Booth-Kewley and Friedman quantitative review. *Psychological Bulletin, 104,* 373–380.

Mathews, K. A., Glass, D. C., Rosenman, R. H., & Bortner, R. W. (1977). Competitive drive, pattern A, and coronary heart disease: A further analysis of some data from the Western Collaborative Group Study. *Journal of Chronic Disease, 30,* 489–498.

Mathews, K. A., Helmreich, R. L., Beane, W. E., & Lucker, G. W. (1980). Pattern A, achievement striving, and scientific merit: Does pattern A help or hinder? *Journal of Personality and Social Psychology, 39,* 962–967.

Maticka-Tyndale, E., Herold, E. S., & Mewhinney, D. (1998). Casual sex on spring break: Intensions and behaviors of Canadian students. *Journal of Sex Research, 35,* 254–264.

Matthews, G., Zeidner, M., & Roberst, R. D. (2002). *Emotional intelligence: Science and myth.* Cambridge, MA: MIT Press.

Maurer, D., & Maurer, C. (1988). *The world of the newborn.* New York: Basic Books.

Mayer, J. D. (1993–1994). A System-Topics Framework for the study of personality. *Imagination, Cognition, and Personality, 13,* 99–123.

Mayer, J. D. (1994). A System-Topics Alternative. *Dialogue: Society for Personality and Social Psychology, 9,* 7.

Mayer, J. D. (1995a). The System-Topics Framework and the location of systems and boundaries within and around personality. *Journal of Personality, 63,* 459–493.

Mayer, J. D. (1995b). A framework for the classification of personality components. *Journal of Personality, 63,* 819–877.

Mayer, J. D. (1998). A Systems Framework for the field of personality psychology. *Psychological Inquiry, 9,* 118–144.

Mayer, J. D. (1998). The Systems Framework: Reception, improvement, and implementation. *Psychological Inquiry, 9,* 169–179.

Mayer, J. D. (1998). A framework for the study of individual differences in personality formations. In J. A. Singer & P. Salovey (Eds.), *At play in the fields of consciousness* (pp. 143–173). Mahwah, NJ: Lawrence Erlbaum.

Mayer, J. D. (2000). Spiritual intelligence or spiritual consciousness? *International Journal for the Psychology of Religion, 10,* 47–56.

Mayer, J. D. (2001a). Primary divisions of personality and their scientific contributions: From the trilogy-of-mind to the systems set. *Journal for the Theory of Social Behaviour, 31,* 449–477.

Mayer, J. D. (2001b). A field guide to emotional intelligence. In J. Ciarrochi, J. P. Forgas, & J. D. Mayer (Eds.), *Emotional intelligence and everday life* (pp. 3–24). New York: Psychology Press.

Mayer, J. D. (2003). Structural divisions of personality and the classification of traits. *Review of General Psychology, 7,* 381–401.

Mayer, J. D. (2004). A classification system for the data of personality psychology and adjoining fields. *Review of General Psychology, 8,* 208–219.

Mayer, J. D. (2005). A tale of two visions: Can a new view of personality help organize psychology? *American Psychologist, 60,* 294–307.

Mayer, J. D., & Bower, G. H. (1986). Learning and memory for personality prototypes. *Journal of Personality and Social Psychology, 51,* 473–492.

Mayer, J. D., & Carlsmith, K. M. (1998). The Systems Framework web site, www.princeton.edu/personality_framework; or www.unh.edu/personality_framework

Mayer, J. D., Carlsmith, K. M., & Chabot, H. F. (1998). Describing the person's external environment: Conceptualizing and measuring the Life Space. *Journal of Research in Personality, 32,* 253–296.

Mayer, J. D., Caruso, D., & Salovey, P. (1999). Emotional intelligence meets traditional standards for an intelligence. *Intelligence, 27,* 267–298.

Mayer, J. D., Caruso, D. R., Zigler, E., & Dreyden, J. I. (1989). Intelligence and intelligence-related personality traits. *Intelligence, 13,* 119–133.

Mayer, J. D., Chabot, H. F., & Carlsmith, K. M. (1997). Conation, affect, and cognition in personality. In G. Matthews (Ed.), *Cognitive science perspectives on personality and emotion.* Oxford: Elsevier.

Mayer, J. D., DiPaolo, M. T., & Salovey, P. (1990). Perceiving affective content in ambiguous visual stimuli: A component of emotional intelligence. *Journal of Personality Assessment, 54,* 772–781.

Mayer, J. D., & Gaschke, Y. (1988). The experience and meta-experience of mood. *Journal of Personality and Social Psychology, 55,* 102–111.

Mayer, J. D., Gaschke, Y., Braverman, D. L., & Evans, T. (1992). Mood-congruent judgment is a general effect. *Journal of Personality and Social Psychology, 63,* 119–132.

Mayer, J. D., & Geher, G. (1996). Emotional intelligence and the identification of emotion. *Intelligence, 22,* 89–113.

Mayer, J. D., & Hanson, E. (1995). Mood-congruent judgment over time. *Personality and Social Psychology Bulletin, 21,* 237–244.

Mayer, J. D., McCormick, L. J., & Strong, S. E. (1995). Mood-congruent recall and natural mood: New evidence. *Personality and Social Psychology Bulletin, 21,* 736–746.

Mayer, J. D., & Mitchell, D. C. (1998). Intelligence as a subsystem of personality: From Spearman's *g* to contemporary models of hot-processing. In W. Tomic & J. Kingma (Eds), *Advances in cognition and educational practice* (Vol. 5: Conceptual issues in research in intelligence) (pp. 43–75). Greenwich, CT: JAI Press.

Mayer, J. D., Perkins, D. M., Caruso, D. R., & Salovey, P. (2000). Emotional intelligence and giftedness. *Roeper Review, 23,* 131–137.

Mayer, J. D., Rapp, H. C., & Williams, L. (1993). Individual differences in behavioral prediction: The acquisition of personal-action schemata. *Personality and Social Psychology Bulletin, 19,* 443–451.

Mayer, J. D., & Salovey, P. (1993). The intelligence of emotional intelligence. *Intelligence, 17(4),* 433–442.

Mayer, J. D., & Salovey, P. (1997). What is emotional intelligence? In P. Salovey & D. Sluyter (Eds), *Emotional development and emotional intelligence: Implications for educators* (pp. 3–31). New York: Basic Books.

Mayer, J. D., Salovey, P., & Caruso, D. R. (2000). Models of emotional intelligence. In R. Sternberg (Ed.), *Handbook of human intelligence* (2nd ed.). New York: Cambridge University Press.

Mayer, J. D., Salovey, P., & Caruso, D. R. (2002). *Mayer-Salovey-Caruso Emotional Intelligence Test (MSCEIT) Users Manual.* Toronto, ON: Multi-Health Systems.

Mayer, J. D., Salovey, P., Caruso, D. R., & Sitarenios, G. (2003). Measuring emotional intelligence with the MSCEIT V2.0. *Emotion, 3,* 97–105.

Mayer, J. D., Salovey, P., Gomberg-Kaufman, M., & Blainey, K. (1991). A broader conception of mood experience. *Journal of Personality and Social Psychology, 60,* 100–111.

Mayer, J. D., & Stevens, A. A. (1994). An emerging understanding of the reflective (meta-) experience of mood. *Journal of Research in Personality, 28,* 351–373.

Mazlish, B. (1973). *In search of Nixon: A psychohistorical inquiry.* New York: Penguin Books.

McAdams, D. P. (1992a). The intimacy motive. In C. P. Smith (Ed.), *Motivation and personality: Handbook of thematic content analysis* (pp. 224–228). New York: Cambridge University Press.

McAdams, D. P. (1992b). The intimacy motivation scoring system. In C. P. Smith (Ed.), *Motivation and personality: Handbook of thematic content analysis* (pp. 229–253). New York: Cambridge University Press.

McAdams, D. P. (1993). *The stories we live by: Personal myths and the making of the self.* New York: William Morrow.

McAdams, D. P. (1995). What do we know when we know a person? *Journal of Personality, 63,* 365–396.

McAdams, D. P. (1996). Personality, modernity, and the storied self: A contemporary framework for studying persons. *Psychological Inquiry, 7,* 295–321.

McAdams, D. P. (1998). Trick or treat: Classifying concepts and accounting for human individuality. *Psychological Inquiry, 9,* 154–158.

McAdams, D. P. (2001). The psychology of life stories. *Review of General Psychology, 5,* 100–122.

McAdams, D. P., & Bowman, P. J. (2001). Narrating life's turning points: Redemption and contamination. In D. P. McAdams & R. Josselson (Eds.), *Turns in the road: Narrative studies of lives in transition* (pp. 3–34). Washington, DC: American Psychological Association.

McAdams, D. P., Diamond, A., de St. Aubin, E., & Mansfield, E. (1997). Stories of commitment: The psychosocial construction of generative lives. *Journal of Personality and Social Psychology, 72,* 678–694.

McAdams, D. P., Reynolds, J., Lewis, M., Patten, A. H., & Bowman, P. J. (2001). When bad things turn good and good things turn bad: Sequences of redemption and contamination in life narrative and their relation to psychosocial adaptation in midlife adults and in students. *Personality and Social Psychology Bulletin, 27,* 474–485.

McAdams, D. P., & West, S. G. (1997). Personality psychology and the case study. Introduction. *Journal of Personality, 65,* 757–783.

McBain, D. A. (1995). Empathy and the salesperson: A multidimensional perspective. *Psychology and Marketing, 12,* 349–370.

McCallum, M., & Piper, W. E. (1997). *Psychological mindedness: A contemporary understanding.* Mahwah, NJ: Lawrence Erlbaum.

McClelland, D. C. (1958). The use of measures of human motivation in the study of society. In J. W. Atkinson (Ed.), *Motives in fantasy, action and society* (pp. 518–552). Princeton, NJ: Van Nostrand.

McClelland, D. C. (1976). *The achieving society.* Princeton, NJ: Van Nostrand. (Original work published 1961.)

McClelland, D. C., Atkinson, J. W., Clark, R. A., & Lowell, E. L. (1992). A scoring manual for the achievement motive. In C. P. Smith (Ed.), *Motivation and personality: Handbook of thematic content analysis* (pp. 153–178). New York: Cambridge University Press.

McClelland, D. C., & Koestner, R. (1992). The achievement motive. In C. P. Smith (Ed.), *Motivation and personality: Handbook of thematic content analysis* (pp. 143–152). New York: Cambridge University Press.

McClelland, D. C., Koestner, R., & Weinberger, J. (1992). How do self-attributed and implicit motives differ? In C. P. Smith (Ed.), *Motivation and personality: Handbook of thematic content analysis* (pp. 49–72). New York: Cambridge University Press.

McCrae, R. R. (1998). An empirically based alternative framework. *Psychological Inquiry, 9,* 158–160.

McCrae, R. R., & Costa, P. T. (1990). *Personality in adulthood.* New York: Guilford.

McCrae, R. R., & Costa, P. T. (1997). Personality trait structure as a human universal. *American Psychologist, 52,* 509–516.

McCrae, R. R., & Costa, P. T. (1999). A five factor theory of personality. In L. A. Pervin & O. P. John (Eds.), *Handbook of personality* (2nd ed.) (pp. 139–153). New York: Guilford.

McEwen, B. S. (1991). Sex differences in the brain: What they are and how they arise. In M. T. Notman & C. C. Nadelson (Eds.), *Women and men: New perspectives on gender differences* (pp. 35–41). Washington, DC: American Psychiatric Association.

McGue, M., Bouchard, T. J., Iacono, W. G., & Lykken, D. T. (1993). Behavioral genetics of cognitive ability: A life-span perspective. In R. Plomin & G. E. McClearn (Eds.). *Nature, nurture, and psychology.* Washington, DC: American Psychological Association.

McGue, M., & Lykken, D. T. (1992). Genetic influence on risk of divorce. *Psychological Science, 6,* 368–373.

McGuire, W. (1984). Search for the self: Going beyond self-esteem and the reactive self. In R. A. Tucker, J. Aronoff, & A. J. Rabin (Eds.), *Personality and the prediction of behavior* (pp. 73–120). Orlando, FL: Academic Press.

McManis, M. H., Kagan, J., & Snidman, N. C., Woodward, S. A. (2002). EEG asymmetry, power, and temperament in children. *Developmental Psychology, 41,* 169–177.

Mead, G. H. (1934). *Mind, self, and society.* Chicago, IL: University of Chicago Press.

Mead, M. (1939). *From the South Seas: Studies of adolescence and sex in primitive societies.* New York: Morrow.

Mebert, C. J. (1991). Dimensions of subjectivity in parents' ratings of infant temperament. *Child Development, 62,* 352–361.

Mednick, S. A. (1962). The associative basis of the creative process. *Psychological Review, 69,* 220–232.

Meehl, P. E. (1975). Hedonic capacity: Some conjectures. *Bulletin of the Menninger Clinic, 39,* 295–307.

Mendelsohn, G. A. (1993). Its time to put theories of personality in their place, or, Allport and Stagner got it right, why can't we? In K. H. Craik, R. Hogan, & R. N. Wolfe (Eds.), *Fifty years of personality psychology* (pp. 103–129). New York: Plenum.

Menninger, K. A. (1930). *The human mind.* Literary Guild of America.

Meyer, B. & Pilkonis, P. A. (2001). Attachment style. *Psychotherapy: Theory, Research, Practice, Training, 38,* 466–472.

Meyer, D., Leventhal, H., & Guttman, M. (1985). Commonsense models of illness: The example of hypertension. *Health Psychology, 4,* 115–135.

Meyer, G. J., Finn, S. E., Eyde, L. D., Kay, G. G., Moreland, K. L., Dies, R. R., Eisman, E. J., Kubiszyn, T. W., & Read, G. M. (2001). Psychological testing and psychological assessment: A review of evidence and issues. *American Psychologist, 56,* 128–156.

Michotte, A. (1963). *The perception of causality* (T. R. Miles & E. Miles, Trans.). New York: Basic Books.

Miech, R., Essex, M. J., & Goldsmith, H. H. (2001). Socioeconomic status and the adjustment to school: The role of self-regulation during early childhood. *Sociology of Education, 74,* 102–120.

Miller, L. C., & Fishkin, S. A. (1997). On the dynamics of human bonding and reproductive success: Seeking windows on the adapted-for human-environmental interface. In J. Simpson & D. Kenrick (Eds.), *Evolutionary social psychology* (pp. 197–235). Mahwah, NJ: Erlbaum.

Miller, S. D. (1989). Optical differences in cases of multiple personality disorder. *The Journal of Nervous and Mental Disease, 177,* 480–486.

Miller, T. Q., Turner, C. W., Tindale, R. S., Posovac, E. J., & Dugoni, B. (1991). Reasons for the trend toward null findings in research on Type A behavior. *Psychological Bulletin, 119,* 322–348.

Miller, W. R., & Taylor, C. A. (1980). Relative effectiveness of bibliotherapy, individual and group self-control training in the treatment of problem drinkers. *Addictive Behavior, 5,* 13–24.

Mills, J., & Clark, M. S. (1982). Exchange and communal relationships. In L. Wheeler (Ed.), *Review of personality and social psychology* (Vol. 3, pp. 121–144). Beverly Hills, CA: Sage.

Milton, J., & Wiseman, R. (1999). Does psi exist? Lack of replication of an anomalous process of information transfer. *Psychological Bulletin, 125,* 387–391.

Mineka, S., Davidson, M., Cook, M., & Keir, R. (1984). Observational conditioning of snake fears in rhesus monkeys. *Journal of Abnormal Psychology, 93,* 355–372.

Mirowsky, J. (1997). Age, subjective life expectancy, and the sense of control: The horizon hypothesis. *Journals of Gerontology: Series B: Psychological Sciences and Social Sciences, 52B,* S125–S134.

Mischel, W. (1968). *Personality and assessment.* New York: Wiley.

Mischel, W. (1973). Toward a cognitive social learning reconceptualization of personality. *Psychological Review, 80,* 252–283.

Mischel, W. (1990). Personality dispositions revisited and revised. In L. Pervin (Ed.), *Handbook of personality: Theory and research* (pp. 111–134). New York: Guilford.

Mischel, W. (1998). *Introduction to personality.* New York: Wiley.

Mischel, W. & Ebbesen, E. B. (1970). Attention in delay of gratification. *Journal of Personality and Social Psychology, 3,* 45–53.

Mischel, W., & Shoda, Y. (1995). A cognitive-affective system theory of personality: Reconceptualizing situations, dispositions, dynamics, and invariance in personality structure. *Psychological Review, 102,* 246–268.

Mischel, W., Shoda, Y., & Peake, P. K. (1988). The nature of adolescent competencies predicted by preschool delay of gratification. *Journal of Personality and Social Psychology, 54,* 687–696.

Miserandino, M. (1996). Children who do well in school: Individual differences in perceived competence and autonomy in above average children. *Journal of Educational Psychology, 88,* 203–214.

Moles, A. (1966). *Information theory and esthetic perception.* Urbana: University of Illinois Press. [Original work published 1958; J. E. Cohen, Trans. English Edition.]

Money, J., & Lehne, G. K. (1999). Gender identity disorders. In R. T. Ammerman, M. Hersen, & C. G. Last (Eds.), *Handbook of prescriptive treatments for children and adolescents* (2nd ed.) (pp. 214–228). Boston: Allyn & Bacon.

Mongar, T. (1976). A cybernetic model of personality structure: A theoretical proposal. *Psychology: A Journal of Human Behavior, 13,* 33–48.

Monte, C. F. (1999). *Beneath the mask: An introduction to theories of personality* (6th ed.). New York: Harcourt Brace College.

Mook, D. G. (1996). *Motivation: The organization of action* (2nd ed.). New York: W. W. Norton.

Moore, K. L., & Persaud, T. V. N. (1993). *Before we are born* (4th ed.). Philadelphia: W. B. Saunders.

Moran, R. A. (1993). *Never confuse a memo with reality and other business lessons too simple not to know.* New York: HarperCollins.

Moravec, H. (2000). Shaper of things to come. *Discover, 21,* 32ff.

Morelli, G., Rogoff, B., Oppenheim, D., & Goldsmith, D. (1992). Cultural variation in infants' sleeping arrangements: Questions of independence. *Developmental Psychology, 28,* 604–613.

Morf, C. C. (2005). Affirming the self, as construct and journal. *Self and Identity, 4,* 97–101.

Morgan, A. H. (1973). The heritability of hypnotic susceptibility in twins. *Journal of Abnormal Psychology, 82,* 55–61.

Morgan, D. M. (1989). *The voyage of the* American Promise. Boston: Houghton Mifflin.

Morgan, W. G. (1995). Origin and history of the Thematic Apperception Test images. *Journal of Personality Assessment, 65,* 237–254.

Morokoff, P. J. (1985). Effects of sex guilt, repression, sexual "arousability," and sexual experience on female sexual arousal during erotica and fantasy. *Journal of Personality and Social Psychology,* 49, 177–187.

Morris, T. W., & Levinson, E. M. (1995). Relationship between intelligence and occupational adjustment and functioning: A literature review. *Journal of Counseling and Development, 73,* 503–514.

Morrison, D. F. (1976). *Multivariate statistical methods* (2nd ed.). New York: McGraw Hill.

Moss, F. A., & Hunt, T. (1927). Are you socially intelligent? *Scientific American, 137,* 108–110.

Motley, M. T., Camden, C.T., & Baars, B. J. (1983). Covert formulation and editing of anomalies in speech production: Evidence from experimentally elicited slips of the tongue. *Journal of Verbal Learning and Verbal Behavior, 21,* 578–594.

Motley, M. T., Camden, C. T., & Baars, B. J. (1983). Polysemantic lexical access: Evidence from laboratory-induced double entendres. *Communication Monographs, 50,* 193–205.

Mroczek, D. K. (2001). Age and emotion in adulthood. *Current Directions in Psychological Science, 10,* 87–90.

Mroczek, D. K., & Kolarz, C. M. (1998). The effect of age on positive and negative affect: A developmental perspective on happiness. *Journal of Personality and Social Psychology, 75,* 1333–1349.

Mullen, B., & Riordan, C. A. (1988). Self-serving attributions for performance in naturalistic settings: A meta-analytic review. *Journal of Applied Social Psychology, 18,* 3–22.

Müller-Lyer, F. C. (1889). Optische Urteilstäuschungen *Dubois-Reymonds Archive für Anatomie und Physiologie,* Supplement-263. [Deception of visual judgment].

Muraven, M., & Baumeister, R. F. (2000). Self-regulation and depletion of limited resources: Does self-control resemble a muscle? *Psychological Bulletin, 126,* 247–259.

Murchison, C. (Ed.). (1930). *Psychologies of 1930.* Worcester, MA: Clark University Press.

Murphy, K. R., & DeShon, R. (2000). Progress in psychometrics: Can industrial and organizational psychology catch up? *Personnel Psychology, 53,* 913–924.

Murray, H. A. (1938). *Explorations in personality.* New York: Oxford University Press.

Murray, H. A. (1951). Toward a classification of interaction. In T. Parsons & E. A. Shils (Eds.), *Toward a general theory of action* (pp. 434–464). Cambridge, MA: Harvard University Press.

Murray, H. A. (1962). The personality and career of Satan. *The Journal of Social Issues, 18,* 36–54.

Murray, H. A., & Kluckhohn, C. (1956). Outline of a conception of personality. In C. Kluckhohn, H. A. Murray, & D. M. Schneider (Eds.), *Personality in nature, society, and culture* (pp. 3–49). New York: Alfred A. Knopf.

Murstein, B. I. (1972). Physical attractiveness and marital choice. *Journal of Personality and Social Psychology, 22,* 8–12.

Myers, D. G. (2000). The funds, friends, and faith of happy people. *American Psychologist, 56,* 56–67.

Myers, D. G., & Deiner, E (1995). Who is happy? *Psychological Science, 6,* 10–19.

Nakamura, J., & Csikszentmihalyi, M. (2002). The concept of flow. In C. R. Snyder & S. J. Lopez (Eds.), *Handbook of positive psychology* (pp. 89–105). New York: Oxford University Press.

Nasby, W., & Read, N. W. (1997). 7. The hero's return. *Journal of Personality, 65,* 1013–1042.

Natsoulas, T. (1986-1987). The six basic concepts of consciousness and William James' stream of thought. *Imagination, Cognition, and Personality, 6,* 289–319.

Newberg, A., Alavi, A., Baime, M., Pourdehnad, M. Santanna, J., & d'Aquili E. (2001). The measurement of regional cerebral blood flow during the complex cognitive task of meditation: A preliminary SPECT study. *Psychiatry Research: Neuroimaging, 106,* 113–122.

Newman, D. L., Caspi, A., Moffitt, T. E., & Silva, P. A. (1997). Antecedents of adult interpersonal functioning: Effects of individual differences in age-3 temperament. *Developmental Psychology, 33,* 206–217.

Nickerson, C. (June 13, 1999). Literary star revisits dark side. *Boston Sunday Globe,* pp. A4–A5.

Nickerson, R. S. (1998). Confirmation bias: A ubiquitous phenomenon in many guises. *Review of General Psychology, 2,* 175–220.

Nisbett, R. E. (1980). The trait construct in lay and professional psychology. In L. Festinger (Ed.), *Retrospectives on social psychology.* New York: Oxford University Press.

Nisbett, R. E., & Wilson, T. C. (1977). Telling more than we can know: Verbal reports on mental processes. *Psychological Review, 84,* 231–259.

Nissel, A. (2001). *The broke diaries.* New York: Villard Books.

Nixon, R. M. (1978). *RN: The memoirs of Richard Nixon.* New York: Grosset & Dunlap.

Nixon, R. M. (1990). *In the arena: A memoir of victory, defeat, and renewal.* New York: Simon & Schuster.

Norcross, J. C., Hedges, M., & Castle, P. H. (2002). Psychologists conducting psychotherapy in 2001: A study of the Division 29 Membership. *Psychotherapy: Theory, Practice, Training, 39,* 97–102.

Norem, J. K., & Chang, E. C. (2002). The positive psychology of negative thinking. *Journal of Clinical Psychology, 58,* 993–1001.

Norem, J. K., & Illingworth, S. (1993). Strategy-dependent effects of reflecting on self and tasks: Some implications of optimism and defensive pessimism. *Journal of Personality and Social Psychology, 65,* 822–835.

Novick, M. R. (1966). The axioms and principal results of classical test theory. *Journal of Mathematical Psychology, 3,* 1–18.

Nowlis, V. (1965). Research with the Mood Adjective Checklist. In S. S. Tomkins & C. E. Izard (Eds.), *Affect, cognition, and personality* (pp. 98–128). New York: Springer.

Nyhus, E. K., & Pons, E. (2005). The effects of personality on earnings. *Journal of Economic Psychology, 26,* 363–384.

O'Connor, T. G., Caspi, A., DeFries, J. C., & Plomin, R. (2000). Are associations between parental divorce and children's adjustment genetically mediated? An adoption study. *Developmental Psychology, 36,* 429–437.

Oliner, S. P., & Oliner, P. M. (1988). *The altruistic personality: Rescuers of Jews in Nazi Europe.* New York: Free Press.

Oliver, M. B., & Hyde, J. S. (1993). Gender differences in sexuality: A meta-analysis. *Psychological Bulletin, 114,* 29–51.

Olweus, D. (1993). Victimization by peers: Antecedents and long-term outcomes. In K. H. Rubin & J. B. Asendopf (Eds.), *Social withdrawal, inhibition, and shyness in childhood* (pp. 315–341). Hillsdale, NJ: Erlbaum.

Orlinsky, D. E., & Howard, K. I. (1986). Process and outcome in psychotherapy. In S. L. Garfield, & A. E. Bergin (Eds.), *Handbook of psychotherapy and behavior change* (3rd ed.) (pp. 311–381). New York: Wiley.

Ornstein, R. (1986). *The psychology of consciousness* (rev. ed.). New York: Penguin Books.

Ornstein, R. (1991). *The evolution of consciousness.* New York: Simon & Schuster.

Ortony, A., Clore, G. L., & Collins, A. (1988). *The cognitive structure of emotions.* Cambridge: Cambridge University Press.

Ortony, A., & Turner, T. J. (1990). What's *basic* about *basic* emotions? *Psychological Review, 97,* 315–331.

O'Sullivan, M., & Guilford, J. P. (1976). *Four factor tests of social intelligence: Manual of instructions and interpretations.* Orange, CA: Sheridan Psychological Services.

Oxenstierna, G., Edman, G., Iselius, L., Oreland, L., Ross, S. B., & Sedvall, G. (1986). Concentrations of monoamine metabolites in the cerebrospinal fluid of twins and unrelated individuals: A genetic study. *Journal of Psychiatric Research, 20,* 19–20.

Oyserman, D., & Markus, H. R. (1990). Possible selves and delinquency. *Journal of Personality and Social Psychology, 59,* 112–125.

Oyserman, D., & Saltz, E. (1993). Competence, delinquency, and attempts to attain possible selves. *Journal of Personality and Social Psychology, 65,* 360–374.

Pajares, F. (1996). Self-efficacy beliefs in academic settings. *Review of Educational Research, 66,* 543–578.

Pancer, K. L., & Pancer, R. J. (1988). The quest, gurus, and the yellow brick road. *Individual Psychology: Journal of Adlerian Theory, Research, and Practice, 44,* 158–166.

Paniagua, C. (2001). The attraction of topographical technique. *International Journal of Psychoanalysis, 82,* 671–684.

Papalia, D. E., Camp, C., & Feldman, R. D. (2002). *Adult development and aging.* New York: McGraw-Hill.

Park, A. (Feburary, 11, 2002). Three U.S. stars. One Gold medal. Get ready for spin city: Not long ago, Sarah Hughes idolized Michelle Kwan. Now she and Sasha Cohen will challenge Kwan's Olympic glory. *Time, 159,* p. 44.

Parker, J. G., & Asher, S. R. (1993). Beyond group acceptance: Friendship adjustment and friendship quality as distinct dimensions of children's peer adjustment. In D. Perlman & W. H. Jones (Eds.), *Advances in personal relationships* (Vol. 4, pp. 261–294). London: Kingsley.

Parkinson, B., & Manstead, A. S. R. (1992). Appraisal as a cause of emotion. *Review of Personality and Social Psychology, 13,* 122–149.

Parrott, G. W. (1993). Beyond hedonism: Motives for inhibiting good moods and for maintaining bad moods. In D. M. Wegner & J. W. Pennebaker (Eds.), *Handbook of mental control* (pp. 278–305). Englewood Cliffs, NJ: Prentice-Hall.

Patrick, C. J., Curtin, J. J., & Tellegen, A. (2002). Development and validation of a brief form of the Multidimensional Personality Questionnaire. *Psychological Assessment, 14,* 150–163.

Paulhus, D. L. (1993). Bypassing the will: The automatization of affirmations. In D. M. Wegner & J. Pennebaker (Eds.), *Handbook of mental control* (pp. 573–587). Upper Saddle River, NJ: Prentice Hall.

Paulhus, D. L., Lysy, D. C., & Yik, M. S. M (1998). Self-report measures of intelligence: Are they useful as proxy IQ tests? *Journal of Personality, 66,* 525–554.

Paulhus, D. L., & Nadine, B. M. (1992). The effect of acquaintanceship on the validity of personality impressions: A longitudinal study. *Journal of Personality and Social Psychology, 63,* 816–824.

Paulhus, D. L., Trapnell, P. D., & Chen, D. (1999). Birth order effects on personality and achievement within families. *Psychological Science, 10,* 482–488.

Paunonen, S. V. (1998). Hierarchical organization of personality and prediction of behavior. *Journal of Personality and Social Psychology, 74,* 538–556.

Paunonen, S. V., & Jackson, D. N. (2000). What is beyond the Big Five? Plenty! *Journal of Personality, 68,* 822–835.

Pavlov, I. P. (1906). The scientific investigation of the psychical faculties or processes in the higher animals. *Science, 24,* 613–619.

Payne, D. (1989). The *Wizard of Oz:* Therapeutic rhetoric in a contemporary media ritual. *Quarterly Journal of Speech, 75,* 25–39.

Pedersen, N. P., Plomin, R., McClearn, G. E., & Friberg, L. T. (1988). Neuroticism, extraversion, and related traits in adult twins reared apart and reared together. *Journal of Personality and Social Psychology, 55,* 950–957.

Pelletier, K. R. (1985). *Toward a science of consciousness.* Berkeley, CA: Celestial Arts.

Pelzer, D. J. (2000). *A man named Dave: A story of triumph and forgiveness.* New York: Penguin.

Pennington, B. F., Filipek, P. A., Lefly, D., Chhabildas, N., Kennedy, D. N., Simon, J. K., Filley, C. M., Galaburda, A., DeFries, J. C. (2000). A twin MRI study of size variations in the human brain. *Journal of Cognitive Neuroscience, 12,* 223–232.

Perry, B. (February, 2001a). *Big questions* Real answers. *Scholastic Choices, 16,* p. 30.

Perry, B. (March, 2001b). *Big questions* Real answers. *Scholastic Choices, 16,* p. 30.

Perry, B. (April, 2001c). *Big questions* Real answers. *Scholastic Choices, 16,* p. 30.

Perry, C., & Laurence, J-R. (1984). Mental processing outside of awareness: The contributions of Freud and Janet. In K. S. Bowers & D. Meichenbaum (Eds.), *The unconscious reconsidered* (pp. 9–48). New York: John Wiley & Sons.

Pervin, L. A. (1990). A brief history of modern personality theory. In L. A. Pervin (Ed.), *Handbook of personality: Theory and research.* New York: Guilford.

Pervin, L. A. (1990). *Handbook of personality: Theory and research.* New York: Guilford.

Pervin, L. A. (1996). *The science of personality.* New York: John Wiley & Sons.

Pervin, L. A. (2003). *The science of personality* (2nd ed.). Oxford: Oxford University Press.

Pervin, L. A., & John, O. P. (Eds.) (1999). *Handbook of personality: Theory and research.* New York: Guilford.

Peterson, B. E., & Stewart, A. J. (1993). Generativity and social motives in young adults. *Journal of Personality and Social Psychology, 65,* 186–198.

Peterson, C. (1991). The meaning and measurement of explanatory style. *Psychological Inquiry, 2,* 1–10.

Peterson, C., & Seligman, M. E. P. (1987). Explanatory style and illness. *Journal of Personality, 55,* 237–265.

Peterson, C., & Seligman, M. E. P. (2004). *Character strengths and virtues: A handbook and classification.* New York: Oxford University Press.

Peterson, C. A. (1997). Tests in print, IV. *Journal of Personality Assessment, 68,* 475–477.

Peterson, G. W., & Rollins, B. C. (1987). Parent-Child Socialization. In M. B. Sussman & S. K. Steinmetz (Eds.), *Handbook of marriage and the family.* New York: Plenum.

Phelps, M. E., & Mazziotta, J. C. (1985). Positron emission tomography: Human brain function and biochemistry. *Science, 228,* 799–809.

Phinney, J. S. (1989). Stages of ethnic identity development in minority group adolescents. *Journal of Early Adolescence, 9,* 34–49.

Phinney, J. S., & Rosenthal, D. A. (1992). Ethnic identity in adolescence: Process, context, and outcome. In G. R. Adams, T. P. Gullotta, & R. Montemayor, R. (Eds.), *Advances in Adolescent Development (Adolescent identity formation), 4,* 145–172. Newbury Park, CA: Sage.

Picard, R. W. (1997). *Affective computing.* Cambridge, MA: MIT Press.

Pietikainen, P. (1998). Archetypes as symbolic forms. *Journal of Analytical Psychology, 43,* 325–343.

Pillemer, D. B. (2000). *Momentous events, vivid memories.* Cambridge, MA: Harvard University Press.

Pillemer, D. B. (2001). Momentous events and the life story. *Review of General Psychology, 5,* 123–134.

Pillemer, D. B., Picariello, M. L., & Pruett, J. C. (1994). Very long-term memories of a salient preschool event. *Applied Cognitive Psychology, 8,* 95–106.

Pinker, S. (1997). *How the mind works.* New York: W. W. Norton.

Plomin, R. (1990). *Nature and nurture.* Pacific Grove, CA: Brooks/Cole.

Plomin, R., DeFries, J. C., & Roberts, M. K. (1977). Assortive mating by unwed biological parents of adopted children. *Science, 196,* 449–450.

Plutchik, R. (1980). *Emotion: A psychoevolutionary synthesis.* New York: Harper & Row.

Plutchik, R. (1984). Emotions: A general psychoevolutionary theory. In K. R. Scherer & P. Ekman (Eds.), *Approaches to emotion* (pp. 197–219). Hillsdale, NJ: Lawrence Erlbaum.

Plutchik, R. (1991). Emotions and evolution. In K. T. Strongman (Ed.), *International Review of Studies on Emotion* (Vol. 1, pp. 37–58). New York: Wiley.

Pohl, F., & Moravec, H. (1993). Souls in silicon. *Omni, 16,* 66–71.

Polivy, J. (1976). Perception of calories and regulation of intake in restrained and unrestrained subjects. *Addictive Behaviors, 1,* 237–243.

Polivy, J., Herman, C. P., Hackett, R., & Kuleshnyk, I. (1986). The effects of self-attention and public attention on eating in restrained and unrestrained subjects. *Journal of Personality and Social Psychology, 50,* 1253–1260.

Poulton, R., Waldie, K. E., Menzies, R. G., Craske, M. G., & Silva, P. A. (2001). Failure to overcome 'innate' fear. A developmental test of the non-associative model of fear acquisition. *Behavioural Research Therapy, 35,* 413–421.

Powell, A., & Royce, J. R. (1981). An overview of a multifactor-system theory of personality and individual differences: I. The factor and system models and the hierarchical factor structure of individuality. *Journal of Personality and Social Psychology, 41,* 818–829.

Powell, B., & Steelman, L. C. (1995). Feeling the pinch: Child spacing and constrains on parental economic investments in children. *Social Forces, 73,* 1465–1486.

Powers, W. T. (1973a). Feedback: Beyond behaviorism. *Science, 179,* 351–356.

Powers, W. T. (1973b). *Behavior: The control of perception.* Chicago, IL: Aldine.

Presson, P. K., & Benassi, V. A. (1996). Illusion of control: A meta-analytic review. *Journal of Social Behavior and Personality, 11,* 493–510.

Pribram, K. H. (1978). Consciousness: A scientific approach. *Journal of Indian Psychology, 1,* 95–118.

Pribram, K. H., & Meade, S. D. (1999). Conscious awareness: Processing in the synaptodendritic web. *New Ideas in Psychology, 17,* 205–214.

Price, D. J. (1963). *Little science, big science.* New York: Columbia University Press.

Price, D. J. (1986). *Little science, big science...and beyond.* New York: Columbia University Press.

Prince, M. (1921/1973). *The unconscious* (2nd ed.). New York: Arno Press.

Prochaska, J. O., & Norcross, J. C. (1999). *Systems of psychotherapy* (4th ed.). CITY: Brooks/Cole Publishing.

Prokop, C. K., Bradley, L. A., Burish, T. G., Anderson, K. O., & Fox, J. E. (1991). *Health psychology: Clinical methods and research.* New York: Macmillan.

Purifoy, F. E., & Koopmans, L. H. (1979). Androstenedione, testosterone, and free testosterone concentration in women of various occupations. *Social Biology, 26,* 179–188.

Putnam, F. W. (1991). Recent research on multiple personality disorder. *Psychiatric Clinics of North America, 14,* 489–502.

Putnam, F. W., & Carlson, E. B. (1998). Hypnosis, dissociation, and trauma: Myths, metaphors, and mechanisms. In J. D. Bremmer & C. R. Marmar (Eds.), *Trauma, memory, and dissociation* (pp. 27–55). Washington, DC: American Psychiatric Press.

Pyszczynski, T., Greenberg, J., & Holt, K. (1985). Maintaining consistency between self-serving beliefs and available data: A bias in information processing. *Personality and Social Psychology Bulletin, 11,* 179–190.

Quain, J. R. (January 21, 2002). Wiseguy. *Popular Science,* 64–68.

Radziszewska, B., Richardson, J. L., Dent, C. W., & Flay, B. R. (1996). Parenting style and adolescent depressive symptoms, smoking, and academic achievement: Ethnic, gender, and SES differences. *Journal of Behavioral Medicine, 19,* 289–305.

Rapaport, D. (1960). The structure of psychoanalytic theory: A systematizing attempt (Monograph 6). *Psychological Issues, 2,* 1–158.

Rapaport, D. (1967). The points of view and assumptions of metapsychology. In M. M. Gill (Ed.), *The collected papers of David Rapaport* (pp. 795–811). New York: Basic Books.

Rapetti, R. (1996). Gauguin, Paul. In J. Turner (Ed.), *The dictionary of art* (pp. 187–196). London: Macmillan.

Raykov, T., & Marcoulides, G. A. (2000). *A first course in structural equation modeling.* Mahwah, NJ: Lawrence Erlbaum.

Read, S. J., & Miller, L. C. (2002). Virtual personalities: A neural network model of personality. *Personality and Social Psychology Review, 6,* 357–369.

Redlich, F., & Bingham, J. (1960). *The inside story: Psychiatry and everyday life.* New York: Vintage Books.

Ree, M. J., & Earles, J. A. (1992). Intelligence is the best predictor of job performance. *Current Directions in Psychological Science, 1,* 86–89.

Reed, T. E., & Jensen, A. R. (1991). Arm nerve conduction velocity (NCV), reaction time, and intelligence. *Intelligence, 15,* 33–47.

Reid, T. (1971). (Facsimile reproduction:) *Essays on the intellectual powers of man.* Scolar Press. [Original work published 1785, Menston, England.]

Reingold, E. M., & Merikle, P. M. (1988). Using direct and indirect measures to study perception without awareness. *Perception and Psychophysics, 44,* 563–575.

Reynolds, C. R., Chastain, R. L., Kaufman, A. S., & McLean, J. E. (1987). Demographic characteristics and IQ among adults: Analysis of the WAIS-R standardization sample as a function of the stratification variables. *Journal of School Psychology, 25,* 323–342.

Reynolds, J. (1966). *Discourses on art.* New York: Collier. [Original work published 1769–1790.]

Richards, R., Kinney, D. K., Lunde, I., Benet, M., & Merzel, A. P. C. (1988). *Journal of Abnormal Psychology, 97,* 281–288.

Richters, J. E., & Cicchetti, D. (1993). Mark Twain meets *DSM-IIIR.*. Conduct disorder, development, and the concept of harmful dysfunction. *Development and Psychopathology, 5,* 5–29.

Riemer, A. (2001). *Hughes.* Sydney: Duffy & Snellgrove.

Rifkin, A., Ghisalbert D., Dimatou, S., Jin, C., & Sethi, M. (1998). Dissociative identity disorder in psychiatric inpatients. *American Journal of Psychiatry, 155,* 144–145.

Roback, A. A. (1928). *The psychology of character; With a survey of temperament.* New York: Harcourt, Brace.

Roberts, B. W., Caspi, A., & Moffitt, T. E. (2003). Work experiences and personality development in young adulthood. *Journal of Personality and Social Psychology, 84,* 582–593.

Roberts, B. W., & Robins, R. W. (2000). Broad dispositions, broad aspirations: The intersection of personality traits and major life goals. *Personality and Social Psychology Bulletin, 26,* 1284–1296.

Roberts, R. D., Zeidner, M., & Matthews, G. (2001). Does emotional intelligence meet traditional standards for an intelligence? Some new data and conclusions. *Emotion, 1,* 196–231.

Robins, R. W., Fraley, R. C., Roberts, B. W., & Trzesniewski, K. H. (2001). A longitudinal study of personality change in young adulthood. *Journal of Personality, 69,* 617–640.

Robins, R. W., John, O. P., & Caspi, A. (1998). The typological approach to studying personality. In R. B. Cairns, L. R. Bergman, & J. Kagan (Eds.), *Methods and models for studying the individual* (pp. 135–157). Thousand Oaks, CA: Sage.

Robins, R. W., John, O. P., Caspi, A., Moffitt, T. E., & Stouthamer-Loeber, M. (1996). Resilient, overcontrolled, and undercontrolled boys: Three replicable personality types. *Journal of Personality and Social Psychology, 70,* 157–171.

Robinson, D. N. (1995). *An intellectual history of psychology* (3rd ed.). Madison: University of Wisconsin Press.

Robinson, J. P., Shaver, P. R., & Wrightsman, L. S. (1991). *Measures of personality and social psychological attitudes.* San Diego, CA: Academic Press.

Rodgers, J. L. (2001). What causes birth order-intelligence patterns. *American Psychologist, 56,* 505–510.

Rogers, C. R. (1951). *Client-centered therapy.* Boston: Houghton Mifflin.

Rogers, C. R. (1954). Towards a theory of creativity. *ETC: A Review of General Semantics, 11,* 249–260.

Rogers, C. R. (1959). A theory of therapy, personality, and interpersonal relationships, as developed in the client-centered framework. In S. Koch (Ed.), *Psychology: A study of a science: Vol. 3: Formulations of the person and the social context* (pp. 185–256). New York: McGraw-Hill.

Rokeach, M. (1960). *The open and closed mind.* New York: Basic Books.

Rokeach, M. (1973). *The nature of human values.* New York: Free Press.

Rorer, L. G. (1990). Personality assessment: A conceptual survey. In L. A. Pervin (Ed.), *Handbook of personality: Theory and research* (pp. 693–720). New York: Guilford.

Rosch, E., Mervis, C. B., Gray, W., Johnson, D., & Boyes-Braem, P. (1976). Basic objects in natural categories. *Cognitive Psychology, 8,* 382–439.

Roseman, I. J. (1984). Cognitive determinants of emotions: A structural theory. In P. Shaver (Ed.), *Review of personality and social psychology: Vol. 5. Emotions, relationships, and health* (pp. 11–36). Beverly Hills, CA: Sage.

Roseman, I. J., & Smith, C. A. (2001). Appraisal theory: Overview, assumptions, varieties, controversies. In K. R. Scherer, A. Schorr, T. Johnstone (Eds.), *Appraisal theories in emotion: Theory, methods, research* (pp. 3–19). London: Oxford University Press.

Rosen, D. H., Smith, S. M., Huston, H. L., & Gonzalez, G. (1991). Empirical study of associations between symbols and their meanings: Evidence of collective unconscious (archetypal) memory. *Journal of Analytical Psychology, 36,* 211–228.

Rosenbaum, D. A. (1991). *Human motor control.* New York: Academic Press.

Rosenbaum, D. A. (2005). The Cinderella of psychology: The neglect of motor control in the science of mental life and behavior. *American Psychologist, 60,* 308–317.

Rosenberg, A. (2000). *Philosophy of science: A contemporary introduction.* New York: Routledge.

Rosenberg, M. (1965). *Society and the adolescent self-image.* Princeton, NJ: Princeton University Press.

Rosenthal, D. (1993). Higher-order thoughts and the appendage theory of consciousness. *Philosophical Psychology, 6,* 155–166.

Rosenthal, D. (2002). The higher-order thought model of consciousness. In R. Carter (Auth. & Ed.). *Exploring consciousness* (pp. 45–47). Berkeley: University of California Press.

Rosenthal, G. G., Evans, C. S., & Miller, W. L. (1996). Female preference for dynamic traits in the green swordtail, Xiphophorus helleri. *Animal Behavior, 51,* 811–820.

Rosenzweig, S. (1941). Need-persistive and ego defensive reactions to frustration as demonstrated by an experiment on repression. *Psychological Review, 48,* 347–349.

Ross, A. O. (1987). *Personality: The scientific study of complex behavior.* New York: Holt, Rinehart, & Winston.

Ross, J. M. (2003). Preconscious defense analysis, memory, and structural change. *International Journal of Psychoanalysis, 84,* 59–76.

Ross, L., Greene, D., & House, P. (1977). The "false consensus effect": An egocentric bias in social perception and attribution processes. *Journal of Experimental and Social Psychology, 13,* 279–301.

Rothbart, M. K. (1981). Measurement of temperament in infancy. *Child Development, 52,* 569–578.

Rothbart, M. K., Ahadi, S. A., & Evans, D. E. (2000). Temperament and personality: Origins and outcomes. *Journal of Personality and Social Psychology, 73,* 122–135.

Rothbart, M. K., & Mauro, J. A. (1990). Questionnaire approaches to the study of infant temperament. In J. W. Fagen & J. Colombo (Eds.), *Individual differences in infancy: reliability, stability, and prediction* (pp. 411–429). Hillsdale, NJ: Erlbaum.

Rothbart, M. K., & Putnam, S. P. (2002). Temperament and socialization. In L. Pulkkinen & A. Caspi (Eds.), *Paths to successful development: Personality in the life course* (pp. 19–45). Cambridge: Cambridge University Press.

Rotter, J. B. (1954). *Social learning and clinical psychology*. New York: Prentice Hall.

Rotter, J. B. (1990). Internal versus external control of reinforcement: A case history of a variable. *American Psychologist, 45,* 489–493.

Rozin, P. (1976). The evolution of intelligence and access to the cognitive unconscious. In J. M. Sprague & A. A. Epstein (Eds.), *Progress in psychobiology and physiological psychology* (pp. 245–280). New York: Academic Press.

Rubin, M. M. (1999). Emotional intelligence and its role in mitigating aggression: A correlational study of the relationship between emotional intelligence and aggression in urban adolescents. Unpublished dissertation, Immaculata College, Immaculata, Pennsylvania.

Ruble, T. L. (1983). Sex stereotypes: Issues of changes in the 1970's. *Sex Roles, 9,* 397–402.

Runco, M. A. (1986). Predicting children's creative performance. *Psychological Reports, 59,* 1247–1254.

Russell, J. A. (1999). On the bipolarity of positive and negative affect. *Psychological Bulletin, 125,* 3–30.

Russell, J. A., & Barrett, L. F. (1999). Core affect, prototypical emotional episodes, and other things called emotion: Dissecting the elephant. *Journal of Personality and Social Psychology, 76,* 805–819.

Russell, J. A., Weiss, A. & Mendelsohn, G. A. (1989). Affect Grid: A single-item scale of pleasure and arousal. *Journal of Personality and Social Psychology, 57,* 493–502.

Rutter, M. (2000). Resilience reconsidered: Conceptual considerations, empirical findings, and policy implications. In J. P. Shonkoff & J. S. Meisels (Eds.), *Handbook of early child intervention* (2nd ed.) (pp. 651682). New York: Cambridge University Press.

Rychlak, J. F. (1981). *Introduction to personality and psychotherapy* (2nd ed.). Boston: Houghton Mifflin Company.

Ryckman, R. M. (2004). *Theories of personality*. Belmont, CA: Wadsworth/Thomson Learning.

Ryff, C. D. (1989). Happiness is everything, or is it? Explorations on the meaning of psychological well-being. *Journal of Personality and Social Psychology, 57,* 1069–1081.

Ryle, G. (1949). *The concept of mind*. New York: Barnes & Noble.

Saad, G., Gill, T., & Nataraajan, R. (2005). Are laterborns more innovative and nonconforming consumers than firstborns? A Darwinian perspective. *Journal of Business Research, 58,* 902–909.

Saarni, C. (2000). The social context of emotional development. In M. Lewis & J. M. Haviland-Jones (Eds.), *Handbook of Emotions* (2nd ed.) (pp. 306–332). New York: Guilford.

Sager, M. (November, 1999). The smartest man in America. *Esquire, 132,* 145–148, 184, 186.

Salovey, P., & Mayer, J.D. (1990). Emotional intelligence. *Imagination, Cognition, and Personality, 9,* 185–211.

Salovey, P., Mayer, J. D., Goldman, S., Turvey, C., & Palfai, T. P. (1995). Emotional attention, clarity, and repair: Exploring emotional intelligence using the trait meta-mood scale. In J. W. Pennebaker (Ed.), *Emotion, disclosure, and health* (pp.

125–154). Washington, DC: American Psychological Association.

Salovey, P., Mayer, J. D., & Rosenhan, D. L. (1991). Mood and helping: Mood as a motivator of helping and helping as a regulator of mood. In M. S. Clark (Ed.), *Prosocial behavior/ Review of Personality and Social Psychology, 12,* 215–237.

Salovey, P., Rothman, A. J., Detweiler, J. B., & Steward, W. T. (2000). Emotional states and physical health. *American Psychologist, 55,* 110–121.

Sampson, E. E. (1989). The challenge of social change for psychology: Globalization and psychology's theory of the person. *American Psychologist, 44,* 914–921.

Sanford, N. (1963). Personality: Its place in psychology. In S. Koch (Ed.), *Psychology: A study of a science* (Vol. 5, pp. 488–592). New York: McGraw-Hill.

Sanford, N. (1970). *Issues in personality psychology*. San Francisco: Jossey-Bass.

Sattler, J. M. (1992). *Assessment of children: WISC-III and SPPSI-R supplement*. San Diego: Author.

Saucier, G. (1992). Benchmarks: Integrating affective and interpersonal circles with the Big-Five personality factors. *Journal of Personality and Social Psychology, 62,* 1025–1035.

Saucier, G., & Goldberg, L. R. (1998). What is beyond the Big Five? *Journal of Personality, 66,* 495–524.

Saucier, G., & Goldberg, L. R. (2001). Lexical studies of indigenous personality factors: Premises, products, and prospects. *Journal of Personality, 69,* 847–879.

Saucier, G., Ostendorf, F., & Peabody, D. (2001). The non-evaluative circumplex of personality adjectives. *Journal of Personality, 69,* 537–582.

Scarr, S. (1981). *Race, social class, and individual differences in I.Q.* Hillsdale, NJ: Erlbaum.

Schank, R., & Abelson, R. (1977). *Scripts, plans, goals and understanding*. Hillsdale, NJ: Lawrence Erlbaum.

Scheflin, A. W., Spiegel, H., & Spiegel, D. (1998). Forensic uses of hypnosis. In A. K. Hess & Weiner, I. B. (Eds.), *The handbook of forensic psychology* (2nd ed.). New York: Wiley.

Scheier, M. F., & Carver, C. S. (1985). Optimism, coping, and health: Assessment and implications of generalized outcome expectancies. *Health Psychology, 4,* 219–247.

Scherer, K. R. Schorr, A., & Johnstone, T. (Eds.) (2001). *Appraisal theories in emotion: Theory, methods, research*. London: Oxford University Press.

Schlaug, G., Jaencke, L., Huang, Y. Staiger, J. F., et al. (1995). Increased corpus callosum size in musicians. *Neuropsychologia, 33,* 1047–1055.

Schlenker, B. R., Weigold, M. F., & Hallam, J. R. (1990). Self-serving attributions in social context: Effects of self-esteem and social pressure. *Journal of Personality and Social Psychology, 58,* 855–863.

Schmitt, D. P., & Buss, D. M. (2000). Sexual dimensions of person description: Beyond or subsumed by the Big Five? *Journal of Research in Personality, 34,* 141–177.

Schopenhauer, A. (1819/1966). World as will and representation (E. F. J. Payne, Trans.). New York: Dover. [Original translation published 1958; Original work published 1819].

Schretlen, D., Pearson, G. D., Anthony, J. C., Aylward, E. H., Augustine, A. M., Davis, A., & Barta, P. (2000). Elucidating the contributions of processing speed, executive ability, and frontal lobe volume to normal age-related differences in fluid intelligence. *Journal of the International Neuropsychological Society, 6,* 52–61.

Schulman, M. (2002). How we become moral. In C. R. Snyder & S. J. Lopez (Eds.), *Handbook of positive psychology* (pp. 499–512). New York: Oxford University Press.

Schultz, D. P., & Schulz, S. E. (2001). *Theories of personality.* Belmont, CA: Wadsworth.

Schultz, L. H., Barr, D. J., & Selman, R. L. (2001). The value of a developmental approach to evaluating character development programees: An outcome study of *Facing History and Ourselves. Journal of Moral Education, 30,* 3–27.

Schutte, N. S., Malouff, J. M., & Simunek, M. (2002). Characteristic emotional intelligence and emotional well-being. *Cognition and Emotion, 16,* 769–785.

Schwartz. D., Dodge, K. A., & Coie, J. D. (1993). The emergence of chronic peer victimization in boys' play groups. *Child Development, 64,* 1755–1772.

Schwartz, D., Dodge, K. A., Pettit, G. S., & Bates, J. E. (1997). The early socialization of aggressive victims of bullying. *Child development, 68,* 665–675.

Schwartz, D., Dodge, K. A., Pettit, G. S., & Bates, J. E. (2000). Friendship as a moderating factor in the pathway between early harsh home environment and later victimization in the peer group. *Developmental Psychology, 36,* 646–662.

Schwartz, G. E., Weinberger, D.A., & Singer, J. A. (1981). Cardiovascular differentiation of happiness, sadness, anger, and fear following imagery and exercise. *Psychosomatic Medicine, 43,* 343–364.

Scott, M., & Lyman, S. M. (1968). Accounts. *The American Sociological Review, 33,* 46–62.

Seabrook, J. (1999). Letter from the Skywalker Ranch: Is the force still with us? In S. Kline (Ed.), *George Lucas Interviews.* Jackson, MI: University of Mississippi Press. [Original published in the *New Yorker,* January 6, 1997, pp. 40–53.]

Sears, R. R. (1950). Personality. *Annual Review of Psychology, 1,* 105–118.

Sears, R. R. (1959). Personality theory: The next forty years. *Monographs of the Society for Research in Child Development, 24,* (Serial No. 74: 37–50).

Segal, N. L. (2000). *Entwined lives: Twins and what they tell us about human behavior.* New York: Dutton/Penguin.

Segal, Z. V. (1988). Appraisal of self-schema in cognitive models of depression. *Psychological Bulletin, 103,* 147–162.

Segal, Z. V., Gemar, M., & Williams, S. (1999). Differential cognitive response to a mood challenge following successful cognitive therapy or pharmacotherapy for unipolar depression. *Journal of Abnormal Psychology, 108,* 3–10.

Segerstrom, S. C. (2001). Optimism, goal conflict, and stressor-related immune change. *Journal of Behavioral Medicine, 24,* 441–467.

Segerstrom, S. C. (2005). Optimism and immunity: Do positive thoughts always lead to positive effects? *Brain, Behavior and Immunity, 19,* 195–200.

Seligman, M. E. P. (1975). *Helplessness: On depression, development, and death.* San Francisco: Freeman.

Seligman, M. E. P., & Csikszentmihalyi, M. (2000). Positive psychology: An introduction. *American Psychologist, 55,* 5–14.

Seligman, M. E. P., & Csikszentmihalyi, M. (2001). Reply to comments. *American Psychologist, 56,* 89–90.

Seltzer, R., & Glass, W. (1991). International politics and judging in Olympic skating events: 1968–1988. *Journal of Sport Behavior, 14,* 189–200.

Shafer, A. B. (2001). The big five and sexuality trait terms as predictors of relationships and sex. *Journal of Research in Personality 35,* 313–338.

Shakespeare, W. (1936). The Merchant of Venice. In W. A. Wright (Ed.), *The complete works of William Shakespeare. The Cambridge edition text.* Garden City, NY: Doubleday & Company. [Original published in c. 1598.]

Shakespeare, W. (1936). Macbeth. In W. A. Wright (Ed.), *The complete works of William Shakespeare. The Cambridge edition text.* Garden City, NY: Doubleday & Company. [Original work published in c. 1606.]

Shakespeare, W. (1936). *The complete works of William Shakespeare* (W.A. Wright, Ed.). Garden City, NY: Doubleday & Company.

Shapiro, D. L., & Bies, R. J. (1994). Threats, bluffs, and disclaimers in negotiations. *Organizational Behavior & Human Decision Processes, 60,* 14–35.

Sharp, S. E. (1899). Individual psychology: A study in psychological method. *The American Journal of Psychology, 10,* 329–391.

Shea, D. L., Lubinski, D., & Benbow, C. P. (2001). Importance of assessing spatial ability in intellectually talented young adolescents: A 20-year longitudinal study. *Journal of Educational Psychology, 93,* 604–614.

Shedler, J., & Block, J. (1990). Adolescent drug use and psychological health: A longitudinal inquiry. *American Psychologist, 45,* 612–630.

Sheldon, K. M., & Kasser, T. (1998). Pursuing personal goals: Skills enable progress but not all progress is beneficial. *Personality and Social Psychology Bulletin, 24,* 1319–1331.

Sheldon, K. M., & Kasser, T. (2001). Goals, congruence, and positive well-being: New empirical support for the humanistic theories. *Journal of Humanistic Psychology, 41,* 30–50.

Sheldon, W. H., & Stevens, S. S. (1940). *The varieties of human physique.* New York: Harper.

Sheldon, W. H., & Stevens, S. S. (1942). *The varieties of temperament.* New York: Harper.

Shepard, R. N., & Metzler, J. (1971). Mental rotation of three-dimensional objects. *Science, 171,* 701–703.

Sherif, M., & Hovland, C. I. (1961). *Social judgment.* New Haven: Yale University Press.

Shill, M. A., & Lumley, M. A. (2000). The Psychological Mindedness Scale: Factor structure, convergent validity and gender in a non-psychiatric sample. *Psychology and Psychotherapy: Theory, Research and Practice, 75,* 131–150.

Shoda, Y., & Leetiernan, S. (2002). What remains invariant? Finding order within a person's thoughts, feelings, and behaviors across situations. In D. Cervone & W. Mischel (Eds.), *Advances in personality science* (pp. 241–270). New York: Guilford.

Shoda, Y., Mischel, W., & Wright, J.C. (1994). Intraindividual stability in the organization and patterning of behavior: Incorporating psychological situations into the idiographic analysis of personality. *Journal of Personality and Social Psychology, 67(4),* 674–687.

Shor, R. E., & Orne, M. T. (Eds.). (1965). *The nature of hypnosis; selected basic readings.* New York: Holt, Rinehart, & Winston.

Shostrom, E. L. (1964). An inventory for the measurement of self-actualization. *Educational and Psychological Measurement, 24,* 207–217.

Showers, C. J. (2002). Integration and compartmentalization: A model of self-structure and self-change. In D. Cervone & W. Mischel (Eds.), *Advances in personality science* (pp. 271–291). New York: Guilford.

Showers, C. J., Abramson, L. Y., & Hogan, M. E. (1998). The dynamic self: How the content and structure of the self-concept change with mood. *Journal of Personality and Social Psychology, 75,* 478–493.

Showers, C. J. & Ryff, C. D. (1996). Self-differentiation and well-being in a life transition. *Personality and Social Psychology Bulletin, 22,* 448–460.

Shweder, R. A. (1975). How relevant is an individual difference theory of personality? *Journal of Personality Psychology, 43,* 455–484.

Shweder, R. A., & D'Andrade, R. G. (1979). Accurate reflection or systematic distortion? A reply to Block, Weiss, & Thorne. *Journal of Personality and Social Psychology, 37,* 1075–1084.

Siegel, J. P., & Spellman, M. E. (2002). The dyadic splitting scale. *The American Journal of Family Therapy, 30,* 117–124.

Siegler, I. C., George, L. K., & Okun, M. A. (1979). Cross-sequential analysis of adult personality. *Developmental Psychology, 15,* 350–351.

Simonton, D. K. (1997). Creative productivity: A predictive and explanatory model of career trajectories and landmarks. *Psychological Review, 104,* 66–89.

Simonton, D. K. (1994). *Greatness: Who makes history and why.* New York: Guilford.

Simonton, D. (1986). Presidential personality: Biographical use of the Gough Adjective Check List. *Journal of Personality and Social Psychology, 51,* 149–160.

Simonton, D. (1988). Presidential style: Personality, biography, and performance. *Journal of Personality and Social Psychology, 55,* 928–936.

Simonton, D. K. (2002). Creativity. In C. R. Snyder & S. J. Lopez (Eds.), *Handbook of positive psychology* (pp. 189–201). New York: Oxford University Press.

Singer, J. A. (1997). *Message in a bottle: Stories of men and addiction.* New York: Free Press.

Singer, J. A. (1998). Applying a Systems Framework to self-defining memories. *Psychological Inquiry, 9,* 161–164.

Singer, J. A, & Bluck, S. (2001). New perspectives on autobiographical memory: The integration of narrative processing and autobiographical reasoning. *Review of General Psychology, 5,* 91–99.

Singer, J. A., & Salovey, P. (1993). *The remembered self: Emotion and memory in personality.* New York: Free Press.

Singer, J. L. (1966). *Daydreaming: An introduction to the experimental study of inner experience.* New York: Random House.

Singer, J. L. (1975). Navigating the stream of consciousness: Research in daydreaming and related inner experience. *American Psychologist, 30,* 727–738.

Singer, J. L. (1984). The private personality. *Personality and Social Psychology, 10,* 7–30.

Six, B., & Eckes, T. (1991). A closer look at the complex structure of gender stereotypes. *Sex Roles, 24,* 64.

Skinner, B. F. (1953). *Science and human behavior.* New York: Knopf.

Skinner, B. F. (1974). *About behaviorism.* New York: Knopf.

Skodak, M., & Skeels, H. M. (1949). A final follow-up of one hundred adopted children. *Journal of Genetic Psychology, 75,* 85–125.

Sleek, S. (1998). Blame your peers, not your parents, author says. *APA Monitor, 29* [Online version: www.apa.org/monitor/oct98/peers.html].

Smith, G. M. (1967). Usefulness of peer ratings of personality in educational research. *Educational and psychological measurement, 27,* 967–984.

Smith, C. A., & Ellsworth, P. C. (1985). Patterns of cognitive appraisal in emotion. *Journal of Personality and Social Psychology, 48,* 813–838.

Smith, M. L., & Glass G. V. (1977). Meta-analysis of psychotherapy outcome studies. *American Psychologist, 32,* 752–760.

Smith, M. L., Glass, G. V., & Miller, T. I. (1980). *The benefits of psychotherapy.* Baltimore: Johns Hopkins University Press.

Smith, R. (September, 2002). Cosmo quiz: Are you open to change? *Cosmopolitan, 234,* 236.

Snow, R. (1995). Foreword. In D. H. Saklofske & M. Zeidner (Eds.), *International handbook of personality and intelligence* (pp. 11–15). New York: Plenum.

Snyder, C. R. (1995). *Coping: The psychology of what works.* New York: Oxford University Press.

Snyder, C. R. & Lopez, S. J. (Eds.) (2002). *The handbook of positive psychology* (pp. 159–171). New York: Oxford University Press.

Snyder, M. & Swann, W. B. (1978). Hypothesis-testing processes in social interaction. *Journal of Personality and Social Psychology, 36,* 1202–1212.

Snyderman, M., & Rothman, S. (1987). Survey of expert opinion on intelligence and aptitude testing. *American Psychologist, 42,* 137–144.

Solomon, R. L., & Corbit, J.D. (1974). An opponent-process theory of motivation: I. Temporal dynamics of affect. *Psychological Review, 81,* 119–145.

Solomon, S., Greenberg, J., & Pyszczynski, T. (1991). A terror-management theory of social behavior: The psychological functions of self-esteem and cultural worldviews. In M. P. Zanna (Ed.), *Advances in experimental social psychology* (pp. 91–159). San Diego: Academic Press.

Sontag, L. W., Baker, C. T., & Nelson, V. L. (1958). Mental growth and personality development: A longitudinal study. *Monographs of the Society for Research in Child Development, 23*(2, Serial No. 68).

Sorce, J. F. & Emde, R. N. (1981). Mother's presence is not enough: Effect of emotional availability on infant exploration. *Developmental Psychology, 17,* 737–745.

Sorce, J. F., Emde, R. N., Campos, J. J., & Klinnert, M. D. (1985). Maternal emotional signaling: Its effect on the visual cliff behavior of 1-year-olds. *Developmental Psychology, 21,* 195–200.

Spaeth, E. B. (1999). What a lawyer needs to learn. In R. J. Sternberg & J. A. Horvath (Eds.), *Tacit knowledge in professional practice: Researcher and professional perspectives* (pp. 21–36). Mahwah, NJ: Lawrence Erlbaum.

Spain, J. S., Eaton, L. G., & Funder, D. (2000) Perspectives on personality: The relative accuracy of self versus others for the prediction of emotion and behavior. *Journal of Personality, 68,* 837–867.

Spearman, C. (1904). General intelligence determined and measured. *American Journal of Psychology, 15,* 201–293.

Spearman, C. (1927). *The abilities of man.* New York: Macmillan.

Spence, J. T., Helmreich, R., & Stapp, J. (1974). The Personal Attributes Questionnaire: A measure of sex-role stereotypes and masculinity and femininity. *Journal Supplement Abstract Service Catalog of Selected Documents in Psychology, 4,* 42 (No. 617).

Spielberger, C. D., & DeNike, L. D. (1966). Descriptive behaviorism versus cognitive theory in verbal operant conditioning. *Psychological Review, 73,* 306–326.

Spiller, H. A., Hale, J. R., & De Boer, J. Z. (2002). The Delphic oracle: A multidisciplinary defense of the gaseous vent theory. *Clinical Toxicology, 40,* 189–196.

Spinoza, B. (2000). *Ethica* (G. H. R. Parkinson, Ed. & Trans.). New York: Oxford University Press. (Original work published 1677).

Spitz, R. (1946). Anaclitic depression. *Psychoanalytic Study of the Child, 2,* 313–342.

Stagner, R. (1937). *Psychology of personality.* New York: McGraw-Hill.

Stanislavsky, K. (1948). *An actor prepares* (E. R. Hapgood, Trans.). New York: Theatre Arts Books.

Statman, D. (Ed.). (1993). *Moral luck.* Albany, NY: State University of New York Press.

Steele, C. M. (1998). Stereotyping and its threat are real. *American Psychologist, 53,* 680–681.

Steele, C. M., & Aronson, J. (1995). Stereotype threat and the intellectual test performance of African Americans. *Journal of Personality and Social Psychology, 69,* 797–811.

Steelman, L. C., Powell, B., Werum, R., & Carter, S. (2002). Reconsidering the effects of sibling configuration: Recent advances and challenges. *Annual Review of Sociology, 28,* 243–269.

Steinberg, L. Lamborn, S. D., Darling, N., Mounts, N. S., & Dornbush, S. (1994). Over-time changes in adjustment and competence among adolescents from authoritative, authoritarian, indulgent, and neglectful families. *Child Development, 65,* 754–770.

Steinsaltz, A. (1987). Soul searchng. In A. A. Cohen & P. Mendes-Flohr (Eds.), *Contemporary Jewish religious thought* (pp. 897–902). New York: Free Press.

Stern, D. (1987). *The interpersonal world of the infant.* New York: Basic Books.

Stern, W. (1914). *The psychological methods of intelligence testing* (G. M. Whipple, Trans.). Baltimore: Warwick and York.

Sternberg, C. R. & Campos, J. J. (1990). The development of anger expressions in infancy. In N. L. Stein & B. Leventhal (Eds.), *Psychological and biological approaches to emotion* (pp. 247–282). Hillsdale, NJ: Erlbaum.

Sternberg, R. J. (1981). Intelligence and non-entrenchment. *Journal of Educational Psychology, 73,* 1–16.

Sternberg, R. J. (1986). A triangular theory of love. *Psychological Review, 93,* 119–135.

Sternberg, R. J. (1987). Liking versus loving: A comparative evaluation of theories. *Psychological Bulletin, 102,* 331–345.

Sternberg, R. J. (1997). Construct validation of a triangular love scale. *European Journal of Social Psychology, 27,* 313–335.

Sternberg, R. J. (1997). The concept of intelligence and its role in lifelong learning and success. *American Psychologist, 52,* 1030–1037.

Sternberg, R. J. (2003). Our research program validating the triarchic theory of successful intelligence: Reply to Gottfredson. *Intelligence, 31,* 399–413.

Sternberg, R. J. (2003). A broad view of intelligence: The theory of successful intelligence. *Consulting Psychology Journal: Practice & Research, 55,* 39–154.

Sternberg, R. J., Forsythe, G. B., Helund, J., Horvath, J. A., Wagner, R. I., Williams, W. M., Snook, S. A., & Grigorenko, E. L. (2000). *Practical intelligence in everyday life.* New York: Cambridge University Press.

Sternberg, R. J., & Grigorenko, E. (2001). Unified psychology, 56, 1069–1079.

Sternberg, R. J., & Horvath, J. A. (Eds). (1999). *Tacit knowledge in professional practice: Researcher and practitioner perspectives.* Mahwah, NJ: Lawrence Erlbaum.

Sternberg, R. J., & O'Hara, L. A. (2000). Intelligence and creativity. In R. J. Sternberg (Ed.), *Handbook of intelligence* (pp. 611–630). Cambridge: Cambridge University Press.

Sternberg, R. J., & Ruzgis, P. (Eds.). (1994). *Personality and intelligence.* Cambridge: Cambridge University Press.

Stevens, A. (2000). Jungian analysis and evolutionary psychotherapy: An integrative approach. In P. Gilbert & K. G. Bailey (Eds.), *Genes on the couch: Explorations in evolutionary psychotherapy.* New York: Brunner-Routledge.

Stevens, R. (1983). *Erik Erikson: An introduction.* Milton Keynes: The Open University Press.

Stevenson, L., & Haberman, D. L. (1998). *Ten theories of human nature*. Oxford: Oxford University Press.

Stewart, D. (1963). Elements of the philosophy of the human mind. Facsimile reprint by University Microfilms International, Ann Arbor, MI. [Original work published 1833, Cambridge: James Munroe.]

Stewart, N. (1947). A.G.C.T. scores of army personnel grouped by occupation. *Occupation, 26,* 5–41.

Stewart, A. J., & Vandewater, E. A. (1999). "If I had it to do over again . . .": Midlife review, midcourse corrections, and women's well-being in midlife. *Journal of Personality and Social Psychology, 76,* 270–283.

Stifter, C. A., & Moyer, D. (1991). The regulation of positive affect: Gaze aversion activity during mother-infant interaction. *Infant Behavior and Development, 14,* 111–123.

Stillion, J. M., & McDowell, E. E. (2001-2002). The early demise of the "Stronger" sex: Gender-related causes of sex differences in longevity. *Omega, 44,* 301–318.

Stocker, S. (May-June, 2002). Finding the future alcoholic. *The Futurist, 36,* 42–46.

Stokes, R., & Hewitt, J. P. (1976). Aligning actions. *The American Sociological Review, 46,* 838–849.

Stone, W. F., & Schaffner, P. E. (1988). *The psychology of politics.* New York: Springer-Verlag.

Storm, L., & Ertel, S. (2001). Does psi exist? Comments on Milton and Wiseman's (1999) meta-analysis of Ganzfield research. *Psychological Bulletin, 127,* 424–433.

Strachey, J. (1960). Editor's introduction. In Freud, S. (1960). *The ego and the id* (pp. ix–xvii). New York: W. W. Norton.

Styron, W. (1990). *Darkness visible.* New York: Random House.

Sulloway, F. J. (1996). *Born to rebel: Birth order, family dynamics, and creative lives.* New York: Pantheon Books.

Svare, B. B. (1983). *Hormones and aggressive behavior.* New York: Plenum.

Swann, W. B., & Pelham, B. W. (2002). The truth about illusions: Authenticity and positivity in social relationships. In C. R. Snyder & S. J. Lopez (Eds.), *Handbook of positive psychology* (pp. 366–381). New York: Oxford University Press.

Swann, W. B., & Seyle, C. (2005). Personality psychology's comeback and its emerging symbiosis with social psychology. *Personality and Social Psychology Bulletin, 31,* 155–165.

Swift, E. M. (March 4, 2002). Head turner: Skating with utter confidence and uninhibited joy, Sarah Hughes soared from fourth place to gold and became the new queen of the ice. *Sports Illustrated, 96,* 48ff.

Tangney, J. P. (2002). Humility. In C. R. Snyder & S. J. Lopez (Eds.), *Handbook of positive psychology* (pp. 411–419). New York: Oxford University Press.

Tart, C. (1972). *Altered states of consciousness.* Garden City, NY: Doubleday.

Taylor, S. E., & Brown, J. D. (1988). Illusion and well-being: A social psychological perspective on mental health. *Psychological Bulletin, 103,* 193–210.

Taylor, S. E., & Brown, J. D. (1994). Positive illusions and well-being revisited: Separating fact from fiction. *Psychological Bulletin, 116,* 21–27.

Tennen, H., & Affleck, G. (1998). Three compulsions of stress and coping research: A Systems Framework cure? *Psychological Inquiry, 9,* 164–168.

Tennen, H., Affleck, G., Armeli, S., & Carney, M. A. (2000). A daily process approach to coping: Linking theory, research, and practice. *American Psychologist, 55,* 626–636.

Terman, L. M. (1917). The intelligence quotient of Francis Galton in childhood. *American Journal of Psychology, 28,* 208–215.

Terman, L. M. (1926). Excerpts from the early writings of young geniuses (Appendix II). In C. M. Cox (Ed.), *Genetic Studies of Genius Volume II: The early mental traits of three hundred geniuses.* Stanford, CA: Stanford University Press.

Tesser, A. (2002). Constructing a niche for the self: A biosocial, PDP approach to understanding lives. *Self and Identity, 1,* 185–190.

Tetlock, P. E., Peterson, R. S., & Berry, J. M. (1993). Flattering and unflattering personality portraits of integratively simple and complex managers. *Journal of Personality and Social Psychology, 64,* 500–511.

Theophrastus (372-287 BC/1929). Demarcated characters. In X. Edmunds (Ed.), *The characters of Theophrastus* (pp. 48–49).

Thomas, A., Chess, S., & Birch, H. G. (1970). The origin of personality. *Scientific American, 223,* 102–109.

Thomas, W. I. (2003). The definition of the situation. In J. A. Holstein & J. F. Gubrium (Eds.), *Inner lives and social worlds* (pp. 80–81). New York: Oxford University Press. [Original work published 1928.]

Thompson, R. A. (1994). Emotion regulation: A theme in search of definition. *Monographs of the Society for Research in Child Development, 59* (2-3, Serial No. 240, 25–52).

Thorndike, E. L. (1906). *Principles of teaching.* New York: Seiler.

Thorndike, E. L. (1920). Intelligence and its use. *Harper's Magazine, 140,* 227–235.

Thorndike, E. L. (1921). Intelligence and its measurement: A symposium. *Journal of Educational Psychology, 12,* 123–147, 195–216, 271–275.

Thorndike, E. L. & Stein, S. (1937). An evaluation of the attempts to measure social intelligence. *Psychological Bulletin, 34,* 275–285.

Thorndike, R. L., Hagen, E. P., & Sattler, J. P. (1986). *Technical manual for the Stanford-Binet Intelligence Scale, Fourth Edition.* Chicago: Riverside.

Thorne, A., & Klohnen, E. (1993). Interpersonal memories as maps for personality consistency. In D. C. Funder, R. D. Parke, C. Tomlinson-Keasey, & K. Widaman (Eds.), *Studying lives through time: Personality and development* (pp. 223–253). Washington, DC: American Psychological Association.

Thurstone, L. L. (1924). *The nature of intelligence.* New York: Harcourt Brace.

Thurstone, L. L. (1938). *Primary mental abilities.* Chicago: University of Chicago Press.

Tice, D. M. (1992). Self-concept change and self-presentation: The looking glass self is also a magnifying glass. *Journal of Personality and Social Psychology, 63,* 435–451.

Tidwell, G. L. (1993). The anatomy of a fraud. *Fund Raising Management, 24,* 58–65.

Tierney, J. (July 21, 1991). Behind Monty Hall's doors: Puzzle, debate, and answer? *The New York Times* (Sec. 1, Part 1), pp. 1ff.

Tomarken, A. J., & Keener, A. D. (1998). Frontal brain asymmetry and depression: A self-regulatory perspective. *Cognition and Emotion, 12,* 387–420.

Tomkins, S. S. (1979). Script theory. In H. E. Howe, Jr., & R. A. Dienstbier (Eds.), *Nebraska Symposium on Motivation, 26,* 201–236. Lincoln, NE: University of Nebraska Press.

Tomkins, S. S. (1983). Left and right: A basic dimension of ideology and personality. In R. W. White (Ed.), *The study of lives* (pp. 388–411). New York: Atherton Press.

Tomkins, S. S. (1984). Affect theory. In K. R. Scherer & P. Ekman (Eds.), *Approaches to emotion.* Hillsdale, NJ: Lawrence Erlbaum.

Tomkins, S. S. (1987). Script theory. In J. Aronoff & A. I. Rabin (Eds.), *Emergence of personality* (pp. 147–216). New York: Springer.

Tooby, J., & Cosmides, L. (1990). On the universality of human nature and the uniqueness of the individual: The role of genetics and adaptation. *Journal of Personality, 58,* 17–67.

Torges, C. M., Stewart, A. J., & Miner-Rubino, K. (2005). Personality after the prime of life: men and women coming to terms with regrets. *Journal of Research in Personality, 39,* 148.

Torrance, E. P. (1972). Career patterns and peak creative achievements of high school students twelve years later. *The Gifted Child Quarterly, 16,* 75–88.

Torrance, E. P. (1975). Creativity research in education: Still alive. In I. A. Taylor & J. W. Getzels (Eds.), *Perspectives in creativity* (pp. 278–296). Chicago: Aldine.

Torrance, E. P. (1988). The nature of creativity as manifest in its testing. In R. J. Sternberg (Ed.), *The nature of creativity* (pp. 43–75). Cambridge: Cambridge University Press.

Totterdell, P. (1999). Mood scores: Mood and performance in professional cricketers. *British Journal of Psychology, 90,* 317–332.

Triandis, H. C. (2001). Individualism-collectivism and personality. *Journal of Personality, 69,* 907–924.

Tsang, J. (2002). Moral rationalization and the integration of situational factors and psychological processes in immoral behavior. *Review of General Psychology, 6,* 25–50.

Tulsky, D., Zhu, J., & Ledbetter, M. F. (Project directors). (1997). *WAIS-III, WMS-III Technical Manual.* San Antonio: Psychological Corporation.

Tulsky, D. S., & Ledbetter, M. F. (2000). Updating to the WAIS-III and WMS-III. Considerations for research and clinical practice. *Psychological Assessment, 12,* 253–262.

Tulving, E. (1972). Episodic and semantic memory. In B. Tulving & W. Donaldson (Eds.), *Organization and memory.* New York: Academic Press.

Tulving, E. (2002). Episodic memory: From mind to brain. *Annual Review of Psychology, 53,* 1–25.

Twenge, J. M. (2002). Birth cohort, social change, and personality. In D. Cervone & W. Mischel (Eds.), *Advances in personality science.* New York: Guilford.

Tyler, L. E. (1965). *The psychology of human differences.* New York: Appleton-Century-Crofts.

Umilta, C., Simion, F., & Valenza, E. (1996). Newborn's preference for faces. *European Psychologist, 1,* 200–205.

U.S. Department of Health and Human Services (2002). *Trends in the well-being of America's Children and Youth.* (http://aspe.hhs.gov/hsp/02trends/index.htm).

Vaillant, G. E. (1971). Theoretical hierarchy of adaptive ego mechanisms. *Archives of General Psychiatry, 24,* 107–118.

Vallacher, R. R., Nowak, A., Froelich, M., & Rockloff, M. (2002). The dynamics of self-evaluation. *Personality and Social Psychology Review, 6,* 370–379.

Vallacher, R. R., Read, S. J., & Nowak, A. (2002). The dynamical perspective in personality and social psychology. *Personality and Social Psychology Review, 6,* 264–273.

Vallacher, R. R., & Wegner, D. M. (1987). What do people think they're doing? Action identification and human behavior. *Psychological Review, 94,* 3–15.

Vallacher, R. R., & Wegner, D. M. (1989). Levels of personal agency: Individual variation in action identification. *Journal of Personality and Social Psychology, 57,* 660–671.

van den Boom, D. C. (1995). Do first-year intervention effects endure? Follow-up during toddlerhood of a sample of Dutch irritable infants. *Child Development, 66,* 1798–1816.

van Lieshout, C. F. M. (2000). Lifespan personality development: Self-organizing goal-oriented agents and developmental outcome. *International Journal of Behavioral Development, 24,* 276–288.

Vandeputte, D. D., Kemper, S., & Hummert, M. L. (1999). Social skills of older people: Conversations in same- and mixed-age dyads. *Discourse Processes, 27,* 55–76.

Vanwesenbeeck, I., Bekker, M., & van Lenning, A. (1998). Gender attitudes, sexual meanings, and interactional patterns in heterosexual encounters among college students in the Netherlands. *Journal of Sex Research, 35,* 317–327.

Varendonck, J. (1921). *The psychology of daydreams.* New York: Macmillan.

Veenhoven, R. (1993). *Happiness in nations.* Rotterdam, Netherlands: Risbo.

Veroff, J. (1992). A scoring manual for the power motive. In C. P. Smith (Ed.), *Motivation and personality: Handbook of thematic content analysis* (pp. 286–310). New York: Cambridge University Press.

Vockell, E. L., Felker, D. W., & Miley, C. H. (1973). Birth order literature: 1967–1972. *Journal of Individual Psychology, 29,* 39–53.

Vogt, D. S., & Randall, C. C. (2005). Assessment of accurate self-knowledge. *Journal of Personality Assessment, 84,* 239–251.

von Bertalanffy, L. (1975a). Theoretical models in biology. In E. Taschdjian (Ed.), *Perspectives on general systems theory* (pp. 103–114). New York: George Braziller.

von Bertalanffy, L. (1975b). A biological world view. In E. Taschdjian (Ed.), *Perspectives on general systems theory* (pp. 115–126). New York: George Braziller.

von Bertalanffy, L. (1975c). New patterns of biological and medical thought. In E. Taschdjian (Ed.). *Perspectives on general systems theory* (pp. 40–52). New York: George Braziller.

von Hoof, A. (1999). The identity status field re-reviewed: An update of unresolved and neglected issues with a view on some alternative approaches. *Developmental Review, 19,* 497–556.

von Knorring, L., Moernstad, H., & Forsgren, L. (1986). Saliva secretion rate and saliva composition in relation to extraversion. *Personality and Individual Differences, 7,* 33–38.

Wagner, R. K. (1987). Tacit knowledge in everyday intelligent behavior. *Journal of Personality and Social Psychology, 52,* 1236–1247.

Wagner, R. K. (2000). Practical intelligence. In R. J. Sternberg (Ed.), *Handbook of intelligence* (pp. 380–395). Cambridge: Cambridge University Press.

Wagner, R. K., & Sternberg, R. J. (1985). Practical intelligence in real-world pursuits: The role of tacit knowledge. *Journal of Personality and Social Psychology, 49,* 436–458.

Wallace, K. A., Bisconti, T. L., & Bergeman, C. S (2001). The mediational effect of hardiness on social support and optimal outcomes in later life. *Basic and Applied Social Psychology, 23,* 267–279.

Wallach, M., & Kogan, N. (1965). *Modes of thinking in young children.* New York: Holt, Rinehart, & Wilson.

Wallechinsky, D., & Wallace, A. (1995). *The book of lists: The '90's edition.* Boston: Little, Brown.

Waller, N. G., Putnam, F. W., & Carlson, E. B. (1996). Types of dissociation and dissociative types: A taxometric analysis of dissociative experiences. *Psychological Methods, 1,* 300–321.

Wampold, B. E., Minami, T., Baskin, T. W., & Tierney, S. C. (2002). A meta- (re)analysis of the effects of cognitive therapy versus "other therapies" for depression. *Journal of Affective Disorders, 69,* 159–165.

Wanderer, J. J. (1987). Social factors in judges' rankings of competitors in figure skating championships. *Journal of Sport Behavior, 10,* 93–102.

Wang, A. Y. (1997). Making implicit personality theories explicit: A classroom demonstration. *Teaching of Psychology, 24,* 258–261.

Wang, Q., & Leichtman, M. D. (2000). Same beginnings, different stories: A comparison of American and Chinese children's narratives. *Child Development, 71,* 1329–1346.

Wang, Q., Leichtman, M. D., & Davies (2000). Sharing memories and telling stories: American and Chinese mothers and their 3-year-olds. *Memory, 8,* 159–177.

Ward, M. J., Lee, S. S., & Lipper, E. G. (2000). Failure-to-thrive is associated with disorganized infant-mother attachment and unresolved maternal attachment. *Infant Mental Health Journal, 2,* 428–442.

Waterman, A. S. (1999). Identity, the identity statuses, and identity status development: A contemporary statement. *Developmental Review, 19,* 591–621.

Watkins, C. E. (1992). Adlerian-oriented early memory research: What does it tell us? *Journal of Personality Assessment, 59,* 248–263.

Watson, D. (2002). Positive affectivity: The disposition to experience pleasurable emotional states. In C. R. Snyder & S. J. Lopez (Eds.), *Handbook of positive psychology* (pp. 106–119). Oxford: Oxford University Press.

Watson, D., & Tellegen, A. (1985). Toward a consensual structure of mood. *Psychological Bulletin, 98,* 219–235.

Watson, D., Wiese, D., Vaidya, J., & Tellegen, A. (1999). The two general activation systems of affect: Structural findings, evolutionary considerations, and psychological evidence. *Journal of Personality and Social Psychology, 76,* 820–838.

Watson, J. B. (1925). *Behaviorism.* New York: W. W. Norton.

Watts, B. L. (1982). Individual differences in circadian activity rhythms and their effects on roommate relationships. *Journal of Personality, 50,* 374–384.

Watzlawick, P., Beavin, J. H., & Jackson, D. D. (1967). *Pragmatics of human communication.* New York: W. W. Norton.

Wechsler, D. (1950). Cognitive, conative, and non-intellective intelligence. *American Psychologist, 5,* 78–83.

Wechsler, D. (1958). *The measurement and appraisal of adult intelligence* (4th ed.). Baltimore: Williams & Wilkins.

Wechsler, D. (1975). Intelligence defined and undefined: a relativistic appraisal. *American Pschologist, 30,* 135–139.

Wegner, D. (1989). *White bears and other unwanted thoughts.* New York: Viking.

Wegner, D. M. (2002). *The illusion of conscious will.* Cambridge, MA: MIT Press.

Wegner, D. M., & Pennebaker, J. W. (1993). Changing our minds: An introduction to mental control. In D. M. Wegner & J. W. Pennebaker (Eds.). *Handbook of mental control* (pp. 1–12). Englewood Cliffs, NJ: Prentice-Hall.

Wegner, D. M., Shortt, J. W., Blake, A. W., & Page, M. S. (1990). The suppression of exciting thoughts. *Journal of Personality and Social Psychology, 58,* 409–418.

Wegner, D. M., & Vallacher, R. R. (1977). *Implicit psychology: An introduction to social cognition.* New York: Oxford University Press.

Wegner, D. M. & Wheatley, T. (1999). Apparent mental causation. *American Psychologist, 54,* 480–492.

Wehr, T. A., & Goodwin, F. K. (1981). Biological rhythms and psychiatry. In S. Arieti & H. K. Brodie (Eds.), *American handbook of psychiatry: Advances and new directions (Vol 7).* New York: Basic Books.

Weinberger, D. A. (1995). The construct validity of the repressive coping style. In J. L. Singer (Ed.), *Repression and dissociation: Implications for personality theory, psychopathology, and health* (pp. 337–386). Chicago: University of Chicago Press.

Weinberger, D. A. (1998). Defenses, personality structure, and development: integrating psychodynamic theory into a typological approach to personality. *Journal of Personality, 66,* 1061–1080.

Weinberger, D. A., Schwartz, G. E., & Davidson, R. J. (1979). Low-anxious, high-anxious, and repressive coping styles: Psychometric patterns and behavioral and physiological responses to stress. *Journal of Abnormal Psychology, 88,* 369–380.

Weinberger, D. A., & Davidson, M. N. (1994). Styles of inhibiting emotional expression: Distinguishing repressive coping from impression management. *Journal of Personality, 62,* 587–613.

Weiner, B., & Graham, S. (1999). Attribution in personality psychology. In L. A. Pervin & O. P. John (Eds.), *Handbook of personality: Theory and research* (pp. 605–628). New York: Guilford.

Weiner, I. B. (1975). *Principles of psychotherapy.* New York: John Wiley & Sons.

Weinstein, E., & Deutschberger, P. (1963). Some dimensions of altercasting. *Sociometry, 26,* 545–566.

Weiskrantz, L. (1986). *Blindsight: A case study and implications.* Oxford: Oxford University Press.

Weiss, L. H., & Schwartz, J. C. (1996). The relationship between parenting types and older adolescents' personality, academic achievement, adjustment, and substance abuse. *Child Development, 67,* 2101–2114.

Weissman, M., & Olfson, M. (1995). Depression in women: Implications for health care research. *Science, 269,* 799–801.

Weissman, A. E., & Ricks, D F. (1966). *Mood and personality.* New York: Holt, Rinehart, & Winston.

Weitzenhoffer, A. M., & Hilgard, E. R. (1992). *Stanford Hypnotic Susceptibility Scale, Form C.* Palo Alto, CA: Consulting Psychologists Press.

Wenzlaff, R. M., & Bates, D. E. (2000). The relative efficacy of concentration and suppression strategies of mental control. *Personality and Social Psychology Bulletin, 26,* 1200–1212.

Wenzlaff, R. M., Rude, S. S., & West, L. M. (2002). Cognitive vulnerability to depression: The role of thought suppression and attitude certainty. *Cognition and Emotion, 16,* 533–548.

Werner, E. E., & Smith, R. S. (2001). *Journeys from childhood to midlife: Risk, resilience, and recovery.* Ithaca, NY: Cornell University Press.

Westen, D. (1990). Psychoanalytic approaches to personality. In L. Pervin (Ed.), *Handbook of personality: Theory and research* (pp. 21–65). New York: Guilford.

Westen, D. (1991). Social cognition and object relations. *Psychological Bulletin, 109,* 429–455.

Westen, D. (1992). The cognitive self and the psychoanalytic self: Can we put our selves together? *Psychological Inquiry, 3,* 1–13.

Westen, D. (1998). The scientific legacy of Sigmund Freud: Toward a psychodynamically informed psychological science. *Psychological Bulletin, 124,* 333–371.

Westen, D., & Morrison, K. (2001). A multidimensional meta-analysis of treatments for depression, panic, and generalized anxiety disorder: An empirical examination of the status of empirically supported therapies. *Journal of Consulting and Clinical Psychology, 69,* 875–899.

White, G. L. (1980). Physical attractiveness and courtship progress. *Journal of Personality and Social Psychology, 39,* 660–668.

Whitehead, A. N. (1929/1978). *Process and reality.* New York: Free Press.

Whyte, W. F. (Ed.). (1946). When workers and customers meet. In *Industry and society.* New York: McGraw Hill.

Wicker, F. W., Brown, G., Weihe, J. A., Hagen, A. S., & Reed, J. L. (1993). On reconsidering Maslow: An examination of the deprivation/domination proposition. *Journal of Research in Personality, 27,* 118–133.

Wickett, J. C., Vernon, P. A., & Lee, D. H. (2000). Relationships between factors of intelligence and brain volume. *Personality and Individual Differences, 29,* 1095–1122.

Wiebe, D. J., & Smith, T. W. (1997). Personality and health: Progress and problems in psychosomatics. In R. Hogan, J. Johnson, & S. Briggs (Eds.), *Handbook of personality psychology.* New York: Academic Press.

Wiedeman, G. H. (1972). Comments on the structural theory of personality. *International Journal of Psychoanalysis, 53,* 307–314.

Wiener, N. (1948). *Cybernetics.* Cambridge, MA: MIT Press.

Wiggins, J. S. (1997). Circumnavigating Dodge Morgan's interpersonal style. *Journal of Personality, 65,* 1069–1086.

Wilbur, K. (1999). The spectrum of consciousness. In K. Wilbur (Ed.), *The collected works of Ken Wilbur* (Vol. 1, pp. 33–414). Boston: Shambhala.

Williams, B. (1993). Moral luck. In D. Statman (Ed.)., *Moral luck* (pp. 35–55). Albany: State University of New York Press.

Williams, G. C., Freedman, Z., & Deci, E. L. (1998). Supporting autonomy to motivate patients with diabetes for glucose control. *Diabetes Care, 21,* 1644–1651.

Williams, G. C., Grow, V. M., Freedman, Z., Ryan, R. M., & Deci, E. L. (1996). Motivational predictors of weight loss and weight-loss maintenance. *Journal of Personality and Social Psychology, 70,* 115–126.

Williams, J. E., & Best, D. L. (1982). *Measuring sex stereotypes: A thirty-nation study.* Beverly Hills, CA: Sage.

Williams, W. (1999). Peering into the nature-nurture debate. *Contemporary Psychology: APA Review of Books, 44,* 267–271.

Wilson, D. S., Near, D., & Miller, R. R. (1966). Machiavellianism: A synthesis of the evolutionary and psychological literatures. *Psychological Bulletin, 119,* 285–299.

Wilson, E. (2001). *The keep.* Iowa City: University of Iowa Press.

Wilson, E. H. (1995). *The genesis of a humanist manifesto.* Amherst, NY: Humanist Press.

Wilson, T. D., & Dunn, E. W. (2004). Self-knowledge: Its limits, value and potential for improvement. *Annual Review of Psychology, 55,* 493–518.

Winter, D. G. (1991). Measuring personality at a distance: Development of an integrated system for scoring motives in running text. In A. J. Stewart, J. M. Healy, Jr., & D. Ozer (Eds.), *Perspectives in personality: Approaches to understanding lives* (Vol. 3, pp. 59–89). London: Jessica Kingsley Publishers.

Winter, D. G. (1992a). Content analysis of archival materials, personal documents, and everyday verbal materials. In C. P. Smith (Ed.), *Motivation and personality: Handbook of thematic content analysis* (pp. 110–125). New York: Cambridge University Press.

Winter, D. G. (1992b). Power motivation revisted. In C. P. Smith (Ed.), *Motivation and personality: Handbook of thematic content analysis* (pp. 301–310). New York: Cambridge University Press.

Winter, D. G. (1992c). A revised scoring system for the power motive. In C. P. Smith (Ed.), *Motivation and personality: Handbook of thematic content analysis* (pp. 311–324). New York: Cambridge University Press.

Winter, D. G. (1996). *Personality: Analysis and interpretation of lives.* New York: McGraw-Hill.

Winter, D. G. (2005). Things I've learned about personality from studying political leaders at a distance. *Journal of Personality, 73,* 557–584.

Winter, D. G., & Barenbaum, N. B. (1999). History of modern personality theory and research. In L. A. Pervin & O. P. John (Eds.), *Handbook of personality: Theory and research* (2nd ed.) (pp. 3–27). New York: Guilford.

Winter, D. G., & Carlson, L. (1988). Using motive scores in the psychobiographical study of an individual: The case of Richard Nixon. *Journal of Personality, 56,* 75–103.

Winter, D. G., John, O. P., Stewart, A. J., Klohnen, E. C., & Duncan, L. E. (1998). Traits and motives: Toward an integration of two traditions in personality research. *Psychological Review, 105,* 230–250.

Wolf, D. P. (1990). Being of several minds: Voices and versions of the self in early childhood. In D. Cicchetti & M. Beeghly (Eds.), *The self in transition* (pp. 183–212). Chicago: The University of Chicago Press.

Wolf, D., & Gardner, H. (1981). On the structure of early symbolization. In R. Schiefelbusch & D. Bricker (Eds.), *Early language: Acquisition and intervention* (pp. 287–328). Baltimore: University Park Press.

Wood, M. (1985). *In search of the Trojan war.* New York: Facts on File Publications.

Wood, W., Tam, L., & Witt, M. G. (2005). Changing circumstances, disrupting habits. *Journal of Personality and Social Psychology, 88,* 918–933.

Woodhouse, M. B. (1984). *A preface to philosophy* (3rd ed.). Belmont, CA: Wadsworth.

Woody, E. Z. (1997). Have the hypnotic susceptibility scales outlived their usefulness? *International Journal of Clinical and Experimental Hypnosis, 45,* 226–238.

Wu, K., Lindsted, K. D., & Lee, J.W. (2005). Blood type and the five factors of personality in Asia. *Personality & Individual Differences, 38,* 797–808.

Wundt, W. M. (1969). *Outlines of psychology* (C. H. Judd, Trans.). New York: G. E. Stechert. (Facsimile reproduction by St. Clair Shores, MI: Scholarly Press. Original English translation 1897; original German publication 1896.)

Wylie, R. (1974). *The self-concept.* Lincoln, NE: University of Nebraska Press.

Yik, M. S. M., Russell, J. A., & Barrett, L. F. (1999). Structure of self-reported current affect: Integration and beyond. *Journal of Personality and Social Psychology, 77,* 600–619.

Zeidner, M., & Mathews, G. (2000). Intelligence and personality. In R. J. Sternberg (Ed.), *Handbook of intelligence* (pp. 581–610). Cambridge: Cambridge University Press.

Zeller, A. F. (1950). An experimental analogue of repression. I. Historical summary. *Psychological Bulletin, 47,* 39–51.

Zevon, M. A., & Tellegen, A. (1982). The structure of mood change: An idiographic/nomothetic analysis. *Journal of Personality and Social Psychology, 43,* 111–122.

Zuckerman, M. (1991). *Psychobiology of personality.* Cambridge: Cambridge University Press.

Name Index